Accession no.
01137008

D0547967

CONSUMER BEHAVIOUR

University of
Chester
Warrington Campus

LIBRARY

Telephone: 01925 534284

This book is to be returned on or before the last date stamped below.
Overdue charges will be incurred by the late return of books.

10 JAN 2006 CANCELLED

1 APR 2006 CANCELLED

CONSUMER BEHAVIOUR

A EUROPEAN PERSPECTIVE

Gerrit Antonides

and

W. Fred van Raaij

Erasmus University, Rotterdam

LIBRARY

ACC. No. 01137008

DEPT.

CLASS No. 658.834 ANT

UNIVERSITY OF CHESTER
WARRINGTON CAMPUS

31 / 08 / 05

JOHN WILEY & SONS

Chichester • New York • Weinheim • Brisbane • Singapore • Toronto

Copyright © 1998 by John Wiley & Sons Ltd,
Baffins Lane, Chichester,
West Sussex PO19 1UD, England

National   01243 779777
International   (+44) 1243 779777
e-mail (for orders and customer service enquiries): cs-books@wiley.co.uk
Visit our Home Page on http://www.wiley.co.uk
or http://www.wiley.com

All Rights Reserved. No part of this publication may be reproduced, stored in a retrieval
system, or transmitted, in any form or by any means, electronic, mechanical, photocopying,
recording, scanning or otherwise, except under the terms of the Copyright, Designs and Patents Act 1988 or
under the terms of a licence issued by the Copyright Licensing Agency, 90 Tottenham Court Road, London,
W1P 9HE, UK, without the permission in writing of the Publisher.

Other Wiley Editorial Offices

John Wiley & Sons, Inc., 605 Third Avenue,
New York, NY 10158-0012, USA

WILEY-VCH Verlag GmbH, Pappelallee 3,
D-69469 Weinheim, Germany

Jacaranda Wiley Ltd, 33 Park Road, Milton,
Queensland 4064, Australia

John Wiley & Sons (Asia) Pte Ltd, 2 Clementi Loop #02-01,
Jin Xing Distripark, Singapore 129809

John Wiley & Sons (Canada) Ltd, 22 Worcester Road,
Rexdale, Ontario M9W 1L1, Canada

Library of Congress Cataloging-in-Publication Data

Antonides, Gerrit, 1951–
  Consumer behaviour : a European perspective / by Gerrit Antonides,
W. Fred van Raaij.
     p.   cm.
  Includes bibliographical references and index.
  ISBN 0-471-97513-3
  1.   Consumer behavior—Europe.   2. Consumption (Economics)—Europe.
  3.   Marketing research—Europe.   I. Raaij, W. Fred van.   II. Title.
  HF5415.33.E85A58 1998
  658.8′34′094—dc21
                                                    97-31193
                                                    CIP

British Library Cataloguing in Publication Data

A catalogue record for this book is available from the British Library

ISBN 0-471-97513-3

Typeset in 11/13pt ITC Garamond by Footnote Graphics, Warminster, Wiltshire
Printed and bound in Great Britain by Martins the Printers, Berwick upon Tweed
This book is printed on acid-free paper responsibly manufactured from sustainable forestry, in which at
least two trees are planted for each one used for paper production.

CONTENTS

PART IV AFTER-SALES PROCESSES

PREFACE

This book about consumer behaviour has been written from a European perspective, with European sociodemographic data and examples. It is a complete work in the sense that all issues that should be considered in a course on consumer behaviour are dealt with. Furthermore, issues omitted from current, mostly American, textbooks on consumer behaviour are included. The differences between this book and the American textbooks require some explanation. This concerns differences in culture, coverage and perspective.

Culture

Until now mainly American textbooks have been used at universities. The authors of this book have also used them for several years. However, reliance on these books has raised more and more difficulties. The American books start from the American situation, from American media and shopping malls and from American brands and products. How many European consumers drink root beer or wine coolers?[1] And how many European students have shopped in an American mall, or know the magazine *Ebony*? In this book, for example, the consumer behaviour of ethnic minorities in Europe is considered. This is not the same as that of the blacks and the hispanics in the USA. European payment systems and banks also differ from American ones. In short, many of the examples used in American books do not form a recognizable part of European daily life.

Coverage

Many American books are incomplete from our perspective. Home production, dealing with products and services, financial behaviour and the externalities of consumption, such as environmental pollution and addiction, are usually

---

[1] Root beer is a soft drink, made from roots of plants and a wine cooler is a mix of white wine and seven-up.

missing. Of the American books, the one by Michael Solomon seems the most satisfying. This book closely follows the developments in views on consumers and consumer research. It contains more information and is less traditional than many other texts entitled *Consumer Behavior*. Also, the German book *Konsumentenverhalten* by Werner Kroeber-Riel is a positive exception in our opinion.

As has been said, this volume covers more topics than other books. The main issues dealt with in American books (such as Engel, Blackwell, and Miniard; Schiffman and Kanuk; Peter and Olson; Mowen; and Wilkie) are also included here. Our book may well replace these frequently used American books.

Perspective

This book has been written from the perspective of the consumer. This too is different from other books, many of which have been written from a marketing perspective. In these books, the consumer is the object rather than the subject. However, from the consumer's viewpoint, the use of the product and its continued functioning without failure are much more important issues than purely its purchase. Marketing-oriented books are often purchase-oriented books. This volume deals with the total consumption cycle: orientation, purchase, usage and disposal of products. Furthermore, innovative issues in this book concern home production, welfare, property and financial behaviour. Goods and services are produced in households too.

This book focuses on consumers, their budgets, acquisitions, usage and disposal or trading-in of goods. Obviously, this is extremely relevant to marketing policy. For the marketeer, it is also relevant and necessary to look beyond the boundaries of marketing and to see how consumers behave and how they deal with products and services. This book is relevant to the consumer policies of government and consumer organizations and education in economics, business, marketing and home economics.

Target audience

This book is intended for students at universities and other institutes of higher education. In addition, it is suitable for marketeers, market researchers, public relations officers and government officials dealing with consumers and consumer policies. The book may be used for self-study, or to accompany lectures and courses.

Transparencies

A set of overhead transparency masters will be provided by the publisher to lecturers who adopt this text book for purchase by their students.

Thanks to . . .

First, we would like to express our gratitude to our students Bas Amesz, Paul Been, Marianne de Groene, Daniëlle de Jong, Vivian de Regt, Chantal de Vette, Ivo Hulscher, Diana Langendoen, Bart Messing, Mariëtte Ooms, Gretta Schoonderbeek, Nico Storm, Michael Sutjiadi, and Angela van Buuren for their help in finding the relevant European statistics on the many subjects considered in the book.

The photographs in this book were taken by Sven van Enckevort, Bart van Raaij, Steve Hardman, Jenny Hayes, Jane Allison and John Freeman.

We thank Susan Douglas, New York University, Peter Verhoef, Erasmus University, Damien McLoughlin, University College Dublin, Helen Woodruffe, Lancaster University, Gordon Foxall, Cardiff Business School, José Bloemer, Limburgs Universitair Centrum, Karin Ekström, Göteborg University and several anonymous reviewers for their comments on earlier drafts.

We would also like to thank Constance Eenschoten, Mikko Larsen and Natasha Stroeker for their assistance in translating parts of our Dutch consumer behaviour textbook into English. We are grateful to Dennis Goedhart and Linda Schijvens who assisted in the technical preparation of the book.

Capelle aan den IJssel, The Netherlands
Alphen, N.Br., The Netherlands

Gerrit Antonides
W. Fred van Raaij

ACKNOWLEDGEMENTS

The publisher wishes to thank the following who have kindly given permission for the use of copyright material. The destination of the reproduced material is indicated in square brackets.

American Marketing Association for:
[Figure 12.1] R.W. Belk (1974) An exploratory assessment of situational effect in buyer behavior. *Journal of Marketing Research* 11, 156–163
[Figure 21.1] A. Parasuraman, V.A. Zeitham and L.L. Berry (1985) A conceptual model of service quality and its implications for future research. *Journal of Marketing* 49(Fall) 4–50

American Psychological Association for:
[Table 7.2] M. Rokeach and S.J. Ball-Rokeach (1989) Stability and change in American value priorities, 1968–1981. *American Psychologist* 44, 775–784
[Figure 10.4] R.A. Rescorla (1988) Pavlovian conditioning. *American Psychologist* 43(3) 151–160

J. Beijk and W.F. van Raaij for:
[Table 8.1] J. Beijk and W.F. van Raaij (1989) *Schemata, Information Processing, Persuasion Processes and Advertising*. Amsterdam: VEA

Brooks/Cole Publishing Company for:
[Figure 8.4] R. Nye (1981) *Three Psychologies: Perspectives from Freud, Skinner, and Rogers.* Pacific Grove, CA: Brooks/Cole Publishing Company

Cambridge University Press for:
[Figure 4.1] A. Deaton and J. Muellbauer (1980) *Economics and Consumer Behavior*. Cambridge: Cambridge University Press, p. 20
[Figure 9.4] R.B. Zajonc and H. Markus (1984) Affect and cognition: The hard interface.
In C.C. Izard, J. Kagan and R.B. Zajonc (eds) *Emotions, Cognition, and Behavior*. Cambridge, MA: Cambridge University Press, pp. 73–102

[Table 19.3] I. Pahl (1990) Household spending, personal spending and the control of money in marriage. *Sociology* 24, Cambridge University Press, p. 124

CBS for:

[Table 4.2] Netherlands Statistics (1982) Statistisch Bulletin, December 12, The Netherlands

[Table 19.9] Netherlands Statistics (1994) Statistical Yearbook 1994 Voorburg: Netherlands Statistics

Elsevier Science – NL for:

[Figure 21.3] D.A. Francken (1983) Postpurchase consumer evaluations, complaint actions and repurchase behavior. *Journal of Economic Psychology* 4, 273–290

[Table 23.12] G. Ger and R.W. Belk (1996) Cross-cultural differences in materialism. *Journal of Economic Psychology* 17, 55–77

ESB for:

[Figure 23.2] W.F. van Raaij and G. Eilander (1983) Consumer economizing tactics. *Economisch Statistische Berichten* 68, 544–547

Euromonitor Plc for:

[Table 2.8, Table 2.9, Table 23.7 and Table 23.8] Euromonitor (1997) *European Marketing Data and Statistics*. London: Euromonitor

[Table 13.5] Euromonitor (1996) *European Marketing Data and Statistics*. London: Euromonitor

Eurostat for:

[Table 2.2, Table 2.3] Based on data supplied by Eurostat

J.F.B. Gieskes for :

[Figure 5.3] J.F.B. Gieskes (1992/1993) Dictaat Kawliteit. University of Enschede.

HarperCollins Publishers for:

[Figure 20.1] J. Piaget (1954) *The Construction of Reality in the Child*. New York: Basic Books

[Figure 20.1] J. Piaget and B. Inhelder (1969) *The Psychology of the Child*. New York: Basic Books

JAI Press Inc. for:

[Table 11.4 and Figure 11.9] S. Trøye (1985) Situationist theory and consumer behavior. In J.N. Sheth (Ed.) *Research in Consumer Behavior*. Greenwich, CT: JAI Press, pp. 285–321.

[Figure 12.2] W.F. van Raaij (1986) Developments in consumer behavior research. In B. Gilad and S. Kaish (eds) *Handbook of Behavioral Economics*. Vol. A. Greenwich, CT: JAI Press, p. 81

Kogan Page Limited for:

[Figure 24.5] J.-N. Kapferer (1992) *Strategic Brand Management. New Approaches to Creating and Evaluating Brand Equity*. London: Kogan Page.

MCB University Press for:
[Table 24.1] Van Raaij, W.F. and Th.M.M. Verhallen (1994) Domain-specific market segmentation. *European Journal of Marketing* 2 8, 49–66

The McGraw-Hill Companies for:
[Figure 21.3] J. Rossiter and L. Percy (1987) *Advertising and Promotion Management*. McGraw-Hill.

The MIT Press for:
[Figure 9.2 and Figure 12.2] A. Mehrabian and J.A. Russell (1974) *An Approach to Environmental Psychology.* Cambridge, MA: MIT Press

NIBE Amsterdam for:
[Table 19.2] C.A. van den Berg (1993) Relationship management. In: *Financial Advising of the Consumer: Fiction or Reality?* Amsterdam: NIBE, p. 21

Prentice-Hall, Inc. for:
[Table 14.4 and Table 14.5] L.G. Schiffman and L.L. Kanuk (1987) *Consumer Behavior*. Englewood Cliffs, NJ: Prentice-Hall, 3rd edn, pp 574, 575

The Reader's Digest N.U. for:
[Table 2.5] Reader's Digest Eurodata (1990)

***Review of Income and Wealth* for:**
[Table 23.4] B.M.S. Van Praag, A.J.M. Hagenaars and H. van Weeren (1982) Poverty in Europe. *The Review of Income and Wealth* 2 8, 345–359

Sage Publications, Inc. for:
[Table 7.4 and Table 7.5] S.H. Schwartz (1994) Beyond individualism/ collectivism. New cultural dimensions of values. In U. Kim, H.C. Triandis, C. Kagitcibasi, S.-C. Choi and G. Yoon (eds) *Individualism and Collectivism: Theory, Method and Applications*. London, UK: Sage, pp. 85–119

Simon & Schuster for:
[Figure 24.5] D.A. Aaker (1991) *Managing Brand Equity*. New York: The Free Press
[Figure 15.4] E.M. Rogers (1983) *Diffusion of Innovations*. New York: The Free Press, 3rd edn

Social and Cultural Planning Bureau, The Netherlands
[Table 3.3, Table 3.4 and Table 3.5] Social and Cultural Planning Bureau (1992) Social and Cultural Report 1992. The Hague: SCP

Statistics Sweden for:
[Table 19.9] Statistical Yearbook of Sweden (1997) Stockholm: Statistics Sweden.

SWOKA:
[Table 23.2] M.H. Feenstra (1991) Less money, less to eat? Report 91. Leiden: SWOKA

Uitgeverij De Vrieseborch for:
[Figure 21.1] J. Lemmink (1992) *Measures for Quality Management. A*

Critical Evaluation of the SERVQUAL Model. Jaarboek van de Nederlandse Vereniging van Marktonderzoekers. Haarlem: De Vrieseborch, pp. 223–235

Universal Media B.V. for:
[Table 17.5] Universal Media B.V., Amstelveen

The University of Chicago Press for:
[Table 13.3] H.L. Davis and B.P. Rigaux (1974) Perception of marital roles in decision processes. *Journal of Consumer Research* 1, 51–61
[Figure 7.2] G. McCracken (1989) Who is the celebrity endorser? Cultural foundations of the endorsement process. *Journal of Consumer Research* 16, 310–321
[Table 13.1] P.E. Murphy and W.A. Staples (1979) A modernized family life cycle. *Journal of Consumer Research* 6, 12–22
[Table 14.3] W.O. Bearden and M.J. Etzel (1982) Reference influence on product and brand purchase decisions. *Journal of Consumer Research* 9, 183–194
[Table 23.11] R.W. Belk (1985) Materialism: trait aspects of living in the material world. *Journal of Consumer Research* 12, 265–280.

R.M. van Kralingen for:
[Table 24.3] P.A.M. Lakatos and R. van Kralingen (1985) *Toward 1990. A Matter of Time and Money*. Amsterdam: Elsevier.

Whitaker's Almanack for:
[Table 2.7] Whitaker's Almanack (1998) London: J. Whitaker and Sons Ltd, p. 782

John Wiley & Sons, Inc. for:
[Figure 4.8] J. Kalbfleisch and R. Prentice (1980) *The Statistical Analysis of Failure Time Data*. New York: Wiley

Every effort has been made to trace and acknowledge ownership of copyright. The publishers will be glad to hear from any copyright holders whom it has not been possible to contact.

INTRODUCTION AND OVERVIEW

1

1.1 Introduction

Consumer behaviour is important from a number of different points of view. From the perspective of marketing, the study of consumer behaviour is important in helping to forecast and understand consumer demand for products as well as brand preferences. From the perspective of consumer policy, it is important to inform consumers about the alternatives open to them and to avoid deceiving them. Consumers also need to gain insight into their own behaviour if they are to spend their income optimally. From the perspective of science, the study of consumer behaviour is a rich domain in which to test economic, cognitive, economic–psychological and social–psychological theories.

The concept of a 'consumer' is only a century old. In an economy of scarcity, the challenge is to 'survive' and to fulfil basic needs. Only if households earn more income than is necessary for their basic needs, do they become free to make choices about how they spend and save. In such cases, we speak of 'discretionary income'. Originally, discretionary income only applied to the higher classes of nobility, the clergy and other wealthy citizens. It was only after the Second World War that most people acquired discretionary income. Consumers held more power because they were able to make choices about their purchases. This increasing freedom of choice makes it important to gain insight into consumer behaviour to help explain preferences for products and brands.

With the development of new interactive media, consumers have acquired even more power. By using the Internet and intelligent search agents, consumers can obtain considerable information on the various prices and qualities of products. Markets become more transparent to them. With new interactive media, consumers can take the initiative to communicate, retrieve the information they want when and where they want it, and then, if they choose, order various products and services.

This chapter continues by giving a definition of consumer behaviour in the next section, which also deals with a variety of individual and collective products and services. In section 1.3, the history of consumer research is considered, progressing from simple descriptions and explanations of consumer behaviour to more detailed models. As previously mentioned, consumer behaviour may be considered from a number of different perspectives. In section 1.4, the perspective of marketing and market research is considered; while the perspective of consumer advice and policy is dealt with in section 1.5. This book uses a descriptive approach based on cognitive, economic and social psychology. Other approaches, including the normative, descriptive and prescriptive approaches are dealt with in section 1.6. Section 1.7 includes an overview of the book, presented as a model of consumer behaviour. Section 1.8 concludes.

1.2 Consumer behaviour

What is consumer behaviour? This is the first question we asked ourselves when preparing for and writing this book. Which behaviours are included and which are excluded? For example, is attending lectures considered to be a form of consumer behaviour? And what about students buying and studying this book? Can we 'consume' art and culture? Is it even appropriate to talk about the consumption of services, since nothing disappears when they are used? For this reason, in any discussion of consumer behaviour, it is necessary to distinguish between goods and services.

Goods and services

Some people think of consumer behaviour as eating and drinking. This is too limited a view. Table 1.1 shows several goods and services, relevant to consumer behaviour. Two dimensions are distinguished: tangible/intangible and individual/collective.

Goods are tangible and concrete; services are intangible and abstract.

Table 1.1 *A classification of goods and services*

	Tangible goods	Mixed	Intangible services
Individual	Food Clothing	Restaurant Car repair	Hairdresser Physician
Household	Washing machine Car	Child care Car rental	Financial advisor Architect
Collective	Street lighting Toll bridge	Education Old-age care	Weather forecast Fire fighting

Figure 1.1 *Food and drink and social interaction*

Frequently, goods also have intangible characteristics, such as the 'personality' of a car, or the exclusiveness of fashion clothing. The functions of goods can be intangible and abstract too, such as the power of a vacuum cleaner or the processing speed of a computer. On the other hand, services frequently include tangible characteristics – a dinner in a restaurant includes the tangible aspect of food in addition to the intangible elements of atmosphere and service. Frequently, one buys or leases a combination of goods and services, as when one leases a car or a photocopying machine. In this case, the tangible product is augmented with (maintenance) services and guaranteed functionality. Many goods and services thus consist of both tangible and intangible characteristics.[1]

Individual goods and services are related to individuals, for example food, clothes and hairdressers' or physicians' services. Household goods and services are related to a group of people who belong to a household, for example, cars, washing machines or paintings. Many services are rendered to households, such as tax advice or decorating. Collective goods and services may be consumed by many people. They are not limited to government goods and services but may also be offered by private firms. Examples of collective goods are street lighting and public roads. A private toll bridge, an environmental service and the presence of a caretaker in a block of flats are all examples of collective goods and services. The consumption of culture, such as a visit to the Prado museum in Madrid or entertainment in Disneyland Paris includes the individual use of collective services. Nature and urban renewal are examples of tangible collective goods.

In this book, we use a broad definition of consumer behaviour. We are all consumers of individual and collective goods and services, of art and culture, of education and television programmes, of order and safety, of nature and architecture. Consumption is not the destruction of production as classic economists have argued.[2] Consumption or rather the positive consequences of consumption (utility) are the aims of production. For this reason, our definition comprises many more aspects than is usual in economics and marketing.

Definition of consumer behaviour

Consumer behaviour concerns

- mental and physical acts (behaviour)
- including their motives and causes
- of individuals and (small) groups
- regarding orientation, purchase, use, maintenance and disposal (consumption cycle)
- and household production (do-it-yourself)
- of (scarce) goods and services
- from the market sector, the public sector, and the household sector
- leading to functionality and the achievement of consumer goals and values
- and thus to satisfaction and well-being
- taking into account short-term and long-term effects
- and individual and societal consequences.

Thus, on the one hand consumption is concrete, physical and observable behaviour like the purchase of a milk-shake. On the other hand, consumer behaviour includes mental operations which are not directly observable, such as the decision to engage in low-fat dieting and to refrain from cakes and snacks. Behaviour may be reasoned and deliberate, as is generally the case with the purchase of a house and the choice of a mortgage. However, it may also be impulsive, such as an order at a bar. Frequently, it is habitual behaviour like buying the same brand every time or taking the same train to work every day.

Not only acts but also their motives and causes are taken into consideration in consumer research. Do displays showing special offers persuade consumers to buy? Do consumers care about the opinions of others? Furthermore, the consequences of behaviour play a part. On the basis of consequences and realized expectations, consumers may feel pleased by their purchase and therefore decide to buy again.

Consumer behaviour not only includes individual behaviour but also group behaviour. In a household, the members communicate, they divide tasks and take decisions mutually. People go to the cinema and on holidays together. Watching a football match on television in a group is more fun than watching alone. Much consumer behaviour takes place on behalf of others and under the influence of others, so buyers and users of a product or service may be different people. For example a single shopper may be buying food for the whole family including Whiskas for the cat and Pedigree Chum for the dog.

Consumer behaviour deals with scarce goods and services. Fortunately, this excludes the breathing of fresh air. Unfortunately, clean drinking water is a scarce good that often has to be paid for. Consumer behaviour frequently includes a cycle consisting of orientation, purchase, use, and disposal. Disposal may imply replacement, thus starting a new consumption cycle.[3]

Goods and services are produced in the market sector, the public sector, and the household sector. The market sector includes profit-seeking firms and entrepreneurs. The government produces social services such as social work and social benefits, and physical goods such as environmental planning and infrastructure. The household sector produces child-care and meals, for example.[4]

The effects of consumption include functionality and the achievement of goals and values.[5] Frequently, consumption is a form of social communication of one's preferences and identity.[6] The ultimate goal is consumer satisfaction and well-being.

Definition

Merit goods are goods providing short-term individual disadvantages and long-term societal benefits. Demerit goods provide short-term individual benefits and long-term societal disadvantages.

Short- and long-term effects of consumption may be distinguished. The short-term effects of alcohol are euphoria and satisfaction; the long-term effects of excessive use are illness, mental deterioration, and social costs. Since the short-term effects are attractive to individuals and the long-term effects are unattractive to society, alcohol is called a *demerit good*. In contrast, *merit goods*, such as a savings account, are unattractive to the individual in the short term and attractive to society in the long term.[7]

1.3 History of consumer research

The history of consumer behaviour is as old as the hills although historically it was not called consumer behaviour. Adam was the first consumer when he ate the apple offered to him by Eve. Humanity has always looked for food, first as a hunter and later as a farmer. In past centuries the nobility and clergy may have had enough to eat, but the ordinary people often went hungry as food was a scarce resource. Only after the industrial revolution, and for many people in Europe only after the Second World War, did a period of affluence arrive.[8]

In this century, consumer behaviour has become a subject of investigation. After consumers no longer had to struggle to survive, and when choice among different alternatives became possible, it became important to producers to investigate the criteria of consumer choice. If household income is more than is needed for the basics of rent, food and clothes, discretionary choice emerges. So, discretionary income is the income a household can spend freely, after covering the basics. Discretionary income first developed in the 'higher' social classes and after that, it became available to the working classes. However, there are still households in Europe with low incomes or high expenses which, in practical terms, do not have any discretionary income at their disposal.

In this section, several stages of scientific research of consumer behaviour are described. In each of these stages, a particular approach, point of view, theory or model prevails.

The pre-scientific approach

The first stage is the *pre-scientific stage* in which consumer behaviour is observed and discussed from a philosophical and socio-critical point of view. This occurred in the period before 1940. Thorstein Veblen dealt with conspicuous consumption in his 1899 book *The Theory of the Leisure Class*.[9] This concerns the demonstration of affluence in clothing, housing, parties and leisure of the upper class. Consumption is an expression of power and status. The members of the 'idle' class compete in this demonstration of richness and extravagance. This explains the consumer behaviour in this class. Veblen lived in the time of immensely rich tycoons such as J. P. Morgan and William Vanderbilt in the United States.

The French philosopher Gabriel Tarde has become known as the father of economic psychology by his books *Les Lois de l'Imitation* (1890) and *La Psychologie Economique* (1902). Tarde too, stressed the role of imitation in explaining consumer behaviour of the French upper classes at that time.

The motivation approach

The second stage includes *motivation research* in the period 1940–1964. Ernst Dichter applied Freud's psychoanalytic theory to consumer behaviour in his *Handbook of Consumer Motivations* (1964), including the concepts of id, ego and super-ego.[10] Dichter and his followers used in-depth interviews with consumers to reveal their deeper, often unconscious motives in purchasing and using goods and services. An interesting example of Dichter's research is baking cakes. Women, he said, frequently take this activity very seriously as if it were the birth of a child. An instant cake mix will not be successful in this case, according to Dichter. By personally adding an egg and other ingredients, a really personalized cake is produced. According to Dichter, men tend to like aromatic cigars; it is a symbol of masculinity. Their convertible sports cars are in one sense their mistresses. Dichter's approach was widely denounced in the 1960s and 1970s, however, it is now recognised as having some validity.[11]

The single-concepts approach

Both during and after the motivational research period, the *single-concepts approach* emerged in the 1960s. The most important concepts included personality, perceived risk and cognitive dissonance. Each of these concepts was used separately to explain and predict part of consumer behaviour.

Personality aspects were studied, for example to find differences between owners of BMWs, Citroëns and Fiats. Personality aspects were drawn frequently from clinical psychology, but they appeared less successful in explaining and predicting consumer behaviour.[12] Personality aspects are too general to be related to specific brand choice. This holds as much for other general aspects, such as socio-demographic characteristics like social class and civil status.[13]

The concept of *perceived risk* is relevant in consumer decisions associated with high costs, physical danger or criticism from other people.[14] Consumer behaviour frequently has unforeseen consequences, some of which may be unpleasant. For this reason, consumers try to reduce the perceived risk.[15]

Cognitive dissonance is experienced when, after having taken a decision, a consumer considers the attractiveness of the non-chosen alternatives. Dissonance reduction may take place by mentally upgrading the characteristics of the chosen alternative and downgrading those of the non-chosen alternative. Cognitive dissonance also arises from knowledge that is inconsistent with behaviour, such as smoking while knowing that smoking is harmful to one's health. In this case, dissonance may be reduced by mistrusting the source of information or even by ignoring the sources that state this harmfulness.[16]

The grand theories

The period of 1966–1972 was characterized by *grand theories*.[17] In these theories, researchers attempted to integrate all existing knowledge into large schemata, summarized by blocks and arrows. The researchers were optimistic about getting a grip on consumer behaviour as a whole.

Andreasen developed a general model of consumer choice behaviour.[18] Information from different sources enters via a 'filter' and influences the key elements of consumer behaviour in the model: opinions, affect and attitudes. Consequently, the elements instigate search behaviour, purchase and ownership of goods. In fact, this is the first 'grand theory' of consumer behaviour.

Nicosia's theory comprises four areas: mass communication, search behaviour, choice and consumption, including feedback to preceding areas.[19] In mass communication, advertising stimuli from the media are received and decoded. The relevant information is included in the information search. On the basis of the information search, the consumer chooses a particular alternative. Finally, consumption and consumption experiences are portrayed. As a result of this, consumers adapt their judgements of producers, products and brands.

Howard and Sheth published the most precise and documented theory, which they called *the* theory of buyer behaviour.[20] They distinguish input, perception, learning and output. The input consists of advertising stimuli, products and other information about products. The stimuli are perceived and evaluated before they are learned and understood. The output includes the actual buying behaviour. This model adequately captured the state of

Figure 1.2 *Store information*

the research by that time and it had the capacity to create new ideas and to stimulate new research. So, the Howard and Sheth model also fulfilled a creative function.

Engel, Kollat and Blackwell (EKB) constructed their theory as a basis of their textbook *Consumer Behavior* (1968), which has since become the precursor and prototype of dozens of textbooks of the same name. The EKB-model does not claim to be *the* model. Primarily, the authors used this model to show the connections between parts of the book. The model assumes a central control unit (CCU) receiving advertising stimuli and recognizing and solving problems. It includes influences from the environment on the CCU and feedback from CCU's actions.

Hansen published the first European book on consumer behaviour.[21] In this text, the focus was on the individual decision process. Consumers experience conflicts between alternatives, between spending and saving and between egoistic and altruistic motives. They try to solve these conflicts by information processing. Another well-known European author on consumer behaviour is Kroeber-Riel.[22]

The information-processing approach

The 1970s may be characterized as the years of *consumer information processing research*. Fishbein and Ajzen's theory of attitude is an information processing theory dealing with characteristics of alternatives rather than the alternatives as a whole. Both consumer opinions regarding characteristics and their evaluations are combined to obtain an overall judgement.[23] Their theory was the basis of the attitude research of the 1970s and has been employed in many studies to predict behavioural intentions and actual behaviour. Jacoby conducted several experiments in which the information supply to consumers was varied.[24] These experiments investigated how much information consumers use and how they use it to arrive at a decision. Bettman published an overview of the latter approach.[25]

The affective approach

In the 1980s, as well as cognition, attention was focused on *affect* or emotion, which had previously been neglected. In fact, the period of information processing research was a cognitive period presenting consumers as rational utility maximizers. However, affect plays a part in many consumer choices and behaviours. Sometimes decisions are taken by affective preferences exclusively: 'I really like this!' or 'I can't eat this.' Almost always, perception and information processing are charged with affect. We do not just look at a house but we see a nice or an ugly house. In Fishbein and Ajzen's attitude theory, the evaluations of an alternative's characteristics are a form of affect.

The experiential approach

The approach of the 1990s may be called the *experiential approach*. The focus is on the symbolic meanings of consumption, hedonism and expressive value. The point of consumption is to obtain experiences and emotions rather than to buy and possess products and brands. Semiotics and the postmodern approach are suggested as qualitative methods of research.[26]

Recent developments in the study of consumer behaviour are categorization and behavioural economics. Categorization is closely related to mental schemata of products, acts and consumers themselves.[27] A mental schema comprises all the kinds of association that a consumer has with these objects.

Behavioural economics concerns the way consumers perceive, evaluate and process information. For example, a product that has just been bought will generally be preferred to the same product before it was bought. A price discount will be perceived as a reduced loss and will be evaluated differently from a commensurate monetary gain. Some consumers simultaneously save and borrow, which is not justifiable economically because of differential rates. However, keeping the savings separate prevents consumers from 'eating up' savings and saves the effort of replenishing the account.[28]

It is not the case that the different approaches can substitute for each other completely. Rather, a new approach emerging at a particular moment builds upon the results and insights gained before. Consumer research frequently fits certain streams in scientific disciplines. For example, motivation research seemed appropriate during the heyday of psychoanalysis, and it has re-appeared during the era of experiential research. The information processing approach emerged during the cognitive revolution in psychological research and is currently of interest in behavioural economics and categorization research.

1.4 The point of view of marketing and marketing research

The study of consumer behaviour is heavily stimulated by the needs of the marketing function. Knowledge of consumer behaviour is essential for marketing management. The marketing point of view is chiefly concerned with the first stages of the consumption cycle: orientation, purchase and brand choice. It is less concerned with the stages of product use and disposal. Recently, after-sales activities have received more attention. Increasing product satisfaction and after-sales service can increase customer loyalty.

Consumer behaviour includes assigning a budget at the generic, modal and specific levels.[29] At the generic level, allocation of the budget to broad groups of savings, and goods and services (consumption domains) takes place.[30] This includes a decision to spend on transport or to save the money, for instance. At the modal level, decisions within the product domain are taken, for example to buy a new car or to use public transport. At the specific level, the brand and brand type will be decided, for example, a Volvo 480 ES sedan. Marketing managers are mainly interested in specific brand choice and frequently neglect the preceding generic and modal choices. This is not justified, as consumers may not only choose between a BMW and an Alpha Romeo at the specific level but also at the generic level between say, a second home or a car.

Definition

Strategic goods are goods that generate a series of complementary purchases.

The available budget is not the only determinant of consumer behaviour. Another important reason and limitation of consumer behaviour is the acquisition of *strategic goods*.[31] These are goods that generate a series of complementary purchases. For example, the purchase of a house induces the acquisition of furniture, decoration and garden tools. Similarly, the purchase of a car results in buying gasoline, maintenance and supplies, insurance and sometimes a caravan.

Consumer behaviour is not limited to buying. It concerns a consumption cycle comprising orientation, purchase, use, and product disposal. Orientation includes problem recognition, information search and evaluating alternatives. The buying process includes brand choice and the actual purchase. Product use concerns the frequency and intensity of use. Disposal includes scrapping, trading-in and/or throwing away products. Combining the allocation levels with the stages of the consumption cycle in table 1.2, the relevant scientific disciplines can be distinguished.

Table 1.2 *Relevant scientific disciplines for areas of consumer behaviour*

	Orientation	Purchase	Usage	Disposal
Generic level	Economics Household economics	Economics Household economics	Household economics Environmental issues	Environmental issues
Modal level	Marketing Household economics	Marketing Household economics	Environmental issues Household economics	Environmental issues
Specific level	Marketing	Marketing	Marketing	–

Marketing mainly deals with modal and specific choices. Do consumers choose holiday travel by car or by airplane (modal level)? And if they choose a flight, which destination, travel operator and airline company do they choose (specific level)? Marketing focuses on the choice of product group, product variety, model and brand. In marketing, the first stages of the consumption cycle (orientation and purchase) are emphasized. Product use and disposal get less attention in marketing research and management. From the point of view of competition and market share, the emphasis is on influencing the consumer's purchase process and the actual purchase.

Marketing is particularly concerned with goods and services in the market sector. In the future, marketing will also be concerned with goods and services in the public and non-profit sectors. For the sake of fund raising, charities deal with the marketing of their image in order to influence donor behaviour. Government services may also profit from knowledge and experience of marketing.

Household economics mainly concentrate on the generic and modal levels. At the model level, the question is which household goods households buy and use. The household is considered to be a small firm in which labour, money, knowledge and capital goods, for instance the cooker, washing machine and refrigerator are used to produce utility and welfare for the members of the household.

The question is how to obtain maximal utility, given the labour, durable goods, financial means and other resources. When is it cheaper to produce goods and services and when is it cheaper to buy them? Cleaning the home oneself is not profitable economically if the person concerned can earn more than the amount paid for domestic help, provided the latter meets certain requirements. Household economics mainly is concerned with the

Figure 1.3 *Demonstration of a sandwich toaster*

generic and modal levels of consumption (see table 1.2). The question is whether the household owns a car, a caravan or a boat and not whether it owns particular brands. The ownership of these goods determines recreation and holiday behaviour. The brand is of secondary importance here.

Environmental issues are mainly raised in the later stages of the consumption cycle: product use and disposal. How can durability be increased by 'better' usage? How can the possibilities for environmentally friendly behaviour be extended to the disposal stage, for example by sorting and separating various types of rubbish? For the rest, the first stages of the consumption cycle are important, as in these stages consumers may include environmental factors in their product choices and purchases.

Under the influence of environmental problems, marketing will pay more attention to the final stages of the consumption cycle. From an environmental point of view, it is important to know whether, and to what degree, consumers are willing to use their cars less or not at all.

1.5 Consumer advice and policy issues

In consumer advice and from the point of view of home economics, the emphasis is on the generic and modal levels of consumption. How do consumers spend their budgets? What levels of consumption and satisfaction do they achieve? Consumer information dealing with product tests may also influence specific choice.

Consumer advice often focuses on the public interest. Advisory services may be provided from the environmental point of view, optimal budget planning, prevention of dangerous situations and accidents in and around the house, healthy food, a healthy life-style and many other perspectives. Consumer interest frequently coincides with the public interest. Healthy food and a healthy life-style are important both for the consumer and for society. Healthy people require less health care provision and are less often absent from work.

Consumer policy will be dealt with in more detail in chapter 5. The emphasis is on health and safety and on the financial situation of the poor. Many other issues, such as product liability are organized between producers and consumer organizations.

1.6 Normative, prescriptive, predictive or descriptive?

The study of consumer behaviour may be approached from a number of different perspectives. Marketing, market research, consumer advice and consumer policy have all been mentioned. But it is also important to distinguish the objectives of consumer behaviour studies. Is the aim to describe and explain consumer behaviour as accurately as possible? Is there an attempt to predict consumer behaviour? Is the purpose to help consumers to make good decisions and to maximize their utility? In these respects, normative, prescriptive, predictive and descriptive approaches to consumer research can be distinguished.

In the *normative* approach to consumer behaviour, it is assumed that structuring the choice problem and the available information will help consumers to take optimal decisions. So, the most important aim is to improve the process of decision making and to prevent consumers from neglecting important information. If consumers are assisted in this way, they learn *how* to decide best and not necessarily *what* to decide.

In economics, normative rules are used to explain consumer behaviour, assuming rationality in decision making. This assumes that people maximize utility or optimize decision making. Obviously, consumers frequently try to behave reasonably and rationally. However, in practice, it appears that consumers do not always behave according to normative rules.

The normative approach is also emphasized in consumer education. Here, consumers are taught how to make the best decisions. Impulsiveness is discouraged in favour of comparing and evaluating alternatives. In consumer advice, too, normative elements appear. The aim of consumer advice is for consumers to spend their budgets 'as effectively as possible'. Marketing also includes normative elements. Sometimes, in advertising, choice rules are suggested to be 'the best' for consumers.

The *prescriptive* approach goes one step further. Here, it is prescribed what consumers should decide, given their budget and their objectives. Budgeting advice frequently makes prescriptive recommendations regarding spending and saving to encourage consumers to make best use of their resources. Consumer advice almost always includes prescriptive elements.

The *predictive* approach mainly deals with predictions of consumer behaviour. For example, how will consumers react to an advertising campaign? Or, what will the market share of a new product be? Economists strongly emphasize prediction, sometimes at the expense of descriptive or explanatory power. Rational hypotheses are formulated and predictions are derived from this.[32] Marketing managers, too, are chiefly interested in the prediction of behaviour rather than the underlying model of consumer behaviour, although an effective underlying model clearly makes it possible to make predictions in new situations.

In this book, the *descriptive* approach of consumer decision making is emphasized. The factors influencing consumer behaviour are described and structured, for instance the decision rules used by the consumer and the social influence exerted on the consumer by the environment. The descriptive approach may form the basis for predictive, normative, and prescriptive approaches as well.

1.7 Model of consumer behaviour

The contents of this book may be summarized by the model shown in figure 1.4. The different subjects are structured in a schema including four main groups:[33]

- A Cultural environment;
- B Social norms, knowledge, attitudes, meaning and consumer objectives;
- C Consumer behaviour and consumption cycle;
- D Satisfaction and complaints.

The main groups (A–D) are influenced by a number of factors. These factors are shown in the left-hand part of figure 1.4. From satisfaction there is feedback to behaviour, knowledge, attitudes and life-style. The chapter numbers are shown in parentheses. The model is definitely not meant as *the* model of consumer behaviour. Rather, it should serve to structure and interlink the chapters of this book.

Block A concerns the general cultural environment that influences consumer behaviour. Mainly sociological, economic and demographic factors play a part here. The macro-environment of consumption includes the culture, subculture, life-style, supply of goods and services, consumerism, and the changing composition of the population.

Block B consists of the mental concepts explaining consumer behaviour. These concepts cannot be observed directly, but they can be measured in research by means of interviews and questionnaires. One could ask whether concepts such as attitude and social norms really exist. We do not know the answer to this question, but they appear to be useful concepts in explaining and predicting human behaviour, in particular consumer behaviour. The concepts of block B are: knowledge, attitude, consumer objectives, meanings of products and brands and behavioural intentions. Also, block B includes learning and decision processes.

Block C comprises the actual consumer behaviour and the consumption cycle of orientation, purchase, use and disposal. Generally, situational factors have a strong influence on behaviour alternatives and on behaviour. Financial behaviour, shopping and household production are all elements of consumer behaviour.

Block D includes processes and effects after the purchase, namely satisfaction and complaints. Satisfaction or dissatisfaction have a feedback effect on behaviour (block C), on knowledge (learning) and attitude (block B) and on life-style (block A). Feedback from satisfaction is an important form of adaptation and learning based on one's own experience.

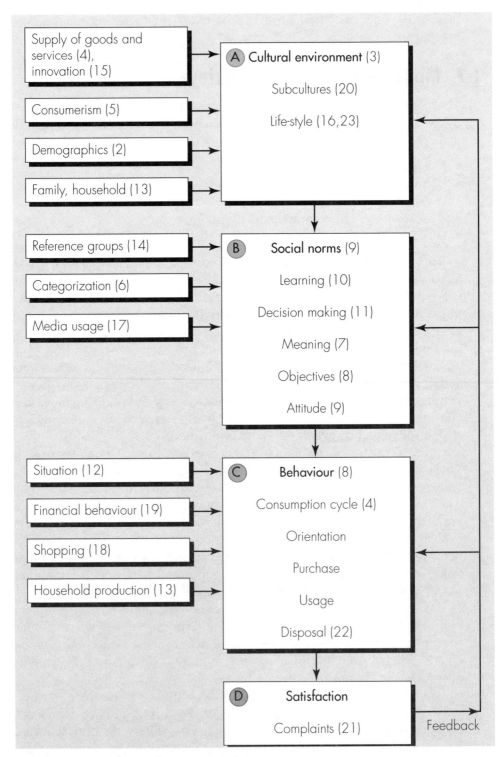

Figure 1.4 *Model of consumer behaviour*

The subjects of chapter 15 (innovations) and chapter 22 (environment) are examples of topics to which the entire model of figure 1.4 is applied.

1.8 Conclusions

In this chapter, consumer behaviour has been defined; and it is much broader than may at first be thought. It deals with goods and services from the market sector, the public sector, and household production. It includes not just the purchase of goods but also their use and disposal.

The history of consumer behaviour research shows periods with changing attention to particular theories, concepts and concept relationships. It is impossible to explain consumer behaviour from a few concepts or from only one perspective. Because of the great variety of sources of supply and the many differences between consumers and their discretionary incomes, explaining consumer behaviour has not become easier. However, consumer behaviour is not totally unpredictable any more, as has been claimed by some pessimists.

In this chapter, several perspectives have been offered from which consumer behaviour can be studied: marketing, household economics and consumer policy. These perspectives have their own approaches, such as the normative, prescriptive, predictive and descriptive approaches. There is also the perspective of the scientific researcher, looking for theories explaining behaviour in more general terms. Consumer behaviour is a rich domain to test social-psychological, micro-economic, sociological and anthropological hypotheses.

The next part of this book considers the macro-factors of consumer behaviour: demographic and cultural developments, supply of goods and services, consumerism and consumer policy (see also block A in figure 1.4). This concerns the backdrop of environmental factors in which consumer behaviour and consumption occurs.

Part II deals with the basic individual and psychological processes of perception and evaluation: categorization of goods and services, motivation of behaviour, levels of behaviour, attribution of causes, knowledge and emotion, attitude, meaning structure, learning and decision processes, the situations in which behaviour occurs. These concepts are shown in block B of figure 1.4.

Part III deals with the social-psychological and sociological processes: interactions within the household, social reference groups, innovation diffusion, media behaviour and shopping, life-style, household production, financial behaviour and consumer behaviour of age groups and ethnic groups. These concepts are shown in blocks B and C of figure 1.4.

Part IV includes after-purchase processes, such as perception of quality, satisfaction and consumer complaints, environmental effects, welfare and possessions. This concerns block D in figure 1.4.

Finally, part V examines the relationships between consumer behaviour research, marketing and market research. Market segmentation, positioning and brand extensions are topics dealt with in this part.

Notes

1. Levitt, T. (1981) 'Marketing intangible product and product intangibles' *Harvard Business Review* May–June, 94–102.
2. Adam Smith, David Ricardo, Thomas Robert Malthus and John Stuart Mill.
3. The consumption cycle will be dealt with in chapter 4.
4. Section 13.6 deals with the relationships between the three sectors.
5. See section 7.4.
6. See chapters 4 and 14.
7. See sections 8.7 and 22.3.
8. See chapter 4.
9. Veblen, T. (1899) *The Theory of the Leisure Class: an Economic Study of Institutions* (New York: The Viking Press).
10. See section 7.4.
11. Callebaut, J. (1994) *The Naked Consumer: The Secret of Motivational Research in Global Marketing* (Antwerp: Censydiam Institute).
12. Kassarjian, H. H. (1971) 'Personality and consumer behavior: a review' *Journal of Marketing Research* 8, 409–418.
13. See chapters 14 and 24.
14. Bauer, R. A. (1960) 'Consumer behavior as risk taking' in: *Dynamic Marketing for a Changing World* (Chicago, IL: American Marketing Association).
15. See chapters 11 and 15.
16. See chapter 21.
17. For an overview, see Zaltman, G., Pinson, C. R. A. and Angelmar, R. (1973) *Metatheory and Consumer Research* (Hinsdale, IL: Dryden Press).
18. Andreasen, A. R. (1965) 'Attitudes and customer behavior: a decision model' in: Preston, L. E. (ed.) *New Research in Marketing* (Berkely, CA: Institute of Business and Economic Research, University of California), 1–16.
19. Nicosia, F. M. (1966) *Consumer Decision Processes: Marketing and Advertising Implications* (Englewood Cliffs, N J: Prentice-Hall).
20. Howard, J. A. and Sheth, J. N. (1969) *The Theory of Buyer Behavior* (New York: Wiley).
21. Hansen, F. (1972) *Consumer Choice Behavior: A Cognitive Theory* (New York: The Free Press).
22. Kroeber-Riel, W. (1992) *Konsumentenverhalten* (München: Verlag Franz Vahlen) (fifth edition).
23. See chapter 9.
24. Jacoby, J., Speller, D. E. and Kohn, D. A. (1974a) 'Brand choice behavior as a function of information load' *Journal of Marketing Research* 11, 63–69. Jacoby, J., Speller, D. E. and Kohn, D. A. (1974b) 'Brand choice behavior as a function of information load: Replication and extension' *Journal of Consumer Research* 1, 33–42.
25. Bettman, J. R. (1979) *An Information-Processing Theory of Consumer Choice* (Reading, MA: Addison-Wesley).

26. See for semiotics Mick, D. G. (1986) 'Consumer research and semiotics: exploring the morphology of signs, symbols and significance' *Journal of Consumer Research* 13, 196–213. For postmodern methods of research, see Sherry, J. F. Jr (1991) 'Postmodern alternatives: The interpretive turn in consumer research' in: Robertson, T. S. and Kassarjian, H. H. (eds) *Handbook of Consumer Research* (Englewood Cliffs, NJ: Prentice-Hall), 548–591.
27. See chapter 7.
28. See chapter 11.
29. See chapter 11.
30. Consumption domains will be considered in chapter 24.
31. Arndt, J. (1979) 'Family life cycle as a determinant of size and composition of household expenditures' *Advances in Consumer Research* 6, 128–132.
32. Friedman even declared that a correct prediction is the only criterion and that the descriptive model is not particularly relevant. Friedman, M. (1953) 'The methodology of positive economics' in: *Essays in Positive Economics* (Chicago: Chicago University Press), 3–43.
33. Van Raaij, W. F. and Verhallen, T. M. M. (1983) 'A behavioral model of residential energy use' *Journal of Economic Psychology* 3, 39–63. They developed a similar model for consumer energy use.

PART I

MACRO-FACTORS IN CONSUMPTION

DEMOGRAPHIC DEVELOPMENT 2

2.1 Introduction

Demographic development constitutes an important determinant of consumer behaviour. The make-up of the European population with respect to age, gender, education, income, labour participation, family composition, social class, residence and other characteristics influences expenditures, savings and life-styles of consumers. 'Greying' and a reduction in the numbers of young people cause a changing distribution of age and needs for products and services.[1] For example, if household size decreases and the proportion of dual-income households increases it can be expected that demand for instant meals and restaurant services will increase.

In general, demographic developments can be predicted with great accuracy. For example, consider the baby boom just after the Second World War. This generation has now reached the age range of 40–49 years old. It also induced a second, smaller baby boom of children now aged 20–29 years old. A third, even smaller baby boom may provide the original baby boomers with grandchildren. With some accuracy it can be predicted when these groups will enter the labour force, form households, have children, and retire. Changing preferences, for example, regarding more education, fewer children or earlier retirement, may cause deviations from predictions.

The aim of this chapter is to provide background information about the socio-demographic composition of the European population as it relates to consumer behaviour.

2.2 Development of the European Union

After a long history of wars between European countries, a number of steps have been taken to accomplish the unification of these countries. The Treaty of Rome in 1957 established a common market in Belgium, France,

Germany, Italy, Luxembourg, and The Netherlands. The Treaty aimed at removing trade barriers between the countries. In 1973, Denmark, Ireland and the UK joined this grouping, followed by Greece in 1981, Portugal in 1986 and Spain, Austria, Finland and Sweden in 1995 to create the European Union (EU). The Single European Act (1986) and the Maastricht Treaty (1992), brought unification closer by lowering the borders between the countries, removing restrictions on worker mobility, establishing a European Currency Unit (ECU), setting a minimum standard of value added tax of 15% in all members states, liberalizing transportation services (no permits or quotas), creating 'level playing fields' for business contracts, technical standards for products and harmonizing food laws. Not all of these aims have yet been fulfilled in all member states. In 1997, the Amsterdam Treaty agreed, among other issues, border removals in the EU, except in the UK, Ireland and Denmark.

Besides the European Union, Iceland, Liechtenstein, Norway and Switzerland belong to the European Free Trade Association (EFTA), which aims to fulfil some but not all of the objectives of the EU. EFTA objectives include free movement of goods, services, capital and people but not (yet) the harmonization of business practices and regulations, nor the harmonization and integration of monetary, fiscal and other macroeconomic policies.[2]

The EU constitutes the largest common market in the West including 370 million inhabitants, as compared with 260 million in the US. Two Asian countries: China and India, include more inhabitants. However, production (GDP) per capita in the EU, USA and Japan is much larger than in China and India (see table 2.1).

Table 2.1 *Large markets in East and West*[3]

Area	Inhabitants (1995) (millions)	GDP per capita (1995) (US$)
EU	372	23,325
US	263	26,444
Japan	125	26,578
China	1221	513
India	936	406

2.3 People and households in Europe

This section deals with the most important demographic developments in Europe such as the number of inhabitants and the structure of the population.

Table 2.2 *Population of the EU in the past and in the future*[4]

Annual average	Inhabitants (millions)	Increase in previous period	Index (1990 = 100)
1950	296		78
1960	316	10.9%	87
1970	340	7.6%	93
1980	355	4.4%	98
1990	364	2.5%	100
2000	375	1.4%	103
2010	375	0.0%	103
2025	368	−1.9%	101
2050	337	−8.4%	93

Number of inhabitants

The number of inhabitants of the EU increased by 23% during 1950–1990, 7% of which occurred during the baby boom in 1950–1960 (see table 2.2). After the baby boom, the growth rate declined considerably until it reached a rate of only 2% per ten years during the 1990s. It is expected that at the beginning of the 21st century the growth rate will be negative, such that in 2050 the EU population will return to its 1970 level.

The growth rate of the population is composed of the differences between births and deaths and between immigration and emigration. Furthermore, the population growth rate in the EU is a weighted average of the growth rates of the member countries. The expected negative growth rate in the EU is mainly due to Italy, Germany, Spain and Greece in which the population is expected to decrease 15–25% by 2050. This cannot be compensated for by expected population increases of 15–20% in Ireland, Sweden and Luxembourg. These expectations are heavily influenced by dramatically decreased birth rates, falling from almost 20 per 1000 inhabitants in the 1960s to slightly over 10 in the 1990s. Birth rates fell below 10 per 1000 inhabitants in Italy and Spain in 1991.[5]

In central Europe, similar differences in population development are found. In Hungary, Bulgaria and the Czech and Slovak Republics, population growth rates varied between −2.8% and 2.6% during 1980–1990. In Poland, Romania and Russia they varied between 5.0% and 7.3%. Their birth rates also decreased generally.

European population age distribution

Birth and death rates influence the age distribution of the population. Although in most European countries the birth rate is still higher than the death rate, both are tending to decrease. The effect of this is a reduction in the number of young people and increase in the number of old people in

Table 2.3 *Greying and de-greening of the population in the EU*[6]

| Year | Age classes (percentage of population in each age class) | | |
	0–19	20–59	≥60
1960	31.8	52.7	15.5
1980	30.0	52.2	17.8
2000	23.4	55.0	21.6
2020	20.4	52.9	26.7

the population, as shown in table 2.3. Although the population in the age bracket 20–59 roughly remains the same in a 60-year interval, the youth population shrinks in proportion to the increase in the 60^+ category. It is also evident that these changes go faster over time. The age distribution in countries characterized by a low birth rate will show a greater increase in the numbers of elderly (greying) and a greater reduction in the numbers of young people in the population (de-greening) than other countries.

De-greening has partially been caused by delay of the first child's birth because of women's emancipation and career building. The later birth of the first child and continuation of the woman's career after birth frequently leads to a smaller number of children in the family. This trend has been visible from the mid-1970s with an average of 27 years at first delivery to the early 1990s with an average age of about 28 years. In The Netherlands and Denmark, the trend is even stronger.

Greying is also influenced by a decreasing death rate in western European countries, leading to a longer life expectancy. In the EU, life expectancy varies between 70 and 72 years for men and between 78 and 80 for women. In central European countries, life expectancy is between 65 and 69 for men and between 73 and 75 for women.[7]

Greying has important consequences for the financing of old-age benefits. In many countries an apportionment system applies in which people with labour income pay premiums for the elderly. Thus, a greying society requires either more premiums or lower retirement benefits. This implies a reduction of discretionary income of the groups concerned.

Despite the greying society, the elderly need not themselves feel as old as they actually are. In one study, it was found, for example, that 20-year-olds consider someone middle-aged at the age of 40, whereas 30-year-olds consider someone middle-aged at the age of 45. The 40-year-olds consider someone somewhat old at the age of 65, whereas the 65-year-olds consider someone somewhat old at the age of 68.[8] In a different study the results were even more striking. People between 40 and 60 years old reported that they felt about 15 years younger than their actual age, on average. This implies that many products need to be positioned for a younger age than the actual target market.[9]

Households

Most people live in households, excluding people living in institutions and prisons, and persons without a permanent residence. Table 2.4 shows the development of households in the EU over a 20-year period. The number of households increases more slowly than the number of inhabitants, leading to a decreasing household size. This is partly due to the increasing proportion of one-person and two-person households. It appears that the traditional family (husband, wife and children) is losing ground. About 40% of the households consist of three or more people and this percentage will decrease further. This has a significant impact on the demand for housing and housing type. Small houses with two or three rooms are in particular demand. Most of these households want a number of durable goods such as a refrigerator, washing machine, television set, car and furniture. Consequently, the demand for these items will increase.

In Ireland, the average household size was 4.1 in 1995. In eastern European countries, the household size is also higher than the EU average running as high as 3.7 in the Russian Federation 1993. However, in these countries, household size will decrease as a result of the falling birth rate.

The consequences of the increasing numbers of smaller households include:

- Decreasing economies of scale: the costs per household regarding rent, mortgage, insurance, telephone connection, and durable goods are increasing.
- Food packaging and other household products will need to be smaller. Alternatively, large packages may contain a number of smaller packages.
- Less people will be at home during the day. Home delivery of goods will be hampered during the day. Also transport demands will increase.
- The marketing of goods and services should be tuned to many more different tastes and needs than in the past. The demand for household services such as caring for the sick, the elderly and even pets will also increase.

Table 2.4 *Statistics regarding households in the EU*[10]

Aspects	1981	1991
Number of inhabitants (millions)	356	365
Number of households (millions)	117	140
Average household size	2.8	2.6
Proportion of one-person households	23%	26%
Proportion of two-person households	28%	30%

Education

Schooling systems differ considerably across countries. For this reason, only the percentage of the population leaving school at the age of 18 years or older is shown in table 2.5.

It appears that in the Scandinavian countries and West Germany most people participated in education up to the age of 18 years. In Portugal, Spain, Switzerland and the UK only a modest proportion participated that long. Since the EU has become a free labour market, this creates unequal opportunities for students to start their careers. Hence, Germany, Denmark and The Netherlands have all taken steps to reduce the length of their study.[11]

An increasing level of education is necessary to keep up with the increasingly skilled nature of jobs. In Western Europe employment in agriculture and manufacturing has decreased to levels around 5% due to automation. In Bulgaria, Greece, Hungary, Poland, Portugal and Russia, it is still around 20%. In Eastern Europe, these countries' levels of unemployment have also risen because of the transition to free-enterprise economies. Employment in social and personal services in Western Europe occupies 26% of the workforce, in manufacturing it is 21% and in commerce and the hotel and catering industry it is 16%.[12] These figures reflect the increasing demand for jobs in services, commerce and the hotel and catering industry and their required educational levels.

An increasing level of education has implications for consumers' information processing abilities. Better educated consumers can handle information more effectively than less educated consumers. Also, better educated consumers demand products and services that are different from those demanded by those who are less educated. Theatre, classical music and books appeal more to the better educated. Educated consumers are better able to formulate complaints and to defend their own interests.[13]

Social class

Social class is a concept that market researchers use to distinguish between groups of people. People in different social classes frequently show differences in their life-styles, consumer behaviour, wealth and leisure

Table 2.5 *Percentage of the population continuing in education beyond the age of 18, 1991*[14]

Denmark	71	Netherlands	53	Italy	34
Norway	68	Greece	46	Portugal	29
Sweden	63	Austria	44	Spain	28
(West) Germany	59	Luxembourg	43	Switzerland	27
Finland	57	France	41	UK	24
Belgium	54	Ireland	34		

pursuits. Also, people of the same social class mix more frequently with others of the same social class than people of different classes. As a result of democratization, class differences have become less important. Earlier, it may not have been acceptable in some countries for women from higher classes to purchase goods at open-air markets. Nowadays, it has become acceptable for everyone. However, higher classes still patronize 'exclusive' shops.

Definition

Social class is a summary of people's ranking in society with respect to profession and education.

Several systems to measure social class exist.[15] Essentially, social class is determined by profession and education. Although social class may be correlated with income, income is not a determinant of social class. For example, an unemployed university graduate may have a lower income than a plumber. Yet, the graduate is assumed to belong to a different social class because of his or her education. The unemployed are categorized according to their last profession or the profession associated with their education.

A common classification by the Joint Industry Committee for National Readership Surveys (JICNARS) is shown in table 2.6. A simplified JICNARS classification has been used in the World Values Surveys of 1981 and 1990. The weighted averages of social classes in eight Western European countries are reported in table 2.6. It appears from these surveys that both A/B and D/E classes have diminished in size, reflecting the effect of democratization. This seems to be partly due to a decrease from 18% to 3% in the A/B classes in West Germany, and to a decrease from 18% to 2% in the D/E classes in France. Also, the skilled working class (C2) in West Germany increased by 30%.

Social classes are considered more or less permanent and homogenous categories in society. The concept of social class shows a rigid image of society implying little social mobility. In past centuries, social class was determined by birth. A working-class child could never belong to the middle classes. New varieties of consumer behaviour (e.g., fashion) primarily emerged in the higher classes and trickled down into the lower classes. In modern times, mobility has increased due to equal rights and equal opportunity of education. Children frequently attain higher educational and professional levels than their parents. For this reason, they frequently belong to higher social classes than their parents and are upwardly mobile. In addition, differences in income and consumption between social classes have become less profound. Nowadays, 'everyone'

Table 2.6 *Socio-economic classification*[16]

Class	Occupation	1981	1990
		(percentage of population in classification)	
A Upper middle class	Higher managerial, administrative or professional	18.5	12.8
B Middle class	Intermediate managerial administrative or professional		
C1 Lower middle-class	Supervisory or clerical and junior managerial, administrative or professional	31.4	36.7
C2 Skilled working class	Skilled manual workers	30.2	36.5
D Working class	Semi-skilled and unskilled manual workers	20.0	14.0
E Those at lowest levels of subsistence	State pensioners or widows (no other earner), casual or lowest grade workers		

can play golf, travel around the world or buy a yacht, although it may be necessary to economize on other expenditures on these items in order to do so. In modern society, the concept social class has become less used and is frequently replaced by other concepts such as lifestyle.

Social class remains however an important determinant of consumption patterns. Several aspects are associated with social class. A positive correlation exists between social class and income and wealth, due to higher salaries being paid in professions requiring higher education. Higher social classes frequently own more goods and also these goods are of higher quality, for example, period furniture and antiques. Higher-class individuals frequently own rather than rent a house, usually in a 'good' neighbourhood. Social class is also associated with prestige. One gets invitations to become a member of the Rotary or Lions Club and to join charity boards. The professions offer possibilities for individual performance and in general give more prestige, for example doctors, military officers, university professors, judges and mayors. Individuals from a certain social class feel attracted to one another and they mix easily. Children's education and schooling may be affected by social class. Higher social classes usually provide better education and a more stimulating environment than lower social classes. Consequently, their children have a better chance of remaining in a higher social class, implying that social class is self-perpetuating to some extent. Higher-class children obtain further advantages in their careers, such as upper class accent, habits and behaviours, and can reap the benefits of advantaged social networks.

Residence

Where a consumer lives partly determines consumption. This may include the nation, the region, the residence, the neighbourhood and the type of housing. The state obviously determines the geographical living conditions, for example, climate, landscape, and economic conditions. The region may be a state, province, county, canton, department, community, which frequently determines living conditions further. The residence may be in a city, suburb, town or village, which impacts the consumption 'infrastructure'. Neighbourhoods may be very different from each other in terms of social conditions and type of housing as well as the availability of facilities such as stores and services. The type of housing may be a detached, semi-detached or terraced house, or a maisonette, flat or farm, which will affect the choice of home decoration, furniture, etc.

European countries greatly vary in degree of urbanization. The population density is the highest in The Netherlands and Belgium (over 300 inhabitants/km^2) and the lowest in the former Soviet Union, Norway, Sweden and Finland (less than 20 inhabitants/km^2). This has a considerable effect on the demand and supply of transport and communication, for instance. In low-density areas, demand for these facilities may be relatively high *per capita*, although total demand—and supply—may be relatively low. In high-density areas, both demand *per capita* and total demand may be high, resulting in relatively high supply.

Another measure of concentration is the percentage of the population living in large cities. In Portugal and Greece (moderately densely populated countries) 60% of the population lives in cities with over half a million inhabitants.[17] In Poland, Germany and the Czech and Slovak Republics less than 20% of the population lives in large cities. Europe's largest cities are shown in table 2.7. Moscow ranks tenth in the list of the world's largest cities. In these cities the variety of tastes is immense, partly due to the ethnic diversity which is typical of big cities. Depending on the wealth of the population, the variety in supply should meet the various tastes. The cities usually have better facilities regarding shopping centres, public transport

Table 2.7 *Inhabitants of the world's largest cities in millions*[1]

Mexico City	15.0	Moscow	8.7
Cairo	13.0	Jakarta	8.5
Bombay	12.6	Delhi	8.4
Calcutta	10.9	Tokyo	8.1
Buenos Aires	10.7	Bogota	8.0
Seoul	10.2	Beijing	7.4
Sao Paulo	9.6	Istanbul	7.3
Paris	9.3	New York	7.3
Shanghai	8.8	Karachi	7.2

[1] Whitaker's Almanac 1998. London: The Stationery Office, p. 782.

and entertainment than the rural areas, which have to rely heavily on private transport.

Religion

In the southern part of western Europe, the Catholic church prevails. In Belgium, Luxembourg, France, Italy, Spain, Portugal and Austria, 70–95% of the population professes the Catholic religion. In the northern part of western Europe, the Protestant churches dominate. In Denmark, Finland, Iceland, Norway and Sweden, 85–95% of the population belongs to the Lutheran church. In the UK and the Netherlands, the non-religious population is the highest, 24% and 33% respectively.[19] Usually, such statistics are based on official church membership data, not necessarily revealing the true preferences and practices of the population. In fact, surveys show large deviations from the above-mentioned statistics. In 11 European countries, 42% of the population reports attending religious services less than once a year or never (except for weddings, funerals and christenings), and 34% reports either to be a non-religious person or to be a convinced atheist.[20]

Religion is firmly incorporated in western culture. Art, welfare, sexuality, labour participation, celebration of Sundays and holidays, and the maintenance of church buildings are all influenced by religion. Religion is associated with norms and values, for example responsibility and respect for nature. Religious values may also affect behaviour, for example

Figure 2.1 *Sunday morning in England*

emphasizing saving and hard work (the 'Protestant ethic'). Sometimes, the type of leisure activities may be restricted by religious beliefs.

Labour and income

In western European countries, roughly 45% of the total population belongs to the labour force (see table 2.8). In Norway, Sweden, Finland, Denmark, and Switzerland, this varies between 49–57%. In the Scandinavian countries, female labour participation is relatively high. All together, 60% of eligible males and 40% of eligible females have a job in the labour market.[21] In eastern European countries, 48% of the total population is working, with Bulgaria taking the lead with 56%. Female participation is also relatively high in these countries—on average 42%. High female participation in the workforce affects, for example, the need for child care, prepared foods, shopping hours and restaurant services.

Gross domestic product and private consumption expenditure (PCE) *per capita* vary widely across countries. In Switzerland and Liechtenstein they are the highest, with private expenditures being $21,602 and $16,129 respectively. This affects the EFTA average positively. In the EU, there is a considerable difference between north and south. Greece, Portugal, Spain and also Ireland have private expenditures *per capita* below $8,000. Expenditure in Eastern Europe is even lower.

Consumer spending

The primary needs of food and shelter take up the largest part of the budget. In addition, because primary needs for food and clothing are fulfilled first, the percentage of a low budget spent on these items tends to be large.[22] Table 2.9 shows that Eastern European countries spend almost half of household budgets on food and clothing, whereas in the west this figure is less than 30%. Expenditure on housing, health and transport tends to be lower in the East, however, and this may be partly due to different prices, climate, and urbanization.

Several types of expenditure are typical for individual countries. For example, spending on alcoholic drinks comprises 16% of the budget in Bulgaria and 12% in Ireland. Swedish consumers spend 33% and the Danish spend 29% on housing and housing fuels. In The Netherlands, Belgium,

Table 2.8 *Labour and income in Europe*[23]

	EU	EFTA	Eastern Europe
Labour participation	42.5%	52.8%	47.6%
Female participation	34.5	45.9	43.3
GDP *per capita* (US$)	22,695	39,560	2,436
PCE *per capita* (US$)	13,562	21,725	1,338

Figure 2.2 *Checking out*

Table 2.9 *Consumer spending on categories in percentage of total spending*[24]

	EU	EFTA	Eastern Europe
Food, drinks, tobacco	18.8%	24.0%	39.3%
Clothing, footware	6.9	4.5	7.8
Housing, housing fuels	20.4	21.3	9.0
Household goods	7.8	4.8	4.8
Health	6.7	9.8	4.8
Transport, communication	15.6	12.2	7.5
Leisure	9.1	9.1	7.3
Others	14.8	14.4	19.6

Switzerland and France, over 10% of the budget is spend on health. In Ireland and Germany, leisure comprises over 11% of the budget.

Average spending figures tell little about the spending of individual households, which may vary according to different tastes, budgets and scale economies. Large households spend relatively little on housing, household appliances and food as compared with small households. In general, it is cheaper per individual to live with four persons in one house, using the same washing machine or television, and preparing one meal than with one or two persons in a household.[25] Usually, social benefit allowances take economies of scale into account. The OECD family equivalence scale implies that the first adult needs 100% of the budget, each additional adult needs 70% and each child (below 14 years of age) needs 50%.[26] For example, a family with two young children needs 270% of the one-person household budget.

2.4 Conclusions

The most important demographic developments in Europe have been considered in this chapter. These include aspects such as the move towards older populations with fewer young people, and shrinking household size. These developments will influence consumer demand because of different needs and greater financial means. Products and services contributing to a more comfortable life will become more popular. Also, the demand for housing, furniture and appliances will increase because of decreasing scale economies.

Furthermore, education, social class, residence, religion, labour participation and income have been dealt with. An increasing level of education may affect demand for cultural events and books. Also, the development of the EU may affect the demand for European issues in the mass media. A trend towards democratization implies that exclusive items will become common property. Communication and transportation will become more important with the development of the EU, increasing the demand for fast railway and airline connections, especially between the major cities. Differences in religion between north and south will sustain differences in norms and values in the EU for a fairly long time. In Scandinavian and Eastern European countries, female labour participation is somewhat higher than in Western Europe (table 2.8), affecting the need for domestic services and time-saving consumables.

The general factors considered in this chapter can be used for market segmentation. The data is often available because statistical agencies gather this type of information on a regular basis. In this way, consumers and households may be easily characterized. This relates to segmentation at the general level. Chapter 24 deals with market segmentation in more detail.

Notes

1. 'Greying' is a term used to describe the increase of people in the 60+ age bracket. (table 2.3). 'De-greening' refers to a reduction in the numbers of young people in the population.
2. Guinness (1994) *The Guinness European Data Book* (London, Guinness Publishing Ltd).
3. Organisation for Economic Co-operation and Development (1997), *National Accounts* Volume 1 (Paris: OECD). IMF (1996) *International Financial*

Statistics (Washington DC: IMF). Eurostat (1997) *Demographic Statistics* 1997 (Luxembourg: Eurostat).

4. Eurostat (1997) *Demographic Statistics 1997* (Luxembourg: Eurostat). United Nations (1995) World Population Prospects. The 1994 Revision. (New York: United Nations).

5. Euromonitor (1994) *European Marketing Data and Statistics* (London: Euromonitor Publications).

6. Eurostat (1992) *Europe in Figures* (Luxembourg: Eurostat) (3rd edition).

7. Euromonitor (1994).

8. Van Praag, B. M. S., Dubnoff, S. and van der Sar, N. L. (1988) 'On the measurement and explanation of standards with respect to income, age and education' *Journal of Economic Psychology* 9, 481–498.

9. Underhill, L. and Caldwell, F. (1983) 'What age do you feel: age perception study' *Journal of Consumer Marketing* (Summer).

10. Eurostat (1997) Yearbook 1996 (Luxembourg: Eurostat).

11. See section 21.5.

12. Readers' Digest Eurodata (1990).

13. Euromonitor (1994).

14. Euromonitor (1994).

15. For an overview, see Chisnall, P. M. (1995) *Consumer Behaviour* (London: McGraw-Hill).

16. Countries: France, UK, W. Germany, Italy, Netherlands, Belgium, Spain, Ireland. World Values Study Group. World Values Survey, 1981–1984 and 1990–1993 [computer file]. ICPSR version. Ann Arbor, MI: Institute for Social Research [producer], 1994. Ann Arbor, MI: Inter-university Consortium for Political and Social Research [distributor], 1994.

17. Euromonitor (1994).

18. Whitaker's Almanac (1998) (London: J. Whitaker & Sons Ltd), p. 782.

19. Guinness (1994).

20. *World Values Survey* (1990) based on Norway and countries from the EU, except Sweden, Austria, Portugal, Greece and Luxembourg. These figures are only 1–3 percent lower than those in 1981.

21. Euromonitor (1996).

22. See section 4.2 on Engel curves.

23. Euromonitor (1997) *European Marketing Data and Statistics* (London: Euromonitor). IMF (1997) *International Financial Statistics*. June (Washington D.C.: IMF). IMF (1996) *International Financial Statistics Yearbook* (Wasington D.C.: IMF).

24. Euromonitor (1996).

25. See section 13.3.

26. OECD (1982) 'The OECD list of social indicators' (Paris: OECD).

CULTURAL DEVELOPMENT 3

3.1 Introduction

Culture includes societal knowledge, values and norms.[1] Culture also includes objects and behaviours that reflect these values and norms. Objects not only include works of art but also services and products, their packaging and advertising. Ancient cultures are studied by examining their remnants—discovered through excavations of towns and villages and by studying the remains of people and animals. Furthermore, writings are also of great importance. Parents and teachers play an important part in the transfer of culture to children. Cultural changes occur by technological and social innovations, by the influence of innovators and by the influx of foreigners from different cultures.

It is useful to consider a number of basic values of Western European culture. These values were developed from the Greek, Roman and Christian cultures. They characterize the current Western cultures in Europe, North America, Central America, South America and Australia/New Zealand.

- *Freedom and democracy*: These values stem from the ancient Greek culture, which featured independent city-states such as Athens with a democratic government. All the male inhabitants of those cities could participate in the city policy-making.
- *Own responsibility and individualism*: these are Calvinist values in Western European culture. Calvinists are responsible for developing their own ethical norms based on Bible study—they cannot refer to statements by clerical authorities. In contrast, faith in a clerical hierarchy exists in the Catholic church: the priest, bishop and pope set rules to which the believers submit. Responsibility for self and individualism are stressed in humanism.
- Mankind is the *steward of nature*. This is a Judaeo-Christian value, stating

that people may use what nature offers but that this carries a duty of care. This value is topical because of current concerns about the environment. Campaigns for saving the environment appeal to this sense of responsibility for nature, which is experienced by many people.

- *Equality of all people* is a value stemming from the French and American revolutions. Brotherhood and humanity were added during the French revolution. Everyone must be given equal opportunities and possibilities. Discrimination based on race, origin, religion or gender must be rejected.
- Since the Age of Reason, Western culture has been characterized by a *linear, exact time perspective*. This suggests growth and continuous improvements of culture, welfare and well-being. Rebuilding Europe after the Second World War, the Marshall Plan and the German Wirtschaftswunder in the 1950s and 1960s created a feeling of progress, but the defeat of certain ideologies has seriously affected trust in progress.[2] In postmodern thinking there is little trust in progress.

In section 3.2, culture is related to consumer behaviour. Section 3.3 deals with the transfer of culture to children and immigrants. Cultural changes may be compared with the diffusion of innovations. Section 3.4 considers the diffusion of culture among (parts of) the population by means of the mass media and intermediaries. This chapter mainly describes economic–cultural development (section 3.5), development of emancipation (section 3.6) and the development of materialism and societal values (section 3.7). Section 3.8 continues with some thoughts on future cultural developments, characterized by postmodernism.[3] Section 3.9 concludes this chapter with a brief summary of the key issues.

The aim of this chapter is to describe culture, the transfer of culture and cultural developments, and to show their relevance to consumer behaviour.

3.2 Culture defined

Cultural changes belong to the external environment of companies and consumers, although both are also parts of that culture. Yet, we consider culture as external, because a consumer or a company alone can hardly exert any influence on cultural development. For marketeers, culture is part of the data to be considered in marketing management. Culture enters the firm by the opinions and behaviour of consumers and employees and by the societal adoption or rejection of government measures. To the consumer, culture forms a basis of judgment, for instance, for determining what is modern or postmodern.

What exactly is culture? Does it include only pieces of art in galleries and museums, or visual and performing art? Does culture belong to the domain of artists? Culture is defined as the totality of societal knowledge, norms and values. A norm is a rule of conduct, a certain sense of what people ought to do in particular circumstances, for example, to let women pass first through a door, except when entering an unknown (and possibly dangerous) situation. A value is a sense of what should be maintained or achieved, for example peace or good health. Culture concerns values and norms shared by many people and determines and sustains social behaviour. So, traditions, habits, procedures, ideologies, styles and symbols are all elements of culture.

Definition

Culture is the entirety of societal knowledge, norms and values.

Culture must be supported by groups of people. A private belief is not a culture. Minority beliefs may form a subculture, such as the subcultures of ethnic minorities in Europe.[4] It is the convictions of a large group that form a culture. This implies that groups of people may change and adapt their culture. Some people form the leading edge or elite by introducing new cultural elements (e.g., fashion and style) which may be accepted or rejected later by larger groups of people.[5] Conversely, the dominant culture influences people's beliefs and behaviour.

Norms and values are part of the 'non-material' culture. Material products such as durable goods, pictures, books, movies and architecture all reflect this underlying culture. Nevertheless, people frequently look at the same product in different ways. To a diplomat, a taxi-driver, a naturalist or a designer, a car may be a different object. To the diplomat, it may be a status symbol; to the taxi-driver, it is an efficient means of transport; to the naturalist, it is a disturber of peace and quiet and an environmental pollutant; and to the designer, it is either a good design or not. Each individual has his or her own interpretation and gives his or her own meaning to the material objects. Certain meanings become dominant whereas other meanings gradually become less important. This is part of cultural change.

Culture has been defined in terms of norms and values. *Norms* are beliefs regarding how to behave (do's) or not to behave (don'ts). People differ in the extent to which they accept and comply with norms. Norms and values create expectations and criteria regarding the conduct of others.

Definition

Norms are group beliefs of how to behave or how not to behave.

Definition

Values are stable beliefs regarding desired behaviour or end states.

Values are core beliefs or standards used to judge one's own behaviour and that of others. Values often have a religious, ideological or humanistic background. From values, *goals* may be derived. Terminal values are values at which human endeavour is aimed. They constitute desired end-states such as 'happiness' or 'peace'. In addition, instrumental values exist, intermediate on the route to the ultimate goal.[6] Terminal values refer to ultimate goals, and instrumental values are the means to achieve these ultimate goals. For example, 'honesty' may be an instrumental value in achieving the ultimate goal of 'world peace'. Honesty may also be a terminal value.

Culture may be dealt with at four different levels (see figure 3.1). Firstly, culture is the totality of norms and values in society (A). This culture co-determines the consumer's sense of what's right, preferences and behaviour (B). Also, the material culture is important (C): the goods, services, ads, organizations and buildings in daily life. They are reflections of the non-material culture.[7] For example, Levi's 501 jeans may be said to symbolize the freedom and independence of the West. Fourthly, the corporate culture of the firm includes the dominant beliefs of the employees (D). The latter type of culture belongs to the internal environment and is frequently called the corporate identity.

Culture is continuously changing. Artists, well-known personalities, innovators and other people may influence cultural developments. Usually, culture changes gradually but noticeably. The cultures of the 1960s ('baby boomers'), the 1980s ('no nonsense'—the new realism) and the 1990s (postmodernist) are clearly different from one another. Culture seems to change faster than before.

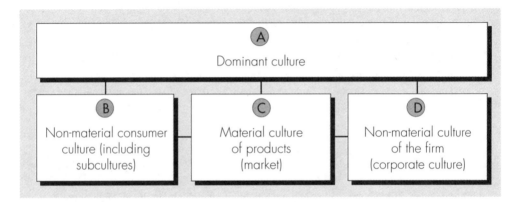

Figure 3.1 *Four levels of culture*

Table 3.1 *Characteristics of premodern, modern and postmodern times*[10]

	Premodern	Modern	Postmodern
Production	Agriculture, handiwork, farming	Industrial production, factory	Information production, office
Society	Feudal	Capitalism	Liberal capitalism
Orientation	Local	National	Global, local
Time perception	Cyclical	Linear	Fragmented, parallel
Culture	Aristocratic	Bourgeois, Mass culture	Fragmented

Three waves

History may be partitioned into three periods: the pre-modern, modern and postmodern times. This coincides with Alvin Toffler's three 'waves' (see table 3.1).[8] In premodern times, agriculture was the most important means of sustaining life. Farmers in that period had a cyclical time perspective of sowing and harvesting. Households comprised three-generation extended families (grandparents, parents and children) and sometimes included uncles, aunts, cousins and nieces. Society was feudal. Landowners, nobility and the clergy were dominant. The 'leisure class', to use Veblen's terms, was recruited from nobility.[9]

In modern times, industrial production became an important source of income. Industry supplies mass products. The time perspective became 'progressive' and linear. Workers moved into cities and the household was reduced to the core family of husband, wife and children. The middle-classes obtained power and dominated the culture. A mass culture emerged in which, especially after the Second World War, more and more people could participate.

Postmodern times are considered in section 3.8.

3.3 Transfer of culture

How does culture change? Is it caused by a brilliant fashion designer or by a convincing publicist initiating the changes? Is there a cultural 'leading-edge' of trend-setters serving as innovators and opinion leaders? Is it a higher social class buying new products and services, copies of which are then purchased by others at a later time (trickle-down)? Or is it a 'trickle-up' process as was the case with the 'mini' and punk fashion? Which agencies transfer culture? These questions are not easy to answer. It is a mix of conservative and innovative forces; of agents benefiting from conservation and of agents striving for changes in norms and values.

> **Definition**
>
> Socialization is the transfer of culture to new generations.

Two main cultural transfer processes are distinguished: socialization and acculturation.

Socialization

Culture is transferred from the older to the younger generation by parents, schools, churches, clubs and other agents. This is called the socialization or education of children. Acceptance of the dominant culture is important to the young generation if they are to function properly in society. Reverse socialization takes place when children educate their parents, for example, showing them how to operate their computers or video recorders, and telling them about new trends in fashion and music.

> **Definition**
>
> Acculturation is the transfer of culture to adults who have grown up in different cultures.

Acculturation

A similar transfer of culture occurs when individuals from a different culture settle into an existing one. This is called acculturation. This concerns people who have grown up and are socialized in a different culture and who then work and live in another country. Acculturation of immigrants is generally only partly successful. Ethnic minorities frequently form their own cultures, including their own habits and consumer behaviour (subculture) within the culture of the country concerned.[11] The variety of subcultures in Europe leads toward a multicultural society.

Socialization agents

Several persons and authorities involved in socialization are listed in table 3.2. In the first place, parents raise their children, teach them good manners, such as eating with knife and fork, and try to prevent the formation of bad habits such as swearing. This way, norms and values are transferred implicitly. Older brothers and sisters and relatives also play a part in this process. Family influence is strongest during early childhood. As mentioned before, some reverse socialization takes place when children are teaching their parents. There is a Dutch saying that men are educated three times: by their mother, by their wife and by their daughter.

When children go to school, friends and peers become important. At this

Figure 3.2 *Chinese or European?*

age, children are conformist and imitate reference individuals, popular peers and older children of importance to them. Generally, they are sensitive to being accepted by others. Wearing the right clothes is important. Certain brands like Nike and Levi's are trendy and children like to wear these brands to feel a sense of belonging.

As an example, starting smoking is mainly determined by parents and children's friends. Parents serve as role models if they smoke at home and offer cigarettes to people at parties and to visitors. If smoking is customary in the circle of friends, young people like to conform: they are offered cigarettes, they then buy cigarettes to hand out and start smoking themselves.[13] Tobacco advertising appears less important than social influence in starting smoking. Not only is culture transferred via social agents but also behaviour is imitated (learning by observation).

Table 3.2 *Agents involved in cultural transfer*

Agents	Age (years)	Most important values[12]
Parents	0	Obedience, cleanliness, honesty
Brothers, sisters	2	Responsibility, social recognition
School, teachers	6	Ambition, capability, logical behaviour
Friends	6	Courage, social recognition
Church	6	Honesty, peace, salvation, forgiveness
(Sport) clubs	12	Ambition, courage
Mass media	12	Pleasure, intellect

The disposition to conform conflicts with the disposition to be unique. Everyone needs to become similar to other people to some extent and to imitate others' behaviours and cultural values, just to be able to function in society. At the same time, however almost everyone wants to be independent and unique, holding individual opinions and behaving independently.[14] The resultant behaviour then constitutes the balance of compliant and independent behaviours and beliefs.

Teachers at school, priests, vicars, sport coaches and musical teachers are socialization agents, who, in addition to specific knowledge and skills, transfer culture and behaviour examples. Especially during puberty their influence becomes important, often at the expense of the influence of the parents.

The mass media show children what is happening in the world by means of television programmes, radio and magazines—political developments, sport news, popular music, movies and information about pop stars, for example. The mass media appeal to intellect (documentaries) and relaxation (game shows and comedies).[15] Pop stars are the idols of many young people, serving as models for their behaviour.

The processes of socialization and acculturation are mainly conservative. It is of great importance to the older generation to transfer their beliefs faithfully to the younger generation or to ethnic minorities. However, the *status quo* is never completely maintained and in this way gradual cultural

Figure 3.3 *Growing up?*

UNIVERSITY OF CHESTER, WARRINGTON CAMPUS

changes occur. Moreover, mass media like MTV go against the dominant culture and initiate renewal. Cultural elements of ethnic minorities also bring about renewal and may eventually be included in the dominant culture, such as for example Turkish and Chinese restaurants.

Art, fashion and technological developments are innovative forces contributing to cultural change. Small groups with great persuasiveness and access to the mass media may influence the dominant culture out of all proportion to their size. Women's liberation is an example of this. Feminists in many West European countries have formed small but influential groups, helped especially by their good contacts with the media. An innovation brought about by a minority may affect the majority of the population.[16] This does not imply that feminism is accepted by all women (and men) in its extreme form. But in a moderated form, it has become part of the dominant culture. This also applies to the peace movement, the environmental conservation movement and consumerism.

Two main groups of cultural changes may be distinguished: the *economic-cultural development* regarding opinions about the economic situation, unemployment and government budget cuts and the *emancipatory-cultural development* regarding opinions about women's liberation, sexuality, marriage and the family. These two developments are separate from each other. Economically-cultural conservative individuals may be emancipatory and sexually progressive.

Both main developments are important to consumer behaviour and will be dealt with separately, in addition to other cultural trends. The latter will be categorized as *materialism and societal opinions* such that three main groups of cultural trends emerge that are important to the study of consumer behaviour.[17]

3.4 Processes of cultural change

Usually, the processes of socialization and acculturation imply a gradual cultural change because transfer agents tend to favour cultural continuity rather than jeopardize their powerful position. In contrast, innovative forces are less conservative. Four processes of change may be distinguished: cohort effects, age effects, democratization and exclusivation.

A *cohort effect* occurs if the acceptance of new values and behaviours begins at a young age and these values and behaviours are retained over the years. So people born between 1960 and 1965 are described as the cohort 60–65. These people were born, raised and have grown up in the same time period. New opinions about sexuality and marriage mainly emerge from young people. These values spread in society because young people grow older and the 'old' values gradually disappear with the extinction of the older cohorts. Thus, a cohort effect implies a slow cultural change, as it may take 25–30 years before the new values are held by a majority of the population, assuming that the cohort constitutes the majority.

An *age effect* occurs if certain values or behaviours are associated with a particular age group. Visiting the nightclub is an example of an age effect. Visitors to clubs are usually from the 15–25 years age bracket. When these visitors grow older, they select another type of leisure. As another example, the use of certain medical and social facilities tends to be limited to the elderly. This constitutes age-bound consumer behaviour.

Cohort effects and age effects may occur simultaneously. Consider the following fictitious example. Table 3.3 shows participation in sport activities. The table shows percentages of people practising sports. It includes four cohorts concerning dates of birth 1941–1945, 1946–1950, 1951–1955 and 1956–1960. There are six intervals in which sport participation has been measured: 1951–1955, 1956–1960, 1960–1965, 1966–1970, 1971–1975 and 1976–1980. It appears that each cohort participates less in sports, the older it grows. The type of sports may also

Figure 3.4 *Roller-blading*

differ. Older people play golf rather than hockey. In addition, it appears that each new cohort practises 5% more sport than does the preceding cohort.[18]

In the sports example both an age effect and a cohort effect can be distinguished. Table 3.4 shows the age effect: every five years a cohort grows older, sporting activities decrease by 5%. Table 3.5 shows the cohort effect. Participation in sport of each new cohort is 5% higher than the preceding cohort.

After adding the percentages of tables 3.4 and 3.5, the percentages of table 3.3 result. The effects are additive. In this example, the age effect is stronger than the cohort effect. Obviously, maximum participation in sports will be somewhere between 90 and 100%, assuming that not everyone will participate. The cohort effect cannot change culture completely.

Democratization means a cultural levelling, in the sense that cultural differences across social classes decrease, perhaps because workers become bourgeois citizens and show the behaviour and consumption pattern of the middle-class. Democratization results from an increasing level of general welfare, the influence of the mass media and the stress on the equality ideal. For that matter, democratization is a Western value. Values may spread quickly, although there are also many examples of slow

Table 3.3 *Participation in sports (in percentages)*

Cohorts	1951–55	1956–60	1961–65	1966–70	1971–75	1976–80
1941–1945	65	60	55	50	45	40
1946–1950		70	65	60	55	50
1951–1955			75	70	65	60
1956–1960				80	75	70

Table 3.4 *Age effect in sports (in percentages)*

Cohorts	1951–55	1956–60	1961–65	1966–70	1971–75	1976–80
1941–1945	60	55	50	45	40	35
1946–1950		60	55	50	45	40
1951–1955			60	55	50	45
1956–1960				60	55	50

Table 3.5 *Cohort effect in sports (in percentages)*

Cohorts	1951–55	1956–60	1961–65	1966–70	1971–75	1976–80
1941–1945	5	5	5	5	5	5
1946–1950		10	10	10	10	10
1951–1955			15	15	15	15
1956–1960				20	20	20

value adoption and diffusion.[19] Democratization occurs frequently, and this implies an increasing use of consumption goods by the lower classes. In addition, as shown in table 2.6, the social classes are converging.

Traditionally it has been stated that cultural goods spread from the higher to the lower social classes.[20] During this process cultural goods are popularized and thus become 'fallen cultural goods'. The work of art becomes a replica and the independent journey becomes mass tourism. In this view, consumption implies imitation of the higher social classes.

Several mechanisms of democratization have been described, including the trickle-down, trickle-up and trickle-across models of spreading.[21]

- The *trickle-down* model states that the lower social classes imitate the higher classes to gain status and recognition. A well-known example is the classical model of the spread of fashion clothes: from fashion designers to boutiques to department stores. During this process, the clothing becomes less exclusive and more of a mass-market product.
- The *trickle-up* model also occurs with fashion, for example the mini-look and punk fashion. These emerged from the youth market and spread, after some adaptation, to other consumers with higher incomes. Drinking beer, buying goods at an open-air market and do-it-yourself activities also show a trickle-up spread from lower to higher classes.
- The *trickle-across* model assumes a combination of mass production, mass media and mass consumption, at the same time allowing everyone to adopt the cultural change. This concerns horizontal rather than vertical spread, implicitly assuming a more or less homogeneous market.[22] The adoption of consumer products such as microwave ovens follows this pattern.

Exclusivation is the reverse of democratization, occurring less frequently in practice. An example is cigar smoking, being relatively common among men in former days. Now it is limited to a small group of both men and women. Exclusivation implies limited social spreading of values, goods and behaviour. It occurs if a cultural change is limited to a certain group, for example the cultural leading edge or elite. Exclusivity is sometimes used as a marketing strategy (the concept of the limited edition) to justify a higher price and to suggest a future increase in value of the good. Also, associations and clubs sometimes purposefully limit their membership (for example, Freemasonry, Rotary and Lions). Cultural and political convictions and also scientific knowledge are sometimes made exclusive by jargon, thus being less accessible to outsiders.

3.5 Economic-cultural developments since 1970

The first part of the 1970s was characterized by pessimism about the environment and economic growth. The Club of Rome's report and the oil crisis were important in this respect.[23] Economic growth stagnated and inflation increased. Consumer confidence in the economy was shocked by the oil crisis of 1973 and increased thereafter. The public sector has grown markedly in these years.

From 1979 on, consumption expenditures decreased. In many countries, governments' budget deficits increased far too much. The first part of the 1980s was characterized by recession. Unemployment increased and the consumer's purchasing power decreased. At the end of the 1980s, budget cuts in the public sector were prevalent.

The recession and increased unemployment in the early 1990s implied that many people in society became dependent on the working population, often for several years. Next to income, time became an important segmentation variable in the marketing of products. Consumers can substitute time and money. They can save money by undertaking DIY projects, and time by using ready-made products.[24]

Demographic development has already been described in chapter 2. The birth rate is declining, causing decreasing numbers of young people.[25] This will become evident on the labour market and in consumption patterns at the beginning of the next century. Fewer young people suggests a reduced cohort effect of cultural change and consequently relatively slow cultural change.[26] In addition, the majority of society consists of older people with their relatively traditional values.

Consumer confidence

Economic-cultural changes can be considered from different points of view. In the *Consumer Survey*, carried out in all EU member countries (except Luxembourg), *consumer confidence* is measured on a monthly basis. Participants in the survey answer questions about the economic situation of the country, inflation and several questions about the possibility and rationality of saving. On the basis of five questions, the Index of Consumer Sentiment (ICS) is computed.[27] The ICS is available in the EU from 1973 onwards: see figure 3.5.

Definition

Consumer confidence summarizes consumers' opinions regarding economic growth, their personal financial situation and the purchasing climate.

The ICS predicted the economic recessions of 1973 (oil crisis), 1979 (second energy crisis) and the early 1990s. In the early 1970s, the ICS was relatively high and optimism prevailed. Soon, however, the ICS decreased rapidly and pessimism was dominant. Thereafter, the ICS recovered until the late 1970s, when a new decline occurred. In the early 1980s the ICS

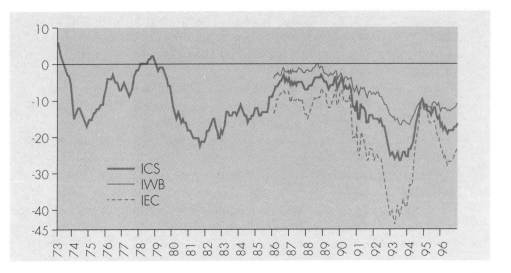

Figure 3.5 *Indicators of consumer sentiment, willingness to buy and economic climate (Source: European Commission, DG II)*

reached an absolute low. In 1983, the index recovered gradually until the late 1980s. In the early 1990s, another decline occurred, which was the forerunner of a new recession from which economies then started to recover.

The ICS can be considered a good indicator of optimism and consumer confidence. Together with income, especially discretionary income, the ICS is a significant predictor of (mainly discretionary) spending and saving.[28] Discretionary expenditures and savings can be delayed or cancelled, or they can be reduced. The mass media can bring about significant changes by reporting optimistic or pessimistic news.

Figure 3.5 shows two more indices: the Index of Willingness to Buy (IWB) and the Index of the Economic Climate (IEC). The IWB is based on three questions and mainly measures buying intentions regarding durable goods. The IEC is based on two questions and measures opinion regarding the economic condition of the country in which the consumer lives. The ICS is the weighted average of the IWB and IEC scores.

Political-economic opinions

Most countries in western Europe have developed more or less as welfare states, in which individuals can rely on social security benefits if they become unemployed, disabled, retired or cannot find a job. This is associated with relatively high levels of taxes and social security premiums which affect the level of wages and after-tax income. Table 3.6 shows that support for the welfare state is not generally high in Western European countries. Individual responsibility for income and wealth is supported more than

Table 3.6 *Opinions on responsibility for income and ownership in Europe (1990)*[29]

	Disagree	Neither agree nor disagree	Agree
Incomes should be made more equal *versus there should be greater incentives for individual effort*	23.4%	41.1%	35.5%
Private ownership of business and industry should be increased *versus government ownership of business and industry should be increased*	39.9%	49.1%	11.0%
Individuals should take more responsibility for providing for themselves *versus the state should take more responsibility to ensure that everyone is provided for*	35.9%	41.5%	22.5%
People who are unemployed should have to take any job available or lose their unemployment benefits *versus they should have the right to refuse a job they do not want*	42.8%	38.0%	19.2%

Note: percentages refer to the second alternative (italicized) in the statements.

state responsibility. Furthermore, income distribution on the basis of individual effort is supported more than equal income distribution. It seems that the political-economic situation is ready for deregulation and self-regulation by employers and employees.

Consequences for consumer behaviour

Economic-cultural changes have important consequences for consumer behaviour. Consumer confidence partly determines expenditure and savings. In the case of prevailing optimism concerning the future, consumers spend more on durables, luxury goods and services than in the case of prevailing pessimism. In the case of optimism, relatively little is saved and relatively more credit is taken. Consumers dare to invest in the future.

In the case of prevailing pessimism, i.e., a low level of consumer confidence, expenditure tends to decrease, especially on discretionary goods and services, such as cars, caravans, holiday trips, antiques, restaurants and luxury clothing. Pessimistic consumers save to have a buffer as a precaution against an uncertain future.

The economic-cultural opinions point to a conservative direction. This is consistent with a decreasing public sector, lower social benefits, privatization and deregulation. This implies less solidarity with the unemployed and disabled, and more stress on individual performance and consequent reward. In this scenario, companies can expect less govern-ment regulation and more self-regulation, for example between producers and consumers, and between employers and employees. A conservative trend strengthens the role and the importance of the business community, but decreases the purchasing power of households dependent on social security. Furthermore, a decreasing public sector may stimulate both the market sector and the household sector. For example, in several countries postal services and utility companies have been sold by the government. Also households are taking up 'caring' tasks, such as taking care of the sick and the elderly.

In this situation, a polarization of households occurs. High-income, two-earner households are concentrated at one extreme whereas at the other extreme we find households dependent on social benefits. In between we find one-earner and one-person households. Except for an increasing income gap, these types of household also differ regarding time available for shopping, housekeeping, consumption and recreation, including media behaviour. On the one hand, there are households with little free time and a limited time budget for housekeeping because of a busy and demanding career. This group demands time-saving, ready-made products and services and long opening hours of shops and banks. On the other hand, there are unemployed households with ample free time and a lifestyle adapted to this situation. This group demands inexpensive DIY products and discount shops. It is expected that shop types, products and services will position themselves differently. One type will focus on service and comfort, whereas the other will focus on low price. Middle-of-the-road shops and products run the risk of appealing to neither of these groups.

3.6 Emancipation

The second main group of cultural developments concerns emancipation, including opinions regarding marriage and role patterns. These develop-ments mainly occur independently from the economic–cultural develop-ments.

In contrast with the swinging 1960s, it seems that family values are more favoured now (see table 3.7). Relatively few people say that marriage is an outdated institution and those who hold this opinion are decreasing in number. The need for children and the family environment for children both obtained more support in 1990 than in 1981. This is consistent with the small increase in birth rate in the early 1990s, considered in chapter 2. In contrast, support for one-parent families, having an extramarital affair and for divorce remained stable or decreased slightly. For marketing, this implies that family issues are becoming more important, for example, joint family activities (eating out, holidays, household fairs, etc.), insurance (child-care, partner policies, etc.) and home products (decoration, bed-

Table 3.7 *Opinions on marriage in Europe*[30]

Opinion-eliciting statements	1981	1990
Marriage is an out-dated institution	18.7%	16.4% (yes)
Do you think that a woman needs to have children in order to be fulfilled or is this not necessary?	41.9%	45.4% (needs)
If someone says a child needs a home with both a father and a mother to grow up happily, would you agree or disagree?	78.1%	88.4% (agree)
If a woman wants to have a child as a single parent but she doesn't want to have a stable relationship with a man, do you approve or disapprove?	42.5%	42.5% (approve)
Can men/women having an affair always be justified, never be justified or in-between?	73.2%	72.4% (never)
Can divorce always be justified, never be justified or in-between?	50.3%	49.7% (never)

Table 3.8 *Opinions on role patterns*[31]

Opinion-eliciting statements	1980	1990
	(percentage agreeing with statement)	
A working mother can establish just as warm and secure a relationship with her children as a mother who does not work.	—[a]	68.5
A pre-school child is likely to suffer if his or her mother works.	—[a]	60.7
A job is alright but what most women really want is a home and children.	—[a]	55.4
Being a housewife is just as fulfilling as working for pay.	—[a]	60.6
Having a job is the best way for a woman to be an independent person.	—[a]	71.0
Both the husband and wife should contribute to household income.	—[a]	73.6
Sharing household chores is very important for a successful marriage.	25.3	20.1

[a] Not available

room, kitchen and bathroom products, etc.). As the number of children is still decreasing in the long run, it seems that the family is capitalizing on quality rather than quantity.

Concerning role patterns, the opinions in Europe reflect the combination of work roles and household roles (see table 3.8). In general, women's paid work is preferred. It seems not to harm her relationship with the children, although pre-school children may suffer.

This implies that many women will participate in the labour market and they will have their own income. Probably, they will decide for themselves how to spend the extra income. It is expected that women will spend more money on themselves—buying items such as personal care, travelling and eating out. At the same time, the needs for child day-care, long opening hours of shops and teleshopping may increase.

Although sharing household chores may be considered as not very important for a successful marriage, female labour participation does require a more flexible role distribution between partners. This might encourage more role specialization and/or more communication and deliberation between husband and wife, e.g., for shopping, household chores, and financial management. Advertising needs to be directed to both partners in many instances. For example, a car is no longer exclusively a man's product. Shopping is no longer exclusively a woman's activity.

3.7 Materialism and societal opinions

The third main group of values includes materialism and societal opinions. This concerns questions regarding economic growth and environmental effects, and individual development and participation in society. In contrast with section 23.4, materialism is considered as a cultural value rather than as a personality trait.

In the 1970s, a shift from materialist values and physical safety to the quality of life was observed in the younger generation. This was based on four surveys held during 1971–1976 in ten Western countries.[32] The pattern of values consisted of several dimensions, the first of which was materialism versus postmaterialism. Postmaterialist values were stronger in industrialized countries, especially for young people. The shift from materialist to postmaterialist values was mainly due to a cohort effect. The World Values Survey included questions regarding the values concerned, several of which were asked both in 1981 and 1990. Table 3.9 shows four values, of which the most important or second most important value was indicated. 'Giving people more to say' and 'Protecting freedom of speech' reflect postmaterialist values, whereas 'Maintaining order' and 'Fighting higher prices' reflect materialist values.

The four values of table 3.9 are representative of the total set, comprising 12 items. It appeared that the shift toward postmaterialist values continued from 1981 to 1990. People found maintaining order in the nation and fighting rising prices less important and giving people more say and protecting freedom of speech more important in 1990 than in 1981.

Other values of concern here refer to possessions, work, technology, individual development, authority, family life and lifestyle. Table 3.10 shows

Table 3.9 *Materialist versus postmaterialist values in Europe*[33]

What's most important?	1981	1990
	(percentage agreeing with statement)	
Maintaining order in the nation	63.7	51.4
Giving people more say in important government decisions	41.0	46.3
Fighting rising prices	48.0	45.2
Protecting freedom of speech	35.8	48.6

Table 3.10 *Opinions about societal issues in Europe*[35]

Suggested changes	1981	1990
	(percentage agreeing with statement)	
Less emphasis on money and material possessions	13.0	14.6
Decrease in the importance of work in our lives	46.1	49.6
More emphasis on the development of technology	19.4	18.5
Greater emphasis on the development of the individual	3.9	3.4
Greater respect for authority	20.4	23.9
More emphasis on family life	3.0	2.5
A simple and more natural lifestyle	4.8	4.7

whether people think positively about changes in these factors. Material possessions, work and technology are favoured slightly less in 1990 than in 1981, consistent with the shift toward postmaterialist values. Individual development and family life are less favoured, pointing to a preference for the development of (non-family) social relationships.[34] At the same time, greater respect for authority is increasingly favoured. Support for a simple and more natural lifestyle is generally low, indicating a preference for the consumption level currently achieved.

3.8 Postmodernism

In the 1970s and 1980s, more people were working in the information industry than in the production of commodities. Managers, teachers, students, accountants, public servants, lawyers, programmers, researchers, politicians are all greater in numbers than workers in factories and agriculture. Services beat production in this respect. This is the 'third wave' or postmodern era. Most professions deal with obtaining, transforming and integrating information and taking decisions on the basis of this information. As everyone can obtain information, (for example, from the Internet) quite individual interpretations of this information may occur. The most important characteristics of the three waves are shown in table 3.1.

Definition

Postmodernism is a cultural episode, characterized by a pluralism of (consumption) styles and ideologies, a need for hyper-reality and self-expression by means of consumption.

Postmodernism is a pluralism of styles and interpretations without one dominant style. Postmodern society is characterized by a form of liberal or social-democratic capitalism. The production system of free enterprise is combined with a system of social security for the elderly, the ill and the disabled. Orientation is global, partly because of the fast and extensive news reports (television) and the use of a military peace force of the United Nations (UN) in case of conflicts and wars. Famines and relief actions obtain worldwide attention. On a worldwide scale, the UN and the Red Cross try to offer help and to negotiate agreement among fighting parties. In addition to this global orientation, a local orientation regarding the own neighborhood and area of living exists. Local transmitters and local news also serve their listeners and viewers.

Postmodern culture is no longer a mass culture but is fragmented. Rather than only one dominant style, different styles exist next to each other. The 'modern' culture included a belief in progress. Ideologies such as communism, socialism, liberalism, anarchism, christianity and feminism each attracted followers and opponents. All of these ideologies aim at achieving a utopia. In postmodern times the ideologies have become less credible.[36] Postmodernism is recognizable in architecture, art and postmodern music.[37] Architecture, visual art and music are characterized by a combination of styles, a collage of modern and classical elements. In postmodern time many styles from the past are revived in adapted form. Modern buildings have Greek pillars and Louis XVI ornaments. Sculptors also make paintings. Separations between varieties of art are removed and intermediate forms emerge.

A second characteristic of postmodern art is parody. Double meanings and self-mockery are characteristic of the times. On a quasi-classical arcade at the Max Euwe square in Amsterdam it is inscribed solemnly: 'Homo sapiens non urinat in ventro'.[38] Art no longer has to propagate an ideological message.

For consumer behaviour, these postmodern technical and cultural changes lead to the following developments.

Fragmentation

Ideologies and consumer groups are fragmenting. The lack of a dominant ideology, culture or fashion obliges consumers to make their own choices and to adopt their own lifestyles. This is a time of secularization and tolerance of others. All styles and core values occur simultaneously or are quickly revived. Eclecticism is the trend to select from earlier styles. Ancient styles and style elements occur higgledy-piggledy. Some even state that consumer behaviour is becoming completely unpredictable. Fortunately, this is not the case, otherwise we could not have written this book. Changes occur faster than before, individualism is growing, brand loyalty decreases, and new criteria for segmentation have to be applied. However, consumer behaviour is far from unpredictable.

Fragmentation not only involves differences across consumers but also the range of behaviour of a single person. Madonna is an example of an artist portraying different images. Experiences regarding work, leisure, hobbies and sports may be very different. People also strive to have different experiences and possibly show a different image in their leisure than at work. The efficient manager is a loving father and a fanatic hockey player, too. Some even speak of a situational consumer and stress the different moods and preferences, depending on the situation.

Hyper-reality

Movies and plays always have dealt with imagination and hyper-reality (or virtual reality). Reality on stage or on the movie screen differs from daily reality. Escape from daily reality is the very reason to visit the cinema or the theatre. IMAX films and 3-D movies strongly involve the spectators in the event. Las Vegas and Disneyland Paris are examples of existing hyper-realities. Shopping malls in Edmonton (Alberta, Canada) and Minneapolis (Minnesota, USA) include amusement parks. MTV programmes and video clips recall hyper-realistic associations. Computer simulations may also create individual hyper-realities, including computer games. The player identifies with the hero of the game influencing the outcome of the situation. Postmodern thinkers consider the possibility that hyper-reality becomes even more important and interesting than reality itself.[39]

Value realization

Value realization tends to occur with the expressive use of products and brands, rather than with their production or purchase. Many consumers identify with their consumption activities, their sports and hobbies, their homes, cars and the brands they are using. The image of the product or brand may be the most important reason for purchase. Consumers may even be considered as 'brands in a market' themselves. In the process of 'self marketing' they position themselves, they maintain and confirm their images and make themselves popular with others. This has been described as self-monitoring.[40] People scoring high at self-monitoring are not so much paying attention to whether their behaviour is consistent with their preferences, norms and values but whether it is consistent with the situation. They behave in a chameleon-like fashion and adapt to others and to the situation.

Paradoxical juxtapositions

Women wearing expensive silk blouses with Levi's jeans are an example of a postmodern paradoxical juxtaposition. In architecture and art, incongruities and style mixtures can be observed. The paradox may even become a parody. In the UK, the cigarette brand Death became popular: a black package showing a skull and an abundantly clear warning against smoking. The package even mentions that 10% of the profit is going to cancer research. The brand ridicules health warnings and attracts smokers who accept that smoking is bad for their health.

Postmodern times seem fatalistic. We are not here to improve the world. So many people have already tried, which has led to totalitarian systems such as fascism and communism. We have to learn to live with one another and with the incongruities of the world. Everything is acceptable and at the same time suspect. On the one hand we are freed of ideologies but on the other hand we do not have any grip or support in our thinking and behaviour. Every protest is absorbed by the market as shown by the way that punk became a fashion style. Even the news is dominated by the market. Voters select attractive party leaders instead of political programmes. Consumers buy images rather than services and durable goods.

3.9 Conclusions

The cultural changes of the three main groups are partly autonomous and partly mutually dependent. There is hardly any connection between the economic-cultural developments and the trend of emancipation. The group of materialism and societal opinions is related to the economic-cultural developments to some extent.

After the dramatic recession at the beginning of the 1980s, consumer confidence and the market mechanism recovered and the government has withdrawn to some extent. Privatisation offers new opportunities for business. However, consumer confidence decreased again in the early 1990s, suggesting that society can hardly be controlled by the market and the government. Recently, consumer confidence has increased again.

Emancipation of workers, women and ethnic minorities creates a more individualistic society with less strict roles and social classes. New ways of living together are accepted. Marketing and advertising should no longer be aimed at men and women in particular social roles, but rather at individuals with many possibilities and task divisions.

Postmodern times do not consist of only one dominant style, fashion or ideology. Many styles and fashions exist next to each other, sometimes in paradoxical combinations. Hyper-reality, images and experiences have become more important at the expense of the striving for an ideal or utopia.

Notes

1. Values are further discussed in chapters 7 and 16.
2. Bell, D. (1962) *The End of Ideology* (New York: The Free Press) (revised edition).
3. Van Raaij, W. F. (1993) 'Postmodern consumption' *Journal of Economic Psychology* 14, 541–563.
4. See section 20.5.
5. This constitutes a form of spreading of an innovation. See section 15.4.
6. Rokeach, M. (1973) *The Nature of Human Values* (New York: The Free Press).
7. Douglas, M. and Isherwood, B. (1980) *The World of Goods* (Harmondsworth, Middlesex: Penguin Books).
8. Toffler, A. (1981) *The Third Wave* (New York: Bantam Books).
9. Veblen, T. (1899) *The Theory of the Leisure Class*.
10. Jencks, C. (1987) *What is Postmodernism?* (New York: Academy Editions), 47.
11. See section 20.5.
12. This table shows the values according to Rokeach (1973. See section 8.3.
13. Van Raaij, W. F. (1990), 'The effect of marketing communication on the initiation of juvenile smoking' *International Journal of Advertising* 9, 15–6.
14. Venkatesan, M. (1966) 'Consumer behavior: conformity and independence' *Journal of Marketing Research* 3, 384–387. Fromkin, H. L. and Snyder, C. R. (1980) 'The search for uniqueness and valuation of scarcity. Neglected dimensions of value in exchange theory' in: Gergen, K. J., Greenberg, M. S. and Willis R. H., (eds) *Social Exchange. Advances in Theory and Research.* (New York: Plenum Press), 57–75.
15. See also chapter 17.
16. Moscovici, S. and Nemeth, C. (1974) 'Social influence II: minority influence' in: Nemeth, C. (ed.) *Social Psychology. Classic and Contemporary Integrations* (Chicago: Rand McNally), 217–249.
17. These three main groups are: economic-cultural; emancipatory-cultural developments, and materialism and societal opinions.
18. These figures stem from the *Social and Cultural Report* (1992) of the Social and Cultural Planning Bureau, The Netherlands, pp. 299–301. The figures have been adapted somewhat to obtain pure cohort and age effects.
19. See sections 15.3 and 15.4 regarding the adoption and spreading of innovations.
20. Naumann, H. (1922) *Grundzüge der deutschen Volkskunde*.
21. Sproles, G. B. (1981) 'Analyzing fashion cycles, principles and perspectives' *Journal of Marketing*, 45, 116–124. See section 15.4.
22. A more extensive analysis of the adoption and spreading of fashion has been given by König, R. (1986) *Menschheit auf dem Laufsteg. Die Mode im Zivilisationsprozess* (München: Carl Hansen).
23. Meadows, D. H., Meadows, D. L., Randers, J. and Behrens III, W. W. (1972) *The Limits to Growth: A Report for the Club of Rome's Project on the Predicament of Mankind* (New York: Universe Books).
24. See section 13.6, table 13.6.

25. See section 2.3.
26. See chapter 2.
27. Katona, G. (1975) *Psychological Economics* (New York: Elsevier). Katona developed the ICS in the United States.
28. Van Raaij, W. F. (1991) 'The formation and use of expectations in consumer decision making' in: Robertson, T. S., and Kassarjian, H. H. (eds) *Handbook of Consumer Behavior* (Englewood Cliffs, NJ: Prentice-Hall), 401–418. Van Raaij, W. F., and Gianotten, H. J. (1990) 'Consumer confidence, expenditure, saving, and credit' *Journal of Economic Psychology* 11, 269–290.
29. *World Values Survey* (1990) including France, Britain, West Germany, Italy, Netherlands, Denmark, Belgium, Spain, Ireland, Northern Ireland, Hungary, Norway, Sweden, Iceland and Finland. Answers on a 10-point agree–disagree scale were combined as follows: agree = 1, 2, 3; neither agree nor disagree = 4. 5. 6. 7; disagree = 8, 9, 10. World Values Study Group. World Values Survey, 1981–1984 and 1990–1993 (computer file). ICPSR version. Ann Arbor, MI: Institute for Social Research (producer), 1994. Ann Arbor, MI: Inter-university Consortium for Political and Social Research (distributor), 1994.
30. *World Values Survey* (1990) as above.
31. *World Values Survey* (1990).
32. Inglehart, R. (1977) *The Silent Revolution. Changing Values and Political Styles among Western Publics* (Princeton: Princeton University Press).
33. *World Values Survey* (1990).
34. This lesser favouring of individual development and family life conflicts with the results shown in table 3.7. From table 3.7 we may conclude that family values are more favoured. This conflict shows that results have to be interpreted in the context of other questions asked in the same questionnaire. In the context of societal issues, individual development and family life seems to become less important (table 3.10). Asked separately (table 3.7), family life seems to become more important.
35. *World Values Survey* (1990).
36. Bell (1962).
37. Van Raaij (1993).
38. In a free translation this means: 'A wise man does not piss against the wind'.
39. Woolley, B. (1992) *Virtual Worlds. A Journey in Hype and Hyperreality* (Oxford: Blackwell).
40. Snyder, M. (1987) *Public Appearances/ Private Realities: The Psychology of Self-monitoring* (New York: Freeman).

SUPPLY AND USE OF PRODUCTS AND SERVICES 4

4.1 Introduction

This chapter gives a short overview of the history of consumption, from initial scarcity to current affluence. The consumption level in western European countries is well above subsistence level. Consumers' willingness to spend and their spending patterns, rather than the ability to produce, now determine the volume of sales. The consumer has become a 'powerful consumer' whose favour is sought by suppliers of goods and services.[1]

Supply is the starting point of the consumption cycle which describes how relationships between the consumers and their products and services evolve. The consumption cycle consists of four stages:

- stage 1: problem recognition and information search
- stage 2: purchase of product or service
- stage 3: use of product or service
- stage 4: disposal or replacement of product or service

Marketing focuses attention on the first two stages of the consumption cycle, while home economics focuses on the third stage. The fourth stage is especially important to environmental researchers as are the earlier stages of purchase and product use.

This chapter starts with the history of consumption in section 4.2. Section 4.3 describes the symbolic meaning of products and services including social exchange. Section 4.4 describes a typology of products. Section 4.5 describes the consumption cycle and distinguishes between duration of use, duration of ownership and the good's lifetime. Section 4.6 concludes with a summary of the chapter.

4.2 From scarcity to affluence

Before the industrial revolution the lower social classes faced a struggle for life. Food and other necessities were scarce and they could not even think of buying luxury goods. Leisure time was limited because working hours were long. Economics could predict the consumption of food, clothing and housing quite accurately because there was little freedom to deviate from the usual consumption pattern. A distinction can be made between necessary, inferior and luxury goods.

- *Necessary goods.* The Engel curve describes expenditure on food as a concave (marginally decreasing) function of household income.[2] With increasing income, the share of expenditure on food decreases. Because food is a necessity, it takes up a large part of the budget of the lower income groups but a smaller part of the budget of higher income groups. In figure 4.1 this is shown by the curve denoted by $\beta < 0$. The x-axis shows the income and the y-axis shows the expenditure. Note that β is the tangent of the angle of the curve with the positive x-axis. If $\beta < 0$ the curve is concave; if $\beta > 0$ the curve is convex.
- *Inferior goods.* As income increases, less is spent on inferior goods. In figure 4.1 this is the segment where the curve denoted by $\beta < 0$ is declining. Examples of inferior goods are potatoes and margarine. Since households with a rising income buy less potatoes and margarine, the absolute expenditure on these goods decreases as income increases. In addition substitution by rice and butter takes place, although the latter may depend on cultural factors either within or across countries.
- *Luxury goods.* As income increases, more is spent on luxury goods. An example is private property. This is shown in figure 4.1 by means of the curve denoted by $\beta > 0$.

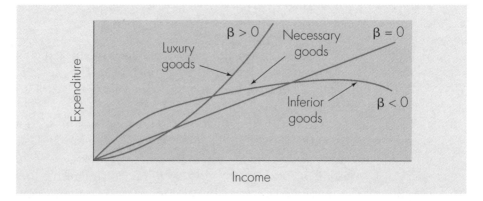

Figure 4.1 *Effects of income on expenditure on inferior, necessary and luxury goods*

During this period of scarcity, the supply of goods mainly served to fulfil the primary needs of life. Primary needs are considered as stable and as having a fixed structure.[3] For instance, the need for food is considered primary, followed respectively by the need for clothing, shelter and other needs. Products were basic, purely functional and produced solely to fulfil the primary needs. At the time, social problems arose primarily when people had not the means to fulfil their basic needs.

Affluence

As a consequence of the industrial revolution, all kinds of goods have become available to the masses. Purchasing power has increased and so has the general standard of living. This has also been associated with a growth in welfare and with social progress. New social problems have arisen— individuals have had to learn how to cope with their increased con- sumption of goods, leisure time has to be filled, the role of the worker has to be combined with that of consumer, and lots of goods have to be sold. Because of the greater freedom of choice and the satisfaction of primary needs, consumers have discretionary incomes at their disposal. This is income that can be spent or saved at free will (i.e., at the consumer's discretion).

In addition to the nature of consumption, the timing of consumption has become discretionary. Formerly, products were only replaced when they were worn out. Nowadays, replacement frequently occurs earlier and the

Figure 4.2 *Mass-produced goods*

timing of replacement is primarily determined by the consumer. Because of this, the dependency relationship between supplier and consumer has been reversed; now the supplier is dependent on the whims of the consumer. The stability of the economy is no longer guaranteed by the control of production, but depends on the willingness of consumers to spend their income. This willingness can be assessed by means of consumer opinion research.

The Index of Consumer Sentiment (ICS) summarizes consumer opinions regarding the development of expenditure.[4] A stable economy is associated with consumer confidence in economic development. Economics has been able to explain and predict consumer spending in times of scarcity. In times of affluence economic psychology is needed to understand and predict consumer behaviour.

Consumer society

The transition from scarcity to affluence has induced a 'consumption culture' in society which is characterized by the following elements.[5]

- The level of consumption is considerably above subsistence level.
- Goods and services are obtained more by acquisition than by household production.
- Consumption is considered to be an acceptable and appropriate activity.
- People are inclined to judge others and possibly also themselves based on their consumption level and style.

A number of factors contributing to the emergence of the consumer society associated with supply, demand and advertising, are examined next.

Supply
Increased production capacity and improved technology contributed considerably to a society of mass consumption. Because of this, goods can be produced more cheaply and in greater quantities, resulting in lower prices and greater affordability for the lower social classes. Furthermore, because of the marketing concept, products are better adjusted to the needs of the consumer. For example, different types and models of cars have become available.

Demand
The rise in income and the lowering of prices both contributed to the increase in consumption. Also, the abundance of goods stimulated demand, in part, as a result of consumer aspirations and the desire to show off. A materialistic mentality, an interest in buying and possessing emerged, which largely resulted from the opportunity to acquire substantial amounts of desirable goods and services, and from the perception that other people are similarly motivated to show off.[6] Consumption is

sometimes considered as a natural human disposition to attract attention. The rise of cities, in which individuals are relatively anonymous, has reinforced this disposition. The large cities with their enormous populations have particularly stimulated the rise of department stores, which have played a crucial role in the spread of the consumption culture. They are 'palaces of consumption; schools for a new culture of buying.'[7]

Advertising
Although there are indications that advertising expenditures follow rather than lead consumption, it is clear that advertising not only stimulates the sales of certain products, but also promotes the entire idea of consumption. It influences not only the pattern of consumption but also its level. Advertising stimulates imitation of influential others (reference groups), such as those from a higher social class, leading edge or trendy consumers. In this way, the consumer hopes to take on to some extent the status of the people imitated and to show off to others, for example, by wearing clothing indicative of a particular status. Because of this phenomenon, consumer behaviour from the higher social classes trickles down to the masses, thus diminishing the distinctions between social layers of the population.[8]

Explanation of consumption

In earlier times, the household budget largely determined consumer spending. Obviously, this is still the case, although credit facilities have expanded. However, it has become more difficult to forecast consumer demand. In general, the economic explanation of consumption—the satisfaction of needs, has become too complex to be described by simple Engel curves. Because of taste differences, the Engel curves may differ across consumers and because of taste changes the Engel curves for the same consumer may differ over time. For example, food not only satisfies primary needs but is associated with a number of higher-order needs such as social contact, prestige and self-realization. The consumption of clothing is heavily influenced by fashion and individual expression. The satisfaction of these needs is not a by-product of consumption but exists independently.[9] Besides the functional utility of products, their societal, expressive and personal meanings play a part in consumption behaviour. For example, a floor lamp not only serves for lighting but also for home decoration. The psychosocial component of consumption has become more important over time. In this way, one's social group has a significant influence on preferences for certain goods but this reference group may also change.[10] Consumers' aspirations are expressed in the products that they buy and, in the absence of clear-cut preferences, they can be manipulated by advertising.

Goods and services, such as a car, television, theatre tickets and financial services, have become available to the masses. This makes the explanation of consumption very complex because the status of many products has changed from that of a luxury to a necessity.

> Goethe still bought sugar in the pharmacy and our grandmothers stored it in lockable boxes of Bohemian glass. Not to mention chocolate. In Europe, thirty years ago ice cream started to become a daily food. In America and England ice cream has been served regularly as a dessert throughout the year. On the European continent thirty years ago ice cream still was something really special and was sold only during the season. Who doubts this will change tomorrow when the last retailer will finally have his cooling equipment and the last working-class housewife her refrigerator?[11]

This 30-year-old quote from Ernest Zahn has proven to be true. In western Europe, the current ownership of refrigerators in several countries exceeds 90%, and in almost all restaurants menus include frozen desserts.

Advertising campaigns no longer promote products by showing their efficiency, utility, and technical perfection but rather by focusing on the design, style, expressive value and personal meaning of the product to the consumer. Suppliers increasingly targeted the tastes and preferences of consumers. Suppliers and consumers are engaged in a dialogue to match supply and demand in the market place.[12] This dialogue takes place by studying opinion leaders, a group of consumers who are decisive in developing the tastes and preferences of the masses.[13] The market researcher attaches a great value to the psychosocial meanings of products and the designer is aware of the tastes of the public and of changes in society. There is the additional possibility of adapting the product to individual consumer needs.

4.3 Symbolic attributes of products and brands

During the transition from scarcity to affluence the psychosocial characteristics of products became more important. While in the earlier period of scarcity, the primary functionality of products was decisive in their acquisition, in a situation of affluence the symbolic and psychosocial characteristics become more important. However, the symbolic meaning of products has a much longer history as historians and anthropologists discovered. For example, the story is told of Cleopatra who dissolved a pearl in order to drink it. Such conspicuous consumption was clearly to show off an immense fortune and had no functional value.

Definition

The symbolic meaning of consumption refers to both the expression of one's personality, culture and history through consumption, and the interpretation of others' consumption with respect to these factors.

Figure 4.3 *Symbolic meanings*

Before the introduction of the money system, the Tiv—a Nigerian tribe–used three types of goods for exchange.[14]

The normal and most frequent transactions concerned domestic goods such as baskets, pots, hoes, cereals and chickens. A more prestigious category included metal products, clothing, guns, slaves, and cattle. These goods were exchanged less frequently at uncommon events (ceremonies, rituals). The third category consisted of the rights over women by a small group of influential men ('elders', heads of lineages). The three categories could not be interchanged—women could only be exchanged for women, guns could only be exchanged for other prestigious goods, and pots and pans could only be acquired in exchange for other 'household' goods. So the goods carried a strongly symbolic meaning.

In contemporary society, the symbolic meaning of goods can still be recognized. For example, rings and gifts at a wedding, flowers and music at a funeral, a certificate at a final exam, a club tie or a uniform. The study of symbolic consumption is important since much consumer behaviour has historic roots.[15] Symbolic consumption may also be based on contemporary symbols such as a popular brand or designer product. Goods are a visible form of culture.[16] A variant of the symbolic meaning of money is mental budgeting—the earmarking of money for particular consumption categories.

Mental budgeting

Consumers frequently set budgets for categories of expenses. They may have budgets for fixed expenditure e.g., rent, insurance, subscriptions, and for discretionary spending, such as clothing and food. Sometimes these budgets are managed by putting money in tin cans, envelopes, glass jars in the cupboard, etc.[17] Premodern societies where urbanization had not yet taken place, were characterized by a rather stable system of financial management, the 'peasant budget' framework, taken from anthropology.[18] In this framework, labour at the farm was not clearly distinguished from the household in financial terms. Much agricultural work entailed male labour whereas housekeeping chores were performed by females. Five budget categories were distinguished which still apply to modern Western society. The peasant funds framework is an attempt to bring some order into the great variety of expenditures on goods for production and consumption. A clear distinction is made between expenditure on functional products and expenditure on symbolic products. Symbolic products are further categorized according to their ceremonial and psychosocial functions. This is summarized in table 4.1.

Rent budget

In former times peasants were obliged to give part of their produce to the land owner. In exchange, they could rent land and were given protection by

Table 4.1 *The peasant budget framework*

	Production	Consumption
Functional	Budget for renting land Replacement budget for capital goods	Rent budget for house Replacement budget for household goods Subsistence budget
Symbolic	Ceremonial budget for acquisition and sale of land	Ceremonial budget for life events Personal budget

the landlord. Nowadays, a similar obligation to the government exists in the form of income tax.

Subsistence budget

The subsistence budget has been defined as the minimal caloric count necessary to keep alive—between 2,000 and 3,000 calories per person per day, depending on the type of labour.[19] Spending on food in Western society usually exceeds the subsistence level. Even for minimum income households the subsistence level is no longer a critical issue because of the network of social security and government welfare programs.

Replacement budget

The replacement budget is the amount that is needed to replace a minimal quantity of goods for production and consumption, for example seeds, equipment, pots and pans. It is not quite clear whether the first purchase of the goods is included. This amount can be substantial given the quantity of goods owned by contemporary consumers. It is not easy to clearly determine the necessity of a given product. Because of increased consumer wealth many luxury goods, such as a telephone, newspapers and a car have become necessities in our society.

Ceremonial budget

The ceremonial budget is allocated to goods that fulfil a social function at rites of passage such as births, weddings and funerals. In contrast with the first three budgets, this budget has a symbolic meaning. In contemporary society, different symbolic goods emerge. In former days the trousseau was part of the bride's dowry; nowadays other goods are considered more appropriate, such as washing machines or microwave ovens. Alternatively, these goods may be given as gifts by the guests at the wedding party. The continuous process of product innovation contributes to the changing symbolism of products. The acquisition and sale of land and the payment of produce was also entailed with some ceremony.

Personal budget

The fifth type of allocation is meant for personal consumption.[20] This has become gradually more important. The symbolism associated with this category—such products as cosmetics and clothing—enhances an individual's personality in the form of self-confidence and prestige. The personal budget has a psychosocial function and is of increasing importance because of an increasing concern with the symbolism in products and personal self-enhancement.[21]

Materialism and symbolism

Consumers show different attitudes toward symbolism in their behaviour.[22] Some people wear a cross, hang a mascot in their car, do not pass underneath a ladder; others refuse medical aid in the case of illness. Symbolism indicates the extent to which individuals invest mental energy in their possessions.[23]

Where a product is not particularly symbolic, then the consumer attaches considerable importance to its functional characteristics, and is concerned with individualism and control, for example a car offers a sense of mastery over distance. The functional use of goods is a central issue and one looks in a pragmatic way at the meaning of goods. This can also be viewed as materialist, not in the sense of possessiveness[24] but in the sense of concern with instrumentality and control. Provided that they are covered by proper insurance, consumers usually find it easy to replace such goods after damage or theft.

In a situation of high symbolism the consumer transcends the material world by building 'spiritual' relationships with goods or by associating them with family, friends, ancestors, future generations, and special events. Types of goods viewed in this way include art, antiques, decorative arts, family heirlooms, and souvenirs from holidays. A postmodern variant is cult-goods. These are products and brands that are worshipped, such as a relic, Elvis Presley's car, a dress worn by Madonna, a soccer shirt of Klinsmann, or the bow tie of one's deceased father. Some may even consider these to be 'sacred' goods. In the case of the loss or theft of these goods people feel seriously deprived as these goods are considered irreplaceable because of their symbolic and nostalgic meaning.

In addition to worshipping goods, places of worship also exist. For example, pilgrims visit Santiago de Compostella in Galicia (Spain). Each year, more than 700,000 people visit Graceland, the former home of Elvis Presley. The true pilgrim surrounds him or herself with Elvis artefacts such as earrings, an Elvis watch and perhaps even a greased quiff.

There are several ways in which the symbolic meaning of goods becomes manifest in society. One of these is via rituals and another via social exchange.

Rituals

Rituals are frequently associated with primitive behaviour or with public events. However, ritualistic behaviour also occurs in relation to ordinary behaviours such as eating, going on holiday, personal care, sports and gift giving.[25] A ritual is an expressive, symbolic activity, comprising a number of behaviours occurring in a fixed order, frequently repeated over time. Ritual behaviour occurs according to a script and is performed with formality, seriousness and inner intensity.[26] Rituals can be short and simple, such as a greeting, or lengthy such as a wedding. Rituals are not the same as habits. For instance, a funeral is a ritual but not a habit. Turning off the light before going to sleep is a habit but not a ritual.

> **Definition**
>
> A ritual is an expressive, symbolic activity, comprising a number of behaviours occurring in a fixed order, frequently repeated.

Rituals are usually made up of four components.[27]

- *Tangible components* are usually goods[28] but sometimes they are mythological characters, icons or logos. For example, the race leader in the Tour de France wears a yellow jersey, whereas the 'king of the mountains' wears a spotted jersey.
- The ritual *script* describes how to deal with tangible components. For example, the winner stands on a platform, sprinkles champagne and is kissed. A script involves a number of individuals who may perform different roles.
- The ritual *role pattern* prescribes how an individual should behave in the ritual.[29] Sometimes a role is explicitly scripted, as in wedding and graduation ceremonies. However, frequently the role allows greater freedom to the actor, e.g., Father Christmas.
- Finally, there is a public ritual performed by *spectators*.

The four components can be used to qualify rituals. In the case of Christmas and birthdays they are clearly present. In the case of Mayday festivities this is hardly the case as they are not usually scripted.[30]

There are four types of rituals in which the symbolism is expressed by means of goods: exchange, possession, care, and disposal rituals.[31]

Exchange

Gifts not only have functional attributes but also convey symbolic meaning. For example, a woman receiving a dress not only receives a piece of material but also a particular image of herself as a woman. Sometimes the gift's meaning is embarrassing. For example, a young man can hardly offer his neighbour a bouquet of red roses without suggesting that he is in love with her.[32] The gift ritual demands a number of acts. The giver removes the price tag from the present. The gift is nicely wrapped and is offered solemnly. The receiver also follows a ritual of unwrapping, surprise and thanking the giver—'You shouldn't have bothered!'[33]

Possession

The ownership of goods frequently conveys a deeper meaning—as a result of associations—which may be shown by the special attention the goods get from those who own or display them. In these cases, the products are usually items which can be shown, compared, discussed and photo-graphed. Associations result in the attachment of a symbolic meaning to the product. Goods become associated with certain dates, places and events. For example when a person might say: 'This is the vase I received from my grandmother six months before she died' or 'This is the bow tie my father always wore.'[34] Sometimes, associations are not formed with a product. The consumer may own a pen but not have any feelings of belonging or any strong associations.

Care

Some rituals are meant to bring to life an item's symbolic meaning. The painstaking ritual of washing the car, which can frequently be observed during weekends, is an act which stresses the symbolic meaning of the car as a status symbol. For many, personal care is a ritual, a transition from the private sphere to the public sphere. One has a bath or a shower, dresses suitably and puts on some make-up. These are acts to make a good impression on others and to gain self-confidence. To many people this means that value (temporarily) is added to one's personality.

Disposal

The symbolic meaning of products is usually personal, so that a change of ownership does not imply a transfer of meaning. Frequently, a person will want to remove the symbolic meaning before disposing of the product, or remove any symbolism from a previous owner before putting a product into use. New paint, new decoration or frequent cleaning is deemed necessary to remove any association with the previous owner. In organ donation, strict anonymity is practised so as to minimize the symbolic transfer.

Exchange processes

The symbolic meaning of goods and services is in part measured by exchange for money, information, status, and love. This not only applies to the goods as such but also to the trade-offs with regard to product characteristics. For example, one person will prefer a prestigious but low-paid job whereas another person will prefer a better-paid job with less status. So, money and status are exchangeable to a certain degree.[35] Six types of resources may be distinguished in an exchange process:

- *Love*: an expression of care, affection, warmth or comfort, for example kissing or caressing.
- *Status*: a value judgement expressing high or low prestige or esteem, for example admiring someone's house or winning an award.
- *Information*: advice, information or education, for example consulting or teaching.
- *Money*: a coin, note or voucher having a standardized exchange value, for example cash money, coupon or gift voucher.
- *Goods*: products or objects, for example clothing or a compact disc.
- *Services*: activities relating to objectives or associated with an individual, for example cleaning someone's house or repairing someone's car.

In social exchange, economic resources, such as money, goods, services and information may be exchanged for the social resources of status and love. However, some resources will be perceived as more similar and more appropriate for exchange with certain other resources. Foa elicited the probabilities of receiving a given type of resource in exchange for certain others in a sample of students.[36] For example, he asked 'What is the proper compensation you wish to receive in exchange for giving information to a person?' Information was most likely to be exchanged for status and money and less likely to be exchanged for love and services. The exchange probabilities can be fitted to two dimensions, capturing the perceptions of the resources. The first dimension distinguishes concrete resources such as goods and services from abstract resources such as information and status. The second dimension distinguishes individual-specific items such as love and affection from general items such as money, goods and information. Particularistic resources are personalized and are strongly associated with the people giving or receiving them, for example a physician or lawyer. General resources are exchanged more easily, for example the services by a bank employee or a cashier. The classification of resources is shown in Figure 4.4.

Each type of resource occupies a certain area in the two-dimensional space. For example, electronic money is considered a type of money, associated with a certain individual. In using electronic money nothing concrete is exchanged but financial information is transmitted. In figure 4.4 electronic money would be located in-between information and cash money.

Cash money and affection are less easily exchanged. Prostitution as an exchange of 'love' for money is deemed unusual or 'abnormal' in most Western countries. Furthermore, it has been found that affection—the type of resource that is most strongly associated with particular persons—is

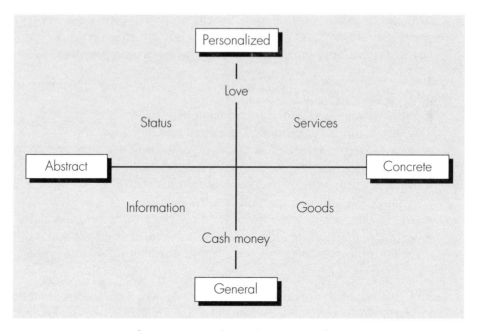

Figure 4.4 *Structure of economic and social resources (from Foa, 1971)*

generally the most preferred resource, irrespective of the resource given in exchange.[37] This has implications for the marketing of products in which the symbolic meaning can be emphasized. For example, flowers may be marketed by stressing the way they can express care and affection. The telephone company may stress the use of a telephone to contact people socially. Deodorants may be associated with success in social relationships. Jewellers may persuade people to buy diamonds to express their feelings for a loved one, e.g., de Beers advertising.

The two-dimensional space of economic and social resources has been found in five different countries and cultures: Israel, Philippines, Mexican Americans, Sweden and the USA.[38]

4.4 Typology of products according to symbolic characteristics

Products and services can be classified in different ways according to the symbolic or psychosocial attributes associated with them.[39]

Symbolic products

Many products have a symbolic or psychosocial meaning.[40] These products appeal strongly to the consumer's ego, for example clothing. Many products such as snacks, ice cream and soft drinks, are purchased because their hedonistic qualities are sometimes irresistible to consumers. These products satisfy needs immediately and are a form of self-gratification. Other products are purchased because of their functional qualities, for example packaged consumer goods and potatoes. These products hardly have any symbolic meaning.

The symbolic products are classified into four groups: prestige goods, status goods, maturity goods and anxiety goods, the first three of which strengthen the consumer's ego. These are transformational goods which add value to life and make the consumer's situation more positive.[41] The anxiety products are informational goods, which make the consumer's situation less negative or prevent it becoming negative. In several cases, the brand rather than the product conveys the symbolic meaning. This may depend on whether the good concerned is classified as a necessity or a luxury good.[42]

The four groups of symbolic products can be defined as follows:

1 *Prestige goods.* Some products or brands not only generate prestige but have become symbols of prestige themselves. A Mercedes is not only a symbol of success but is the proof of it. Products belonging to this category are villas, art, antiques and several brands of cars, clothing, furniture, and magazines. The function of these products is to enhance the consumer's ego.
2 *Status goods.* Consumers frequently like well-known brands because of the status they provide. Often these products are not qualitatively better than others but they are positioned as status objects by means of advertising. Examples are Nike sporting shoes, Lacoste shirts and Coca-Cola. Prestige goods are mainly associated with leadership; status goods are mainly associated with group membership.
3 *Maturity goods.* Some products symbolize maturity and are not meant for the young. Hence, these products have become attractive to them. Examples are cigarettes, cosmetics, coffee and alcohol. The functional value of these goods is not a factor, at least not in the early stages of use.
4 *Anxiety goods.* The function of the fourth group is to avoid or solve social problems, to defend the ego by preventing or overcoming personal or social threats. Examples in this category are soap, toothpaste, deodorants, mouthwash, perfume, shaving and health products. They change a situation of insecurity, worry or fear into a situation of self-confidence, relief and safety.

Several products or brands cannot be classified unequivocally as symbolic goods. For example, soap can be considered as a purely functional product without realizing that not using it can be quite embarrassing. Also, the symbolic value may be different to different people. For example, a business person may consider a Mercedes to be a convenient car which takes him or her to clients reliably and quickly. However, for many people a Mercedes signals prestige.

The symbolic meaning of brands develops mainly by learning and by advertising.[43] For example, by observing successful people, one gets to know the signs of success. Then, by imitating successful people's consumption, one hopes to be associated with success. The image of this type of consumption is enhanced by advertising, frequently associating brands and status.

4.5 Consumption cycle

So far, this chapter has dealt with the supply and symbolic meaning of goods. Next, the demand for goods is considered in relation to the consumption cycle. The consumption cycle is distinct from the product life-cycle.[44] The product life-cycle is concerned with the introduction, development of sales and improvement of a product in the marketplace and the final stage in which the product is taken from the market. The product life-cycle is driven by the producer. The consumption cycle concerns the consumption of the product in the household, from the moment of acquisition up to and including its disposal. The stages of the consumption life-cycle are prepurchase activities—problem recognition and information search—purchase, use and disposal. After disposal, the cycle starts again in the case of product replacement. If a product is sold on the second-hand market a second consumption cycle starts with the new user; see figure 4.5.

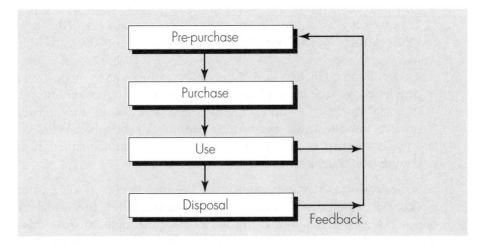

Figure 4.5 *Consumption cycle*

Duration of use, ownership and lifetime

The consumption cycle concerns durable and non-durable consumption goods and the duration of ownership of a good by the household. For non-durable goods, the end of the consumption cycle coincides with the end of use. Strictly speaking, non-durables are used only once. However, sometimes non-durables are used more than once, for example, disposable plastic cups may be used several times. So, the border between durable and non-durable goods is not always clear-cut. The duration of product use is usually shorter than the duration of ownership. The product lifetime in many cases is longer than the duration of ownership because the product may be used by a second owner or it may perform a different function, for example a glass food jar may be used as a container for nails. In summary, the following sequence should hold:

lifetime > duration of ownership > duration of use.

The consumption cycle is only partly determined by product characteristics. A product with a potentially long lifetime, for example a car, may be discarded prematurely by the owner. In addition, not only the duration of use but also the lifetime is determined by the consumer. For, not selling a

Figure 4.6 *Flea market*

product implies the end of its lifetime. For a durable, such a decision also has implications for the environment because the product becomes trash.[45]

There are three reasons why consumers terminate the duration of ownership of a good (implying three types of product obsolescence):

- *Technical obsolescence*: the product is worn out and no longer functions properly.
- *Economic obsolescence*: products have come onto the market that perform the function concerned more efficiently or more effectively.
- *Psychological obsolescence*: better designed products or a new style or fashion have emerged on the market.

The consumer's influence on the consumption cycle and on the lifetime of a product is associated with its symbolic value.[46] In former days, product functionality was of central importance and products were used until wear-out (technical obsolescence). Because of economic and societal developments products have obtained a different meaning. Psychological obsolescence implies that after some time consumers no longer like the products and want to replace them with more fashionable brands. New clothing fashions are an example of psychological obsolescence.[47]

Pre-purchase activities

The move towards the purchase of a new or second-hand product can be described as having two processes: the recognition of a need and the search for alternatives to satisfy the need.[48] The need to purchase or to replace a product arises if dissatisfaction with the existing situation becomes too great. This may occur for several reasons:

- The current state of consumption is no longer satisfactory, for example, because a product functions inappropriately (technical obsolescence).
- Different or better product innovations have become available in the market place (economic obsolescence).
- The aspirations, and objectives of the consumer have changed.

The three possibilities are shown in figure 4.7. The different factors are judged and compared. If the product satisfies current consumption needs and product innovations and aspirations remain unchanged, no need for a new product arises and the *status quo* is maintained. Otherwise a need arises and a search process is activated.

The current state of consumption
The product may not satisfy current needs because the functional product characteristics are deteriorating. This may be evident from failure, noise or increased energy consumption (technical and economic obsolescence). Sometimes the product functions as before, but the user's needs have

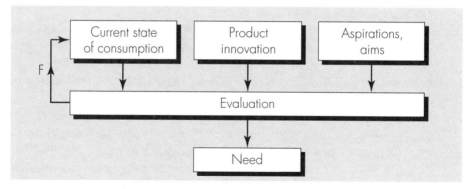

Figure 4.7 *Rise and recognition of a need*

changed, for example, a vacuum cleaner becomes too heavy for an elderly person.

The psychosocial characteristics concern the appearance of a product. A dilapidated product may still function but one feels embarrassed in the presence of neighbours, friends or relatives. This may especially be true for products which are conspicuously consumed such as cars, clothing and houses. Some needs arise because of stock depletion, for example light bulbs and fuses.

Product innovation
Needs may also arise because of new technological developments such as the CD player. Although the old record player still functions well, the characteristics of the new products are attractive enough to stimulate an acquisition need. The record player has become economically obsolete. Acquisition of an innovation generates demand for complementary products. For example, the acquisition of a CD player stimulates demand for CDs, CD storage racks and a new stereo cabinet. In this case, the CD player is called a *strategic product* influencing the consumption of other goods.[49]

Aspirations
Many needs arise from consumer aspirations, as a result of changed circumstances or from the consumer's personality. Changed circumstances frequently involve rites of passage such as marriage, bearing children, and house or job moves, changing the consumer's preferences. The aspiration level is also dependent on the family life-cycle and the economic expectations of the household.[50] Young households and households with optimistic economic expectations, in general, have higher expectation levels. Another relevant personal characteristic is the willingness to innovate and change behaviour.[51] The need for new stimuli or sensations may encourage new aspirations if an existing consumer solution has lasted for some time.[52]

Consumption ladder

As durable consumer goods usually are acquired in a certain sequence, this can be viewed as a *consumption ladder*.[53] The more goods in one's possession, the greater the chance of acquiring a good higher on the ladder. This indicates that aspirations are partly bred from the rung a household has reached on the ladder.

Frequently, a product is acquired because a budget restriction has been lifted, for example, because of an income increase. Preferences may change because of a change in budget restrictions or availability of product innovations.[54] An income change not only changes budget restrictions but also influences the preferences, aims and aspirations of a consumer. For example, higher incomes can lead people to think their housing is inadequate and to acquire aspirations for larger and more attractive living rooms.

Evaluation

The current consumption situation is evaluated based on availability of product innovations and aspirations. (See the feedback loop F in figure 4.7.) If these factors are considered important enough, a need will be triggered. This implies a threshold value of the factors below which a need will not be triggered but also that factors may cancel out or reinforce one another. For example, the aspiration to buy a bigger refrigerator may be cancelled out by the fact that the old brand still performs excellently. This is unlikely to trigger a need. However, if the old brand performs less well, both factors will reinforce each other , triggering a need.

Needs

The need then has to be specified. The consumer thinks about which functions the new product has to perform. For example, what are we going to use the car for? To commute, to take the children to school, to transport sport and hobby articles, to pull the caravan during weekends and holidays, or to transport bicycles? After the evaluation stage, the search process will start, eventually leading to a purchase.[55]

Acquisition

Needs do not always lead to a buying intention nor to the purchase of a good or service. Restrictions may be present, preventing the purchase. In addition to the consumption ladder and the wearing-out of goods in one's possession, economic expectations and situational circumstances also influence the purchasing process.

Buying intentions

Attitude models assume that a buying intention precedes a purchase and that it follows the formation of an attitude.[56] Researchers have long attempted to measure buying intentions in order to predict purchases.[57] In the case of low-priced products which are immediately consumed, a statistically non-linear relationship exists between intentions and purchases.[58] However, other processes affect purchasing behaviour. Intentions generally give less reliable predictions of durable goods purchases, partly because people are unable to predict a long time ahead. Economic expectations of consumers and situational circumstances may change purchase intentions. In addition, consumers often acquire goods and services without planning to do so.

Economic expectations

Economic expectations concern the consumer's confidence in the general economic development and the financial situation of the household.[59] In addition to consumption possibilities—determined by restrictions— the willingness to consume plays a part in the prediction of consumer behaviour.[60] Several investigations show that the Consumer Sentiment Index, together with constraining factors such as income, forecasts expenditure on durable purchases rather well.[61]

Constraining factors

These factors include money, time, physical and cognitive capacity of consumers, technology, norms and self-imposed constraints.[62]

- Economic theory explains consumption based on the maximization of the utility function under an (intertemporal) budget constraint. This implies that a household during its lifetime can never spend more than it earns. Frequently, the budget constraint induces the formation of a consideration set including brands and products which one can afford. Purchasing choices are limited to this set.[63]
- Consumption activities are also restricted by the time available. This implies utility maximization subject to a time constraint.[64]
- The consumer's capacity refers to the amount of physical and mental effort a consumer is willing to expend on consumption. For example, information overload occurs when the consumer is required to process too much information.
- Technical constraints for instance include the need for transportation, which is eliminated in teleshopping; social constraints, for instance, include the enforced closing times of shops and pubs.
- Norms include the social pressure to consume or not to consume, such as using personal care products or not using heroin or pornography.[65] Codified norms consists of laws, regulations and trading agreements.
- Self-imposed constraints include measures to protect oneself against too much consumption, for example, setting up a standing order to transfer money to a savings account in order to limit current spending.[66]

Product use

In the usage stage of the consumption cycle, the product has to be integrated in the household's stock of products. The product has to be put somewhere in the home. For example, the refrigerator has to be put in the kitchen. Perhaps another appliance has to be moved or replaced. In the initial stage, usage may be restricted. For example, the children are not permitted to play the CD player and the dog is not allowed to sit on the new couch. The owner of a new car may keep the plastic covers on the seats for months.

The use frequency of products may vary considerably across households. The use of products is influenced by three factors: the type of product, the environment and the user(s).[67] Some products are continuously in use (for example, refrigerators and freezers), others are only used at certain times of the day (for example, heating and lighting) or at certain seasons (for example, skates, gardening equipment, barbecues).

Product usage further depends on the environment. The climate—temperature, precipitation, wind, sun—among others may influence the use of heating, lighting, mode of transportation, maintenance of the house and clothing. The type of home—size, location, lay-out—may influence heating, maintenance and cleaning of the home.

Finally, the household itself—size, composition, preferences, habits—greatly influences product use. Washing machines are used five times per week on average.[68] The number of washes is about proportional to the household size.

Life-cycle costs

Product use leads to energy consumption and the acquisition of supplies such as gasoline and detergents. Buyers of mobile telephones tend to underestimate the costs of using this equipment. Furthermore, frequent use increases the chances of defects and may shorten the product's lifetime. This has led to attempts to estimate life-cycle costs concerning acquisition, installation, supplies, repairs, maintenance, insurance, guarantees, taxes and product disposal. Acquisition costs are the most important. Energy consumption may be substantial depending on the brand and type of product. Frequently, lower energy consumption is associated with a higher acquisition price. In this case, the pay-back period indicates the desirability of purchasing a more expensive product.[69] Consumer bodies frequently report running costs, for example car driving expenses. For example, a Lada usually has a lower purchase price but higher fuel consumption than a Nissan.

Maintenance and repairs

The duration of use and ownership may be considerably extended by more effective product maintenance. Maintenance prevents problems and repairs

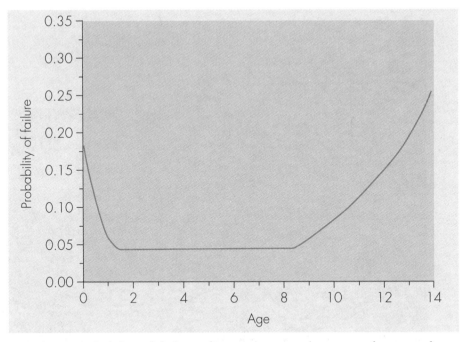

Figure 4.8 *Probability of failure of a washing machine as a function of age ('bath-tub' shaped function)*

and may also lead to energy saving. The use of a product is associated with the probability of failure. In general the probability of failure shows a nonlinear (bath-tub) shape during the time of use[70] (see figure 4.8). In the beginning of the use period, the probability of failure is relatively high because of teething troubles and improper use, partly caused by consumer inexperience. In the middle period of the lifetime the probability of a failure stabilizes at a low level. In the final period it increases steadily because goods wear out.

Because initial failures are usually covered by product guarantee, repair costs tend to increase over the product's lifetime. The frequency of failure increases with older products and is higher for households in which the product is used more often. In general failure frequency is higher where the purchase price is lower (assuming lower quality).[71] Finally, wear-out and inadequate performance lead to the end of the lifetime.

Disposal

Both the consumer and the condition of the product ultimately determine the end of ownership. A number of ways of discarding old products have been identified.[72] The three main groups of disposal options include: keeping the product and putting it to another use, temporary disposal and permanent disposal. Keeping a product may include using it in another function such as using jars and cans to store nails. Parts may be re-used;

Figure 4.9 *TV repair man*

products may be stored in a barn or attic, possibly to be used again later. The technical state of the product is important, which is shown by the reasons for product disposal.[73] Frequently mentioned reasons include 'the product is worn-out', 'the product is old and unreliable' or 'a more fashionable product is desired'.

The motives for disposal decision can be categorized as factors concerning the old product, the new product and personal factors.

The old product
The product in use (strictly speaking the product need not be old) performs a number of functions of importance to the consumer. The technical function of the product refers to the purposes for which it has been designed, together with reliable and safe performance. If this function is no longer fulfilled properly, the product is technically obsolete. The appearance of the product, the model and the usage possibilities are important, too. If this performance is out of date, psychological obsolescence occurs. In addition to the performance function, usage costs play a part. Considered economically, if usage costs are increasing, a consumer may calculate a time point at which it is rational to replace the product.[74]

Two biases—to be discussed in section 12.5—may influence the disposal decision. Because of the bias towards the *status quo* consumers are psychologically attached to the products they own.[75] This bias may reduce the need for product disposal. A related bias, the endowment effect[76] captures the way that goods that people own are more highly valued than similar goods that they do not own. This bias leads people to demand relatively high offers to sell their goods second-hand[77] and consequently, a relatively high probability of keeping the product in use. As most products are used at home, a direct comparison with other consumers' products is often impossible. Because of this, a product's obsolescence will not be easily noticed in many cases.

If a product functions adequately, disposal may not be economically rational although there may be a hidden need for it. This need may become manifest in the case of a specific event such as product failure.[78] Indeed, the direct cause of disposal is product failure in many cases (see table 4.2). Product failure may lead to repair if there is no other motive to dispose of the product.

The new product
Although a product may function well, new products may come onto the market that perform the same function better than the old product. In this case replacement may be attractive. This especially occurs in domains with frequent product innovations, such as computers, cameras and clothing. Lower operating costs of new products may also contribute to the early replacement of the product. The consumer makes a cost-benefit analysis both for the old and for the new brand.

Personal factors
Household income is important in the disposal or replacement decision. The higher the income, the earlier a product will be replaced. Obviously, more frequent replacements are associated with higher life-cycle costs, which can be paid more easily from a high income. Since a durable purchase implies an investment which is paid back by the product's performance over its lifetime, the consumer's *time preference* plays a part. A positive time preference implies an attitude to spend on consumption as

Table 4.2 *Product failure and wear-out as a percentage of reasons for replacement*[79]

Product	Percentage claiming failure as reason for replacement
Washing machine	90.1
Colour television	80.2
Black-and-white television	74.3
Dishwasher	67.1
Refrigerator	66.2
Freezer	61.4

quickly as possible; one is inclined to replace products relatively fast. Since replacement costs are paid in the present, less money will be available in the future. Positive time preference implies low weight given to future consumption.

The desire for newness or innovations is an important personality factor influencing the weight given to the new product in the evaluation of alternatives. This is discussed further in section 15.5.

Environmental concerns might play a part in the postponement of replacement, although empirical results are lacking.[80] It is more likely, however, that environmental concerns play a part in choosing the disposal alternative. It is possible to throw away, give away, sell, exchange or store the old product.[81]

The above-mentioned disposal factors are evaluated jointly and in the presence of a specific event, such as a product failure, will lead to a decision to keep or to discard the product.[82]

4.6 Conclusions

This chapter has shown the historic development from scarcity and poverty to the current affluent society. Necessary and inferior goods have become less important than luxury goods carrying symbolic meaning. Symbolic meaning has a psychological meaning for the individual and a social meaning in people's relations with others. These meanings are also called the impressive and expressive values of goods and values, respectively.

In marketing, the first stages of the consumption cycle are of primary importance—pre-purchase and purchase. From the consumer's perspective, all stages are important, especially product use and reliable functioning. Consumers optimize money and effort on the one hand and benefits on the other. This process and its results determine product satisfaction and possible repeat purchases of the product or brand.

For the consumer, the life-cycle costs are very important although few consumers have a precise idea of these costs. Frequently, the purchase price dominates the decision and little is known about the product's usage costs. Consumers with high incomes are generally more willing to pay a higher purchase price if this will be paid back by lower usage costs, for example an energy-efficient car or heater. Consumers with low incomes may lack the financial means to make such investments.

Three kinds of depreciation may cause replacement and disposal. In an economy of scarcity and few product innovations, technical obsolescence usually constitutes the reason for disposal. Where there is rapid product innovation, economic obsolescence usually causes replacement. In the case of fashion and design, psychological obsolescence prevails. In general, highly innovative consumers replace durables earlier than less innovative consumers.

Notes

1. Katona, G. (1964) *The Mass Consumption Society* (New York: McGraw-Hill).
2. The Engel curve was named after Ernst Engel (1857).
3. Zahn, E. (1964) *Soziologie der Prosperität* (Deutscher Taschenbuch Verlag). For a hierarchy of needs, see figure 8.7.
4. Katona, G. (1975) *Psychological Economics* (New York: Elsevier). See also figure 3.5.
5. Rassuli, K. M. and Hollander, S. C. (1986) 'Desire—induced, innate, instable?' *Journal of Macromarketing*, 6, 2, 4–24.
6. Rassuli and Hollander (1986).
7. Porter, S. B. (1979) 'Palace of consumption and machine for selling: The American department store, 1880–1940' *Radical History Review* 21, 199–221.
8. See section 3.4 for other models.
9. Zahn (1964).
10. See chapter 14.
11. Translated from Zahn (1964).
12. Zahn (1964).
13. See section 14.4.
14. Bohannan, P. (1955) 'Some principles of exchange and investment among the Tiv' *American Anthropologist* 57, 60–70. Also reported in: Douglas, M. and Isherwood, B. (1978) *The World of Goods: Towards an Anthropology of Consumption* (New York: Basic Books).
15. Hirschman, E. C. (1985) 'Cognitive processes in experiential consumer behavior' in: Sheth, J. (ed.) *Research in Consumer Behavior* (Greenwich, CT: JAI Press), 67–102.
16. Douglas and Isherwood (1978).
17. Heath, C. and Soll, J. B. (1996) 'Mental budgeting and consumer decisions' *Journal of Consumer Research* 23, 40–52.
18. Wolf, E. R. (1966) *Peasants* (Englewood Cliffs, NJ: Prentice Hall); Roberts, S. D. and Dant, R. P. (1991) 'Rethinking resource allocation in modern society: a meaning-based approach' *Journal of Economic Psychology* 12, 411–429.
19. This is equivalent to 8,444–12,667 kJ per day.
20. Roberts and Dant (1991) add this type to the classification by Wolf (1966).
21. Hirschman (1985).
22. Hirschman (1985).
23. Czikszentmihalyi, M. and Rochberg-Halton, E. (1982) *The Meaning of Things: Domestic Symbols and the Self* (Cambridge: Cambridge University Press).
24. Belk, R. W. (1985) 'Materialism: trait aspects of living in the material world' *Journal of Consumer Research* 12, 265–280.
25. Rook, D. W. (1985) 'The ritual dimensions of consumer behavior' *Journal of Consumer Research* 12, 251–264.
26. Rook (1985).
27. Rook (1985).
28. Douglas, M. and Isherwood, B. (1978) *The World of Goods: Towards an Anthropology of Consumption* (New York: Basic Books).
29. This is a script, a series or pattern of consecutive, inter-related behaviours.
30. An example of scripted Mayday festivities could be seen in the former Soviet Union.

31. McCracken, G. (1982) 'Culture and consumption: a theoretical account of the structure and movement of the cultural meaning of consumer goods' *Journal of Consumer Research* 9, 71–84.
32. The symbolism of flowers varies from country to country.
33. The script for receiving a gift may vary from country to country. For example, in Japan gifts should not be opened in the presence of the giver. In European countries, at weddings and christenings, when many presents are received, gifts are not opened in the presence of the giver.
34. B. Small, St Andrews University, England, at the *Advances in Consumer Research Conference* (Amsterdam, 1993).
35. Foa, U. G. (1971) 'Interpersonal and economic resources' *Science* 171, 345–352.
36. Foa (1971).
37. This has been found both by Foa (1971) and Brinberg, D. and Wood, R. (1983) 'A resource exchange theory analysis of consumer behavior' *Journal of Consumer Research* 10, 330–338.
38. Foa, U. G., Salcedo, L. N., Tornblom, K. Y., Garner, M., Glaubman, H. and Teichman, M. (1987) 'Interrelation of social resources' *Journal of Cross-cultural Psychology* 18, 221–233.
39. The classification by Woods, W. A. (1960) 'Psychological dimensions of consumer decisions' *Journal of Marketing* 24, 15–19, refers to psychological value. Firat, A. F. (1987) 'Towards a deeper understanding of consumer experiences: the underlying dimensions' *Advances in Consumer Research* 14, 342–346, has a rather sociological-historical classification.
40. Woods (1960).
41. Rossiter, J. R. and Percy, L. (1987) *Advertising and Promotion Management* (New York: McGraw-Hill).
42. See section 14.2.
43. See chapter 10.
44. See chapter 15.
45. See chapter 22.
46. See section 4.3.
47. So psychological obsolescence is partly instigated by product innovations. See chapter 15.
48. Search processes are described in section 11.2.
49. Arndt, J. (1976) 'Reflections on research in consumer behavior' *Advances in Consumer Research* 3, 213–221.
50. Schmölders, G. and Biervert, B. (1972) 'Level of aspiration and consumption standard: some general findings' in: Strümpel, B., Morgan, J. N. and Zahn, E. (eds) *Human Behavior in Economic Affairs* (Amsterdam: Elsevier).
51. Midgley, D. F. and Dowling, G. R. (1978) 'Innovativeness: the concept and its measurement' *Journal of Consumer Research* 4 (March), 229–242. Rogers, E. M. (1995) *Diffusion of Innovations* (New York: The Free Press).
52. Zuckerman, M. (1979) *Sensation Seeking: Beyond the Optimal Level of Arousal* (Hillsdale, NJ: Lawrence Erlbaum).
53. Pyatt, F. G. (1964) *Priority Patterns and the Demand for Household Durable Goods* (Cambridge: Cambridge University Press). Kasulis, J. J., Lusch, R. F. and Stafford, E. F. Jr (1979) 'Consumer acquisition patterns for durable goods' *Journal of Consumer Research* 6, 47–57. See also section 23.2.

54. Elster, J. (1983) *Sour Grapes* (Cambridge: Cambridge University Press).
55. See section 11.2.
56. Ajzen, I. and Fishbein, M. (1980) *Understanding Attitudes and Predicting Social Behavior* (Englewood Cliffs, NJ: Prentice Hall).
57. For example, Theil, H. and Kosobud, R. F. (1968) 'How informative are consumer buying intentions surveys?' *Review of Economics and Statistics* 50, 50–59, and McNeil, J. (1974) 'Federal programs to measure consumer purchase expectations, 1946–1973, a post mortem' *Journal of Consumer Research* 1, 3, 1–10.
58. According to Ehrenberg, A. S. C. (1966) 'Laws in marketing: a tail piece' *Applied Statistics* 15, 257–267, intention has a marginally decreasing effect on purchasing.
59. Katona (1975).
60. See section 3.5.
61. Mueller, E. (1963), 'Ten years of consumer attitude surveys: Their forecasting record' *Journal of the American Statistical Association*, 58, 899–917. Van Raaij, W. F. and Gianotten, H. J. (1990) 'Consumer confidence, expenditure, saving, and credit' *Journal of Economic Psychology* 11, 269–290.
62. Lesourne, J. (1979) 'Economic dynamics and individual behavior' in: Lévy-Garboua, L. (ed.) *Sociological Economics* (London: Sage), 29–47. Frey, B. S. and Foppa, K. (1986) 'Human behavior: Possibilities explain action' *Journal of Economic Psychology* 7, 137–160.
63. See section 11.3.
64. Becker, G. S. (1965) 'A theory on the allocation of time' *Economic Journal* 75, 493–517.
65. See chapter 14.
66. Thaler, R. H. (1980) 'Toward a positive theory of consumer choice' *Journal of Economic Behavior and Organization* 1, 39–60.
67. Lund, R. T. (1978) 'Life-cycle costing: A business and social instrument' *Management Review* (April), 17–23.
68. Antonides, G. (1990) *The Lifetime of a Durable Good: An Economic Psychological Approach* (Dordrecht: Kluwer Academic).
69. Hausman, J. A. (1979) 'Individual discount rates and the purchase and utilization of energy-using durables' *Bell Journal of Economics* 10, 33–54. Cunningham, W. H. and Joseph, B. (1979) 'Energy conservations, price increases and payback periods' *Advances in Consumer Research* 5, 201–205.
70. Kalbfleish, J. and Prentice, R. (1980) *The Statistical Analysis of Failure Time Data* (New York: Wiley).
71. Antonides (1990).
72. Jacoby, J., Berning, C. K. and Dietvorst, T. F. (1977) 'What about disposition?' *Journal of Marketing* 41, 2, 22–28.
73. Pickering, J. F. (1975) 'Verbal explanations of consumer durable purchase decisions' *Journal of the Market Research Society* 17, 107–113. DeBell, M. and Dardis, R. (1979) 'Extending product life: technology isn't the only issue' *Association for Consumer Research* 6, 381–385. Bayus, B. L. (1991) 'The consumer durable replacement buyer' *Journal of Marketing* 55, 42–51. Bayus, B. L. and Gupta, S. (1992) 'An empirical analysis of consumer durable replacement intentions' *International Journal of Research in Marketing* 9, 257–267.

74. Su, T. T. (1975) 'Durability of consumption goods reconsidered' *American Economic Review* 65, 148–157.
75. See section 12.5.
76. Kahneman, D., Knetsch, J. L. and Thaler, R. H. (1991), 'The endowment effect, loss aversion, and status quo bias' *Journal of Economic Perspectives* 5, 193–206.
77. Purohit, D. (1995) 'Playing the role of buyer and seller: the mental accounting of trade-ins' *Marketing Letters* 6, 101–110.
78. Hanson, J. W. (1980) 'A proposed paradigm for consumer product disposition processes' *Journal of Consumer Affairs* 14, 49–67.
79. Central Bureau of Statistics, The Netherlands, *Statistisch Bulletin*, December 12, 1982.
80. See section 22.4.
81. Jacoby *et al.* (1977).
82. Antonides (1990).

CONSUMERISM AND CONSUMER POLICY

5

5.1 Introduction

In the Middle Ages, Thomas Aquinas and later Martin Luther and John Calvin criticized the misleading practices of some business people, including charging exorbitant interest rates and inflated prices. For this reason, we could call Aquinas, Luther and Calvin the first consumerists. Desiderius Erasmus also did not think much of businessmen, judging by his statement:

> But the most foolish and sordid of all are your merchants, in that they partake in the most illicit business by the most illegal means they can find. Sometimes they lie, they perjure themselves, they steal and cheat, and they impose on the public. Yet they consider themselves important men because they have gold rings on their fingers.
>
> Desiderius Erasmus (1517) *The Praise of Folly*. Translated by J. P. Dolan (1964) in *The Essential Erasmus* (The New American Library, p. 137)

However, these philosophers restricted themselves to ethical statements and, except for hunger riots, extensive social movements to protect the consumers' interests were not established. The current concept of the consumer did not exist at that time.

Consumerism arose this century. It is a social movement driven by the interests of the consumer and aiming at gaining more information, protection, rights and guarantees for consumers. Consumerism attempts to strengthen the rights and power of buyers relative to those of the sellers.[1] Consumerism may be considered a 'countervailing power' against the mighty business world[2] and government services. It is predominantly a social movement, although it includes individual consumer actions.

Consumerism as a social movement arose in the USA at the beginning of this century and developed in Europe after the Second World War with the rise of consumer organizations, such as the Arbeitsgemeinschaft der

Verbraucherverbände founded in Germany in 1953 and the Consumers' Association founded in the UK in 1957. Most governments in the European Union implement consumer policies to protect consumer interests and to further general societal aims such as an equitable distribution of consumption[3] and fight against exploitation and environmental pollution. However, many governments have withdrawn to some extent from consumer protection because of deregulation and have left matters to the consumer organizations. For this reason, consumer policy has gradually become the policy of consumer organizations debating with commercial organizations and firms. The role of the government is twofold. On the one hand, the government provides goods and services, for example passports and health care, on the other hand the government implements consumer policy to protect the consumers' interests, even in the case of the goods and services that it provides.

Consumerism belongs to the cultural environment of consumers. It affects the supply, distribution and promotion of consumer products at the aggregate level. At the individual level, it facilitates consumer choice and redress. For this reason, we are discussing this topic as one of the macro-factors of consumption rather than as one of the after-sales processes.

This chapter describes the history of consumerism and consumer organizations, both in the USA (section 5.2) and in Europe (section 5.3). The causes of consumerism and most important points of action are described in section 5.4. The consumer policy of the firm is described in section 5.5, and section 5.6 offers a conclusion.

5.2 Consumerism in the USA

The establishment of the first Consumers' League in New York City in 1891 is usually known as the official starting point of consumerism in the USA. At the beginning of this century, attempts were made to develop legal rights in the area of food purity. The National Consumers' League, founded in 1899, was involved. These attempts only succeeded after Upton Sinclair published *The Jungle* in 1905.[4] He described abuses in the meat industry in Chicago. This book had such a strong influence on public opinion that Congress approved the Meat Inspection Act and the Food and Drugs Act. The Food and Drugs Administration (FDA) was established in 1906 to combat dangerous and ineffective drugs. The Federal Trade Commission (FTC) was established in 1914 to investigate and to ban unfair, illegal and misleading trade activities, such as monopolies. This was the first wave of US consumerism. This wave did not cause many reactions from the business community and partly because of the First World War interest in consumerism declined.

Thirty years later a second wave of consumerism emerged. Again, public opinion was influenced by several books: in 1927 Chase and Schlink published *Your Money's Worth*[5] and in 1933 Kallet and Schlink published *100,000,000 Guinea Pigs*.[6] These authors stated that 100 million American consumers were used as guinea pigs for unsafe products. They exposed misleading advertising and unsafe products and proposed to supply the consumer with reliable product information. Chase and Schlink got so much reaction to their book that the local White Plains Consumer Club (New York) was extended into a new consumer organization in 1929, Consumers' Research, which was the precursor of the Consumers' Union, publisher of *Consumer Reports*. The American Council on Consumer Interests (ACCI) also stems from this period. Attention was once more paid to unsafe drugs and cosmetics. The Second World War distracted attention from consumer problems and the interest in consumerism almost disappeared again.

Thirty years later the third wave emerged triggered by Vance Packard's *The Hidden Persuaders* (1957)[7] and Ralph Nader's *Unsafe at any Speed* (1965).[8] Vance Packard criticized advertising and stated that consumers were being influenced subliminally and against their will. Ralph Nader attacked General Motors and its unsafe cars, especially the Chevrolet Corvair.[9] In 1966 the National Traffic and Motor Vehicle Safety Act was enacted to regulate car safety. The problem of unsafe drugs also received attention.

In 1962 President John F. Kennedy formulated four fundamental consumer rights in his Consumer Message: the right to be informed, freedom of choice, safety, and the right to be heard. On the basis of these fundamental rights an impressive amount of consumer legislation was enacted in the USA. Following Kennedy's approach the government guarantees consumer rights by legislation.

In the 1980s consumerism in the USA was characterized by deregulation; the government withdrew and enabled the market parties—industry and consumer organizations—to make agreements to safeguard consumers' interests. Deregulation is associated with the privatization of government services.[10]

In this century waves of consumerism in the USA have occurred every thirty years. Characteristic of the third wave in the 1990s is that consumer organizations and industry are negotiating to secure consumer rights by means of self-regulation. Table 5.1 summarizes the history of consumerism in the USA.

5.3 Consumerism in Europe[11]

In several states, consumer legislation already existed before the formation of the European Community. For example in Germany, the Act of Parliament (1894) includes a law that obliges the seller to refund any instalments

Table 5.1 *History of consumerism in the USA*

Wave	Date	Development
Around 1900	1891	Consumers' League, New York
	1899	National Consumers' League
	1905	Upton Sinclair *The Jungle*
	1906	Federal Drugs Administration
	1914	Federal Trade Commission
Around 1930	1927	Chase and Schlink *Your Money's Worth*
	1929	Consumers' Club
	1930	American Council on Consumer Interests
	1933	Kallet and Schlink *100,000,000 Guinea Pigs*
Around 1960	1957	Vance Packard *The Hidden Persuaders*
	1962	John Kennedy's consumer rights
	1965	Ralph Nader *Unsafe at any Speed*
	1966	Traffic and Motor Vehicle Safety Act
Around 1990	Deregulation and self-regulation	

already paid by the buyer, if the seller withdraws from the contract because the buyer has ceased to pay the instalments. Of course the buyer has to return the delivered goods in this case. In 1909 the German Act against Unfair Competition came into force, in Sweden this occurred in 1943. In The Netherlands, the Commodities Act, dealing with product safety and consumer health, was introduced in 1935.

In the 1960s and 1970s, national consumer legislation in different states developed rapidly.[12] Topics covered by the law included product safety, product liability, misleading advertising, doorstep selling, consumer credit and unfair contracts. European states in this era can be split into three groups:[13]

- high level of consumer protection and organizations: The Netherlands, UK, France, Germany, Norway and Sweden;
- moderate level of consumer protection: Belgium, Italy and Spain;
- little consumer legislation: Greece, Portugal and Switzerland.

In 1973, two important steps in institutionalizing consumer representation were made: a service was installed at the European Commission which dealt with problems of the environment, nuclear energy and consumer protection, and the former Consumer Contact Committee was transformed into the Consumer Consultative Committee (CCC), charged with giving advice on consumer affairs at the EC level by request of the Commission. In 1995, the CCC was transformed into the Consumer Committee, consisting of 20 representatives of national consumer organizations. In 1975, a resolution was adopted that included five consumer rights inspired by

Figure 5.1 *Consumer Committee*

the Kennedy declaration: the right to protection of health and safety, protection of economic interests, redress, information and education, and representation.

Article 100A of the Single Act (1987) contains an express reference to consumer protection and removes the unanimity rule in the adoption of directives in numerous matters relating to consumer protection. The Treaty on the European Union (1992) includes a separate article (129A) devoted to consumer protection, which states:

> The Community shall contribute to the attainment of a high level of consumer protection through: a) measures adopted pursuant to Article 100A in the context of the completion of the internal market and b) specific action which supports and supplements the policy pursued by the member states to protect health, safety and economic interests of consumers and to provide adequate information to the consumers.

Furthermore, a new Directorate General of consumer policy (DG XXIV) was established with the following mission:

- to develop a consumer policy at the level of the European Union;
- to ensure that the interests of consumers are given due consideration in the development of the other European Union policies;
- to improve the safety of consumer products and services sold in the European single market;
- to improve consumer confidence, by ensuring consumers are given more complete and effective information;
- to develop a system of dialogue and consultation between the Commission and organizations representing consumers.

EC Directives

Since its formation, the European Commission has issued a number of Directives to improve consumer protection:

- In 1984, a directive concerning misleading advertising was adopted. However, unfair advertising is excluded and the directive does not protect a consumer who has concluded an agreement on the basis of misleading advertising.
- A product liability directive appeared in 1985 in which a producer is considered liable for damage, loss or injury caused by a defect in the product.
- A directive on door-to-door selling (1985) concerns contracts between a trader and a consumer during an organized excursion, during a visit to the consumer's home or place of work and where the visit does not take place at the express request of the consumer. Consumers must be given written notice of their right of cancellation within a special period (the 7-day 'cooling-off' period). The directive does not apply to insurance contracts or contracts concerning immovable property, nor to contracts for supply of goods by regular roundsmen. Subject to certain conditions, sales from catalogues are also excluded.
- A directive on general product safety appeared in 1987 and was revised in 1992. This concerns all products offered for sale which endanger the health or safety of consumers. Safety is defined in broad terms as regarding all products which, under normal or reasonably foreseeable conditions for usage, are durable and do not pose any risks or only low risks in normal use.
- A consumer credit directive (1987) provides minimum requirements for consumer credit agreements, i.e., requiring advertising not to be misleading or unfair and to show the total cost of credit, indicating any rate of interest or charge. Credit agreements must be in writing and must state the essential terms. Mortgages are excluded because they form a distinct market in which the techniques of lending are different from ordinary consumer credit agreements.
- A package travel, package holiday and package tours directive (1990) contains provisions concerning the information that travel operators must provide. This includes information about travel arrangements, accommodation, passports, visas, cancellation arrangements etc.
- A directive concerning unfair contract terms (1993) seeks to harmonize the laws and practices of the EC nations in order to avoid unequal treatment of EC citizens. Besides the recognition of the importance of freedom to contract and negotiating the terms, the directive aims to protect consumers who are not aware of what they are signing or are ignorant of the precise meaning of the terms.

These EC directives have been implemented in almost all of the member states.

EC Consumer Policy 1996–1998

On 8 November 1995, the Commission's consumer policy for the next three years was presented.[14] The program consists of the following parts, which may be summarized into five categories: increasing market transparency, stimulating market competition, consumer protection, activating consumers, and assistance to countries outside the EU.

Increasing market transparency

This element of the program is aimed at improving consumer education and the quality of information on offer. The EC will stimulate academic research to develop knowledge regarding a variety of consumption issues. Furthermore, the EC will support member states in their efforts to inform consumers, by making the fullest possible use of electronic and audio-visual resources, and to help consumers become familiar with a series of issues, including nutrition, the information society, and market mechanisms.

Increasing market transparency and consumer protection

To enable consumers to make the most of the information society, the EU has formulated the action plan: 'Europe's Way to the Information Society', which has created an Information Society Forum and an expert group on the social and societal aspects of the information society (i.e., voice telephony, data protection and distant selling). Particular attention will be paid to the accessibility of the system to everyone, training consumers in the new technologies and the security of electronic payment systems.

Stimulating market competition

Consider, as an example, the consumer aspects of financial services. Financial service companies are now free to offer services across member states' borders and the requirements for setting up branches in different member states have been liberalized in order to stimulate competition and provide consumers with a wider range of choices. Furthermore, the consumer credit market and notably the role of credit intermediaries is to be scrutinized. In particular, attention will be paid to consumer debt and mortgage credit. Also, various aspects of payment cards, e.g., conditions of use, price, will be considered.

Consumer protection

The aim is to complete, review and maintain the framework needed to ensure that consumers' interests are fully taken into account in the internal market. This part deals with the proper implementation of internal market legislation, including access to justice, guarantees and after-sales service.

Part of this is a commitment to protect consumers' interests in the supply of essential public utility services. Essential public utility services have to meet the citizens' needs, and that means providing an adequate guarantee of universal service. The EU has done much to hasten liberalization in this area. Competition in the supply of these services will certainly benefit consumers.

There are also plans to take measures to improve consumer confidence in foodstuffs. This part will focus on measures concerning the effectiveness of food safety/purity control systems and the possibility of extending product liability to include primary products.

Activating consumers

The aim here is to encourage a practical approach to sustainable consumption.[15] Consumer habits will have to change for consumption to become sustainable. Identified groups of consumers are committed to addressing this problem. The Commission's surveys show that the general public is becoming increasingly sensitive to environmental issues. Through their choices consumers can exercise considerable pressure towards the design, production and marketing of products and services with a reduced environmental impact. Moreover, they can themselves play a part by participating in recovery and recycling schemes. However, consumers can only make fully informed and rational choices if they have access to impartial and reliable information. This is why sensitization and education measures are top priority. For how otherwise can consumers determine precisely the merits and demerits of individual products?

Part of this process means strengthening and increasing consumer representation. An estimated four million citizens belong to consumer associations throughout the EU. Because the most highly organized groups are located in the northern member states, the Commission has endeavoured to strengthen the movement in the southern countries. The constitution of the Consumer Committee by national representatives of organizations from each member state has already been mentioned. In addition, the Commission is making increased use of market research techniques to sample opinions and to study consumer habits and attitudes throughout the EU.

Assistance to countries outside the EU

The EU aims to help the Central and Eastern European Countries (CEEC) to develop consumer policies. Fundamental reforms to promote consumer interests in economies that are in transition have already been achieved or are in the pipeline in all CEEC countries. However, consumer legislation is often patchwork and subordinate to other political objectives, and the laws that do exist are often not enforced. Legal and technical assistance is thus required to overcome the remaining hurdles.[16]

The EU also aims to contribute to the introduction of consumer policies in developing countries. Up to now consumer policies as such have not been included as parts of development policy. Even though consumer policy is potentially of central importance in situations of abject poverty where malnutrition and exclusion are key issues, it has been seen as relevant to developing markets only. However, the European Parliament voted for the first time in 1995 for an amendment putting consumer policy actions into the budget lines for developing countries. Starting with pilot projects, the Commission intends to redouble its efforts to provide them with real assistance.

Every member state in the EU recognizes the need and the importance of consumer protection. Consumers play important economic and political roles in society. The EU countries have developed policies whose objective is to defend the specific interests of consumers. The underlying objectives of these consumer policies are to reduce inequalities, guard against unfairness, promote health and safety, and improve the overall standard of living.

With the emergence of the single market, many different approaches pose practical problems for consumers and also businesses. It is difficult for consumers to obtain satisfaction in cross-border transactions since the rules, the jurisdiction of national courts and regulatory authorities are so different.

The existence of diversity in regulations and structures justifies the development of a consumer policy at top level which is designed to ensure that all consumers have sufficient confidence to play an active role in the single market, whilst enjoying the highest level of consumer protection.

Consumer organizations

In general, we can divide the organization of consumer interests into four groups: private consumer organizations, indirect organizations, semi-public and public organizations.

- *Private consumer organizations*: these are organizations formed by individuals to promote their common interests as consumers. There may be different reasons why individuals join such organizations. Usually, the members expect some service and are willing to pay a membership fee to get it. The most attractive service has been the subscription to a magazine of comparative product testing. Similar to the USA, private consumer organizations are often formed around testing activities. Table 5.2 shows an overview of private consumer organizations in Europe and it clearly shows the advanced organization in the Northern European countries relative to those in the south.
- *Indirect organizations*: as table 5.2 shows, in several countries umbrella organizations exist in which a number of private consumer organizations and trade unions are joined.
- *Semi-public and public organizations*: due to the weakness of some of the existing consumer organizations and the difficulty of organizing the

Figure 5.2 *Product tests*

consumer's interests, the governments in some EU countries have deemed it necessary to provide for representation of consumers' interests on a semi-public basis. The government usually employs the organizational patterns available under private law and sees to the financing of these organizations. Several international organizations exist:

- Bureau Européen des Unions de Consommateurs (BEUC), Brussels;
- Comité des Organisations Familiales auprès des Communautés Européennes (COFACE);
- Communauté Européenne des Cooperatives de Consommation (EUROCOOP);
- Consumers International (CI), London.

5.4 Determinants and forms of consumerism

In fact, the development of post-war consumerism is a paradox. Never before have incomes been so high, never before has there been such an abundance of choice and never before have we lived as long as we presently do. However, it has not made us happier.[17] Not only the means to satisfy our needs but also the needs themselves have proliferated. The abundance of goods may have left us more comfortable but their possession also has created worries. The more goods a household possesses, the greater the chances of problems and complaints will be.[18] Also, the increased product

Table 5.2 *Private consumer organizations in Europe*

Country	Organization	Year of founding	Membership 1996 (×1000)
Austria	Verein für Konsumenteninformation	1961	101[a]
Belgium	Verbruikersunie, Association des Consommateurs	1957	265[a]
Denmark	Forbrugerstyrelsen, Statens Husholdningsrad	1988	74[b]
France	Union Fédérale des Consommateurs	1951	201
	Ass. Fédérale des Nouveaux Consommateurs	1975	40
Finland	Kuluttajavirasto	1990	20
Germany	Stiftung Warentest	1964	776
Greece	EKPIZO, Association 'Quality of Life'	1988	4
Ireland	Consumers' Association of Ireland	1966	10
Italy	Editoriale Altro Consumo	1973	273[a]
The Netherlands	Consumentenbond	1953	662
Norway	Forbrukerradet, Consumer Council	1953	90[b]
Portugal	Edideco, Editores para Defasa do Consumidor	1974	200
Russia	KonfOP International	1989	85
Slovenia	Zveza Potrosnikov Slovenije	1990	8
Spain	Edocusa, Organizacion de Consumidores y Usuarios	1975	250
Sweden	Konsumentverket, Consumer Council	1973	162[b]
Switzerland	Konsumentinnenforum	1960	33[a,b]
	Fédération Romande des Consommateurs	1959	42
UK	Consumers' Association	1957	800

[a] Estimated readership of magazine
[b] Umbrella organization

complexity has introduced new possibilities for malfunctioning. Thus, even though the failure rate has declined or has been held constant, the total number of product failures has increased because of the growth in the quantity and complexity of products. Many consumers feel confused and express a general dissatisfaction with the quality of the products they buy.[19]

In addition, well-being and satisfaction not only depend on the stock of material possessions but also on the comparison of one's belongings with those of others.[20] Consumers in particular become dissatisfied if comparable others—reference people—own more goods than they own themselves. Dissatisfaction may also result from attribution processes if consumers attribute problems with products or services to retailers or producers rather than to themselves.

Furthermore, dissatisfaction may result from a critical attitude toward production and concern about the environment and the depletion of energy supplies.[21] Also, the increased level of education may be indicated as a cause. Consumers have become more critical; they seek and require more information because of a better education. They are deceived less easily and they are more inclined to seek redress from retailers or to seek support from consumer organizations.

Types of consumerism

Several types of consumerism can be distinguished based on the political and societal opinions of consumers:[22]

- *Liberal consumerism*. According to this view, the consumers' knowledge and capacities need to be extended to increase their market power. Consumers may then form an opposing ('countervailing') power against the power of producers and traders. In fact, liberal consumerism stimulates the free market economy by strengthening a weak market party.
- *Responsible consumerism* puts consumerism into a wider context of societal responsibility. It is not only value for money that determines consumer choice but also factors such as extended durability, lower levels of pollutant emission, more efficient use of energy, less noise pollution and the use of recycled materials. In short, negative external effects should be avoided. Some producers take this responsibility into account and speak of societal marketing. Examples include the Body Shop which does not sell products associated with animal experiments, and Visa which transfers part of the spending on the Panda card to the World Wildlife Fund.
- *Critical consumerism* is a more structural type of consumerism, questioning the consumption system. Products need to become better and more safe. 'Unnecessary' products may be prohibited. The consumer's position needs to be strengthened, both by consumer actions and by legislation and government measures.
- *Radical consumerism* considers consumerism as suppressing symptoms, since the weak position of the consumer results from the inequity of the societal system. This ideology is anti-capitalist and sees consumer organizations as merely fighting the symptoms rather than the root cause of problems. Consumer boycotts, such as the anti-Shell actions because of the Brent Spar oil platform and the boycott of French wine during the nuclear tests in the Pacific, can be considered as radical consumerism.

5.5 Quality management and social responsibility

Company-level consumer policy is evidenced by the development of products and services on the basis of consumers' wants and desires. Marketing can be blamed for the development of consumerism and the need for government-level consumer policy. Consumer policy at company-level includes quality management, social responsibility and the avoidance of negative external effects of production and products. This also applies to the products and services of the government.

Quality management

Total quality management includes product development, advertising, distribution and maintenance. Interest in continuous quality control in the production and distribution of products has been strongly influenced by Japanese companies success.

Quality management has passed through several stages. In each of these stages, the scope of the concept has broadened. See figure 5.3.

The first stage of quality management comprised *quality inspection* or *quality control* after the fact. Products failing to meet the norm were not sold. This fall-out and its eventual correction implied an important financial loss.

In the second stage of quality management quality was not only considered an inspection problem but also as a *production control* problem. Each link in the chain of design, production, logistics and sale was organized so as to ensure high product quality.

The beginning of the 1980s saw the third stage in which *quality guarantees* had become central. Quality norms, inspection and quality circles served to motivate employees to deliver quality products and services. Quality handbooks including norms and standards appeared. The ISO standards were developed in this period.

The fourth stage comprised *total quality management*. Quality management is considered a problem of total control within the organization in all stages of production and supporting processes. In the fifth stage of *strategic quality management*, quality is considered as a strategic tool to obtain differential advantages and to increase the profit of the firm. The consumer is considered the final judge of the product as he or she

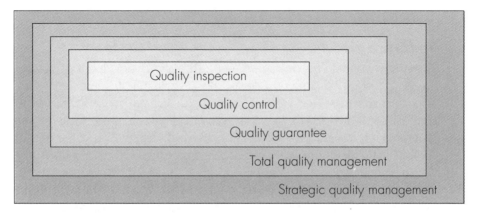

Figure 5.3 *Stages in quality management*

compares it with competitors' alternatives and evaluates the product during its whole lifetime.[23]

Quality management also has to cover product management. In the case of certain product failures, the relevant products have to be recalled according to a European directive. This implies that the defective or unsafe product parts have to be replaced by the producer. For example, Heineken had to recall its green export bottles because the bottle neck could splinter when it was opened. In such cases, communication with consumers has to be truthful and informative. Guarantees and safeguards have to be clear and should not be set up exclusively to the advantage of the producer. The firm has to set up an efficient type of complaint handling, for example, the department of Consumer Affairs at Philips, the department of Customer Service at Ikea or an Ombudsman in the case of life insurance. Freephone numbers also facilitate the acquisition of information and the filing of complaints.

Social responsibility

Consumer policy can be considered within the framework of social responsibility of a company. Companies not only have to produce products and services which are relevant to society in an acceptable way, but they are also responsible for the physical and social consequences of the use of these products and services. Profit-making is not their only economic responsibility. A new definition of the marketing concept is: socially responsible marketing based on a consumer orientation, supported by an integrated marketing approach and aimed at consumer satisfaction and long-term well-being as the key to profit margins.

Research has been carried out concerning the acceptability of social responsibility by US firms.[24] It was found that stores with close links to their customers accepted social responsibility most, while producers accepted less social responsibility. Other firms frequently showed defensive behaviour, in that they denied problems or only paid lipservice to consumerism.

External effects

Socially responsible companies will attempt to develop environmentally friendly and safe products. The socially responsible firm also plays a part in the local situation, for example by subsidizing and sponsoring local clubs and local initiatives. The firm acts as a good citizen in the local community. This also has advantages in terms of boosting the public profile of the firm.

External effects may concern the entire industry. Organizations of manufacturers may consider product standards and quality norms with regard to the environmental effects of production and usage of their products. The marketing concept starting from the consumers' desires is extended to a marketing concept starting from societal needs. Consumerism not only should aim at strengthening the position of the consumer but also at a greater social responsibility of the firm.

5.6 Conclusions

Consumerism in Europe in the 1980s and 1990s has been relatively institutionalized. Consumer organizations have found their places in discussion platforms such as the Consumer Committee. Consumer organizations directly negotiate with producers and distributors to ensure purchase and delivery conditions which are acceptable to the consumers. Consumerism is not declining but has established a firm position as a countervailing power in the consumption system in our society.

The government has only a limited task in constructing legislation. Only in the case of severe physical and financial risk to consumers is the government willing to establish legal rules and to impose sanctions. Most consumer protection is arranged by mutual agreement between consumer organizations and producers. Companies that act in a socially responsible way may gain competitive advantage, as firms which have adopted an ethical, socially responsible stance, such as The Body Shop and The Co-operative Bank, have shown. As consumers become more aware of the external effects of consumption, they will be more critical when making their purchases.

Obviously, consumerism and consumer policy have ethical aspects, i.e., the norms and values to which product development, marketing, advertising and marketing research have to adhere. Market researchers, advertisers and other professionals dealing with consumers are usually required to follow a code of conduct imposed by their organizations. Misleading and/or manipulating of consumers is prevented as far as possible by these codes of conduct.[25]

Notes

1. Kotler, P. (1972) 'What consumerism means for marketers' *Harvard Business Review* 50, 48–57.
2. Galbraith, J. K. (1958) *The Affluent Society* (Harmondsworth, UK: Penguin). Galbraith, J. K. (1973) *Economics and the Public Purpose* (Harmondsworth, UK: Penguin). Galbraith coined the term 'countervailing power' to indicate that with more consumer power opposing business power a 'better' equilibrium could be reached.
3. The distribution of consumption equals the tertiary income distribution, i.e., the distribution of income after deduction of taxes and premiums. This is the income that can be used for consumption.
4. Sinclair, U. (1905) *The Jungle* (New York: Viking) (Reprinted 1946 and 1972).
5. Chase, S. and Schlink, F. J. (1927) *Your Money's Worth* (New York: Macmillan).
6. Kallet, A. and Schlink, F. J. (1933) *100,000,000 Guinea Pigs* (New York: Vanguard).

7. Packard, V. (1957) *The Hidden Persuaders* (New York: David McKay).
8. Nader, R. (1965) *Unsafe at any Speed* (New York: Grossman).
9. Later it appeared that the Chevrolet Corvair was actually safer than Ralph Nader claimed. The Corvair is now a collector's item.
10. Feldman, L. P. (1980) *Consumer Protection. Problems and Prospects* (St Paul, MN: West Publishing Company) (second edition).
11. This section benefits from a thesis by Sutjiadi, S. M. (1996), 'Consumer protection and satisfaction in the European community'. Master's Thesis Erasmus University, Rotterdam.
12. Reich, N. and Micklitz, H. W. (1980) *Consumer Legislation in the EC Countries: A Comparative Analysis* (translated by S. Geis) (New York: Van Nostrand Reinhold).
13. Maier, L. (1993) 'Institutional consumer representation in the European community' *Journal of Consumer Policy* 16, 355–374.
14. Commission of the European Community 1995. This is the third three-year programme.
15. See also chapter 22.
16. The 1995 White Paper pays special attention to this issue. The Phare programme, started in 1994 and continued in 1995 also aims to encourage the development of consumer policy in these countries.
17. Easterlin, R. A. (1974) 'Does economic growth improve the human lot? Some empirical evidence' in: David, P. A. and Melvin, W. R. (eds) *Nations and Households in Economic Growth* (Palo Alto: Stanford University Press) 89–121.
18. Francken, D. A. and Van Raaij, W. F. (1985) 'Socio-economic and demographic determinants of consumer problem perception' *Journal of Consumer Policy* 8, 303–314.
19. Aaker, D. A. and Day, G. S. (1978) *Consumerism. Search for the Consumer Interest* (third edition) (New York: Free Press).
20. This constitutes the relative income hypothesis, *cf.* Duesenberry, J. S. (1949) *Income, Saving and the Theory of Consumer Behavior* (Cambridge, MA: Harvard University Press). See also chapter 15.
21. Aaker and Day (1978).
22. Van Raaij, W. F. (1974) *The Dutch Consumers' View of the Consumption Scene* (Tilburg, The Netherlands: Tilburg University).
23. Garvin, D. A. (1988) *Managing Quality: the Strategic and Competitive Edge* (New York: The Free Press).
24. Webster, F. W. (1973) 'Does business understand consumerism?' *Harvard Business Review* 51, 89–97.
25. See also section 25.8.

PART II

BASIC PROCESSES

PERCEPTION AND CATEGORIZATION

6

6.1 Introduction

Consumers vary in the way they perceive products, brands, and stores. Each individual has a subjective view of reality. People differ in their perception of reality depending on their own experiences, life histories, and personal situations. These differences result from both variations in the psychophysics of perception and the cognitive biases and distortions that occur when perceiving people, products and brands. Although there may exist an 'objective' reality, a lot of perceptual differences exist between people.

Four types of reality may be distinguished (see figure 6.1):

- The objective reality of people, products, and brands;
- The reality as constructed and represented in advertisements, usage instructions, information given out by consumer organizations, and information from other sources;
- The reality of other consumers, their experiences and judgments;
- The subjective reality (perception) of consumers.

One's own observation of the objective reality of other people, other people's behaviours, products, shops and advertisements influence one's perception or subjective reality (A). This perception is also influenced by the representation of reality in advertisements and (public, institutional) information (B) and by the experiences of other people, i.e., social information (C). In these three realities, images are of major importance.[1] The realities of advertising and (public) information provision and the experiences of other people are representations in which written and spoken texts and pictures play a role.

Categorization interacts with perception, namely the way consumers classify products, stores, services, and brands. Which product classes or categories do they distinguish? Which products and brands do they regard

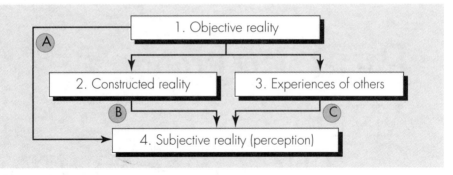

Figure 6.1 *Three levels and four types of reality*

as substitutes for each other? At what level of differentiation do consumers regard the supply of goods and services? The experiences of consumers themselves, advertisements and the experiences of others all contribute to the formation and differentiation of categories.

In this chapter schemas are discussed in section 6.2. Schemas play an important part regarding perception, categorization, and the structuring of meaning. In section 6.3 the perception processes are described. The meaning structure and functions of categorization are discussed in, respectively, sections 6.4 and 6.5. Categories can be formed on the basis of the same function and meaning of products. Consumers form categories on the basis of a prototype or a sample of the category (section 6.6). As one becomes more familiar with a category or product class, more refined and differentiated categories are usually formed (section 6.7). Certain sequences in categorization may appear, for instance in types or brands. One application of this is market partitioning. Two processes are instrumental in differentiation: assimilation and accommodation (section 6.8). Some conclusions are drawn in section 6.9.

The aim of this chapter is to show the relevance of consumer perception to the study of consumer behaviour. Perception does not exist without the ability to perform primary information processing such as categorization. Categorization is both the result of perception and also helps to structure perception. In new situations, people perceive objects and try to classify these objects into meaningful categories. In other situations, categories are used in perception—the world is perceived through existing categories. Perception and categorization influence other processes and the behaviour of consumers. The supply of goods and services exists in the perceptions of consumers.

6.2 Schemas

Consumers easily find their way around shopping centres and stores they frequently visit. They also know the properties and advantages of products they frequently use. These characteristics of stores, products and brands are stored in their memory as schemas. Schemas are networks of associations (images, characteristics, functions, values and feelings) with a product, brand, shop or another object.[2] These associations with each object exist (or are formed) in the memory of the consumers.[3]

Definition

A schema is a network of associations with a product, brand, shop or another object.

In a schema, a product or brand is associated with a number of positive and negative characteristics and experiences. Muesli for instance is associated with nutrition, health, and a good physical condition. As soon as consumers hear or see the word 'muesli', these associations come to their minds. The first muesli product was muesli breakfast cereal, followed by muesli bread, cookies, biscuits, and even candy bars. By means of extending the concept 'muesli', these products are associated with nutrition and health. Figure 6.2 gives an example of a schema.

Schemas are formed on the basis of individual's own experiences, the experiences of other people and information from advertisements and personal advice. The images and associations give meaning to the original object. The concept of a 'schema' is an old one. In the eighteenth century

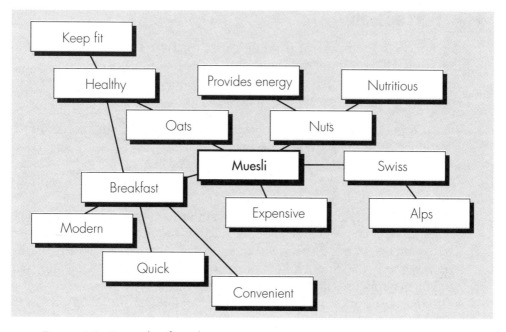

Figure 6.2 *Example of a schema*

the philosopher Immanuel Kant used the schema concept to describe a cluster of information held in memory.[4] Schemas act as an observational and interpretational framework. The things that one expects to see are more likely to be noticed. The things that one does not want or expect to see are less likely to be noticed.

Through the observation of an object, mental schemas that are connected with this specific object are activated. A colour or a smell may activate schemas that contain this colour or smell. This is called the activation or dispersion theory of the brain. When a part of the network is activated, then other elements of the network will be activated too. So, for example, if you cannot remember the name of a certain person, it is advisable to think about where you met this person before, where he or she works or lives. This activates part of the network and makes it more likely that the name will come into your mind all of a sudden.

In this chapter and the next two chapters, the following types of schemas will be discussed:

- Frames or observation schemas in perception.[5]
- Category schemas, characteristic attributes of a category of products.[6]
- Product and brand schemas; knowledge and feelings of consumers about products and brands.[7]
- Self-schemas, schemas consumers have about themselves.[8]
- Scripts or action schemas.[9]

6.3 Perception

Perception is an important psychological process and is also significant in the study of consumer behaviour. It concerns the observation of the surroundings, of people and objects, of sounds, smells, movements and colours. The five senses are essential to consumer perception:

- *Visual* perception plays an important role in judging situations, shops, products, brands, and advertisements.
- *Auditory* perception is of importance regarding radio and broadcast messages. Background music influences consumer judgment of shops and products and buying behaviour.[10]
- *Olfactory* (smell) perception often happens quite unconsciously. The slight fragrancing of certain products can make them more attractive to consumers, without the consumers being consciously aware of the difference.[11] In supermarkets, a 'manufactured smell' of baking may stimulate appetites and thus increase food buying activities.
- *Tactile* observation includes touching, handling and holding products. Think of consumers squeezing a pack of coffee to see whether or not the vacuum is intact, or feeling fruit to find out whether it is fresh or ripe.

Tactile observation is important regarding clothes and materials. Is the sweater comfortable and does the material feel soft and supple?
- Consumers can taste food products at product demonstrations. The judgement of wine, coffee and food is strongly based upon the sense of taste.

Visual observation concerns the spatial observation including foreground and background, depth and distance, and the stability of objects, seen under different angles and different kinds of lighting. Person and object perception concerns the way we observe the attributes of persons and objects. A short introduction to psychophysics is given next, and following that the observation of people and objects is discussed.

Psychophysics

Dogs react to a dog whistle with a high pitch that human beings cannot hear. This means that perception thresholds exist which differ between human beings and animals. A sound may have a pitch that is too low or too high for human ears to hear it. This also holds for the observation of colours. Some people see differences in colours where others do not. These differences in observation are part of the field of psychophysics. In this way the objective (physical) stimulus is related to the subjective (psychological) observation or sensation.

Both absolute and relative perception thresholds exist. An *absolute perception threshold* is a limit or marginal value above or below which a stimulus can only be observed 50% of the time. The pitch of a sound can be so high that it can only be heard in half the cases, or so low that it can only be heard in half the cases. The limit or marginal value holds for sounds, images and smells. The characters of an advertisement on the outside of a cab, for instance, may be so small that they can only be read by passing motorists half the time.

A *relative perception threshold* also exists. Differences between stimuli may be too small to be observed. Expensive audio-systems often give better sound contrasts than cheap systems. However, if these differences are not perceptible to the human ear, it is unnecessary to buy the expensive audio-systems. One speaks of 'just noticeable differences' (jnd's). A *just-noticeable difference* is one in which there is a 50% probability that the difference in the strength or intensity of a sound or light will be noticed.

According to Weber's law, the jnd (δI) is a constant fraction (k) of the intensity of the original stimulus (I): $\delta I/I = k$. Suppose the constant fraction k equals 0.05. A difference between I = 500 and I + δI = 525 lumen can just be perceived. It follows that a difference between 1000 and 1050 lumen can also just be noticed.

Stimuli that fall below the perception threshold are called subliminal. Subliminal 'perception' takes place when the stimulus is below the observation threshold. According to psychophysics, perception cannot take place in more than 50% of these cases. However, many people believe that subliminal stimuli have an effect on the buying behaviour of consumers. In September 1957, the following experiment was carried out in a drive-in movie in New Jersey (USA). In the movie *Picnic* pictures were inserted every 5 seconds showing 'Drink Coca-Cola' or 'Eat Popcorn'. These pictures were shown for 1/3000 seconds—far below the perception threshold. The consumption of Coca-Cola was 60% higher than normal, and also 20% more popcorn was sold. These results caused a lot of excitement.[12] It seemed possible to influence people without them being aware of it. These striking results were not found when the same experiment was repeated. In the first experiment no check or control was done for the weather, the content of the movie and other factors that might explain the increased sales of Coca-Cola and popcorn. Later the researcher, Jim Vicary, admitted that the experiment was a fraud.

In another experiment the words 'meat' and 'cheese' were subliminally supplied. This appeared to activate the appetite of people who were exposed to these stimuli, while people who were not exposed to these stimuli showed little or no appetite at all.[13]

The possibility of subliminal influence has caused great anxiety. Consumers, after all, cannot defend themselves against this form of persuasion. And it is not clear how the process works. In many countries, subliminal advertising is expressly forbidden.[14]

Selective and transformed perception

We have a network of associations (schemas) about many things in our lives present in our minds. These schemas are not innate, but have been and are being constructed according to our own needs based on the available information. Schemas regarding brands, products, organizations, countries and people exist. As soon as a brand name is mentioned, the corresponding schema is activated. Mention Volkswagen, and we might think of: Germany, solid, durable, Lederhosen, and other associations. Marketing communication and other forms of promotional communication aim at developing a positive schema (positive associations) about a brand or company name.

Schemas facilitate information processing, which implies the intake, storage in memory, recognition and recall of information. Schemas that influence the perception of the incoming information, are called 'frames' or observation schemas. A frame is a window or filter in the mind.

The working of frames can be illustrated by means of the Müller–Lyer illusion; see figure 6.3. Most people think that the lower line segment with the arrows is shorter than the upper line segment, though they are equal in length. This is caused by the fact that people in the Western world are used to rectangular forms. That is why they associate the sloping points on the

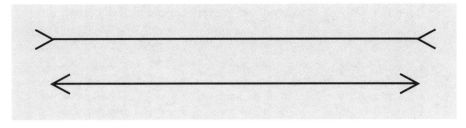

Figure 6.3 *The Müller–Lyer illusion*

line segments with angles of rectangular objects. The arrows might suggest a projecting (outer) angle, in the direction of the observer, while the upper line segment is regarded as a backward extending angle, away from the observer. The lower line segment is regarded as closer than the second line segment, and should therefore, according to our experience, be smaller than the line-segment that seems to be further away.[15] This is an example of a frame or perception schema (all kinds of associations with rectangular objects) that influences the observation (lengths of line segments).

In the Zulu culture, in which the people are more used to open spaces and to bent structures, people seem to be less influenced by the Müller–Lyer illusion. They have no association with inner and outer angles. That is why they can estimate the lengths of the line segments much better.

An example in the consumer area is the 'halo effect' of completing perception, in which a certain schema of a product, such as a fast, shining, expensive BMW can lead to an over-estimation of a characteristic, such as the interior space of a car.[16]

Definition

Consumer orientation is the direction, purpose or goal of consumer behaviour.

A clear relationship exists between a frame and the *orientation* of people. An orientation is a direction, a purpose or goal of the behaviour of the consumer. Sometimes, we concentrate on information processing (instrumental orientation). The dominant frame then determines on which form and which type of information we concentrate and how we observe this information. Sometimes we concentrate on leisure activities and having fun (hedonistic orientation). The dominant frame in this case is that we search for and take note of leisure activities. See table 6.1.

Table 6.1 shows the most important concepts concerning perception. Prior knowledge, orientation, circumstances and cognitive style are determinants which can bring about certain intermediary conditions for

Table 6.1 *Determinants, intermediary states and effects of perception*

Determinants	Intermediary states	Perception effects
1 Prior knowledge	Schemas	7 Completing perception
2 Orientation	Frames	8 Selective perception
3 Situation	5 Expectations	9 Biased perception
4 Cognitive style	6 Involvement	10 Differentiation

observers, such as expectations and involvement. These conditions lead to perceptual transformations, distortions such as completing perception (Gestalt), selective perception, biased perception, and perceptual differentiation.

The determinants and intermediary conditions that play a part regarding perception are discussed in more detail in the following subsections.

1   Prior knowledge

People who have certain prior knowledge frequently observe phenomena in a more differentiated way than people without this knowledge. Experienced chess players do not observe separate pieces, but observe combinations on the chess board. They 'see' positions on the chess board in a more differentiated way than novice chess players. Experienced chess players often immediately see the strong and weak points of a position and the possible moves. Furthermore, they can think ahead more moves than novice chess players.[17]

Prior knowledge and experience result in the creation of more elaborated and qualitatively different schemas and, as a result of this, different expectations. Also, prior knowledge leads to involvement with the topic, for example one feels an increased interest in news about a country or area one has visited.

2   Orientation

The orientation of the consumer activates certain frames and leads to a more selective observation of the environment.[18] Examples are the instrumental and hedonistic orientation of consumers. Consumers who are considering buying a car, see more advertisements for cars than consumers who are not making this choice.[19] Consumers needing some relaxation may be more interested in TV soaps or sport items.

3   Situation

Situational conditions also influence perception. When time is limited, circumstances are distracting or there is too much information, the opportunity for information processing is reduced. Selective and biased perception and perceptual differentiation take place. In these conditions, people are less able to concentrate on the work they are doing and are more inclined to make simplifications in order to form an opinion or make a decision. Another condition is deprivation. In a state of hunger people notice more objects having to do with food than under normal circumstances. Perceptions can be coloured or biased by the circumstances of a situation.

4 Cognitive style

A personality characteristic that influences perception, and especially perceptual differentiation, is cognitive style. This concerns a style of observation that to a certain degree depends on the context of the observable object. A field-dependent cognitive style implies that one is strongly influenced by one's environment and shows little interest in the differences between products. A person with this cognitive style may be strongly affected by advertising. A field-independent cognitive style implies that one is less influenced by one's environment and one brings more differentiation to the perception of products.[20] Some people naturally devise for themselves broad categories and arrange many objects in each category ('leveling'). Others create small categories and place only a few objects in each category ('sharpening'). This is also an example of cognitive style.

5 Expectations

Schemas form a *window* or filter on reality. It is a window, because we largely see what we expect to see. Information that is available, but does not fit into the schema, has only a small probability of being observed. Information that is less available, but does fit into the schema and thus is expected, is more likely to be observed. Football supporters are severely biased in their perception of the reality of the football game and the decisions of the referee.

We expect to hear positive news about a company that has a positive image. In an ambiguous situation we would probably select the positive aspects rather than the negative ones. We would also tend to view bad news about such a company as an exception and not as a rule.

In advertisements positive expectations are created concerning products and brands. This makes it more likely that consumers will pay attention to these products and brands than products that are not advertised. Likewise, it holds that products and services are observed against this background. The expectation creates a standard against which the observation of stimuli is positioned. This is consistent with the adaptation theory of observation.[21]

Schemas form a window, filter, colouring, or bias of our observation. Any observation is influenced by what we know and feel. Colouring the observation is mainly affective or emotional. Many aspects are ambiguous. Intuitively, a favourable or unfavourable interpretation is formed. An example of a biased observation is the fact that the size of valuable coins is often overestimated, while the size of low-value coins is under-estimated.[22]

6   Involvement

If someone is deeply involved in a subject or situation, then he or she will be more knowledgeable and his or her perception will be more differentiated. Greater involvement usually leads to more thinking, more information processing and less superficial perceptions. Gradations in perception mainly appear when substantial involvement is combined with more thinking about the subject. Consequently, involvement and prior knowledge are often highly correlated.

Definition

Involvement is the level of a consumer's personal relationship with a product or service including perceived importance, value and risk.

However, high involvement combined with little thinking may lead to undifferentiated, extreme, and one-sided perceptions and even totally biased opinions, such as in the case of football supporters and visitors to pop concerts.

Four forms of perception

Based on prior knowledge, circumstances, expectations, involvement, and cognitive style, four forms of perception can be distinguished: completing, selective, biased perception, and perceptual differentiation. See the last column of table 6.1.

7   Completing perception

People are inclined to 'complete' their observations. They want to create a complete, well-structured whole—a Gestalt.[23] Missing elements that fit into the whole are completed, even if they are not present or are ambiguous. A complete and consistent form is easier to remember than an irregular form. We like people or not. We ascribe more positive characteristics to people whom we like than to people whom we do not like. This is called the 'halo-effect'.[24] Missing product information is also often completed in this way. If a product is good on three product attributes, consumers tend to assume that the product will be good on a fourth attribute as well.

The Gestalt principles are: completion, similarity, and figure/back-ground. In figure 6.4 a few examples of the Gestalt principles are shown. Identical or similar elements are taken together in the observation. Figures are distinguished from the background, like the vase and the faces in figure

Figure 6.4 *Gestalt principles of closure, similarity and figure/background*

6.4. The figure can be white with a dark background (vase) or dark with a white background (faces).

8   Selective perception

Perception can be a selective observation or reality. We actually see what we want to see and expect to see, even if it is not there. We do not see what we do not expect or want to see. Selective perception implies that people observe different aspects of reality and do not see other aspects. Especially in the case of information overload or deprivation, people are urged to use information in a selective way and only to observe and use part of the available information.

9   Biased perception

Everyone has a different view on reality. Because of differing life histories, circumstances, moods, tasks and goals we each perceive reality differently. It is as though we all look at life through differently coloured glasses. We may ask ourselves whether an objective reality actually exists. In a cheerful mood, we see positive aspects of reality ('The sun is shining'). In a bad mood, we see other aspects ('It is too hot'). Moods and feelings can strongly influence what we observe.

10   Perceptual differentiation

Differentiation in perception implies that more aspects are included in the judgement and that more categories are formed to classify phenomena. When one knows more about a topic, one can identify more aspects and will probably arrive at a more differentiated image of reality. Highly involved consumers, in general, see greater differentiation between products and brands than less involved consumers. Perceptual differentiation can lead to one forming precise categories with which to classify reality. When differentiation is substantial, objects have to be more similar to be classified into the same category than when there is little differentiation. In the case of high differentiation, 'narrow' categories are formed.

Selective memory

Apart from selective perception there is selective memory. Even if we correctly observe something, we may selectively only remember what fits into our pre-existing schemas and expectations. In this way, the effects mentioned above do not only exist in perception but also in memory. Thus the effects of selective perception may be compounded by the additional factors of biased and completing memory.

6.4 Categorization

The world is chaotic, full of objects, people, noises, colours, smells, temperatures and ideas. For instance, it is possible to distinguish 7 million colours. We do not even have names for all these colours. A shopping street with people, store windows, billboards, direction signs, automobiles and tramcars has a high degree of complexity. Furthermore, people and objects change over time. How do we know whether today somebody or something is still the same person or the same thing as they were yesterday? People have to impose order onto this chaos to be able to survive.

People appear to be provided with certain inborn observation categories (dimensions) of space and time.[25] We observe all objects and persons in three spatial dimensions and in a time dimension. However, these categories are not enough to handle objects and persons appropriately and efficiently. Further categorization is also needed.

A *category* is a collection of objects with one or more common characteristics or functions. A product class like 'wine' is a category. But more specific categories also exist, such as Bordeaux or Chablis wines. The refinement or differentiation of the category wine into its subcategories is dependent upon the knowledge and involvement of a person.

By means of *categorization* it is possible to collate a large collection of objects and people under a common denominator. Objects and people possess characteristics and functions that distinguish them from other people and objects. A category is a collection of people, e.g., citizens of Denmark, with the shared characteristic that they live in Denmark. Do Danes living in a country other than Denmark also belong to this category? The category 'soft drinks' possesses the characteristics of being liquid and refreshing and containing no alcohol. The colour blue is a category of colours that reflect a certain spectrum of lightwaves. According to some people turquoise belongs to this category. According to others turquoise is more green than blue. 'Villa' is a category of houses standing alone surrounded by a garden. According to some estate agents semi-detached and terraced houses may also belong to the category of 'villas.' If this happens a category inflates too much and a new category is needed for the 'real' villas.

Consumers organize and categorize incoming information.[26] They develop a schema of expectations regarding a category.[27] The schema of a drink, for instance, consists of the following associations: liquid, thirst-quenching and refreshing. In this way, the category of 'drinks' is determined. Within this category the subcategory of 'fruit juices' exists, characterized by the same associations plus the associations made from fruit, being pure and healthy. Within the subcategory fruit juices, apple juice and orange juice exist. Orange juice can be thick and may contain solid parts of pulp. When apple juice contains pulp, this may be seen as an indication of low quality.

The first element of order concerning categorization is *identification*. People and things change, but still retain some characteristics. Identification is stating whether or not something or somebody is still the same.[28] A collection of photographs of a boy of ten years to a man of 25 years[29] shows that a lot changes, but he is still the same person (face and posture show

Figure 6.5 *Brand logos*

development, but also similarity). In different states of life and under different circumstances, we regard somebody or something as identical. The moon stays the same even as it waxes and wanes. Brands have their own identity, although the brand images have developed in time (Agfa, IBM, Lego, Shell). Drastic changes of a brand image disturb its identity. Only when a new identity is desired or when the introduction of the new logo is supported in a good way, can a sudden change like this be recommended. The Trustee Savings Bank in the UK made such a major change to TSB to get away from the savings bank image and to position itself as a mainstream bank. British Home Stores repositioned itself in the high street by becoming BHS.

The second element of order concerning categorization is *equivalence*. People and objects are equivalent if they have one or more similar characteristics. Motorized vehicles for the transport of one to five persons are called 'cars', which should be distinguished from motor bikes, scooters, buses, vans, trains, and lorries. Although a number of different cars exist, we normally know, without much difficulty whether something is a car or not. Is a Reliant on three wheels a car? And is a Renault Espace a car or a van? And is alcohol-free Miller Light a real beer or a soft drink? These are interesting categorization questions. Which characteristics have to be associated with Miller Light so that consumers put it in the category 'beer' and not in the category 'soft drinks'?

Categorization is a general psychological phenomenon. Part of perceiving an object is determining to which category it belongs. Categorization is a conceptual activity, as when we think about objects and define new categories. Conceptual categories, once they are formed, have their effect on perception and serve as a frame or a perceptual schema. After categories are formed, people try to fit as many observations as possible into the formed categories. This leads to a simplification and transformation of reality.

An object that fits easily into an existing category, has a better chance of being observed. The Whorfian hypothesis states that language and thinking are related. We have difficulty or cannot think about something, if we have no word (concept) for it.[30] According to this hypothesis, infants cannot think in an abstract way, because they have insufficient mastery of language. Appointing a striking word to a category often initiates a conceptual thinking process. Think of the concept 'yuppie' for a category of people or households with certain characteristics (young, urban, professional). Yuppies, in practice, do not seem to exist in large numbers. However, the conceptual category remains.[31] Affective, functional and formal categories may be distinguished.[32]

Affective categories
Affective categories are collections of objects and/or people who have similar affective (emotional) relationships for somebody. Everything that

reminds us of our last summer holiday has an affective loading for us. Thus, it can be a very diverse collection of objects and/or people: souvenirs, pictures, books and anything taken on a holiday. It is difficult to describe this affective relationship. Brands from our childhood (Lego, Playmobil, Singer) may belong to such an affective category. They originate from childhood, long before a conscious categorization is developed. There are substantial differences between consumers probably because of individual differences in experiences.

Affective categorization is not much differentiated and often makes a simple distinction between good and bad. Cognitively simple, field-dependent and uninvolved consumers often limit themselves to such a dichotomy of brands and types. Differentiation within a category is often affective too, for instance when we distinguish between good and bad restaurants or nice and terrible music.

Affective categorization may be crucial in the choice process of consumers. Brands and types we reject because of affective reasons are often not carefully considered, even though they might rationally have been the 'best choice'. If we categorize desserts into fattening and low calorie desserts, we may prefer desserts from the latter category. Cake and ice-cream are fattening; fruit and yoghurt are not. And what to do with yoghurt ice-cream and fruit ice-cream? Should these desserts be categorized in the fattening or the low calorie category?

Functional categories
Functional categories are easier to define, because the common element is part of the object itself. All objects fulfilling the same function belong to the category. For instance, the categories of diet products and contraceptives exist. Cars, helicopters and sailing boats belong to the category transport vehicles, but each is a subcategory. Functional categories often correspond with product classes.

Functional categories often concern the 'technical' function of products, as in the examples mentioned above. However, products can also be functional because they have the same instrumental value(s). Diet products do not only provide fewer calories (technical), but also lead to being slim and attractive (values). Toyota decided to give their more expensive cars the brand name Lexus. These cars compete with BMW and Mercedes and may not be associated with the category 'small cars'. The functional categorizations of consumers will often deviate from the categorizations that are made by producers and distributors. For marketing communication and the layout of goods in stores, it is important to know the functional categorization of consumers. A functional category is characterized by a schema of a few determining variables. Is Heinz sandwich spread something you eat on your bread or is it a party sauce? And where in the store do you find Heinz sandwich spread?

Figure 6.6 *Spread for bread?*

Formal categories
Formal categories are used in science and therefore have a more precise description than the terms that are used in daily language. Brands can also be regarded as formal categories. Producer brands or retailer (private label) brands contain all the emotional values the brand built up in time, such as goodwill and reputation. Formal and functional categories do not necessarily correspond. Virgin is an airline carrier, but the Virgin brand is also used for hotels, train services, and insurance services.[33] These are four different functional categories. Private-label brands, such as St Michael, have a large assortment of products in their formal category. The common element here is a certain quality level or a high-value image of the store.

6.5 Functions of categorization

What are the functions of categorization for consumers, producers and distributors? The following functions can be distinguished:

- *Reduction of complexity*. Categorization creates order and grouping out of chaos. According to Newtonian ideas, categories are given in nature and only needed to be discovered. According to modern ideas we make our categories ourselves to map a complex world.[34] Of all possible categorizations we choose one or a few as an acceptable way to reduce the complexity of reality.

- *Identification of objects* in the perception of reality. In the perception, phenomena and objects should be quickly classified in a category in order to react adequately. Is the strange, cracking noise caused by a burglar or by the storm? Is leasing a form of renting or buying, or is it a new category? Is BT a Danish, Dutch, or British company?[35] Logos and brand names are sometimes mixed up by consumers and categorized incorrectly.
- *Reduction of continuous learning.* Without categorization we would have to study all objects again every time to find out whether they are of any use to us or not. Using categories and characteristics we can classify objects quickly. Advertisements, brands and packaging are quickly classified this way and sometimes incorrectly rejected. A first positive recognition[36] and categorization is a good basis for further information processing about a product or brand.
- *Ordering of categories.* Categories have mutual (causal) relations. The category 'matches' has a relationship with the category 'fire.' Alcohol has a relationship with road safety, smoking with lung cancer, and driving a car with ecology, as suggested by information campaigns.
- Categorization gives *direction to behaviour* and to the way one reacts to new objects and persons. Affective categorization implies attraction or rejection. Functional categorization gives direction to the use of the product. Formal categorization implies that brands can have affective and symbolic values for consumers.
- *Substitution.* When a product or brand is sold out in the store, other products or brands in the same or similar category serve as substitutes, for instance Pepsi Cola for Coca-Cola and margarine for butter. The latter substitution is only feasible for broad categorizers.

A first categorization of objects in terms of dangerous *versus* safe, poisonous *versus* edible, or important *versus* unimportant facilitates a quick and adequate reaction. This is often an affective categorization. Categorization is often oriented towards the future and is not only a classification after the event. It is also a quick way to identify objects and people, although it carries the risk of stereotyping. One may judge too quickly and group things together that are actually quite different.

Criteria

Consumers have some criteria at their disposal to determine whether the chosen categorization is correct. Three of these four criteria come from attribution theory. Attribution theory is a theory about searching for causes of phenomena. People try to find out why something happened, why someone does something, or, in this case, how items should be categorized.[37]

Final criterion

To determine whether a mushroom is poisonous, we can eat it. To determine whether someone belongs to the category of solvent debtors, we could deliver goods without prepayment. This is, however, looking for validation after the event, while we usually want to know beforehand to which category something or somebody belongs.

Distinctiveness

When an object possesses no distinctive characteristics compared to similar objects, it is easy to classify the object in a category. Is Becel Gold a real or an imitation cheese? The packaging, the colour and the smell point towards 'cheese', but it is not written anywhere on the package. Or does Becel Gold belong to the new category of imitation cheeses? It is easiest to classify Becel Gold in the category of cheese and to use where otherwise 'real' cheese would be used. In the communication about Becel Gold the emphasis could be put on vegetable fats and it could be advertised as 'more healthy' than real cheese made of animal fat. Consumers could possibly form a new subcategory of 'vegetable cheeses'. Also should Yofresh yogorine be categorized as a type of margarine or as a subcategory of yoghurt-based margarines?[38]

Consistency

In general, we can be more certain of a categorization, if we can classify the object in a class on the basis of more than one attribute. A Miele or a Bosch washing machine is only good, when it seems to be good on a range of different characteristics. This is a form of affective categorization. A restaurant is only really good, when both the service and the food are good. Consumers use indicators to determine the quality of a product or a service. If all indicators point in the same direction, there is consistency.

Consensus

In general, we are more certain about a categorization, if different people, independently of each other, reach the same verdict. There are some passengers, who ask two or more other passengers who are independent of each other, whether this is the train to Brussels or not. They also examine the indicators on the platform. Only when the other passengers and indicators agree that this is the train to Brussels, do they dare to get on the train. Consumers talk to each other to test and validate their categorizations. Is *The Phantom of the Opera* a good musical? Can you have a nice meal at a TGI Friday restaurant? Consumers often test their opinion against those of others and against those of reviewers.

Clear categorization

According to attribution theory a category can be defined clearly and confidently when distinctiveness, consistency and consensus are all high. If

Becel Gold has several distinctive characteristics in the packaging and the product itself pointing in the direction of 'cheese' and a lot of people say it tastes like cheese, Becel Gold will be classified in the category 'cheese' or the subcategory 'vegetable cheese.' We could call 'tasting' the final criterion.

Categorization is the first step in giving meaning to objects and people.[39] We find it frustrating when we cannot classify an object and the object thus has less or no meaning for us. The discovery of where the object fits in gives a feeling of relief. We try to place a 'new' object in an existing category whenever possible. Only after a long period of hesitation will we decide to form a new category for a 'new' object. The easier an innovation can be categorized, the more likely it is to succeed.[40]

In many studies concerning consumer perceptions and decisions only one or a few brands are the subject of research. The categorization approach has the important advantage that products and brands are regarded in their context of substitution and complementarity. Changes in the market, the introduction of a new brand or the repositioning of an existing brand have consequences for the total market.

6.6 Rules of categorization

How do individuals allocate objects to categories? How do they remember which objects or persons belong to which category? Distinctive character-istics are important here. All objects possessing a certain characteristic or a combination of characteristics belong to a category. Consumers often remember a category on the basis of a *prototype*, a common or typical example of the category.

Categories may be defined and remembered in four different ways. The criteria according to attribution theory have already been discussed in section 6.5. The other three methods use a specimen, prototype or a decision rule.

A *specimen* is an 'example' of the collection of objects in a category. Several somewhat different specimens may exist in a category. A new object is compared to one or more specimens in order to decide whether the object belongs to the category. The ease of digging up a specimen from memory and imagining it, determines the choice of specimen that will be used.[41] These specimens determine the category in this way. As time passes new specimens are chosen and old specimens are not used any more: the specimen method is changeable. As examples of the 'space wagon' one can imagine the Renault Espace or the Chrysler Voyager, but in some years' time the specimen will probably be another brand or type.

A *prototype* is an 'ideal representation' of the collection of objects in a category. The prototype schematically combines the most characteristic properties of a category. A prototype is a Gestalt that does not have to exist in the real world. A new object is globally compared with the prototype and, on the basis of this comparison, it is determined whether the object belongs to that specific category or not. It is possible to question which critical properties are important and how strong the similarity between the object and the prototype has to be for the object to be placed in a category. Wrongly applying the probability rules could place a product in an incorrect category.[42]

For instance, for many individuals Blue Band is the prototypical margarine, the IBM PC is the prototype of a personal computer, and the MG is the prototype of a sports car. The prototype and its characteristic properties are remembered as a schema, a cognitive structure with associations and expectations concerning the category.[43] A prototype is more constant than a specimen.

An example of a wrong application of a prototype is the following. The prototype of a car in poor condition (a 'lemon') is a car with an ugly appearance, rusty and full of dents. In reality dents are removed from second-hand lemons in the showroom and they are given a new coat of paint. The consumer buys a car that looks in mint condition and doesn't recognize it as a lemon because it does not fit the lemon prototype.

In the classical approach to categorization, consumers use *decision rules*. This implies that consumers trace which characteristics products should possess to be classified in a certain category, or not be classified in any existing category at all. Necessary and sufficient characteristics are distinguished here. The presence of wheels for instance is a necessary but insufficient condition for an object to be categorized as a car. Bikes and buses also have wheels. Using decision rules is a conscious process of weighing up attributes.[44]

In practice, consumers will use combinations of the above-mentioned methods to determine whether an object belongs to a category. The specimen method is a good method for a first selection, the prototype method can be used for a more precise determination, while the decision rule method makes the most precise, almost scientific, determination possible. The last method is the most long-winded and time-consuming in its application.

It may be expected that visual information concerning new products can be processed more easily with the exemplar or prototype method than with the decision-rule method. Written information on the other hand, such as the inspection report of a car, can be processed more easily with the decision-rule method.

6.7 Differentiation

The more experience one has with a certain product group, the more precise categorizations one can make. Inuit,[45] Swiss and Austrian people distinguish different types of snow, whereas French, Italian and Spanish people generally only have one word for snow. In many African languages the word snow does not even exist. With increasing expertise, the differentiation in words and categories increases.

Producers and distributors have a lot of experience with their products and services. In general, they have a more precise differentiation than consumers. They use professional jargon. Furthermore, they often differentiate categories on the basis of technical characteristics and substantive arguments. Consumers may deviate from this. Consumers often base their categorization upon cues, i.e., indicators that have little to do with the content. Producers in the snack market give explicit names to crisps, whereas consumers call them all 'crisps' or use another categorization, for instance on the basis of the packaging, colour, taste, usage situation or target group. Producers distinguish (isotonic) sports drinks from normal lemonades. Consumers often do not make this distinction.

The quality indicators or cues of consumers can be different from those used by the producer. For many consumers an orange which is orange-coloured is perceived as being ripe and good to eat, while an orange that is slightly green is judged as inferior. However, choosing colour as a indicator of quality may be a mistake, as oranges are often 'coloured' by the suppliers. The official criterion for safe driving in many cities is the maximum speed of 30 mph. For many car drivers, the criterion may be different, namely the speed at which the car still feels 'under control.'

Differentiation does not only concern the number of categories, but also the number of characteristics or attributes, on the basis of which a category is formed. Greater differentiation corresponds with a larger degree of cognitive complexity, and probably with a more accurate reflection of reality. Cognitively complex people use less affective and more functional categorizations.[46] Cognitively complex consumers will more easily accept that products can possess both positive and negative characteristics and they will probably reject a product less easily on the basis of a single poor characteristic.

Differentiation leads to a hierarchy of categories and subcategories, i.e., subcategories are distinguished within a category and also at different levels. Examples are hierarchies of drinks[47] such as lemonade, juices, dairy products, beer, wine, and spirits, and a hierarchy of yoghurt-like desserts, such as normal, live yoghurt and Yakult. To which category does cottage cheese belong: cheese or yoghurt? Is it for salads, sandwiches or is it a dessert? Is yoghurt first categorized on taste (natural, strawberries, raspberries) and secondly on brand (Danone, Ski, Loseley)? Or is it categorised the other way around? In the supermarket the assortment is often grouped on the basis of brands and within the brands a distinction into taste or variants is made. The hierarchy of categories or partitioning of the market is relevant for competitive structures.[48]

The decision structure of consumers is important here. How do consumers, for instance, choose a car? Do they first choose the variant or type (saloon, hatchback, coupé, estate, multi-purpose vehicle or off-roader) and then the brand, or do they first select the brand and then the variant?[49] This depends on the type of market partitioning.[50] Both types of market partitioning can be found in figures 6.7 and 6.8. Market partitioning is a subjective categorization of the market.

If 'strong' brands exist within a category, consumers usually choose on the basis of brand names. Consumers purposefully select Coca-Cola or Pepsi Cola. If no strong brands exist, one normally chooses on the basis of taste. Consumers choosing tonic or bitter-lemon normally do not have a particular preference for Schweppes or Royal Club. For strong brands the partitioning is brand-based, while for weak brands the partitioning is often variant-based.

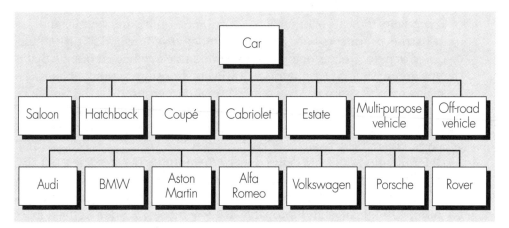

Figure 6.7 *Variant-based market partitioning*

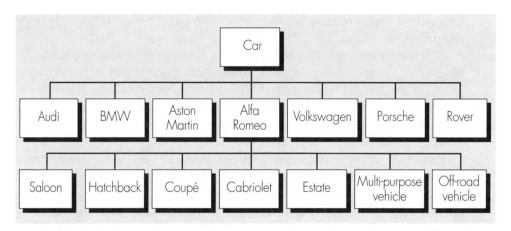

Figure 6.8 *Brand-based market partitioning*

The degree of cognitive complexity (differentiation or partitioning) depends upon the following factors:

- *Complexity of the product class.* If the product class is complex, consumers are forced to include a certain degree of complexity in their judgement. Consumers, in general, use less complex and differentiated judgements than the producers of goods. Producers understand the differences in the way that goods are produced and thus come up with categorizations that consumers do not use.
- *Degree of experience* with the product class. With increasing personal experience and prior knowledge, cognitive complexity and differentiation increase too.[51] This is often the case with specialized consumption domains.
- *Involvement* of the consumer. As a consumer becomes more involved with a certain product class, cognitive differentiation increases. A high degree of involvement is often accompanied by a higher level of ability and motivation. A music fan has a much more complex cognitive model regarding audio equipment than a person who only listens to music occasionally.
- *Ability* of the consumer is important. Consumers who are more capable of information processing and who show field independence,[52] also show greater differentiation.
- *Motivation* to process information, such as the 'need for cognition'[53] can determine the degree of cognitive complexity. There are consumers who enjoy thinking about something, to read and see, to differentiate, and to understand information.
- *Cognitive style* of the consumer. Broad categorizers ('levellers') show less differentiation and cognitive complexity than narrow categorizers ('sharpeners'). Field-independent consumers use more differentiation than field-dependent consumers.

Consumers who use broad categories, see little differences between products and brands and, generally, take larger risks. These broad categorizers accept new products more easily. Consumers who use narrower categories are more differentiated in their perception and see many differences between products and brands. These narrow categorizers are generally more cautious and risk-averse which in turn makes them less willing to accept new products.[54]

The Pollyanna hypothesis argues that a universal tendency exists to evaluate in positive terms.[55] We would rather speak of 'underdeveloped' or 'developing' than 'undeveloped', and 'weakly talented' rather than 'backward'. Some people even go so far as to replace 'disabled' with 'other-abled.' Negative differentiation probably goes together hand-in-hand with the tendency to judge in positive terms.

6.8 Assimilation and accommodation

An object that is congruent with an existing category, is placed in that category. For incongruent objects it is necessary to place them in an existing category or to create a new category. When a new and incongruent object is under consideration, two processes operate to fit the new object into an existing categorization: assimilation and accommodation. Assimilation occurs when a new object is fitted in the schema of an existing category. Accommodation occurs when a schema of a new (sub)category is formed for the object.[56]

Assimilation

If an object slightly deviates from the schema of a category, a process of assimilation takes place. The generic schema of the category is applied to the object. If the assimilation is complete, one speaks of a 'me-too' product. The product is more or less identical to existing products in the category. Absent or unknown characteristics are automatically 'borrowed' from the generic schema. Consumers thus complete the schema with characteristics of the category. When Hyundai is seen as a Japanese brand, Hyundai is endowed with all the characteristics of Japanese cars, such as quality and reliability.[57]

Definition

Assimilation is the categorization of an object into an existing schema.

Characteristics that are unique to particular objects are added as tags. For example, the Nissan 300ZX may be described by the schema of a sports car with the tags 'Japanese' and 'fairly priced'. Miller Light or Clausthaler are defined by the schema of beer with the tag 'without alcohol'. The 'schema plus tag' model indicates that assimilation appears for those characteristics of the object which are the same as the generic characteristics of the category. Only the tagged characteristics are different.

The introduction of a muesli-Mars bar could bring the consumer into categorization problems. Mars bars belong to the category of chocolate bars, associated with taste, sugar and energy, but are also considered unhealthy. Muesli belongs to the category of healthy products. So, a muesli-Mars bar is difficult to categorize for consumers. The most probable outcome of the assimilation process is that the Mars brand would be perceived as more healthy if such a product were to be introduced. However, even then a muesli-Mars bar would still be difficult to categorize.[58]

Two processes take place over time. The first is that any tag characteristics are forgotten or transformed (it is easier to transform the tag characteristics than the generic characteristics of the category). The tag characteristics are not cramped in the schema of the category. This is the process of assimilation. The second process is to fill in any unknown characteristics of the object with the generic characteristics of the category. This implies that the original positioning of the brand or type in a category is of crucial importance. After this the object is gradually assimilated into the category, as any tag characteristics are forgotten or transformed and the generic characteristics of the category are ascribed to the object.

Not only are the characteristics of a brand influenced by assimilation, but also the affective (emotional) judgement is influenced by the schema of the category. Feelings or emotions that are associated with the category, are transferred to the specific brand. That is why it is positive for a producer to associate a new product with a positively judged category.

Accommodation

If a product strongly deviates from an existing category, the process of accommodation or 'subtyping' takes place. A new (sub)category is formed for the product. When this happens, no assimilation takes place. The unknown characteristics are not completed with those of the category. The deviating aspects of the (sub)category are remembered very well. Furthermore, little transformation of affect of the general category to the (sub)category takes place.

Definition

Accommodation is the adaptation of an existing schema to an object to allow it to be categorized.

Assimilation and accommodation are closely related with the process of innovation.[59] For a discontinuous ('real') innovation accommodation is needed, as that implies forming a new category. For continuous innovations, such as variants and line extensions, assimilation suffices.

The process of accommodation, however, may create a broader range of category. The subcategory 'space wagon' creates more differentiation and variation of the category of cars. This also applies to forming subcategories such as buggy, jeep, and truck. The process of accommodation becomes stronger over time. Gradually, different categories evolve, each with their own schema. For interested consumers the category car is then replaced by a number of (sub)categories of automobile variants.

6.9 Conclusions

It is important to distinguish objective from subjective reality. People 'perceive' reality in their own ways. For the study of consumer behaviour it is important to take this subjectivity into account and to start from the reality as it is observed by consumers.

Subjective perception is selective. Relevant and remarkable items are selected and other items are not observed. This selectivity is necessary to survive in a world that offers an overload of information. However, such selective perception does make it possible to miss out on less remarkable, less eye-catching, but nevertheless relevant information.

Giving meaning to something is a process consisting of several steps of categorization and differentiation. When introducing a new product or brand, one needs to discover in which category consumers position or should position the product or brand. This means finding out which characteristics consumers pay attention to and which prototype or samples exist for that category.

Differentiation enables the formation of broad or narrow categories. Highly involved consumers often develop a high degree of differentiation and will consequently categorize brands and products precisely and narrowly. The process of assimilation reduces the number of categories. The process of accommodation, on the other hand, enlarges the number of categories.

Perception and categorization are the first steps in the process of giving meaning to products and brands; in the next chapters we discuss this subject further.

Notes

1. Kroeber-Riel, W. (1993) *Konsumentenverhalten* (München: Verlag Franz Vahlen) 5th edition.
2. Alba, J. W. and Hasher, L. (1983) 'Is memory schematic? *Psychological Bulletin* 93, 203–231.
3. Neisser, U. (1967) *Cognitive Psychology* (Englewood Cliffs, NJ: Prentice Hall). Posner, M. I. (1973) *Cognition: An Introduction* (Glenview, IL: Scott Foresman). Others also believe in the schematical model of the memory.
4. Kant, I. (1787), *Kritik der Reinen Vernunft*, Königsbergen, Germany.
5. Section 6.3.
6. Section 6.4.
7. Section 7.6.
8. Section 8.3.
9. Section 8.6.
10. Milliman, R. E. (1982) 'The effect of background music upon the shopping behavior of supermarket patrons' *Journal of Marketing* 46, 86–91. Milliman,

R. E. (1986) 'The influence of background music on the behavior of restaurant patrons' *Journal of Consumer Research* 13, 286–289.

11. Cox, D. F. (1967), *Risk Taking and Information Handling in Consumer Behavior*. (Boston, MA: Harvard Business School).

12. This story about subliminal perception can be found in Packard, V. (1957) *The Hidden Persuaders* (New York: David McKay).

13. Byrne, D. (1959) 'The effect of a subliminal food stimulus on verbal responses' *Journal of Applied Psychology* 43, 249–251.
    Spence, D. P. (1964) 'Effects of a continuously flashing subliminal verbal food stimulus on subjective hunger ratings' *Psychological Review* 15, 993–994. Another famous book is: Key, W. B. (1973) *Subliminal Seduction* (Englewood Cliffs, NJ: Signet).

14. For more information about subliminal perception see: Moore, T. E. (1982) 'Subliminal advertising: what you see is what you get' *Journal of Marketing* 46, 38–47.

15. Gregory, R. L. (1978) cited by Gross, R. D. (1987) *Psychology* (London: Hodder & Stoughton).

16. See 'completing perception' in this section.

17. De Groot, A. D. (1965) *Thought and Choice in Chess* (The Hague: Mouton).

18. Consider Gorn, G. J. (1982) 'The effects of music in advertising on choice behavior: A classical conditioning approach' *Journal of Marketing* 46, 94–101 (in section 10.2).

19. A good overview of possible forms of information acquisition can be found in Bettman, J. R. (1979) *An Information-processing Theory of Consumer Choice*, (Reading, MA: Addison-Wesley).

20. Witkin, H. A., Goodenough, D. R. and Oltman, P. K. (1979) 'Psychological differentiation: current status' *Journal of Personality and Social Psychology* 37, 1127–1145.
    Pinson, C. (1978) 'Consumer cognitive styles: review and implications for marketing' in: Topritzhofer, E. (ed.) *Marketing. Neue Ergebnisse aus Forschung und Praxis* (Wiesbaden: Gabler) 163–184.

21. Helson, H. (1964) *Adaptation Level Theory* (New York: Harper & Row).

22. Bruner, J. S. and Goodman, C. C. (1947) 'Value and need as organizing factors in perception' *Journal of Abnormal and Social Psychology* 42, 33–44.
    Ginsburg, N. and Courtis, R. (1974) 'The effect of value on perceived numerosity' *American Journal of Psychology* 87, 481–486.
    Smith, H. V., Fuller, R. G. C. and Forrest, D. W. (1975) 'Coin value and perceived size: a longitudinal study' *Perceptual and Motor Skills* 41, 227–232.

23. Gestalt psychology is the theory of observation in which a whole (a gestalt) is observed from separate stimuli. An advertisement with lights going on and off systematically, for instance, gives the idea of motion. All movie pictures are based on the Gestalt principle. Furthermore, there is a tendency to complete incomplete figures.

24. A 'halo' is the aureole around the head of a saint.

25. Kant (1787).

26. In order to simplify and to structure reality.

27. Bettman (1979).

28. Note that 'identification' is used differently than the use of this concept by Kelman, H. C. (1958) 'Compliance, identification, and internalization: three processes of attitude change' *Journal of Conflict Resolution* 2, 51–60 (see section 14.3).
29. Sheldon (1950) cited in: Bruner, J. S., Goodnow, J. J. and Austin, G. A. (1956) *A Study of Thinking* (New York: John Wiley) 3.
30. Whorf, B. L. (1940) 'Linguistics as an exact science' *Technology Review* 43, 61–63.
31. Solomon, M. R. (1992) *Consumer Behavior* (Boston: Allyn and Bacon).
32. Bruner *et al.* (1956).
    See also: Rosch, E. and Lloyd B. B. (Eds) (1978) *Cognition and Categorization* (Hillsdale, NJ: Lawrence Erlbaum).
33. These are examples of brand extensions.
34. These modern opinions were also proposed by Immanuel Kant (1787).
35. BT can stand for *Berlingske Tidende*, a Danish newspaper, Bührmann-Tetterode (a Dutch company), or British Telecom (a British company).
36. Affective categorization: primary affective reaction.
37. Van Raaij, W. F. (1986) 'Causal attributions in economic behavior' in: MacFadyen, A. J. and MacFadyen, H. W. (Eds) *Economic Psychology: Intersections in Theory and Application* (Amsterdam: North-Holland) 353–379. See also section 21.3.
38. (Sub)categorization is an important part of positioning. See section 24.7.
39. Bartlett, F. C. (1932) *Remembering* (Cambridge: Cambridge University Press).
40. Sections 15.2 and 15.3.
41. This is the heuristic of 'availability'. Tversky, A. and Kahneman, D. (1973) 'Availability: a heuristic for judging frequency and probability' *Cognitive Psychology* 5, 207–232.
    Sherman, S. J. and Corty, E. (1984) 'Cognitive heuristics' in: Wyer Jr, R. S. and Srull, T. S. (Eds) *Handbook of Social Cognition* part 1 (Hillsdale, NJ: Erlbaum) 189–286.
42. This is the heuristic of 'representativeness'. Tversky and Kahneman (1973); Sherman and Corty (1984).
43. Alba and Hasher (1983).
44. Cohen, J. B. and Basu, K. (1987) 'Alternative models of categorization: toward a contingent processing framework' *Journal of Consumer Research* 13, 455–472. See also chapter 11.
45. Inuit is the official name of the Eskimo population in Greenland and Canada.
46. Scott, W. A. (1963) 'Cognitive complexity and cognitive flexibility' *Sociometry* 26, 405–415.
47. Meyers-Levy, J. and Tybout, A. M. (1989) 'Schema congruity as a basis for product evaluation' *Journal of Consumer Research* 16, 39–54.
48. Rossiter, J. R. and Percy, L. (1987) *Advertising & Promotion Management* (New York: McGraw-Hill) 46–51.
    Waarts, E. (1996) 'Analysing competitive links in marketing' Unpublished doctoral dissertation, Erasmus University, Rotterdam.
49. Compare information processing activity with regard to an alternative and an attribute. See section 11.5.

50. See also Rossiter and Percy (1987) 46–51.
51. Linville, P. W. (1982) 'Affective consequences of complexity regarding the self and others' in: Clark, M. S. and Fiske, S. T. (Eds) *Affect and Cognition* (Hillsdale, NJ: Lawrence Erlbaum) 79–109.
52. Field dependence is a cognitive style in which people let environmental factors affect their judgements.
53. Cacioppo, J. T. and Petty, R. E. (1982) 'The need for cognition' *Journal of Personality and Social Psychology* 42, 116–131.
54. Donnelly, J. H. and Etzel, M. J. (1973) 'Degrees of product newness and early trial' *Journal of Marketing Research* 10, 295–300.
55. Boucher, J. and Osgood, C. E. (1969) 'The Pollyanna hypothesis' *Journal of Verbal Learning and Verbal Behavior* 8, 1–8.
56. Pinson, C. R. A. (1978) 'Consumer cognitive styles: review and implications for marketing', in: Topritzhofer, E. (ed.) *Marketing. Neue Ergebnisse aus Forschung und Praxis* (Wiesbaden: Gabler) 163–184.
    Sujan, M. and Bettman, J. R. (1989) 'The effects of brand positioning strategies on consumers' brand and category perceptions: some insights from schema research' *Journal of Marketing Research* 26, 454–467.
57. Hyundai is a South Korean automobile brand.
58. This is a fictitious example of a brand extension. See section 24.8.
59. See chapter 15.

7 Meaning Structure and Values

7.1 Introduction

Values and meanings related to products, services and brands are discussed in this chapter. These combine to form a central theme that is referred to in several other chapters of this book, particularly in the chapters on behaviour, lifestyle, market segmentation, positioning and brand extension.

Categorization is the first step in giving meaning to products. Products, services and brands partly derive their meaning from the category they are placed in. As a second step, products, services and brands derive meaning from the related networks of associations (schema) that develop in the minds of consumers.[1] These associations arise from people's experiences, the opinions of others, and from a range of types of communication. The meaning can be functional or psychosocial and relates to product benefits and values.

Consumption is also a kind of communication. By using products and brands consumers communicate meanings to others and show who they are or would like to be. Many children and adults pay a lot of attention to wearing the 'correct' clothing brands and sports shoes. Others wonder whether they visit the 'right' restaurant. Many consumers show that they are successful and wealthy by their choices of brand and type of car.

Semiotics, the science of meaning is discussed in the second section of this chapter. One particular schema is the means–end chain of the meaning structure (section 7.3). Means–end chains are discussed further in section 7.4. Section 7.5 is concerned with values. Some conclusions are drawn in section 7.6.

The objective of this chapter is to demonstrate the process and functions of meaning structures for consumer behaviour. Meaning structures are essential to the relationships between consumers and the products and services they use.

7.2 Semiotics

Semiotics is concerned with the meaning of objects. Semiotics was developed in the first half of the century, particularly in France, Italy and Switzerland.[2] In semiotics, people's interpretations and the meanings of signs for them are studied. A sign (S) refers to an object (O), so for example, the m-sign refers to McDonald's and a flag with a red maple leaf refers to Canada. The sign has to be interpreted by a consumer—the interpretant (I). These relationships are shown in figure 7.1. The relationship between a sign and an object (S–O) is called semantics. The relationship between the sign and the interpretant (S–I) is called pragmatics. The relationship between the signs (S–S) is called syntax.

A sign can be related to an object (semantics) in three ways:[3]

1 *Iconic signs* are non-abstract signs that represent the object by drawing on a similarity of appearance, such as a photograph, a drawing or other graphic image as a sign of an object. A picture of the product package in an advertisement ('a packshot') is an iconic sign of the product. The girl that is dressed and made-up just like a Spice Girl is an iconic sign of the real Spice Girls.

2 *Indexical signs* refer to an object or event because of the connection or causal relationship with the object. Tracks of a car are an indexical sign that a car has been driven there. In an advertisement for Lean Cuisine meals slim women are shown as indexical signs of the way that Lean Cuisine concerns 'slim products'.

3 *Symbolic signs* are signs that are related to an object based on an agreement or convention. The black-yellow-red flag is a symbolic sign for Belgium. No similarity or causal relationship exists between this flag and the state of Belgium. The Lego logo is a symbolic sign for Lego toys.

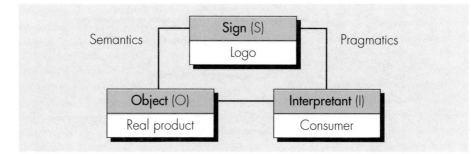

Figure 7.1 *Sign, object and interpretant*

Advertisements may contain iconical, indexical and symbolic signs for the advertised product or brand. If the product is shown in a picture, the advert contains an iconic sign. It includes indexical signs if conclusions can be drawn about the product characteristics from it. It includes a symbolic sign if the logo or the brand name is shown or mentioned.

Meaning transfer

Symbolic signs have to be learned. In advertising, symbolic signs can be matched with products and brands. In this way, the black-and-white cartoon figure of Fido Dido is a symbolic sign for Seven-Up. Just as with Seven-Up, Fido Dido needs no colour. The blue air and the swan are indexical signs for KLM. The blue air and the swan after all have a causal relationship with flying.

In figure 7.2 this transfer of meaning is shown. Pepsi Cola has already got a certain meaning through its past marketing communications. A famous person, for instance Michael Jackson, has a certain meaning for consumers. Michael Jackson is used by Pepsi Cola and by association transfers some of his meaning to the brand. The brand image, in this way, becomes young, dynamic and popular. Consumers who use this brand, in turn, receive these meanings (impressions) and transfer these to others (expression).

The transfer of meaning is not limited to people. Animals and symbols can also transfer meanings to brands. In an advertisement for Andrex toilet paper a labrador puppy signals the softness of the toilet paper.[4]

7.3 Meaning structure

Products can have different values and meanings for consumers. A product, first of all, has physical characteristics, like the cylinder size of a car and the ingredients of a meal. Added to this are psychosocial functions, such as comfort and good taste. The benefits of the usage can be functional, such as driving a car economically. The benefits may also be psychosocial, such as

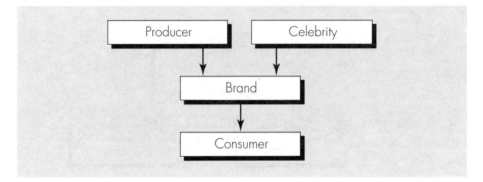

Figure 7.2 *Transfer of meaning*[5]

eating healthy food or doing sports. A product may also express the (desired) values of the consumer. The car is not only a means of transport, but the brand of the car also says something about its owner. The functional (technical) difference between a Volvo and an Opel is no doubt smaller than the psychosocial difference might suggest. And the quality of a Lacoste shirt might not differ at all from the quality of an unknown brand. However, it does say something about the person wearing the shirt. Lacoste signals exclusivity and fashion. Brands have their own schemas. Brand names refer to this and add meanings to products that satisfy the users.

Products and brands often have an outer-directed meaning, a meaning that is directed towards others. Products and brands are means to self-expression. Besides this expressive meaning, a product or brand can have an inner-directed meaning. An alarm installation may give a safe feeling and a book or a glass of Rémy Martin may give somebody a nice evening ('impression').

The functions and meaning of a product can be shown in a 'means–end' chain or ladder. This is called a meaning structure, (see figure 7.3[6]). The means–end chain starts with a *brand sign*—the characteristic packaging, the logo and other characteristics of the brand. Consumers recognize the brand in the store by the brand sign. The brand sign 'stands' for a number of product characteristics such as quality and status. Producers have invested many marketing communication campaigns in famous brands such as Coca-Cola, IBM, Sony, Porsche and McDonald's. Brands are important to producers, because consumers rely on these brands.[7]

Definition

A means–end chain captures the meaning structure of a brand, including the brand sign, product attributes, benefits and values.

We speak of means–end chains, because product characteristics lead to consequences (advantages or benefits), and these consequences lead to the realization of values. The characteristics are means to an end, namely the consequences or advantages. The consequences are, in turn, means to realizing values. Consumers have values. Product characteristics and consumer values are connected by the consequences. For instance, a car with petrol-injection (attribute) that uses less petrol (functional consequence), is especially important for consumers that are environmentally conscious or thrifty (values).

Consumers buy products and services to realize positive consequences and benefits for themselves in this way. When making a sales pitch, a salesperson will stress the benefits of using the product to the client.[8] The benefits, product advantages and functions are usually the starting point of

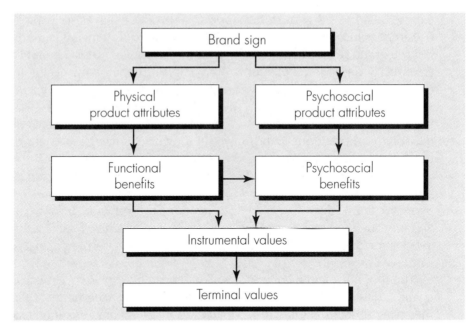

Figure 7.3 *Means–end chain*

product positioning and communication with the target group. In an advertisement, the benefits for the consumer can be shown or suggested by the product characteristics. Or the consumer is addressed with values, and it is demonstrated how the benefits lead to the realization of these values.

The importance of the characteristics, benefits and values differs between product classes. Products like a drill and a washing machine are mainly bought because of their functional consequences. Consumers are mainly concerned with what these products achieve in a technical sense. However, for other products the psychosocial or symbolic meanings are the most important. A ring, a tie, or a painting have no or hardly any functional characteristics. The psychosocial or symbolic meaning of these products is more important. Perfumes and jewellery have a high psychosocial meaning. Charles Revlon said: "In the factory we produce cosmetics, but in the stores we sell hope." This implies both psychosocial consequences and the realization of values. The brand shows the social environment of the users something about their prosperity and good taste. And it also gives the user a feeling of being stylish and rich.

Instrumental values are 'modes of conduct' that one adheres to in order to reach terminal values. Somebody can be polite and friendly in order to receive appreciation and trust from others. Products such as perfume can contribute to reaching instrumental values such as imagination and feelings such as falling in love. *Terminal values* are concerned with an end goal such as happiness, peace and a clean environment. Products such as a catalytic converter in a car can contribute by means of instrumental values (cleanliness) to reaching desired terminal values (a world of beauty, happiness).[9] Personal goals are related to terminal values.[10]

In practice, it is important to determine the relative importance of functional and psychosocial meanings. Even a product that seems only functional at first sight, often has a psychosocial meaning as well. A washing powder is primarily meant for washing clothes. However, it is also a way of showing others that one devotes enough care to the household and the environment.

Consumers may buy products primarily for their functional character-istics. For the brand decision they may let the psychosocial differences between the brands play a role. One buys a soft drink to quench thirst. But in deciding between Coca-Cola and Pepsi Cola the psychosocial differences between both brands are most important. These psychosocial differences become more important when the functional differences are small.

From generic to potential product

In the first stages of the means–end chain the physical product or service plays the central role. The physical product characteristics lead to the functional consequences. This is called the 'core product'. Psychosocial product characteristics lead to psychosocial consequences. The psycho-social or symbolic product characteristics are associated with the product and are ascribed to the product. They are part of the 'augmented product' and obtain their meaning by means of the packaging, advertisements and distribution.[11] See figure 7.4.

The generic product is unbranded, has physical characteristics, but no added value. It is the product as it comes from the factory. The core product has a brand name, a certain quality and is known because of this. A higher price is asked for the core product compared to the generic product. Psychosocial characteristics belong to the augmented product. Consumers experience the psychosocial consequences of product usage and connect these, just like the functional consequences, to their own instrumental

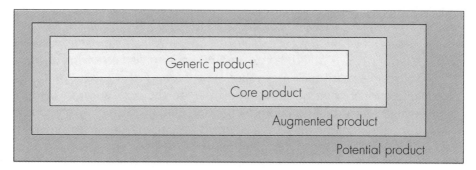

Figure 7.4 *From generic to potential product*

values and terminal values. The augmented product has an even higher price. The potential product shows the possibilities for a further development of the branded product, brand extensions, such as new variants and new applications.

A shampoo that is produced without a brand name, is an example of a generic product. With a brand name the product becomes known and, based on the brand's reputation, a certain quality may be assumed (core product). The advantage for the consumer is mainly the physical effect of the shampoo. The augmented product has a reputation and often an expressive value, for instance Timotei shampoo. The potential product is all the future possibilities of Timotei such as new fragrances and other additions, and even a complete Timotei product line for personal care.[12]

7.4 Means–end chains

Figure 7.5 shows six means–end relationships, marked A–F. Relationship A is situated within the product domain. Relationships B, C and D are situated at the interaction of the product domain and the domain of the consumer. Relationships E and F are situated within the consumer domain. These relationships imply the following:

A The relationship between physical product characteristics and the functional consequences is the primary functionality of the product or service. A vacuum cleaner has to have a number of technical characteristics in order to suck up dirt. Does the product fulfil the function for which it is bought? And to what extent is this function fulfilled?

B The relationship between psychosocial product characteristics and its consequences shows to what degree the product attributes that are ascribed to the product are actually experienced. A good design gives aesthetic pleasure to the user. Do consumers experience these consequences of characteristics that are ascribed to the product? Is the augmented product superior compared with the core product? Do consumers experience the augmented product as a consequence of advertising and tradition?

C Functional consequences may lead to psychosocial consequences. When a product functions satisfactorily, this leads to satisfaction and appreciation. This is called the secondary functionality. A car that always starts, is reliable. With such a car, a lot of problems are avoided.

D Functional consequences play a part in the realization of instrumental values. A car that functions well gives self-control. A car with good brakes provides safety and thus security. Safety is an instrumental value, whereas security is a terminal value.

E Psychosocial consequences also contribute to the realization of values. A product that gives aesthetic pleasure may contribute to the values

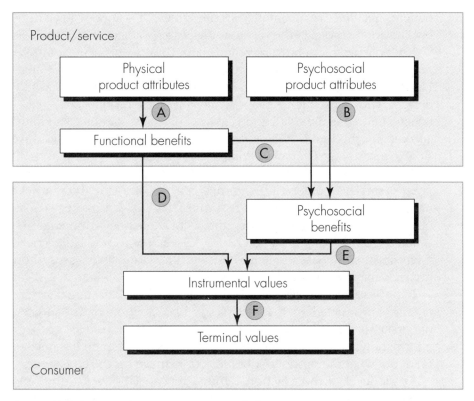

Figure 7.5 *Relationships in a means–end chain*

'cheerfulness' and 'imagination'. The ease and comfort of a dinner in a restaurant can give status and prestige and thus increase self-respect.

F Products and brands are often chosen to realize instrumental values. Instrumental values which contribute to the realization of terminal values, such as capability, may lead to self-respect.

Three of the six relationships are situated on the border of the domains of the product and the consumer. Here, the interaction takes place between product and consumer. On the grounds of these relationships a quality judgement is given and products and services are selected. When groups of consumers can be formed with certain characteristics and values (market segmentation), products and services could be designed with certain characteristics (product differentiation), that appeal to these segments of consumers.[13]

Meaning giving

The utility of products is not so much contained in product characteristics, but in benefits.[14] These functional and psychosocial benefits are important for the realization of values. The benefits are often affective in nature. The benefits get affective meaning from the values: 'It is good when a car is safe' or 'The good service in the restaurant gives a feeling of satisfaction.'

Not only products, but also brands have these levels of meaning. A brand is mainly a collection of characteristics. Philips evokes the schema with: Eindhoven, Dutch, electronics, good availability, reasonable price and good design. The consequences of buying a Philips product are: reasonable quality, middle of the road, good service and a long lifetime. The values that accompany the brand Philips for instance are: technically innovative, but slow in marketing. The brand Philips is a sign of these benefits and values.

At the level of physical and psychosocial *characteristics*, the brands possess similar or different technical characteristics or ingredients. A Volvo has airbags but a Fiat does not. Assuming that 'more is better', consumers place the products in a category and will favour one brand over another. When the difference in characteristics (e.g., safety) is very large, consumers might form two classes: safe and unsafe cars. Distinctiveness is often temporary. Characteristics of brands can often be quickly imitated.

In professional journals directed towards professional target groups only technical product characteristics need to be mentioned. The target group understands the utility and function of these characteristics. In other cases, information at the level of benefits or values is desired and it is necessary to point out what the product or brands could mean for the consumer.[15]

At the level of the functional and psychosocial *benefits*, the emphasis is on the consequences of the use of the brands: for instance ease of handling, quality, comfort and sociability. It concerns the consequences, the promises, the benefits for the user. Advertising should show which advantages the product has for the consumer and in which way the brand is better than its competitors.

At the level of *values*, instrumental and terminal values are important.[16] The lifestyle and the personal goals of the users play a role. Which personal goals, lifestyle, instrumental and terminal values can be realized with brands and products?

Problem solving and enrichment of meaning

A distinction can be made between problem solving and enrichment of meaning.[17] Central to problem solving is that the product prevents or solves a problem. Something negative such as damage or a headache is neutralized. For enrichment of meaning, the product must add value to the life of the consumer. Something neutral becomes positive, for instance a holiday trip or a nice car could make life more pleasant. Alternatively, problem solving products are classified as informational and enrichment products as transformational.[18] Products and services can also fulfil both meanings. By going on holiday tiredness and boredom are removed (problem solved) and life is enriched. A soft drink quenches thirst and the brand can make life more pleasant for the drinker.

Table 7.1 *Levels of meaning*

	Problem solving	Enrichment
Attributes	1 Hygienic inhibition	4 Motivational facilitation
Consequences	2 Relief respite relaxation	5 Excitement pleasure joy comfort
Values	3 Anxiety, dismay rest, peace security safety inner harmony	6 Social recognition status, prestige pride happiness

Three levels may be distinguished for both forms of meaning, i.e., different types of characteristics, consequences and values. The options are shown in table 7.1.

Considering cell 1 of table 7.1, products and services such as aspirin, insurance, and lawyers are mainly problem-solving. The attributes of these products or services are mainly judged on the basis of their effectiveness to prevent and solve problems. These are called *hygienic* characteristics. When the characteristics are lacking or insufficient, a negative consequence develops. When these characteristics are present, a positive consequence may not necessarily develop. Travellers with the SNCF are not really satisfied when the train runs on time. This is normal. They are only dissatisfied when the train is too late. The characteristic of 'punctuality' is an inhibition factor. When it is not satisfied, the consumer cannot be satisfied, even if the train is comfortable and the conductor friendly.[19]

Concerning cell 2 of table 7.1, the consequences of the use of problem-solving products are relief, respite and relaxation when the problem is prevented or solved. The danger is past or the negative consequences one was afraid of, did not occur. In advertisements, the consequences can be shown in a negative or a positive way. Sometimes the negative consequences in the case of non-usage are shown, such as a headache at the moment that visitors are arriving. Sometimes the positive consequences of actual usage are shown such as the ease of paying with a credit card. Advertisements with contrasts, such as the past/the present (grandmother washed in that way and granddaughter washes in this way), before/after (before and after a cure) and one/the other (two people who borrowed money, of which one is better off than the other) are examples.

In cell 3, products and brands may also solve problems that are concerned with values. By saving at the Co-operative Bank one prevents money being used for environmentally harmful purposes. By buying a safe car, one hopes to prevent oneself from getting seriously injured in the case of an accident. Thus, problem-solving has also to do with values. Products and brands can help prevent negative values from becoming reality. In advertisements values can be shown in a negative and positive way: fear and horror versus relaxation and peace of mind.

In cell 4, products and services such as soft drinks, holidays and cars are mainly enriching. The characteristics of these products are mainly judged on their effectiveness in making life more pleasant. These are called *motivational* characteristics. When these characteristics are present, a positive consequence develops. When these characteristics are absent, a negative consequence does not necessarily develop. Diners at a restaurant are satisfied when the dinner meets their expectations, and delighted when a special dessert is served.

Concerning cell 5, when meanings are enriched, the consequences are nearly always positive: excitement, pleasure and joy. The products and services make life more easy, pleasant and interesting.

In cell 6, enriching products and brands leads to the realization of positive values such as status, prestige, happiness, pride, self-esteem, and social recognition. The positive values are normally shown or suggested in advertisements.

7.5 Values

The behaviour of people is partly determined by culture, norms and values. Values are important, especially when they concern behaviour in the long run. Values give meaning and direction to behaviour. A value is a permanent belief that certain ways of behaviour or end states are preferred to the opposite ways of behaviour or end states.[20] Values are often structured in a value system. A value system is a more or less permanent organization of beliefs concerning preferred ways of behaving and end states. People have a limited number of values, so it is possible to map human values through research. Value systems of groups of consumers can be compared.

From the definition it appears that a value is a type of belief about how one should behave, such as honestly and correctly, and it also concerns desirable end goals, such as freedom and security. Values are more or less permanent. This implies that the values of people hardly, if ever, change. A value is a prescriptive belief, which means that it concerns desired behaviours and end goals.

Values differ from attitude. Attitudes concern objects. The object of an attitude can be a behaviour, person, idea or thing. We have an attitude towards something, for instance towards Benetton or shopping. Values are not directly related to objects. At most, objects are judged regarding the extent to which they can contribute to reaching values. In this way food and sports might be judged according to their contribution to health.

Figure 7.6 *Food and health*

Values play an important part in Christianity and West European culture.[22] Values give direction to the life that one strives for. From long-term values, short-term goals can be derived. Goals are the motives for concrete behaviours and for the attitudes and interests that concur with these behaviours.[23] Note that values and goals give direction to knowledge, attitude and behaviour. Values are more general than attitudes because one value can give direction to several attitudes because values are not directly linked to specific objects.

In addition to the distinction between instrumental and terminal values made earlier, a distinction can be made between personal and social values. Personal instrumental values are concerned with competence. Personal terminal values are concerned with self-realization. Social instrumental values are moral values. Social terminal values are concerned with society at large. Four groups of values can be identified as shown in table 7.2. In this table, examples of instrumental and terminal values are included.

More dimensions can be distinguished from the values of table 7.2 than just instrumental/terminal or personal/social. Some values can be realized immediately, such as pleasure and a comfortable, exciting life. Postponed realization is more likely to occur with values such as wisdom and inner harmony. Some values are self-restricting, such as obedience, politeness, and honesty. Other values are self-enhancing such as capability and imagination.

From table 7.2, it appears that the moral values of honesty, responsibility, forgiving others and broadmindedness are among the top five instrumental values in the USA. From repeated surveys, it has appeared that this ranking is highly stable over time.[24] The societal values of a world at peace, family security and freedom constitute the top three terminal values. It appears that both social and societal values obtain the highest ranks in

Table 7.2 *Four groups of Rokeach values*[21] (rank orders in parentheses)

	Instrumental values	(1971)	Terminal values	(1971, 1981)
Personal	**Competence**		**Self-realization**	
	ambition	(3)	self-respect	(5, 4)
	courageousness	(6)	happiness	(6, 5)
	capability	(9)	wisdom	(7, 6)
	cleanliness	(10)	salvation	(9, 9)
	self-control	(11)	a sense of accomplishment	(11, 7)
	cheerfulness	(13)	inner harmony	(12, 13)
	being intellectual	(15)	a comfortable life	(13, 8)[a]
	imagination	(16)	pleasure	(16, 17)
	being logical	(17)	an exciting life	(18, 15)[a]
Social	**Morality**		**Societal**	
	honesty	(1)	a world at peace	(1, 2)
	taking responsibility	(2)	family security	(2, 1)
	forgiving others	(4)	freedom	(3, 3)
	broadmindedness	(5)	equality	(4, 12)[a]
	helpfulness	(7)	national security	(8, 11)[a]
	being loving to others	(8)	true friendship	(10, 10)
	independence	(12)	mature love	(14, 14)
	politeness	(14)	a world of beauty	(15, 16)
	obedience	(18)	social recognition	(17, 18)

[a] A significant change occurred between 1971 and 1981.

value surveys. This seems to be consistent with product positioning in advertising.

Despite their general stability, several changes in the ranks of terminal values have been found. Equality and national security have obtained lower ranks in 1981 than in 1971 in favour of a sense of accomplishment and an exciting life. This seems to reflect the change from materialist to post-materialist values, considered in chapter 3.

Research shows that most of the Rokeach values can be classified into seven domains.[25] In table 7.3 these seven domains are shown in combination with the List of Values (LOV). The LOV values concern only five domains.

Table 7.3 *Seven domains of Rokeach and LOV values*

Domain	Rokeach values	LOV values
Pleasure	Pleasure a comfortable life happiness cheerfulness	Pleasure an exciting life
Security	Family security national security a world at peace freedom	Security
Achievement	A sense of accomplishment social recognition ambition capability courageousness	Accomplishment being respected
Independence	Imagination independence being intellectual being logical	Self-esteem self-realization
Maturity	Wisdom mature love true friendship a world of beauty inner harmony	Belonging good relationships with others
Conformism	Obedience politeness cleanliness self-control	
Social	Equality helpfulness forgiving others being loving to others taking responsibility	

LOV

The List of Values (LOV) is an alternative to the Rokeach values with the nine values shown in table 7.3.[26] It seems that LOV values are easier to apply for market segmentation purposes than Rokeach values. LOV values are closer to the reality of everyday life of consumers and products.

On the basis of the Rokeach values and a number of other values from the literature, an attempt has been made to organize values in two-dimensional space.[27] One dimension should capture whether the values serve individual or collective interests—individual autonomy (self-directedness) versus conservatism. This also implies that values serving the same interest are more closely correlated than those serving different interests. The second dimension distinguishes hierarchy and mastery values from egalitarian commitment and harmony with nature. The two dimensions also imply that some values conflict with each other. Seven value domains have been distinguished empirically in 86 samples of teachers from 38 nations. Teachers were selected because they are considered to be important agents in transmitting cultural values to new generations. They were asked to rate the importance of 56 values using a scale of 7 (of supreme importance) to 0 (not important) and −1 (opposed to my values). It appeared that 45 values had equivalent meanings across the samples, which were selected to form the final domains. They are derived from biologically based needs, social interaction requirements for interpersonal cooperation and social institution demands for group welfare and survival.[28]

The seven value domains are:

- *Conservatism domain.* This domain includes values associated with maintaining the *status quo* and common interests of individuals and society, i.e., social order, honouring elders, preserving public image, politeness, reciprocation of favours, self-discipline, devotion and respect for tradition. This domain also includes the Rokeach values of family security, national security, obedience, wisdom, cleanliness and being forgiving.
- *Affective autonomy domain.* This domain is associated with the emotionally self-directed individual valuing an enjoyable, varied life and pleasure. Rokeach's value of an exciting life is also included.
- *Intellectual autonomy.* This domain captures the intellectually self-directed individual valuing curiosity and creativity. The Rokeach value of broadmindedness is also included.
- *Hierarchy domain.* This domain includes values of social power, authority, wealth, influence and humility. No Rokeach values correspond with this domain.
- *Mastery domain.* This domain includes successfulness, daring, capability and choosing own goals. Rokeach's values of independence and ambition are also included.

Figure 7.7 *Norms and values*

- *Egalitarian commitment domain.* This domain captures social justice, loyalty and accepting one's lot. The Rokeach values of equality, responsibility, freedom, honesty, helpfulness and world peace are also included.
- *Harmony domain.* This domain includes protecting the environment and unity with nature. The Rokeach value world of beauty is also included.

A sketch of the seven domains in two-dimensional space is shown in figure 7.8. The sketch shows adjacent domains (for example, egalitarian commitment and harmony) and opposite domains (for example, autonomy and conservatism). Tables 7.4 and 7.5 show the average scores of different samples from Europe, USA, Japan and Australia. It appears that Eastern European countries find conservative values more important than Western European countries. As autonomy values contrast with conservatism, so these values of autonomy are more important in Western than in Eastern Europe. The other parts of the world score in-between. With respect to the hierarchy and mastery values and the egalitarian commitment and harmony values no clear pattern emerges. Turkey scores the highest and Italy the

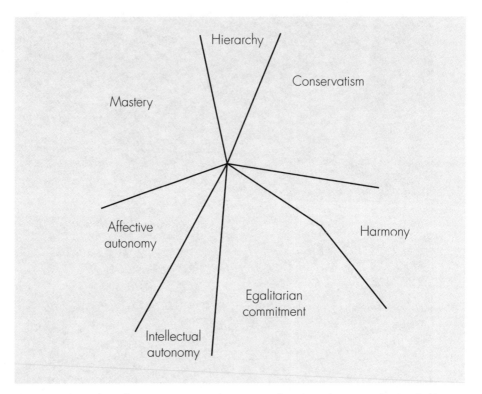

Figure 7.8 *Value domains in two-dimensional space (source: S. H. Schwartz (1994))*

lowest with respect to hierarchy values. The USA, Japan, Portugal and Greece score the highest on mastery values whereas Estonia and Finland score the lowest. The USA scores relatively low on harmony values.

Using an earlier vision of the value system, a Danish study has found positive correlations between harmony, egalitarian commitment and intellectual autonomy values and favourable attitudes toward the environment, negative correlations between conservative and hierarchy values and favourable attitudes toward the environment and no relationship with mastery and affective autonomy values.[29] This result indicates that general values have implications for specific attitudes.

Functions of values

Some functions of values have already been mentioned. These functions may be ordered systematically into five categories:[32]

- Values have a *justification function*. People strive for goals and values in life and choose activities and interests based on values that are important to them. Religion, humanism, and ideologies like socialism, liberalism and feminism are important value systems.

Table 7.4 *Average importance of conservatism and autonomy values in various countries*[30]

	Conservatism	Affective autonomy	Intellectual autonomy
Bulgaria-Turks	4.43	3.13	3.78
Estonia-Rural	4.37	3.03	3.69
Poland	4.31	3.13	4.09
Slovakia	4.28	2.76	4.03
Slovenia	4.27	3.76	5.03
Turkey	4.27	3.25	4.12
Estonia-Urban	4.26	3.08	3.93
Hungary	3.97	3.34	4.44
Finland	3.84	3.51	4.62
Italy	3.82	2.95	4.60
Portugal	3.76	3.54	4.12
Greece	3.68	3.96	4.09
Netherlands	3.68	3.51	4.44
Denmark	3.64	4.01	4.58
East Germany	3.50	4.16	4.47
West Germany	3.42	4.03	4.75
Spain	3.42	3.97	4.90
France	3.35	4.41	5.15
Switzerland (Fr)	3.25	4.24	5.33
USA	3.90	3.65	4.20
Japan	3.87	3.54	4.68
Australia	4.06	3.50	4.12

- Values have a *knowledge function*. People look for the reason and meaning of life, they search for insight and clarity. Their value system can be instrumental in reaching this insight. Values order attitudes and bring consistency to our opinions. From some central values attitudes regarding products and brands can be derived. People strive for consistency (also a value!) and therefore bring about a more unified framework for their values and attitudes.
- Values are *instrumental*. Goals, attitudes and objectives for behaviour can be derived from values. Terminal values such as self-realization are 'supergoals' that never can be fully achieved, but for which we strive our whole lives.
- Values are *ego-protecting*. People can support their opinions with values. Authoritarian people put much emphasis on being clean, orderly, and honest. Democratic people value imagination, freedom and friendship as important. Sometimes we rationalize our own behaviour by thinking out values for this behaviour after the fact. An unkind remark may be rationalized as being 'honest'.
- Values are also criteria for appreciation and can act as standards for judging our own behaviour and the behaviour of others. Values are thus

Table 7.5 *Average importance of hierarchy, mastery, egalitarian commitment and harmony values in various countries*[31]

	Hierarchy	Mastery	Egalitarian commitment	Harmony
Turkey	3.30	3.90	5.12	4.26
Bulgaria-Turks	3.07	4.04	4.83	4.32
East Germany	2.69	4.16	5.29	4.08
Poland	2.53	4.00	4.82	4.10
Hungary	2.42	3.96	4.87	4.51
West Germany	2.27	4.07	5.37	4.42
Netherlands	2.26	3.98	5.39	3.98
Switzerland	2.20	4.18	5.19	4.50
Estonia-Rural	2.18	3.64	5.02	4.53
France	2.16	3.89	5.45	4.31
Slovakia	2.11	4.09	4.98	4.40
Portugal	2.08	4.25	5.62	4.29
Spain	2.03	4.11	5.55	4.53
Finland	2.03	3.63	5.26	4.54
Greece	2.01	4.53	5.35	4.39
Estonia-Urban	2.00	3.73	4.96	4.65
Denmark	1.86	3.97	5.52	4.16
Slovenia	1.76	3.76	4.36	4.72
Italy	1.69	4.08	5.57	4.80
USA	2.39	4.34	5.03	3.70
Japan	2.86	4.27	4.69	4.07
Australia	2.36	4.09	4.98	4.05

normative. Do others act in accordance with general acceptable norms and values? And it can be questioned as to whether our own behaviour is always in accordance with our values.

7.6 Conclusions

A central issue in this chapter is the meaning of products and brands. This meaning is historically based on consumers' personal experiences, the experiences of others and on promotional communications. The meaning can be seen as a meaning structure, i.e., the means–end chain.

Consumers do not only use products for their functional consequences or benefits, but also for their psychosocial consequences. They communicate with others by means of the products and brands that they own and use. However, it is a particularly postmodern idea that people evaluate others on the basis of product/brand ownership and usage and not only on aspects such as personality, behaviour and contribution to society.

Even daily consumer behaviour is concerned with values. We do not always realize this when buying washing powder or driving our cars. Every purchase or every usage of a product can make the realization of values easier or harder. Sometimes this is clear, for instance when an adult buys his or her first house and thereby realizes the value of independence. Sometimes, this is not so clear, as in the case of impulse buying.

Notes

1. See chapter 6.
2. Peirce, C. S. (1960) *Collected papers of Charles Sanders Peirce* (Cambridge, MA: Harvard University Press).
   F. de Saussure, F. (1966) *Course in General Linguistics* (New York: McGraw-Hill).
3. Dingena, M. (1994) *The Creation of Meaning in Advertising* Doctoral dissertation, Erasmus University, Rotterdam.
4. The process of meaning-giving can be explained by classical conditioning. See section 10.3.
5. McCracken, G. (1989) 'Who is the celebrity endorser? Cultural foundations of the endorsement process' *Journal of Consumer Research* 16, 310–321.
6. Reynolds, T. J. and Gutman, J. (1984) 'Advertising is image management' *Journal of Advertising Research* 24, 27–36.
7. The importance of a brand to the brand owner is called brand equity. See Aaker, D. A. (1991) *Managing Brand Equity* (New York: The Free Press).
8. Floor, J. M. G. and van Raaij, W. F. (in preparation) *Marketing Communication Strategy* (Hemel Hempstead, UK: Prentice Hall).
9. See section 8.2.
10. See section 7.5 on values.
11. Levitt, T. (1986) *The Marketing Imagination* (New York: The Free Press). Levitt speaks of 'core products' and 'augmented products'.
12. This is called brand extension. See section 24.8.
13. See chapter 24.
14. Cude, B. J. (1980) 'An objective method of determining the relevancy of product characteristics' *Proceedings of the American Council of Consumer Interests*, 111–116. The economist distinguishes characteristics and 'services' of products. A product delivers a 'service' by means of a combination of characteristics. In this way an automobile delivers the functional service of 'transportation' by means of a combination of a motor and wheels, and the psycho-social service of 'status' by means of brand, size, and price.
15. Maheswaran, D. and Sternthal, B. (1990) 'The effects of knowledge, motivation, and type of message on ad processing and product judgments' *Journal of Consumer Research* 17, 66–73.
16. See section 7.5.
17. Rossiter, J. R. and Percy, L. (1987) *Advertising & Promotion Management* (New York: McGraw-Hill).
18. Rossiter and Percy (1987).
19. The distinction between hygiene and motivational factors comes from Herzberg's theory of job satisfaction. See Herzberg, F., Mausner, B. and Snyderman, B. (1959) *The Motivation to Work* (New York: John Wiley), 2nd edition.

20. Rokeach, M. (1973) *The Nature of Human Values* (New York: The Free Press) 5.
21. Rokeach, M. and Ball-Rokeach, S. J. (1989) 'Stability and change in American value priorities 1968–1981'. *American Psychologist* 44, 775–784.
22. See chapter 3.
23. See figure 8.1.
24. Rokeach, M. and Ball-Rokeach, S. J. (1989). Inglehart, R. (1985) 'Aggregate stability and individual-level flux in mass belief systems: the level of analysis paradox' *American Political Science Review* 79, 97–116.
25. Kahle (1984); Kahle, L. R., Beatty, S. E. and Homer, P. (1986) 'Alternative measurement approaches to consumer values: The List of Values (LOV) and Values and Lifestyles (VALS)' *Journal of Consumer Research* 13, 405–409.
26. Kahle (1984).
27. Schwartz, S. H. and Bilsky, W. (1987) 'Toward a universal psychological structure of human values' *Journal of Personality and Social Psychology* 53, 550–562.
28. Schwartz, S. H. (1994) 'Beyond individualism/collectivism. New cultural dimensions of values' in: Kim, U., Triandis, H. C., Kagitcibasi, C., Choi, S.-C. and Yoon, G. (Eds) *Individualism and Collectivism: Theory, Method and Applications* (London, UK: Sage) 85–119.
29. Grunert, S. C. and Juhl, H. J. (1995) 'Values, environmental attitudes, and buying of organic foods' *Journal of Economic Psychology* 16, 39–62.
30. From Schwartz (1994).
31. From Schwartz (1994).
32. Katz, D. (1960) 'The functional approach to the study of attitudes' *Public Opinion Quarterly* 24, 163–204. He distinguished the instrumental, ego-protective, value-expressive, and knowledge functions of attitudes. See section 9.3. The instrumental, ego-protective, and knowledge functions can also be applied to values.

MOTIVATION AND CONSUMER BEHAVIOUR

8

8.1 Introduction

Identity, motivation, consumer goals and consumer behaviour are the central issues in this chapter. The reader might ask why 'consumer behaviour' is not discussed in the first six chapters of this book. After all, the whole book is about consumer behaviour. The other chapters focus on the determinants and the consequences of consumer behaviour. This chapter focuses on the 'real' behaviour, and its motivational factors.

In figure 8.1 the most important concepts of this chapter are summarized in a model that is derived from the general model of this book.[1] Values, identity and needs lead to goals and behaviour. This does not imply that all behaviours can be derived from somebody's values or personal identity. Many needs and goals arise without a direct relationship with values, such as impulse-buying behaviour. The effects of the behaviour are judged by people themselves and by others. This judgement feeds back into behaviour, goals, needs and values. An example may clarify this. Consumers wanting to save energy, may put on a sweater and turn down the thermostat (behaviour). They will observe effects from this behaviour, namely a lower energy bill. They may adjust their behaviour and goals in reaction to this. The consequences of behaviour also have a feedback effect on needs and values.[2]

As well as identifying the concepts within the model, figure 8.1 also shows in which sections of the book these concepts are discussed. The identity and image of consumers is discussed in section 8.2. Section 8.3 deals with motivation and needs. People are motivated by 'push' factors, their inner pressures, or by 'pull' factors from outside themselves. Needs also arise from discrepancies between the desired and actual status. In section 8.4 the personality factors 'need for cognition' and 'self-monitoring' are discussed. In section 8.5 the goals of consumers are considered. These

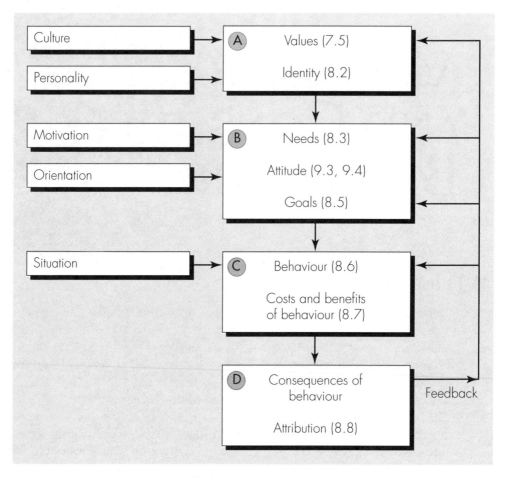

Figure 8.1 *Motivation and behaviour*

goals are closely related to consumer behaviour as discussed in section 8.6 and the costs and benefits of behaviour is considered in section 8.7. After a short introduction to attribution theory in section 8.8, some conclusions are drawn in section 8.9.

The objective of this chapter is to give insight into consumer behaviour as such, in addition to motivation, identity, personality, and consumer goals. The chapter concerns the behaviour itself and the motivational factors that determine the behaviour.

8.2 Identity and image

Self-schema

In the networks of associations (schemas) in our brain the self-schema or personal identity takes a dominant position.[3] It is built on experiences from

Figure 8.2 *Desired identity?*

the past, especially those resulting from one's own behaviour and feedback from the outside world. The self-schema or identity includes detailed information concerning one's actual, perceived and desired identities.

Sometimes people imagine themselves in future situations and they foresee the reactions of others to these situations. For example, a person may daydream about being the owner of a nice house and an expensive car. Advertising stimulates these thoughts and dreams about oneself and about the future. Self-schemas are sometimes fantasies and daydreams, sometimes realistic possibilities for self-development. The repertoire of possibilities goes from strongly idealized self-schemas such as being rich, good looking, famous and being admired, to negative self-schemas which one would like to avoid, such as being poor, lonely, contemptible, or ill.

Information concerning the self is more easily recognized and more readily available in memory than information not concerning the self. Incoming information will first be tested with regards to its meaning or implications for oneself. Is the information personally relevant? This also happens when the attention is not focused, as in the 'cocktail party phenomenon'. When one is speaking to somebody at a party, it is practically impossible to hear anything of other conversations. However, when one's name is mentioned in a nearby conversation, the chances of hearing it are large, because the self-schema is activated.[4]

Identity

Consumers often buy products and brands that match their *identities*. Identity is the idea one has about oneself, about characteristic properties, one's own body and about the values one considers to be important. Achievements and consumer goods contribute to the construction of this self-schema. Someone who thinks he or she is sports-minded will choose a 'sports car' or a 'sporting holiday'.

Definition

Identity is a self-schema, consisting of associations with one's characteristic properties, one's own body and one's values.

People think about themselves. They themselves are the 'object' (me) of their thinking: 'Who am I?' 'How am I?' 'What impression do I make on others?' At the same time they are the 'subject' (I) and they are the people who do the thinking.[5]

The identity or self-schema is broader than values; it is a meaning structure with a means–end chain of personal characteristics, conse-

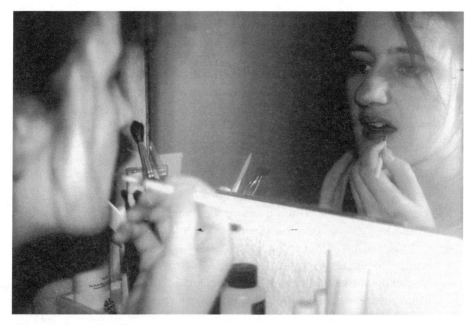

Figure 8.3 *High self-monitoring?*

quences and values. Two examples may clarify this. A personal characteristic is for example intelligence. A consequence of this characteristic is a better performance at school and at work. This stimulates self-confidence and self-respect.[6] Physical attractiveness leads to valuation and acceptance by others, which leads to an increase in self-confidence and self-respect.

The body is an important part of the identity. People think about it a lot and regard themselves as being pretty or ugly, fat or thin, masculine or feminine, sexy, attractive or ordinary. The feminine ideal of good-looking has changed in time: the pin-up girl of the 1940s, Marilyn Monroe in the 1950s, Brigitte Bardot in the 1960s, Twiggy in the 1970s, Madonna in the 1980s and the Spice Girls in the 1990s.

It is important to distinguish between the actual and desired identity: see figure 8.4. The *identity* or personality is the way someone sees him or herself with his or her characteristics and values. The *desired identity* is the person he or she wants to be. Plans for the future, goals in life and aspirations are related to the desired identity. Consumer decisions are often made in an attempt to bring this identity closer. Which man or woman does one want to be? Advertisements often refer to the desired identity or ideal self-schema. Advertisements for the perfume Seduction suggest that after using it fantasies of attractive men in speedy sports cars sweeping one away may even become reality.

Both desired self-schemas, that are possible and attainable, and identities that should be avoided motivate behaviour. Products and services can contribute to reaching the possible identities or avoiding the unwanted ones. Cosmetics, clothes and cars are expressive means of building a desired identity.

Image

The image is how others see and judge a person. The image may differ by the role one plays, by the evaluator, or by the target group. One can have a good image as a father, but a poor image as an employee. A company can have a favourable image on the financial market, but a poor image on the consumer market.

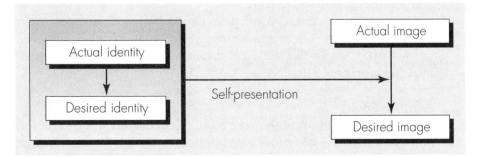

Figure 8.4 *Actual and desired identity: actual and desired image*[7]

Definition

Image is the perception of a firm, brand or another person.

The image is a function of social interaction. Everybody is concerned with self-presentation to a certain extent and with questions like: 'How do others see me?' and 'What do others think of me?'[8] Consumption is a way of self-presentation. By means of self-presentation one tries to improve one's image in the desired direction. This is the *desired image* or the ideal social self-image. Persons scoring high on self-monitoring, mainly strive to evoke a positive image of themselves.[9]

The desired identity and the desire image are continually developing. In terms of the hierarchy of needs this concerns the 'higher' needs of recognition, and self-realization. Also for firms and brands, identity and image are important and figure 8.4 applies. Shop images are discussed further in section 18.3.[10]

8.3 Motivation and needs

Motivation

What motivates people's behaviour and in particular consumer behaviour? Somebody who starts eating may be motivated by hunger, but he or she may just be polite, when having lunch with a business partner. Motivation thus cannot be directly inferred from behaviour.[11] Motivation is an activation, an incentive or reason to start or to maintain behaviour. Motivation determines the strength and the direction of behaviour.[12] People are motivated to escape from something that is negative and to avoid problems (negative motivation). Negative motivation is directed towards problem solving. People are also looking for something positive or worthwhile, something new that makes their lives better and more interesting (positive motivation). Positive motivation is directed towards making things better and adding value to something.

Motivation is a central concept in psychology and in the study of consumer behaviour. There are many different approaches and levels of motivation. A list of the most important motivation theories is presented next (see also figure 8.6).[13]

Basic instincts

At a primitive level of motivation, one speaks of *instincts or passions*, the innate motivations of animals and people. The direction of instincts and drives is biologically determined. Instincts and drives are mainly internal push factors and tell little about the external pull of the goals that are strived for. Hunger and thirst are examples of biologically determined needs. In extreme situations such as wars these needs get a vital meaning.

In psycho-analytic theory, personality consists of three layers, the id, the ego and the superego. The id is the source of physical energy, which is searching for immediate satisfaction. For Freud, the id is the libido— sexuality. The id is unconscious and obeys the instant gratification principle.

The ego deals with the psychic energy in a more realistic way. It transforms the immediate needs into socially acceptable modes of conduct. The ego obeys the reality principle. The ego may be partly unconscious, subconscious and conscious: see figure 8.5.

The superego is one's conscience, i.e., a set of internalized rules, norms and values which are used to judge one's behaviour in terms of good and bad. It serves as a benchmark for the ego. The superego may punish the ego for bad behaviour, thus inducing guilt, or it may reward good behaviour, leading to pride. The superego is mainly formed during socialization in early childhood. It is partly unconscious, subconscious and conscious.

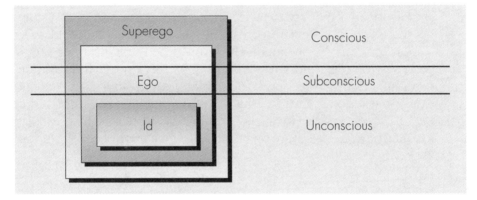

Figure 8.5 *Id, ego and superego*[16]

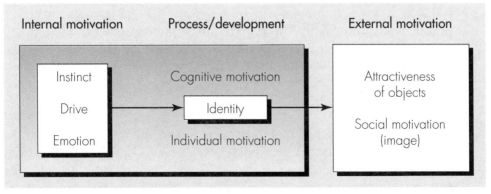

Figure 8.6 *Context of motivation theories*

The ego manoeuvres between the hedonistic demands of the id and the moralistic constraints of the superego. In this respect, the id and the superego may be viewed as similar to the 'doer' and 'planner', respectively, to be considered in section 19.4.

The unconscious includes ideas and concepts that can only be made conscious in therapeutic sessions by using methods such as free association and hypnosis. Sometimes unconscious desires express themselves in slips of the tongue or mistakes and they can play a part in consumer behaviour.[14] Certain events and traumatic experiences are possibly repressed in the unconscious and they might influence conscious functioning. Making these traumatic, repressed experiences conscious has a liberating and therapeutic effect. This is the basis of psycho-analysis.[15]

Homeostasis

Motivation can also concern keeping and maintaining a *balance*. People strive for an optimal level of stimulation. If the stimulation is perceived as being too little or too much, people take action to regain the desired level.[17] People looking for sensation are usually in an environment with too little stimulation and they try to increase the level of stimulation. By going out, getting involved in social interests or sports, boredom and a low level of stimulation can be avoided. However, when the level of stimulation becomes too high and stress develops, we disconnect from the environment in order to decrease the level of stimulation. This equilibrium situation is called homeostasis, a term from physiology. All sorts of physiological processes strive for a level of equilibrium, such as the preservation of a certain body temperature, by perspiring when it is hot and shivering when it is cold.

Emotional factors

Emotions such as anxiety and pleasure can motivate behaviour. Emotions are usually aroused in reaction to a certain state or event. Emotions mobilize energy and may lead to escaping, fighting or consumption. For instance, a sudden danger can evoke fear or anger and an increased production of adrenaline. This is necessary to fight against the danger or to avoid it (fight or flight).[18] Alternatively, emotions can be expressed less directly and consumers may ease their frustration with a problem by going shopping.

'Pull' factors

The attraction of goods, persons, situations and behaviours can be motivating. Consumers want to possess certain goods, visit certain holiday destinations, reach certain situations and imitate certain other people. The motivation develops externally, as a 'pull' factor. The benefits of these goods have a positive motivational effect. The (benefits of the) objects can be rewarding and thus attractive. As examples, consider operant conditioning and learning by imitation, where rewards are employed to strengthen behavioural responses.[19] Materialism is also based on the attractiveness of owning goods.

Social pressures

Social motivation. Social motives include the need for social contacts (affiliation), being accepted by others, and having power over others. These aspects can help people reach certain goals. It can be handy to have friends and acquaintances who can 'fix' things for you, including consumer goods and services.

Cognitive factors

Cognitive motivation is a broad category of concepts that have found their applications in consumer behaviour. The theories concern ways of thinking that lead to behaviour. Examples are:

- Cognitive balance theory: inconsistencies between values and behaviour lead to action to reduce these inconsistencies.[20] Values and behaviour can be adapted to reach the balance.
- The theory of the *reduction of cognitive dissonance* is similar to cognitive balance.[21] When knowledge and behaviour are inconsistent, there is a behavioural tendency to change one of them in order to reach consistency or consonance. A well-known example is smoking and the knowledge that smokers may get lung cancer. To solve this dissonance, one should either stop smoking or stop seeing or getting information about lung cancer.
- People are motivated to understand their own behaviour and that of others. People play the role of a lay-scientist. *Personal constructs* play a role in explaining behaviour.[22] Personal constructs are a set of polar traits to evaluate a person.
- Attribution theory fulfils the same role. Human motivation is partly driven by the causes we ascribe to phenomena and behaviour of ourselves and others.[23]

Individual issues

Individual motivation also includes many concepts that are important for consumer behaviour:

- *Internal locus of control* is the tendency to take the future into one's own hands and not to await passively for what circumstances or other people will bring.[24] The extreme case of external control is 'learned helplessness'—a dependency on others. This may be the case, for instance, for institutionalized patients or people in problematic debt situations.[25]

- *Achievement motivation* is the motivation to fulfil difficult tasks and to achieve a better performance every time.[26] The level of achievement motivation of entrepreneurs is connected with economic growth. The achievement motivation of consumers can be concerned with looking for the lowest price or best quality. Consumers may look for something in particular for a long time before actually finding it.
- *Self-realization* is the highest need in figure 8.7. Many people are motivated to use their abilities and talents in a good way.[27]
- *Time preference* is the motivation to consume in the present or in the future. A positive time preference increases the probability of present consumption. One is impatient and desires immediate gratification. A negative time preference increases the probability of future consumption. One is prepared to delay gratification in favour of greater satisfaction later. Time preference has consequences for the saving and spending behaviour of consumers.[28]
- *Need for cognition* is a personality characteristic which explains why some people are motivated to think about the solutions to problems and to mull over purchase decisions.[29]
- *Self-monitoring* is a personality characteristic concerned with self-presentation and adaptation to situations and to others. Individuals strongly inclined to self-monitor try to behave in a way that they think will be approved of by others.[30]

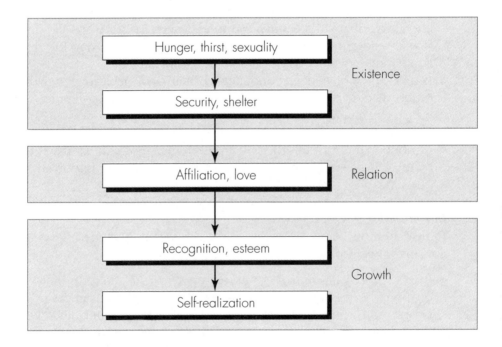

Figure 8.7 *Hierarchy of needs*

Results-driven motivation

The first and oldest motivation theories assume an inner motivation for behaviour. The later and newer theories assume the external attraction of objects or persons. Much behaviour is motivated by a feed-forward process. Here, one anticipates a certain effect or result before one decides to undertake a certain behaviour. The behaviour is adjusted if the desired result is not reached. For instance, the results of cooking can be disappointing. Consequently, one can look for other dishes and recipes and for another way of preparing food, for example, more herbs and less salt. Somebody can buy a present for a birthday anticipating how the receiver will appreciate the present. Pleasure for the receiver also implies pleasure for the person giving the present. It is possibly a contribution to a good relationship between giver and receiver. When the present is not greatly appreciated, next time the giver will look for something else that will be appreciated more.

Recent motivation theories focus on the interaction between motivation and situation.[31] Many people show a high level of achievement motivation in their paid work. But do they also show a high level of achievement motivation in household work? Personal identity maybe strongly defended against others, but how does one treat one's partner? This implies that behaviour may depend both on internal motivation, and on external motivation associated with the situation.

Needs

A need results from experiencing a shortage. The experience of a need motivates someone to remove this shortage. Thus, needs are motivating. Needs should be distinguished from wants, wishes and desires. Needs are general. The need to eat and drink can be satisfied by a number of types of food and drinks. Wants, wishes and desires are much more specific and related to concrete objects. Wants, wishes and desires are, in principle, unlimited. Consider, for example the 'wants lists' that people prepare for their birthdays or for Christmas. During a famine, water and bread are sufficient to satisfy the needs. In luxurious situations, people wish to have champagne and caviar.

Definition

A need is the lack of something necessary for survival or well-being.

Needs can be ordered in successive levels or categories. In the ERG-model a categorization into three parts is sustained: the first level of existence or survival (E), the second level of relationships or social contacts (R), and the third level of growth and self-realization (G).[32] The well-known five-level categorization by Abraham Maslow[33] can be fitted into this categorization (as shown in figure 8.7).

Definition

A want is the particular form of consumption chosen to satisfy a need.

The first level (existence) includes the needs concerning the 'body' and physical existence, such as the physiological needs, hunger, thirst and sexuality, and the needs for safety such as shelter and protection. When these needs are not satisfied (deprivation), the life of a person is threatened. The need for sexuality here is mainly a physiological need. Of course this need is closely connected with the need for relationship with others at the second level.

A human being cannot be alone for a very long time. At the second level (relationships) the needs have to do with social relationships, such as contacts with others, affiliation, affection, and love. We live together with others and need them to help us reach our goals.

The third level is called 'growth'. Recognition, being accepted, respect, and esteem are of major importance. Self-realization implies that someone's talents and possibilities are fulfilled and that someone's 'potential' is realized. Power can be a part of it. By means of power one can arrange things and realize the desired goals.

Definition

A hierarchy of needs assumes that higher needs only show up after the fulfilment of the lower needs.

In this model, it is assumed that the 'lower' needs should be satisfied before a 'higher' need can be accounted for. When a lower need remains unsatisfied (deprivation), a fixation on this need exists and further development is slowed down. 'Backsliding' is also a possibility.[34] While in normal times only a few consumers worry about the daily needs of life, these needs are brought back to the fore in times of stress and war. Consumers often hoard in these times to create a security of food for themselves. However, exceptions exist, such as a mother giving scarce food to her child and not keeping it for herself.

A need leads to behaviour to satisfy the need. People set themselves goals to satisfy their needs. A woman may feel lonely and have a need for social contacts. She becomes a member of the music or sports club to meet other people. She could also call a chatline by telephone, join one on the

Internet, or put a 'lonely hearts' ad in the regional paper. Thus, several ways exist to satisfy the need for social contact. As soon as a goal (more social contacts) is set, ways have to be chosen to reach that goal.

8.4 Personality

Personality characteristics are more or less permanent and stable—they are independent of the situations that people find themselves in, although their expression may vary according to the situation. Personality characteristics, like values, play a part at the general level of consumer behaviour. Personality characteristics have played an important part in the development of consumer research. Researchers tried to distinguish the personalities of Ford and Chevrolet drivers and to explain consumer behaviour generally by using personality characteristics. However, personality characteristics did not provide an explanation of specific consumer behaviour, for instance the differences between brand users.[35] An explanation for this lack of success is that personality characteristics are measured at a general level, whereas the behaviour to be explained is domain-specific.

Personality characteristics are permanent and fundamental characteristics that show up in many situations. However, in personality psychology, the approach assumes more and more an interaction of personality and situation.[36] Personality characteristics mainly show themselves in situations that fit the characteristic. A lot of personality characteristics that were used in consumer research were drawn from clinical psychology and while relevant to deviant behaviour, were less useful when trying to understand 'normal' consumer behaviour.

Types or traits

In personality research, two approaches dominate: the 'traits or features' and the 'types' approach. In the traits approach, character traits or personality characteristics are measured and people are scored on a number of personality dimensions. In the types approach, personality types are defined, such as introvert and extrovert types. In the first approach one assumes that the scores on the underlying dimensions do not necessarily have to lead to separate groups (types). In the second approach, one assumes that a number of discrete (non-overlapping) groups can be formed. In general, the traits approach gives a better reflection of reality than the types approach. Personality characteristics (traits or features) that are helpful in understanding the behaviour of consumers, include the need for cognition, self-monitoring, locus of control, etc.

Need for cognition

Need for cognition (NfC) is the motivational tendency to engage in cognitive effort and to experience pleasure from this effort. A characteristic statement of the NfC-scale is: 'I really enjoy a task in which one has to offer new solutions to problems'. Individuals with a strong NfC base their choice more on a comparison of alternatives than those with a weak NfC. This implies that individuals with a strong NfC will follow the central route of information processing more often than people with a weak NfC.[37] In general they will collect more external information and process more information. Individuals with a weak NfC will more often follow the peripheral route of deciding on the basis of cues. They will gather and process less external information.

> **Definition**
>
> Need for cognition is a personality trait representing the tendency to engage in cognitive effort and to experience pleasure from this effort.

People with a strong NfC are often directed towards technical–instrumental elements in an advertising message, but may concentrate on the 'image' elements as well. Consumers can think extensively about the quality of the offered product or about the appropriateness of the product for their own lifestyle or specific situations. A strong NfC leads to a stronger correlation between attitude and behaviour. In general, these persons act consistently with their beliefs and thoroughly think things through. The need for cognition as a personality characteristic is relatively stable over different situations.

Self-monitoring
Self-monitoring is a personality characteristic that is concerned with the self-presentation of a person.[38] Some people are chameleon-like and strive to adapt their behaviour to each situation they are in. It is important for them to behave in the right way in every situation. People high in self-monitoring are extremely sensitive to any cues that can help them to find the suitable or appropriate behaviour. They are strongly directed towards others.[39] They use a kind of 'self-marketing' to 'sell' themselves to others and to reach their goals. As a consequence of other-directedness they tend to leave different impressions, depending on the situation. Because of their sensitivity to their image in every situation, they are particularly directed towards any information that gives them the opportunity to create or strengthen an image. They have a preference for image-directed advertisements. These people score high on the self-monitoring scale.

People with low scores on the self-monitoring scale are less sensitive to the opinion of others. They act in accordance to their inner values, attitudes and opinions, and these do not change according to the situation ('inner-directedness'). The correlation between their attitude and behaviour is strong and consistent. In general, they behave consistently in different situations. As consumers they are sensitive to information about product attributes because this easily fits their values and attitudes. For instance, if they drink a certain brand of whisky, it is because of the superior taste and not because of the image of the brand. They show a preference for advertising aimed at product characteristics and product benefits.

Definition

Self-monitoring is a personality trait representing the tendency to adapt one's behaviour to a particular context.

Self-monitoring is associated with conformism.[40] High self-monitoring consumers conform to the ideas and product choices of others. They agree with an idea if this gives them a positive image and leads to them being accepted by others. Conformism is mainly instrumental in reaching benefits and lasts as long as it provides benefits to consumers in social situations. As soon as these benefits disappear, the preference for the product or brand disappears. Take, for instance, the popularity of certain brands of sporting shoes, such as Nike, New Balance and Reebok. Brand loyalty and brand preference concur with high self-monitoring as long as the brand is popular.

Low self-monitoring is associated with internalization.[41] Agreement with the message only happens when the message is in accordance with the already existing schemas, opinions, attitudes and values. The popularity of the brand for other people is less important in this case. As a result, brand loyalty and brand preference are more stable for persons with a low degree of self-monitoring.

In an experiment, advertisements were designed for three types of products: whisky, cigarettes and coffee. The visual material was similar for the three products. By means of the accompanying text an image- or quality-directed campaign was simulated. In the quality-directed advertising, physical product characteristics and functional benefits of the product were emphasized. The participants, who were divided into high- and low-monitoring groups on the basis of prior research, had to give a comparative evaluation of the two versions. As expected, the high self-monitoring group gave a more positive evaluation regarding the image-directed advertisement. The low self-monitoring group, on the other hand, gave a more positive evaluation regarding the quality-directed advertisement.[42]

In subsequent research, high self-monitoring persons were more prepared to try a product and to pay more when the advertisement is image-directed. Low self-monitoring persons, on the other hand, show the same tendency with regard to the quality-directed advertisement. Image-directed messages evoke more cognitive responses with high self-monitoring respondents.

The high or low self-monitoring character of the target group can also be derived in an indirect way, for instance from the subscription to magazines. Magazines such as *Cosmopolitan* and *Vogue* will probably attract more high self-monitoring readers than hobby magazines, that are specifically directed towards people who are very interested in computers or music systems.

Self-monitoring is concerned with the expression of lifestyle: recognition and being accepted by others is of major concern. Important value domains for self-monitoring people are: pleasure, maturity, conformism, and sociability. For people with low self-monitoring important value domains are: security, achievement, and independence.

The combination of self-monitoring and need for cognition (NfC) leads to four combinations. See table 8.1. Persons with a weak NfC and low self-monitoring keep old habits and ignore others (apathetic). Persons with a weak NfC and high self-monitoring are unstable in beliefs and behaviour, and conform to others without much thinking. Persons with a strong NfC and a low self-monitoring like to think about the characteristics and functional advantages of products. The combination of high self-monitoring and strong NfC means that these consumers think a lot about the impression they make on others. Their behaviour is determined by this to a large extent.

The quality of arguments has a clear influence on the opinion of persons with a high NfC-score.[44] The influence is lacking for those with a low NfC-score. Low NfC-scorers, in contrast, are easily influenced by cues and the number of arguments, and less by the content of these arguments.[45] Since NfC is correlated with the level of education, high NfC-scorers are often highly educated.

Open and closed minds

Self-monitoring and need for cognition are not the only personality characteristics that are relevant to the study of consumer behaviour. The distinction between open and closed minds offers perspectives as well. Open-minded people are directed towards reaching clarity in uncertain situations.[46] New and uncertain products and brands are challenges they

Table 8.1 *Information processing as a function of self-monitoring and need for cognition*[43]

Need for cognition	Low self-monitoring	High self-monitoring
Weak	Habit formation (apathy)	Unstable beliefs (conformism)
Strong	Stable beliefs, thinking about products (quality)	Thinking about social situations (image)

feel attracted to. Closed-minded people, on the other hand, strive for the maintenance of the *status quo*. They avoid uncertain and new situations. The majority of the population is oriented towards certainty. They will avoid changes, and are not interested in the arguments used. They will follow the people they perceive as authorities, without weighing the quality of their arguments.[47]

8.5 Consumer goals

Values, desired identity and needs need to be realized and satisfied. Consumers will seek ways to realize these objectives or goals. A goal is an intention to realize a desired state. Based on their values, people are triggered to try to realize their goals. Many behaviours of people are directed towards a goal: collecting information, buying and using products, or relaxing with an easy and entertaining television programme. Goals are often ordered hierarchically. The hierarchy of consumer goals is shown in figure 8.8.

Definition

A goal is an intention to realize a desired state.

If somebody's value pattern is strongly directed towards a better environment, many ways can be derived to reach this goal. This consumer might not buy tropical hardwood, he or she might travel by train rather than car, and might not book flights to distant countries. At a simple level, needs lead to goals. A visitor wandering about at a festival for hours might like to

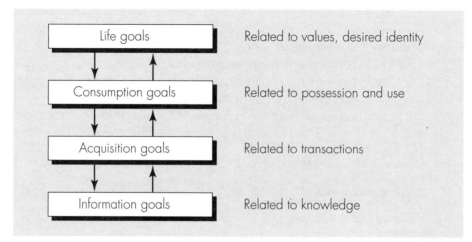

Figure 8.8 *Hierarchy of consumer goals*

have a snack and might be looking for a shop with, for instance, Mexican tacos. Here, the (short-term) goal is to get something to eat.

People have *life or personal goals*. These are states or situations they want to reach, such as a good career, a nice family, happiness, possessions, and interesting experiences. Some people are strongly oriented towards performance at work, others towards going out and having fun. A third group may be directed towards home, family and children.[48] Reaching a certain position, having a nice family or having fun can be life goals for these groups. Life goals are directed towards the realization of values and the desired identity. A nice family as a life goal leads to the value of happiness.

From these life goals, concrete *consumption goals* can be derived such as ownership and usage of products. Such goals might include going on holiday with the whole family, buying a new car, and nicely furnishing the nursery. These are all desired states and consumption goals that fit a certain life goal. Consumers cannot realize all consumption goals within their limited budgets. They have to set priorities and decide what is most important to them.[49]

To realize a consumption goal, a product or a service has to be purchased. Thus *purchasing goals* are transactions such as booking a journey, buying a car, and ordering furniture for the nursery. The consumer may have to save up or borrow money to be able to fulfil the purchasing goal. Alternatively, the product could be made by the consumer, or borrowed or rented.

As part of and preparation for a purchasing goal *information goals* exist. An information goal is the plan of a consumer to retrieve more information about a certain product class, often with the objective of making a purchase, but this is not always necessary. Some consumers like to know what is available. Others like to read leaflets and advertisements concerning PCs to keep informed (a high need for cognition). The information goal is then to find ways to retrieve this information. Which magazine should be read to find out about international economic politics? *The Economist, Times, Financial Times* or *Business Week*? To reach this information goal one has to read one or more of these magazines.

Sources that can be consulted to realize information goals, are commercial, neutral or social, respectively advertisements, consumer reports, and friends and acquaintances. See table 8.2. Consumers learn brand names and brand knowledge from advertisements. From neutral sources con-

Table 8.2 *Observed expertise and trustworthiness of information sources*

Information source	Expertise	Trustworthiness
Commercial	+	−
Neutral	+	+
Social	−	+

sumers learn the characteristics and qualities of brands. From friends and acquaintances they learn judgements, preferences, abilities and behaviour.

Commercial and neutral sources are generally seen as more professional (expert) than social sources, since they contain more technical product information. Social sources, however, often have usage experience with products in the same circumstances as the consumer who has to make a choice. People also learn from social sources by imitation. Neutral and social sources are usually more trustworthy than commercial sources, since they have no clear self-interest in giving biased or partial information.

Consumers actually pass along the hierarchy of goals in figure 8.8 twice. The first time they go from top to bottom, from life goals to information goals. From a life goal, respectively, consumption, purchasing, and information goals are derived. The second time the hierarchy is passed from bottom to top. After the information goal is reached, the purchasing, consumption and life goals can be realized. However, this does not always happen. Many decision processes are quick and impulsive or based on habits. Frequently, separate goals can hardly be distinguished. Consumers may only spend a long time thinking about how they can reach important life goals by means of subgoals.

Producers also have a similar hierarchy of goals: organization, action and communication goals. They are similar to the goals of consumers. The communication goals of producers and advertisers are directed towards the information goals of the consumer. The action goals of producers (selling) are directed towards the purchasing goals of consumers. And the marketing goals of producers are directed towards the consumption goals of consumers. In addition to this, producers also act as consumers, as they buy office equipment, catering services, parking space, etc.

8.6 Consumer behaviour

It seems self-evident to ask 'What is behaviour?' and more particularly 'What is consumer behaviour?' One answer could be that behaviour is what people do, and what can be observed. However, behaviour that is not observable exists, such as thinking and feeling. Behaviour is more complex than it might at first seem. In psychology, more attention is usually given to the explanation of behaviour than to the behaviour itself. Studies concerning attitudes, intentions and decision processes can try to explain and predict behaviour. The consequences of behaviour such as satisfaction receive the attention they deserve in this type of research. The behaviour itself, however, is often under-reported.

Behavioural domain

A behavioural domain is a whole group of connecting behaviours that in most cases lead to a certain goal such as, for example, saving energy.

Behaviours belonging to this domain include: turning the thermostat down, putting on a sweater, installing double glazing, insulating the loft and taking notice of the energy consumption of equipment when buying it. A behavioural domain is often directed towards the realization of values, such as a clean environment. 'The boat' or 'the garden' for many people refer to behavioural domains with a number of behaviours, directed towards relaxation or a certain achievement.

Definition

A behavioural domain is a set of behaviours frequently organized around a common goal.

Aspects of behaviour

A number of aspects of behaviour can be distinguished.[50] These aspects are important for a better understanding of behaviour.

Control of behaviour
People strive to control their immediate environment. In fact behaviour for people mainly means control over their environment, situations and possibly also over other people. People try to stay 'in control' and pursue things in a direction that is positive for themselves and their family. Behaviour is often directed towards maintaining one's own position or that of others or making it stronger.

Objective versus subjective
At first sight behaviour seems to be objectively measurable. One can observe and measure behaviour. However, it is less objective than one thinks. Although behaviour may consist of a number of single acts, it is often difficult to observe these acts without one's own interpretation. It is, for instance, possible to observe the behaviour of consumers in the store. They walk through the supermarket. They take things from the shelf, look at the packaging and either put them in their trolley or back on the shelf. Many things that shoppers do can be readily understood by the observer, but there are also behaviours that remain incomprehensible to the observer. For example, why does a consumer choose a different brand than he or she used in the preceding couple of weeks? Only when the consumer is asked for the meaning of his or her behaviour, does it become clear why somebody does something (and not always then).[51] Thus, for a full explanation and interpretation of behaviour, subjective insights are needed.

Observation and description of behaviour are only part of the reality: the 'objective' part. By self-reporting another 'subjective' reality appears which must be included to be able to interpret and understand the behaviour.

Scripts

Behaviours do not stand on their own, but form a connected sequence. Behaviour is sequential. Going out shopping is a behaviour made up of a large number of separate behaviours, such as going to the supermarket, getting the trolley and pushing it forward, getting products from the shelf and putting these into the trolley, waiting at the check-out counter, putting the products on the counter, paying, and putting the products into the shopping bag. It is a 'script' of behaviours, that together combine to form 'shopping'. It is a routine or a habit, a set sequence of behaviours to reach a certain result. A script is a schema of the order in which certain behaviours or acts and conversations in general (and sometimes in a stereotypical way) take place.[52]

Definition

A script is a schema regarding an ordered sequence of connected behaviours.

Scripts appear quite often. Think of how you behave at the post office, in an exclusive restaurant or at McDonald's, at the doctor's, or when driving a car. The connection between acts is often goal-oriented. The behaviours are performed to achieve something and therefore have to be performed in a certain order. The script of having a meal at McDonald's clearly deviates from that of an exclusive restaurant. It is useless to sit at a table at McDonald's and wait until somebody comes to take the order.

Feedback

Behaviour almost always provides feedback to knowledge, attitudes, goals, needs or values. People want to know how they perform and whether they reach their goals. And on the basis of this information they can modify their behaviour (see figure 8.1). The following functions of feedback can be distinguished:[53]

- *Learning function*. By discovering the results of behaviour, it is possible to distinguish between effective and less effective behaviours. In this way consumers can learn, by means of feedback, the consequences of their behaviours. They can then direct their behaviour in a better way towards the desired goal.[54]
- *Habit formation*. Feedback can help to form and strengthen habits. When consumers deviate from their routines and this leads to negative consequences, they are more likely to stick to their previous routines and keep on doing this.

- *Internalization*. Feedback confronts consumers with the consequences of their behaviour. From these effects attitudes can be formed and changed. The consequences of behaviour are the motivation to change attitudes and the internalization of those attitudes.[55]

Means–end chain of behaviour
Behaviour, in most cases, is ordered hierarchically. To reach something, certain acts or behaviours have to be performed in order. Acts or behaviours are a means to an end, which is often a step towards a higher goal or reaching a value.

Definition

A means–end chain of behaviour specifies the behavioural steps reducing the distance between a state and a goal.

When one sees somebody turning the thermostat down and one asks: 'What are you doing?' The answer can be given at four different levels, dependent on the degree to which the person thinks about his/her own behaviour:

- Observable, *single acts* such as 'I am turning the thermostat down'.
- A behavioural domain such as 'I am saving natural gas'.
- *Goals* such as 'I am trying to cut my gas bill by ten per cent'.
- *Values* such as 'I want to behave in an energy-conscious and environmentally friendly way'.

The four levels can also be stated in terms of goals.[56] These goals run from concrete to abstract. At the most concrete level, behavioural goals are identical to behavioural intentions. For instance:

- 'I plan to eat no more snacks.'
- 'I want to lose weight.'
- 'I want to look good.'
- 'I want to be accepted by others.'
- 'I want to be happy.'

Three questions concerning behaviour can be asked in principle:

- *What?* This is the question regarding actual behaviour: 'I am saving gas' or 'I watch my weight'.
- *Why?* This is the question for reasons, causes, antecedents and consequences: 'I act in an energy-conscious way' or 'I want to be slim'.
- *How?* This is the question about the way one acts and how one tries to reach the goals: 'I turn the thermostat down' or 'I do not eat snacks any more'.

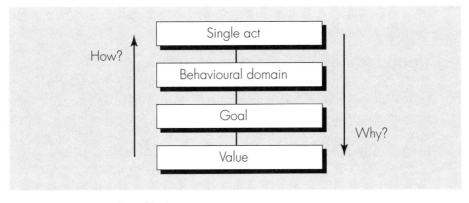

Figure 8.9 *Hierarchy of behaviour*

In figure 8.9 the means–end hierarchy or means–end structure of single acts, behavioural domains, goals and values is shown.[57] When behaviour is defined as a single act, one can ask the question: 'Why do you do that?' In this way one comes to, respectively, the behavioural domain, the goal and the value. One goes top-down. This can be seen as the right-hand side of figure 8.9. One can also repeat the question 'How do you do that?' to find out respectively, the behaviour goal and the behavioural domain. One goes bottom-up, from the bottom to the top. This can be seen on the lefthand side of figure 8.9. Subgoals and main goals, instrumental and terminal values may be distinguished.

The 'how'-question asks for a specific explanation of behaviour. It requires an interpretation about how to handle or act concretely in terms of single acts; what to do and what not to do. Often there are several ways to reach a goal. With the 'how' question one gets an answer to the question about which way the goal is striven for and hopefully will be reached. To save energy one can, for example, insulate the house, put in double-glazed windows, put on a sweater at home in winter, turn down the thermostat, or not heat the bedrooms. There are many more behaviours or acts by which energy can be saved.

The 'why' question asks for an abstract explanation of behaviour. It requires the reasons, (sub)goals and values as to why one does or does not do certain things. The 'why' question is most often the question about the motivation of behaviour. There are many reasons why somebody acts in a certain way. Consumers for instance may save energy because they are concerned about the environment, because of thriftiness or because other people do it.

Of course, one can also give a double-sided explanation of behaviour, both concerning single acts and goals and values.[58] One saves energy for instance, by turning the thermostat down while thinking about the hole in the ozone layer and the environment in general. Or one gets fitter by jogging, while thinking about good health.

Concrete and abstract behaviour

Single acts, as shown at the top of figure 8.9, have a high degree of concreteness and include only a small domain. For instance, it may only include eating less fat. A single act often has little explanatory power for other behaviours. When somebody eats less fat, this says little about other health-related behaviours.[59]

Goals and values such as 'living healthily' are more abstract and include a large domain. Goals and values in general have a high level of predictive value for behaviour, although it is not known in which way a person will want to reach a desired goal.

Goals and values can be reached in a number of ways. When, as an example, the goal of 'losing weight' is adopted, there are several ways to reach this goal, including dieting, doing exercise, sports and massage. When the behavioural domain 'dieting' is taken, there are several ways to go on a diet, such as the Hay diet, an all fruit diet, not eating snacks between meals, or not eating snacks at all. 'Eating no snacks at all' is an example of a single act.

8.7 Costs and benefits of behaviour

In many cases, it is useful to distinguish the benefits (advantages) and costs of behaviour. In attitude models, costs are usually excluded.[60] However, the distinction between benefits and costs does give a better insight into why consumers act in certain ways and do not act in other ways. Consumers act economically in the sense that they try to maximize benefits and try to minimize costs. In general, an act is undertaken if the benefits are larger than the costs.[61]

The perception of benefits and costs may differ with regard to concreteness and time (short- and long-term consequences). There is also a difference in perception whether the benefits and costs apply to the individual or to society.

Concreteness of benefits and costs
The benefits of behaviour are generally defined at an abstract level. 'How happy would I be, if I only got my diploma!' The costs of getting such a diploma are defined at a concrete level. It concerns concrete acts, money, time and effort to study for the diploma. Thus, there are financial costs, both the out-of-pocket costs of the course and the opportunity costs of lost income and time when one is attending the course. Time and effort can be seen as behavioural costs.[62] The ideal is often set at an abstract level. Otherwise one might not even start. The realization is at a concrete level,

Table 8.3 *Level of abstraction of merit and demerit behaviour*[63]

Level of abstraction	Merit behaviour	Demerit behaviour
Concrete	Costs	Benefits
Abstract	Benefits	Costs
Examples:	Energy conservation, education	Smoking, drinking

the operational level of acts, effort, and time expenses. One becomes aware of the time and effort costs only after the behaviour has started, such as attending an evening course.

With costs at a concrete level and benefits at an abstract level, one speaks of 'merit behaviour.' This is behaviour that is desired by the individual and by society, for instance environmentally friendly behaviour or education. The opposite is called 'demerit behaviour'. At a concrete level there are benefits while at an abstract level costs exist. Smoking and drinking are examples of this. The actual usage of cigarettes and alcohol is attractive, while the costs of poor health or unhappiness are more abstract and general, and come as a consequence of the behaviour. This is shown in table 8.3.

Time difference between benefits and costs
In the examples of smoking and drinking not only the levels of identification of benefits and costs differ, but also a difference in time exists. The joy of smoking and drinking comes immediately, while the consequences and the costs come several years later. This type of behaviour is a result of positive time preference. The long-term consequences are weighted less heavily than the short-term benefits. Environmentally unfriendly behaviour may bring the consumer short-term advantages, such as speed and comfort, but brings society long-term disadvantages, such as degradation of nature. The feedback of unpleasant effects comes after a long time interval.

Individual benefits and societal costs
Listening to music from a ghetto-blaster on the beach can bring the owner advantages or benefits such as relaxation and stimulation. For others it brings loud noise, annoyance and disturbance. Thus, individual benefits and societal costs exist here. This is often the case concerning environmentally relevant behaviour. The individual benefits should be traded off against societal costs.

8.8 Observed causes of behaviour

Attribution is the act of ascribing or attributing causes to behaviour. When a student passes an exam, this can be ascribed to internal or external causes.

Intelligence, insight and effort are examples of internal causes. External causes include an easy exam, good luck and coincidence. Some of these causes are stable; others are unstable. This is shown in table 8.4. Stable causes are highly predictive of future behaviour. If a person passed the exam because of intelligence, the chance is high that this person will pass other exams as well. Intelligence is thus a stable cause. If somebody passes an exam by effort and hard work, it is less certain whether this person will work as hard and pass the exam the next time. Effort is thus an unstable cause. If the exam is easy, the chance is high that many students will pass. An easy exam is thus a stable cause. If somebody passes the exam because of good luck or coincidence, the chance that this person will pass another exam is small. Good luck is thus an unstable cause.

Table 8.4 can be applied to energy saving, as shown in table 8.5. Older people and babies need a higher ambient temperature than other people. The need for heat or warmth is a more or less permanent personal characteristic. Being ill is an occasional incident. Therefore, it is an unstable characteristic. Winter temperature is an external, stable characteristic. An extremely low outside temperature and a severe winter both result in energy use, but are unstable and less predictive of behaviour in the next season.

People are often prejudiced. When they are successful, they tend to ascribe this to their own expertise or effort (internal causes). When they fail, they tend to ascribe this to the circumstances or bad luck (external causes). Often people associate themselves with winners and dissociate themselves from losers. In the case of a victory, supporters of a football club may say: 'We won', thus identifying themselves with the players. However, in the case of a lost match they may say: 'They lost', thus dissociating themselves from the players.

Table 8.4 *Stable and unstable, internal and external causes of success and failure*[64]

	Stable	Unstable
Internal	Ability, competence	Effort
External	Task difficulty	Chance, luck

Table 8.5 *Stable and unstable, internal and external causes of energy use*

	Stable	Unstable
Internal	Need for heating	Being ill
External	Winter temperature	Extreme winter

> **Definition**
>
> The fundamental attribution error is the tendency to overestimate the importance of personal factors relative to environmental influences on a person's behaviour, but not on one's own behaviour.

We may also ascribe the behaviour of others to internal or external causes. Here, a distinction between the person and the situation is often made. We can look for the cause of the behaviour of another person in that person him or herself, or in the situation/circumstances of that person. We tend to overestimate personal factors at the cost of situational factors. This is called the fundamental attribution error or bias.[65] Another prejudice or bias is that we often ascribe the success of others to circumstances. Their failure we ascribe to personal factors such as lack of expertise or effort.

Internal attribution of the causes of one's own behaviour is predictive of future behaviour, as said before. It is important for our motivation and for reaching our goals. It implies information feedback about one's own achievements. If somebody is successful, he or she gets more self-respect and dares to undertake more difficult tasks. If he or she ascribes results to circumstances, good luck and coincidence, there will be little increase in his or her achievements or performance.

Tasks should have an average level of difficulty to have a learning effect and to produce an increase in performance. If tasks are too easy, practically everybody can do them. If tasks are too difficult then hardly anyone can do them. Too easy and too difficult tasks both lead to external attribution in most cases. Tasks with an average level of difficulty lead to internal or external attribution. These tasks thus give better information about one's own performance.[66]

8.9 Conclusions

The central issues of this chapter are motivation and behaviour. Values, identity, needs and goals were discussed as direct causes of behaviour. The effects of behaviour and attribution processes were discussed as consequences of behaviour with an effect on future behaviour.

Motivation determines the direction and intensity of behaviour. Motivation can be an inner impulse ('push' factors) to fulfil a certain need. Consumers can also be motivated by persons and objects outside themselves ('pull' factors), such as attractive products, brands, persons, and situations.

Consumer behaviour is more complex than it seems. Sometimes it is concrete and observable, and sometimes it is abstract. Levels of abstraction can be distinguished, linked by (causal) means–end relationships. Concrete acts are means (*how*) to reach behavioural goals. Goals and values are (abstract) reasons (*why*) to act in a certain way or to perform certain behaviours.

Behaviour can be corrected and managed by means of feedback. From feedback we learn the effects of behaviour and whether or not these effects are desired and expected. This mainly works for tasks with an average degree of difficulty.

The perception of costs and benefits of behaviour varies according to the level of abstraction, i.e., short-term and long-term consequences, and individual and societal outcomes. The benefits usually dominate at the outset of a behaviour, whereas the costs are only appreciated during the execution of the behaviour. Many consumers tend to let the individual benefits dominate the societal costs. This can make it hard and complicated to initiate and sustain environmentally friendly consumer behaviour.

Notes

1 See chapter 1, figure 1.4.
2 Van Houwelingen, J. H. and van Raaij, W. F. (1989) 'The effect of goal setting and daily electronic feedback on in-home energy use' *Journal of Consumer Research* 16, 98–105.
3 H. Markus (1977) 'Self-schemata and processing information about the self' *Journal of Personality and Social Psychology* 35, 63–78.
4 Alba, J. W. and Hasher, L. (1983) 'Is memory schematic?' *Psychological Bulletin* 93, 203–231.
5 James, W. (1907) *Psychology: The Briefer Course* (New York: Holt).
6 Compare the means-end chain for products. See section 7.3.
7 Floor, J. M. G. and van Raaij, W. F. (in preparation) *Marketing Communication Strategy* (Hemel Hempstead, UK: Prentice Hall).
8 Goffman, E. (1959) *The Presentation of Self in Everyday Life* (New York: Double Anchor).
9 See section 8.4 for self-monitoring.
10 For images of firms, see van Riel, C. B. M. (1995) *Principles of Corporate Communication* (London: Prentice Hall).
11 The 'revealed preference' concept in economics assumes that preferences can be derived from the behaviour. According to the authors this is often incorrect.
12 Motivation is not the only determinant of behaviour. Restrictions and situational circumstances also influence behaviour. See section 4.5 and chapter 12.
13 Based on MacFadyen, H. W. (1986) 'Motivational constructs in psychology' in: MacFadyen, H. J. and MacFadyen, H. W. (Eds) *Economic Psychology: Intersections in Theory and Application* (Amsterdam: North-Holland) 67–108.
14 Freud, S. (1952) *A General Introduction to Psychoanalysis* (New York: Washington Square Press) (original work published in 1917).
15 Consumer research based on psychoanalytical concepts can be found in Dichter, E. (1964) *Handbook of Consumer Motivations* (New York: McGraw-

Hill) and in Callebaut, J., Janssens, M., Lorré, D. and Hendrickx, H. (1994) *The Naked Consumer* (Antwerp, Belgium: Censydiam Institute). Callebaut and his co-authors belong to the marketing research agency Censydiam at Antwerp, Belgium, which is mainly based on the 'individual psychology' of Alfred Adler (1927) *Practice and Theory of Individual Psychology* (New York: Harcourt Brace Jovanovich).

16 Nye, D. (1981) *Three Psychologies: Perspectives from Freud, Skinner, and Roger* (Monterey, CA: Brooks/Cole) 18.

17 See section 9.2; Raju, P. S. (1980) 'Optimal stimulation level: its relationship to personality, demographics and exploratory behavior' *Journal of Consumer Research* 7, 272–282. Berlyne, D. E. (1963) 'Motivational problems raised by exploratory and epistemic behavior' in: Koch, S. (Ed.) *Psychology: A Study of a Science* 5th edition (New York: McGraw-Hill) 284–364.

18 Pieters, R. G. M. and van Raaij, W. F. (1988) 'The role of affect in economic behavior' in: van Raaij, W. F., van Veldhoven, G. M. and Wärneryd, K.-E. (Eds) *Handbook of Economic Psychology* (Amsterdam: North-Holland) 108–142.

19 See sections 10.4 and 10.5.

20 Heider, F. (1958) *The Psychology of Interpersonal Relations* (New York: John Wiley).

21 Festinger, L. (1957) *A Theory of Cognitive Dissonance* (New York: Harper & Row). See also section 9.5.

22 Kelly, G. A. (1955) *The Psychology of Personal Constructs* (New York: Norton). A construct is a set of polar traits like warm–cold or friendly–hostile. People use these constructs to evaluate persons.

23 See sections 8.8 and 21.3.

24 Rotter, J. B. (1966) 'Generalized expectancies for internal vs. external control of reinforcement' *Psychological Monographs* 80, 1–28.

25 Seligman, M. E. P. (1975) *Helplessness. On Depression, Development, and Death* (San Francisco: Freeman).

26 Atkinson, J. W. (1964) *An Introduction to Motivation* (Princeton, NJ: Van Nostrand). McClelland, D. C. (1987) *Human Motivation* (Cambridge: Cambridge University Press).

27 Maslow, A. H. (1954) *Motivation and Personality* (New York: Harper & Row).

28 See sections 19.4 and 19.5.

29 Cacioppo, J. T. and Petty, R. E. (1982) 'The need for cognition' *Journal of Personality and Social Psychology* 42, 116–131. See also section 8.4.

30 See section 8.4.

31 Mischel, W. (1968) *Personality and Assessment* (New York: John Wiley).

32 The ERG-model: Alderfer, C. P. (1972) *Existence, Relatedness, and Growth* (New York: The Free Press).

33 Maslow (1954).

34 Wahba, M. A. and Bridwell, L. G. (1976) 'Maslow reconsidered: a review of research on the need hierarchy theory' *Organizational Behavior and Human Performance* 15, 212–240.

35 Kassarjian, H. H. (1971) 'Personality and consumer behavior: a review' *Journal of Marketing Research* 8, 409–418.

36 Mischel (1968).

37 See section 9.6.

38 Goffman (1959).
    Snyder, M. (1987) *Public Appearances/Private Realities. The Psychology of Self-Monitoring* (New York: Freeman).
    Snyder, M. and de Bono, K. G. (1985) 'Appeals to image and claims about quality: understanding the psychology of advertising' *Journal of Personality and Social Psychology* 49, 586–597.

39 'Other- and inner-directedness' are concepts used by Riesman, D., Galzer, N. and Denney, R. (1960) *The Lonely Crowd* (New Haven, CT: Yale University Press).

40 Kelman, H. C. (1958) 'Compliance, identification, and internalization: Three processes of attitude change' *Journal of Conflict Resolution* 2, 51–60. See also section 14.3.

41 Kelman (1958). See section 14.3.

42 Snyder and De Bono (1985).

43 See section 8.4 for more discussion on the 'need for cognition.'

44 Cacioppo, J. T., Petty, R. E. and Morris, K. J. (1983) 'Effects of need for cognition on message evaluation, recall, and persuasion' *Journal of Personality and Social Psychology* 45, 805–818.

45 Chaiken, S. (1987) 'The heuristic model of persuasion' in: Zanna, M. P., Olsen, J. M. and Herman, C. P. (Eds) *Social Influence. The Ontario Symposium* Vol 5 (London: Lawrence Erlbaum).

46 Sorrentino, R. M. and Hancock, R. D. (1987) 'Information and affective value: a case for the study of individual differences and social influence' in: Zanna, M. P., Olson, J. M. and Herman, C. P. (Eds) *Social Influence. The Ontario Symposium* Vol. 5 (London: Lawrence Erlbaum). This was inspired by Rokeach, M. (1960) *The Open and Closed Mind* (New York: Basic Books).

47 This is the peripheral route in the ELM. See section 9.6.

48 Ferber, R. and Lee, L. C. (1974) 'The role of lifestyle in studying family behavior' Working paper, College of Commerce and Business Administration, University of Illinois at Urbana-Champaign.

49 See section 23.3 on the consumption ladder.

50 Pieters, R. G. M. and Verplanken, B. (1991) 'Changing our mind about behavior' in: Antonides, G., Arts, W. A. and van Raaij, W. F. (Eds) *The Timing of Consumption and the Consumption of Time* (Amsterdam: North-Holland) 49–65.

51 Wells, W. D. and Lo Sciuto, L. A. (1966) 'Direct observation of purchasing behavior' *Journal of Marketing Research* 3, 227–233.

52 Abelson, R. P. (1976) 'Script processing in attitude formation and decision making' in: Carroll, J. S. and Payne, J. W. (Eds) *Cognition and Social Behavior* (Hillsdale, NJ: Lawrence Erlbaum) 33–45.

53 Annett, J. (1969) *Feedback and Human Behaviour* (London: Penguin).

54 Van Houwelingen, J. H. and van Raaij, W. F. (1989) 'The effect of goal setting and daily electronic feedback on in-home energy use' *Journal of Consumer Research* 16, 98–105.

55 See for internalization section 14.3. The adaptation of the attitude to the behaviour is called self-perception. See section 22.4. Bem, D. J. (1967) 'Self-perception theory' in: Berkowitz, L. (Ed.), *Advances in Experimental Social Psychology* Vol. 6 (New York: Academic Press) 1–62. Scott, C. A. (1977)

'Modifying socially-conscious behaviour: The foot-in-the-door technique' *Journal of Consumer Research* 4, 156–164.

56 Pieters, R., Baumgartner, H. and Allen, D. (1995) 'A means–end chain conceptualization of consumers' goal structures' *International Journal of Research in Marketing* 12, 217–244.

57 This is comparable with the means–end chain. See section 7.4.

58 Compare section 24.7 on positioning.

59 Vallacher, R. R. and Wegner, D. M. (1985) *A Theory of Action Identification* (Hillsdale, NJ: Lawrence Erlbaum). They use the concept 'identification level of behaviour.' Single acts have a low level of behaviour identification, this implies that they have little predictive power for other behaviours. Goals and values have a high level of behaviour identification. They predict other behaviours better.

60 Fishbein, M. and Ajzen, I. (1975) *Belief, Attitude, Intention and Behavior: An Introduction to Theory and Research* (Reading, MA: Addison-Wesley).

61 Homans, G. C. (1961) *Social Behavior* (New York: Harcourt, Brace & World).

62 Verhallen, T. M. M. and Pieters, R. G. M. (1984) 'Attitude theory and behavioral costs' *Journal of Economic Psychology* 5, 223–249.

63 Compare section 1.2. Alternatively, merit behaviour can be considered a virtue and demerit behaviour can be considered a vice. See Read, D., Loewenstein, G., Kalyanaraman, S. and Bivolaru, A. (in press) 'Mixing virtue and vice: the combined effects of hyberbolic discounting and diversification' *Journal of Behavioral Decision Making*, and Wertenbroch, K. and Carmon, Z. (1997) 'Dynamic preference maintenance' *Marketing Letters* 8, 145–152.

64 Weiner, B. (1980) *Human Motivation* (New York: Holt, Rinehart & Winston).

65 Ross, L. (1977) 'The intuitive psychologist and his shortcomings: distortions in the attribution process' in: Berkowitz, L. (Ed.) *Advances in Experimental Social Psychology* Vol. 10 (New York: Academic Press) 174–220.

66 Atkinson (1964). Section 21.3 shows an example concerning an application of attribution theory to consumer satisfaction.

9 ATTITUDES AND EMOTIONS

9.1 Introduction

Some people get a romantic feeling listening to a Chopin nocturne. Others become ecstatically enthusiastic at a performance by Nigel Kennedy. Still others fall in love with a VW Golf Cabriolet or an artistic necklace. On the other hand, certain products can also bring about negative feelings. For example, some people dislike baked beans. Other people cannot stand opera or convertible cars. These examples show that consumers experience all kinds of feelings for goods and services, and that consumption is not just a question of the available budget, functional benefits and price of the product. The experiences mentioned are called emotions because they may be quite intense and depend on a given product or situation. An emotion is a feeling of excitement (activation or 'arousal' of the central nervous system) with a positive or negative experience. Positive emotions include, for example, anticipation, relief and pleasure. Negative emotions include fear, sorrow and disgust.

Emotions usually fade after some time, but can leave behind a trace in the form of a certain mood. Positive and negative emotions and moods are jointly referred to as *affects*.[1] Both can have an influence on consumer behaviour. Emotions are brief by nature, moods usually last longer. Some people are often in a good mood and happy; others have changing moods; and still others are usually in a relatively unpleasant mood and unhappy. Long-term mood traces may be called temperament, and can be seen as personality traits.[2]

Affect may create a certain attitude towards products and services. Models of emotion are discussed in section 9.2, and section 9.3 examines the concept of attitude. Attitude is an important concept in the explanation of consumer behaviour, and this is also the topic of section 9.4. Attitude change is a central theme of providing consumers with persuasive and other information and is discussed along with cognitive dissonance in section 9.5. The Elaboration Likelihood Model (ELM) of attitude change is dealt with in section 9.6. Some conclusions follow in section 9.7.

The objective of this chapter is to point out the importance of affective factors and the role of attitude in consumer behaviour.

9.2 Models of emotion

Emotions are positive or negative, but not both. Primary emotions are pleasure, acceptance, fear, surprise, sorrow, disgust, anger and anticipation. These primary emotions can be shown in a circle as shown by figure 9.1.[3] Mixed emotions occur through combinations, for example love as a combination of pleasure and acceptance. Emotions are often opposites, like acceptance *versus* disgust, and pleasure *versus* sorrow. Finally, emotions may vary in intensity.

Besides categorizing emotions, researchers have also tried to find their underlying dimensions.[4] These dimensions are:

- Pleasure (P)—positive, attractive (P+) and negative, unattractive (P−) emotions.
- Activation (A) or 'arousal'—active (A+) and passive (A−) emotions.
- Dominance (D)—the perception of control over an emotion by self (D+) or by others (D−).

The PAD dimensions form a three-dimensional space in which emotions can be placed. In figure 9.2, several emotions are placed in the two-dimensional space, formed by the dimensions of pleasure and arousal.

Figure 9.1 *Primary emotions according to Plutchik*

For insight into consumer behaviour, it would be useful to know which emotions are brought about by products, services, and purchase situations. Consumption situations have been judged with respect to the emotional dimensions of the PAD model. In this way, medical services, for example, score low on the dimensions pleasure (P−) and dominance (D−), but high on activation (A+). Medical services would be associated with the emotion 'afraid' because this emotion is characterized similarly in the PAD model. The purchase of clothing would score high on pleasure (P+) and dominance (D+), but low on activation (A−). Purchase of clothing would be associated with the emotion 'satisfied.'

Both physiological and cognitive theories exist on the nature of emotion. The physiological theory concerns the relationship of the nature of the emotion and certain physiological reactions.[5] In this way, the breathing rate increases with fear, but this is not the case with anger. With anger the galvanometric skin resistance (transpiration) increases, but this does not occur with fear.[6] On seeing attractive objects, the pupils dilate.[7] The physiological reactions serve as indicators for the expression of an emotion. Sometimes the physiological reactions are observable, such as shivering, becoming pale with fear, or red with anger or shame. They are expressions of emotion which can barely be suppressed. In commercial research, galvanometric skin resistance and pupil dilation are used to measure the physiological–emotional reactions to advertisements.[8]

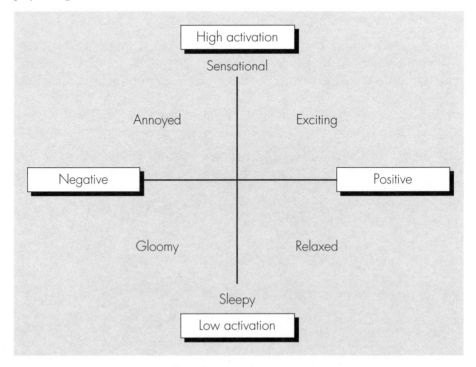

Figure 9.2 *Some emotions placed in two-dimensional space*

Figure 9.3 *Emotional audience*

Emotions have three representations: activation, experience, and expression. These three representations are shown in figure 9.4.[9] *Activation* or arousal is the physiological representation, somatic but not necessarily perceivable by others, for example a faster heart rate. This activation is experienced by the person, attributed to something or someone, interpreted and in this way experienced as emotion (A). *Experience* is a mental representation. After interpretation of one's state of arousal, a positive or negative emotion is experienced. This emotion is somatically *expressed* in, for example, pupil dilation, transpiration, blushing or becoming pale. A strong experience of emotion, for example in sexual fantasies, goes together with activation and expression (B). Expression is the somatic representation which is perceivable to others. An actor who tries to express an emotion in a play can be so activated that he or she really experiences this emotion (C).

The three representations show that aspects of emotion can be measured in three ways. A physiological measurement is, for example, that of galvanometric skin resistance. The experience can be measured by asking the subjects afterwards: 'What did you feel when you saw this advertisement?' The expression can be observed, for example when people blush, go pale or speak in shaky voice.

The cognitive theory of emotions is based on the assumption of a higher state of physical activity, alertness or excitement. This is a general reaction to a sudden change in the environment, for example, seeing a nice suit in a

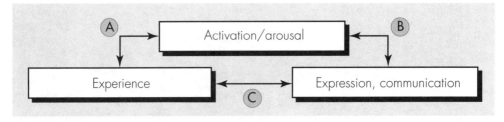

Figure 9.4 *Representations of emotion*

shop window. According to the cognitive theory, the consumer will consequently try to explain the feeling of excitement. Activation is experienced and a cause is searched for (attribution). An obvious interpretation in this example is desire. Another example concerns the situation wherein the consumer notices the price of the suit. If this is higher than normal, activation occurs which may be termed as fear (of not having any money left over for other purchases).[10]

Affect fulfils different functions for the consumer:

- it gives an interpretation and organization of the environment;
- it gives direction to choice behaviour;
- it is a means of communication with others;
- it gives information on the achieved level of activation.[11]

Interpretation and organization of the environment
Affect can contribute to distinctions between products and services. People may associate certain products with certain emotions, for example, visiting a theme park can be associated with joy and pleasure, and visiting the cinema with surprise or sensation. Most products serve to arouse positive feelings, they transform a neutral state into pleasure, for example, a new dress. Other products serve to solve or avoid problems, for example aspirin.[12] Emotions can also be associated with products, for example, anticipation at the purchase of a present or fear as a reason to install a burglar alarm.

The mood of the consumer partly determines the storage and retrieval of information about products and services in memory. In a good mood, usually more positive information is stored, which is the reason why commercials aim to get consumers in a good mood in order to achieve a favourable image of a product in the mind of the consumer. A good mood also contributes to remembering positive information about products and brands.

Orienting consumer choice
Affect has a direct influence on the choice of products and services. The probability of consumption is partly dependent on the association of

products with positive and negative emotions and moods. Likewise, attention given to commercials will be partly determined by these associations.[13]

In a positive mood, one is more optimistic about future events than in a negative mood. The chance of dying is estimated as smaller and one has more positive expectations about the economic situation. This has implications, amongst other things, for buying insurance or setting up saving plans.[14]

Finally, a joyful mood can lead to optimism and simple decision making, whereby one does not take all information on other products into account.[15] In a more pessimistic and depressed state, one would be more inclined to a thorough, but rather defensive form of decision making.

Communication
Affect can be expressed in posture and movement, aided by facial expressions or verbally. Through the expression of emotion, one can perceive the feelings of others and express one's own feelings. This is important in commercials and observational learning.[16]

Activation
In general, people have a need for variation, and this is also true for consumption. Variation generally increases the level of activation. If the variation is too great, a person will try to reduce it. Individuals strive towards optimal levels of stimulation and activation.[17]

The link between a person's affect and the level of variation in the environment ('arousal potential') is shown in figure 9.5. The two dimensions are similar to pleasure and arousal in the PAD model, shown in figure 9.2. With an average level of variation, the affect reaches its highest level. This is the optimal level of stimulation.[18] With too little as well as too much variation, the affect is negative. The behaviour in each of the four areas can be explained as follows.

In area 1, there is too little variation in the consumption pattern. It is improbable that in the current pattern new stimuli will be found. The most likely behaviour is the search for a more stimulating consumption pattern. An example of this situation is someone who watches television every night. Sooner or later the variation in this consumption pattern will be too small and he or she will look for a more varied pattern, for example by taking up a hobby or joining a sports club.

In area 2, the affect is positive, but the variation is still too small. Stimuli in the current consumption pattern can probably be found which lead to more variation, for example switching to another channel to watch another programme.

In area 3, the affect is also positive, but there is somewhat more variation. The consumption pattern is too complex. One will look for a simpler

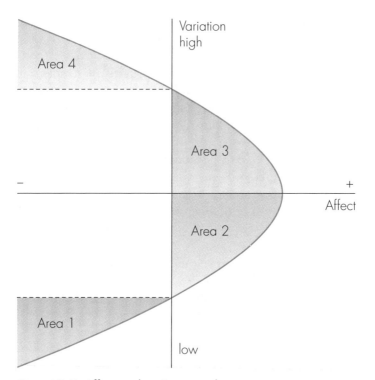

Figure 9.5 *Affect and variation in the consumption pattern*

pattern, or one will try to accustomize oneself sufficiently enough with the complex pattern whereby it becomes simpler. In the preceding example, one could see a large number of satellite TV channels as superfluous. By staying with the terrestrial channels, the situation remains simple. This corresponds with the situation of information overload.[19]

In area 4, the affect is negative due to an excess of variation ('arousal potential') in the consumption pattern. After a while this can lead to stress. Within the pattern, simplifications are hardly possible, so that one will probably look for a simpler pattern. In the example, one could turn on the radio instead of television, whereby the quantity of stimuli decreases.

Not every individual has the same affect curve as shown in figure 9.5. People have differing tastes for variation and there are also differences in the intake capacity of the amount of stimuli. It is to be expected that people with a taste for variation are more able and willing to process information, tend to experience less information overload and use more complex decision rules.

The taste for variation may depend on several factors, for example age and whether one lives in a city or in the countryside. On average, younger people and urban citizens have a higher optimal level of stimulation. This may raise the question of causality with respect to the optimal level of stimulation. On the one hand, the optimal level of stimulation may be selected by an individual. On the other hand, it may be possible that people adapt to their environment, for example city-dwellers may get used to a faster pace of life. The former is characterized as a short-run process, whereas the latter affects people in the long run.

9.3 Attitude models

Attitude formation

Emotional associations can have an influence on the assessment of products and services. Under the influence of simple learning processes, associations lead to a certain *attitude* with regard to the product.[20] An affect can be linked through associations to a certain characteristic or benefit of a product or commercial message. Nice music can be associated in a commercial with a certain brand or product. In this way the brand or product is evaluated in a relatively positive manner (route A in figure 9.6). Attribution can also give occasion to the forming of (a part of the) attitude.

> **Definition**
>
> An attitude is the individual predisposition to evaluate an object or an aspect of the world in a favourable or unfavourable manner.

Attitudes can briefly be described as likes and dislikes with regard to products, services, people, ideas, behaviours and other attitude objects.[21] This attitude will generally be related to a global notion of the product. If one always gets a kick out of buying a CD (a positive emotion), a positive attitude regarding this behaviour will develop.

However, an attitude usually arises as a result of cognitive processes, which can be, but do not have to be, related to the affect. If a consumer is in

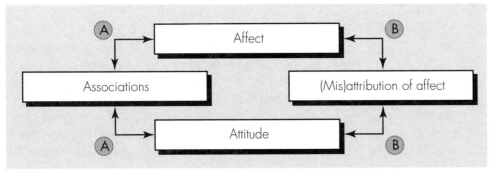

Figure 9.6 *Relations between affect and attitude*

an emotional state or in a certain mood, this mood can be associated with a certain product or service (route B in figure 9.6). An attribution is then made which leads to a particular attitude towards the product. If one is often in a good mood in the afternoon after having a plentiful lunch, one can make the attribution that a plentiful lunch helps to put one in a good mood.[22] One then gets a positive attitude towards a plentiful lunch. This attribution does not necessarily have to take place, however. The attribution can also be false, in which case we speak of a misattribution. If one has a conversation with a sales representative after lunch, it is possible to attribute one's good mood to the conversation and not to the lunch. This could lead to a false interpretation of the products which are being sold by the representative.[23]

Definition

Cognition refers to the mental processes concerned with the acquisition and manipulation of knowledge, including learning, perception and thinking.

This argument indicates a connection between affect and attitude, with associative learning processes and attribution as linking elements. Attitudes can also be formed without any affect, but under the influence of cognitive or social processes. In this way a negative attitude towards cars can be developed through awareness of the effects of car driving on the environment. The social environment can also contribute to the development of a certain attitude towards cars, for example the political party of which one is a member. This information about objects and ideas contributes to the formation of attitudes and the resulting affect which one experiences through these objects and ideas. It is a 'reasoned' opinion of objects and ideas—see figure 9.7. Notice that the process of figure 9.7 is opposite to that of figure 9.6. However, in figure 9.6, the affect may be unrelated to the object (for example, mood), whereas in figure 9.6 the affect is directly associated with the object (for example, dislike of cars).

Functions of attitude

Attitudes, like values and affect, fulfil different functions for people: knowledge, instrumental, value-expressive, and ego-protective functions.[24]

The *knowledge function* of attitudes is to strengthen the correspondence between the consumption of goods and services and all sorts of knowledge elements. A negative attitude towards meat consumption is consistent with the knowledge that many animals are kept in very small spaces, and the fact that animal fat is bad for one's health, and that there are alternative sources of protein.

The *instrumental or utilitarian function* of attitudes is to provide

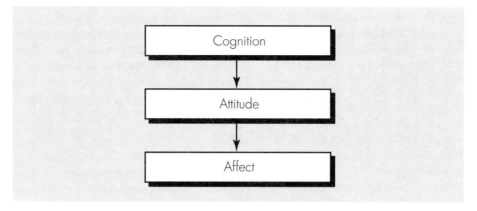

Figure 9.7 *Cognitive antecedents of attitude and affect*

direction to the choice of the consumer. Buying products and services towards which one has a positive attitude takes one nearer to desired goals. If one has a positive attitude towards the aroma of coffee, the purchase of aromatic coffee will lead to the desired goal: the delightful smell of coffee. Some goals, like a clean environment or a slim body, will not be brought about by a single purchase, but demand more behavioural changes. Still, the purchase of certain products will be able to contribute to these goals.

The *value-expressive function* fulfils the need to express one's own values in terms of attitudes towards products and services. This is important in the expression of satisfaction with a product. The expression of a positive attitude with regard to a product just bought strengthens the correctness of one's own behaviour. For example, a person could tell friends and colleagues how she liked the concert she heard last night.

The *ego-protective function* of attitudes is the strengthening of the consumer's self-confidence. A consumer with a positive attitude towards the use of cosmetics will feel secure using cosmetics. A feeling of self-confidence can also be achieved by a positive attitude towards conspicuous consumption and the purchase of 'conspicuous' products.

Development of the attitude concept

The concept of attitude has developed from a global to an increasingly differentiated concept.[25] Attitude is now seen as a combination of cognitive and evaluative components, which each bear a relation to a characteristic of a product or service. The cognitive components concern convincing consumers of the presence or absence of a product characteristic or benefit. For example, does a colour television set offer stereo sound? Sometimes one is not sure about the presence, and the belief is based on a probability, for example that a colour television set lasts for ten years. The evaluative components of an attitude concern the evaluation of product characteristics for a consumer. This is often shown in a quality judgement of a product characteristic, for example, Nicam stereo is a favoured characteristic of a colour television set, or a life-span of at least ten years is desirable.

The total attitude regarding a product is equal to the weighted sum of the opinions and evaluations of all relevant product attributes. In the attitude model of Fishbein and Ajzen this is formalized as follows:[26]

$$A = \Sigma_i \, B_i \times E_i$$

The summation is valid for all relevant attributes i ($i = 1,\ldots,N$). N is the total number of beliefs. The ith belief is represented by B_i, the ith evaluation of the belief by E_i. The beliefs and evaluations can be measured in consumer research with the use of Likert scales or semantic differentials.[27]

An example may help clarify this idea. Three holiday destinations, Greece, Italy and Spain, are known for the beliefs that these countries are suitable for an active holiday, that the weather is nice, that there is an interesting culture to be experienced, that there is good food, and that one meets interesting people over there. These scores are given as probabilities between 0 and 1. See table 9.1. For example, Greece has the highest chance (0.8) of good weather. The evaluations of these beliefs are also given in table 9.1, for both students and older people. The evaluations are given on a scale from −3 to +3. Older people find nice weather more desirable than students.

Based on the information in table 9.1, the attitudes of students and older persons can be calculated for the three holiday destinations. Which country scores the highest on culture? Which belief is a negative point for older people? For which country do students have the most favourable belief? And which country do older people prefer?[28]

Attitude models contain cognitive components: beliefs (B). These beliefs are strongly dependent on the perception or estimation of the consumer. These have little to do with affect. The evaluative components, evaluations of beliefs (E) reflect value judgements on which affect can have a direct or indirect influence. If, for example, the smell of coffee has a positive affective

Table 9.1 *Beliefs and evaluations with relation to three holiday destinations*

| | Beliefs | | | Evaluations by | |
	Greece	Italy	Spain	students	older perons
Active holiday	0.7	0.5	0.6	+2	0
Nice weather	0.8	0.5	0.6	+1	+2
Culture	0.7	0.9	0.5	−1	+1
Good food	0.5	0.8	0.7	−1	+2
Meeting people	0.7	0.4	0.8	+2	−2

association, this will be directly expressed in a positive evaluation of this characteristic of coffee.

The attitude model by Fishbein and Ajzen is an example of a compensatory decision rule. This means that a negative belief or a negative evaluation regarding a certain characteristic or attribute can be compensated by another (positive) belief. This is not the case with simplified decision rules in which either not all attributes are considered or trade-offs between attributes are excluded.[29]

Researchers into consumer behaviour have often measured attitudes and have tried to estimate their effect on purchase behaviour. This does not imply, however, that consumers calculate a weighted sum of a vector with opinions and a vector with evaluations, as if their brains function like computers (performing mental algebra to arrive at decisions). These models are therefore not descriptive. One can accept that most consumers have beliefs about product characteristics (be it only a few) and that they evaluate some characteristics or attributes more favourably than others. The linear attitude model seems to be easily capable of explaining and predicting the total judgement of a product on the basis of these components.[30]

Relationship of attitude, affect and values

For the relationship between attitude, on the one hand, and values and affect, on the other hand, we need to distinguish between global and differentiated attitudes.[31]

A *global attitude* concerns an overall attitude towards a product or brand, without separate attributes playing a role. The link between a global attitude and affect usually arises through associations, for example via advertising, and, to a limited degree, by cognition (route A in figure 9.6). The link between attitudes and values is, to a certain extent, cognitive. For example, car ownership may contribute to the achievement of the value 'independence'. The realization of mobility and freedom makes the car 'valuable.'

A *differentiated attitude* is a combination of beliefs (cognitive) and evaluations or weights. The beliefs concern the perceived characteristics of products. The evaluative components can be connected with affect and values. Just as with a whole product, one can associate a positive or negative affect with a certain product characteristic, for example with the delicious smell of freshly baked bread. This leads to a high value of the evaluation of the traits 'smell' and 'freshness' of bread. Evaluations have a cognitive link with values. One will positively evaluate a product characteristic if this characteristic contributes to reaching a value. A beautiful design of a car can for example contribute to the value 'beauty'.

The functions of attitude, affect and values resemble each other strongly as a consequence of the underlying connection (table 9.2). Affect and

Table 9.2 *Functions of attitude, affect and values*

Attitude	Affect	Values
Instrumental, utilitarian	Orientation in choice first impressions	Instrumental values, modes of conduct
Knowledge	Interpretation, organization	Knowledge, meaning, intellectual mastery
Value-expressive	Communication	—
Ego-protective	Ego-protective	Ego-protective
—	Activation	—
—	—	Normative

values each have an extra function, an activation and a normative function, respectively. An example of the ego-protective function of affect is the protection that negative emotions of mourning, like sorrow and distress, may offer against further attacks on the survival of a person. The functions of attitude, affect and values are thus very similar.

9.4 Attitudes and behaviour

Under certain conditions the behaviour of consumers can be predicted from their attitudes towards products, services and brands. There are many ideas about the relationship between attitude and behaviour. Two different attitude models have already been discussed in section 9.3. The interaction is also related to the way in which attitude is measured, and to factors other than the attitude which are linked to behaviour.

Measurement of attitude

Ajzen and Fishbein give some conditions for the measurement of attitude to optimally predict behaviour.[32] These conditions apply to the action (behaviour), the subject of the action, the situation, and the time of the action. By action we usually mean purchasing behaviour. The subject of the action is the product or service being purchased. If one tries to predict the purchase of a single good or service, the measurement of attitude needs to agree with the behaviour on at least the first two points. The measurement then needs to deal with the *purchase* (act) of the *product or brand* in question (the subject of the act). An example is the measurement of an evaluative component: 'How important is the life-time of a colour television set for you when you buy one?' The prediction can be improved by including a reference to the situation and the time of the act. An example of this is the measurement of the belief component: 'If I buy a Philips colour television set next week, I expect it to have a life-time of at least ten years.'

In the prediction of complex behaviour, like environmentally friendly car driving, a reference to the subject of the behaviour is in principle enough to predict the behaviour. Environmentally friendly use of cars consists of a complex group of acts, like the purchase of a car with a catalyzer, economic fuel consumption, using unleaded petrol, not driving at high speed, and accelerating slowly. Such behaviour can be predicted by an attitude measurement with a reference to the subject, for example: 'How important is environmentally friendly car use for you?' If needed, other questions may be asked about the different elements of environmental car use.

Other factors in the explanation of behaviour

Behavioural intention is a mediating variable in the explanation of behaviour. This implies that the intention to purchase directly predicts the behaviour, and that the intention is explained by the attitude. The attitude alone has less predictive value than the behavioural intention.

In the extended model by Fishbein and Ajzen, the influence of the social norm (SN) is included along with attitude. The social norm indicates to what extent the social environment agrees with the behaviour of the individual. The social norm is a system of weighted opinions of different groups in the social environment, such as the normative beliefs of family members, weighted according to the extent to which one complies with these normative beliefs (motivation to comply). Compliance with the normative beliefs of others is a form of conformism. Besides family members, normative beliefs of other reference people like friends, acquaintances and colleagues, can also play a role. In fact, it is not so much the *actual* normative beliefs of reference people but the normative beliefs which are *attributed to them*. The social norm is the weighted sum of the normative beliefs and motivation to comply with these norms.

The extended model is shown in figure 9.8. As mentioned earlier, one's own attitude consists of beliefs and the evaluations of these beliefs. In a similar manner, the social norm consists of normative beliefs (NB) and the extent to which one complies with the normative beliefs (motivation to comply, MC). A weighted combination of attitude and social norms gives the behavioural intention (BI). The behavioural intention is a predictor for the actual behaviour (B). A woman might have a positive attitude towards the use of contraceptives, but know that the social norm of her reference group is negative. The relative weight of her own attitude (w_1) and of the social norm (w_2) then determines whether or not she will use contraceptives.[33] Note that $i = 1,..., N$ for N beliefs and $j = 1,..., M$ for M reference persons.

This can be shown as follows:

$$B \approx BI = w_1 \times A + w_2 \times SN = w_1 \left(\Sigma_i B_i \times E_i\right) + w_2 \left(\Sigma_j NB_j \times MC_j\right) + w_3 \times PBC$$

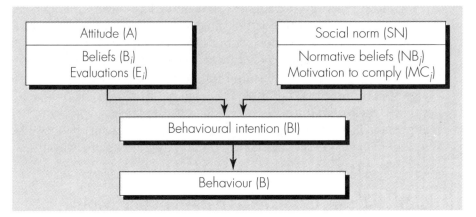

Figure 9.8 *Extended attitude model for the prediction of behaviour*

In the extended attitude model of figure 9.8 it is assumed that subjects have some degree of freedom and control of their behaviour. They can choose between a number of alternatives and weigh these alternatives against each other. This is called the perceived behavioural control.[34] Perceived behavioural control (PBC) may be regarded as a third component.

The social norm can be seen as a factor in the purchase of a product. Consumers take it into account to a certain extent. Other factors are behavioural limitations such as the financial situation of the consumer and the available time. Self-applied norms and values are largely represented in personal attitudes. Purely on the basis of these restrictions consumer behaviour can be reasonably well predicted.[35] Within these limitations, the extended model by Fishbein and Ajzen can improve predictions.

Habits may have their own influence on purchasing behaviour, besides that of attitude and social norms.[36] In this way the purchase of tomato ketchup could be led by the brand one always buys (habit), the attitude regarding a certain brand (brand loyalty; the weighted judgements pertaining to the taste, price, thickness and other characteristics) and the social norm (the opinion of others about the purchase of the brand of ketchup by the consumer in question).

In the model by Triandis, behaviour is explained by the behavioural intention and habits, multiplied by certain facilitating factors.[37] The behavioural intention is explained, just as in the model by Fishbein and Ajzen, by the attitude and the social norm. In the example above, the purchase of tomato ketchup is explained by the buying intention and the brand one has always bought, for example Heinz, while the strength of these factors is influenced by facilitating factors, like the frequency of purchase. With a high purchase frequency the habit will have more influence.

Besides intention and habit, situational factors may also have an effect on purchasing behaviour. If Heinz ketchup is coincidentally sold out, or another brand is being discounted, the purchase of Heinz will be less probable.[38] Apart from this, emotions can also be seen as situational determinants of behaviour.[39] Many emotions and moods are unpredictable. They are strongly dependent on the situation, place, time and preceding experiences of the individual.

Personality factors may contribute to purchasing behaviour. The need for cognition (NfC) is a personality trait which contributes to a more differentiated attitude and to a strong influence of the attitude on behaviour.[40] Self-monitoring is a property which contributes to social norms strongly influencing behaviour. People with a high level of self-monitoring are more sensitive to the social consequences of their behaviour. People with low self-monitoring are more likely to behave how they feel.[41] Furthermore, the action orientation of the individual influences how far attitudes and social norms can predict behaviour. For people who are strongly inclined to convert preferences into action, attitude has a relatively strong influence on purchasing behaviour. People less inclined to take action are more influenced by the social norms.[42]

9.5 Attitude change

In communication and information provision, attitude change in favour of a certain brand or a certain behaviour is often the objective. This can be achieved in different ways by making use of the functions of attitudes, as described in section 9.3.[43]

The instrumental function of attitudes can be used to change attitudes with the help of marketing communication and information extension. Information extension means that the desirable attributes of products can be accentuated, for example, grocers might emphasize the amount of vitamin C in oranges, the aim being to strengthen this belief about this positive attribute of oranges. The evaluations of product attributes can be improved, for example by stressing the health value of vitamin C. The less desirable attributes of a product obviously get less attention from the marketer, who may try to de-emphasize these attributes.

The ego-protective function can be used by appealing to the self-perception of the consumer, for example: 'How can you go on without the radiance of the X beauty mask?' The suggestion is made that the ego is unprotected without the use of this product.

The value-expressive function plays a large role in marketing communications that confirm the correctness of a purchase made by a consumer. Much advertising has the function of convincing consumers of the value of the purchase. Confirmation of value can be provided to encourage and reassure the consumer to continue this behaviour.

The knowledge function of attitudes can be adapted by providing information which indirectly involves the product. For example, the desirability of drinking milk can be strengthened by pointing to the ingredients of milk and the useful functions they have in the body, to the long history of the use of milk, the value of milk products for preventing malnutrition, the effect on growth, weight, and perhaps the life expectation. In this way, the attitude towards milk becomes a part of a substantial network of associations and is thus better protected against change.

Cognitive dissonance

The theory of cognitive dissonance concerns the contradiction between an opinion or attitude and a certain behaviour, or the contradiction between attitudes. Cognitive dissonance is experienced as an internal conflict between two attitudes or between attitude and behaviour. In general, people strive towards consonance (agreement) of their attitudes and behaviour. Unless there are good reasons, they will not act in a way that contradicts their beliefs, or hold beliefs that are contrary to their behaviour, nor beliefs which are contrary to each other.[44] So people will swap from their current choice of brand, if a new brand appears on the market that has much better characteristics.

Definition

Cognitive dissonance is a kind of tension or uneasiness we feel when our behaviour is inconsistent with our attitudes or when our attitudes are inconsistent with each other.

In a classic experiment, a group of women were asked to state their preferences for a number of products on an 8-point scale, for example a stopwatch or a portable radio.[45] As a reward, they were allowed to choose from two of these products (A or B). A and B were either very similar or rather dissimilar. Some women had the choice between two products which differed by only 1–1½ points on the scale (condition with high dissonance). Because the preferences for products A and B were almost equal, they experienced dissonance if they chose A and thereby could not have B, or if they chose B and could not have A. Some other women were asked to choose between two products which differed 3 points (condition with low dissonance). After the choice, the women were given more information about the products and asked to evaluate them again. In the condition with high dissonance, the women showed an increased preference for the chosen product and a decreased preference for the product not chosen. In the condition with low dissonance, there was no significant difference between the evaluations before and after the choice. In the control condition, where the researcher did not ask the women to choose, but simply gave them one of the two products, no attitude change took place.

In the condition with high dissonance, there is a contradiction between the choice for product A and the (almost) equally large preference assigned to product B. The women solved this contradiction by changing their evaluation of both products. In other words, the act of choosing precipitated a change in attitude. In the condition with low dissonance, there is no need to alter the evaluation, because the choice does not create conflict with the preferences. This cognitive strategy can be used in marketing by encouraging people with a negative attitude towards a product to use the product, for example by giving out a free sample or lending it out for use. People are then more willing to change their attitudes towards the product in a favourable direction.

A part of cognitive dissonance theory is the prediction that people try to avoid cognitive dissonance by ignoring information which conflicts with their choices and paying attention to information which confirms their choices. People are more willing to accept opinions with which they already agree. That is why people tend to pay more attention to advertising about brands they possess than others.[46] For this reason, after-sales service is important in strengthening and confirming the attitude towards the purchased product or service. Many user instruction booklets start with the congratulations that one has chosen a good brand/product. This is helpful for consumers in avoiding or overcoming cognitive dissonance.

Another effect of cognitive dissonance is that the more effort one has to put into obtaining a product, the more this product is valued in retrospect. For example, people who overcome a difficult introductory period to become members of a student society are then more satisfied with their membership than those who did not face such an introductory period. The logic is a form of self-perception: 'If I put so much effort into it, it must be valuable'. The behaviour (participation in an introductory period) and attitude (normal evaluation of a student organization) are at first in conflict. This dissonance can be reduced by valuing the organization more. The reduction of cognitive dissonance can therefore bring about attitude change.

9.6 Elaboration likelihood model

The Elaboration Likelihood Model of persuasive communication (ELM) concerns the chance that the recipient of a message engages in cognitive information processing. Two routes are identified in the ELM that lead to attitude change. Attitude change via the *central route* is based on information processing whereby the advantages and disadvantages of a product and/or the arguments in a message are extensively weighed against each other. Attitude change via the *peripheral route* takes place via limited information processing. In this route, the largest influence takes the form of simple 'cues' in the message or the environment of the message, for example the number of arguments in a message (rather than the quality of the arguments), the status and attractiveness of the source, and the number of times that the message is repeated. The central route presupposes a more extensive and deeper level of information processing than the peripheral route.

Definition

Elaboration likelihood refers to the probability of information processing, depending on the motivation, ability and opportunity to engage in such behaviour.

Attitudes which are formed or changed via the central route, are generally more stable than attitudes which are formed via the peripheral route. Often consistency, persistence and resistance are distinguished. Attitudes which are formed or changed via the central route are in general more consistent with other attitudes and schemas in memory. They are also more persistent, which is to say, they are more stable and remain intact longer. Thirdly, they are more resistant to change as a result of new information.

An important condition in ELM is the *motivation* to process the message. This is strongly dependent on the involvement of the receiver with the message. A second condition is the *ability* of the recipient to process the message. Knowledge and level of education play a role. Complicated messages require more knowledge and insight than simple messages. If the recipient does not comply with these two conditions (motivation and ability), an attitude change can still take place by the presence of cues (see figure 9.9). A third condition is the opportunity to process the information. This condition is not explicitly distinguished in the ELM. These three conditions for behaviour to occur form the MAO model: motivation, ability and opportunity.[47]

Motivation
One of the conditions which determines whether persuasion and choice processes go via the central or the peripheral route is the involvement of the recipient with the message or product. Highly involved consumers are usually more motivated to follow the central route, whereas consumers with a low involvement tend to choose the peripheral route. Consequently it has been found that the attitude of consumers who were strongly involved with a certain product (in this case disposable razor blades) was

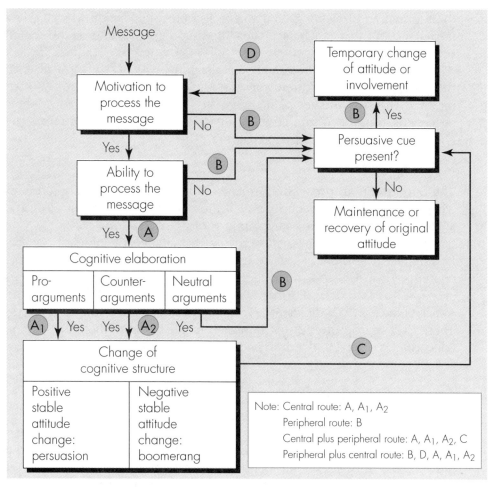

Figure 9.9 *Central and peripheral routes to attitude change*

mainly determined by the strength of the arguments in the message.[48] The attitude of consumers who were not strongly involved with the product, was mainly determined by the status of the presenter of the message. In the experiment 'professional golf players' were used as presenters. They brought about a more positive attitude change than the (unknown) 'inhabitants of Bakersfield' as presenters.

The need for cognition (NfC) can also contribute to a motivation to process the information via the central route. However, NfC does not reflect ability, it only relates to the person's need for a certain kind of information processing.[49]

Ability

The knowledge, education and intelligence of the recipient of a message determine the ability to process the message. Sufficient ability is required for information processing via the central route. Specific knowledge about the subject of the message facilitates information processing via the central route.

The ability to process information is also influenced by the form wherein the message appears: written, verbal (radio) or visual (television). Written information gives the recipient longer to process the message. A short processing time, for example with television commercials, increases the chance of using cues (peripheral route).

Opportunity

The opportunity to process information is also a factor which determines whether the central or peripheral routes are followed. Motivation and ability are personal factors, while opportunity is a situational factor.

Repetition of the message increases the chance of information processing, because there is a more frequent opportunity to think about the contents. However, too much repetition leads to overexposure and thus aversion and boredom. Furthermore, external events, such as noise and social interaction, can distract the recipient of a message from processing it. There is less opportunity for information processing when the person concerned is placed under time pressure.

Cognitive responses

Cognitive processing concerns pro-, counter- and neutral arguments. Consumers, after a confrontation with a message, think of arguments which support the message (pro-arguments), arguments which go against the message (counter-arguments), and neutral arguments (which are neither for nor against the argument). The development of these arguments is the elaboration after which the ELM is named. In a Rémy Martin commercial viewers think of the good taste of the cognac (pro-argument), the high price (counter-argument) and/or that Rémy Martin is available at the local off-license (neutral argument). With many pro-arguments, advertising has a positive effect on persuasion. Advertising may also evoke counter-arguments. With many counter-arguments, advertising has a boomerang effect. The opposite of what the advertiser meant is then achieved. If, for example, in a reorganization of a company, many people lose their jobs, a commercial of that company may evoke negative associations and the counter-arguments of consumers. Analysis of cognitive responses is a widely used type of advertising research.[50]

In the Elaboration Likelihood Model only cognitive responses are included. But there are also affective responses in reaction to a message, in the form of both pro- and counter-affective responses. These affective responses also determine the effect of advertising and information extension: a persuasive or a boomerang effect.

Cues

If the recipient is neither willing nor able to process information cognitively, attitude change may take place via the peripheral route. According to this route, the recipient is influenced by cues or signs which have little or nothing to do with the contents of the message. These cues may be the source or the presenter of the message, the style of the message, the topic of the message, and the medium. See table 9.3.

Presenter of the message
The attractiveness of the presenter has a positive effect on the attitude towards the product or service that is the subject of the message. An unattractive person can even have a boomerang effect, whereby the recipient develops an attitude contrary to the message.

The expertise of the presenter has a positive effect on attitude, for example a doctor, dietician, biologist or scientist. The status and fame of the presenter is also important. An actor, top sportsman or popular television presenter is more convincing than people who have a lower status or are less famous. The credibility of the messenger has a positive effect on the attitude. Neutral presenters are more convincing than those who have a personal interest in the message. A notary who recommends his own services or a shop owner who emphasizes the value of his own goods, is less believable than someone who delivers such a message without a personal interest, such as a consumer spokesperson.

The number of communicating sources influences the attitude. If the Consumer Association (*Which*), the neighbour and the salesperson all recommend a Zanussi washing machine, the consumer is likely to develop a positive attitude towards Zanussi.

Message

The number of arguments for a certain product or a certain service has a positive effect on the attitude, just like the number of sources. If the arguments are brought forward in a personal conversation, this is more convincing than a message broadcast on the radio or television. In personal interaction, an insurance salesman can respond to the consumer with eye contact, facial expressions, and posture, and is better able to adapt the message and to react to counter-arguments. What also counts is that the more attractive the form of the message, the more positive the attitude is.

Emotions in the message can contribute to a positive attitude, because they are more striking and are better remembered. A very emotionally charged message can be threatening, and can, for example cause *anxiety*. In a classic experiment, information about dental care was given in three ways: one which was likely to provoke a high level of anxiety (examples of harmful effects of bad tooth care); one likely to result in an average anxiety

Figure 9.10 *Connoisseurs?*

level; and one aimed at producing a low anxiety level (factual information and examples of the positive effects of good tooth care).[51] In the condition with a low anxiety level, the influence on dental care was largest. In the condition with a high anxiety level, it may be the case that dissonance occurs between the message and the behaviour of the target group. This dissonance can be reduced by denying the contents of the message. The effect of the message is thus reduced.

Anxiety as an emotion is regularly used in advertising and promotional information related to health and insurance. Usually there are three phases. In the first phase a terrifying situation is created. In the second phase it is made clear that this situation can occur in the target group. In the third phase the comfort is given that no anxiety is needed if the recommendations are followed. A high level of anxiety increases the attention given to the message, but also produces boomerang effects, like dissonance reduction. In general, a ∩-formed relationship is found between the anxiety level and the effect of the message. The message has the strongest effect when it produces an average anxiety level.[52]

Explicit messages, in which clear conclusions are drawn, are less effective than implicit messages from which the consumer him or herself has to draw the conclusions. By making personal effort to understand, one elaborates the message. This increases the chance of the message being remembered.

Table 9.3 *Cues in attitude change, and examples of persuasion without arguments*

Traits	Cues	Example
Source	Attractiveness	Photo model in advertisement
	Expertise	Doctor, scientist
	Status	Top athlete
	Credibility	Independent sources
	Number of sources	Signatures on a petition
Message	Number of arguments	Elaborating product benefits
	Personal	Sales representative
	Explicit, implicit	Suggestion in advertisement
	Design	Humour
Product	Price	Price as quality indicator
	Design	Fashionable design
	Country of origin	Japanese (electronics)
		French (wine)
		Belgian (beer)
		German (machines)
Medium	Speed of information transfer	Radio, television
	Umfeld, context	Television programmes around commercial
	Expertise	*The Economist*
	Authority	Government agency
	Attractiveness	Full-colour magazine

Explicit messages are, however, more effective for less motivated or less intelligent people, because they may not draw the proper conclusions from implicit messages.

Product

Some product properties can serve as peripheral cues. For many consumers a high price is an indicator or cue of high quality. Sometimes this really is the case and the price can be seen as an argument in the central route. The price can also contribute to a higher involvement, and thus a willingness to follow the central route. The same applies to the brand, the design, and the country of origin of a product. Sometimes this information gives good arguments for the purchase of a product, but it is often only a cue.

Medium

The speed of the information transfer has implications for the thoroughness of information processing. Compare this with the type of the message above. Slow transfer promotes the processing; fast transfer obstructs it.

The 'Umfeld' or context of the medium influences the effectiveness of the message. Joyful programmes around the commercial broadcast contribute to the forming of a positive attitude relative to the message. This is possibly a consequence of mood, as discussed in section 9.2.

The expertise of the medium is not the same as the expertise of the source. An article in *The Economist* about new products will contribute better to attitude formation than an article in *The Daily Mirror*, although the author may be the same. Expertise is often the basis for authority, but not always. If the government (high authority) warns against the consumption of spinach after a nuclear disaster, this will lead to a different attitude than if someone sends a letter on this matter to a newspaper. The attractiveness of the medium also influences attitude formation. Messages printed in colour are generally more attractive than black-and-white advertisements in a newspaper.

Consumers do not just follow either the central or the peripheral route. It is possible for them to follow both routes. This is shown by line C in figure 9.9. It means that the design or other cues in the commercial message have an extra effect besides the attitude change via the central route.[53] After the peripheral route the central route can be followed, shown by line D in figure 9.9. The advertisement can, for example, be attractive and arouse interest in the message. Consumers then decide to follow the central route. For the advertiser this is the ideal situation, but it does not often occur in practice.

It may be expected that research into the conditions under which consumers follow the central or peripheral routes to attitude change, will not only produce further insights into the mechanisms of advertising and information extension, but also into product choice and product use by consumers. Consumers who are motivated and able to follow the central route, spend more time and attention on the information, and notice more aspects, often including the technical, instrumental attributes of the products. Consumers who follow the peripheral route, give less time and attention to the information and often notice form (rather than content) and other peripheral aspects. Or consumers trust habit and show brand and store loyalty. Reading magazines and viewing television programmes can send messages via both the central and peripheral routes.

9.7 Conclusions

In this chapter, both emotions and attitudes were discussed. These are the emotional and evaluative aspects of consumer behaviour which have been disregarded in research for years, although affect and cognition play a large role in the development of preferences and in consumer decisions. Emotions may be even more important than cognitions. Emotions about products, services and brands and their characteristics may be at least as important as knowledge.

Emotion and cognition can be distinguished, but are difficult to separate. Cognition has emotional aspects. Consider, for instance, the strain you feel when solving a difficult problem. Emotion goes together with thinking. If you experience arousal, you try to identify its cause. Are you really in love with that person, when you heart beats faster every time you see him or her?

Attitude is a central concept in social psychology and in the study of consumer behaviour. The relationship of attitude to behaviour remains a topic of research. The ELM offers a theory about the formation and change of attitudes. This model also explains which attitudes are stable or unstable.

If attitudes and behaviour do not correspond, we speak of cognitive dissonance. This dissonance is usually experienced as unpleasant and people strive to reduce it. They may do this by changing their behaviour or their attitude.

Notes

1 Cohen, J. B. and Areni, C. S. (1991) 'Affect and consumer behavior' in: Robertson, T. S. and Kassarjian, H. H. (Eds) *Handbook of Consumer Behavior* (Englewood Cliffs, NJ: Prentice-Hall), 188–240.

2 See Costa, P. T. and McCrae, R. R. (1980) 'Still stable after all these years: personality as a key to some issues in adulthood and old age' in: Baltes, P. B. and Brim Jr, O. G. (Eds) *Life Span Development and Behavior* Vol. 3 (New York: Academic Press) 65–102. They describe happy and unhappy people as the consequences of extraversion and neuroticism.

3 Plutchik, R. (1980) *Emotion: A Psychoevolutionary Synthesis* (New York: Harper & Row).

4 Mehrabian, A. and Russell, J. A. (1974) *An Approach to Environmental Psychology* (Cambridge, MA: MIT Press). See also section 12.3.

5 This theory is developed by James, W. (1950) *The Principles of Psychology* (New York: Dover) (first published in 1890) and Lange, C. (1922) *The Emotions* (Baltimore: Williams and Wilkins). The theory is therefore also called the James–Lange theory of emotions. See also Ax, A. F. (1953) 'The psychological differentiation of fear and anger in humans' *Psychosomatic Medicine* 15, 433–442; Ekman, P., Levenson, R. W. and Friesen, W. V. (1983) 'Autonomic nervous system activity distinguishes among emotions' *Science* 221, 1208–1210.

6 A galvanic skin response is a change in electrical resistance of the skin. This is determined with the use of a galvanometer.

7 Hess, E. H. (1965) 'Attitude and pupil size' *Scientific American* 212, 46–54. Krugman, H. E. (1964) 'Some applications of pupil measurement' *Journal of Marketing Research* 1, 15–19.

8 Floor, J. M. G. and Van Raaij, W. F. (1998) *Marketing Communication Strategy* (Hemel Hempstead, UK: Prentice Hall).

9 Zajonc, R. B. and Markus, H. (1984) 'Affect and cognition: the hard interface' in: Izard, C. C., Kagan, J. and Zajonc, R. B. (Eds) *Emotions, Cognition, and Behavior* (Cambridge: Cambridge University Press) 73–102.

10 A classic experiment is described in Schachter, S. and Singer, J. E. (1962) 'Cognitive, social and physiological determinants of emotional state' *Psychological Review* 69, 379–399.

11 Pieters, R. G. M. and Van Raaij, W. F. (1988) 'The role of affect in economic behavior' in: Van Raaij, W. F., Van Veldhoven, G. M. and Wärneryd, K.-E. (Eds) *Handbook of Economic Psychology* (Dordrecht, The Netherlands: Kluwer Academic Publishers) 108–142.

12 These goods and services are referred to as transformational and informational, respectively. See Rossiter, J. R. and Percy, L. (1987) *Advertising and Promotion Management* (New York: McGraw-Hill). See section 7.4.

13 Compare the primary affective reaction (PAR), described in section 12.3. The PAR partly determines the further attention given to messages. See Russo, J. E., Metcalf, B. L. and Stephens, D. (1981) 'Identifying misleading advertising' *Journal of Consumer Research* 8, 119–131.

14 Johnson, E. and Tversky, A. (1983) 'Affect, generalization, and the perception of risk' *Journal of Personality and Social Psychology* 45, 20–31.

15 This concerns decision rules. See section 11.6.

16 See section 10.5.

17 Berlyne, D. E. (1963) 'Motivational problems raised by exploratory and epistemic behavior' in: Koch, S. (Ed.) *Psychology: A Study of a Science* Vol. 15 (New York: McGraw-Hill) 284–364.
Raju, P. S. and Venkatesan, M. (1980) 'Exploratory behavior in the consumer context: A state of the art review' *Advances in Consumer Research* 7, 258–263.

18 Optimal level of stimulation (OLS).

19 See section 11.8.

20 Compare the experiments of Gorn, G. J. (1982) 'The effects of music in advertising on choice behavior: a classical conditioning approach' *Journal of Marketing*, 46, 94–101, described in section 10.3.

21 From Gross, R. D. (1987) *Psychology* (London: Hodder & Stoughton).

22 For the attribution process, see sections 8.8 and 21.3.

23 This line of argumentation is in accordance with the cognitive theory of emotion.

24 Katz, D. (1960) 'The functional approach to the study of attitudes' *Public Opinion Quarterly* 24, 163–204.

25 Antonides, G. (1989) 'An attempt at integration of economic and psychological theories of consumption' *Journal of Economic Psychology* 10, 77–99.

26 Fishbein, M. and Ajzen, I. (1975) *Belief, Attitude, Intention, and Behavior: An Introduction to Theory and Research* (Reading, MA: Addison-Wesley).

27 A *Likert scale* consists of five response options:
strongly agree; agree; neither agree, nor disagree; disagree; strongly disagree.
A *semantic differential* consists of a number of adjectives (good/bad, strong/weak, active/passive) on which the product attributes are evaluated. On a 7-point scale the positive adjective gets the highest score (7) and the negative adjective the lowest score (1). In the Fishbein model only the evaluative scale (good/bad) is applicable.

28 Italy scores the highest on culture. Older people find meeting people the least favourable. The attitude of students towards Greece is 2.4, Italy 0.6, and Spain 2.2. Greece is therefore the most popular. The attitude of students towards

Greece is calculated as follows: $(0.7 \times +2) + (0.8 \times +1) + (0.7 \times -1) + (0.5 \times -1) + (0.7 \times +2) = 2.4$. The attitude of older people towards Greece is 1.9, Italy 2.7 and Spain 0.5. Italy is therefore the most popular for older people.

29 See section 11.6.

30 See for instance Dawes, R. M. (1979) 'The robust beauty of improper linear models in decision making' *American Psychologist* 34, 571–582. Dawes, R. M. and Corrigan, B. (1974) 'Linear models in decision making' *Psychological Bulletin* 81, 95–106.

31 Antonides, G. (1989).

32 Ajzen, I. and Fishbein, M. (1977) 'Attitude-behavior relations: theoretical analysis and review of empirical research' *Psychological Bulletin* 84, 888–918.

33 Fishbein, M. and Jaccard, J. J. (1973) 'Theoretical and methodological considerations in the prediction of family planning intentions and behavior' *Representative Research in Social Psychology* 4, 37–51.

34 Ajzen, I. and Fishbein, M. (1980) *Understanding Attitudes and Predicting Social Behavior* (Englewood Cliffs, NJ: Prentice-Hall).

35 See Frey, B. S. and Foppa, K. (1986) 'Human behavior: possibilities explain action' *Journal of Economic Psychology* 7, 137–160.

36 Bagozzi, R. P. (1981) 'Attitudes, intentions and behavior: a test of some key hypotheses' *Journal of Personality and Social Psychology* 41, 607–627. Bentler, P. M. and Speckart, G. (1981) 'Attitudes "cause" behaviors: A structural equation analysis' *Journal of Personality and Social Psychology* 40, 226–238.

37 Landis, D., Triandis, H. C. and Adamopoulos, J. (1978) 'Habit and behavioral intentions as predictors of social behavior' *Journal of Social Psychology* 106, 227–237.

38 See chapter 12 for situational influences.

39 See section 12.3.

40 Petty, R. E. and Cacioppo, J. T. (1986) 'The elaboration likelihood model of persuasion' in: Berkowitz, L. (Ed.) *Advances in Experimental Social Psychology* Vol. 18 (New York: Academic Press) 123–205. See sections 9.5 and 8.4.

41 Self-monitoring is discussed in section 8.4.

42 Bagozzi, R. P., Baumgartner, H. and Yi, Y. (1992) 'State versus action orientation and the theory of reasoned action: an application to coupon usage' *Journal of Consumer Research* 18, 505–518.

43 Antonides, G. (1996) *Psychology in Economics and Business* (Dordrecht: Kluwer Academic Publishers) Chapter 6.

44 Festinger, L. (1957) *A Theory of Cognitive Dissonance* (New York: Harper & Row). Cooper, J. and Fazio, R. H. (1984) 'A new look at dissonance theory' in: Berkowitz, L. (Ed.) *Advances in Experimental Social Psychology* 17, 229–266.

45 Brehm, J. W. (1956) 'Postdecision changes in the desirability of alternatives' *Journal of Abnormal and Social Psychology* 52, 384–389.

46 Ehrlich, D., Guttman, L., Schonbach, P. and Mills, J. (1957) 'Postdecision exposure to relevant information' *Journal of Personality and Social Psychology* 54, 98–102.

47 See also section 11.8.

48 Petty, R. E., Cacioppo, J. T. and Schumann, D. (1983) 'Central and peripheral routes to advertising effectiveness: the moderating role of involvement'

Journal of Consumer Research 10, 134–148.

49 Petty, R. E., Unnava, R. H. and Strathman, A. J. (1991) 'Theories of attitude change' in: Robertson, T. S. and Kassarjian, H. H. (Eds) *Handbook of Consumer Behavior* (Englewood Cliffs, NJ: Prentice Hall) 241–280.

50 See for cognitive response analysis: Brock, T. (1967) 'Communication discrepancy and intent to persuade as determinants of counterargument production' *Journal of Experimental Social Psychology* 3, 296–309.

51 Janish, I. L., and Feshbach, S. (1953) 'Effects of fear-arousing communications' *Journal of Abnormal and Social Psychology* 48, 78–92.

52 Ray, M. L., and Wilkie, W. (1970) 'Fear: The potential of an appeal neglected by marketing' *Journal of Marketing* 34, 54–62.
Sternthal, B. and Craig, C. S. (1974) 'Fear appeals: Revisited and revised' *Journal of Consumer Research* 1, 22–34.

53 Petty, R. E., Cacioppo, J. T. and Schumann, D. (1983) 'Central and peripheral routes to advertising effectiveness: the moderating role of involvement' *Journal of Consumer Research* 10, 134–148.

LEARNING PROCESSES

10

10.1 Introduction

Different forms of basic learning are discussed in this chapter. Basic learning means that consumers are not actively involved. Often these learning processes occur more or less subconsciously.

First of all, classical and operant conditioning are learning processes in which simple associations between stimuli are made. Advertising makes frequent use of classical conditioning. Products and brands are associated with attractive people and situations. This way, the advertised products and brands gain in desirability.

Operant conditioning mainly occurs during and after the use of products and services. This learning process makes use of reward and punishment. A favourable product experience is a reward and has positive effect on consecutive purchases and on social communication. An unfavourable product experience is a punishment and works negatively against repeat purchases and on the content of social communication between consumers.

A third form of basic learning takes place through observation and imitation of other people. Consciously or subconsciously we imitate people whom we admire: their posture, behaviour, use of language, and the products and brands they use.

Consumers often learn and choose in situations of low involvement. This is certainly the case with regard to routine purchases which carry little risk. People do not always watch television consciously, instead they let many programmes and commercials wash over them. Basic learning processes take place which, after many repetitions, influence behaviour.

The different learning processes are discussed in section 10.2. Sections 10.3 and 10.4 deal with classical and operant conditioning, respectively. In section 10.5 observational learning is discussed, and learning with low involvement is covered in section 10.6. Some conclusions follow in section 10.7.

The objective of this chapter is to offer insight into the learning processes of consumers, namely the less conscious and often passive learning processes about products, services, stores and brands.

10.2 Types of learning processes

Learning processes can be separated into routines and more elaborate learning processes.

Routines

Much of consumer behaviour occurs without extensive consideration and reflection like shopping in a supermarket, grabbing a snack from around the corner, or going out to the movies. These forms of consumption are routine, in contrast with, for example, the purchase of a television set or a car. For these products extensive information processing takes place. Routine consumption implies a learning process, whereby thinking and actions are shortened more and more until a script or scheme is formed which can be recalled as soon as a purchase needs to be made.[1] These learned scripts and schemes are exceptionally useful in daily life because more time and energy is left for behaviour for which no structure yet exists, like social interactions, studying, and the planning of activities. The difference between routine and problem solving is evident in the following example. The purchase of a loaf of bread is routine for most people. It consists of a number of sequential actions (script): Get money, go to the bakery, stand in line, place order, pay and bring home the bread.[2] Buying a loaf after arriving in Tokyo is a problem: How much money do we need? Is there a bakery? Where is the bakery? Is there a system of waiting in line or something else? Does bread exist and how is this word pronounced in Japanese? Will the bread taste the same as at home?

Learning processes

Routines help to ensure efficient consumer behaviour and grow out of the influence of a number of different processes which are discussed next. One well-known type of learning is conditioning, whereby behaviour becomes dependent on certain events (stimuli) in the environment. When, after a few visits to a store a consumer notices that this store is cheaper than other supermarkets, this store will function as a stimulus to go shopping there. Clearly, it can be time-consuming to try new behaviours out, so it may be easier to observe and imitate more experienced people. For example, when someone moves into a new neighbourhood, he or she might ask the neighbours where they do their shopping. This last form is known as observational or social learning. Finally, it is possible to acquire certain behaviour by means of insight into a situation. For example, a consumer may learn to associate a certain variety with a lower price, or that it is cheaper to go shopping at a discount shop.[3]

To understand consumer behaviour, it is important to know how the different learning processes take place. Based on this knowledge, a marketer may try to influence this behaviour, for example, by using particular types of marketing communication. Consumer organizations and educational institutes, on the other hand, can make consumers more aware of the processes that lead to their behaviour. Finally, learning processes play a very important role in raising children. Understanding them can help parents to comprehend and, if necessary, guide the consumption behaviour of their children.

10.3 Classical conditioning

The starting point of classical conditioning is an unconditioned stimulus (US) followed by a natural, spontaneous reaction: the unconditioned response (UR). The classical example is that of the dog, which, upon seeing food (US) starts to salivate (UR). The Russian physiologist Ivan Pavlov originally studied this phenomenon of salivation as a reflex. The classical conditioning process is shown schematically in figure 10.1. The instinctive behaviour of a hungry dog is to salivate on seeing or smelling food (figure 10.1a). Pavlov discovered that the dog, after a certain period of time, began to drool as soon as it saw Pavlov and heard him rattling his food bowl.[4] A dependency or association developed between the signal of the approaching food and the reflex (figure 10.1b). The development of this association is the learning process known as classical conditioning. After a while the dog started to salivate at the rattling sound of the food bowl (figure 10.1c). The signal is the conditioned stimulus (CS) and the learned reaction is the conditioned response (CR). Unlike the unconditioned response (UR), the conditioned response can be activated without seeing the food (US). The CR is identical to or strongly resembles the UR.

Definition

Classical conditioning is a process in which a previously neutral stimulus acquires the ability to elicit a response by repeated association with a stimulus that naturally produces a similar response.

This Pavlovian example can be substituted by a contemporary example of classical conditioning. A girl with long blond hair in a white dress at a farm and a pump with clear water (US) brings the association of naturalness and purity (UR). Timotei shampoo (CS) is associated in a commercial with

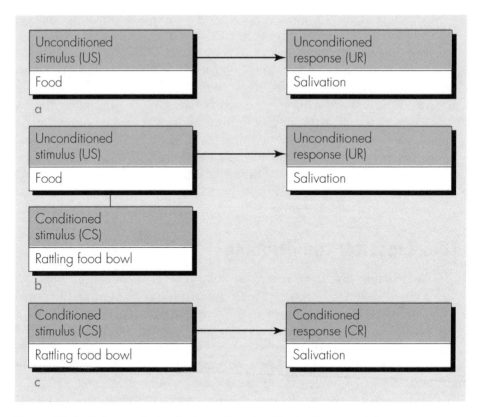

Figure 10.1 *Scheme of classical conditioning (Pavlov's example)*

the blond girl and also acquires an image of naturalness and purity. This applies to Western Europe where the old farming way of life is associated with nature. This commercial was also used in Russia, but there farming was associated with backwardness, and this led to unintentional and undesirable associations for Timotei shampoo being created.

Much consumer behaviour is learned under the influence of classical conditioning. After some visits to McDonald's one might react to the McDonald's logo (with salivation?) without necessarily even seeing a hamburger. In consumption, brand names and logos play the role of the conditioned stimulus (CS). Associations are built between US and CS. The induction of associations is often seen in advertising.

Stimulus association

An important element in classical conditioning is the association of the CS to the US. Experiments show that the best learning result is given by a CS which just precedes a US (forward conditioning). The presentation of a CS following a US (reverse conditioning) gives less good results.[5] The strength of the CR can be measured both as the frequency and amount of consumption. The lesson for McDonald's marketing policy is therefore: produce as many McDonald's signals as possible before consumption takes place. This message is apparently well understood.

Stimulus generalization

Definition

Stimulus generalization is the phenomenon in which stimuli similar to a conditioned stimulus elicit a similar response without prior learning.

The CS does not have to be identical to the stimulus associated with behaviour during the learning process. A similar signal (for example a Burger King) is also capable of bringing to mind the CR (the buying of a hamburger), albeit to a lesser extent. This is known as stimulus generalization. The more a signal differs from the original CS, the weaker the CR will be. To prevent another manufacturer from taking over the logo of an existing product, these names and logos are protected by law. Nevertheless, it can be interesting for the competing producers to incorporate as many external characteristics of the product of the market leader in order to take maximum advantage of stimulus generalization. In Shanghai (China) imitation McDonald's stores exist, hoping to acquire the same associations as the real McDonald's.

Stimulus discrimination

The consumer in an affluent society has a hard time finding the most satisfactory products due to the small differences between products and brands. By paying close attention to these differences, stimulus discrimination can be achieved. A price reduction has to be large enough to be distinguished (discriminated) by consumers. Discounts of less than 10% are often not seen as 'real' advantages. In general, 'special offers' must have a price/value improvement above a certain level to be perceived as improvements.

Definition

Stimulus discrimination is the process in which the organism responds only to the exact, original conditioned stimulus and not to similar stimuli.

Incidentally, a situation where one must choose between many similar brands can be an unpleasant experience. Consumer organizations can be helpful in supplying clear overviews. In experimental situations, where dogs are asked to identify increasingly subtle distinctions in the CS, the dogs eventually become neurotic.[6]

Application to advertising

Classical conditioning is widely used in advertising. Brands, products, and services (CS) are often associated with enjoyable stimuli (US), such as pleasant music, colours, attractive-looking people, and humour. The idea is that consumers learn to associate brands and logos with positive feelings. From stimulus generalization of the brand in the commercial to the brand on the shelf, learning will contribute to a more positive attitude towards the purchase of the respective products and services. It is also probable that the information obtained about a product, is viewed more positively once the learning process has taken place.

Phases in the learning process

In classical conditioning, different phases may be distinguished. In the first phase, the connection between the CS and US is established, after which the CR occurs on presentation of the CS. If consequently the US lags several times after the CS is provided, the CR will decrease (extinction). In the third phase, no presentation of stimuli takes place (resting phase). It seems that the learned behaviour is now forgotten. However, if in the fourth phase the CS is presented again, a spontaneous recovery of the learned response, the

Figure 10.2 *Conditioning or association?*

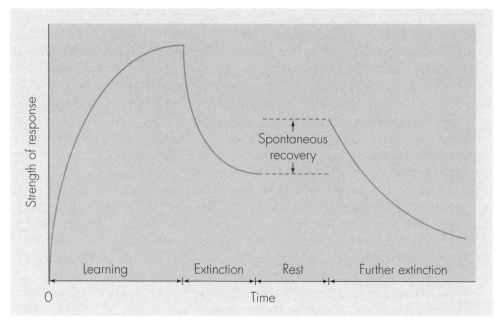

Figure 10.3 *Learning and extinction of a conditioned response*

CR, occurs. After further extinction, this will disappear again; see figure 10.3.

For advertisements to be effective, the learning phases have certain implications. In the establishing phase, the advertisements should be shown several times. To prevent extinction of the response the advertisements must be repeated every now and then. It is important to note that the connection between the CS and US brings about a learning process, but not necessarily one that leads to a purchase. Purchasing is, after all, different behaviour with different consequences (US) than the learning process. In case the product has consequences that are not comparable with the UR in advertising, stimulus discrimination could occur. Consumers might find the products attractive in the advertisements, but not when they see them in the store.

Explanation of classical conditioning

It is easy to explain the principle of classical conditioning as a substitution of a CS for a US in order to elicit a certain behaviour (CR) from the consumer. The process takes place subconsciously. Reactions of the autonomous nervous system can be conditioned using classical conditioning. This is why we get goose bumps at the sound of a dentist's drill. There are indications, however, that there is a certain amount of thinking activity in the development of the learning result.[7]

New insights into classical conditioning underline the informative value of the CS for the appearance of the US. The dog 'knows' that food is on its way when someone is rattling the food bowl. An association of CS and US is only meaningful if the US does not occur when the CS is lacking. So no food should be given if there is no rattling of the food bowl. Figure 10.4a shows a simultaneous association of CS and US, but the US also occurs without a CS. It is therefore not immediately clear whether the CS has anything to do with the US. In these cases classical conditioning will not occur. In figure 10.4b the informative value of the CS is much larger, and conditioning is observed. The degree of conditioning is dependent on the probability that the US takes place in the presence of the CS.[8]

The modern view of classical conditioning assumes that people strive towards obtaining a reward (US). To this end, they look for the best predictor of the US. This will be the CS which most often covaries with the US. This is called covariation of the CS and US. In other words, in classical conditioning, individuals cognitively interpret stimuli as predictors of reward. In this respect, the learning process is related to the attribution process whereby the covariation principle is also applied.[9] If two phenomena regularly occur at the same time, a causal relationship is inferred. If the CS often occurs without the US, the informative value of the CS decreases.[10]

Applied to advertising for the car brand Opel (CS), this means that the US (positive sensations in the advertisement) will have little effect because Opels in reality often come without the US. Classical conditioning will therefore be most effective at the introduction of a new type of car that is rarely seen without the US.[11] On the other hand, the US should not occur frequently without the brand name. Thus, the US should be selected that is uniquely associated with the CS, for example, a jingle exclusively connected to the brand.

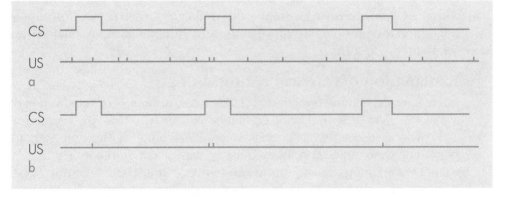

Figure 10.4 *Schemes of relationships between conditioned and unconditioned stimuli, CS and US respectively*

Factors in classical conditioning

Cognition plays a role in different ways in classical conditioning processes. Several cognitive factors have an influence on the learning result.[12]

Consumer characteristics

If the stimuli in the conditioning process are largely visual (as they tend to be in advertising), the visualization capacity of the consumer will influence the extent of conditioning. Furthermore, unconditioned stimuli can have different meanings for different consumers. A jingle based on a Michael Jackson song will be associated by many people with a number of experiences which have nothing to do with the product. The same applies to the effect of Beatles music on forty-year-olds. Such music does not necessarily have to be associated with the product in the commercial (CS), whereby the informative value of the US is lost.

Stimulus characteristics

The saliency of a stimulus has a large influence on the learning process. In this way, a salient US, e.g., a loud noise, can overshadow a more subtle US (a soft sound). In advertising one must therefore make sure the US can be clearly distinguished.

Well-known stimuli are not suited as US for several reasons. Firstly, there is a pre-exposure effect. This effect is based on the fact that well-known stimuli may become boring and are not experienced positively. For example, in direct mail-shots, promoters often make an offer which is only valid if the consumer buys 'today'. This is a stimulus which becomes boring and is no longer capable of bringing about a positive association with the product.

Another effect is the blocking of association. This may occur if there already exists an association between CS_1 and US and one tries to connect a CS_2 with the US. The existing connection now blocks the conditioning of the CS_2. If for example a connection exists between H&M (CS_1) and a famous model as Linda Evangelista (US), then if Esprit (CS_2) also employs Linda consumers may be blocked from making the connection. As trusted stimuli have existing connections with conditioned stimuli, they are much less feasible as unconditioned stimuli in a new conditioning process.

If two brands use the same advertising themes, brand confusion may result. If Pampers and Peaudouce both use the theme of walking and playing babies, the brand (CS) is no longer uniquely associated with walking and playing babies (US). A brand must distinguish itself from the competition and build unique associations.

Nature of the conditioned response

The conditioned response (CR) in a classical conditioning process is usually the evaluation or attitude in relation to a conditioned stimulus (CS), and not the completion of a task with regard to the stimulus.[13] This rests on the instrumental function of attitudes,[14] which means that after learning whether stimuli are good or bad, one can deal better with the situation. At the same time, the attitude will affect a wide scale of responses, while an act is only related to one response. This argument is part of attitude theory where attitudes are predictors of different, but related behaviours.[15]

Technical aspects of the conditioning
A number of technical factors can influence the conditioning process. These conditions concern the number of associations needed to achieve the learning result, the time between associations and the time taken up by each association. The latter is usually limited: the airing time for commercials is expensive, so that association time lasts for only 20–30 seconds. The number of associations corresponds with the contact frequency of a person with a commercial message. The time between the associations corresponds with the interval between two contacts (contact interval). To achieve fast conditioning, the contact frequency needs to be high and the intervals to be kept short. This is a 'burst' or concentration condition. To maintain the effect, the intervals can be longer. This is called 'spreading' or a condition of constant presence.[16]

Problems with research in classical conditioning

Some problems exist in the research in classical conditioning.[17] Subjects are sometimes capable of guessing the goal of the experiment and may behave according to the expectations of the researcher. The results of the experiment are then not purely a result of the conditioning process. By minimalizing the information about the learning result, the researcher is more likely to find out whether the classical conditioning really takes place.

Because conditioning is an unconscious process, subjects are not able to explain why a certain reaction (CR) is given in response to a certain stimulus (CS) after the conditioning process. Despite the unconscious process subjects come up with all sorts of explanations for the learned behaviour. People are used to giving explanations and justifications for their behaviour, although these do not have to be the real causes of the behaviour. This gives the impression of a cognitive learning process, where information processing about the product leads to the behaviour. Classical conditioning can be overlooked in such instances. It may seem as though no conditioning has taken place.

The unconditioned stimuli (US) in a learning process can make subjects pay more attention to the product information. The learning result is then strengthened by the cognitive effort. Researchers wishing to focus on conditioning need to minimize the information provided with the stimulus so that the learning result cannot be attributed to information processing and can only be attributed to conditioning.

Finally, the simple revelation of a conditioned stimulus (CS) can change a subject's disposition. This is called the effect of 'mere exposure'. The 'mere exposure' effect implies that with an increased perception of a stimulus, it becomes more attractive. This can be confused with the effect of conditioning. By including negative unconditioned stimuli the 'mere exposure' effect can give no explanation of a (negative) learning result.[18]

Conditioning through advertising

In experiments researchers have tried to exclude the above-mentioned alternative explanations of the learning result.[19] In one experiment, subjects were told that an advertising agency had been given the task of finding the right music (US) for the commercial for a ballpoint pen (CS). The ballpoint pen looked cheap and cost 49 cents. While showing the ballpoint pen on a slide, the music was played for one minute. There were four groups (conditions) each comprising about 60 students. In each group, 'attractive' (music from the musical 'Grease') or 'unattractive' music (Indian music) was used with a blue or beige ballpoint pen. The conditions were the following:

1 attractive music and a blue ballpoint pen;
2 attractive music and a beige ballpoint pen;
3 unattractive music and a blue ballpoint pen;
4 unattractive music and a beige ballpoint pen.

After the presentation, the subjects were given the choice between a blue and a beige ballpoint pen as a reward. The results of the experiment were as follows: in conditions 1 and 2 with attractive music 79% chose the ballpoint pen of the same colour as on the slide which they had seen, while in conditions 3 and 4 with unattractive music only 30% chose the ballpoint pen with the same colour. So the use of an unconditioned stimulus (music) can significantly influence the response. In this case the result can hardly be attributed to product information, because none was given. It was not the case that subjects always chose the colour they had seen ('mere exposure'), as the product shown with unattractive music was chosen less frequently. Finally the learning result was determined by a choice which had no under-lying rationalization. The individuals were asked to explain why they had chosen the blue or beige ballpoint pen. None of the subjects noted that the choice was based on the music. They were therefore not aware of the con-ditioning which had taken place. They did think of all sorts of reasons such as 'blue is my favorite colour' to justify their behaviour.

The *orientation* of the consumer often determines which commercial is accepted in a certain situation. People who have to make a choice between alternatives, are in a *utilitarian* orientation. Informative advertising fits with this orientation because this form of advertising provides information which can be used in making the choice. People who do not need to make a choice, often find themselves in a *hedonistic* orientation. They look at advertising in a relaxed fashion and especially value funny and attractive commercials.

In a second experiment, the role of product information and the relevance for consumer decision-making was investigated.[20] A group of students was told that their help was needed by an advertising agency to determine whether air-time should be bought for a commercial in a television programme. It concerned two ballpoint pens produced by different manufacturers (A produced a beige ballpoint pen and B produced a blue ballpoint pen). As a reward for their help, the students were told that after the experiment they could choose between a set of ballpoint pens of brands A and B (this is the decision process). Brands A and B had different advertising strategies. The students saw the ballpoint pen of brand A along with attractive music (from 'Grease'), and then the ballpoint pen of brand B with product information (the pen is smooth, never leaks and is durable). After the slides the students watched a television programme ('Drugs and Teenagers') and were asked their opinions about the purchase of air-time for the commercial in this programme. Finally the students were told that after the lecture (70 minutes later) they could hand in their answers and select their pens. This was done to simulate a real situation where some time passes between commercial appearance and purchase. Another group of students underwent exactly the same procedure, but were not told until after the lecture (when no stimuli were being presented) that they could choose between the two kinds of ballpoint pens (the non-decision-making condition).

Product information is important in a utilitarian orientation if a decision has to be made. In a hedonistic orientation, mostly attractive advertising is valued, for example with nice music. Conditioning, as an unconscious process, occurs more easily in a hedonistic orientation. In the decision-making condition (utilitarian orientation) of the experiment, 71% chose the brand accompanied by product information. In the non-decision-making condition (hedonistic orientation), 63% chose the brand accompanied by music. The fit of the commercial to the orientation of the consumer determines to a large extent to which aspects attention is directed. Conditioning apparently has less effect in a utilitarian orientation, compared with a hedonistic orientation. This means that advertising can bring about a conditioning process without product information. The product information should then be given at the point of purchase.

10.4 Operant conditioning

Different from classical conditioning, the process of operant or instrumental conditioning rests on the giving of an unconditioned stimulus (US), *after* certain behaviour is shown. The American psychologist Burrhus Skinner is known as the 'discoverer' of operant conditioning.[21] The US is then a positive or negative reinforcement of the performed behaviour. The effect of operant conditioning is the strengthening or weakening of the performed behaviour. A positive stimulus (reward) leads to a larger chance that the given behaviour will be performed again (strengthening). A negative stimulus (punishment) leads to a smaller chance that the given behaviour will be performed again (weakening).

Definition

Operant conditioning is a type of learning in which the consequences of behaviour lead to changes in the probability of that behaviour's occurrence.

Operant conditioning involves the consequences of behaviour. For example, a person could behave in three ways: behaviours A, B or C (see figure 10.5). Behaviour A is followed by a reward and is thereby strengthened. For example, a woman using White Linen eau de toilette gets many compliments for it. She will therefore use it more often. Behaviour B is followed by 'punishment'. One evening she wears too strong a perfume and is laughed at. This weakens her desire to use this perfume again. Behaviour C is neither punished nor rewarded and will therefore not be strengthened or weakened.

Purchasing behaviour can be influenced by operant conditioning. If the product provides enough benefits and one is satisfied with the product, this is a positive reward which increases the chance of repeat purchase (A). If one is dissatisfied, the chances of a repeat purchase decrease (B). In principle, any kind of behaviour is susceptible to operant conditioning, even the unconscious behaviour of the autonomic nervous system like the heart beat.

The following experiment is a marketing example.[22] There was a jewellery shop in a Texas town of 22,000 inhabitants. Recent customers of the jewellery shop were divided into three equal groups. The first group was called and thanked for the purchase they had made. The second group

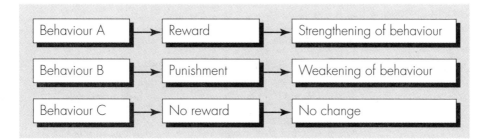

Figure 10.5 *Three types of reinforcement in operant conditioning*

was also thanked and made aware of a special offer. The third group was not called. The callers introduced themselves by name and the name of the shop and gave their message. The interviewers were well-mannered and continued the conversation as the customers wished. Some customers immediately hung up; others were happy with the call. Most customers reacted neutrally and did not show any intention to make new purchases. However, the results were that on average over the three groups 27% more sales were realized in the test month than in the same month of the previous year, while in the preceding year sales had been 25% below average. By this experiment the negative trend had been turned into a positive one. The first group was 70% responsible for the rise in sales, the second group responsible for 30% of the increase. The third (control) group behaved as before. With this experiment it is shown that in practice a positive experience (reinforcement) *after* a purchase increases the chance of a repeat purchase. The difference is greatest if the positive experience occurs without any obvious commercial intentions. This could be the result of cognitive dissonance which is higher in group 1 than in group 2.[23]

Reward schedules

In the operant conditioning process it is not necessary to reward the behaviour each time. A reward ('reinforcement') that is only given occasionally is more effective than one given each time. Ratio and time schedules have been described for different marketing requirements. See table 10.1.

If a reward is given for some behaviours, we speak of a ratio reward. The ratio reward can be given continuously after a fixed number of times (fixed ratio schedule or fixed ratio reinforcement) or after a continuously changing number of times (variable ratio schedule or variable ratio reinforcement). Reward systems of stamps or sales coupons are examples of a fixed ratio schedule. When the savings card is completed, one obtains the reward. Brand and store loyalty are thereby strengthened. Lotteries, prize questions and arcade machines with a chance of reward are examples

Table 10.1 *Fixed and variable ratio and time schedules with examples and implications*

	Ratio schedule	Time schedule
Fixed	Fixed ratio schedule supermarket value stamps → brand and store loyalty	Fixed time schedule discounts → bargain hunting
Variable	Variable ratio schedule national lottery, fruit machine → continuation of behaviour	Variable time schedule 'mystery shopper' → constant behaviour

Figure 10.6 *Operant conditioning*

of a variable ratio schedule. Some people keep putting money in fruit machines, because they expect to win something eventually.

The clearest example of operant conditioning is the arcade machine, for example the 'fruit machine', also called the 'one-armed bandit'. The player sometimes wins. The ratio of won-to-lost games is rewarding to such an extent that many players continue playing. The spreading of winning games over time is also important. The player should win with a certain regularity, but not in a fixed pattern. With 'normal' fruit machines, a regular, but not large reward is given. At the so-called 'peak machines' the player is not rewarded for quite a long time, but then may enjoy a short period of large rewards. These 'peak machines' seem to be strongly addictive and are therefore forbidden in many countries.[24]

A time schedule rather than a ratio schedule of reinforcement is often followed. It is possible to have a fixed time schedule ('fixed-interval reinforcement'), for example, a once-a-year sale. This attracts bargain-hunters, who may not return until the next sale. There are also variable time schedules ('variable-interval reinforcement'), for example price cuts at unexpected moments. Some companies employ 'mystery shoppers' to go shopping at unexpected moments to test the service, expertise and friendliness of the personnel. Mystery shoppers are employees of a research agency who act as customers. Mystery shoppers report their experiences to the retail company. The reviewers of the *Michelin Guide* visit restaurants at unexpected moments without identifying themselves. These reviewers determine whether a restaurant obtains or loses a star. Mystery shoppers make use of a variable time schedule. It encourages the shop and restaurant personnel to pay constant attention to the quality of the service.

It is found that a variable ratio schedule of small rewards for bus travel was just as effective as a fixed ratio schedule.[25] In the variable ratio schedule, one out of every three bus passengers got a 10 cent coupon and a short text thanking the passenger for taking the bus. In the fixed ratio schedule, each passenger got a coupon. A variable ratio schedule is less expensive to apply than a fixed ratio schedule.

Shaping

Shaping is the gradual forming of certain behaviour using operant conditioning. A reward is given after a small change of behaviour in the desired direction. This is how circus animals are trained to do certain tricks. There are also applications in consumer behaviour. Take for example a car dealer, who wants to make a deal with a customer. First, coffee and biscuits are presented to everyone who enters the business. Then ten euros are paid to each customer with a driver's licence who wishes to take a test drive. Finally, a 500 euro discount is given on the price of a car.[26] In this way, a customer can gradually (in steps) be tempted to make the purchase. Shaping is a process by which a customer, via intermediate steps, is induced to perform the intended behaviour or to go from a limited to a full use of a product.

> **Definition**
>
> Shaping is the process of rewarding sequential approximations to desired behaviour that encourage the person to perform the desired behaviour eventually.

Shaping looks like the 'foot-in-the-door' technique, but is based on steps in rewards. The 'foot-in-the-door' technique rests on a continuous decrease in the tension between attitude and behaviour.[27] A gradual change in attitude can also take place as a result of shaping.

Habituation

Habituation is related to shaping. In shaping, the desired behaviour is reached via an approximation with gradual steps. In habituation, the desired behaviour is created directly by offering gradually decreasing discounts. For example a consumer receives a free sample of the new (fictitious) dish-cleaning detergent 'Supershine'. On the package there is a coupon for 50% off the next purchase. At the third purchase, the full price must be paid. The rewards in habituation are decreasing and intended to stimulate continuation of the behaviour.[28]

Shaping and habituation are often applied in sales promotion. A free trial period for a product, like a trial subscription for a newspaper, is a kind of habituation. Giving an advance balance for the opening of a savings account, is shaping. The selling of a product at a very low price ('loss leader' or bait) serves to get customers into the store. If these customers consequently buy other products, this is a form of shaping. An ad at the entrance of a shop and a free sample of a product are also forms of shaping.[29] If there is a discount every week (a fixed time schedule), habituation in revisiting the shop occurs.

In the practical examples in this section, a positive experience is linked with the behaviour, so that the information content of the stimulus is high. The information content of a reward ('reinforcement') in operant conditioning will largely be determined by the same factors as with classical conditioning.

Primary and secondary reward

A distinction can be made between primary and secondary reinforcers. A primary reinforcer satisfies basic needs, like hunger and thirst. Secondary reinforcers have attained their value by association with primary reinforcers, like for example when the rattling of the food bowl was associated with food. Secondary reinforcers can strengthen the behaviour in a second-order conditioning situation. If, for instance, the rattling of the food bowl was associated with a flash of light in a conditioning situation, eventually the flash of light on its own will provoke the conditioned behaviour (salivation). See figure 10.7.

> **Definition**
>
> A secondary reinforcer is a stimulus that has become reinforcing through previously being associated with a reinforcing stimulus.

Practical examples of secondary reinforcers are compliments, value coupons, and money. These reinforcers have attained their rewarding value through association with primary reinforcers like food, candy or gasoline. The secondary reinforcers can themselves be used in a second-order learning process, for example, school kids are rewarded with compliments, value coupons can be acquired through the purchase of certain products, and money acts as a reinforcer for many different behaviours. Secondary reinforcers are often very general by nature, that is to say, they can reinforce many more behaviours than those reinforced in the first-order process.

Secondary reinforcers often satisfy 'higher' needs like status and recog-

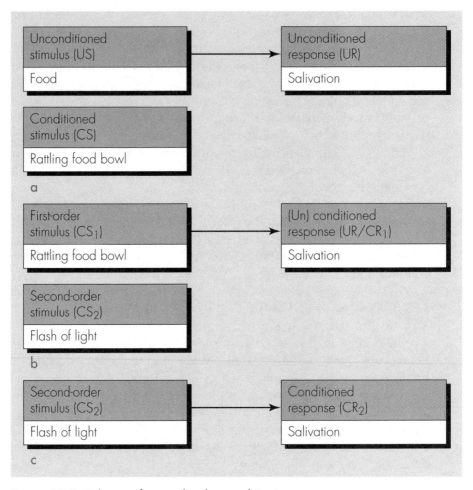

Figure 10.7 *Scheme of second-order conditioning*

nition: for example, consider compliments. Primary reinforcers of the drinking of beer are the quenching of thirst and joviality. Secondary reinforcers are social recognition and acceptance by others, for example in a student organization.

Secondary reinforcers are frequently applied in token economies. Token economies are relatively closed social systems where tokens (coupons, chips, receipts or tickets) are used as rewards for behaviours or services. The tokens (secondary reinforcers) can be exchanged for good or services which are valuable to the owner (primary reinforcers). Examples are psychiatric institutions, jails, schools, and countries or situations where the money system no longer functions properly. Even animals can be taught the value of coupons. Chimpanzees can learn to work for poker chips instead of food. With the chips the animals could get food out of a dispenser, the 'Chimp-o-mat'.

Behaviourism

Classical and operant conditioning belong to the school of behaviourism. This is a school within psychology which aims to make as little use as possible of mental concepts like attitude and intention. In behaviourism, behaviour is explained by stimulus–response relationships as well as the strengthening and weakening of these relationships. Skinner was the protagonist of behaviourism and developed a social vision based on behaviourism in his novel *Walden Two*.[30]

10.5 Observational learning

The conditioning processes can be seen as more or less mechanical, where the cognitive aspect is mainly concerned with the information content of the stimuli. Another form of learning rests on social aspects and involves imitation of the behaviour of other people, i.e., following a 'model'. A model is a person serving as an example and he or she becomes a behavioural goal for the followers. Observational learning is extremely important in giving instructions and demonstrations, for example about the use of a product. 'Modelling' and social learning are other names for observational learning. At the turn of the century, Gabriel Tarde in France pointed to the role of imitation in consumer behaviour.[31]

Observational learning rests on the imitation of the behaviour of a model, because this behaviour may result in optimal use of a product. Instructions or demonstrations might show certain behaviour, like a demonstration of vacuum cleaners at a trade fair or a television programme about DIY jobs around the house. Alternatively, a videotape of a cooking course may be presented. Here the proper execution of the steps is of central importance. The learning process can occur much faster through imitation than by trial and error.

Another principle of observational learning is the identification with the model being observed. According to this principle one will have the tendency to identify oneself with an attractive model who uses a certain perfume in a commercial. The suggestion is made that through the use of that perfume one will become just as attractive as the model. This stimulates the purchase of the perfume. In an advertisement, models are also used to fix one's attention on the advantages of the product, for example by having women talk about the problems of stain removal in the laundry and providing a solution to the problem with Ariel Ultra.

In observational learning, the difference between a learning result and the actual imitation of behaviour is very important. After all, something could have been learned without being directly expressed in behaviour. The actual performance of the learned behaviour is partly dependent on the situation and on the expectation of the result of the behaviour. The learning result is also dependent on whether the model is rewarded for the observed behaviour.[32] An example is the choice between a new and a popular soft drink.[33] Children who have seen their friends choose the new soft drink, will choose the new drink more often than those who have not. The new soft drink is also more frequently chosen if the model (or the research co-ordinator) shows observable pleasure in the choice made.

The influence of peer pressure in a day-care centre on children's choice between two different menus has also been researched.[34] The children sat in groups of four at a table and could choose between two menus. It was arranged so that the one menu would be preferred by only one child (A) and the other menu by the other three children. On the first day, child A was allowed to choose first; and to choose last on the second, third and fourth day. The result was that the child chose the preferred menu on the first day, but was influenced by the choice of the other children on the other days. On the other days, child A chose the non-preferred menu more often. The choice of the one child could be significantly influenced by the decisions made by the other children. The implication of these experiments is that seeing a purchase stimulates a purchase. To stimulate the purchase of a certain product, 'pace-makers' could be employed to act as examples to other customers. Stall-holders at fairs sometimes use accomplices as pace-makers to encourage onlookers to buy. A more honest way to promote social learning is to say how many of a certain product have been sold. This is why McDonald's tells its US consumers 'Billions and billions sold'.

The experiments involving decision behaviour give the same results as experiments on group conformism. In a classic experiment by Asch a subject together with six other people is faced with the following task.[35] The researcher shows the group two cards at a time. On one card a standard line with a certain length is shown. On the other card three lines with different lengths are shown. The researcher asks everyone in turn which of the three lines has the same length as the standard line. The six other members of the group are in fact accomplices of the researcher, but the 'real' subject does not know this. At the first and second set of cards, everyone agrees which of the lines has the same length as the standard line. At the third set of cards the five accomplices choose the same wrong line before the 'real' subject is asked to make a choice. The latter is greatly confused by the group's consensus and experiences a pressure to conform to the group's decision. The result is that in 30% of the cases the subject conforms to the (wrong) verdict of the group.

Characteristics of a model

Not all observed behaviours lead to imitation by the observer. Some models have more success than others. A number of characteristics of the model are important for the imitation of behaviour.[36]

- Similarity between the model and the observer makes imitation more likely. A model of the same sex will more often be imitated than a model of the opposite sex. The social learning process is also enhanced by a similar age.
- Warm, friendly people are more likely to be imitated than unfriendly people. In an experiment with children at play, the behaviour of a woman sitting on the ground responding enthusiastically and sensitively was more often imitated than that of a woman sitting in a corner at a table.
- Dominant people and people with power are more often imitated than others. Parents are usually the dominant people in a family and are often observed. If one of the parents is dominant, this parent is more often imitated. In a group of children, the most dominant children are the most imitated ones. In advertising, celebrities are used as models in the hope that more imitation will take place.

Characteristics of the behaviour

Not all behaviours are easily imitated.[37] The suitability, relevance and consistency of the behaviour and the reward the model receives all play a role.

The *suitability* of the behaviour is an important factor. Aggressive behaviour by a male model is more likely to be imitated than the same behaviour by a female model. In many commercials, the prevailing role pattern is used to guarantee the suitability of the behaviour. In this way, advertising for detergents and household products usually uses a female model, and that for cars, tools and financial issues usually uses a male model.

The *relevance* of the behaviour is also of importance for the social learning process. As the observed behaviour increases in importance for the observer, it will be imitated more often. This is also associated with the prevailing role pattern.

The *consistency* of the behaviour of the model adds to the learning result. A presenter who is seen in a commercial for a better environment one day and in a car advertisement the next day, can hardly be called consistent, and is therefore less credible.

Finally, the *reward* for the observed behaviour is an important factor in the learning process. The reward is offered to the model and not to the observer during the learning process. This is called *vicarious reinforcement*. Rewarded behaviour is followed by more imitation than punished or non-rewarded behaviour. In advertisements, negative reinforcements are usually used to enhance the contrast between the product to be promoted and other products. For example, the man in the commercial who took out a loan from the 'wrong' bank looks sad, whereas the man with the 'right' loan looks happy and prosperous.

Even with negative vicarious reinforcement the observer can be brought to imitate the behaviour if the expected results are positive. An example is information about tax-paying. One will not imitate the tax-paying model if the chances of being caught not paying tax are small. On the other hand, a positive vicarious reinforcement does not always have to lead to imitation if the expected results for the individual are negative. Therefore, in social learning, the learning result is distinguished from the actual imitation. An example of not imitating a model is the person who realizes that the expected wins in a lottery are lower than the price of a ticket. This person will probably not respond to advertisements which feature a prize-winner explaining the advantages of the lottery.

Definition

Vicarious reinforcement is the process by which the strength of a response is increased when a model is observed who is rewarded for performing the response.

There are plenty of examples of socially learned behaviour. Addictions to smoking, drinking and drug use are often socially learned. Most of these users have parents, relatives or friends who also use.[38] An important aspect of consumption behaviour which can be socially learned, is the refusal of immediate satisfaction of needs in order to have greater satisfaction later (delayed gratification). The following experiment is an example of this idea.[39] Children observed an adult who could choose between a chess game with plastic pieces and one with wooden pieces. The wooden pieces were not going to be available until two weeks later. In the one condition of the experiment, the plastic pieces were chosen and the adults made comments like: 'Chess pieces are chess pieces. I might as well use the plastic pieces at once'. In the other condition, the wooden pieces were chosen with the comments: 'The wooden pieces are much better. Usually I find life more fun if you can wait for good things'. Consequently, the children were left to make similar choices with objects more suitable for children. The choice of the children was strongly influenced by the behaviour of the adult. The influence was also long-lasting and was still recognizable in choice behaviour four weeks later.

Stages in the observational learning process

Four stages of the observational learning process can be distinguished: attention, learning, reproduction, and reward.[40] These stages are shown in figure 10.8.

Attention
Attention for an observed behaviour can be influenced in several ways. Salient activities, accompanied by striking sounds and objects attract more

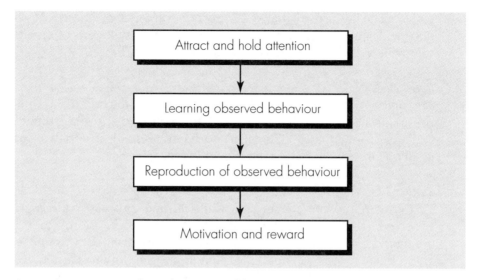

Figure 10.8 *Stages of an observational learning process*

attention than less salient behaviours. The better the observed behaviour corresponds with the knowledge, experience and expectations of the observer, the more attention it gets. The details of a product demonstration might be overlooked by a less experienced customer but not by an experienced one. Attention levels will also be greater the more relevant the behaviour is to the observers, for example, because they will soon be carrying out the behaviour themselves. Attention can be retained by frequently noting the relevance to the consumer.

Moreover, the reputation and the attractiveness of the models and the consequences of their behaviour will affect the attention of the observer. The attention can further be enhanced by the style of the observed behaviour, for example, using the voice and style of Orson Welles in the Sandeman commercial. The contrast between a good or poor results of an action may increase the attention, for example the retaining and spoiling of colours after washing with Dreft or another detergent. Some actions occur too quickly to get enough attention. Attention can be focused by showing the behaviour in slow motion, for example, showing a tennis serve in slow motion. Modern communication techniques expand the spectrum of observed actions and can strengthen the attention of the observer.

Learning
Observed behaviours are stored in memory in a special way. Nobody exactly remembers all observed actions. The ease with which an observation can be stored in memory, will partly determine how well it is remembered. Easily visualized or verbalized behaviour is coded faster. Colours and simple forms are probably quickly visually coded, rhyming words are quickly verbally

coded. The individual makes an abstraction or a prototype of what is observed, and this determines the ease with which the observation is remembered and recollected.

Reproduction
The actions of a model will not always be correctly imitated. This is linked to the abilities of the observer. Children are smaller in size and strength than adults and may find it difficult to correctly imitate the motor actions of adults. This may be true for older people too.

Reward
Vicarious reinforcement in a social learning process consists of the observed results of model's behaviours. However, these rewards are compared to standards held by the individuals themselves. This implies that an everyday reward will not be enough to bring about the learning result. If one is used to exuberant reactions to an observed behaviour in a commercial, a less exuberant reaction will no longer be seen as a positive reward. Consumers use a standard of fairness of rewards. This is to say, the rewards must be comparable to a reasonable standard.[41] The reward works as a motivation to keep performing the learned behaviour.

10.6 Low-involvement learning

Television viewers confronted with commercials and magazine readers looking at advertisements on the page are not usually consciously processing the information. Advertising is often uninvited and imposed on consumers. Consumers are not thrilled and often not involved. Advertising should therefore be striking if it is to grab attention. Do consumers actually learn something from these intrusive confrontations? In most cases not, but sometimes they do. A model of learning under low involvement is therefore necessary.

Television advertising is usually not focused on extensive information processing. This is not possible in the 20–30 seconds of a commercial. The aim is to bring about primary associations with the brand. Brand awareness and a positive brand attitude are often the objectives of the advertiser. Classical conditioning and observational learning are learning processes which occur here. Repetition plays an important role. Learning under low involvement is a form of learning with small, sometimes almost unnoticeable steps.

There are many possible exposures to advertising. Three exposures to the same advertisement is optimal.[42] The first time, consumers see the advertisement, they may think 'What is this?' and/or 'Do I like this?' It is a form of identification and categorization to assign the message to a product category. Consumers who see a commercial for Becel Gold determine that it deals with a kind of cheese. It is also a primary affective reaction and a judgement of likeability.[43] On the second exposure, consumers ask themselves: 'Is this something for me?' 'Is this a good, filling, or healthy cheese?' Or 'Is this real cheese?' By the third time the consumers see the advertisement, it might seep through that it is about cheese that is not made from milk, and thus not a dairy product, but it looks healthy. It is on this third exposure that consumers understand the real message. After that, further exposure is needed to stop people from forgetting the message. These later exposures are mainly reminders.

The three-step exposure model is an example of an advertising strategy.[44] Some messages are so simple that one exposure is enough. If consumers are strongly involved in a topic, one exposure is often sufficient. For complex messages, further exposure might be necessary to convey the full message. But as mentioned, the medium of television is less suited to complex messages, especially for an audience with low involvement. If three exposures are enough, this does not mean that the commercial only needs to be shown three times. The frequency of broadcasting needs to be ten times or higher in order to achieve a contact frequency of three with a large proportion of the target group.

In the primary affective reaction, there is little or no comparison of pros and cons, the assets and liabilities, the advantages and disadvantages. It is about a global attitude in terms of beautiful–ugly, good–bad, and attractive–unattractive. The level of product involvement influences the chance that an elaborated attitude will be formed by the consumer's processing of information. If involvement is low, the consumer is not likely to be ready to put a lot of effort into processing the relevant information. Cues and other peripheral elements will then play a role in attitude formation.[45]

The relevancy question is often posed by consumers. Irrelevant advertising will be ignored. Commercial messages often do not bear an immediate relationship to the situation and the needs of the moment. Consumers mostly watch television out of the desire for relaxation (hedonistic orientation). Advertising which strongly appeals to active learning is not suitable. A jovial and amusing commercial is more fitting in such a situation. However, the message could be relevant in the future, and this is one reason why not all messages are ignored.

The effects of low-involvement learning are that the brand attains a kind of passive identity. Consumers may not actively think about it, do not even remember the commercial, but may recognize the brand in the shop. It is also linked to some positive associations in their minds. This increases the probability that consumers buy the brand in the shop and try it at home. Only after that does the real learning begin. Does the product satisfy? Does it deliver the benefits for a reasonable price? Product knowledge and a more elaborated attitude are usually not formed prior to use. With

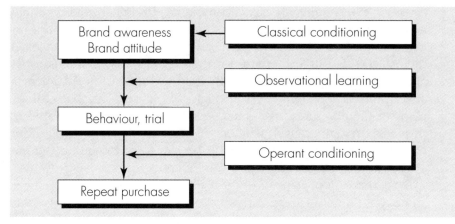

Figure 10.9 *Learning hierarchy under low involvement*

positive usage experience a kind of operant conditioning takes place. Favourable experiences are rewarding and unfavourable ones are 'punishing'. In the case of favourable experiences, this will lead to repeat purchases. For the users, advertising becomes a confirmation of the favourable experiences. This model of learning under low involvement is known as the ATR hierarchy (awareness, trial, reinforcement/repeat):[46] see figure 10.9.

Classical and operant conditioning and observational learning are the basic forms of learning under low involvement. Classical conditioning leads to associations being formed between brand name and positive situations and people. Observational learning occurs if consumers imagine themselves behaving and being just as attractive as the advertising model. Unconsciously the model is imitated and the commercial message is related to the desired situation. Operant conditioning occurs in the form of a reward after favourable product experiences. This leads to a strengthening of the behaviour.

10.7 Conclusions

Learned behaviour has significant advantages for the consumer. Otherwise one would have to spend a lot of time in supermarkets and department stores to make the right choice. There is a disadvantage of learned behaviour, namely that one is no longer aware of the alternatives to the learned ones. A change in this learned behaviour will only arise with difficulty because a new learning process would have to take place. All this leads to brand loyalty and a barrier against behavioural changes.

There are however, important human characteristics that can break routine behaviour, and these are boredom and curiosity. People have a need for change and variation, and look for new impulses if these are lacking.[47] Brand choice can change, and for a producer a broad range of products seems to be the solution. The good qualities of the brand can thereby be combined with the need for variation. Somewhere between the chaos of extensive problem solving for each product and the boredom of single-tracked consumption, the consumer will look for an optimum level of stimulation: here the consumer feels most comfortable.[48]

In consumption we find routines and little problem-solving behaviour. This implies that a change in choice is hard to achieve. People do not tend to be sensitive to information and arguments, probably because they have developed routines not to have to bother themselves with the choice anymore. According to the Elaboration Likelihood Model there is another way to get people to change their minds.[49] Where the probability of making a cognitive evaluation of information is small, people still often react in a non-cognitive way under the influence of cues. Classical and operant conditioning and observational learning all make use of these cues.

Although some cognitive aspects of these learning processes are dealt with in this chapter, they are still not based on the processing of the content of a cue, but rather on the meaning of a cue for events in the environment. In other words, the conditioned stimuli, the actions of a model and the vicarious reinforcement can be cues for behavioural change.

The effectiveness of stimuli which can influence behaviour is dependent on the *Zeitgeist*, the 'spirit of the time.' If the tendency to conformism in society decreases, stimuli which appeal to individuality will more strongly influence behaviour.[50] If emancipation and liberation are prevalent, stimuli which break through existing role patterns will be more effective, as for example, in advertising for participation of women in traditionally male occupations. In shorter periods of time, seasonal influences can make themselves felt. 'Wintry' stimuli like ice, snow and skiing heroes dominate in the winter. Whereas in the summer, the sun, beach resorts and tennis players become more dominant. We see other differences between stimuli during the day and during the evening, on weekdays and in the weekend, and between countries and regions.

Learning is often not a conscious process. Unconsciously and after many repetitions we end up a little wiser. In many cases, we only learn a brand name and some associations. This is often enough to choose an insurance policy from a number of insurance brands, providing that the conditions of these policies do not differ too much. With convenience goods, we learn from users' experience, imitate and repeat the purchase, providing no shocking changes in the environment take place like a striking ad campaign for another brand which succeeds in making it appear familiar and attractive.

Notes

1 A script is a sequence of characteristic acts. Compare the planning of a sequence of events based on a memory schema in Barsalou, L. W. and Hutchinson, G. W. (1986) 'Schema-based planning of events in consumer contexts' *Advances in Consumer Research* 14, 114–118.
2 This is also called a script.
3 See chapter 11.
4 Pavlov, I. P. (1927) *Conditioned Reflexes* (New York: Oxford University Press).
5 McSweeney, F. K., and Bierley, C. (1984) 'Recent developments in classical conditioning' *Journal of Consumer Research* 11, 619–631.
6 Pavlov (1927).
7 Rescorla, R. A. (1988) 'Pavlovian conditioning: it's not what you think it is' *American Psychologist* 43, 151–160.
Shimp, T. A. (1991) 'Neo-Pavlovian conditioning and its implications for consumer theory and research' in: Robertson T. S., and Kassarjian, H. H. (Eds) *Handbook of Consumer Behavior* (Englewood Cliffs, NJ: Prentice-Hall) 162–187.
8 Rescorla, R. A. (1968) 'Probability of shock in the presence and absence of CS in fear conditioning' *Journal of Comparative and Physiological Psychology* 66, 1–5.
9 Heider, F. (1958) *The Psychology of Interpersonal Relations* (New York: John Wiley).
10 McSweeney and Bierley (1984) give an incorrect interpretation of Rescorla's idea.
11 Compare McSweeney and Bierley (1984).
12 Shimp (1991).
13 Shimp (1991). In operant conditioning the act is central in the learning process. See section 10.4.
14 Katz, E. (1960) 'The functional approach to the study of attitudes' *Public Opinion Quarterly* 24, 163–204.
15 Ajzen, I. and Fishbein, M. (1980) *Understanding Attitudes and Predicting Social Behavior* (Englewood Cliffs, NJ: Prentice-Hall). See chapter 9.
16 See chapter 16 of Floor, J. M. G. and van Raaij, W. F. (1998) *Marketing Communication Strategy* (Hemel Hempstead, UK: Prentice Hall).
17 Gorn, G. J. (1982) 'The effects of music in advertising on choice behavior: a classical conditioning approach' *Journal of Marketing* 46, 94–101.
18 Zajonc, R. B. (1968) 'Attitudinal effects of mere exposure' *Journal of Personality and Social Psychology* 9, 1–27.
19 Gorn (1982).
20 Gorn (1982).
21 Skinner, B. F. (1938) *The Behavior of Organisms* (New York: Appleton-Century-Crofts).
Skinner, B. F. (1974) *Walden Two*.
Skinner, B. F. (1976) *About Behaviorism* (New York: Vintage Books).
22 Carey, J. B., Clicque, S. H., Leighton, B. A. and Milton, F. (1976) 'A test of positive reinforcement of customers' *Journal of Marketing* 13, 98–100.
23 See section 9.5. Customers of group 1 received a telephone call without a

commercial purpose. This friendliness may create dissonance and imbalance in the customers. They felt obliged to do something in return, for instance, buying again with the jewellery shop.

24 For gambling addiction see section 23.5.

25 Deslauriers, B. C. and Everett, P. B. (1977) 'Effects of intermittent and continuous token reinforcement on bus ridership' *Journal of Applied Psychology* 62, 369–375.

26 Peter, J. P. and Nord, W. R. (1982) 'A clarification and extension of operant conditioning principles in marketing' *Journal of Marketing* 46, 102–107.

27 Scott, C. A. (1977) 'Modifying socially-conscious behavior: the foot-in-the-door technique' *Journal of Consumer Research* 4, 156–164. See section 22.4.

28 Scott, C. A. (1976) 'The effect of trial and incentives on repeat purchase behavior' *Journal of Marketing Research* 13, 263–269.
    Rothschild, M. L. and Gaidis, W. C. (1981) 'Behavioral learning theory: its relevance to marketing and promotions' *Journal of Marketing* 45, 70–78.

29 Nord, W. R. and Peter, J. P. (1980) 'A behavior modification perspective on marketing' *Journal of Marketing* 44, 36–47.

30 Skinner (1974).

31 Tarde, G. (1890) *Les Lois de l'Imitation (The Laws of Imitation)* (Paris: Alcan).
    Tarde, G. (1902) *La Psychologie Economique (Economic Psychology)* (Paris: Alcan, two parts).

32 This point concerns a perceived strengthening (reinforcement) of the behaviour in the commercial, and not a form of payment to the actor in the commercial.

33 Barnwell, A. K. (1965) 'Potency of modeling cues in imitation and vicarious reinforcement situations' *Dissertation Abstracts* 26, 7444.

34 Birch, L. L. (1980) 'Effects of peer models' food choices and eating behaviors on preschoolers' food preferences' *Child Development* 51, 489–496.

35 Asch, S. E. (1956) 'Studies of independence and submission to group pressure: 1. a minority of one against a unanimous majority' *Psychological Monographs* 70, No. 416.

36 Mazur, J. E. (1986) *Learning and Behavior* (Englewood Cliffs, NJ: Prentice-Hall).

37 Gross, R. D. (1987) *Psychology* (London: Hodder & Stoughton).

38 Mazur (1986).

39 Mischel, W. (1966) 'Theory and research on the antecedents of self-imposed delay of reward' *Progress in Experimental Personality Research* 3, 85–132.

40 Bandura, A. (1986) *Social Foundations of Thought & Action. A Social Cognitive Theory* (Englewood Cliffs, NJ: Prentice-Hall).

41 Compare Adams, J. S. (1963) 'Toward an understanding of inequity' *Journal of Abnormal and Social Psychology* 67, 422–436.

42 Krugman, H. E. (1977) 'Memory without recall, exposure without perception' *Journal of Advertising Research* 17, 4, 7–12.

43 Russo, J. E., Metcalf, B. L. and Stephens, D. (1981) 'Identifying misleading advertising' *Journal of Consumer Research* 8, 119–131.

44 Krugman (1977).

45 For instance, the peripheral route of the ELM model. See section 9.6. Conditioning may also take place.

46 Ehrenberg, A. S. C. (1974) 'Repetitive advertising and the consumer' *Journal of Advertising Research* 14, 2, 25–34. See also section 18.5.

47 Zuckerman, M. (1978) 'Sensation seeking' in: London, H. and Exner Jr., J. E. (Eds) *Dimensions of Personality* (New York: John Wiley) 487–559.
McAlister, L. and Pessemier, E. (1982) 'Variety seeking behavior: an interdisciplinary review' *Journal of Consumer Research* 9, 311–322.

48 Berlyne, D. E. (1963) 'Motivational problems raised by exploratory and epistemic behavior' in: Koch, S. (Ed.) *Psychology: A Study of a Science* Part 5 (New York: McGraw-Hill) 284–364.

49 Petty, R. E. and Cacioppo, J. T. (1986) 'The elaboration likelihood model of persuasion' in: Berkowitz, L. (Ed.) *Advances in Experimental Social Psychology* Part 18 (New York: Academic Press) 123–205.

50 Bandura (1986).

DECISION PROCESSES

11

11.1 Introduction

Some basic learning processes, such as classical and operant conditioning were reviewed in the previous chapter. These are less conscious learning processes that cause changes in behaviour. Observational learning is a learning process in which one observes and imitates the behaviour of others. In this chapter, conscious learning processes are discussed. In table 11.1 these learning processes are ranked from less conscious to fully conscious. Conditioning is called behavioural learning.[1] Observation and imitation imply a small degree of cognitive activity. Cognitive learning is a conscious mental activity of comparing and trading off factors, which plays a role in information processing and the solution of (consumption) problems.

In the case of attitude formation and change, conscious and less conscious processes may also be distinguished, respectively the central and peripheral routes to attitude change.[2]

Information processing and decision processes play an important role

Table 11.1 *Types of learning processes*

Learning process categories	Level of consciousness	Specific processes	Behavioural indicators
Behavioural learning	Less conscious	Classical conditioning Operant conditioning	Forming associations Preference, habit formation
Observational learning		Social conditioning	Observation, imitation
Cognitive learning	Fully conscious	Information processing Decision processes	Understanding Problem solving

in consumer behaviour. These processes consist of the comparison of alternative products, services or brands with the aim of making a choice. These processes take place at different levels. First, the generic choice of saving or spending on product categories such as clothing, drinks and food is made. Then, for example, within the category of drinks, follows the modal choice between products such as milk, beer and soft drinks. Finally, the specific choice of a brand or type within the product range follows, e.g., Heineken or Kronenbourg. At each of these steps the consumer has to choose from several alternatives or decide to choose none of them. Although only three levels of choice are identified in figure 11.1, finer gradations may be distinguished. For example, specific choices could be separated into decisions about the type of car (e.g., saloon, estate, convertible, etc.), the brand and the dealer. It should be remarked that these decision processes take place in cases of high involvement. In the case of impulse purchases and low involvement, one spontaneously chooses a product or brand without first thinking about the generic choice.

As for the choice between saving or spending, the moment of consumption plays an important role. Here the freedom exists to delay or advance consumption. In adverse situations and with negative expectations, for example, in a recession, spending can be delayed. This also has important repercussions for the financial services of banks in connection with saving and lending. The generic choice is closely linked to domestic budget management with such questions as: 'How much should we spend on groceries?', 'How much money has to be put aside for regular bills?' and 'How much pocket money shall I give to the children?'[3] For modal and specific choices, the consumer gets help from consumer programmes in the media, e.g., comparative product testing and information extension.

How do such decision processes take place? How are choice alternatives found? How do consumers compare the alternatives? Do consumers acquire a lot or little information about the alternatives? If so, how much

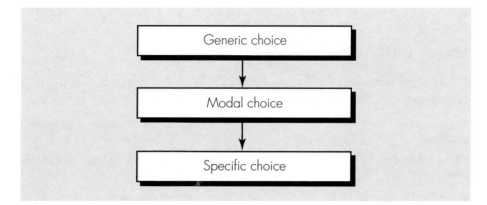

Figure 11.1 *Levels of decision and choice processes*

information do consumers gather to make a better choice? And do consumers with a lot of information make better choices than those with little information?

For some decisions information from memory is sufficient to make a choice. This is the case with well-known alternatives for repeat purchases. When information from memory is not sufficient, consumers may seek additional information by reading advertisements, leaflets or *Which?* magazine, by looking at shop windows, by asking friends and by visiting stores. The consumer has to decide whether more information leads to a better decision and whether it pays to collect more information in view of an expected better choice. With choices in which consumers perceive a large risk or uncertainty, additional information can help to decrease the sense of risk or uncertainty.[4] In fact, the consumer has to weigh the time and effort to collect more information against the value of a possibly better choice.

Section 11.2 of this chapter deals with information and product search. The choice alternatives consumers know and consider, are discussed in section 11.3. The functions of information processes with regard to consumer decision making are considered in section 11.4. Then follows a description of the internal representation of information (section 11.5). An outline of the most important decision rules is given in section 11.6, and the sequential use of these rules in section 11.7. In section 11.8, the possibilities and restrictions on human information gathering and processing are discussed on the basis of the MAO model. In section 11.9 some conclusions are drawn.

The objective of this chapter is to give insight into the way information is processed, namely the conscious learning and decision making of consumers.

11.2 Search

If consumers become aware of a need, want or problem, they start to look for ways to satisfy the need or solve the problem. This does not always mean that a product will be bought. In many cases, services or products already in possession can be used. For instance, if a student needs a textbook, this book can be bought or borrowed from the library or from a friend. A certain function has to be fulfilled, i.e., studying a book, but these functions can be fulfilled by a number of different approaches.[5]

Internal versus external search processes[6]

Internal search
Often, the first place that consumers look to solve a problem is internally. Consumers may derive solutions from their own experience. This means that relevant information is retrieved from memory. The availability

heuristic may play a role here. The available option and habits are most easily retrieved from memory. Often these options will suffice to solve the problem.

Search processes are often not optimal. Simplified search processes often imply the concept of *satisficing*. A satisfactory or 'good enough' solution is adopted. Simplified searches may follow a certain pattern. The availability heuristic consists of processing information that can be retrieved most easily from memory, for instance a nearby store, a frequently purchased, or heavily advertised brand. These brands belong to the top-of-mind awareness (TOMA) set. Asking a sample of consumers for fast-food brands, brands like Burger King and McDonald's are likely to be mentioned. A high TOMA score is good news for the producers concerned.

The extension of the cognitive network (the number of cognitive elements) may determine the success of internal search. If one wants to move from A to B, one may search one's memory for options. If one habitually takes the car (directly available), one may tend to select this option. There are other options that are not directly available such as taking a taxi or bus. Some options may be forgotten—for instance a train connection to B. Experienced consumers may solve many problems using internal search. Consumers with little experience, or experienced consumers in new or changed situations may use external search.

External search
If search takes place outside the consumer's own knowledge and experience, it is called external search. Social sources, media, stores, databases, the Internet, and observing others may provide information. Information is not always sought to solve a problem. Many people like

Figure 11.2 *High risk purchase?*

shopping without necessarily buying anything, but just to keep aware of new products and prices. This type of search is internally motivated. Searching for the solution to a problem may be externally motivated.[7] A number of characteristics of the search process may be distinguished.[8]

Characteristics of the search process

Characteristics of the search process are: sources (where to search), search intensity (degree of search) and intentionality of search.

Sources

Information sources are the brands that are searched, the stores visited, the product characteristics, and the media that are consulted. Information sources play an important role. These information sources may be categorized in personal/impersonal and commercial/non-commercial sources, as shown in table 11.2.

Salespeople constitute a commercial personal information source, especially for products about which consumers need extensive help. Salespeople play different roles in 'push' and 'pull' marketing strategies. A 'pull' strategy is based on the attractiveness of the product itself. A 'push' strategy is based on the persuasive power of the retail channel and depends more on sales personnel.

Advertising and product information in the store is impersonal and commercial. If a consumer needs something, then he or she is usually more receptive to advertising for products that may satisfy this need. Types of product information in the store include displays and informative labelling on the package (for instance a declaration of ingredients). Low-income and less educated consumers make less use of informative labelling. This is certainly not the purpose of policy-makers. Policy-makers aim to help households with lower incomes and education levels.

Social sources such as friends, relatives, and colleagues are non-commercial, personal sources that may simplify search processes considerably. Using these sources may be seen as a heuristic in decision making, if a consumer relies on friends for solutions.

Non-commercial, neutral sources and media are impersonal, for example, consumer programmes on radio and television, articles in mag-

Table 11.2 *Examples of personal and impersonal, commercial and non-commercial sources*

	Personal source	Impersonal source
Commercial source	Salesperson	Advertising, displays
Non-commercial source	Friend, colleague (social source)	*Consumer Reports* (neutral source)

azines and newspapers, and the publications of consumer organizations. Consumers consider these sources as more reliable. These sources can have a strong impact on consumer decision making and choice, especially with regard to negative information and warnings about products.

Search intensity
The intensity of consumer search can be judged by looking to the number of brands that a consumer considers, the number of stores visited, the number of product characteristics considered, the number of information sources consulted, and the amount of time spent on search. Search intensity differs according to the type of decision process used.[9] With routine problem solving, intensity is low, with extensive problem solving, the intensity is high. Extensive and routine problem solving are discussed in section 11.7.

Search intentionality
Information is not always gathered intentionally. Consumers also encounter information they are not looking for, but learn incidentally (unintentionally and unmotivated) from advertisements and from products observed and used by others. People are, however, more sensitive to incidental information when they are on the verge of taking an important decision or solving a problem.

11.3 Consideration and rejection of alternatives

When gathering information, comparing and choosing between alternatives, it is important to know which alternatives play a role. Which alternatives does the consumer know? And which alternatives does the consumer weigh when making a choice? When a product, type or brand is not included in the choice set, it cannot play a role. It is therefore important for the consumer to know the proper alternatives and to choose from the right set of alternatives. Manufacturers have to make sure their brand is included in the set of options considered.

For example, in the market there are options or choice alternatives A–K. These alternatives can be brands (Volkswagen) or different types of cars (VW Golf). The 'awareness set' consists of alternatives which a particular consumer knows from the start. The TOMA set (top-of-mind awareness) is a subset of the awareness set. The awareness set of figure 11.3 consists of alternatives D, E, F, G, I and J.

The consideration set or 'shortlist' consists of those alternatives a consumer considers at the point of purchase: F, G, and H.[10] In this example the consumer already knew about alternatives F and G, and after seeking information, was able to add brand H. Brand H was not part of the original awareness set, but was included after the information search, thus

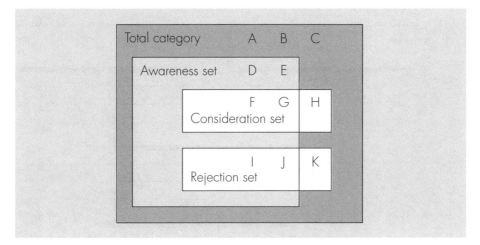

Figure 11.3 *Relation between different sets of choice alternatives*

increasing the awareness set. In general, increasing brand reputation serves to have the brand included in the awareness sets of as many consumers as possible. The chances of the brand being considered at the point of purchase will then increase. Brand H has been added to the consideration set of this consumer following his or her information search.

The rejection set consists of alternatives that do not play a role, such as alternatives I, J and K in figure 11.3. Brand K was only included in the rejection set after information search, thus increasing the awareness set. The rejection set consists of those brands that are consciously rejected in the way some consumers consciously reject German or Japanese cars because of their experiences during the Second World War. Alternatives A, B and C are and remain unknown by the consumer. Alternatives D and E are known but neither considered nor rejected and take a position in the middle between the consideration and rejection set.

The situation of figure 11.3 is a step in a process. By information search and processing the contents of the sets change, as has happened with alternatives H and K, which have appeared in the awareness set. The consideration set has developed out of brands the consumer already knew about and brands that have been added after information search. The ultimate brand is selected out of the consideration set. Figure 11.4 shows this process.

When consumers are asked to name car brands (awareness set) they might name: BMW, Fiat, Lada, Mercedes, Rover, Peugeot, Skoda and Toyota. When asked to name car brands they possibly choose they might name Fiat, Rover and Peugeot. When asked which brand they would reject, they might possibly name Lada and Skoda.[11]

Before a consumer starts to collect information, the awareness set may

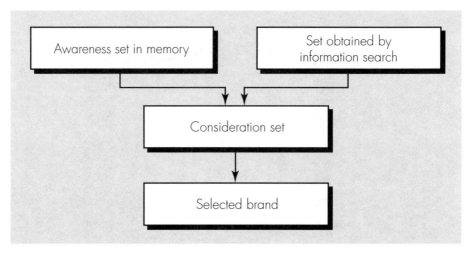

Figure 11.4 *Position of the consideration set in the process of information search*

be small. It is possible the consumer only knows a few brands and types at that stage. After collecting information, the awareness set nearly always grows, as do the consideration and rejection sets.

11.4 Functions of information processing

Information processing has several functions for consumers:

- Consumers expect to make better decisions after obtaining and processing information about the alternatives.
- Consumers expect to reduce the perceived risk and uncertainty by obtaining a lot of information, although their decisions do not necessarily gain by this.
- By seeking and evaluating information, difficult decisions can be postponed for some time.
- Information can serve as justification afterwards when the actual decision has been made or a preference for a specific alternative already exists.
- Consumers may perceive information processing as an investment in knowledge about products to be used at a later stage when a purchase is imminent.

Perceived risk

Decision makers often experience risk and conflict in their decisions.[12] The outcome of a choice is often uncertain. Even non-selected alternatives have attractive qualities. Some cognitive dissonance can hardly be avoided. The degree of risk is related to four factors: the number of selected alternatives, the perceived equivalence of the alternatives, the importance and similarity of the alternatives. The more important an option is, for example, when a product is expensive, the more similar the alternatives are, and the more difficult it is to compare the alternatives, then it follows that the more difficult it is to make a choice.

Four types of risk can be identified. These are perceived risks.[13] Thus, it is important to consider them the way consumers experience them.

- *Physical risk*: This can result from choices made regarding physical well-being, as with the use of medicines, medical services, alcohol, tobacco, drugs, car driving, and sports activities.
- *Financial risk*: This can result from choices made for future expenditure such as the maintenance and repair of durable goods and unforeseen extra expenses. 'Money back' guarantees may reduce the consumer's perception of financial risk.
- *Social risk*: This can result from choices made concerning social relations and the prestige of the consumer. How will others evaluate his or her choices? Information from social sources may reduce this risk.
- *Time risk*: This can result from choices made about the future time expenditure of the consumer. How much time will the use and maintenance of particular goods take? How much time will be spent on repairs? How often does the dog have to be walked? Will the computer programme provide the data in time? Postponement of the decision also has a time risk, namely the delayed use of the product.

Figure 11.5 *Baby food is not low risk!*

In general, consumers not only try to reduce the risk by seeking information, e.g., shopping, but also by brand and store loyalty; trusting the recommendations of friends, sales personnel and experts; buying well-known brands in stores with favourable images; buying the most expensive product of its kind; and asking for money-back guarantees.

Information may decrease the subjective uncertainty about the choice alternatives, because the consumer more clearly understands the risk being taken, for example, the consumer may ask about the probability of success of an operation. The risk itself does not diminish, but the uncertainty about the level of the risk does reduce. Risk R is the product of the probability P and the seriousness of the consequence C, i.e., $R = P \times C$. Most forms of risk reduction are based on the probability (P) that negative results can be prevented. The money-back guarantee diminishes the negative outcome (C) of a risky decision.

Confidence

A lot of consumers trust a decision after they have collected a lot of information, even if they did not use this information to its fullest extent when making their decision. Consumers trust foodstuffs with labels that show detailed ingredient listings, although they do not always understand this information completely. The danger exists that consumers think they are making the right decision when they do so on the basis of a great deal of information. However, research has shown that more information does not necessarily lead to a better decision, sometimes it can lead to an inferior one. This is true in the case of *information overload*.[14] Figure 11.6 shows that confidence in the quality of a decision increases in line with the quantity of information, but decision quality actually only increases to a certain level.

Definition

Information overload is a situation in which too many stimuli overload a person's ability to process them effectively.

Conflict

Choice situations are often connected with psychological conflict. Not making a choice can also be viewed as an alternative which is in conflict with the making of a decision. Conflict between choices is frequently associated with cognitive dissonance. Consumers doubt if they are able to choose the right alternative. We identify four types of conflict, see also table 11.3.[15]

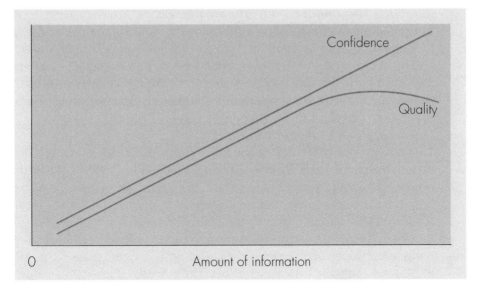

Figure 11.6 *Confidence in a decision and the actual quality of a decision as functions of amount of information processed*

Table 11.3 *Overview of conflict situations*

Alternative 1	Alternative 2	Type of conflict
1 Positive	Positive	Approach conflict
2 Negative	Negative	Avoidance conflict
3 Positive/negative	—	Approach-avoidance conflict
4 Positive/negative	Positive/negative	Double approach-avoidance conflict

Approach conflict
Here a choice has to be made from alternatives with attractive properties and results, for example, cycling or sailing? film or music? London or Paris? This particularly concerns the alternatives in the consideration set, since here the differences are small. This is a sort of luxury conflict, since the result of the choice is pleasant anyhow. It is possible to go to London in the future, even if the choice is made to go to Paris now.

Avoidance conflict
In this case the choice concerns alternatives with mostly negative properties and results: 'choosing between a rock and a hard place'. For example: if I need money, shall I deliver newspapers or wash dishes in a restaurant? Choices like that often are delayed to the last moment, till the need for money is very strong.

Approach–avoidance conflict (or ambivalence)
This concerns a choice of one alternative with both positive and negative consequences. For example: we are having such a good time, do we have one more drink? If an extra round is chosen, then the chances of a hangover are greater. In this example the short-term benefits have to be weighed against the longer-term costs. Benefits and costs can exist simultaneously.

Double approach–avoidance conflict
This conflict resembles the single approach-avoidance conflict but now the choice has to be made between two or more alternatives, each with both positive and negative consequences. For example: working or studying both have positive consequences (immediate income or a good career) and negative consequences (performing labour or working for exams).

Strictly speaking, most consumer decisions belong to the fourth of the types listed above, as for the use of goods and services (positive) a price has to be paid (negative). However when the price is of less concern or is the same for both alternatives, the decision can be seen as an approach conflict. When negative results prevail, it is an avoidance conflict.

Costs and benefits of information search and processing

Information collection and processing often involves financial and time costs. The financial costs include travel and telephone costs. Time and effort sometimes have to be invested to be able to make a choice; they count as the behavioural costs of a decision. The financial costs and behavioural costs are weighed against the expected advantages of a better decision.[16] The 'cost of thinking' is linked, just as the perceived risk is, to the complexity and similarity of the choice alternatives. Often it is not possible or feasible to process all information. In that case, the decision process is simplified by applying less complex decision rules, although then the best alternative may not be selected.

Definition

Satisficing is the behaviour in which the individual does not strive for the best alternative by optimally using all available information but is satisfied with the first alternative that meets his or her requirements.

In many choice situations, it is impossible to select the best alternative, for example, when all the information is not available at the same time. Although motivated to choose the best alternative, the possibility to do so may not exist. The term *satisficing* has been introduced to describe this situation. It means selecting the first alternative to meet certain criteria, for instance, the minimum requirements of quality or price. Even if it is possible to select the best alternative, but the consumers concerned do not want to maximize utility, satisficing will occur.[17] The decision maker formulates certain criteria for the alternatives. These criteria are based on the expectations the decision maker has about the characteristics of the alternatives. This can be a minimum level of quality or a maximum price. As soon as an alternative has been found that satisfies these criteria, this alternative is selected without looking for any further alternatives. If too many alternatives satisfy the criteria, the decision maker may develop stricter criteria. When no available alternatives meet the criteria, the decision maker may relax the criteria.

An example of non-simultaneous availability is the purchase of a house. In a particular week, a certain number of houses are for sale, and a prospective buyer does not know which houses will become available next week or which will be sold. Prospective buyers can maximize their expected benefit by calculating the optimal moment of purchasing.[18] To avoid complex calculations the first house that meets the buyer's criteria is accepted (satisficing). The buying of shoes is also often satisficing behaviour, because one store does not carry all types and sizes. It is not worth visiting all the shoe stores in an area to find the best pair of shoes. The expected search costs have to be set against the expected benefits of a pair of better or cheaper shoes.[19]

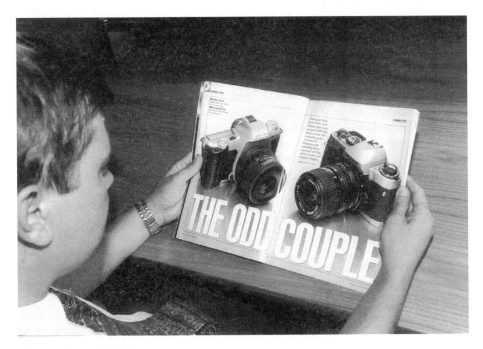

Figure 11.7 *Which?*

Justification

A neglected function of information is the justification or legitimization of the choice afterwards. In a lot of cases, the decision has to be defended against partners, colleagues, friends, relatives, and oneself. Information is needed to explain why a specific alternative was chosen. For this reason consumers quite often read advertisements about a product after they have bought it, to find arguments to justify the purchase both to themselves as well as to others.[20] This can also be seen as an attempt to reduce the dissatisfaction and cognitive dissonance of the purchase. The positive characteristics of the chosen alternative are emphasized and the negative characteristics of the chosen alternative as well as the positive characteristics of rejected alternatives are 'forgotten' or suppressed.

The objective of a lot of information search is to legitimize a decision that has already been taken. Information therefore not only has a role before the decision is made, but afterwards too. Often, this retrospective justification has a positive effect on repeat purchases.

11.5 Cognitive elaboration

Most models of human information processing state that information search and processing precedes the evaluation and judgement of the alternatives. Here 'cognition' (knowledge of choice alternatives) precedes 'affect' and 'attitude' (judgement of alternatives). We therefore pay attention to cognitive elaboration, memory, and internal representation.

Levels of cognitive elaboration

Cognitive elaboration is the process of more detailed information processing of alternatives selected by internal and external search. The level of cognitive elaboration is relevant to being able to assure whether information has been understood and will be integrated into information already held in memory.

At a superficial level, information is only viewed at a glance. The information is stored as 'loose facts' in memory, sometimes only in the short-term memory. This means that little or no linkages are made with other information already stored in memory. Information in the short-term memory is quickly forgotten, as happens with a telephone number after dialling.

A deep level of information processing implies that the decision maker spends more time and effort, with resultant higher behavioural costs, on information processing. The consumer tries to understand the meaning of the information offered. Information processed at a deep level is stored in memory in an integrated way, i.e., linked to existing information in (long-term) memory. A deep level of information processing is generally necessary to understand information, to learn from it and to remember it later.[21]

Information stored in an integrated manner is related to other information in memory. This is called a cognitive structure or schema. A cognitive structure is usually introduced as a neurophysiological network. The concepts are the junctions (nerve synapses) in the network and the relations between the concepts are the connections (nerve links) between the junctions. The distribution theory of memory states that junctions are activated through internal or external stimulation. From the activated junctions the neural activity spreads to adjoining junctions. In this way, connections are strengthened. New junctions and connections can also be formed. With the integrated (deep) level of information processing, new connections are formed and existing connections strengthened. The meaning structure is an example of a schema.[22]

Memory

As shown above, cognitive elaboration relates to memory. In a popular model of memory, a distinction is made between sensory registers, short-term and long-term memory (STM and LTM, respectively). Information via the senses (A) enters a sensory register for a very short time. When no attention is paid to it, it disappears within a fraction of a second. If attention is paid to it, the information enters STM, a kind of working memory with limited capacity. Information can only remain in STM if it is processed. Processes include categorization, repeating, coding, and association. When the information has been processed sufficiently, it can be stored in LTM. LTM has an almost unlimited capacity. Figure 11.8 represents these types of memory.

STM functions together with LTM. Information is coded in STM and then stored in LTM. This is the process of 'transfer'. Information can also be taken from LTM into STM (recollection or 'retrieval'). New information is linked to existing information in LTM. Categorization, for example, is a process by which new information is put into existing categories. When LTM is activated, it is a matter of deep level information processing. The results of these processes are, for example, recognition, recall, perception and evaluation.

Internal representation

Impression formation is important for subsequent information processing. People very quickly form a primary affective impression of persons, objects and situations, often only based on 'first impressions', i.e., on little information.[24] A positive first impression can strongly affect subsequent information processing. With a positive first impression about a choice object, the cognitive elaboration will emphasize positive characteristics of the object. With a negative first impression, more emphasis will be placed

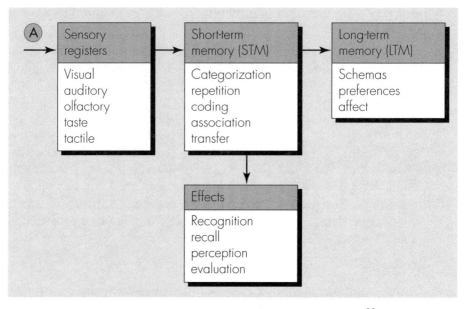

Figure 11.8 *Sensory registers, short-term and long-term memory*[23]

on negative characteristics of the object.[25] When consumers like a brand, they will emphasize the positive characteristics of the brand and negate or 'forget' the negative characteristics.

The multitude of shops, brands, and advertisements would lead to enormous confusion and chaos, if we were not able to categorize these objects, i.e., classify them into groups with similar characteristics or functions.[26] People try to maintain a once-made categorization for as long as possible, out of some sort of conservatism or because behavioural costs have to be paid to develop a new categorization. Consumers who have classified a specific brand as negative, are not easily prepared to change this affective classification. This means producers have to avoid a bad reputation as much as possible, since a bad reputation is difficult to change. According to this view, a good reputation has a certain stability in the affective classification of the consumer.

11.6 Decision rules

Consumers can be limited in their motivation and competence to process information. A lot of situations do not allow it and there is often no opportunity. This means that complex and detailed considerations and calculations ('mental algebra') are more often the exception than the rule. Only in the case of high involvement and important decisions do consumers extensively collect and process information.

In this section, decision rules are discussed. In a descriptive sense, a decision rule is a means to process information in order to compare alternatives. In an operational sense, it is a formula to compute the outcome of a decision process. Sometimes a decision rule specifies the choice criterion, i.e., the grounds for choosing an alternative.[27] Seven decision rules are discussed here. The first decision rule is compensatory, while the other six are non-compensatory. With a compensatory decision rule a negative value of one characteristic can be compensated with the positive value of another characteristic.

Linear-compensatory rules

Linear compensatory decision rules are relatively complex.[28] The choice alternatives are described by different characteristics. Each characteristic (attribute) is weighted with respect to importance or desirability. How important or desirable is the safety of a car to you? How relevant is car safety to you? To what extent do you think a Nissan Micra or a Renault Mégane is safe? The attitude model of Fishbein and Ajzen is an example of a linear-compensatory decision rule.[29] Because the weighted characteristics are added, the decision rule is linear. The decision rule is compensatory because the 'weak' or negative characteristics can be compensated by 'strong' or positive characteristics.

The compensatory decision rule is the most rational of the decision rules. It offers the best chances of obtaining the 'optimum' alternative. At the same time this rule is complex and requires high behavioural costs (in terms of time and effort) from the consumer. An example of a compensatory rule is: 'I have chosen the PC that came out best after comparing and weighing the pros and cons of several PCs.'

The other decision rules are non-compensatory. This implies that a less desirable value of the characteristic can lead to rejection of an alternative without being compensated for by the desirable value of another characteristic.

Affect referral

This is the simplest decision rule. Acting on a first impression, recognition, familiarity or primary affective reaction the consumer chooses an alternative (without cognitive processing). In fact the consumer hardly uses any information but immediately selects or recognizes an attractive or familiar alternative. In this way consumers will choose their familiar coffee brand. An example is: 'Everything this firm does is fantastic. I have therefore chosen a PC made by them.'

Conjunctive decision rules

With conjunctive decision rules minimum or maximum values (cut-off scores) are required for one or more characteristics. The alternatives have to meet these requirements in order to be chosen. With the help of a conjunctive rule a separation between acceptable and unacceptable alternatives is made. The awareness set thus is reduced to the consideration set. When two or more alternatives are acceptable, another decision rule is necessary to choose the 'best' alternative from the consideration set. For example: 'I have selected the PCs without negative characteristics.'

For a lot of individual sports, the selection of athletes for the Olympic Games is a conjunctive selection. Only athletes who meet certain criteria are selected. This is related to the satisficing concept, in the way that an alternative meeting the minimum requirements is selected.[30] The conjunctive rule is non-compensatory.

The criteria the alternatives have to meet in order to be selected are also a basis for rejection. If one of the attributes does not meet the criterion (cut-off score), the choice for this alternative is blocked. A coffee maker may be attractive and cheap, but without an electrical safety mark a lot of consumers will not buy it. The absence of the safety mark is the rejection factor.[31]

Disjunctive decision rules

These rules are based on a striking or outstanding (very positive) value of a characteristic. An alternative is selected because of at least one superior attribute value, irrespective of the other attribute values. Consumers sometimes choose an option because it has one outstanding characteristic, irrespective of all other characteristics. This can be seen when people buy a home because of a beautiful fireplace, or a PC is selected because of its graphics card. The disjunctive decision rule is non-compensatory. An example is: 'I have chosen this PC because of its exceptional design.'

Lexicographic decision rules

These rules assume that characteristics are ranked and arranged according to their importance. The options are judged on the first and most important characteristic. If some alternatives are superior according to this first characteristic, then these will be selected. These alternatives are then judged on the second characteristic, and so on. The lexicographic decision rule emphasizes information processing by characteristics and is non-compensatory. A consumer picking a bunch of flowers at a flower stall may look for chrysanthemums first. Then he or she may look for colour. When two types of yellow chrysanthemums are available, he or she may pick the yellow chrysanthemums with the highest quality or the lowest price. Another consumer looking for a car may compare cars first on price. Cars below or above a certain price range will not qualify. The remaining cars (acceptable in price) are then compared on engine power and after that on a third characteristic like handling or safety.[32] Information processing per characteristic happens often. An example is: 'I checked the most important features of a PC for myself and I have chosen the PC that is satisfactory on these features.'

Sequential elimination
Sequential elimination is conjunctive in the way that minimum values are required for each characteristic. Alternatives are eliminated because of one insufficient attribute value. An example is the choice university students have to make. Study programmes may be eliminated because of their negative characteristics, such as expected unemployment, expected programme difficulty and future income. The programme which has no apparent negative characteristics is selected. In research it was found that consumers with a lack of time or with a lot of distracting activities often use negative elimination to make decisions. They reject alternatives one at a time if and when they find something negative about them.[33]

Additive differences
The decision rule of additive differences is a sequence of paired comparisons of choice alternatives. The differences between two alternatives (weighted or unweighted) are added. The 'winner' of a paired comparison is then compared with another alternative and the loser once again rejected. With N alternatives the consumer has to make $N - 1$ paired comparisons and this decision rule has high behavioural costs. A tennis tournament is an example. Two players play a match and the winner goes to the next round. An example is: 'I visited five PC shops. In the second shop I found a PC which was better than the one in the first shop. No PCs in the other three shops were better than the second one, which I then bought.'

Decision rules are not necessarily a description of the choice process. Decision rules can also be used to predict and explain the outcomes of decision processes. These rules then simulate the choice processes of consumers.

11.7 Sequential use of decision rules

Preselection and choice

As discussed above, decision rules are often used in sequence, in a sequential or phased strategy. Conjunctive decision rules are often used at the beginning of the process to separate acceptable from unacceptable alternatives. This is a form of *preselection* to obtain a consideration set or shortlist of acceptable alternatives. A compensatory decision rule is mostly used in the second part of the decision process to choose the 'best' alternative from the preselected ones.

An example of a phased strategy is shown in figure 11.9. Here the conjunctive rule is used in the preselection stage. If no alternative is acceptable, consumers will have to find new alternatives or lower their criterion values. If one acceptable alternative exists, this alternative is chosen and the decision process is finished. If more acceptable alternatives exist, consumers may see whether one alternative distinguishes itself positively from the others. In that case this alternative is selected (disjunctive rule). The final choice between acceptable alternatives can be made with a compensatory rule.

The choice rule concerns the number of alternatives selected, often just one alternative. However, several alternatives can also be chosen as is the case when putting together a supply of stock or selecting a team of players.

Consumers do not always follow such an extensive decision-making strategy (figure 11.9). Often a condensed strategy is used of only a conjunctive, disjunctive, lexicographic, sequential-elimination or additive-differences rule. The following sequences may occur with the conjunctive rule in the preselection stage:

- conjunctive and then a disjunctive rule;
- conjunctive and then a compensatory rule;
- conjunctive and then sequential elimination;
- conjunctive and then additive differences.

With impulse purchases, the procedure is probably even shorter and is made up of a quick evaluation of the acceptability of the alternative, for example, affect referral.

Problem-solving behaviour

Three types of problem-solving behaviour may be distinguished: routine, limited and extensive problem solving. Extensive problem-solving consumer behaviour will take place at the beginning of the product life-cycle.[34] In later phases, limited and routine problem solving occur as well. In table 11.4 these three types of problem-solving behaviour are compared. For example, if frequency of purchase is high, search behaviour is very limited. If involvement is high, the decision rule will be compensatory.

Brand loyalty

Brand and store loyalty have been mentioned as part of routine decision-making behaviour. However, brand loyalty does not only occur with low involvement and low perceived risk. It may also occur with high commitment and high perceived risk. There are two aspects of brand loyalty: purchase behaviour and attitude.[36]

Brand loyalty is a type of *behaviour*: the regular buying of a specific brand. With convenience goods consumers may be loyal to brands through habit or because it is not worth comparing the characteristics of different

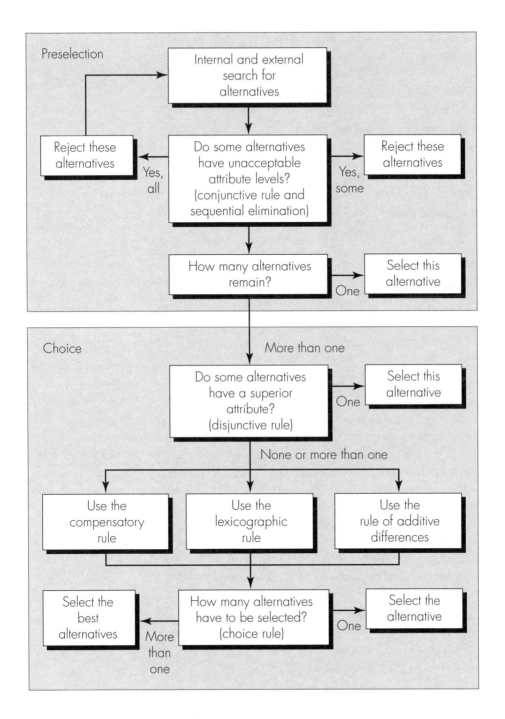

Figure 11.9 *Model of sequential use of decision rules in preselection and choice*

Table 11.4 *Three types of problem-solving behaviour*[35]

	Problem-solving behaviour		
	Routine (RPB)	Limited (LPB)	Extensive (EPB)
If (conditions):			
Frequency of purchase	High	Average	Low
Purchase price	Low	Average	High
Involvement	Low	Moderate	High
Product familiarity	High	Moderate	Low
Perceived risk	Low	Moderate	High
Then (consequences):			
Search behaviour	Very limited	Limited	Extensive
Decision rule	Routine Recognition Impulse Affect referral	Non-compensatory	Compensatory

brands. Consumers may show substantial brand loyalty to a make of rubbish bags. This is because they detect little risk and are not very interested in the purchase. In the past, brands may have been compared and because of this a specific brand chosen. Brand loyalty then becomes routine purchase behaviour to avoid having to compare all alternatives again. 'Brand loyalty' is forced if a store carries only one brand, for example, one brand of long-life milk. In this case consumers are forced to purchase this specific brand.

Brand loyalty can also be based on a positive *attitude* towards a specific brand. Brand loyalty as an attitude is strong with expressive products such as cigarettes and cosmetics and weak with non-expressive products such as milk, paper tissues and rubbish bags. A loyal BMW driver has a clear preference for BMW and is therefore loyal to the brand. A loyal BMW driver considers no other brands than BMW when buying a car.

Definition

Brand loyalty is characterized by a series of repeat purchases of the same brand, frequently accompanied by a positive attitude towards the brand.

Obviously, attitude and behaviour quite often concur and brand loyalty is a repeated purchase of a specific product because of a preference for that product. In such circumstances brand loyalty is both a behaviour and an attitude. This is the case with the BMW driver. The same goes for store loyalty. Some consumers always shop at Benetton or Marks & Spencer.

11.8 Determinants of decision making

Consumers are not computers, and even computers have their limitations. The limitations in decision making may be linked to the limitations in information supply, human limitations, and individual differences. The factors determining information processing are summarized in the MAO model. This stands for three main groups of factors: Motivation, Ability and Opportunity.[37]

Motivation includes the tendency and interest of consumers to process information. Ability is the degree to which consumers are competent to process the information. Opportunity refers to the circumstances to process the information. Personal characteristics are the general characteristics which affect different situations. As specific characteristics they depend on the information supplied.

The factors in the three main groups have been listed in table 11.5. In the Elaboration Likelihood Model only motivation and capacity are described as determinants of attitude change via the central or peripheral route.[38] However, capacity includes both ability (a personal factor) and opportunity (a situational factor). In this way the determinants of ELM can be said to correspond with the MAO (motivation, ability and opportunity) model.

Motivation, ability and opportunity have consequences for information processing. In addition, interactions exist between these three main groups. For example, consumers with a limited procedural capacity are more damaged by poor information supply than consumers with a high procedural capacity. As another example: consumers with high motivation

Table 11.5 *Motivation, ability and opportunity to process information*

MAO model	General (product independent)	Specific (product or domain dependent)
Motivation	Need for cognition Opinion leadership	Personal relevance Involvement
Ability	Self-schema Intelligence Procedural competence Optimal level of stimulation	Expertise Prior knowledge
Opportunity	Information supply Status-quo tendency	Level of stimulation Information supply Framing Time pressure Distraction Medium, context

are not bothered by distractions as much as consumers with low motivation.

Motivation

Consumers are not always motivated to maximize their utility. Rational behaviour of consumers is more often the exception than the rule, since rationality includes considerable behavioural costs in the form of information search, processing and selecting the 'best' alternative.[39] Habits and routines have considerably lower costs and tend to prevail when it comes to convenience goods.

Motivation can both be general and specific. The need for cognition is a personality characteristic and because of that a general motivation factor.[40] Commitment and personal relevance may differ according to domain and are therefore product-specific. Some are interested in clothing; others in wine, or holiday travel.

Motivation may be social as well. Some consumers like to inform and warn other consumers about new products. If their advice is appreciated, they become opinion leaders and communicate information from the mass media and their own experiences to other consumers. They are also more often asked for advice about the options.[41] Opinion leadership is both general and specific. Some consumers tend to be opinion leaders in many domains, whereas others only in one or two domains.

Ability

Ability can be divided into general and specific factors. Self-schemas, intelligence, procedural ability, and optimal level of stimulation are personality factors and therefore general. Expertise and prior knowledge are domain-specific. Consumers do not have expertise and prior knowledge in all product domains.

Procedural ability

Not only is the information held in memory important; knowledge of decision rules and 'procedural rationality' is perhaps even more so. Some knowledge of facts has its merit, but knowledge about how to collect and process relevant information is more important in new situations.

In experiments with experienced consumers more information processing was found than with students.[42] When information is offered in a matrix structure, however, students more often process information by attributes. The rather abstract task of processing information offered in a matrix structure is done more easily by students than by experienced consumers. These differences are related to levels of education, the daily experiences of consumers and students, and to procedural ability. This is an indication that it is necessary to be careful when generalizing results from experiments with small or specific groups. Results from small and non-representative consumer surveys are too easily falsely generalized to the general population.

Prior knowledge

It seems reasonable to expect that information sought externally is complementary to prior knowledge. Decision makers who know little or nothing about a particular product class or problem on which a decision has to be made, should spend more time and effort to compensate for this lack of knowledge. However it is also possible to state the opposite hypothesis. Consumers with prior knowledge are well equipped to collect new information since they possess the basic categories and criteria with which they can judge any new information. They are probably more interested in new information about the product class or may want to test the validity of their knowledge.

Do consumers with prior knowledge seek more or less information? It is likely that most information will be sought by consumers with an average level of knowledge. A ∩-shaped relationship exists between prior knowledge and information sought. This relationship is shown in figure 11.10.

Information currently held in memory normally guides both the new information sought and the way it is interpreted. The manner in which coding and storage of information in memory takes place determines the required supplementary information. The categories used and the internal representations probably lead to preferences for alternatives suitable to

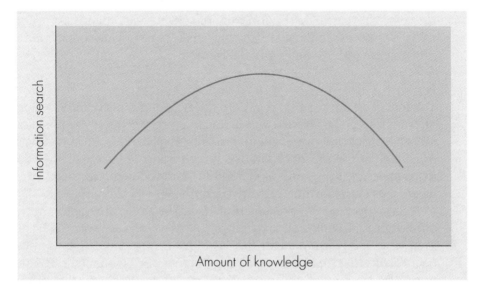

Figure 11.10 *Relationship between amount of prior knowledge and information search*

these categories, and an aversion against alternatives that are difficult to place or cannot be placed in these categories.

Opportunity

Opportunity includes both general and specific factors. The quality of information supply is a general factor. Situational factors (which are considered in section 12.5) are specific factors associated with opportunity.

The structure, format, amount, and comprehensibility of information are important supply factors and determinants of the decision process.

Structure
The structure of information can take several forms:

- Information matrix, such as the presentation of comparative product tests, or information on package tours in travel guides.
- Information per separate alternative, such as advertisements, brochures and leaflets.
- Information per attribute, such as mortgage rates and stock exchange on the Internet.
- Non-simultaneous structuring, where not all information is available at the same time.

Information in a matrix or presented by attribute/characteristic makes information processing by attribute easier, for example, using a lexico-graphical decision rule. Information that is already structured and presented by separate alternative makes it easier to process on an alternative-by-alternative basis, for example, using a compensatory decision rule. Non-simultaneous structuring makes satisficing behaviour more probable, as with a conjunctive decision rule.[43]

Format
The format of information relates to the type and units of information. The information can be given in metric units such as price and weight, in ordinal units such as hotel or restaurant classifications in stars, or in dichotomous units such as the presence or absence of certain characteristics. In the UK, the octane level of petrol is marked in stars for example, 2-star or 4-star, whereas in Germany numbers are used (95, 98, 101).

Information can be presented as 'facts' or as 'evaluations'. A price in euros is factual, while a label that says 'low price' or 'expensive' is evaluative. Well-informed consumers are able to transform factual data into evaluative data. Obviously, this is easier for experts than for beginners.[44] The distinction between factual and evaluative formats is similar to the distinction between product characteristics and benefits. For that matter it is interesting to check in what way decision makers classify product characteristics in evaluative categories as part of their internal models of the products.

Amount of information
Situations can be rich or poor in relevant information. A large amount of information may lead to the problem of information overload. This means that too many alternatives or too many characteristics demand attention from the consumer. Too much information can diminish the quality of the decision, especially when irrelevant information obscures relevant information. An overload of alternatives proves to be more harmful to the quality of a decision than an overload of characteristics. To combat or prevent information overload it is better to reduce the number of alternatives than the number of characteristics.[45]

Comprehensibility
The clarity of information is important. New information must be integrated into the existing network of information in memory. When new information is difficult to classify in existing categories, the decision maker is less susceptible to this information and it becomes more difficult to understand, memorize, and recall.[46] Incompatible information can only be understood and processed at substantial behavioural cost. This requires a high level of consumer motivation.

Standard product information

The packaging of products often contains a lot of information. Sometimes this information is legally required; sometimes it is there because of self-regulation of a particular industry. When all producers within a particular industry use the same product information system, it is called standard product information (SPI). This information is often presented in a standard format. The following information can be found on packages:

- Product name, e.g., butter.
- Brand name, e.g., Lurpak.
- Composition of the product in the form of a declaration of ingredients. The ingredients are listed in decreasing order of content. With catalysts or additives such as aromatic substances, colourings, flavourings and preservatives, E-numbers are given. All additives allowed by the European Union have an E-number.
- Alcohol, nicotine and tar content, if applicable.
- Expiry date of perishables or last date of use is given.
- Net volume in litres or grammes. Sometimes the symbol "e" (estimate) is given when small fluctuations in volume are allowed (on average, consumers are getting the right weight).
- Name, address and sometimes telephone number of the producer or

supplier. The telephone number is the customer services, complaint or advice line of the producer or supplier.

- Usage directions, storage instructions, and sometimes recipes.
- Uniform article coding (UAC; bar codes) for scanning purposes.

Additional information that may also be listed on the packaging includes:

- Sales price and price per standard amount (PPS), per 100 g, per 1 kg or per litre. PPS facilitates price comparison of different package sizes. Some stores display PPS information on the shelf.
- Declaration of nutritional values with an overview of fats, proteins, carbohydrates, vitamins and minerals per 100 g of the product. The energy value in kilojoules or kilocalories may also be listed. The standard form of this is called the nutritional value indicator.
- Some products list a quality class such as 'extra fine'.
- A health warning as with tobacco and alcohol.
- Country of origin, for example, 'made in Germany'.
- Textile products require a label that gives the composition of the fabric, listing the percentages of the different materials or fibres used.
- Although not mandatory, textile products often also include a laundry instruction label. This gives the correct temperatures for washing and ironing, use of bleach, detergents, and the use of the dryer.
- Symbols for substances dangerous to the environment and health are mandatory, e.g., symbols for flammable, toxic and other harmful substances.
- Quality marks too can be printed on packaging, e.g., the symbol for electric safety and the eco-label for natural and environment-friendly products. Producers and suppliers may use their own quality mark such as the woolmark (pure wool) and leathermark (real leather). In the future, an environmental symbol will be mandatory such as the 'blue angel' in Germany and the 'white swan' in Scandinavia.

Apart from standard product information, packaging also holds marketing information about quality, usage possibilities, and an occasional sales-promotion message. Consumers can only process a limited amount of this information in the store. This information may be read when the consumer is using the product and it may affect repeat purchase. By no means does everyone read this information carefully. Some Dutch researchers tested to see how many buyers actually read the ingredients listing on six consumer goods. The results are shown in table 11.6. The information about product content was hardly ever read for products like sugar and soft drinks. Information about jam was read more often, but mostly at the breakfast table and not in the store. As a general point, information is most often read when the package is kept and available at the moment of use, as is the case with breakfast products like jam, peanut butter and chocolate sprinkles.

Table 11.6 *Percentages of consumers that read ingredient declarations on the package*[47]

	Always	Sometimes	Never
Jam	16	51	32
Peanut butter	9	54	37
Chocolate sprinkles	9	40	50
Apple sauce	7	41	52
Soft drink (in bottles)	5	31	64
Sugar	3	20	75

The packages of sugar and soft drinks are often not seen at the moment of use.

Mass media, professional journals, fairs and meetings with other consumers are often rich sources of information. Discussions with other consumers (social sources) also provide a lot of information. The disadvantage of these information-rich surroundings, however, is that they offer too much information in too short a period of time. The result is information overload and, because of this, less opportunity for effective information processing and learning.

11.9 Conclusions

An important aspect of consumer behaviour is information search to select the 'best' alternative from a set of options in a product class. This is especially true for important decisions which tend to have high consumer involvement. The study of consumer decision processes has identified a number of decision rules. We have used these decision rules to describe the decision processes of consumers, but it is also possible to use the decision rules to predict and simulate the results of decision processes, or to teach the consumer how to make better decisions. Decision rules can be used in a descriptive way (how consumers make decisions), in a predictive way (likely outcomes of consumer decisions), and in a prescriptive or normative way (how consumers should make better decisions). For predictive purposes, these rules can be used in the micro-simulation of consumer choices.

Human limitations (motivation and ability) and circumstances (opportunity) affect consumer decision making and choice. Situations with time pressure and distraction force the consumer to use simple decision rules so as to eliminate alternatives quickly and make a choice. Consumers spend more time and effort on more important decisions. The sequential use of decision rules was also discussed. In the first phase of the process, acceptable alternatives are separated from the unacceptable alternatives. The acceptable alternatives constitute the consideration set. In the second phase, the most suitable option is selected from the set of acceptable alternatives.

Involvement plays an important role in the decision process. This chapter has largely focused on decision processes with high involvement. In these circumstances consumers are prepared to devote a lot of time and effort to making the right choice. However, the extensive weighing of pros and cons of alternatives is more the exception than the rule. Many daily consumer decisions are routine decisions.

The decision process is influenced by the characteristics of the consumer, the set of available and known alternatives, the presentation of the information (its structure and format), and the choice situation. Human limitations and individual differences are related to prior knowledge, expertise, ability to process information and personality characteristics such as the need for cognition.

Notes

1 See for behavioural learning chapter 10.
2 See section 9.6.
3 See chapter 19.
4 Risk involves situations in which the probability of possible results is known. Uncertainty involves situations in which these probabilities are unknown or even impossible to define. See Deaton, A. and Muellbauer, J. (1980) *Economics and Consumer Behaviour* (Cambridge: Cambridge University Press).
5 Lancaster, K. (1979) *Variety, Equity and Efficiency* (New York: Columbia University Press).
6 See Engel, J. F., Blackwell, R. D. and Miniard, P. W. (1990) *Consumer Behavior* (Chicago: The Dryden Press) 6th edition.
   Schmidt, J. B. and Spreng, R. A. (1996) 'A proposed model of external consumer information search' *Journal of the Academy of Marketing Science* 24, 246–256.
7 Mischel, W. (1968) *Personality and Assessment* (New York: John Wiley).
8 Engel, Blackwell and Miniard (1990).
9 See section 11.6.
10 Howard, J. A. and Sheth, J. N. (1969) *The Theory of Buyer Behavior* (New York: John Wiley). They use the concept of 'evoked set' corresponding to the consideration set. With other authors evoked set corresponds to the awareness set.
11 The method used here is recollection or 'recall'. The list would be greater with recognition. Here the consumers get a list of car brands and then indicate which names on the list they know.
12 Cox, D. F. (1967) *Risk Taking and Information Handling in Consumer Behavior* (Boston, MA: Harvard Business School). Cox introduced the concept 'perceived risk' with decisions. Hansen, F. (1972) *Consumer Choice Behavior. A Cognitive Theory* (New York: The Free Press). Hansen introduced the concept 'conflict', based on Berlyne, D. E. (1963) 'Motivational problems raised by exploratory and epistemic behavior' in: Koch, S. (Ed.) *Psychology: A Study of a Science* part 5 (New York: McGraw-Hill) 284–364.

13 Roselius, T. (1971) 'Consumer rankings of risk reduction methods' *Journal of Marketing* 35, 56–61. He distinguishes these types of risks and describes the possible types of risk reduction.

14 Oskamp, S. (1965) 'Overconfidence in case-study judgments' *Journal of Consulting Psychology* 29, 261–265. He showed that in the selection of applicants, decision makers are more confident with more information in making the right decision whereas the quality of the decision with more information is not necessarily better, sometimes even worse.

Jacoby, J., Speller, D. E. and Kohn, D. A. (1974a) 'Brand choice behavior as a function of information load' *Journal of Marketing Research* 11, 63–69.

Jacoby, J., Speller, D. E. and Kohn, D. A. (1974b) 'Brand choice behavior as a function of information load: replication and extension' *Journal of Consumer Research* 1, 33–42.

Van Raaij, W. F. (1977) *Consumer Choice Behavior: An Information-processing Approach* (Tilburg University, dissertation).

These authors conclude from experimental research that consumers only use a small part of available information. They have more confidence in their decision when a lot of information is available.

15 Saccuzzo, D. P. (1987) *Psychology* (Boston: Allyn and Bacon), 372.

Kroeber-Riel, W. (1992) *Konsumentenverhalten* [*Consumer Behaviour*] (in German). (München: Verlag Franz Vahlen) 5th edition, 153–159.

16 See Shugan, S. M. (1980) 'The cost of thinking' *Journal of Consumer Research* 7, 99–111.

Schmidt, J. B., and Spreng, R. A. (1996).

Ratchford, B. T. (1980) 'The value of information for selected appliances' *Journal of Marketing Research* 17, 14–25.

17 Simon, H. A. (1976) 'From substantial to procedural rationality' in: Latsis, S. J. (Ed.) *Method and Appraisal in Economics* (Cambridge: Cambridge University Press) 129–148.

18 The optimal moment of purchase can be calculated with regard to 'optimal shopping rules' in operations research. See Wagner, H. M. (1975) *Principles of Operations Research*. (Englewood Cliffs, NJ: Prentice-Hall). Possible outcome has to be evaluated and the probability of the occurrence estimated.

19 Simon (1976) developed the concept of 'satisficing'.

Ölander, F. (1976) 'Can consumer dissatisfaction and complaints guide public consumer policy?' *Journal of Consumer Policy* 1, 124–137. This article describes the satisficing choice situation.

Shugan (1980) described 'the costs of thinking' and developed a confusion index for the cost of information processing, in his case a coupled comparison of alternatives.

20 Ehrlich, D., Guttman, L., Schonbach, P. and Mills, J. (1957) 'Postdecision exposure to relevant information' *Journal of Personality and Social Psychology* 54, 98–102.

21 Craik, F. I. M., and Tulving, T. (1975) 'Depth of processing and the retention of words in episodic memory' *Journal of Experimental Psychology: General* 104, 268–294. They made the distinction between superficial and profound (deep) levels of information processing. Superficial level information is stored in the memory in an isolated and episodic way, with the result that 'retrieval'

(retrieval of the information from memory) at the right time becomes less feasible. With a profound level of information processing the information is stored in an integrated way in the memory, i.e., linked to other information.

22 See sections 7.3 and 7.4.

23 Figure 11.8 is taken, with some adaptation from: Atkinson, R. C. and Shiffrin, R. M. (1971) 'The control of short-term memory' *Scientific American* 225(August), 82–90.

24 Asch, S. E. (1956) 'Studies of independence and submission to group pressure: 1. A minority of one against a unanimous majority' *Psychological Monographs* 70, No. 416. Kelly, G. A. (1955) *The Psychology of Personal Constructs* (New York: Norton). They varied the adjectives 'warm' and 'cold' in person descriptions and found significant differences in evaluation of persons by reviewers. Obviously the dimension warm–cold influences the evaluation of other dimensions.

25 Compare the primary affective reaction (PAR). Russo, J. E., Metcalf, B. L. and Stephens, D. (1981) 'Identifying misleading advertising' *Journal of Consumer Research* 8, 119–131.

26 Bruner, J. S., Goodnow, J. J. and Austin, G. A. (1956) *A Study of Thinking* (New York: Wiley). The authors describe the process of categorization. See chapter 6.

27 A more extensive overview of these decision rules can be found in Bettman, J. R. (1979) *An Information-processing Theory of Consumer Choice* (Reading, MA: Addison-Wesley). Svenson, O. (1983) 'Decision rules and information processing in decision making' in: Sjöberg, L., Tyszka, T. and Wise, J. A. (Eds) *Human Decision Making* (Bodafors, Sweden: Doxa) 131–162.

28 Non-linear compensatory decision rules are even more complicated. See for example the multiplicative compensatory rule and the use of the Minkowski metric. Wilkie, W. L. and Pessemier, E. A. (1973) 'Issues in marketing's use of multi-attribute attitude models' *Journal of Marketing Research* 10, 428–441.

29 See sections 9.3 and 9.4.

30 Simon, H. A. (1955) 'A behavioral model of rational choice' *Quarterly Journal of Economics* 69, 99–118.

31 See section 21.3.

32 A special case of sequential elimination is 'elimination by aspects' by Tversky, A. (1972), 'Elimination by aspects: a theory of choice' *Psychological Review* 79, 281–299. An aspect gets selected with a probability that is proportional to the weight or importance of the attribute. All alternatives with insufficient attribute values are eliminated.

33 Wright, P. L. (1974) 'The harassed decision maker: time pressure, distractions, and the use of evidence' *Journal of Applied Psychology* 59, 555–561. He describes the 'harassed decision maker', who has to make decisions under time pressure or distraction.

34 See section 15.4.

35 This table is compiled on the basis of Engel, Blackwell and Miniard (1990). Solomon, M. R. (1992) *Consumer Behavior: Buying, Having and Being* (Needham Heights, MA: Allyn and Bacon).

36 Jacoby, J. and Chesnut, R. W. (1978) *Brand Loyalty, Measurement and Management* (New York: Ronald Press).

37 Batra, R. and Ray, M. L. (1986) 'Situational effects of involvement and message content on information processing intensity' *Journal of Consumer Research* 12, 432–445.
    De Bont, C. J. P. M., Poiesz, T. B. C. and Van Venrooij, M. G. E. (1997) 'Direct and indirect advertising effects of opportunity: an empirical study' in: Antonides, G., Van Raaij, W. F. and Maital, S. (Eds) *Advances in Economic Psychology* (Chichester, UK: John Wiley) 97–111.
38 See section 9.6.
39 Etzioni, A. (1986) 'Rationality is anti-entropic' *Journal of Economic Psychology* 7, 17–36. He states rather provocatively that rational behaviour is 'anti-entropic'.
40 See section 8.4.
41 See section 14.4.
42 Van Raaij (1977).
43 See Van Raaij (1977, 1988) for a description of the structure and format of information.
44 Maheswaran, D. and Sternthal, B. (1990) 'The effects of knowledge, motivation, and type of message on ad processing and product judgments' *Journal of Consumer Research* 17, 66–73.
45 See Jacoby, J., Speller, D. E. and Kohn, C. A. (1974) 'Brand choice behavior as a function of information load' *Journal of Marketing Research* 11, 63–69. See also the criticism of this study by Wilkie, W. L. (1974) 'Analysis of effects of information load' *Journal of Marketing Research* 11, 462–466.
46 See sections 6.4 and 6.5.
47 Kroesbergen, H. T., Visser, W. and Glerum-Van der Laan, C. (1985) 'Attention to package labels' (in Dutch) *Voeding* 46, 106.

12 SITUATION AND BEHAVIOUR

12.1 Introduction

Consumer behaviour is a function of the characteristics of the person and the situation.[1] Behaviour is influenced by consumers themselves and by the situation—by internal and external factors, respectively. *Internal factors* refer to such personal characteristics as a consumer's moods, interests, involvement, knowledge and attitude. These characteristics have a strong influence on behaviour. Most people try to be consistent and stable with regard to themselves and others. They try to behave consistently in as many situations as possible.[2] *External factors* refer to the situation, the environment in which the consumer acts and makes decisions. This could restrict the range of options available to the consumer. Other people who influence the consumer's behaviour are also considered to be part of the environment.

To understand and be able to predict consumer behaviour accurately requires a situational perspective.[3] This statement indicates that understanding the situation in which behaviour takes place is important if we wish to understand, explain and predict consumer behaviour (and behaviour in general).

Consumer behaviour at home or elsewhere takes place in an environment or situation that involves interacting with products and other people. The consumer sits in an airplane, lies on the beach, stays in a hotel, visits a bank or a store, works in the kitchen, or sits at the breakfast table. These environments exercise influence on the consumer's behaviour. Is it possible to chart the influence of the environment and show how this influence develops? We try to answer this question in this chapter.

Many situations have an affective value. Think, for example, of your parents' home, the school you attended, bars and clubs you like to visit, the view over the Alps, the places where you may have had a romantic experience. The situation can play an emotional part in helping to determine behaviour. Memories and expectations are often connected to situations. One may imagine how it would feel to have a holiday in the Bahamas. Or one may imagine how it would be to attend a performance of *Swan Lake* in the Bolshoi theatre in Moscow.

This chapter starts with some definitions and characteristics of situations in section 12.2. Section 12.3 looks at the way that situations influence behaviour through primary affective reactions and cognitive bias. The situational aspects are discussed for the prediction of behaviour from attitudes and intentions in section 12.4. Frequent consumer situations including shopping, purchasing, communicating and product usage are considered in section 12.5. In section 12.6 some conclusions are drawn.[4]

The objective of this chapter is to emphasize the importance of situational factors in consumer behaviour. The range of available alternatives and the situation have more influence than consumers often realize. Consumers often have the illusion that they completely control their own behaviour. They do not realize how much they are influenced by circumstances.

12.2 Characteristics of the situation

It is useful to define some concepts that will be used in this chapter. A *location* is a point in space, for instance a road crossing or the location of a McDonald's restaurant in Moscow. A *situation* is a point in space and time. It is a location with a time dimension. Think for a moment about a typical traffic situation, such as crossing the street. People move through space and time. They encounter numerous slight changes in circumstance. In consumer behaviour the situation often corresponds with a single act taking place at the particular point in space and time. A situation may be experienced, perceived or imagined. An imagined situation could include a new holiday destination or even a science-fiction situation on another planet, as in *Star Wars*.

Definition

A situation is a point in space and time. It is unrelated to consumer and product characteristics.

The time and space dimensions are essential aspects of transport. Airlines and railways provide spatial displacements as the main purpose of their service. It is still a strange experience to fly non-stop for 18 hours from Europe to Japan. For some (post)modern consumers it may be quite normal to fly from London to Sydney in less than 20 hours.

Figure 12.1 *Speed of air travel*

A *behavioural setting* is a broader unit of analysis than a situation. 'Going to a restaurant' or 'commuting' are examples of behavioural settings occupying an interval in space and time in which a certain behaviour is expected irrespective of the people present in the setting.[5] The behaviours in a setting constitute a behavioural category because of the common nature, goal or value of these behaviours.[6]

Situations and behavioural settings are parts of the environment. The *environment*, in the context of consumer behaviour, may be defined as 'all factors in a particular place and time (situation) that are not the effect of personal and stimulus characteristics'.[7] Based on this definition, the following five groups of environmental characteristics may be distinguished:

- The *physical environment* consists of objects, colours, smells, noises, light, temperature, weather and signs. For example, the home, the store with an assortment of goods, the airport, the motorway, the city, and the landscape.
- The *social environment* comprises people with their characteristics, behaviours, roles and interactions. Seen from person A's perspective, these people may cooperate with A (co-actors) or may be observers.[8]
- The *time perspective* comprises the time of the day, week, month and season. Aspects such as the duration of an event, time restrictions and deadlines belong to this category. A time restriction occurs when a limited amount of time is available for an activity; for instance a lecture may not be longer than 50 minutes. A consumer may have to shop under time constraints. A deadline might for instance be that the vouchers in a sales-promotion campaign must be returned within two weeks to receive the free gift.

- The *task definition* comprises the task orientation and definition for oneself or others including such aspects as intention and role. A policeman in his function as police officer walks through a shopping mall in a different way than when he is off-duty. Someone looking for a particular product, looks around purposefully and perceives other things than someone who is simply window shopping or casually browsing.
- *Prior situations* and tasks may result in moods, feelings, fatigue and illness. These psychological states influence an individual's perception and evaluation of the environment. In a happy mood, more pleasant elements of the environment are perceived. In an unhappy mood, one is more likely to see unpleasant elements.[9]

Internal factors such as personality and the current state of the person, do not belong to the environment, but lie within this environment. This is represented in figure 12.2.[10]

The environment in its broadest and most abstract sense comprises the historical, cultural, legal and economic environment. It is an abstract, almost metaphorical use of the concept 'environment'. The physical, social and temporal environments are concrete, close and observable. Therefore these environments are more relevant and easier to study within the context of consumer behaviour. We focus on these environments in this chapter.

Within these environments, people, objects and situations are 'situated'. Note that the objects that are part of the physical environment form the background. The objects identified in figure 12.2 are the objects with which a person deals directly. The sequence person-object-situation in

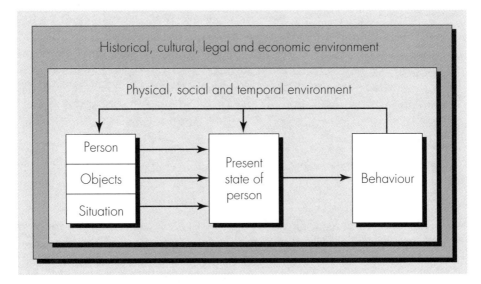

Figure 12.2 *Environment, situation and behaviour*

figure 12.2 is, for instance, a student underlining sentences of this book sitting at his or her desk. The physical environment may be his or her room in the dormitory.

12.3 Influence of situations on behaviour

There is much research about the effect that the situation, the person or the consumer, and the type of product have on the intention to buy particular products.[11] In these studies, a number of situations are presented to the participants. They are then asked whether they are willing to buy particular products in these situations. For instance, buying drinks (coffee, soft drinks, beer or wine) for regular use, for a party, or for the visit of a friend. The variance of the buying intention depends for only a small part on the effects of people and situations. The most important effects are the particular products, and the interactions between people and products, and between products and situations. This means that the probability of a purchase mainly depends on:

• The product: snacks are selected more frequently than caviar.
• The interaction of people and products. Some people buy snacks more often, whereas others buy caviar more often.
• The interaction of products and situations: in some situations, consumers buy snacks more often, in other situations they buy caviar more often.

In these studies the situation is shown to have an effect, but mainly in combination or interaction with the product.

Characteristics of the environment may evoke emotions. Do people feel that they control the environment or are they overwhelmed by it?[12] The PAD-model is considered in section 9.2: the importance of this model is that primary affective responses are assumed to intervene between a person and the environment on the one hand, and behaviour on the other hand.[13] Researchers showed respondents a few hundred different situations and asked them to rate them on a number of scales.[14] In a factor analysis of the scale scores three factors were obtained, that were interpreted as:

• Pleasure (P): a judgement of the situation in positive or negative terms.
• Activation (A): such as 'arousal', vigilance, interest and action tendency.
• Dominance (D): perceived control of the environment.[15]

This three-dimensional model of emotions is called the PAD model based on the interpretation of the three factors. The PAD model indicates three dimensions of emotion that play a role not only in the evaluation of situations but also more generally in the evaluation of advertisements, products, services and consumption experiences.[16]

Situations are evaluated using all three PAD dimensions. A boring situation scores low on all three dimensions. A hostile situation gives a high score on activation and low scores on pleasure and dominance. In this way, emotions may be classified, and also the situations that lead to these emotions. For instance, someone shopping for a dinner for important guests, may be in a situation with high activation.[17]

Although the primary affective responses can be defined separately, they control the behaviour in combination with other factors.[18] There are studies on the role of primary affective responses in different situations.[19] High levels of activation are perceived as more attractive in pleasant environments, whereas low levels of activation are perceived as more pleasant in 'difficult' situations. Most consumer situations are in the middle, neither pleasant nor unpleasant. An average level of activation is reached, for instance, a not too boring store, with a good assortment of products in an orderly layout. In pleasant situations, such as in a restaurant, new stimuli are easily accepted, for instance, a different menu.[20] The tendency to be part of the group is present in pleasurable situations in which dominance is evoked, for instance, in educational situations or in some student clubs. Activation strengthens this tendency in pleasant situations, but weakens it in unpleasant situations. These findings provide a framework that can be applied in the design of store environments and predicting consumer behaviour in such environments.[21]

Colours evoke pleasure to different degrees. For most people, blue is a favourite colour; then green, violet, red and yellow. The strongest activation is evoked by red; then orange, yellow, violet and green. Environments differ to the degree of evoked pleasure and activation. Green plants in a room and background music tend to increase the pleasure. The living room may evoke activation by its design and colour scheme. In this way the room feels cosy and encourages social interaction. The interiors of bedrooms and study rooms are normally less dramatic and evoke less activation. Cats and fish evoke less activation and are restful pets, whereas, dogs and parrots are activating pets.[22]

Coherence between parts of the environment

People bring their characteristics and prior states into the environment. Together with the objects and the situation these factors influence their behaviour. People are not necessarily victims of the situation. According to the interactionist perspective, people select, avoid and create situations for themselves and others.[23] The result of this behavioural feedback influences the person and his or her momentary state.

The five groups of environmental characteristics described at the beginning of this chapter are useful for defining the environment in terms of the relevant physical, social and temporal characteristics. These variables may be objective or subjective. The objective physical environment is the situation as it might be recorded by a camera, before it is interpreted by the consumer. The subjective environment is perceived, defined and interpreted by consumers. In general, consumer behaviour is more influenced by the subjective than by the objective environment. Some environmental influences such as subtle cues (smell, temperature) play an almost subliminal role.[24]

The characteristics of the situation may be related to behaviour in two ways.[25] Their direct effect takes place almost without delay. Situational characteristics influence behaviour: different situations may directly lead to a different allocation of free time or to a different choice of products. An example is the purchase of an umbrella when it rains. Delayed effects occur if a consumer, at a particular point in time, takes a decision that is influenced by future events and situations, for example, purchasing a birthday present to give later, or instant coffee to be used only if the regular coffee runs out. In the latter case it concerns an anticipated situation.

Three main characteristics of a situation influence behaviour: task definition, anticipation, and environmental effects.[26] Environmental effects have already been discussed at the beginning of this chapter.

Task definition
The consumer may have a number of different tasks including the evaluation of the differences between products and the actual purchase. Beliefs and evaluations combine to constitute the consumer's attitude to a product or brand.[27] This attitude may differ according to the stage which the consumer has reached, whether it be the search for alternatives, the decision to collect more information about various alternatives, the determination of the consideration set, or the final choice of the right option to buy.[28]

Anticipation
The evaluation of information about products may differ according to the usage situation: does one need the product now or later? Information about saving and pension plans may be seen as irrelevant to a young consumer, while this information may be seen as very relevant to someone of more mature years. The occasion for which the purchase is made may lead to a different evaluation of product information. It may happen that the required information about the perceived risk of a purchase differs, depending on whether the product is for personal use or is a gift.

Environmental effects
Both physical, social and temporal characteristics of the environment (context and time) may influence consumer behaviour. These characteristics are discussed earlier in this section.

12.4 Situations and the prediction of behaviour

Attitudes are used to explain and predict behaviour. Attitudes together with other factors influence behavioural intention.[29] The relationship between intention and behaviour may be confounded by a change of situation or by the fact that measurement of intention is not accurately focused on the situation in which the behaviour takes place.[30]

It makes a difference whether the behaviour being predicted is specific, such as the purchase of the book *Consumer Behaviour* for a marketing course, or more general, such as the purchase of any kind of book. The measurement of the attitude or behavioural intention should be more specific in the first case than in the second case.

To explain a specific behaviour, the intention should be operationalized in terms of the corresponding act, goal, situation and time.[31] In other words, situational characteristics (situation and time) are important for predicting behaviour. The behavioural intention of a consumer to have a Magnum ice-cream in the afternoon (time) on the beach (situation) is a better predictor of the actual behaviour in the afternoon on the beach than the behavioural intention to have a Magnum, without an indication of place or time.

To explain more general behaviour, it is sufficient to measure the attitude in terms of the corresponding goal. The attitude of a consumer with regard to textbooks could reasonably well predict the purchase of textbooks in general, without regard for the situation, time or act. Situational characteristics are less important for the explanation of general behaviour.

In the well-known study by LaPiere,[32] the correspondence of a measured behavioural intention and the actual behaviour was tested. In the 1930s, LaPiere travelled for several months across the USA in the company of a Chinese couple and, except in one case, they were always admitted into hotels and restaurants. Afterwards, in a survey, LaPiere asked the hotel and restaurant owners whether they would accept Chinese people as guests in their establishments. Their answers were all, except in one case, negative. This measurement of behavioural intention was a poor predictor of actual behaviour.

This example is typical of the fact that intentions are often poor predictors of behaviour. Observed actual behaviour and behavioural outcomes provide more valid measures. Behavioural outcomes include for instance 'garbology', inspecting rubbish bins to assess product use or rubbish separation.

According to the rule of corresponding elements in measurement and behaviour, the measurement of behavioural intention is not sufficient for predicting behaviour. The relationship between intention and behaviour might have been expressed differently, if the question asked was as follows: 'Would you accept as a guest in your establishment a young, well-dressed, pleasant, self-confident and well-to-do Chinese couple accompanied by an adult, well-dressed, mature European gentleman?'[33]

Intentions are often unstable. Prediction of behaviour thus leaves much to be desired. The intention to quit smoking next month may change after a month into an intention to quit tomorrow. Generally, the predictive power of intentions is greater if the time interval between the intention measurement and the behaviour is shorter.

Finally, perceived behavioural control affects the predictability of behaviour.[34] The perceived behavioural control is greater if the behaviour is not dependent on others. For the purchase of a product, consumers are dependent on others such as the retailer, the wholesaler and even their employers paying their salary so they can pay for the purchase. The perceived behavioural control may also be blocked by non-human causes, such as a car that will not start due to bad weather.

12.5 Consumer situations

How does the environment affect cognition, affect and behaviour? Is the environment causing the behaviour? Does the environment permit the behaviour? Does the environment facilitate or trigger the behaviour? Does the environment direct the behaviour?[35] Does a store display force the customer to buy? Or is this an exaggeration of the direct effect of the environment on behaviour? It is likely that environmental effects are created through interaction with other variables. For the consumer several situations are important: the communication situation, the information situation, the shopping situation, the buying situation, the situation at home, the product usage situation and the disposal situation. The most important behaviours and some examples are given in table 12.1.[36]

Communication situation
The communication situation is either personal or impersonal. Personal communication implies interaction between the customer and salesperson in the store or by telephone, between the customer and the insurance agent at home, and between customers. Impersonal communication pertains to most advertising, flyers and brochures, but also interaction through modern communication media such as teletext and the Internet. Personal communication is to be preferred over impersonal communication.[37] Impersonal communication and advice provides more privacy, often costs less time and money, but is often less specific to the individual consumer.

The communication situation in the contact with media is called the 'confrontation situation'.[38] Crowding and distraction in the confrontation situation determine the degree to which consumers are influenced by

Table 12.1 *Consumer situations*

Situations	Behaviour	Examples
Communication situation	Advertising confrontation, social communication	Observing outdoor advertising, talking about the vacation trip
Information situation	Outcome evaluation with respect to a reference point	Endowment effect, status-quo bias, mental accounting, spending, product bundling
Shopping situation	Checking the assortment, comparing alternatives	Looking at store windows, trying clothing
Buying situation	Transaction	Paying at the checkout counter
Situation at home	Household production	Preparing a meal
Usage situation	Using a product or service	Dinner in a restaurant
Disposal situation	Separating household waste	Returning bottles to bottle banks

television and other media. With high levels of crowding and distraction there is little opportunity to direct the consumer's attention to the message. Consumers understand that the message may be incomplete and do not grasp the details. In the case of a commercial, the characteristics and benefits of the product may escape the notice of the viewers. The effects of crowding and distraction also lead to less extreme evaluations by consumers (both positive and negative).

The *context of a medium* also constitutes a situation.[39] The information in the media is often mainly editorial, but frequently contains commercial elements (advertisements). The environment of the message in the medium is relevant. Too much advertising at the same time ('advertising clutter') hinders information processing. The message may then not reach its effect. Take for instance the situation of information overload. The context of a message (Umfeld) determines whether and partly how a message is perceived. A relaxed context, for instance, a soap on television or the sports section in a newspaper, facilitates the recall of an advertising message. A serious context, for instance the news, may hinder this.[40]

Information situation

Information can be presented in different ways with different effects on consumer behaviour. An important way of framing information is by presenting outcomes of behaviour either as gains or losses with respect to a certain reference point. In prospect theory, it has been shown that gains are evaluated differently than losses.[41] In general, gains are evaluated according to a relatively flat, concave function, whereas losses are evaluated according to a relatively steep, convex function. Consequently, losses are perceived as more serious than commensurate gains. Several effects are based on this idea, including the endowment effect, status-quo bias, mental accounting, spending, and product bundling.

Endowment effect   The endowment effect refers to the economic valuation of a product, which is higher after possession than before.[42] This effect is related to prospect theory since before possession the acquisition is considered a gain from the reference point of no possession, whereas after acquisition the eventual loss of the commodity is considered from the reference point of possession. Thus, the endowment effect implies a shift of the reference point. Usually, the endowment effect is measured by asking people to state their willingness to pay for the acquisition of a commodity (*WTP*) and their willingness to accept the loss of the commodity after possession (*WTA*). Both *WTP* and *WTA* are expressed in terms of money. Alternatively, people may be asked to accept or reject a given *WTP* or *WTA*.[43] In a number of different surveys and experiments, the ratio of *WTA* to *WTP* was in the 1.4–16.5 range.[44] This is explained by the fact that losses are weighed more heavily than gains.

Definition

The endowment effect refers to an individual's economic valuation of a product, which is higher after that person has taken possession of it than before.

It has been found that in trading-in a car, people care more about obtaining a high price for their used car (*WTA*) than about paying a high price for the new car (*WTP*).[45] This preference is consistent with the endowment effect.

In market experiments, the median reservation prices of sellers and buyers, expressed by their bids, have a ratio exceeding 1.5 in a number of experiments, resulting in substantial undertrading.[46] This effect may also be present in second-hand markets.

A further example in consumer behaviour is badly exposed pictures, which have nevertheless been processed. Although customers do not need to buy these pictures, they may buy them once they have the pictures in their hands.[47] Product trials with a money-back guarantee provide another example. In the first instance, the tendency to buy such products will be high. In the second instance, they will be inclined to keep the products because the purchase price was lower than their *WTA*s. Possibly, the endowment effect also plays a part in shop-lifting and borrowed items that are not returned.

In contingent valuation studies, either the *WTP* or the *WTA* is used in measuring the value of outcomes relevant to society. It is clear that the choice of the reference point, i.e., whether one considers a situation as an endowment or not, determines the type of measure used and the consequent result.[48] Policy measures are evaluated more favourably if they are known to restore a previous (better) state of the world than if they are just improving the current state.[49] This accords with the notion that the reference point determines whether the measures are considered as reducing a loss or obtaining a gain.

Status-quo bias   The status-quo bias has been defined as 'doing nothing or maintaining one's current or previous decision'.[50] Since the status quo may be different for different people, preferences for the same commodities may be different due to the bias. This has been shown with respect to energy consumption. Consumers' preference for taking account of the frequency of electric power cuts when compiling the bill were elicited by a survey.[51] More frequent power cuts were offset by a lower bill. The researchers compared the answers from a group characterized by approx- imately three power cuts per year with those from a group experiencing 15 power cuts per year. Of the first group, 60.2% preferred the status quo (3 power cuts per year) to the alternative combinations offered and 58.3% of the latter group preferred their status quo (15 power cuts). Although the reliability of electricity was quite different in the two groups, both preferred the situation they were accustomed to. Hence, the status-quo bias may also be indicated as a 'habit' effect.

Definition

The *status-quo* bias is a tendency to do nothing, or a tendency to maintain one's current or previous decision.

Further evidence of the status-quo bias comes from questionnaires examining hypothetical situations.[52] For example, people are told a story in which they have inherited a large sum of money from their great uncle, invested in a particular way (the status quo). They are asked to select one of four investment opportunities to invest their inheritance (one of which was to maintain the status quo). A strong bias toward the status-quo alternative was found in general.

The status-quo bias is sensitive to a reference point, which may be manipulated by the way the information is presented (or framed). Different 'frames' of car insurance information presented to consumers in real life have been investigated.[53] In New Jersey, the default option is coverage excluding the right to sue, which may be purchased additionally. In

Pennsylvania, the default option is coverage including the right to sue, which may be redeemed. In New Jersey, only 20% acquired the full right to sue, whereas in Pennsylvania, 75% retained the full right to sue. Thus, the economic impact of the status-quo bias can be considerable.

The status-quo bias is related to prospect theory and the endowment effect, as giving up the status quo incurs a loss, whereas adopting an alternative constitutes a gain. From prospect theory, we know that losses are weighted more heavily than gains, with the result that the statuo quo is frequently maintained.

Mental accounting   Mental accounting refers to the idea that consumers may use different mental accounts to evaluate different events. For example, it is quite common for people to save money for a second house and to buy a car on credit. They have separate mental accounts for these items. Economically, it would be more sensible to buy the car using the money in the savings account because of the high cost of credit. However, this would disturb the mental separation of the two accounts. Likewise, windfall income is more easily saved than money derived from a pay-rise because it is mentally accounted in a different way.[54] Mental budgeting, as considered in section 4.3, provides another example of mental accounting.

> **Definition**
>
> Mental accounting implies that consumers use either the same or different mental accounts in evaluating events. This is particularly relevant to the evaluation of gains and losses.

Prospect theory may also have implications for the evaluation of combined events. Two different combination rules can be identified: the *integration rule* comprising the evaluation of joint outcomes of events and the *segregation rule* combining the separate evaluations of different events.[55] It appears that different combination rules may result in different preferences, depending on the shape of the value function.

Multiple gains are generally preferred when received separately rather than together. For this reason, the advantages of consumer products and bonuses should be presented separately to consumers. Trading stamps and air miles are examples of separate gains.

Multiple losses are generally preferred integrated rather than segregated. For example, by using a credit card all expenditure over a period is pooled. The latter implication has been qualified after discovering that people sometimes appear to have difficulties integrating losses.[56] Examples of integrated losses are packages of several theatre shows for one price,

Figure 12.3 *Merry-go-round*

annual membership fees for clubs, and theme parks with free entrance to all attractions once the main entrance charge has been paid.

Withholding premiums implies that a loss is integrated with a benefit resulting in a positive balance (a mixed gain). In effect, one obtains less income. Segregation would imply that one gets income and pays the premiums later. The former is psychologically different and preferred to the latter. In market transactions, the expenditure is immediately offset by the benefit of the product purchased (compensated). Advance payment is undesirable according to this rule because it segregates the benefit from the loss.

In the case of mixed losses when the gain is small relative to the loss, segregation seems to be preferred, for example, rebates in price pro-motions. The rebate reduces the loss of spending, which is more important than an equivalent gain. However, relative price information—discounts and price increases as percentages of list prices—reverses the preference for mixed gains and mixed losses.[57]

Many retailers use product prices that are just below rounded numbers, for example 99.95 euros rather than 100 euros. The 5 cents hardly make any difference to the purchase price, but cognitively the consumer will recognize this price as cheaper than 100 euros. It reduces the loss by 5 cents. This phenomenon is a form of 'framing'. In framing, product characteristics can be used freely with respect to a specific reference point, whereby they are judged better than when described at random. The energy use and lifespan of an energy saving lightbulb can be expressed as kWh, and burning hours, however, the announcement that 'This lightbulb uses five times less energy and burns three times longer than a regular lightbulb' is psychologically more effective.

Spending 'Penny-wise and pound-foolish' behaviour can be explained from the convex shape of the value function for losses.[58] This kind of behaviour may occur if people go to a different shop to obtain a discount of 1 euro on a cheap product but refrain from doing this to obtain the same discount on an expensive product. Since the value of a loss marginally decreases with its size, the discount is valued more for low expenditure items than for high expenditure items. This kind of behaviour has also been investigated for spending on small items in connection with high expenditure.[59] The same kind of explanation applies. It has been found that:

- students spend more on extra items in a bookstore, if they spend more on required supplies;
- people are willing to spend more on headphones, if they have already spent more on a stereo sound system;
- volunteers from Catholic churches donate more money if they are told that other people donate $400 per year than if told that others donate $33 per month;
- students are willing to spend more on headphones if presented with a situation in which a stereo sound system costs $1,200 than with a situation involving 12 monthly payments of $100.

Several of these outcomes show that the spending effect may be framed.

Product bundling An application of mental accounting is the combined offer of two or more products that are somehow related: product bundling. Examples include a camera with a roll of film and a wide-screen television with a video movie. The small extra product increases the total value, usually to the advantage of the main product. It has been found that an excellent video movie may compensate for the lower quality of a television set disproportionately.[60] However, this effect was not found if the small product was unrelated to the main product, for example an electric typewriter with a calculator.

Definition

Product bundling refers to the fact that special offers that combine products may be preferred to separate product offers.

An interesting way of product bundling is the connection of consumption with charity.[61] By combining small donations with consumption of particular items, marketers may provide the opportunity for consumers to feel good because of the donation. For the consumer, the total value in this case may be greater than if the two were separated. In a group of students, 28% preferred the donation of a dollar to charity in their name to the receipt of a dollar in cash. A second group of students was asked to state their preference for either a $20 gift coupon for chocolate truffles or a $20 gift coupon for chocolate truffles plus a donation of a dollar to charity in their name. Seventy four per cent of the students preferred the second alternative. This result was typical for a number of different combinations of a donation and a frivolous product (on average, 68% preferred the donation in combination with the product, whereas only 31% preferred the donation without the product). In other words, the willingness to donate was more than doubled by its combination with a frivolous product. Hedonistic products provide immediate satisfaction, for example, a dinner at a fine restaurant, theme park, large bag of M&Ms, chocolate brownie and movie pass. If the donation was combined with a practical product, such as a mountain bike, toothpaste, textbooks or pocket dictionary, the effect was smaller: 55% preferred the combined alternative on average.

Shopping situation
The attractiveness of shopping centres is shown by the number of shoppers attracted to them. Among other factors this depends on the size and the travel time of the consumer, and the range of products that are available at the centre.[62] The location of the stores, in a crowded or less crowded street, in the centre or in a suburb, is also a determinant of customers' visits. Parking and accessibility by public transport are also situational.[63] Some shopping centres are true consumption paradises and thus act as strong stimulants to buying activity. Note that 'shopping' need not necessarily result in buying. Shopping may simply be only an orientation toward the assortment of stores.

Buying situation
The buying situation is determined by many factors. What information is present? Are there many distractions and thus less emphasis on purchasing? Store atmosphere and time pressure also play a part. The store environment and its layout may largely determine purchasing behaviour.

Presence of information   Product information is particularly important for products where brand and type differences play a role, thus leading to additional costs or risks for consumers. For example, information about the energy usage of refrigerators, about the total monthly running costs of cars, about the price per kilogramme of groceries and about ingredients of food products, is important. The way in which product information is given in the store affects buying behaviour.[64] Information about the price per standard unit may lead for instance to a choice of cheaper products and larger quantities.[65] The information should not be too extensive (because of 'information overload'), should have an easy-to-understand format (preferably ordered by the way in which the consumer needs the information, for instance prices per brand), and in a form that one could easily interpret, such as indications with plusses and minuses rather than for instance calories per gramme.[66]

Store atmosphere   Store atmosphere is determined by a large number of factors: store layout, music, colours, temperature, point of sale, crowdedness and sales personnel. Manipulation of these factors affects sales: displays at crowded places, for instance at elevators and escalators, bakery products with their pleasant smell at the entrance, and warm colours (red and yellow) in the store windows to attract consumers. The politeness, expertise, dress and behaviour of the store personnel are also factors that affect sales.

The effect of background music on behaviour in stores and restaurants has been investigated.[67] Many consumers like to hear music in a store. Consumers stay longer in the store under these circumstances and spend more money. The speed of the music affects the speed of the 'traffic' in the store. Background music is relaxing and affects the ambience and atmosphere of the restaurant, airport, train station and other public places.

Distraction   Consumers tend to pay less attention when there are many distractions. In these circumstances, consumers tend to attribute a lot of weight to negative evidence to eliminate alternatives. Distraction happens when too many different activities take place simultaneously. Crowding in the store can have the same effect. This is not desired by the marketeer who wants the marketing communication to be effective. It is also a negative aspect for consumers who are distracted from the products and services they came for. Distraction can be prevented by arranging for non-distracting situations, for instance, an insurance agent may telephone clients in the evening, or by eliminating the cause of the distraction, for instance by taking a customer to a quiet room.

Time pressure   Apart from the role that timing can play in the sales of products (for instance toys and gifts in December) time also plays a role in the decision making of consumers. Information processing under time pressure leads to reduced information search and the use of simplified decision rules.[68] Time pressure can occur if a consumer goes shopping just before closing time. The effect of the consumer's perception of the time horizon is also important. Women who have to decide about a means of contraception tend to use a decision rule with negative evidence when there is a short-term horizon (immediate use). However, they are more likely to adopt a compensatory decision rule when there is a long-term horizon (later use).[69]

Competition Purchase situations may differ considerably. In situations where there is little or no competition prices are usually considerably higher, for example, ice cream on the beach, coffee during the interval of a theatre performance, products in a camping shop or an umbrella during a sudden rainstorm. The impulse to buy these goods in these situations is stronger.

Situation at home
Consumer behaviour often occurs at home. For example, consider mail-order purchases, teleshopping, telebanking, information search on the Internet, or ordering from direct-mail-shots. Consumers are exposed to the media and advertising at home. Products such as washing machines, are mostly used at home. Situational factors such as the house type, the rooms and the style of the home may all influence behaviour.

Usage situation
The usage situation consists of the social environment, time of the day, day of the week, season, and the interaction between person and situation.

Social environment The use of consumption goods is often determined by the social environment. Increasingly, for instance, smokers are not allowed to smoke in public places. Clothing and cosmetics get more attention in social situations. The behaviour and possessions of referent people in the social environment may be imitated.[70]

Time and season The eating of meals is strongly related to time. There may be fixed meal-times (lunch-time at work), but often they are determined by habit. The use of durable goods is often time-dependent. Gardening and painting tools are used in the summer, washing machines are used at night in areas with cheaper electricity at night. This is because the utility of these consumption means is larger at particular times.[71] The marketing of products may be tuned to the time that these goods are the most useful for particular types of consumption.

Interaction of person and situation Often the utility of products is not only dependent on the usage situation, but also on the person using the product in the situation. For instance, racing bikes may be popular for outdoor recreation with young men, but not with older people or women. They might prefer another type of recreation.

Disposal situation
The disposal situation is the moment to decide what to do with worn-out and superfluous products. The options are selling, giving away, throwing away or otherwise disposing of products. This will be discussed in chapter 22 on consumption and the environment.

The choice of a product or brand is partly determined by the situation. Some even go so far as to speak of 'momentary consumption', i.e., consumption that is triggered by the situation and moods in which consumers find themselves at a particular moment. The choice of a magazine may be situational. On some occasions you may want to read *Cosmopolitan* and at other times you may prefer *Reader's Digest*. This type of segmentation starts with the frequency of a particular situation or mood of consumers. Some consumers always prefer *Cosmopolitan* and may become subscribers. Others are only in a 'Cosmo mood' sometimes. They are more likely to buy separate issues of the magazine.

12.6 Conclusions

The most important characteristics of situations influencing consumer behaviour are discussed in this chapter. The situation is a partial determinant of behaviour, often in interaction with the product. In some situations you may order a glass of beer, but in other situations you prefer a glass of orange juice. Knowledge of the situation is thus necessary to explain and predict consumer behaviour.

The primary evaluation of situations is affective on the dimensions of pleasure, activation and dominance (the PAD model). This has an effect on the experience and judgement of situations. Consumers experience new situations such as a shopping centre, a new store, a bar, a restaurant, a hotel, an office and an airport, almost immediately as either pleasant or unpleasant, interesting or boring, controllable or overwhelming. Depending on this primary affective response, consumers behave in a certain way in the situation. They may be relaxed, irritated, in control or submissive.

Interactions between situation and person and between situation and product have been distinguished. Depending on the situation people behave in a certain way and select products and brands. Behaviour and product choice are thus not only dependent on one's own preferences, but also on the circumstances. Preferences are not independent of the situation either. On a sunny terrace one may prefer a cola with ice. In winter, after a long walk on the beach one may prefer a hot chocolate. The situation determines and restricts the available choice alternatives.

The (post)modern consumer tends to be influenced by situations. Some consumers think it is important to show the 'right' behaviour in the situation: the 'correct' suit and jewelry, talk about the 'right' things and have the 'right' friends. It seems that one's own 'real' preference, if any, should be hidden from others. One 'sells' oneself as well as possible, because it is important to be popular. The person who plays the role best fitted to the situation is the winner of the party.

Recently, there is more emphasis on 'momentary consumption'. People are not always stable in their preferences. Situations and moods may determine which magazines are preferred or which 'consumption' one selects in a particular situation. Moods may be dependent on the situation as is described in this chapter.

Notes

1 Kurt Lewin stressed this in his 'field theory'. Actually, it is more complex. Lewin's concept of 'environment' is similar to our concept of 'situation'. Lewin's concept of 'situation' is a kind of 'occasion'. An occasion is an incentive or opportunity for behaviour. See Lewin, K. (1936) *Principles of Topological Psychology* (New York: McGraw-Hill) 11.

2 These people score low on a self-monitoring scale. See section 8.4.

3 Kakkar, P. and Lutz, R. J. (1981) 'Situational influence on consumer behavior: A review' in: Kassarjian, H. H. and Robertson, T. S. (Eds) *Perspectives in Consumer Behavior* (Glenview, IL: Scott Foresman) 204.

4 This chapter is partly based on Hackett, P. M. W., Foxall, G. R. and Van Raaij, W. F. (1993) 'Consumers in retail environments' in: Gärling, T. and Golledge, R. G. (Eds) *Behavior and Environment: Psychological and Geographical Approaches* (Amsterdam: Elsevier) 378–399.

5 Belk, R. W. (1975) 'Situation variables and consumer behavior' *Journal of Consumer Research* 2, 157–164.

6 Verhallen, T. M. M. and Pieters, R. G.M. (1984) 'Attitude theory and behavioral costs' *Journal of Economic Psychology* 5, 223–249.

7 Belk (1975) defines the environment as 'all those factors particular to a time and place of observation, which do not follow from personal (intra-individual) and stimulus (object or choice alternative) attributes and which have a demonstrable and systematic effect on current behaviour' (p. 158). In our view, the addition of the demonstrable and systematic effect on behaviour is not necessary and even not desirable. It leads to a circular definition of 'situation'. It is an empirical question whether these factors affect consumer behaviour. See also Hansen, F. (1972) *Consumer Choice Behavior. A Cognitive Theory* (New York: The Free Press), chapter 3.

8 See section 14.1.

9 Pieters, R. G. M. and Van Raaij, W. F. (1988) 'The role of affect in economic behavior' in: Van Raaij, W. F., van Veldhoven, G. M. and Wärneryd, K.-E. (Eds) *Handbook of Economic Psychology* (Amsterdam: North-Holland) 108–142.

10 Trøye, S. (1985) 'Situationist theory and consumer behavior' in: Sheth, J. N. (Ed.) *Research in Consumer Behavior* (Greenwich, CT: JAI Press) 285–321. Trøye integrates the systems of Belk and Russell and Mehrabian.
   Belk, R. W. (1974) 'An exploratory assessment of situational effects in buyer behavior' *Journal of Marketing Research* 11, 156–163.

Mehrabian, A. and Russell, J. A. (1974) *An Approach to Environmental Psychology* (Cambridge, MA: MIT Press).
Figure 12.2 is based on this integration. See Hackett *et al.* (1993).

11   Belk (1974; 1975). Lutz, R. J. and Kakkar, P. (1975) 'The psychological situation as a determinant of consumer behavior' *Advances in Consumer Research* 1, 439–453.

12   Mehrabian and Russell (1974). The primary affective response (PAR) is the first response to a confrontation with advertising. See van Raaij, W. F. (1989) 'How consumers react to advertising' *International Journal of Advertising* 8, 261–273.

13   Mehrabian and Russell (1974); Russell, J. A. and Mehrabian, A. (1975) 'Task, setting and personality variables affecting the desire to work' *Journal of Applied Psychology* 60, 518–520; Russell, J. A. and Mehrabian, A. (1976) 'Some behavioral effects of the physical environment' in: Wapner, S., Cohen, S. and Kaplan, B. (Eds) *Experiencing the Environment* (New York: Plenum) 138–154.

14   Mehrabian and Russell (1978).

15   These three dimensions show a large similarity with the dimensions of the semantic differential. See Osgood, C. E., Suci, G. J. and Tannenbaum, P. H. (1957) *The Measurement of Meaning* (Urbana-Champaign, IL: University of Illinois Press). These three dimensions are: evaluation (pleasure), activity (arousal) and potency (dominance). See Kakkar, P. and Lutz, R. J. (1981). See for perceived control: Hui, M. K. and Bateson, J. E. G. (1991) 'Perceived control and the effects of crowding and consumer choice on the service experience' *Journal of Consumer Research* 18, 174–184.

16   Havlena, W. J. and Holbrook, M. B. (1986) 'The varieties of consumption experience: comparing two typologies of emotion in consumer behavior' *Journal of Consumer Research* 13, 394–404.

17   Contrary to Berlyne, D. E. (1963) 'Motivational problems raised by exploratory and epistemic behavior' in: Koch, S. (Ed.) *Psychology: A Study of a Science* Part 5 (New York: McGraw-Hill) 284–364. Mehrabian and Russell do not relate pleasure to activation. Berlyne states that people prefer an average level of activation and do not like a high or low level of activation.

18   Mehrabian and Russell (1974).

19   Russell and Mehrabian (1978).

20   Compare Berlyne (1963).

21   Other affective reactions in analogy with Mehrabian and Russell are defined by Foxall, G. R. (1990) *Consumer Psychology in Behavioural Perspective* (London: Routledge). The classification of emotions by Plutchik is studied in relation to consumer behaviour. See Plutchik, R. (1980) *Emotion: A Psycho-evolutionary Synthesis* (New York: Harper & Row). Havlena and Holbrook (1986) conclude that the PAD model of Mehrabian and Russell is better suited to the description of consumption experiences than the eight emotional categories of Plutchik.

22   Kroeber-Riel, W. (1992) *Konsumentenverhalten* [Consumer Behavior] (München: Verslag Franz Vahlen) 5th edition, 433.

23   Bowers, D. S. (1973) 'Situationism in psychology: an analysis and a critique' *Psychological Review* 80, 307–337.

24   Subliminal means 'below the perception threshold'. It concerns influence of

which one is not aware that it is taking place. See Moore, T. E. (1982) 'Subliminal advertising: what you see is what you get' *Journal of Marketing* 46, 38–47.

25 Trøye (1985).

26 Trøye (1985).

27 See section 9.3.

28 Compare the experiment of Gorn (1982) in section 10.3.
    Gorn, J. G. (1982) 'The effects of music in advertising on choice behavior: a classical conditioning approach' *Journal of Marketing* 46, 94–101.

29 See section 9.4.

30 Fishbein, M. and Ajzen, I. (1975) *Belief, Attitude, Intention, and Behavior* (Reading, MA: Addison-Wesley).

31 Fishbein and Ajzen (1975).

32 LaPiere, R. T. (1934).

33 Fishbein and Ajzen (1975), 374–375.

34 See section 9.4.

35 Trøye (1985).

36 Hansen (1972, figures 2.2 and 3.1) also gives a classification of situations.

37 Antonides, G. and Van Raaij, W. F. (1993) 'Financiële advisering en relatiebeheer' [Financial advice and relationships] in: *Financiële adviserung aan de consument: Fictie of realiteit?* [Financial Advice to the Consumer: Fiction or Reality?] (Amsterdam: NIBE) 33–66.

38 Pieters, R. G. M. and Van Raaij, W. F. (1993) *Reclamewerking* [Advertising Processing] (Leiden: Stenfert Kroese), Chapter 20.

39 Pieters and Van Raaij (1992), Chapter 19.

40 Soldow, G. F. and Principe, V. (1981) 'Response to commercial as a function of program context' *Journal of Advertising Research* 21, 2, 59–65.

41 Kahneman, D. and Tversky, A. (1979) 'Prospect theory: an analysis of decision under risk' *Econometrica* 47, 263–291.

42 Thaler, R. H. (1980) 'Toward a positive theory of consumer choice' *Journal of Economic Behavior and Organization* 1, 39–60.
    Kahneman, D., Knetsch, J. L. and Thaler, R. H. (1990) 'Experimental tests of the endowment effect and the Coase theorem' *Journal of Political Economy* 98, 1325–1347.

43 Knetsch, J. L. and Sinden, J. A. (1984) 'Willingness to pay and compensation demanded: Experimental evidence of an unexpected disparity in measures of value' *The Quarterly Journal of Economics* 99, 507–521.

44 Kahneman *et al.* (1990).

45 Purohit, D. (1995) 'Playing the role of buyer and seller: the mental accounting of trade-ins' *Marketing Letters* 6, 101–110.

46 Tietz, R. (1992) 'An endowment effect in market experiments' in: Lea, S. E. G., Webley, P. and Young, B. M. (Eds) *New Directions in Economic Psychology* (Aldershot: Edward Elgar) 99–121.
    Kahneman *et al.* (1990).

47 Thaler (1980).

48 Knetsch, J. L. (1996) 'Choosing a measure of welfare change: Disparities, legal entitlements, and reference positions' Paper prepared for the Western Regional Science Association Annual Meeting, Napa, CA.

49 Gregory, R., Lichtenstein, S. and MacGregor, D. (1993) 'The role of past states in determining reference points for policy decisions' *Organizational Behavior and Human Decision Processes* 55, 195–206.

50 Samuelson, W. and Zeckhauser, R. (1988) 'Status quo bias in decision making' *Journal of Risk and Uncertainty* 1, 7–59.

51 Hartman, R. S., Doane, M. J. and Woo, C.-K. (1991) 'Consumer rationality and the status quo' *The Quarterly Journal of Economics* 106, 141–162.

52 Samuelson and Zeckhauser (1988).

53 Johnson, E. J., Hershey, J., Meszaros, J. and Kunreuther, H. (1993) 'Framing, probability distortions, and insurance decisions' *Journal of Risk and Uncertainty* 7, 35–51.

54 Thaler, R. H. (1990) 'Saving, fungibility and mental accounts' *Journal of Economic Perspectives* 4, 193–205.

55 Thaler, R. H. (1985) 'Mental accounting and consumer choice' *Marketing Science* 4, 199–214.

56 Thaler, R. H. and Johnson, E. J. (1990) 'Gambling with the house money and trying to break even: The effects of prior outcomes on risky choice' *Management Science* 36, 643–660.
Linville, P. W. and Fischer, G. W. (1991) 'Preferences for separating or combining events' *Journal of Personality and Social Psychology* 60, 5–23.

57 Heath, T. B., Chatterjee, S. and France, K. R. (1995) 'Mental accounting and changes in price: The frame dependence of reference dependence' *Journal of Consumer Research* 22, 90–97.

58 Thaler (1980).

59 Christensen, C. (1989) 'The psychophysics of spending' *Journal of Behavioral Decision Making* 2, 69–80.

60 Gaeth, G., Levin, I., Chakraborty, G. and Levin, A. (1991) 'Consumer evaluation of multi-product bundles: an information integration analysis' *Marketing Letters* 2, 81–84.

61 Strahilevitz, M. and Myers, J. G. (1997) 'Donations to charity as purchase incentives: How well they work may depend on what you are trying to sell' (*in press*).

62 Huff, D. L. (1962) 'A probabilistic analysis of consumer spatial behavior' in: Decker, W. S. (Ed.) *Emerging Concepts in Marketing* (Chicago: American Marketing Association) 443–461.

63 See sections 18.3 and 18.4.

64 The content of the information is not included. This is an external factor. The way information is given is the structure and the format of information. Compare with section 11.8.

65 Russo, J. E. (1977) 'The value of unit price information' *Journal of Marketing Research* 14, 193–201.

66 See section 11.8.

67 Milliman, R. E. (1982) 'The effect of background music upon the shopping behavior of supermarket patrons' *Journal of Marketing* 46, 86–91.
Milliman, R. E. (1982) 'The influence of background music on the behavior of restaurant patrons' *Journal of Consumer Research* 13, 286–289.

68 See sections 11.5 and 11.8.

69 Wright, P. L. and Weitz, B. (1977) 'Time horizon effects on product evaluation strategies' *Journal of Marketing Research* 14, 429–443.

70 This is observational learning; see section 10.5.

71 Winston, G. C. (1988) 'The time-shape of transactions' in: Maital, S. (Ed.) *Applied Behavioural Economics* Part 2 (Brighton: Wheatsheaf) 593–609.

PART III

SOCIAL PROCESSES

FAMILIES AND HOUSEHOLD PRODUCTION 13

13.1 Introduction

This chapter concerns the household. Many decisions regarding schooling, labour, purchases, moves, leisure, and transportation are taken jointly by members of the household. The influence of husband, wife and children will be considered here. However, the multi-person household or family is not just an economic decision-making unit, it also creates a sense of security and belonging for its members. One can relax and recover from the strain of the job and pay attention to the home, garden and children. This behaviour is called 'cocooning'.[1]

The term 'household' may be distinguished from the family. A *family* is a group of two or more persons cohabiting by means of marriage, partnership, blood relationship or adoption. A household may consist of one person, for example a student living on his or her own. A household may also consist of many people, such as a residential home or community. The traditional household consists of a husband, wife and children. Non-traditional households are emerging such as one-person households, one-parent households and cohabitating homosexual couples. A *household* is defined as a person or a group of cohabitating persons who jointly manage time and money budgets.

A flexible function of the household is *prosumption*,[2] which is a combination of production and consumption. This concerns unpaid private production and consumption by the household. For example, a housewife or a househusband produces a meal by combining purchased food, time, effort and capital goods such as a cooker and pans. Home production includes all the activities of the household members to produce unpaid goods and services and to add value for their own profit.

Section 13.2 deals with the advantages of multi-person households. Section 13.3 considers the household life-cycle and child rearing. Family decision making and conflict resolution are considered in section 13.4. Section 13.5 deals with household production and section 13.6 considers its relation with the market sector and the public sector. Section 13.7 concludes.

13.2 Advantages of multi-person households

The multi-person household has some advantages over that of a single person. These concern the ability to combine activities for household production and also economies of scale and psychological advantages.[3]

Combination of activities

Partners with different abilities can complement each other's activities. In the traditional household the husband carries out the DIY activities whereas the wife prepares the meals. If these activities agree with the capacities of the partners, this implies efficiency through specialization. Each of the partners carries out the activities which fits them best. Other specializations include working in a paid job, child care, financial management, gardening and negotiating with traders, among others. If the activities of the partners do not agree with their abilities, specialization efficiency will not be achieved. An accountant without affinity to child care and a child-care worker without affinity to financial matters do not obtain specialization efficiency if the accountant looks after the children and the child-care worker manages financial matters. However, they may learn from each other, which might lead to a different kind of mutual advantage. Alternatively, they may consider the household tasks as a variation on their daily routine. Obviously, child care is not exclusively a business matter for the parents.

Economies of scale

Durable goods, such as a home, home decoration, car, washing machine, refrigerator and drill, are used by several members of the household. In general, joint use is cheaper than individual use. This is called economies of scale.[4] It is cheaper for two persons to cook together than for each person to cook for him or herself. The economies of scale may become even larger if more households are using the same goods, such as a drill or a lawn mower.

Many types of consumption concern so-called public goods, from which several members of the household may benefit without diminishing the consumption of the other members.[5] Examples of public goods are a tidy house, a nice garden and even children. Economies of scale constitute the basic reason for the OECD equivalence scale in which the two-person budget equals only 143% per cent of the one-person budget.[6]

Figure 13.1 *Economies of scale?*

Psychological advantages

Besides economic advantages the household offers psychological advantages such as love, affection and friendship. Also, marriage or partnership frequently provides social status, protection and a satisfactory sex life.[7] A different psychological advantage concerns the pleasure one may derive from the consumption by one's partner. For example, a husband might enjoy buying a dress as a gift for his wife. The consumption of the dress is a mutual benefit because both take pleasure from it.

Unfortunately cohabitating also has disadvantages. One has to negotiate about all kinds of issues and exercise consideration for one another. There may also be negative external effects, for example if one partner smokes and the other does not. Finally, opportunity costs may arise such as the loss of a potentially more successful relationship. The mutual advantages have to be distributed equally between the partners, such that one partner is not favoured over the other. As long as the advantages are greater than the disadvantages for both partners, the relationship is likely to survive. In general, the disadvantages of multi-person households coincide with the advantages of one-person households.

13.3 Household life-cycle and child rearing

Many families evolve in similar stages over time. The family life-cycle stages are distinguished by age, presence or absence of children and paid or unpaid employment. The stages of the family and their typical patterns of spending are shown in table 13.1.[8]

Each family type has its own needs and restrictions. For example, young families have a need for housing and decoration but they have limited financial means. In this respect, the family life-cycle is similar to the economic life-cycle.[10] The modernized life-cycle includes divorced (either without children or single parents in table 13.1), remarried and homosexual couples (respectively, married and unmarried in table 13.1).[11]

Definition

The family life-cycle describes the consecutive stages the family passes through over time.

An important task of the family is to raise children. For children, the family is a very important socializing agent.[12] During socialization, norms and values are transferred to the children and several psychological motivations and information processing styles are shaped. This is highly dependent on the parental style of child rearing. An important distinction of parental style is authoritarian versus democratic.[13] Democratic parents are the most active in consumer socialization. They communicate more

Table 13.1 *Typical spending in family life cycle stages*[9]

Stage	Typical items of expenditure
Young, single adult	Clothing, entertainment, car
Unmarried couples	Low-cost furniture, budget travel
Newly married family, without children	Furniture, appliances, entertainment
Married without children	Design furniture, entertainment, smaller homes, sports cars, career clothing
Family with young children at home	Insurance, medical expenses, children's clothing, toys, larger homes
Family with older children at home	Personal electronic items, holidays, family size packages, larger homes
Single parents	Low-cost housing, discount food, inexpensive clothing
Divorced couples without children	Apartments, small packages, dating service, clubs
Family, children left home (empty nest)	Travel, hobbies, home improvement
Family, main breadwinner retired	Medical expenses, retirement homes, cosmetics, jewellery
Solitary survivor	Medical expenses, restaurants, apartments

with their children regarding consumption, have more consumption goals for them and engage in co-shopping and co-viewing television more frequently than authoritarian parents. Furthermore, parental style influences the attention given to children's opinions, the weight given to children's opinions and the influence of children in the family decision making process.[14]

> **Definition**
>
> Parental style describes the characteristic way of raising children, frequently divided into authoritarian versus democratic styles.

Parental style may be indicated by the love and respect parents demand from their children, regardless of the qualities and faults of the parents, and the value attached to obedience, independence and feelings of responsibility in child rearing. Based on these indicators, it has been found that the Nordic countries, The Netherlands, Germany, Austria, Bulgaria and Hungary practise a relatively democratic parental style, whereas Portugal, UK, France, Slovenia, Czech and Slovak Republics, Ireland, Spain, Belgium, Russia and Italy practise a relatively authoritarian parental style. Table 13.2 shows several family life-cycle groups and their parental styles on the democratic–authoritarian dimension. Shortage of time was associated with a more democratic parental style.[15] Children with busy parents, i.e., dual-income families and one-parent households with a working parent, are raised in a more democratic parental style than children with at least

Table 13.2 *Parental style in several family life-cycle groups (Europe 1990)*

Life-cycle group	Percentage of population	Parental style[a]
Single, no children, age <40 years old	19.2	5.88
Cohabitating, no children, age <40 years old	6.2	5.75
Cohabitating, children at home, non-working parents	3.0	6.31
Cohabitating, children at home, one working parent	10.7	6.24
Cohabitating, children at home, husband working	16.5	6.11
Cohabitating, children at home, wife working	1.7	5.87
Cohabitating, children at home, both parents working	10.0	5.90
Single parent with job, children at home	2.4	5.80
Single parent, no job, children at home	2.3	6.18
Cohabitating, children left home	14.4	6.21
Single, children left home	6.5	6.43
Cohabitating, no children, age ≥40 years	2.8	6.41
Single, no children, age ≥40 years	4.2	6.42

[a] 2 = very democratic, 8 = very authoritarian

one non-working parent. Presumably they are more frequently left on their own and are given more responsibility, stimulating their independence in consumer behaviour. Furthermore, it appears that the traditional family (husband, wife and children) comprises only 42% of European households.

13.4 Family decision making and conflict resolution

The whole family plays a part in household decision making. How does decision making proceed? How much influence do the various parties have on the final decision? How are conflicts resolved in the family? This section deals with the issues raised by these questions.

The members of a household take decisions about the purchase and the use of products and services. Sometimes decisions are taken autonomously, sometimes jointly, especially in the case of important purchases. In traditional households, husbands are usually dominant in deciding about the car and financial matters, whereas the wife dominates in the purchase of food and clothing. Several goods, such as home decoration, family holidays and children's education are usually decided upon jointly (syncratic). Autonomous decisions (each for oneself) are usually taken regarding such goods as gardening equipment, cosmetics and alcoholic beverages.[16]

However, the influence of the members may be different in different stages of the decision making process. Decision making consists of several stages: problem recognition, information search, alternative evaluation, and choice or purchase. In the traditional family, role patterns are generally

Figure 13.2 *Buyer, payer, user . . .*

Table 13.3 *Influence of husband and wife in decision making*[18]

	Problem recognition	Orientation	Decision
Husband-dominant	8%	12%	8%
Wife-dominant	24%	28%	20%
Autonomous	40%	36%	20%
Syncratic	28%	24%	52%

used in decision making. As the wife takes care of many household affairs, she frequently recognizes a problem and tries to find solutions. During the decision making process, the husband participates in alternative evaluation and choice or purchase: see table 13.3. In the decision making stage, autonomous and dominant behaviour—frequently shown in the earlier stages—is often replaced by syncratic behaviour. The type of decision making remains constant in about two-thirds of the cases. The influence in family decision making has been found to depend on sex role orientations in the households.[17]

The influence of children on household decision making may vary according to product type and decision stage.[19] Children have a relatively strong (but not decisive) influence on decisions regarding breakfast cereal, sandwich filling, toothpaste, bicycle for child, child clothing and holidays, and a relatively weak influence regarding cars, household appliances, furniture, and adult clothing.[20] Regarding holidays, sandwich filling and clothing, the influence of children was found to be greater in the alternative evaluation and choice stages than in the problem recognition and information search stages.[21] For other products, this may be different, however.

The respective influences of household members on the decision making process are associated with their respective roles.[22]

- The *initiator* is active in the problem recognition stage and may suggest the need to make a purchase and may choose a particular brand, for example a Grundig CD-player.
- The *influencer* may approve or disapprove the suggestion by the initiator. The influencer guides the choice process in the stage of alternative evaluation and may suggest a brand, for example to buy a Philips CD-player instead of the Grundig.
- The *decision maker* takes the decision to make or not to make a purchase.
- The *buyer* goes to the shop to buy the product that was selected. At this stage, it is significant whether the buyer is still allowed to make a brand choice or not.
- The buyer usually pays for the purchase. However, in mail order purchases or buying on account, someone else may be the *payer*. The

payer transfers the money and keeps track of the (large) household expenses.

- The *users* may be different from the people mentioned before, for example, children or pets. Their preferences will usually be taken into account in the decision making process.
- The *complainant* takes action in case of a consumer problem and may be yet another person, for instance the complainant may be the most assertive household member.

In addition, the role of 'specialist' has been distinguished, who makes decisions in a particular household product domain.[23] Usually, the specialist owes this role to expertise, as perceived by the other household members. The role distribution in the household is important to advertising. Who needs to be informed in the problem-recognition stage, who will evaluate the alternatives and who will make the final decision?

Although the decision process described above suggests that family decision making is a well-structured process, this is often not the case. Many purchases are unplanned and many purchase plans are not carried out.[24] In addition, the above-mentioned roles may be different across different consumption domains and they may change over time.

The importance of the decision may affect who has influence in the decision-making process. If importance is high, more influence is needed.[25] It appears that children are relatively influential with regard to the products that are relevant to them. The children's influence is likely to depend on the parental style considered in section 13.2. In democratic families, the children have more influence in the problem recognition stage than in authoritarian families.[26] The decision making process in traditional families differs from the modern process.

Several other factors influence decision making.[27]

- *Social class*. The middle classes more often take decisions jointly than either the higher or lower classes. In the higher classes, frequently each of the partners has an income, a budget and a car, leading to more autonomous decision making. If the income is high, this diminishes the pressure for optimal spending. In the lower classes, the role distribution of the partners is more strict. Hence, less adjustment and communication is necessary and less syncratic decision making occurs.
- *Role orientation*. A strict orientation of male and female roles induces specialization, less communication and less syncratic decision making. Role orientation may also concern the stages of the decision making process. For example, one partner may gather the information, which the other partner may use in decision making.
- *Family life-cycle*. Just-married or cohabiting couples usually need much deliberation to arrive at a decision. Role distributions are still loose. Later, distributions of roles and tasks make the decision process less

syncratic. Also, in second marriages, less syncratic decision processes are likely to take place, as the partners already have experience with decision roles.

- *Perceived risk* normally induces syncratic decision making. The risk frequently concerns all family members, causing joint decision making. Financial, physical, social and temporal risk may be involved.[28] Perceived risk also is associated with the importance of the decision.
- *Time pressure* reduces the opportunity of deliberation and joint decision making. The family types shown in table 13.2 reflect different time scales, consequently affecting the type of decision making.

Conflict resolution

The resolution of conflict in the household can be accomplished in different ways. Conflict can be resolved by means of authority, rules (e.g., according to roles), negotiation or habit. Either explicitly or implicitly, power may be involved in the process of reaching an agreement. Parents can exert power over their children and spouses can exert power on each other in different ways, leading to different outcomes.[29] Several factors play a part in this process.

Resources
The resources available to households include:

- *Income*. The main income earner frequently has the most important say in spending. The wife's influence generally increases if she has income herself. This may induce more autonomous behaviour.
- *Education*. The partner with the highest education frequently has the most influence. This may be based on expertise in problem solving, knowledge of alternatives and persuasiveness.
- *Labour participation*. Working partners may use their labour activities— effort, working time and status—to demand compensation in household negotiation. A job frequently requires special skills or knowledge, which may be used to exert power on the other partner.

Personal attributes
The personal attributes of the partners, such as intelligence, need for cognition and cognitive style may result in a power imbalance. One partner may be smarter than the other.

Culture and tradition
Cultural tradition may determine power differences. The traditional husband-dominant role pattern prevails in European ethnic minority households.[30] In these households the wife usually needs permission from her husband to make a large purchase, whereas the husband does not need

permission from his wife.[31] In the lower social classes the wife usually has more say in housekeeping matters and in some countries the husband transfers his entire income or part of it to his wife, in exchange for 'pocket-money'.

Duration of partnership
If the relationship lasts for a long time, a power imbalance is more likely. Age may also lead to psychological superiority as older people usually have more experience and insight. Where there are children in the household, the mother often represents them in the decision making process.

Involvement
Involvement with a product or service generally leads to substantial influence in decision making in that subject area.[32] Involvement is frequently related to the use of the product concerned, for example, the household member who does most of the laundry will probably have a high degree of involvement with the purchase of a washing machine. Self-concern may influence the decision-making process, for example, by reducing the number of concessions on offer. In addition, role preferences may influence the process, for example a husband may not be willing to take care of the children because this is inconsistent with his image of the 'male role'.

Past behaviour
The *orientation with respect to previous negotiation* may influence the decision making process. If one has always been cooperative and trustful in making agreements, one is likely to persist in this kind of behaviour, thus creating a favourable negotiation climate. Old 'wounds' may negatively influence the climate.

Cohesion
Cohesion refers to the degree of harmony in the household, indicated by the degree of interest in each other and in joint decision making.[33] Cohesive families decide less egotistically and rely less on coalition formation among their members. Mutual understanding, emotional support, and special attention make individual decisions, such as whether the mother works, a matter for the family as a whole.

Other ways of resolving conflict include:

- problem solving by rational arguments and seeking new information;
- compromising or trading issues, for example an outing to an amusement park, desired by the children, may be negotiated in exchange for the children cleaning their rooms;
- utility debts or book-keeping of satisfaction and dissatisfaction with earlier agreements (this is similar to compromising over time);

- persuasion or insisting, for example on choices that avoid debt;
- strategic behaviour, including threats and coalitions.

13.5 **Household production**

Before we consider the relations between household production, the market sector and the public sector, the factors that distinguish between the three sectors are discussed—see table 13.4. Activities can be divided according to whether or not the work is paid. If production and income is included in the official statistics, it belongs to the formal economy, otherwise it belongs to the informal economy.

The *formal economy* comprises activities included in the National Accounts. This is paid work on which value added tax, income tax and social security premiums are levied. Homework belongs to the formal economy if it is paid and taxed. Homework may vary from such activities as sewing clothes and doing car mechanics to writing books or articles. Although the work is carried out at home, it is not considered household production. A special type of homework is telework based on a telephone/computer connection with the organization one is working for.

The *black economy*[35] includes paid work on which no tax or premium has been paid. The income and turnover are both concealed from the tax authorities. This informal economy may be connected to the formal economy as part of the purchases or sales that are not officially accounted for, although it may also contribute to the formal economy, such as an illegal clothing 'sweatshop' supplying the clothing industry. Theft and the

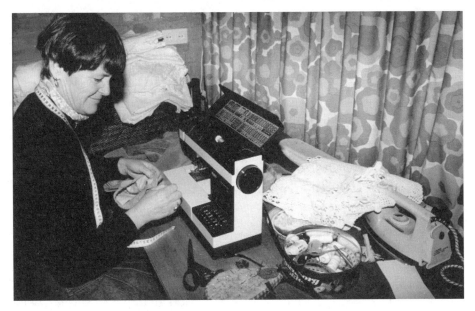

Figure 13.3 *Household production*

Table 13.4 *Distinctions between formal and informal economies*[34]

Types of work	Paid?	Legal?	Formal?	Example
Formal economy	yes	yes	yes	Paid job
Black economy	yes	no	no	Smuggling
Household production	no	yes	no	Housekeeping
Volunteer work	no	yes	no	Work for charity

fencing of stolen goods also belong to the black economy. Such work is illegal and is not accounted for in the Gross National Product.

Household production includes the unpaid production and value addition created for the householder's own benefit, i.e., for direct consumption by the household. This includes among others cleaning, shopping, preparing meals, and DIY activities such as painting the house and fixing the car. Household production usually takes place at home. However, shopping is an example of household production outside the home. Household production is not paid and it is excluded from the National Accounts and the Gross National Product.

Voluntary work is unpaid work that is sometimes carried out at home and sometimes outside the home, such as providing help for neighbours and relatives, clubs, foundations, churches, political parties and charity. The difference between voluntary work and household production is that the former is not for one's own profit. Voluntary work is based on societal responsibility, to acquire social contacts or to gain experience which may be used in paid labour later, for example being the treasurer of a sports club. As voluntary work is not paid, it is excluded from the National Accounts. The borderline between voluntary work and leisure often is hard to draw, for example in the case of amateur drama clubs.

The informal economy includes household production and voluntary work. Because the informal economy is excluded from the National Accounts, a country's economic activity is underestimated by the official statistics.[36] Several methods can be used to estimate the value of household production.

Value of household production

Household production makes use of several production means:

- labour, effort and time;
- knowledge and skills, such as product knowledge, financial insight and craftsmanship;
- capital goods, such as a sewing machine, drill, car, dishwasher, caravan, refrigerator, microwave and washing machine;
- raw and processed materials, such as food, detergents, textiles, wood and nails.

Figure 13.4 *DIY*

The production means are combined to produce consumables, such as meals, clean clothes and a tidy house. Production means may be purchased or hired, for example, a domestic help, advice or appliances. Labour and capital goods are substitutes to some extent, for example a dishwasher saves the effort of cleaning the dishes manually. Labour and materials can also be substituted for each other to some extent, for instance ready-made dishes need little preparation time.

The value of household production can be estimated by means of *output methods*: the income evaluation method, the contingent valuation method and the market cost methods. It can also be estimated by *input methods*: the opportunity cost method and the market replacement cost method.[37]

The *income evaluation method* starts from a subjective income evaluation, for example, an income may be described as 'good'. Households which have a large amount of household production may need less money than households with smaller amounts of household production. The difference equals the monetary value of household production.[38] A dual-income family usually needs more income than a one-earner family because it has little time for household production. Moreover, there is little time for bargain hunting and housekeeping.

The *contingent valuation* method is based on direct measurement of the willingness to pay (WTP) for a release from housework. The WTP equals the amount at which one is indifferent to doing housework or hiring a worker to do the job.[39] However, in behavioural economics substantial differences have been found between the WTP and the willingness to accept (WTA), i.e., the amount at which a consumer is indifferent to not doing the work or doing the work for pay.[40] This casts doubt on the validity of contingent valuation.

The *market cost method* comprises the monetary valuation of services and goods produced by the household at market prices minus their production costs. For example, the value of home-made curtains equals the price of the ready-made curtains from the shop minus the value of the textile, rail, hooks and gliders. This method is time consuming because all home-produced goods and services have to be evaluated at market prices and all the production costs have to be subtracted.[41]

The *opportunity cost method* focuses on household production time which can be measured by means of time budget surveys. The price of household production time may be fixed at the hourly wage that could be earned by the householders on the labour market. The income foregone by doing household production gives a value for that production. Using this method, the value given to an hour of household production is greater for a doctor than for a nurse.

The *market replacement cost method* is similar to the opportunity-cost method although the price of household production time depends on the wage rates associated with the different activities practised by the household. For example, the cost of one hour's cooking activity is equal to what a cook would be paid for the hour, whereas the price of an hour's child care equals the hourly pay of a child care worker. A problem with this method is that the productivity of a professional may be different from that of a household member. A second problem is that different wage rates may exist, for example in the market sector and in the public sector. A simplified market replacement cost method uses a general wage rate associated with household activities: the wage rate of a housekeeper. Table 13.5 shows the average household production times of men and women in different

Table 13.5 *Household production time and its value per capita for several European countries (1995)*

	Household production (hours per week)			Hourly cost of a house-keeper (Ecu)	Per capita value of annual production (Ecu × 1000)	Percentage of National Income
	Men	Women	Total			
Denmark	11.3	21.7	33.0	10.3	4.75	25
France	18.8	32.9	51.7	8.4	7.08	44
Germany	18.2	33.8	52.0	5.5	5.54	36
Italy	8.4	38.5	46.9	6.4	5.58	38
The Netherlands	15.5	32.4	47.9	5.5	4.86	33
UK	12.0	20.0	32.0	5.9	3.49	26

countries, the hourly cost of a housekeeper and the *per capita* value of household production according to the simplified market replacement cost method.

It appears that on average women spend about twice as much time on household production as men. Furthermore, in Denmark and the UK less time is spent on household production than in France, Germany, Italy and The Netherlands. The monetary value of household production comprises 25–44% of the National Income. This means that actual economic productivity is much larger than the National Accounts indicate.

The valuation of household production is relevant to insurance companies in estimating the cost of domestic help. If the person taking care of the household and the children becomes ill or dies, domestic help has to be found and paid for. In a family with young children, the cost of home help may be very high. Also the valuation of household production is relevant in understanding household decision making in labour supply, do-it-yourself activities and the demand for market substitutes.

13.6 Relationships between economic sectors

The neglect of the household sector in economic accounts causes a biased image of a country's welfare, economic growth and unemployment. It also hampers welfare comparisons across countries. For example, in developing countries the household sector is large as compared to West European countries. It is useful to investigate the relationships between the household sector, the market sector and the public sector, as shown in figure 13.5. The relationships may be either substitutional or complementary. In the case of substitution, household production is replaced by the market

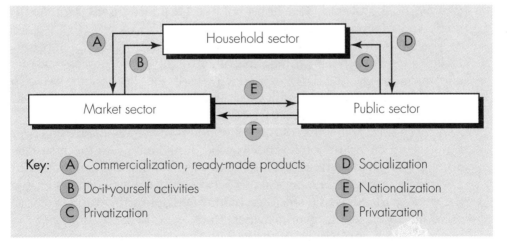

Figure 13.5 *Relationships between three economic sectors*

sector and vice versa. In the case of complementarity the household sector adds value to products and services from the market sector.

Several shifts may occur between the three sectors. The shift from the household sector to the market sector is called commercialization (A), for example by means of ready-made products or commercial services in the area of household production. The reverse shift comprises DIY activities (B). The shift from the household sector to the public sector is called socialization (D), for example the government taking care of the elderly. The reverse shift is privatization (C). The government is giving up tasks to be carried out by the household sector, for example local residents taking care of public gardens. Figure 13.5 shows two kinds of privatization, from the public sector to the household sector (C) and from the public sector to the market sector (F). The government taking over (nationalizing) industry is shift E.

Several theories explain the relationships between paid labour in the market sector and the public sector and the paid or unpaid work in the household sector. In premodern times the household sector dominated the economy. During the industrial revolution the market sector emerged. Later, in Western countries the public sector grew. In the postindustrial era the household sector is important again, because the wages and social premiums in the market sector and the public sector have increased so much that household production becomes profitable again.[42]

Substitution between the sectors is related to the economic situation.[43] In times of prosperity more paid labour is demanded—both in the market sector and in the public sector—than during a recession in which demand for unpaid labour—in the household—is relatively high. For example, during a recession the unemployed become more active in household production, thus partly compensating for the decrease of purchasing power. During an upswing the household sector shrinks because more paid jobs become available. The household sector functions as a *buffer* to compensate for changes in the economic situation.

The stock of capital goods in the household has increased and now includes items such as: washing machines, dryers, food processors, cars and, as a result, the labour productivity of the household has also increased.[44] In earlier days, doing the laundry took a whole day, whereas today it takes a few hours and less effort.

A psychological function of the household is to help employees recover from the strain of the job so they can be 'exploited' again the next day, according to Marxist dogma. More subtly we say that the family has an affective function. The emotional ties between the family members enable the workers to reduce the tensions accumulated during the working day, to relax and to engage in joint activities. Here, we observe a compensation between work and leisure, between effort and relaxation. A satisfactory family life generally will facilitate job achievements.

Table 13.6 *Transfer of products and services between the market and the household sector*

Market sector	←——→	Household sector
Visiting the cinema		Watching television
Playing compact disks		Making one's own music
Buying ready-made clothes		Making one's own clothes
Going to the hairdresser		Doing one's hair
Dining out		Cooking own meals
Buying furniture		Building furniture from a kit
Hiring a party service		Organizing one's own party
Buying a travel package		Organizing travel independently
Desk money transaction		Using an automatic teller machine
Maintenance by a building contractor		Doing one's own maintenance

A two-way exchange of activities occurs between the household sector and the market sector. On the one hand, the increased labour costs in the market sector have stimulated transfer of services to the household sector, for example, DIY products. On the other hand, the increased household income has stimulated transfer to the market sector, for example dining out. The choice between household production and 'farming out' depends on available time, household income and the price of the market service.[45] Table 13.6 shows several examples of exchange of goods and services between the market and the household sector. Several products and services from the market sector are purchased less to the benefit of others. For example, demand for public transport has decreased whereas demand for cars has increased. In general, time consuming and boring household activities are replaced by the market substitutes that offer the greatest relative advantages and efficiency.

To market these goods and services, it is important to know which type of households may be interested in replacing or complementing household production by market substitutes. Which households consider shopping time consuming and boring enough to be interested in teleshopping or home delivery of goods? Are dual-income 'yuppy' families interested in a party service or domestic catering? And which service characteristics make dining out attractive enough to replace a home-made meal?

13.7 Conclusions

Many consumption decisions in the household are taken jointly, making the household an important economic unit. The household offers economic and psychological advantages, in addition to its societal function as a buffer to the labour supply.

The traditional family life-cycle is changing into a greater set of co-habitation varieties. Also parental style may change according to different family patterns, leading to different interactions and decision-making processes in households. Family decision making is influenced by power, cohesion and role patterns. Furthermore, several circumstances influence autonomic or syncratic decision making. In advertising and advisory services, it is important to understand these processes in order to target messages to the right people or groups.

Many products such as kitchen appliances are used as means of production in households. Products, combined with time, effort, knowledge and skills are used in household production, and this comprises a substantial part of economic activity. Household production can be measured in different ways, although this has not been carried out on a regular basis. The neglect of the household sector implies an underestimation of national income.

The value of consumption is not realized by the producer or retailer but by the consumer who uses the products and who derives functional and psychosocial utility from them. The value or utility is not only generated during production and purchase but particularly during product use. Much of the value of products and services from the market sector is added by means of household production.[46]

Notes

1   Popcorn, F. (1992) *The Popcorn Report* (New York: Doubleday).
2   Toffler, A. (1980) *The Third Wave* (New York: Bantam Books).
3   Antonides, G. and Hagenaars, A. J. M. (1989) 'The distribution of welfare in the household' *Papers on Economic Psychology* 81 (Rotterdam: Erasmus University).
4   Kooreman, P. and Wunderink, S. R. (1997) *The Economics of Household Behavior* (London: Macmillan).
5   Public goods should not be confused with publicly consumed goods. See section 14.3.
6   See section 2.3.
7   Tullock, G. and McKenzie, R. B. (1985) *The New World of Economics* (Chicago, IL: Irwin).
8   Based on Wells, W. D. and Gubar, G. (1966) 'Life cycle concepts in marketing research' *Journal of Marketing Research* 3, 355–363.
9   Adapted from Murphy, P. E. (1984) 'Family and household changes: developments and implications' in: Roberts, M. L. and Wortzel, L. H. (Eds) *Marketing to the Changing Household* (Cambridge, MA: Ballinger) 4.
    Murphy, P. E. and Staples, W. A. (1979) 'A modernized family life cycle' *Journal of Consumer Research* 6, 12–22.
10 See section 19.2.
11 Gilly, M. C. and Enis, B. J. (1982) 'Recycling in the family life cycle: a proposal for redefinition' *Advances in Consumer Research* 9, 155–162.
12 See section 3.3.
13 See Carlson, L. and Grossbart, S. (1988) 'Parental style and consumer socialization of children' *Journal of Consumer Research* 15, 77–94.

Moschis, G. P. (1985) 'The role of family communication in consumer socialization of children and adolescents' *Journal of Consumer Research* 11, 898–913. He distinguishes socially-oriented communication (stressing children's obedience) and concept-oriented communication (stressing children's independence).

14 Carlson and Grossbart (1988).
McLeod, J. M. and Chaffee, S. H. (1972) 'The construction of social reality' in: Tedeschi, J. T. (Ed.) *The Social Influence Process* (Chicago: Aldine-Atherton).
Holdert, F. and Antonides, G. (1997) 'Family type effects on household members' decision making' *Advances in Consumer Research* 24, 48–54.
Grossbart, S., Carlson, L. and Walsh, A. (1991) 'Consumer socialization and frequency of shopping with children' *Journal of the Academy of Marketing Science* 19, 155–162.
Foxman, E. R., Tansuhaj, P. S. and Ekstrom, K. M. (1989) 'Adolescents' influence in family purchase decisions: a socialization perspective' *Journal of Business Research* 18, 159–172.

15 Antonides, G. and De Regt, V. (1997) 'Parental styles in 35 countries' *Papers on Economic Psychology* 146 (Rotterdam: Erasmus University).

16 Davis, H. L. and Rigaux, B. P. (1974) 'Perception of marital roles in decision processes' *Journal of Consumer Research* 1, 51–61. In this study, 73 households in Louvain, Belgium, were investigated. Most of the goods in their study were decided upon autonomously.

17 Qualls, W. J. (1987) 'Household decision behavior: the impact of husbands' and wives' sex role orientation' *Journal of Consumer Research* 14, 264–279.

18 From Davis and Rigaux (1974).

19 Belch, G. E., Belch, M. A. and Ceresino, G. (1985) 'Parental and teenage child influences in family decision making' *Journal of Business Research* 13, 163–176.

20 Belch *et al.* (1985); Holdert and Antonides (1997); Foxman, *et al.* (1989).

21 Holdert and Antonides (1997).

22 Davis and Rigaux (1974).
Kirchler, E. (1988) 'Diary reports on daily economic decisions of happy versus unhappy couples' *Journal of Economic Psychology* 9, 327–357.

23 Davis, H. L. (1976) 'Decision making within the household' *Journal of Consumer Research* 2, 241–259.

24 See Foote, N. (1974) 'Unfulfilled plans and unplanned actions' *Advances in Consumer Research* 1, 529–531. Olshavsky, R. W. and Granbois, D. H. (1979) 'Consumer decision making—fact or fiction?' *Journal of Consumer Research* 6, 93–100. Whan Park, C. (1982) 'Joint decisions in home purchasing: a muddling-through process' *Journal of Consumer Research* 9, 151–162. See also section 18.5.

25 Belch *et al.* (1985).
Foxman *et al.* (1989).
Corfman, K. P. and Lehmann, D. R. (1987) 'Models of cooperative group decision-making and relative influence: an experimental investigation of family purchase decisions' *Journal of Consumer Research* 13, 1–13.
Beatty, S. E. and Talpade, S. (1994) 'Adolescent influence in family decision making: a replication with extension' *Journal of Consumer Research* 21, 332–341.

26 Holdert and Antonides (1997).
27 Sheth, J. N. (1974) 'A theory of family buying decisions' in: Sheth, J. N. (Ed.) *Models of Buyer Behavior* (New York: Harper & Row) 17–33.
28 Wagner, W., Kirchler, E. and Brandstätter, H. (1984) 'Marital relationships and purchasing decisions—to buy or not to buy, that is the question' *Journal of Economic Psychology* 5, 139–157.
    Scanzoni, J. and Polonko, K. (1980) 'A conceptual approach to explicit marital negotation' *Journal of Marriage and the Family* 42, 31–44.
    Antonides and Hagenaars (1989).
29 Wagner *et al.* (1984); Scanzoni and Polonko (1980); Antonides and Hagenaars (1989); Qualls (1987).
30 European ethnic minorities are quite different from those in, for example, the USA. In black households in the USA, the wife-dominant role pattern prevails. See also section 20.5.
31 Wagner *et al.* (1984).
32 Belch *et al.* (1985); Foxman *et al.* (1989); Corfman and Lehmann (1987); Beatty and Talpade (1994).
33 Kirchler, E. (1989) 'Diary reports on daily economic decisions of happy versus unhappy couples' *Journal of Economic Psychology* 9, 327–357.
34 Mevissen, J. W. M. (1990) 'What is informal economics?' in: Van Hoof, J. J., Mevissen, J. W. M. and Renooy, P. H. (Eds) *Informal Economics: Marginal Phenomenon or Daily Reality?* (Deventer: Kluwer) 11–19.
35 The black economy is sometimes also called the black circuit or underground economy.
36 Carter, M. (1984) 'Issues in the hidden economy' *The Economic Record* 60, 209–221.
37 See Homan, M. E. (1988) 'The allocation of time and money in one-earner and two-earner families: an economic analysis' (Doctoral dissertation. Erasmus University Rotterdam).
38 Homan (1988).
39 Quah, E. (1987) 'Valuing family household production: a contingent evaluation approach' *Applied Economics* 19, 875–890.
    Kooreman and Wunderink (1997).
40 Kahneman, D., Knetsch, J. L. and Thaler, R. H. (1990) 'The endowment effect, loss aversion, and status quo bias' *Journal of Economic Perspective* 5, 193–206.
41 See also Fitzgerald, J. and Wicks, J. (1990) 'Measuring the value of household output: a comparison of direct and indirect approaches' *Review of Income and Wealth* 36, 129–141.
42 Burns, S. (1975) *Home Inc. The Hidden Wealth and Power of the American Household* (Garden City, NY: Doubleday); Toffler (1980).
43 Kuznets, S. (1946) *National Income. A Summary of Findings* (New York: National Bureau of Economic Research).
44 Gershuny, J. I. (1977) 'Post-industrial society: the myth of the service economy' *Futures* 9, 103–114.
45 Becker, G. S. (1965) 'A theory on the allocation of time' *Economic Journal* 75, 493–517.

46   Baudrillard (1975; 1981) states that only during the very use of goods and
     services is 'sign value' derived.
     Baudrillard, J. (1975), *The Mirror of Production* (St Louis. MO: Telos).
     Baudrillard, J. (1981), *For a Critique of the Political Economy of the Sign* (St
     Louis, MO: Telos).
     See also Van Raaij, W. F. (1993) 'Postmodern consumption' *Journal of
     Economic Psychology* 14, 541–563.

14 REFERENCE GROUPS

14.1 Introduction

> If a hen is fed grain in sufficient amount, she will start eating, eat for a while and then
> stop. If another hen is introduced and is similarly fed, the first hen will start eating
> again, and stop after some time. If a third hen is introduced and fed after the first two
> hens have both stopped eating, the latter will start again.[1]

In the above example, the effect of *social facilitation* is demonstrated, which means facilitation of a particular behaviour by the presence of others. Behaviour can also be hampered by the presence of others. Think about a pianist who knows the musical score very well but gets nervous when there are listeners. The latter is an example of *social inhibition*.

Social facilitation can be caused by several processes. Imitation is considered a social learning process by which an individual acquires new behaviour by observing another individual's behaviour.[2] The mere presence of other people may influence one's behaviour indirectly, as a result of the effect of social norms. Social pressure may be exerted more directly by other people demanding compliance with their norms. Finally, competition may trigger the desire to achieve, thus influencing one's behaviour. These processes may be of different importance in different societies. For example, in Japan social norms are relatively important determinants of social effects, whereas competition may be more important in Western societies. Imitation is relatively important in children's behaviour.

Social facilitation and social inhibition have an effect on both the performance of behaviour and the quality of the performance. So, there are four possibilities, as shown in table 14.1. Other people's behaviour may be a reason for some people to imitate it (the 'bandwagon effect') and it may be relatively easy to do. Furthermore, involvement may increase and because of this, the level of the performance of behaviour may improve. Social

Table 14.1 *Social facilitation and inhibition*

	Performance	Quality of performance	Examples
Social facilitation	Imitation, Bandwagon effect	Co-action effect, Positive public-action effect	Drinking at a bar with friends
Social inhibition	Taboo effect	Negative public-action effect	Buying soft-porn videos

inhibition occurs when others do not implement the behaviour concerned or even reject it. Inhibition is most likely in connection with taboo behaviour, for example visiting a sex club.

Social facilitation is a type of social influence and can be distinguished into a co-action effect and a public action effect.

The co-action effect concerns actions undertaken together with others. It has been found that work, done in the presence of other workers yields a better result than work done alone. A cyclist often rides faster when racing with other cyclists than when riding against the clock. The co-action effect may even occur when the other workers are visibly absent, but it is known that others are doing the same work elsewhere.

The public action effect concerns behaviour in the presence of others. It may result in a positive effect on behaviour shown in the presence of other people who do not perform the same behaviour, for example washing a car in the presence of neighbours. In such a case, people work harder and the quality of their behaviour improves. The positive public-action effect affects motivation, especially for simple behaviour. However, if other people are watching one perform, one may become too nervous to implement the behaviour as planned (stage fright). This is a negative public-action effect. It affects the performer's ability, especially with regards to complex or difficult tasks.

Social facilitation and social inhibition both imply the influence of other people. What causes this effect? There are many different explanations of social influence. In most situations where such effects arise, there is a social group influencing individual behaviour. We talk about a reference group, for example a group of subjects in an experiment, a bridge club, students during a lecture, a political party, or the neighbours. These groups can exert their influence by means of group norms, group values, and spreading information.

The following topics will be discussed in this chapter. Social reference is dealt with in section 14.2 and the social influence on product purchases is explained in section 14.3. The phenomenon of 'opinion leader' and the flow of information among consumers is very important and is described in section 14.4. Section 14.5 discusses social communication—the usual communication between consumers about product purchases and product use. This communication takes place in social networks. Rumours about products are also considered. At the end of this chapter, some implications for marketing are highlighted and conclusions drawn; see sections 14.6 and 14.7.

The objective of this chapter is to provide insight into the processes of social comparison and social influences on consumer behaviour. The most relevant aspects include social communication, observation and imitation of behaviour.

14.2 Social reference

Within many groups, information is exchanged by imitation and observational learning, among others. By this, a group culture is developed implying its own norms and values.

Group norms

Norms concerning perceptions, opinions, attitudes and behaviours frequently develop within a group. A group norm is an opinion about how people should behave in a particular situation. The group norm may either be obligatory—'people should do this'—or less obligatory—'people might do this'. Even without sanctions on judgements that deviate from those of the group, there is still a tendency to conform to group norms. This tendency is illustrated by the experiments conducted by Asch.[3]

Another example concerns experiments on group members' judgements about the distance of a light moving in a dark room.[4] In a dark room it is very difficult to estimate distances because a frame of reference is lacking. Actually, the light in the experiment is stationary. The fact that people still think it moves is based on the autokinetic effect, caused by movements of the eye and the missing frame of reference. When four individuals are left in the room separately, they might say that the light is moving over a distance of, say 3, 5, 1 and 9 cm respectively. However, if they are in the room together and can hear each other's estimates, the reported distances will converge, for example 4, 5, 4 and 5 cm respectively. Apparently, a group norm has developed, which will be taken into consideration by the respondents even when they have to state their judgements separately again.

These experiments illustrate the existence of a social reality, which may deviate from the objective reality, especially if the objective reality is ambiguous. Judgements and opinions concerning subjective issues may be influenced by group norms in a similar way. The motivation to conform to the group norm has to do with the psychological costs and benefits of nonconformism. People may be afraid of being laughed at for having a different opinion—psychological costs in the form of group sanctions—but people also want to maintain their own identity and they want to be more or less unique—psychological benefits. One tries to find a balance between conformism and individuality. Trading off these costs and benefits determines the individual's attitudes and behaviour. The lack of any motivation to conform is indicated as *anomy*. In situations without group affiliation, people often feel 'lost', for example, when alone in an apartment building or in a crowd.

Definition

A reference group is a group of people that an individual refers to for comparison when making judgements about his or her own circumstances, attitudes and behaviour.

The following factors contribute to the influence of reference groups:

- cultural pressure, for example the Japanese culture;
- fear of deviancy—people may have the impression that different behaviour and opinions will be punished;
- involvement with a group, for example 'groupies' following a rock band;
- group power—a sect may exert power by threatening hell and damnation so that the group members comply through fear of the consequences.

For consumer behaviour, group norms are relevant insofar as they influence the requirement for information about products and services, and the consumer's attitudes and purchasing behaviour.

Group values

Some groups represent certain values without exerting any group pressure, for example Greenpeace supporters. One may feel the need to associate with the values of Greenpeace, for example by wearing badges or signing petitions. Some groups represent values which can be shown only by one's appearance or behaviour, for example the rave or rasta subcultures.

Information

Besides norms and values group influences may become apparent by the way members communicate. People who like to try new products, are acquainted with new products or express a new trend, may be considered as information sources for others. These people transmit information about new products and new social trends. Alternatively, people asking for information may be identified as a separate group. Some groups supply information regarding a certain domain, for instance fashion, but not about other domains, for instance household appliances. Thus it is possible to belong simultaneously to a group of information suppliers and to a group of information gatherers.[5]

Figure 14.1 *Conformism*

Group types

Several types of groups may be distinguished that are relevant to consumer behaviour. These groups are described here as opposite or complementary pairing: comparison and normative groups, formal and informal groups, primary and secondary groups, and aspiration and dissociation groups.

Comparison and normative groups

Comparison groups are groups to which the judges themselves do not belong.[6] This reference group serves as a standard for self-assessment. The members may derive aspirations and satisfaction from it. The comparison group may be involved in the individual evaluation of income.[7] On the one hand, people from a lower income group usually look at higher income groups to help determine their aspirations. On the other hand, a comparison with lower income groups may lead to greater satisfaction with one's own income.

The normative group constitutes a source of norms and values for the individual whether or not he or she belongs to this group. Normative authorities such as the church and political parties exert this type of influence.

This influence is called social comparison. Consumers compare themselves with other consumers to see whether they are dressed correctly, are behaving in the right manner and whether they themselves have good taste. People often prefer to compare themselves with those who are just one step higher on the social ladder. The comparison person or group will often change as people climb this ladder. Consciously or unconsciously one hopes to appear favourably as a result of this comparison and to be better off than others.[8]

Formal and informal groups

Formal groups have a clear structure and a well-ordered organization. Such groups may have membership directories, for example the Consumer Union or a trade organization. Consumer organizations are tied by common interests rather than by norms and values. In contrast, trade organizations are frequently committed to setting norms and values so that the group effect plays a part in the mode of conduct. Information plays an important part in these groups. Informal groups have less structure and are often based on friendship or collegiality.

Primary and secondary groups

A primary group consists of members having much personal contact and a strong coherence. The members are motivated to belong to the group and exert much influence on each other's behaviour. Examples are the family, a group of colleagues and the regular customers of a pub. The members of a secondary group also have personal contacts but less frequently so and they exert less influence on each other's behaviour. Examples include professional organizations, unions, and community organizations.

Aspiration and dissociation groups

The aspiration group has a need to imitate the norms, values and behaviour of others, for instance children who aspire to look similar to older friends, or the less well-off who try to imitate the consumption behaviour of the wealthy. Many advertising campaigns by American Express and Diners Club show a life-style which is aspired to by many people. The desired identity is expressed in these campaigns.[9]

In contrast, the dissociation group is motivated *not* to belong to a certain group, for instance young people withdrawing from the older generation or counter-culturists turning their backs on the lifestyle of materialistic consumption.

Mixed groupings

The above-mentioned social group types partly overlap and they are not exhaustive. Frequently, people belong to a group that can be indicated in different ways, for example an informal, primary, dissociative group of homeless people or a formal, secondary group of Visa card owners. Usually one belongs to more than one group at the same time, for example a family (primary group), union (secondary group), and the second team of the soccer club (aspiration group).

Table 14.2 *Social effects on consumption*

	Bandwagon effect	Veblen effect	Snob effect
Behaviour	'Keeping up with the Joneses', imitating the reference group	Conspicuous consumption, showing off	Ownership of scarce goods, high aesthetic quality
Group	Normative group	Comparison group	Aspiration group
Meaning	Conformism	Success and achievement	Distinction, uniqueness
Example	Drinking at a bar with friends	Buying an expensive car	Buying a sea-going yacht

Social effects

Social effects on consumption include bandwagon effects, Veblen effects and snob effects.[10] These three social effects are summarized in table 14.2. They imply materialism and conspicuous consumption, based on a longing for the possession of goods and a desire for showing off, respectively.[11]

The *bandwagon effect*[12] implies that the more people who own a product, the more pressure is exerted on non-owners to purchase the product. Consumers want to 'keep up with the Joneses', they imitate others' behaviour and conformism appears. For instance, when more and more households owned a colour television set, intellectuals could not lag behind and also bought sets. However, if more and more people buy the same products, the individual need for uniqueness may become stronger. Consequently, one may reject the product concerned.

Definition

Conspicuous consumption is the purchase and public display of luxury goods in order to show off to other people.

The *Veblen effect* concerns the purchase of expensive products associated with high status to show off one's wealth and to impress others. This is also called conspicuous consumption. For example, one seeks to impress others by owning an expensive car and a villa.

The *snob effect* implies that products become more attractive the fewer people own them. One may think of antiques, art and sea-going yachts. Such scarce goods—usually of high aesthetic quality—are called positional goods.[13] Their ownership sets people apart from others.

Figure 14.2 *Conspicuous consumption*

14.3 Social influences on purchasing

The visibility of behaviour plays an important part in social influence. Visibility increases the motivation for group conformity and shows the norms more clearly. The status of purchases also plays a part because of the chance to demonstrate success and achievement. However, products already owned by many consumers do not increase status as much, although the brand choice within a product group may yield status. On the basis of these factors, a typology of products has been developed.[14] Visibility is strongly associated with the domain of product use, i.e., public or private use. In public use, the product is observed by others, whereas in private use it is not. The status of product use is strongly associated with the necessity or luxury of the product. Combining these factors, a fourfold product classification emerges: see table 14.3.

Table 14.3 *Examples of public and private use of necessary and luxury goods*[15]

	Public use	Private use
Necessary goods	watch, car	refrigerator, mattress
Luxury goods	golf clubs, skis	pool table, computer game

Public use of necessary goods
Examples of this category are a watch and a car. Because it concerns necessary goods, the influence of the reference group on product choice is small. Because product use is perceived by others, the reference group's influence on brand choice may be large.

Private use of necessary goods
Examples of this category are washing machines, refrigerators, lamps, mattresses and blankets. As it concerns necessary goods, the influence of the reference group on product choice is small. As the products are not usually observed by others, the reference group's influence on brand choice will also be small.

Public use of luxury products
Examples of this category are golf clubs, tennis rackets and skis. As it concerns luxury goods, the influence of the reference group on product choice will be large. As the product use is perceived by others, the reference group's influence on brand choice will also be large. In advertising, reference groups are frequently used for the marketing of luxury goods.

Private use of luxury goods
Examples of this category are a pool table and a computer game. As it concerns luxury goods, the influence of the reference group on product choice will be large. However, as the products are not usually observed by others (at least not by others outside one's home), the reference group's influence on brand choice will be small.
Research shows that the reference group influences the choice of luxury products, but not the choice of necessary goods. Furthermore, the reference group influences the brand choice of publicly used goods, but not the brand choice of privately used goods.

Modes of influence of the reference group

The influence of the reference group on consumer behaviour may be accomplished in different ways: compliance, identification and internalization.

Compliance
The influence of the reference group is subtle, in that consumers do not comply with a detailed choice of a product or brand. Within the group norms, there is usually some freedom for individual choice, for instance the choice of a colour or shape. The following experiment indicates that group

compliance depends on individual opinions rather than on conformity shown by the group members.[16] In groups of four, participants were asked to examine three suits—A, B and C—and to judge which one was the best. The circumstances of the judgement were similar to the Asch experiment,[17] i.e., only one of the four people was a participant. The other three were stooges. In one condition, the first stooge did not seem to be certain but judged suit B to be the best. The second stooge also was in doubt and said: 'I agree with person 1.' The third stooge said that he was uncertain but did not want to be a spoil-sport. He chose B too. So, the three stooges were not really convinced of their preferences and did not choose on the basis of their own judgement. In these circumstances, compliance with the group norm did not occur. The 'real' participants did not judge suit B to be the best as frequently as the stooges did.

This indicates that group pressure as such has no effect, in contrast to the Asch experiment in which the actual judgements of the group members converge. Alternatively, compliance may only involve a superficial agreement with the behaviour of the reference group, without actually leading to compliance with the norms and opinions of that group. One may appear to comply with the group out of opportunism or for convenience sake.

Individualism and group compliance may be considered as two points on a collative stimulus dimension,[18] being attractive in different ways to people with different needs for sensation seeking.[19] Group compliance may be preferred by low sensation seekers, whereas individualism may be preferred by high sensation seekers.

Identification

Identification goes further than compliance. The reference group may be an attractive group one would like to join and identify with. The reference group may also have available a certain know-how one would like to use. In addition, this know-how is reflected by all of the group members. Here too, opportunist considerations may be present. One may attempt to improve one's position by identifying oneself with particular opinions or a particular group, for example a political party.

Internalization

Internalization goes further than identification, because values, opinions and behaviour may be transferred to and accepted by consumers. Eventually, these opinions become their own. This may be the aim of governmental policy, for instance in encouraging the population as a whole to internalize environmental values. Consumers 'believe' in these values and opinions and behave accordingly. In marketing communication, testimonials of declaredly satisfied consumers are frequently used. In such cases, internalization is only suggested.

14.4 Opinion leadership

Although opinion leaders are not the only ones involved in social communication, attempts have been made to identify this group in order to influence their opinions in marketing and consumer advice. The information would then spread from opinion leaders to opinion followers. The publisher of John Naisbitt's *Megatrends*[20] has sent free samples of the book to important decision makers in business. These people read the book and used it in their conversations, thus stimulating others to buy and read the book as well.

Definition

An opinion leader is a person who is knowledgeable about at least one product domain and who is consulted for advice by other consumers, who are sometimes called opinion followers.

People who frequently provide information to others and who are asked for advice by others are called *opinion leaders*. Frequently, they are among the first to know about innovations and new trends and they disseminate this information among others. They may also socially approve other consumers' choices, thus enabling the latter to buy with more confidence. What motives exist for passing on information to others? The following motives have been distinguished.[21]

- *Involvement* appears to be a reason to talk about products. For example, after one has just bought a new CD-player one is enthusiastic to talk about it with others.
- *Self-enhancement* may be a motive. By talking about products one creates the impression of being an expert, having information first-hand. 'Lately, I've discovered a new Thai restaurant. I can recommend it!' or 'The new HD-TV really is an improvement on the old system.' With such conversation, one attracts attention and gains esteem and status. This motive generally results in positive information.
- Giving information to others is a form of *altruism*—an unselfish concern for others. One wishes to help others and to guard them against wrong decisions. For example: 'You should not visit that shop because you will not be served well.' This motive generally results in negative information.
- Sometimes a consumer needs to talk after a purchase to rationalize a decision. If uncertainty after the purchase exists, a certain tension is felt which can be removed by reassurance. *Dissonance reduction* may occur if other people also buy the product.[22] However, significant dissatis-

faction will result in consumers dissuading others from buying the product.

- Some consumers are *interested in advertising* and want to talk about it, especially in the case of unusual advertising, such as the Benetton advertisements and Pepsi commercials.

Opinion leadership may not be the same across consumption domains. An opinion leader in fashion may not be an opinion leader in audio equipment. Although there is some indication that opinion leadership extends to associated areas,[23] several unrelated opinion leadership domains have been distinguished: (1) clothing, food articles and external care products, (2) vacation trips, audio–video equipment and leisure time hobbies, and (3) media.[24] Opinion leaders serve as references for others and are characterized by:[25]

- high involvement with a certain product class, category or domain, e.g., cosmetics;
- high familiarity and expertise with respect to a category or domain, e.g., audio equipment;
- high exposure to mass media, especially in the domain of their interest, e.g., financial services;
- openness to new and different ideas and behaviours, for example fashion;
- sociability and need for social contacts and social activities.

Furthermore, opinion leaders have certain demographic characteristics. Young women are frequently opinion leaders in fashion and movies. Mothers with many children are often consulted about medical issues. Experts such as accountants are consulted about financial matters.

Leaders and followers

Opinion leaders do not exclusively form opinions. Opinion leaders may be opinion followers in other areas and even in the same area they may be both opinion leaders *and* followers. For example, at one time an individual may give away information about a new Mercedes Benz model whereas at a different time the same individual may be given information on a new BMW model. Substantial correlations have been found between opinion leadership and opinion followership in the same consumption domain.[26] It may be more useful to speak of the strength of interest in communication about a certain product group than to speak of leadership and followership.

Opinion leaders frequently participate in extensive social networks in which they spread information and are asked for advice. Table 14.4 shows four possible relationships between opinion leaders and followers. Consumers scoring high on opinion leadership and followership are called socially integrated (1). In certain domains they provide information to

Table 14.4 *Relationships between opinion leadership and followership*[27]

Opinion leadership	Opinion followership	
	Strong	Weak
Strong	1 Socially integrated	2 Socially independent
Weak	3 Socially dependent	4 Socially isolated

Table 14.5 *Examples of relationships between opinion leaders and followers*[28]

	1 Socially integrated (%)	2 Socially independent (%)	3 Socially dependent (%)	4 Socially isolated (%)
Razor blades	14	4	35	47
Detergents	21	6	35	38
Cosmetics	22	4	40	34
Diet food	28	16	21	35
Women's fashions	32	18	18	32
Novels	38	24	8	30
Audio equipment	51	14	25	10

others, whereas in other domains or at different times they ask others for information. Consumers who provide information but do not ask for it are socially independent (2). Consumers who predominantly ask rather than give information are socially dependent (3). Consumers who neither give nor receive information are socially isolated (4). Table 14.4 gives a more realistic picture of the situation than models in which opinion leaders and followers are strictly separated, i.e., ones that suggest that consumers are either opinion leaders or followers.

Since opinion leadership may be different across product groups, the distribution of the population over the four categories in table 14.4 may be different across product groups. In the case of audio equipment, 51% of the consumers appear to be socially integrated. In the case of razor blades, it is only 14%. Table 14.5 shows examples concerning different product domains.

One- and two-step flows of communication

Opinion leaders get to know of new products chiefly via the mass media. They read a lot and keep themselves posted on what is new and what may be purchased. The followers are informed by the opinion leaders, i.e., via social contacts. The theory of the *two-step flow of communication* is based on these two phenomena.[29] The first step (A_1) flows from the mass media. The second step consists of word-of-mouth between consumers themselves. This is shown by the route A_1–A_2 in figure 14.3.

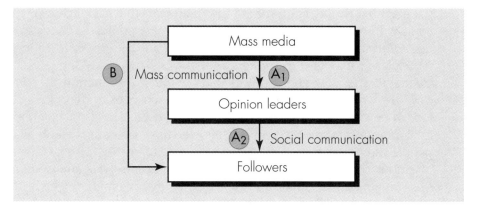

Figure 14.3 *One-step and two-step communication flows*

In fact, the theory of the two-step flow of communication is too simple. Opinion leaders are not the only ones influenced by the mass media, and followers are not only influenced by opinion leaders; they may be influenced by the mass media (route B). Consequently, they may ask opinion leaders for further information (reverse A$_2$). Opinion leaders are important in innovation diffusion. Their positive or negative advice can make or break an innovation.

Advertising may serve as an agenda-setting device. In social communication, opinion leaders may direct the followers' attention to advertising campaigns for new products (A$_2$). Consequently, the followers will pay attention to the innovation (reverse B).

Because mass communication and social communication interact, it may be better to speak of the multi-step flow of communication. Summarizing, the three routes in figure 14.3 may be described as:

- A$_1$–A$_2$, the two-step flow of communication model—an indirect effect of mass communication on followers via the opinion leaders;
- B–A$_2$, a direct effect of mass communication on followers with confirmation by the opinion leaders;
- A$_2$–B, a direct effect of mass communication on followers upon signalling by the opinion leaders.

Several methods exist to assess the nature and the extent of social networks and the quality and amount of their information and influence. The *socio-metric method* amounts to asking people to say which individuals they consult when taking a certain type of decision. In one study, all a piano tuner's customers were asked how they found out about him. As a result referral paths and opinion leaders could be traced down.[30] In this study 4% of those who were referral sources were classified as opinion leaders. Frequently, it suffices to assess the number of social contacts of someone in the neighbourhood, family or at work. It appears that people having mutual contact frequently use the same products and brands.[31] The *method of key informants* means asking people who are the opinion leaders in a particular group. The *self-designation method* means asking people how frequently they talk about products, how much information they give, to how many people they give information, the chances of them being asked for advice and how often they chat with relatives, friends or neighbours.[32] Analogously—to assess opinion followership—one may ask how often people listen, receive information, etc.[33] As a follow-up it is possible to ask questions concerning their personal situations, life-styles and opinions. In this way images of opinion leaders and followers emerge, which may be used in market communication.

14.5 Social communication

Much influence on buying decisions takes place by word-of-mouth, i.e., by communication via the consumer's social network. This is especially true if the following conditions apply:

- Insufficient information is available from other sources, such as consumer magazines and leaflets.
- Information is available but difficult to retrieve or to understand.
- Credibility and reliability of written information may be insufficient, for example the media during the Second World War.
- The consumer is not able to process written information and attempts to acquire oral information from other consumers. In the lower social classes a culture of talking rather than reading prevails.
- Much product information is general and does not apply to specific usage situations. For this reason, consumers in comparable circumstances may serve as reference persons because of their specific product knowledge and experience.
- It can be enjoyable to talk about important and interesting purchases and product experiences such as those relating to a new car or a holiday trip.

Networks and social communication

Frequently, consumers participate in a network of relationships in which they talk about products and services. Networks may include:

- colleagues and business relationships;
- friends and acquaintances in general;
- club members and members of societies;
- family members and relatives;
- neighbours.

Different networks may be used to communicate about different consumption domains. For example, local shopping experiences may be discussed with one's neighbours, whereas financial affairs may be discussed with one's friends.

Lower class individuals mainly go about with relatives, neighbours and colleagues.[34] Because their relatives usually live in the same neighbourhood, their network is local or regional. Products appealing to the lower social classes are often distributed locally by means of promotions and advertising campaigns in regional newspapers and door-to-door magazines.

Higher social classes usually show more diverse life-styles and mainly go about with colleagues and business acquaintances, friends and people who belong to the same clubs and societies. They meet less often with relatives and neighbours. Their network is less regional and extends nationally and sometimes even internationally. Products appealing to the upper classes are often distributed internationally. The media used in advertising campaigns aimed at this group are news magazines, business magazines, controlled-circulation magazines and national newspapers.[35]

How are these networks constructed and how does social communication flow in these networks? A useful distinction is between interpersonal relations—the network—and the information flowing through the network.[36] In figure 14.4, persons A, B and C have strong relationships and form a so-called 'clique', indicated by means of connecting lines. They may be friends living in the same neighbourhood. Persons E, F and G also form a clique. They may be colleagues working at the same firm. In this way, information concerning a new product flows from A to B and D; from B to C and E; and from E to F and G. Figure 14.4 shows these information flows by means of arrows.

Definition

A clique is a group of persons in a social network characterized by relatively intensive communication (strong ties), and similar types of information exchange (homophilous communication).

The relations within the cliques, i.e., between A, B and C and also between E, F and G, are called 'strong ties' because members of a clique exchange much information. The relations between B and E and between A and D are called 'weak ties' in the network because relatively little information is exchanged. However, the relation B–E is an important weak tie because this weak tie transmits information from the A–B–C clique to the E–F–G clique. The weak ties connecting cliques are of great importance for the spread of information in social networks.[37] Person D is socially dependent in this network. D only receives information from A and does not transmit information to others.

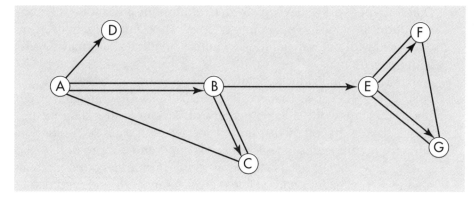

Figure 14.4 *Relationships between individuals in a network*

Weak ties are important for fast word-of-mouth communication in a network. The more weak ties connecting the cliques, the faster the information is spread among the population. Strong ties are also important, as they can encourage opinion formation and changes of attitudes and behaviour.

A strong tie frequently implies a relationship between highly similar individuals. This is called a homophilous relationship. Homophily is the extent of similarity of persons regarding age, gender, education and social status. In general, people prefer to mix with highly similar people. Strong ties frequently are homophilous, whereas weak ties frequently are heterophilous. Heterophily is characterized by dissimilar individuals.

The influence of the reference group is usually homophilous, that is, information is transmitted between groups with similar characteristics, such as age, social class, education and other demographic characteristics. In contrast, heterophilous communication occurs between groups with dissimilar characteristics. The latter frequently yields richer information because heterophilous groups often possess more diverse information than homophilous groups. The effect of heterophilous groups is not usually normative because there is no need to belong to another group. The other group is not a reference group in this case.

A club or society may set up a campaign in which members are asked to bring in new members, for example, book clubs and credit card companies which practise relationship marketing. In this case, members and potential new members may resemble each other. Thus, the success of the campaign will be limited to homophilous cliques. The probability that the campaign is successful outside the cliques is generally low. However, if the members are asked to provide addresses of potential members, the probability of addresses outside the cliques will be considerably higher.

'Word-of-mouth' topics

How much do consumers talk about products and services? How extensive is social communication? In the theory of agenda setting it is assumed that advertising and consumer advice may put topics 'on the agenda' and stimulate conversation between consumers.[38] This conversation may be routine with a social aim, only now and then including product and brand experiences. If product involvement is high, the conversation may turn into a 'real' talk. Then, conversation becomes more intentional, including information exchange and look for a solution to a certain problem.

Information from other consumers ranks second in importance after information from the shops but before advertising in the mass media. Social communication plays a part in important purchases such as a car, home decoration, audio–video equipment and household appliances. It appears that this conversation is positive about the product in most of the cases (59%) and negative in some cases (10%). Negative conversation frequently deals with the replacement of durable goods. Apparently, when consumers feel dissatisfied with a product they want to talk about the replacement product and brand. Thirty per cent of conversations deal with advertisements, usually in a positive sense. For the rest, social talks and intentional conversations appear almost equally relevant. Consumers consider their conversations as an important factor in opinion formation and behaviour.

Vividness of social communication

Social communication is particularly effective because it is generally more vivid than written information. In an experiment, a number of participants were given information about a new PC under four different conditions.[39] Across the conditions, both the information about the PC's quality and the form of the information were varied. The form of the information either concerned a printed text describing the PC or an oral message concerning the PC's quality from the experimenter's assistant. The printed information either described the PC as ranking third, or 17th regarding quality in a comparative product test of 20 PCs. Furthermore, the attributes of the PC were described in positive or negative terms. In the social communication condition, the research assistant said: 'It is the best PC I ever had. It is easy to operate and I did not have any problem with it.' Or the assistant said: 'It is the worst PC I ever had. It is difficult to operate and I have had nothing but problems with it.' Next, the participants evaluated the PC's attributes.

In the positive information conditions, the PC was evaluated considerably more positively when the information was given personally than when the information was provided in print. In the negative information conditions, the PC was evaluated considerably more negatively when the information was given personally as compared with the printed information. So, word-of-mouth communication proved more effective than printed information. The effect was ascribed to the vivid and personal way of presenting information, in contrast to the printed information. These results suggests that a more vivid form of printed information or information given using different media is more effective than a straightforward printed text.[40]

Rumours

Related to the research into conversation about products is the research regarding product rumours.[41] It was investigated how negative and false rumours about products disseminate, such as rumours that a well-known soft drink could remove rust from nails, that a certain detergent would be suitable for glueing PVC tubes and that an international firm's profit would go to a Satanic cult. Sometimes, consumers strongly believed these rumours and behaved accordingly. Rumours are fruitful topics of conversation at parties and social gatherings and provide colour to a dull life. Many rumours are evidently incorrect and are really pure gossip. A producer suffering from a negative and incorrect rumour is advised to disseminate counter-arguments, showing the incorrectness of the rumour. McDonald's in 1990 conducted an advertising campaign against rumours concerning the origin of the meat in its hamburgers, the environmental effects of its packaging, and its methods of personnel management.

14.6 Implications for marketing and consumer advice

If opinion leaders can be identified, marketers and advisors can approach them in several ways. Professional groups, businessmen and clubs are easy-to-reach target groups for marketers. Except for marketing communication, for instance direct marketing, one may approach such a group by means of free samples. Physicians frequently obtain free medicine or medical care samples. Directors and managers sometimes have new models of car placed at their disposal for free. The producer may then attempt to obtain favourable quotes regarding the product from these people, for example in speeches or commercials.

Negative word-of-mouth, for example in the media or in rumours, can strongly influence sales. In the case of calamities like aircraft crashes, and production failures like polluted mineral water,[42] the truth has to be revealed in the media in a convincing way and incorrect rumours have to be denied. If the rumours are correct, this has to be admitted and everything possible has to be arranged to remedy the mistake. The bottles of mineral water have to be recalled from the shops and consumers have to be warned not to consume the product.

Fighting incorrect rumours is not an easy task. Some time ago there was a rumour about the French actress Isabelle Adjani having contracted Aids. Obviously this was likely to diminish her chances of obtaining new contracts. To squash the rumours she went out of public view for several months. The rumour became worse: 'Isabelle has died of Aids.' Finally, she unexpectedly appeared in a popular television show, thus spiking the rumour about her death. In the television programme, a well-known dermatologist declared that Isabelle did not have Aids. This statement squashed the first rumour. This is an example of increasing the rumour in the first place and disproving it more convincingly.[43] However, in general it is ill-advised to increase a rumour.

The number of people having a negative opinion about a product is less important than the number of different groups to which they belong. In an experiment the subjects were presented with the case of a baby that had been burned by an allegedly defective vaporizer.[44] The parents were suing the manufacturer for damage. The subjects were inclined to side with the mother but in the course of the experiment they heard six opinions all blaming the mother for the incident and absolving the firm. The subjects were then asked to express their own judgements. If the opinions were presented as stemming from three groups each consisting of two individuals, the subjects more frequently blamed the mother than if the opinions stemmed from one group of six people. This indicates that a set of independent people has a stronger influence on opinion formation than a group even if it includes the same number of people. The independent opinions appear to create a credible consensus effect.[45]

The results of the experiment could be applied in the case of negative word-of-mouth regarding a product. A number of small organizations expressing negative opinions would be more detrimental to the manufacturer than one large organization. It seems to be in the interest of the manufacturer to keep the number of independent organizations spreading negative word-of-mouth as small as possible. Many firms keep track of consumer complaints and deal with them as effectively as possible. This may help prevent negative word-of-mouth at an early stage.

14.7 Conclusions

This chapter has considered several social influences on consumer behaviour. People try to make a positive impression on others and they tend to behave differently in public than in private. This may be accomplished either by conforming to the behaviour and beliefs of the social environment or by distinguishing oneself from others by one's behaviour, beliefs and possssions. Most consumers select a mixture of conformism and individualism. On the one hand, they conform to establish good relations with other people. On the other hand, they distinguish themselves to feel superior or to obtain admiration from other people.

People do not usually admit that they are influenced by others. Readers of newspapers and magazines are frequently unaware of the extent of the influence these publications exert on them. The social influence is internalized and transformed into personal opinions. The source of the information may even be repressed or forgotten in order to sustain the illusion that an opinion is one's own or that a behaviour took place independently. This is a kind of 'sleeper' effect, a striking example of which is the positive effect of irritating commercials.[46] In this case, the source of the message is forgotten but the message is stored.

Social communication may have underestimated effects. A neighbour's personal and lively experiences with his or her car sometimes outweighs a comparative product test involving a thousand consumers. To the consumer, the averaged and tabularized consumer reports have a less vivid appeal than personal and colourful stories.

A special kind of social communication occurs between opinion leaders and followers. The opinion leader 'translates' the information from the mass media and his or her own experiences with a product for other consumers. Social networks between consumers, in particular their weak ties, are of great importance for the dispersion of information. Recommendations and dissuasions can make or break a new product. Enthusiastic reports by visitors to Disneyland Paris are likely to generate new visits. Social communication then reinforces marketing communication and consumer advice.

Notes

1 D. Katz, 1937, quoted by K.-E. Wärneryd (1988) 'Social influence on economic behavior' in: Van Raaij, W. F., van Veldhoven, G. M. and Wärneryd, K. E. (Eds.), *Handbook of Economic Psychology* (Dordrecht: Kluwer Academic Publishers) 206–248.
2 Bandura, A. (1977) *Social Learning Theory* (Englewood Cliffs, NJ: Prentice Hall).
3 See section 10.5.
4 Sherif, M. (1936) *The Psychology of Social Norms* (New York: Harper and Row).
5 See section 14.4 on opinion leadership.
6 Kelly, G. A. (1952) 'Two functions of reference groups' in: Swanson, G., Newcomb, T. M. and Hartley, E. L. (Eds) *Readings in Social Psychology* (New York: Holt) 410–414.
7 Van Praag, B. M. S., Kapteyn, A. and van Herwaarden, F. (1979) 'The definition and measurement of social reference spaces' *The Netherlands Journal of Sociology* 15, 13–25.
8 Festinger, L. (1954) 'A theory of social comparison processes' *Human Relations* 7, 117–140. Rijsman, J. B. (1974) 'Factors in social comparison of performance influencing actual performance' *European Journal of Social Psychology* 4, 279–311.
9 See section 8.2.

10 Leibenstein, H. (1950) 'Snob and Veblen effects in the theory of consumers' demand' *Quarterly Journal of Economics* 64, 183–207. For the Veblen effect, see the information about Veblen in section 1.3.

11 Mason, R. S. (1981) *Conspicuous Consumption. A Study of Exceptional Behavior* (New York: St Martin's Press). For materialism, see section 23.4.

12 The 'bandwagon' was originally the music wagon in a parade.

13 Hirsch, F. (1977) *Social Limits to Growth* (London: Routledge and Kegan Paul).

14 Bearden, W. O. and Etzel, M. J. (1982) 'Reference group influence on product and brand purchase decisions' *Journal of Consumer Research* 9, 183–194.

15 Bearden, W. O. and Etzel, M. J. (1982).

16 Venkatesan, M. (1966) 'Consumer behavior: Conformity and independence' *Journal of Marketing Research* 3, 384–387.

17 Section 10.5.

18 Collative stimuli are unexpected, new and surprising stimuli. The word 'collative' means that two or more aspects are brought together for the first time ('newness').

19 See section 9.2.

20 Naisbitt, J. (1984) *Megatrends. The New Directions Transforming our Lives* (London: Macdonald & Co, Futura).

21 Engel, J. F., Blackwell, R. D. and Miniard, P. W. (1989) *Consumer Behavior* (Chicago: The Dryden Press), 6th edition.

22 See section 9.5.

23 King, C. W. and Summers, J. O. (1970) 'Overlap of opinion leadership across product categories' *Journal of Marketing Research* 7, 43–50.
Summers, J. O., and King, C. W. (1971) 'Overlap of opinion leadership: a reply' *Journal of Marketing Research* 8, 259–261.

24 Myers, J. H. and Robertson, T. S. (1972) 'Dimensions of opinion leadership' *Journal of Marketing Research* 9, 41–46.
Antonides, G. and Asugman, G. (1995) 'The communication structure of consumer opinions' *European Advances of Consumer Research* 2, 132–137.

25 Chan, K. K. and Misra, S. (1990) 'Characteristics of the opinion leader: a new dimension' *Journal of Advertising* 19, 3, 53–60.

26 Antonides and Asugman (1995).

27 Schiffman, L. G. and Kanuk, L. L. (1987) *Consumer Behavior* (Englewood Cliffs, NJ: Prentice-Hall) 3rd edition, table 16.4, p. 574.

28 For more details see Schiffman and Kanuk (1987), table 16.5, p. 575.

29 Lazarsfeld, P. F., Berelson, B. R. and Gaudet, H. (1948) *The People's Choice* (New York: Columbia University Press).

30 Reingen, P. H. and Kernan, J. B. (1986) 'Analysis of referral networks in marketing: methods and illustration' *Journal of Marketing Research* 23, 370–378.

31 Reingen, P. H., Foster, B. L., Johnson Brown, J. and Seidman, S. B. (1984) 'Brand congruence in interpersonal relations: a social network analysis' *Journal of Consumer Research* 11, 771–783.

32 Flynn, L. R., Goldsmith, R. E. and Eastman, J. K. (1994) 'The King and Summers opinion leadership scale: revision and refinement' *Journal of Business Research* 31, 55–64.

33 Antonides and Asugman (1995).

34 Komarovsky, M. (1961) 'Class differences in family decision-making on expenditures' in: Foote, N. (Ed.) *Household Decision Making* (New York: New York University Press) 255–265.
Coleman, R. P. (1983) 'The continuing significance of social class to marketing' *Journal of Consumer Research* 10, 265–280.

35 A controlled circulation magazine is distributed (often for free) among individuals meeting certain criteria, such as belonging to a certain profession. Examples are the house magazine *Expression* of American Express and magazines aimed at members of professional institutions or societies.

36 Johnson Brown, J. and Reingen, P. H. (1987) 'Social ties and word-of-mouth referral behavior' *Journal of Consumer Research* 14, 350–362.

37 Granovetter, M. S. (1973) 'The strength of weak ties' *American Journal of Sociology* 78, 1360–1380.

38 McCombs, M. E. (1981) 'The agenda-setting approach' in: Nimmo, D. D. and Sanders, K. R. (Eds) *Handbook of Political Communication* (Beverly Hills, CA: Sage) 121–140.

39 Herr, P. M., Kardes, F. R. and Kim, J. (1991) 'Effects of word-of-mouth and product-attribute information on persuasion: an accessibility-diagnosticity perspective' *Journal of Consumer Research* 17, 454–462.

40 For the liveliness effect: Taylor, S. E. and Thompson, S. C. (1982) 'Stalking the elusive "vividness" effect' *Psychological Review* 89, 155–181.

41 Kapferer, J.-N. (1990) *Rumors. Uses, Interpretations, & Images* (New Brunswick, NJ: Transaction Publishers).

42 In 1990, benzene was detected in bottles of Perrier mineral water in the USA. This resulted in the recall of 180 million bottles. This is one of the largest product recalls in history.

43 See section 21.4.

44 Wilder, D. A. (1977) 'Perception of groups, size of opposition, and social influence' *Journal of Experimental Society Psychology* 13, 253–268.

45 The consensus effect is one of the effects in attribution theory. It means that the same information obtained from different source is considered believable.

46 Pratkanis, A. R., Greenwald, A. G., Leippe, M. R. and Baumgardner, M. H. (1988) 'In search of reliable persuasion effects: III. The sleeper effect is dead. Long live the sleeper effect' *Journal of Personality and Social Psychology* 54, 203–218.

INNOVATION 15

15.1 Introduction

Four out of every five new products introduced on the market fail and are taken off the market several months after their introduction.[1] Usually, this means a substantial financial loss to the producer. However, product innovation is vital for producers to remain ahead of competitors and to keep their brands and ranges up to date. How can the risk of failure be minimized? Usually, innovations are considered as useful and necessary developments of the supply of goods and services. But is each innovation really useful and necessary when considered from the consumer's point of view? Is it not the case that consumers are frequently presented with quasi-innovations?

What should consumer researchers pay attention to with regard to the introduction of innovations? Innovations not only include new products and services, but also ideas and behaviours, i.e., culture. Innovations differ in their degree of newness (see section 15.2). A completely new product in a sense causes a turning point or discontinuity in consumer behaviour.

Adoption is the process by which consumers or households decide to accept or reject a new product or behaviour (see section 15.3). Adoption can be distinguished from diffusion—the penetration of a new product into the market (see section 15.4). Diffusion is based on adoption by individual consumers and is studied at the sociological and geographical (macro) level. Consumers differ in the degree and speed of new-product adoption. For this reason, section 15.5 deals with a classification of consumers regarding the adoption of innovations. In section 15.6 some conclusions are drawn.

The aim of this chapter is to clarify the diffusion and the adoption of innovations—new products and services. This concerns both the process of diffusion and the characteristics of products, services and consumers in relation to the diffusion and adoption of innovations.

15.2 Characteristics of innovations

Innovations can be described on the continuity–discontinuity dimension and as purchase-related or behaviour-related. Table 15.1 shows the possibilities.

The continuity or discontinuity of an innovation is an important dimension. It is a dimension on which the newness of the innovation can be graded. A *discontinuous* innovation concerns a completely new product that offers different possibilities from existing products. New functions can be performed and new benefits can be obtained. Consumer behaviour is really changed by this. Television, the fax machine, the personal computer, electronic mail and contraceptive pills are all examples of 'real', i.e., discontinuous, innovations.

Compared with the black-and-white television, colour television is a *semi-continuous* (or dynamic continuous) innovation. A semi-continuous innovation performs the same functions as the old product in a better way and offers important quality advantages. Semi-continuous innovations can perform existing functions considerably faster and more effectively, for example, mobile telephones, automatic teller machines, and electric toothbrushes.

A detergent that contains a new additive or is put in different packaging constitutes a *continuous* innovation. Consumer behaviour does not really change. Sometimes consumers hardly notice the difference from the old product, for example, high-speed trains, wide-screen television, and ABS brakes.

Another useful distinction concerns purchase-related and behaviour-related innovations.[2] In the area of energy saving, purchase-related ways of energy saving include, for instance, home insulation, buying an energy-saving heater or clock-thermostat. A purchase-related innovation, for example solar energy panels, has money costs, but usually requires little adaptation of consumer behaviour. A behaviour-related innovation is energy saving by turning the thermostat down when absent or at night.

Table 15.1 *Examples of innovation types*

	Purchase-related	Behaviour-related	Cognitive schema
Continuous	Improved detergent	Energy saving	Assimilation
Semi-continuous	Colour television	Salt-free diet	Assimilation/ accommodation
Discontinuous	Personal computer	Changed life-style	Accommodation

Behaviour-related innovations require constant attention.

In the area of health, behaviour-related ways of keeping fit are more difficult because time and again one has to decide, for example, whether to eat or to abstain from fatty food. Behaviour-related health innovations, for example 'jogging' in the 1980s, usually do not cost money but they are associated with behavioural costs—time, effort and exertion to perform the new behaviour.[3]

Discontinuous innovations may elicit high consumer involvement and sometimes also considerable resistance. They are turning points in the development of consumption. In postmodern times more and more discontinuous—and for this reason unpredictable—changes will appear. Discontinuous innovations spread with difficulty but may have far-reaching consequences for consumers and society. A discontinuous innovation demands accommodation of the consumption schema since a new category and a new behaviour are involved.[4] The ownership of a personal computer for most consumers implies a discontinuous behaviour change. It is a break with the past and it leads to important changes of possibilities and behaviour.

Continuous innovations demand assimilation and little adaptation of behaviour. A new packaging, a new product additive, a new colour or taste are examples of continuous innovations. Assimilation implies categorizing the innovation in an existing category of products and behaviours, possibly including a new characteristic.[5] Lowering the thermostat a few degrees is

Figure 15.1 *Continuous innovations*

a continuous behavioural change. It demands attention, assimilation and perhaps a warm sweater. Driving in a more economical way also implies a continuous innovation.

Innovation characteristics

The following characteristics of innovation facilitate the adoption and diffusion of innovations.[6] These are characteristics and benefits as perceived by the consumer.

Compatibility refers to the degree of fit of the new product with the consumer's life-style. Continuous innovations are often compatible with existing behaviours but the relative advantages may be negligible. For example, home insulation is compatible with a consumer life-style of comfort and concern for health. Clairol in the USA introduced a new shampoo 'A touch of yoghurt'. This became a failure. People found the idea of yoghurt in their hair to be in disagreement with their norms and values, even if it was good for the hair. Compatibility may also depend on one's need for variety, as variety seekers will adopt incompatible innovations relatively easily.

The perceived financial, physical and social *risks* of an innovation also determine the speed of its adoption and diffusion. New products, deemed to be too expensive, dangerous to one's health or not accepted by others, spread with difficulty or do not spread at all among consumers. Genetically manipulated food is not yet considered safe by the general public. Activities such as bungee jumping—jumping from a high level tied to an elastic rope—will never become widespread throughout society simply because of the perceived risk. Possibly the objective risk of skiing down a hill is greater than that of bungee jumping. Yet, more people are skiing than tying themselves to elastic ropes.

Visibility is especially important to the familiarity and social acceptability of an innovation. New fashions, e.g., body piercing, new cosmetics and new cars are highly visible whereas energy saving heaters are fairly invisible. Solar panels and windmills for electricity generation are highly visible innovations. Noticeable innovations will spread faster than invisible ones. This explains why double-glazing has become popular faster than cavity wall insulation for home energy saving. The tazos rage[7] constitutes an example of visibility, since tazos are used in children's play and for exchange. Although the consumption of crisps may occur privately, the tazos—packed within the crisp bags—connect it to the public scene.

The *relative advantage* of an innovation comprises its advantage compared to existing products. Assuming that it costs effort to adopt a new product, the new product should provide sufficient advantages so that its benefits are greater than the behavioural costs. Automatic teller machines (ATMs) are a success for banks. It would seem that consumers consider not being committed to the bank's opening hours and the option of getting cash at any time as important advantages. Other examples include fax and email.

If an innovation *fulfils a latent need*, the probability of success is high. In this case, the product offers more than just a relative advantage; it offers a completely new possibility to satisfy an existing need. Usually this concerns a discontinuous innovation such as the answering machine or contraceptive pills.

Trialability refers to the degree to which an innovation can be tried without any risks and obligations. A trial subscription to a weekly magazine may persuade people to try the product without committing themselves and they can then decide later whether or not to subscribe. Lincoln introduced the 'Town Car' in the USA in collaboration with Budget Rent-a-Car. Consumers could rent this car at a moderate rate. For many consumers, this experience gave them a reason to buy a Lincoln Town Car. Trialability seems to make use of the endowment effect.[8]

The *complexity* comprises the degree to which an innovation can be easily understood or used. A product requiring much explanation and which is difficult to handle will have a long period of adoption or will be rejected by many consumers. The personal computer and the Internet are examples of such complex innovations. Many computers given away by firms to their employees end up unused because people do not accept the behavioural costs of learning how to use the equipment or the software.

Large-scale *availability* speeds up the diffusion of an innovation. This facilitates the conversion of buying intentions into buying behaviour. For this reason, large-scale distribution is important to producers of fast-moving convenience goods. With fast-moving consumer goods, this boils down to having the products on the shelves of all main supermarket chains. Widescreen television sets still suffer from a lack of programmes broadcast in the widescreen format.

The *expense* of an innovation may hamper its diffusion. In order to use electronic bank services, consumers have to possess a PC, modem and software. There may be additional charges in the form of a subscription fee. This cost dissuades many consumers from using these services. In this case a low subscription fee is necessary to encourage enough participants to make electronic banking a success (penetration pricing). The latter is not true for the development of the Internet. The world-wide scale of the Internet guarantees its success. However, consumers still have to buy a modem and pay subscription fees.

For other innovations—especially in the early stage—a high price is set. In this way the manufacturer can earn back the costs of research and development. This is called market skimming. The high introduction price makes the product exclusive and because of this it becomes attractive to some people.[9] The manufacturer knows that a group of consumers exist who are so interested in the innovation that they are willing to pay the high

Figure 15.2 *Availability*

price. The first videocassette recorders were very expensive, difficult to use and had many failures in their early lives. However, for a small group of innovators, this was not an objection to experimenting with the equipment. Videocassette recorders have since become cheaper and—because of this—more attractive to large groups of consumers.

An effective *marketing campaign* is necessary to promote the innovation. The characteristics of the innovation have to be communicated to the target market. Both the relative advantage and the possible risks have to be explained. For example, how about the compatibility of the innovation? A complex innovation requires much explanation and demonstration. And how and where is the innovation available?

From the above, it should be clear that there are four key ingredients in the marketing mix that are important in the case of an innovation. These are known as the four Ps:

- **Product** or service—the innovation proper, its relative advantage, risk, complexity, visibility and compatibility;
- **Price**—low or high introduction price of the innovation;
- **Place**—distribution and availability of the innovation;
- **Promotion**—marketing communication to explain the relative advantages with regard to other products and other relevant characteristics.

15.3 A model of adoption

Adoption is an individual, psychological (micro) process of consumers of trying and repeatedly buying a product. For convenience goods, the criterion is usually repeat buying and brand loyalty. For durable goods which are purchased with an interval of several years, the criterion of adoption is the first purchase. The forces against adoption are resistance to change and constraints such as insufficient income.

Definition

Adoption of an innovation is the psychological process of trying and repeatedly buying a new type of product.

The adoption of innovations can be shown by means of the general model in the first chapter (figure 1.4). In figure 15.3 the general model has been applied to innovations. This model includes the factors applicable to the adoption or rejection of an innovation. Regarding a discontinuous innovation most factors will play a part; in the case of a continuous innovation, perhaps only a few factors.

Block A includes the cultural environment. In a (post)modern environment, innovations will be adopted more easily than in a traditional culture. Cultures placing a high value on innovativeness, such as in the USA, will tend to adopt innovations more easily than for example in the UK or France. In a modern culture, the innovators are often opinion leaders, too, transmitting information to other consumers. Furthermore, innovations are more easily accepted if they are compatible with the prevailing life-style. Energy-saving equipment is more easily accepted than energy-saving behaviour.

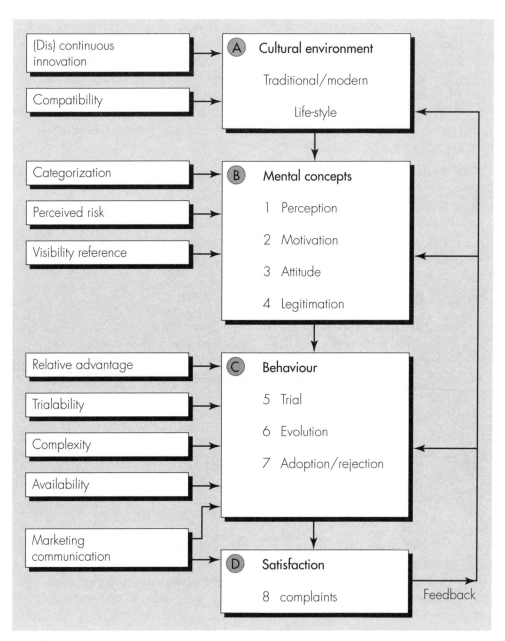

Figure 15.3 *Model of adoption of innovations*

Cultural barriers against the introduction of new products may elicit strong resistance. The example of yoghurt shampoo has already been mentioned. Black & Decker attempted to introduce DIY equipment in Latin-America. However, in these Latin-American countries consumers who can afford drills and working-benches do not work with their hands. Whereas the labourers cannot afford the Black & Decker products.

Many errors are made with respect to cultural norms and language in marketing communication. Brand names sometimes have less desirable connotations in different languages and cultures, such as Schwarzkopf shampoo and the Chevrolet Nova.[10]

Block B includes mental concepts. This concerns perception, motivation, attitude and legitimation. Block C includes behavioural factors—trying, evaluating, adoption and rejection. Finally, block D includes satisfaction and eventual complaints. Satisfaction has a feedback effect on behaviour, mental concepts such as motivation and attitude, and on life-style.

The numbers in figure 15.3 agree with the numbering of the concepts in this section.

1 Perception

In the perceptual stage, consumers categorize the innovation as continuous or discontinuous. It is important that consumers know the product, not only the brand name but also the benefits of the new product as compared with existing products. Also, consumers will have to become familiar with the innovation by means of advertising, advice and editorials in newspapers and magazines, particularly the early adopters, or by the observation of other consumers using the product—particularly the late adopters. In these stages, the issues of selective attention and selection retention (memory), are important. They are barriers to consumer perception because of which new products and product improvements may be incorrectly categorized and not perceived or recalled. In addition, consumers do not always correctly assess the important advantages of a new product or the major drawbacks of an old one.

2 Motivation

In the motivational stage, consumers have to be prepared for a behavioural change. For discontinuous innovations this may be very difficult or may have far-reaching consequences, for example, the introduction of the contraceptive pill. If the new product has a clear advantage over existing products and behavioural change is hardly necessary, the probability of fast adoption is maximised. The relative advantage of an innovation may also depend on the consumer's level of satisfaction with existing solutions.[11] For continuous innovations, in these stages habit formation and brand loyalty are important. To what extent are consumers committed to existing habits and brands and to what extent can they break with these habits and brand loyalty to change to the new product?

3 Attitude

In the attitude stage consumers form an opinion about the innovation. Is it really worthwhile? What advantages does it offer? Is the innovation really better than traditional alternatives? At this stage, rumours may prevent the development of a positive attitude.[12] Beliefs about the advantages of the new product are especially important at this stage. For a new technology is at stake rather than the change of values or weights regarding product characteristics. Consumers may ask themselves if they are able to judge the innovation adequately and to actually use the new product. Consumers may believe that they cannot do this (illusion of impotence). According to the elaboration likelihood model an innovation may be adopted under these circumstances if consumers rely on cues, for instance the environment in which the product is demonstrated such as a fashion show.[13]

4 Legitimation

Legitimation describes the justification of consumer purchases to other persons, the normative groups or agencies. Many intellectuals in the 1970s wondered whether it was acceptable to have a colour television set. Now, this is no longer an issue. It has been completely legitimized. However, is it still acceptable to watch black-and-white? Some consumers exclusively buy products that fit the prevailing social norm. Is it acceptable to go on holiday to South Africa? This is an example of a question of legitimation. It concerns what others say or do.

Legitimation depends on the environment and on people who approve or disapprove of the innovation. Disapproval by others causes a delay or even a complete rejection of the new product. At the outset, the use of the contraceptive pill was strongly dependent on the approval by parents and friends. The Roman Catholic church is an opponent of contraceptives and for this reason the pill has not been legitimized for some people.

Legitimation may be less important for privately consumed products than for publicly consumed goods. For example, individuals need not admit to using contraceptives and no one will know about it.[14]

5 Trial stage

In the trial stage it is how the consumers feel about trying the product that is important. Consumers may simply observe others who are trying the product.[15] However, one's own experience is a stronger source of learning than the observation of others. A new detergent or a new soft drink may be tried easily; trying a new home is not. In the latter case, a show house may give an impression of what the house will look like. A new car may be leased before it is bought. Sometimes hire purchase is possible: the product is rented but may still be purchased with the deduction of the paid instalments. A second-hand product may also serve for inspection. If the product suits, a new brand may be purchased. Computer software is often copied illegally for people to try it out. Only if it is useful will people buy the software; sometimes they never do. By way of introduction, many software dealers offer cut-down legal versions of the program for free—'lite' versions which may then tempt the consumers to buy the full program.

In the trial stage, the confidence of the consumer plays an important part: do I use the product correctly? Can I operate the product well? Can I actually judge the benefits of the product?

6 Evaluation stage
After trying out an innovation, the affective component becomes important in the evaluation stage. Global and specific evaluations of the new product play a part in communication between actual and potential users. Frequently, a new product only succeeds after a positive evaluation from a number of consumers. In the evaluation stage, uncertainty may elicit resistance. Can I judge the value of the product properly? Have I really obtained the advantages promised? Am I satisfied with the product?

7 Adoption stage
The stage of adoption or rejection is the crucial point of the process. Is the innovation adopted incidentally or permanently? For convenience goods the percentage of repeat purchases is the criterion of a successful innovation. A high percentage of repeat purchases indicates habitual behaviour. Another criterion is the time-lapse between the introduction and the adoption of the innovation.

8 Satisfaction
In the stage of satisfaction or dissatisfaction, adaptations are made following the adoption or rejection of the innovation. One such adaptation is the reduction of cognitive dissonance. The life-style has to be adapted and the alternatives selected or rejected have to be re-evaluated. A feedback to earlier stages of the process occurs.

Resistance against adoption

Resistance against the adoption of innovations may exist because of cultural and social barriers. Failures in the marketing of new products, especially communication failure, may elicit resistance, too. At each stage of the model in figure 15.3, certain types of resistance may counteract adoption and diffusion of an innovation. These types of resistance have already been discussed for stages 1–6.

Microwave oven
An example is the introduction of microwave ovens several years ago. Imagine that a family discovers the existence of these ovens and the (perceived) differences with conventional ovens. Both partners are working and on weekdays there is little time for cooking. So the family is motivated to find out more about these time-saving ovens. Gradually the partners form an attitude toward the advantages of a microwave oven. How much time do they save? How large are these ovens? Would one fit in the kitchen?

How are they operated? Is the radiation harmless? Information is obtained and other people's opinions sought (legitimation). Perhaps the family can use the microwave oven for a week on trial or maybe they can have dinner with friends who already own a microwave oven (trial stage). After the trial stage, one can evaluate the microwave oven properly. Are the benefits large enough? Is the microwave oven too expensive? Does the food prepared in the oven taste good? Is it acceptable that quiches are not crusty? After the purchase they verify how often they use the microwave oven and how satisfied they are with it. They even adapt their lives and start to cook using microwave dishes with recipes from a microwave cookbook. They discover that they can defrost deep-frozen products very easily in the microwave oven.

15.4 Diffusion process

In the process of diffusion, groups of consumers are identified according to the speed of adopting an innovation. This also applies to cultural change. The following categories of adopters can be identified according to the speed of adoption of innovation:[16]

- Innovators, 2.5% of the market;
- Early adopters, 13.5% of the market;
- Early majority, 34% of the market;
- Late majority, 34% of the market;
- Laggards, 16% of the market.

In figure 15.4 the distribution of these groups is assumed to be normal. The borders between the groups lie one and two standard deviations from the mean respectively. As a consequence of the differences in speed of adoption, a cumulative frequency curve emerges showing the ultimate market share and the speed with which it is reached: see figure 15.5. In this figure it is assumed that after some time all consumers adopt the innovation, implying 100% penetration of the total market. The steepness in the shaded area indicates the success of the innovation. If the adoption in the shaded area drops less steeply, the innovation is probably less successful. The market potential may be considerably less than the total market, so penetration of the total market may be substantially less than 100%.

The spread of an innovation depends on the degree of social imitation or personal influence, the distribution of personal opinions about the

Definition

Diffusion of an innovation is the large-scale process of penetration of a new type of product on the market.

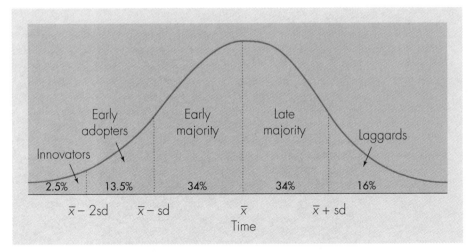

Figure 15.4 *Distribution of adopter categories*

innovation in the population and the learning processes preceding the adoption of the innovation. Different assumptions regarding these factors lead to different shapes of the diffusion curve (a normal or an exponential curve).[17]

Figure 15.5 is similar to the product life-cycle curve. This shows the connection between the adoption and penetration of a product.[18]

In the above-mentioned categories, social networks are very important, especially for the early adopters and early majority. The diffusion process may be started off by a producer in the first stage by means of product advertising and free samples. In the second stage of the process, social communication among consumers in a network becomes more important.[19]

Critical mass

The theory of critical mass states that some innovations will succeed only if there are enough adopters. A critical mass of users is necessary for the innovation.[20] An example is the introduction of the Internet. The Internet only becomes an interesting medium if there are many users. By enlarging the scale, the price goes down and more services can be offered. This can be seen as a 'chicken-and-egg' problem. For consumers, the Internet becomes interesting only if there is plenty of information available. For information suppliers, the Internet becomes interesting only if there are enough users.

The early adopters of such an innovation contribute much to the supply of a public good, whereas the majority of the population contributes little or nothing at the start. The early adopters of the Internet enjoy few immediate advantages from their adoption. The only advantage is that they have information at their disposal that other people do not have, for

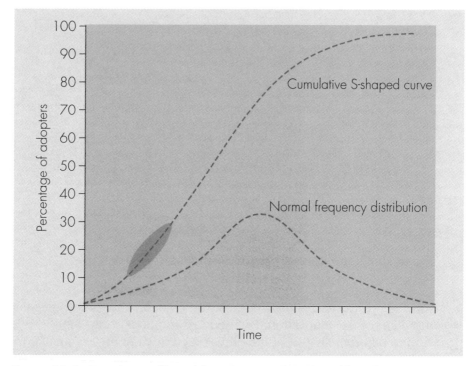

Figure 15.5 *Cumulative effect of the adoption of an innovation*

Figure 15.6 *Private or public?*

example on-line stock prices. A disadvantage is that at this stage few services are offered on the Internet. In addition, few opportunities for communication with other users are available. The advantages to early adopters emerge if the early majority adopts the Internet. The critical mass should not be reached too late, otherwise the early adopters may give up.

15.5 Adopter characteristics

Although most consumers will go through all the stages of the model shown in figure 15.3, great differences in the speed of this process exist. Some consumers will never adopt an innovation; sometimes they will even reject it.

The perception of an innovation may differ strongly across consumers. Innovators and early adopters learn more quickly about the availability of a new product on the market than the late majority and the laggards. Also, early adopters tend to know more characteristics and benefits of new products than the late majority and the laggards.

Innovators and early adopters[21]
Innovators distinguish themselves by their sense of adventure, their sensitivity to new things and their ability to think autonomously and to acquaint themselves with new developments via the mass media. Innovators and early adopters like to try new things. They are more likely to see the positive aspects of new products.

Definition

An innovator is a consumer who belongs to the 2.5% segment of the population that adopts new products first.

Innovators and early adopters are not necessarily interested in all product categories. In fact, this is impossible. Some are innovators in the domain of fashion, others know everything about cars, motorbikes or computers. They are innovators in a specific domain of goods and services. Their innovative behaviour is domain-specific. In fact, evidence suggests that involvement with the product category is a more important determinant of new product adoption than innovativeness as a personality characteristic.[22]

To the producer of a new product, the early adopters (13.5%) supply a substantial part of the return on investment. In addition, the adoption of the innovation by the early adopters is a sign of the success of the innovation (see the shaded area of figure 15.5).

Much research has been conducted into the characteristics of early adopters and innovators. The main attributes may be summarized as follows.

Socioeconomic characteristics
It appears that consumers who are highly educated and have a high socioeconomic status, and people who are young and upwardly mobile, are more likely to adopt an innovation. Innovators and early adopters also earn a higher than average income. The high income is needed because of the typically high price of innovations and the opportunity cost of failure. Large households are more likely to adopt an innovation than small households.

Social behavior
Early adopters usually have an extended network of social contacts and they relatively often take part in meetings and social groups. Frequently, they are opinion leaders for other people.[23] Furthermore, they have a cosmopolitan attitude and are interested in world news.

Personality characteristics
Summarizing, we may state that consumers with high aspirations and achievements tend to be innovators and early adopters. These are people who want to achieve something, who have broad interests and are, cosmopolitan with many social contacts. Intelligence, rationality, abstract and autonomous thinking and a positive attitude regarding education appear to have a positive effect on the adoption of innovations. Innovators and early adopters in general are more disposed to change and more tolerant of uncertainty. A commercial orientation and a positive attitude to credit is favourable to the adoption of an innovation. Possibly the innovation has to be purchased on credit.

Perception of new products
Innovators and early adopters perceive more benefits and less problems of new products. In general, they state more positive judgements concerning the characteristics of an innovation as listed in this chapter.

Strong communicators
The *communication behaviour* of innovators and early adopters includes social contacts and media usage. Integration in the social network appears to be positively linked to early innovation adoption. Early adopters look actively for information themselves. Innovators and early adopters obtain more information from the mass media and from their social contacts than the majority. Innovators and early adopters also are opinion leaders more often than average.

Heavy users

The *purchase and consumption behaviour* of innovators and early adopters is different. Frequently, they are heavy users of the product. Consumers buying a new type of telephone frequently have high telephone bills. Innovators and early adopters may be heavy users but in general they are not brand loyal. A new innovation soon draws their attention.

Differences between innovators and early adopters

Sometimes innovators are singular fanatics, having extended knowledge about computers, motorbikes, fashion or whatever. Innovators are not necessarily opinion leaders. In a traditional culture, innovators are outsiders and they may have little influence on the majority. In postmodern culture the chances are greater that innovators are also opinion leaders.[24]

Early adopters are more integrated in social networks and respected by their environment. Early adopters are often opinion leaders, having strong influence on the 'followers' who show much interest in the opinions of the opinion leaders.

Early majority

The early majority includes many followers. They wait for the experiences of the early adopters and then decide whether or not to try the product. By the adoption of an innovation by the early majority the critical mass for the success of the adoption may be attained.

Late majority

The consumers of the late majority are the sceptics. They do not need the innovation that much. Their media usage is less than average and they are less integrated in social networks. Finally they will adopt the product, especially if the critical mass works to their disadvantage. If most consumers own a television set and important information is spread via this medium, the late majority has to adopt television, although they might be reluctant to do so.

Laggards

In general, the laggards have a traditional and conservative attitude. For them, existing norms and values are difficult to break. In many cases they will never adopt the innovation. The term 'laggard' in some cases is misplaced. In part they may be active rejectors of the innovation. For instance, they are frequently opponents of contraception. This explains why an innovation seldom reaches 100% of its potential market.

For the late majority and the laggards income restrictions may also play a part. For this reason, these consumers are forced to wait until the purchase of the innovation becomes cheaper or they can buy a second-hand product.

15.6 Conclusions

This chapter considered the diffusion of innovations. The characteristics of innovations enabling and speeding up adoption and diffusion have been examined. The adoption and diffusion of discontinuous innovations is relatively difficult and fundamental for consumers. In general, adaptation of behaviour and lifestyle is needed for such a discontinuous innovation.

Consumers differ in the speed of adopting an innovation. For this reason, it is sensible to direct marketing and advisory services to innovators and early adopters in the first place. These groups include many opinion leaders.

Innovators may be fanatics who deal with the adoption because of their hobby. They are prepared to invest much effort and time in it. They do not mind spending hours solving the problems arising in the early stages of an innovation themselves. The first PC users were fully fledged programmers who were motivated to invest much knowledge, effort and time in their PCs. The early adopters are more practical. They want to see benefits and a favourable price-value trade-off before adopting the innovation. Innovators are not usually opinion leaders because of their special characteristics. Early adopters are more likely to be opinion leaders. They may explain and recommend the innovation to other consumers.

Diffusion of innovations is a process that takes place via communication in social networks. Advertising campaigns and consumer advice may guide but not control this process. In this chapter, the factors starting and reinforcing the process have been indicated. Finally, it is the consumers who decide whether or not an innovation becomes a success. For not every innovation contributes to a better world and a happier consumer.

Notes

1 Booz, Allen and Hamilton, Inc., USA.
2 Van Raaij, W. F. and Verhallen, T. M. M. (1981) 'A behavioral model of residential energy use' *Journal of Economic Psychology* 3, 39–63.
3 Van Raaij and Verhallen (1983).
4 See section 6.8.
5 See section 6.8.
6 Gatignon, H. and Robertson, T. S. (1985) 'A propositional inventory of new diffusion research' *Journal of Consumer Research* 11, 849–867.
7 Tazos are round plastic chips showing Warner Bros comic characters. They were very popular among children between 1994 and 1997.
8 See section 12.5.
9 See section 14.2.
10 Schwartzkopf can be translated as 'black head'. In Spanish, Nova is associated with 'no va' (does not move).

11 Compare the attitude toward the existing product in disposal behaviour. See section 4.5.
12 See section 14.5.
13 For ELM, see section 9.6.
14 Compare the influence of reference groups on consumption, considered in section 14.3.
15 See section 10.5.
16 Rogers, E. M. (1983) *Diffusion of Innovation* (New York: The Free Press) 3rd edition.
17 Gatignon and Robertson (1985).
18 See section 4.3.
19 See Foxall, G. R. and Goldsmith, R. E. (1994) *Consumer Psychology for Marketing Managers* (London: Routledge).
20 See Markus, M. L. (1987) 'Toward a "critical mass" theory of interactive media' *Communication Research* 14, 491–511.
21 Based on Foxall and Goldsmith (1994).
22 Foxall, G. R. (1994) 'Consumer initiators: adaptors and innovators' *British Journal of Management* 5 (Special Issue), S3–S12.
23 See section 14.4.
24 See section 14.4.

16 LIFESTYLE AND CONSUMPTION OF TIME

16.1 Introduction

As the classical criteria of categorizing consumers, e.g., social class, income, education, religion, region or neighbourhood, professional status, and family life-cycle have gradually become less useful to explain and predict consumer behaviour, 'lifestyle' has become popular in consumer research. Consumers can be less easily categorized or they may change categories continuously, depending on fiscal and social norms, rules and advantages. Workers start studying again; unemployed people find jobs; men and women will work either more or less depending on the family situation; people start cohabiting or start living apart after a divorce; single-parent families are no longer exceptional. In fact the socio-demographic and economic variables used earlier were never totally accurate, although at the time they were rather efficient approximations of preferences for expenditure, consumption patterns, brand and media choice.

By using social class and the other variables, researchers attempted to construct more or less homogeneous groups of consumers regarding their purchasing behaviour, product usage, shopping, media usage, and other types of consumer behaviour. In previous times, society was highly rigid: from birth onwards, one belonged to a particular church and social class and usually stayed that way for one's whole life. Only occasionally did someone move away from his or her native region. One's situation at birth largely determined one's possibilities in life. Social mobility was limited, for example going to college was reserved for those who could pay for themselves. At the time the consumer behaviour of a particular social class was rather homogeneous and stable but this has changed through the levelling of incomes, democratization, and the influence of the mass media.

In most countries, professions or positions have lost much of their distinctive features. Norms and values of parents, the church and social classes have become blurred. Differences in social class have been superseded. Lately, church membership has become a distinctive characteristic again as church membership is based now more on belief than in the past. Consumers want to be unique and they want to distinguish themselves. However, at the same time they want to belong to a group, be similar to other people and gain security by complying with norms and values. The mix of uniqueness and conformism[1] creates new categories in society—lifestyle groups.

Current society is dynamic and flexible. In principle, everyone may achieve their aspirations. Nowadays, personal characteristics rather than birth determine one's potential. In such a flexible society, lifestyle becomes an important way of describing consumer's behaviour and their choices of shops and media. The target group of marketing policy regarding products, services and media now is largely determined by the lifestyle group. It is even conceivable to develop and extend a lifestyle group by means of a magazine. In this case, the medium gives further substance to the lifestyle group. On the one hand, one complies with the preferences of the lifestyle group concerned; on the other hand, the editors of the magazine define the preferences regarding fashion clothing, cosmetic, travel stories, new cars, developments in the areas of literature, expressive arts, and dining.

Why is lifestyle important? Lifestyle is distinctive. Lifestyle enables people to belong to attractive groups. It is possible to imitate the lifestyles of attractive or famous people. Lifestyle is a form of self-expression. Lifestyle shows who you are or who you want to be. For the consumer, lifestyle is a type of membership of an invisible group which endorses key values.[2] Lifestyle is somehow similar to a subculture. While the traditional values and norms of religion, politics and ideology are becoming blurred, lifestyle is emerging as a completely new set of norms and rules of conduct.

The involvement of consumers is also evident from the specialization of consumption. One feels involved with some particular product domains and one is prepared to spend much time, attention and money in these domains, whereas other product domains get less attention in terms of time and money. Because of time and budget restrictions it is impossible to fully participate in all domains. Some consumers know everything about photography and spend much time and money on this hobby. Others are more interested in travelling abroad or in a particular sport. Media fulfil a double role here; they are both a group of products themselves and they refer to product groups in editorials and in advertising. Frequently, magazines are segmented according to a certain specialization such as *Vogue* for those interested in fashion and *Amateur Photographer* for keen users of cameras.

Lifestyle is defined as the entire set of values, norms, interests, opinions and behaviour in section 16.2. Sections 16.3 and 16.4 deal with value

Figure 16.1 *Looks and lifestyle*

systems and lifestyle groups. Consumption of time is a method to assess consumer lifestyle. Examples of time consumption and activities are shown in section 16.5. Section 16.6 draws some conclusions.

The aim of this chapter is to categorize consumers' lifestyles and values and to provide some insight into consumer time consumption.

16.2 Consumption patterns

Chapter 4 has already described the symbolic meaning and the historical development of consumption. Symbolic meaning is closely related to the characteristics of the goods and services one consumes. They determine the status and the personality one derives from a product or brand and they represent the motives of the consumer and the society's culture. The meaning of products is not random but fits a general consumption pattern.[3] Since contemporary culture and history of a society are roughly the same for all consumers, the distinctive consumption patterns will converge to a pattern that dominates society. On the basis of an analysis of societal developments, the prevailing consumption pattern can be characterized as individualistic, private, alienated or passive.[4] This conclusion is based on four dimensions of the consumption pattern in society: social relations, availability of goods, participation and activity. These four aspects are discussed in the following.

Social relations
In society there is a trend from extended to 'nuclear' families, thus diminishing the collectivity of consumption. This is also a trend towards individualizing consumer activities. The development of commodities such as single-family dwellings, cars, television sets, refrigerators, and washing-machines enables households to live and to survive on their own. Hence, the need for interaction and social relationships between consumers is minimized. Individualization has not yet been finished, given the trend of an individual television set, (mobile) telephone set and car for each family member.

Availability of goods
Many goods have gradually become available to individual households and consumers and become individualized. The public telephone has been replaced by the telephone at home and in the car and is further individualized by mobile telephones. The bank branch is being replaced by ATMs and online banking. The cinema has been replaced by television and pay-TV. A move from public to private is evident. Although many goods and services are only publicly available, their consumption may be individual. Public transport, movies, theatre, museum and public parks are consumed individually, without interaction with the other consumers who are present at the same time.[5]

Participation
Many consumers may have imagined that their social needs could be satisfied by the consumption of mass products. Mass products obviously are standardized and hence the similarity of consumption patterns has increased in the 1960s and the 1970s. Consumer life patterns showed little variation in nature and quality. Because of the rise of mass products people have become alienated from the production of goods and services. In postmodern times, after the 1980s, fragmentation has occurred. By product

differentiation and extended choices the consumption patterns have diverged. Consumers cannot participate in everything but they have to choose certain product domains and to specialize.[6] Hence consumer participation increases in domains in which they have specialized.

Activity
Many consumer activities have been mechanized and automated, hence consumers have become physically and mentally passive. For example, the washing-machine has eliminated much hand washing; the dish-washer the washing up of the dishes; and the television the visit to the cinema. Increased television watching is also associated with less reading, especially among the young. Although there is a health trend for more physical activity, in consumption people remain dependent on activity-saving household equipment.

The typology of consumption patterns has been investigated in consumer research.[7] First, 200 people were asked to make a list of products and consumer activities from three different periods: before 1850, 1850–1950 and after 1950. From the list, 22 products were selected for the second stage of the research including 240 different consumers. These consumers were shown two-dimensional pictures in which they had to indicate the positions of the 22 products. Each picture included a horizontal axis with two end-points, for example individual–collective, and a vertical axis also including two end-points, for example active–passive. Two other dimensions were private–public and alienated–synergistic. In total, there were six pictures, each including a different combination of two dimensions. Obviously, the dimensions were the same as in the typology of the consumption pattern.

The result of the investigation was that currently popular products were systematically positioned at the individual–private–alienated–passive endpoint of the axes, for example the microwave oven, dish-washer and freezer meals. Products and activities positioned at the other ends of the axes included for instance folklore, community theatre, community kitchen and family picnic, which occurred in the past.

16.3 Lifestyle

We define lifestyle as the entire set of values, interests, opinions and behaviour of consumers, insofar as they influence consumer behaviour. This is shown in figure 16.2. So lifestyle comprises behaviour, knowledge and attitudes—both what consumers do and what they feel. Lifestyle is a complex variable composed of many different elements. For this reason, we cannot provide a lifestyle categorization *a priori*, but we have to investigate this empirically in each product domain. Lifestyle categorizations are typically not the same across product domains but they are stable to some extent. However, time and again lifestyle categorizations and the sizes of lifestyle segments found in earlier research have to be verified.

Definition

Lifestyle is the entire set of values, interests, opinions and behaviour of consumers.

Values and norms

Values and norms are quite general; they constitute a general basis for behaviour. Instrumental values such as honesty, accuracy and friendliness concern the quality of daily behaviour. In addition, terminal values exist such as happiness, salvation, equality and security. Terminal values indicate people's aspirations in terms of targets. Norms are beliefs about what is permitted and what is not. Values and norms are rather stable; they are almost like personality characteristics. If values change, they usually do so very slowly. The most important cultural changes in recent years concern the role of the government, emancipation regarding marriage and sexuality, health and the environment. Well-known US studies regarding lifestyle, values and consumer behaviour are VALS (values and lifestyle) and LOV (list of values).[8]

The generality of values is useful for describing, explaining or predicting behaviour in general terms. Producers, public-relations officials, reporters and creative advertising teams have to take into account the values of their target groups. They can hardly change these values but they have to adapt

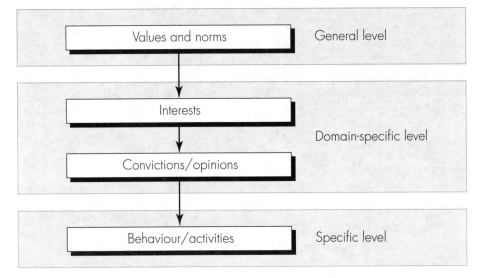

Figure 16.2 *Lifestyle components*

the contents of their messages to the prevailing values and norms. Consider the level of protest against Bennetton's advertising campaigns which portrayed an Aids patient or a mafia murder.

Value systems such as the categorizations by Rokeach, Schwartz, LOV and VALS are important for a general description of consumer groups and their development. They are background variables at a general level. At the domain-specific level, interests and opinions are important. They are linked to the benefits consumers obtain by using products, services, stores and media.[9] Product characteristics and concrete consumer actions are situated at the specific level. The connection of product characteristics and values may be accomplished by means of meaning-structure analysis and laddering research.[10] Starting from values, consumers set goals and product benefits become important.

Interests

Compared with values, interests concern more concrete domains and areas of activities such as politics, sports, culture, gastronomy, hobbies, travelling, and social contacts. The interests are reflected in all kinds of subjects and columns in magazines. Interests imply preferences regarding the consumption of time. Also paid work in many cases is a field of interest. Interests are determinants of lifestyle because they indicate preferred consumer activities, both in acting and in reading. Consumers interested in a partic-

Figure 16.3 *Interests are determinants of lifestyle*

ular area of activities are more involved in these activities, they read more and they talk more about them with others. Media are often segmented with regard to fields of interest such as politics, sports, hobbies, travelling, and music.

Opinions

Opinions are more specific than interests. They relate to phenomena, issues, persons, products, firms, government, politicians, countries, shops, newspapers and magazines. In contrast with values, opinions relate to objects, i.e., people have an opinion about something, for example about abortions, the euro, *The Sun* newspaper or whatever. Opinions are more variable than values. A message in the newspaper, a talk with a friend or an article in a magazine may change one's opinion. Opinions usually fit a field of interest in the sense that opinions within a field of interest are structured more, are better founded on information and sometimes also are more extreme. Advertising capitalizes on consumer opinions regarding commercial objects (products and services).

Several examples of opinions have already been mentioned in chapter 3 with regard to cultural developments, dealing especially with opinions regarding marriage, emancipation, variants of cohabitation, materialism, health, and the environment.[11]

Behaviour

Lifestyle is partly characterized by a behaviour pattern. Lifestyle can be measured concretely on the basis of one's activities. How do consumers use their time? What hobbies do they have? What types of recreation and sports do they practice? How much time do they spend on mass media, on shopping and going out, on maintenance of the house, the garden and the car, on travelling and on visiting friends and relatives? Activities have an objective and perceived reality. Differences between men and women manifest themselves clearly in research on time use, for example regarding the time spent on household duties and paid labour, on media usage and leisure in general. Some of these differences are shown in section 16.4.

16.4 Value systems and lifestyle groups

Lifestyle variables are measured by means of psychographic research, i.e., by means of (usually long) questionnaires regarding values, interests, opinions and activities.[12] As a result of these investigations, typologies have been developed, and men, women and the young have been categorized into lifestyle groups. These typologies are only crude approximations of reality. In fact, it is impossible to categorize consumers into types that are valid for all product domains.

Obviously a number of demographic and socioeconomic characteristics co-determine the lifestyle, such as the composition of the household, gender and the life-cycle stage.

In the first place, the concept of lifestyle comprises the type of activities and how much time one spends on them. This is the *behavioural* part. Furthermore it comprises the interests and involvement of consumers with these activities—the prevailing *opinions*. In the third place the *values* of consumers belong here. And finally it deals with the type of products, services, magazines and brands consumers use in these activities.

Values are an important part of the lifestyle categorizations used in consumer behaviour research. On the basis of the values consumers adhere to, clusters or consumer lifestyle groups can be constructed.[13] In this section several value systems are considered which are used as a basis for lifestyle categorizations and lifestyle segments.

It is important to distinguish between traits and types. Here, we primarily start from consumer traits such as values, attitudes and personality characteristics. Using these characteristics and the situational attributes, behaviour can be explained and predicted to some extent. The authors of this book have reservations with respect to using typologies in the sense of: there are six types of men or eight types of tourists. Usually, these typologies are based on arbitrary and unstable categorizations. The authors have particular reservations when it comes to typologies at a general level, valid for all types of consumers. The VALS typology is the only general typology considered by this book, not because the authors believe in VALS or because it is applied in practice, but because this typology has been frequently cited in articles and books.[14]

VALS

The VALS typology is based on the acceptance of values, and it produces a categorization at the general level, resulting in eight consumer groups. The VALS typology is shown in figure 16.4.[15] The eight types are distinguished on the basis of two main dimensions: resources on the vertical axis and self-orientation on the horizontal axis. Resources not only comprise income but also other resources such as education and skills.[16] Groups with few resources are situated at the top of figure 16.4, and groups with substantial resources are placed at the bottom. The categorization suggests that, starting with few means, there are three ways to reach the group characterized by high self-realization and considerable means.[17] The three ways or self-orientations are: principle, status and action. The name of each group shows its most important value or aim.

The VALS typology is useful for distinguishing consumer types, from minimum income households who are in debt or can just make ends meet, to wealthy consumers who are happy with themselves and with the world. It constitutes a segmentation at the general level.[18] It says something about one's way of life, one's home, holidays, leisure and possession of goods.

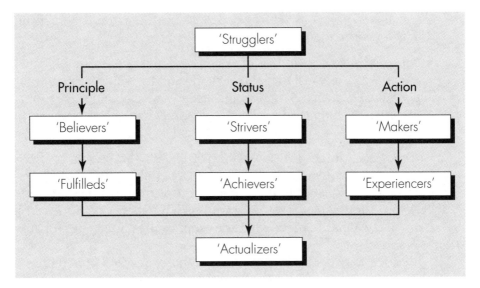

Figure 16.4 *The eight groups of VALS-2*

The category headed *principles* indicates a functional and practical disposition, attaching importance to confidence and security, for example well-known brands. The category headed *status* describes the way of hard work, achievement, career and the achievement of a certain status of importance to some consumers. The category headed *action* describes consumers who believe in fixing things themselves and getting experience. These consumers fix their own cars, build their own houses, grow their own vegetables and enjoy various experiences. Some differences between countries have been pointed out.[19] For example, in Sweden and the UK the strugglers consist of two groups: an older group similar to the USA and a young group, mainly unemployed. In Germany, economic strugglers are virtually absent but they exist in a psychological sense.

The objection to the VALS typology is that consumers can only fall into one of the eight categories. However, in practice a person or household may be a struggler in one domain but an actualizer in another. For example, a poor artist who can just make ends meet but produces top-flight artistic achievements. A domain-specific segmentation is preferable to this general segmentation of consumers.

16.5 Time use

As argued before, the study of the way consumers spend their time provides insight into the actual behaviour, activities and lifestyles of consumers. The use of time is both part of the lifestyle and an indicator of values, norms, interests and opinions. How do people use their time? Four main time 'budgets' can be identified:[20]

- *contracted time*, including work and commuting to work;
- *committed time*, including housework, child care and shopping;
- *personal care*, including sleeping, eating and grooming;
- *free time*, including educational, social, recreational and communication activities.

The latter three activities are particularly important to consumer behaviour. Chapter 13 examined time committed to work, household duties and personal care; this section deals with spending free time. Table 16.1 shows free time for several groups in a number of countries, in several years. These data are based on diaries kept by the participants for at least 24 hours.

Besides a general increase in free time, marked differences across countries exist. In the USA, UK and Norway people have less free time available than in The Netherlands and Denmark. The increase in free time may be partly due to the decreasing birthrate, a decreasing family size and an increasing availability of household appliances in these countries. To the

Table 16.1 *Free time by country and year for different groups*[21] *(hours per week)*

	USA			UK		
	1965	1975	1985	1961	1974	1984
Men						
Full-time employed	32.8	35.6	35.4	33.2	36.9	38.1
Part-time employed	48.2	63.3	55.5	36.1	45.8	48.3
Unemployed	69.2	56.9	57.6	58.4	62.6	63.2
Women						
Full-time employed	27.2	29.8	33.6	30.2	32.8	35.1
Part-time employed	39.0	38.5	40.4	32.1	37.8	36.0
Unemployed	39.8	46.8	48.9	39.9	46.6	49.9

	Netherlands		Denmark		Norway	
	1975	1980	1964	1981	1971	1981
Men						
Full-time employed	45.6	46.3	48.7	46.2	33.7	39.8
Part-time employed	75.3	70.8	62.3	55.1	50.8	55.4
Unemployed	63.6	66.4	71.7	67.4	64.2	68.3
Women						
Full-time employed	50.5	49.4	46.1	43.2	31.1	37.6
Part-time employed	59.8	56.6	46.4	45.5	33.3	41.1
Unemployed	48.5	48.0	53.7	56.8	38.6	51.6

Table 16.2 *Free time spent on activities by country for different groups[24] (hours per week)*

	USA (1985)		UK (1984)		Netherlands (1980)	Denmark (1975)	Norway (1981)
	Men	Women	Men	Women			
Full-time employed							
Education	1.7	2.8	0.4	0.7	4.3	0.5	0.3
Social life	9.1	10.0	7.4	9.1	11.3	15.5	11.9
Recreation	4.7	3.6	3.6	2.8	5.9	3.9	3.5
Communication	19.8	17.2	23.6	19.3	22.4	22.1	19.5
Part-time employed							
Education	10.2	2.7	0.0	0.2	15.0	0.5	7.5
Social life	11.0	12.1	8.1	7.5	11.3	19.1	13.8
Recreation	3.4	4.7	30.2	3.3	9.8	3.7	5.2
Communication	30.8	20.9	30.2	22.0	29.9	27.2	24.6
Unemployed							
Education	5.4	3.7	6.2	3.2	0.5	5.1	9.8
Social life	10.4	9.8	9.0	8.5	15.4	18.2	13.8
Recreation	7.5	6.1	5.4	5.2	10.3	5.8	7.4
Communication	34.1	28.8	39.1	29.5	37.5	35.6	32.3

extent that free time is chosen by free will, the differences across countries reflect cultural differences.

Table 16.2 shows a subdivision of free time per country in the most recent year reported. Social activities include visiting and entertaining, attending movies and other cultural events, and time spent in pubs, bars, cafés, etc. Recreational activities include playing sports, walking and hobbies among others. Communication activities include television, reading and conversations with others. By far the most popular way of spending free time is 'communication', most of which is watching television.[22] Social activities come in second place, followed by recreation and education. This reflects a preference for passive spending of free time, especially for men. A passive spending of free time is consistent with the compensation hypothesis, stating that free time will be used for relaxation in order to be fit to work.[23]

An important way of spending free time is tourism. In the European Union, 130 billion euros was spent on tourism, and tourist movements have increased by 50% from 1985 to 1995.[25] Other indicators of free time use are borrowing books from libraries, visiting museums and attending cinemas, reported in table 16.3 for a number of European countries. It appears that in the southern European countries, book stocks in libraries are relatively small. In Austria and France, the museums attract relatively many visitors. Ireland and Iceland score relatively high on cinema visits. These ways of spending free time are relatively cheap.

Table 16.3 *Consumption of free-time related services*[26]

	Library book stocks per capita	Museum visitors per annum per capita	Cinema visitors per annum per capita
European Union			
France	1.57	2.47	1.54
Germany	1.58	1.65	1.62
Italy	0.48	0.10	1.62
UK	2.29	0.32	1.94
Belgium	2.98	0.51	1.89
Luxembourg	1.62	—	2.53
Netherlands	2.75	1.36	1.00
Denmark	6.28	1.96	1.93
Finland	7.17	0.80	1.19
Sweden	5.18	1.76	1.84
Portugal	0.40	0.38	0.81
Spain	0.70	0.05	2.25
Austria	1.05	2.47	1.54
Greece	0.73	0.30	—
Ireland	3.11	0.29	3.39
EFTA			
Iceland	7.11	—	3.79
Norway	4.64	1.43	2.56
Switzerland	4.12	1.34	2.31
Eastern Europe			
Albania	1.30	—	1,26
Bulgaria	6.69	0.89	1.22
Croatia	0.97	0.21	0.89
Czech/Slovak Reps	3.67	1.02	1.99
Hungary	4.77	0.96	1.07
Romania	—	0.09	1.53
Slovenia	2.65	0.50	1.01
Poland	3.53	0.63	0.39
Estonia	7.06	—	1.97
Latvia	7.91	—	0.77
Russia	5.96	—	2.56

More expensive ways of spending free time include the consumption of goods available on the market. Table 16.4 shows the consumption statistics for a number of these goods. It appears that books, toys and games, and magazines are popular items related to free time. Consumption of compact disks, toys and games, video cassettes, books and bicycles has increased substantially. Consumption of blank audio cassettes and cameras has decreased. The latter result indicates less active types of free time, although the increased consumption of bicycles points to more active use of free time.

Table 16.4 *Consumption of free time related goods in Europe (1995)*

	Per capita value in US$ 1995	Percentage change 1990–1995	Per capita volume 1995	Percentage change 1990–1995
Toys and games	54.36	41		
Bicycles			0.047	18
Cameras	6.99	−15	0.035	−15
Films (rolls)			1.6	1
Pre-recorded cassettes			0.4	−41
Blank audio cassettes			1.2	−9
Compact disks			1.7	123
Blank video cassettes			1.2	24
Books	72.22	22		
Daily newspapers			0.25	7
Non-daily newspapers			0.21	6
Magazines			4.5	4

16.6 Conclusions

This chapter has dealt with the concept of lifestyle. Some argue that studying lifestyle is out of fashion and irrelevant to explaining consumer behaviour. This is generally not true. At a general level, lifestyle provides insight into the behaviour and opinions of large consumer groups. From this, areas of consumer interest and general preferences at the meso-level can be derived. However, lifestyle is less relevant in explaining specific brand preferences. To this end, the domain-specific segmentation methods of chapter 24 are more appropriate.

A personality factor associated with lifestyle is self-monitoring. For persons who score highly on self-monitoring, the expressive value of lifestyle is important. They have a need to express themselves by means of consumption. In this respect, lifestyle is related to value systems. However, lifestyle consists of interests, opinions and behaviour, so one may consider lifestyle as the interface between general consumer variables and behaviour. The latter has been dealt with regarding the use of free time.

It appears that free time has increased generally and that large differences across countries exist. On the one hand, the differences across countries reflect different cultures and lifestyles but on the other hand, different levels of income restrict the consumption possibilities.

Notes

1 Fromkin, H. L. and Snyder, C. R. (1980) 'The search for uniqueness and valuation of scarcity. Neglected dimensions of value in exchange theory' in:

Gergen, K. J., Greenberg, M. S. and Willis, R. H. (Eds) *Social Exchange. Advances in Theory and Research* (New York: Plenum Press), 57–75.

2   See section 14.2.

3   Firat, A. F. (1987) 'Towards a deeper understanding of consumption experiences: the underlying dimensions' *Advances in Consumer Research* 14, 342–346.

4   Firat (1987).

5   See section 17.3.

6   See section 16.1.

7   Firat (1987).

8   See also the values in Rokeach, M. (1973) *The Nature of Human Values* (New York: The Free Press) and section 7.5, tables 7.2 and 7.3.

9   For segmentation based on the three levels, see chapter 24.

10 Reynolds, T. J. and Gutman, J. (1984) 'Advertising is image management' *Journal of Advertising Research* 24, 27–36. See also section 7.3.

11 See sections 3.6 and 3.7.

12 Wells, W. D. (1975) 'Psychographics: a critical review' *Journal of Marketing Research* 12, 196–213.

13 It is possible to characterize consumers on the basis of acceptance of these values. The nine LOV values are easier to apply than the 36 Rokeach values (cf. section 7.5). The clustering of consumers on the basis of the LOV values produces a segmentation which in marketing can be used to categorize consumers at the general level (cf. section 24.3).

14 In chapter 24 segmentation is applied to the domain-specific level. The typology in this case varies across product domains in principle.

15 This is the typology according to VALS-2: Riche, M. F. (1989) 'VALS 2' *American Demographics* July, 25. For VALS-1, see Mitchell, A. (1983) *Nine American Lifestyles: Who We Are and Where We Are Going* (New York: Macmillan).

16 See section 4.3, figure 4.4.

17 In VALS terminology, the 'way' is called 'self-orientation'.

18 See section 24.3.

19 Mitchell, A. (1984) 'Nine American lifestyles: values and societal change' *The Futurist* 18 (August), 4–13.

20 Robinson, J. P. (1991) 'Trends in free time: A cross-national comparative analysis for seven industrial countries 1961–1985' in: Köhler, E. and O'Conghaile, W. (Eds), *The Changing Use of Time: Report from an International Workshop* (Luxembourg: Office for Official Publications of the European Communities) 123–151.

21 Robinson, J. P. (1991).

22 See chapter 17.

23 See section 13.6.

24 Robinson, J. P. (1991).

25 Euromonitor (1997) *European Marketing Data and Statistics* (London: Euromonitor). Tourist movements are measured as arrivals at frontiers.

26 Euromonitor (1997). Most of the data refer to the early 1990s.

MEDIA USE 17

Introduction

The media are important sources of information and entertainment for consumers. Many consumers spend more than 20 hours per week watching, listening to or reading the media, especially television, radio, newspapers and magazines. Media provide information for those who seek information to support a planned holiday trip, plans for recreation, or the purchase of durables and daily goods. Media offer entertainment for those who want to escape from reality.

After sleeping, media use occupies the most time (measured in hours). Although many associate free time with outdoor recreation and sports, more time is actually spent on using media at home than on outdoor recreation. Consumers spend hours watching television or reading books. Many people spend an hour a day reading a newspaper.

In section 17.2, the characteristics and functions of media are discussed, in connection with the general model of consumer behaviour of chapter 1. There are developments from public to personal media, and from public use of media to use at home (section 17.3). The time spent on watching television increases, while the time spent on print media decreases (section 17.4). The reach of media and messages in the media is discussed in section 17.5. The processing and effects of media are not discussed in this chapter, but information about this can be found in chapter 11. In section 17.6, some conclusions are drawn.

The objective of this chapter is to provide insight into the functions and use of the media, both as sources of information and entertainment for consumers.

17.2 **Characteristics and functions of media**

Media developed from clay tablets and papyrus scrolls to handwritten and printed books. Later, newspapers and magazines developed. In the last century, photography and film were invented. In this century, radio and television have flourished. Recently, electronic interactive media have been developed, such as the Internet. The reach of these media has increased dramatically. More than 1.5 billion people watched the television coverage of the 1990 Football World Championship in Italy. Sports, pop music and politics become global affairs via the media.

Some media constitute a unity: a book and a movie cover one topic. This is also true for pamphlets and CDs. Other media are more diverse: newspapers and magazines cover many topics. Radio and television broadcast different programmes about a diverse range of topics. These 'diverse' media often contain 'news' and other events.

Media may be categorized in different ways: print media, broadcast media, outdoor media and interactive media.[1] In this chapter, we discuss print media such as books, newspapers and magazines; audiovisual media such as film, television and radio; and interactive media such as the Internet. Table 17.1 shows this categorization.

Pacing

Print and audiovisual media differ in their control of speed and sequence ('pacing'). Pacing is the control of the use of the medium by the sender or by the receiver. Obviously, consumers are free to determine whether they switch on the television set and which channel they select. Within the programme, the producer determines the speed and sequence of the topics. The control of the consumer is restricted to the remote control and 'zapping' (switching channels). The most important concepts are summarized in table 17.2.

Table 17.1 *Media and their unity, diversity and pacing*

Characteristics	Print media	Audiovisual media	Interactive media
Unity	Book, pamphlet	Film, CD	CD-ROM package, CD-I concert
Diversity	Magazine, newspaper	Radio, television	Telephone, the Internet
Pacing	Internal	External	Internal or mixed

Table 17.2 *Internal and external pacing of media*

	Internal pacing	External pacing
Medium	Passive	Active
Controlled by	Receiver	Sender
Preferable for	High involvement	Low involvement
Documentation	Easy	Less easy

Definition

Pacing is the control of the use of a medium by the sender (external pacing), the receiver (internal pacing) or both sender and receiver (mixed pacing).

Internal pacing

In the case of print media, consumers determine the sequence and the speed at which the contents of printed publications are read or viewed. These media are passive. The reader controls the medium. This is called 'internal pacing'. The Internet is a medium that is also largely controlled by consumers. They decide what to see and how to browse and surf through the medium. If consumers are highly involved with the subject matter, internal pacing is preferable. Involved consumers may then devote a lot of attention to the topic. They may read the message several times, study, clip and keep the message. Consumers can easily keep advertisements, price lists, e-mail and Internet addresses, and telephone numbers. Print media offer a good source of documentation.

Most interactive media have internal pacing. Consumers may find the information themselves in databases (machine interaction). With respect to these interactive media, consumers take the initiative to consult the media. The information on Internet sites is available to browsers and should be relevant, up-to-date and attractive if it is to be visited and consulted more than once.

External pacing

In the case of audiovisual media, the sender takes the initiative and determines the speed, sequence of the messages and topics covered by the programme. These media are active. The sender controls the medium. This is called 'external pacing'. If consumers are not involved in the subject matter, external pacing is preferable for the advertiser. Uninvolved consumers are more or less forced to pay attention to the message, because the message is on the screen in front of them. Consumers may however switch channels or direct their attention to something else in their environment.

If television is not to become boring to young and 'postmodern' viewers it needs to feature quick cuts between programme segments. Long monologues and complex arguments do not 'fit' in a television programme. This leads to television programmes in which reality is simplified with a loss of nuances in the discussion. On the other hand, new nuances are created in the form of close-ups of people and situations.

Mixed pacing
Using interactive media, consumers sometimes have to follow a pre-determined sequence to trace the required information, for example, going through teletext pages. The telephone also offers mixed pacing as an interactive medium. Both parties influence the speed and the sequence of topics to be discussed.

For highly involved consumers, media with external pacing are not always preferred, because the topics are discussed at a speed and in a sequence determined by the sender. They cannot save the message to read it again. Providing addresses and telephone numbers on television is not always a solution, because viewers do not always have paper and pencil at hand. Teletext may be a solution to this problem. Audiovisual media are problematic with regard to documentation: a collection of videotapes is more difficult to browse than a collection of magazines. Videotapes with information on how to use products or how to do jobs such as car repair, may be better than printed information, because certain skills can be better demonstrated than described. This is a type of observational learning.[2]

Functions of media
Media have different functions for people. In this complex and fast-changing society and with increased information needs, media become more important. From a customer's perspective, the media have the following functions.[3] (See also figure 17.1.)

General information
Through the use of media, people remain up-to-date on what happens in their country and the rest of the world. Media provide 'news' on politics, economic and social developments and also provide background and interpretation of the news. In particular, newspapers, radio and television are important. The media also satisfy curiosity about the lives of film and pop stars. From the media consumers can learn what is fashionable, how to behave in certain circumstances, and discover the opinions of others. On the basis of this general information, for example, on the state of the environment, consumers may form general intentions to behave in a more environmentally friendly way.

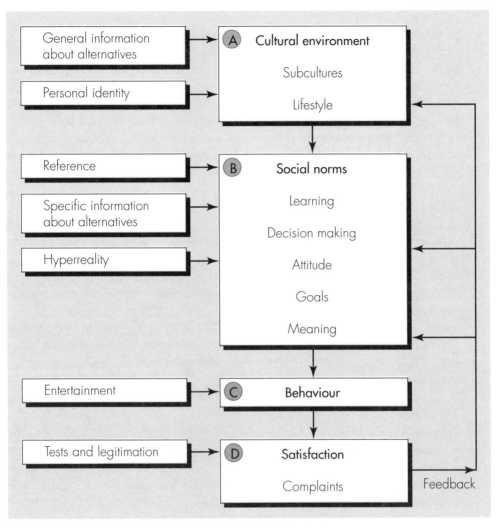

Figure 17.1 *Functions of media and consumer behaviour*

Specific information

Media also provide information on practical things such as how to fill out tax forms and about new products and their prices and qualities. Consumers with a general intention to behave in a more environmentally friendly way, need concrete and specific information about the costs and benefits of alternative ecological behaviours. Newspapers, magazines and leaflets consulted the most. Many people get a feeling of certainty and trust after consulting information from the media. As seen before, more certainty and trust does not necessarily lead to a better decision.[4] Information overload is largely caused by the media.

Personal identity

In newspaper and magazine articles and programmes on television, people may recognize and realize their personal norms and values. Media play an important role in the socialization of children and the acculturation of foreigners living in a country.[5] Through the media, the dominant values and identification with other people are learnt. From observational learning, people may learn how to behave in a particular situation and how to use products.[6] Many media are segmented and represent a particular lifestyle or subculture. Consumers select magazines and a lifestyle that fits them best and with which they can identify themselves.

Reference

Through the media people may understand the situation of others (empathy). Through identification with other people one may get the feeling of belonging to a group. Media provide the opportunity for awareness of and social comparison with other people. Media put topics on the agenda for conversation between people and provide information for this conversation. This is called 'agenda setting'.[7] Reports of national and sports events give the feeling that people belong to the nation. People may feel part of the nation on special days, even if they are abroad. The BBC World Service and other international radio stations are important for this.

Hyper-reality

The media may be even a substitute for personal experiences and relations with other people. This is called cultivation theory.[8] Television has such a central place in the life of many people that their world view comes from what they see on the television screen. Reality for many people is what the television shows. Television selects images from reality on the basis of news value and aesthetics. Thus people get a 'biased' and fragmented view of reality. It is possible that television images cause people to perceive reality via these images ('frames').[9] A postmodern idea is that the media offer a reality that is more interesting than the 'real' reality.[10] Theatre, film, books and other media have always offered an escape to another and more interesting reality.

Entertainment

Media provide entertainment and diversity to escape from daily problems. Media may provide a cultural and aesthetic function. A medium such as television fills time that otherwise may be boring. Television is the story-teller of our time. In different forms, largely the same stories are told.[11] Emotional and sexual arousal may occur while reading *Playboy* or *Penthouse* and watching pornographic videos. These forms of entertainment are a type of hyper-reality.

Test and legitimation

Media, and especially consumer programmes, report on comparative tests of products and services. These programmes also function to structure the product experience of consumers. With ambiguous product experiences consumers compare their own experiences with those of others and with messages in the mass media to ascertain whether they are satisfied or not. Suppose you visit Disneyland Paris and you do not know whether you like it or not. In such a case, a positive article in the newspaper may tip the balance to 'like'. This can be compared to the function of product information after the purchase, in the way that it reduces cognitive dissonance.[12]

17.3 From public to personal entertainment

Entertainment has now taken on a totally different character. The word 'entertainment' implies attractive experiences, interesting information and escape from the daily routine. In earlier times, the fair, the revue, the cinema and the theatre were the occasions for entertainment and meeting other people. Families played games together. People visited each other for birthdays. In many towns and villages there was little else in the way of entertainment.

Television has changed the scope of entertainment. We only have to press a button on the remote control and movies, theatre, quizzes, and talk shows appear on the screen. We do not play games any more—we watch others doing so. We do not talk with each other, but watch a chat show. We do not leave home to go to the movies, but select a movie from the video shop or watch one being broadcast by the many TV stations.

Active sports, recreation, tourism and other outdoor activities are increasingly ways of spending free time. Events such as football games, theatre, concerts and cinema have seen decreasing attendances. These activities are partly replaced by media use at home, as these media provide greater freedom and control than actually going to these events.[13] If the show is not interesting, we can switch off the television set. On the other hand, it is frustrating to leave a disappointing pop concert. During a concert on television we may have a drink and do other things, while in the concert hall at a 'live' performance the audience is expected to remain silent and attentive. There are advantages to attending a live concert including the uncertainty as to whether the musicians will give a good performance without mistakes and the pleasure of being part of an audience. Attending a live concert means having an 'evening out' and a change of routine.

With regard to the use of media and participation in events, the following trends may be distinguished: substitution, increased consumer competence, immediate gratification, individualization, and self-service.[14] Events include visiting museums, concerts, theatre, opera, musicals, film and other forms of cultural participation.

Substitution

As said before, passive participation in events is partly replaced by media use. The public event that one attends with others, becomes a private and personal event in the home on the screen or via the CD-player. Explanations for this substitution include:

- The greater freedom and control that media offer compared to 'live' events.
- Gratification through the media is perceived as quicker and more effective than waiting for a 'live' show.
- The often higher quality of the television coverage compared to the 'live' event. The television camera provides a better view of the goals and the action than a seat in the football stadium. Goals on television are shown in slow motion and from several angles a number of times and expert commentary is added. The stadium offers atmosphere and the experience of 'being there', as well as a break in the daily routine.
- Fear of trouble on the streets or in the stadium may prevent people from going to an event like a football match.
- People may prefer the home over the public space. Watching a video at home may feel more enjoyable than going to the cinema and mixing with other people. To retreat into the home is called 'cocooning'.

The substitution hypothesis is true for media use, but not for other domains. There has been an increase in the use of kitchen equipment in households over the last few years. According to the substitution hypothesis, this should lead to more dinners at home. However, the number of restaurant visits has also increased, despite the improved equipment now present in many household kitchens. In the same way, there was no decrease in museum or gallery visits, even after books with perfect art reproductions came onto the market. Obviously, kitchen machines and art books are insufficient substitutes for visits to restaurants and museums. Another possibility is that the 'substitutes' increase the wish to experience the 'real thing.'

Increased competence

As a consequence of the increased level of education, people understand more and are more able to cope with 'difficult' media such as the Internet and 'difficult' events such as Le Nozze di Figaro or a Shostakovich symphony. Increased consumer competence leads to greater participation in cultural events. This increased participation could also be explained by a higher level of need gratification, once the simple needs are satisfied.[15] Postmaterialism provides the latter explanation.

Increased competence explains why people read quality newspapers, use the Internet, read literature, visit theatres and museums, and make cultural trips. However, participation in cultural events did not increase in all segments.

Immediate gratification

People have less time available and look for immediate gratification and 'easy' entertainment. Long training periods, concentration and exercises beforehand are not possible or not appreciated. A superficial hedonism is the norm for many people. Thanks to the new technology, the 'harried leisure class' may easily consume large quantities of entertainment.[16] Explanations for this are:

- Because of lack of time, people look for quick and efficient entertainment and avoid activities that take time and patience. This leads to superficial participation.
- Immediate sensations are preferred over long and 'boring' efforts.[17]
- There is a preference for quick 'piecemeal' information over complex arguments. There is a preference for images over words. Pessimists may assert that television has a detrimental effect on society and that future generations will not be able to understand complex reasoning any more.[18] In this vision, print media will lose out to television.
- Programmes need to attract and keep viewers' attention. Shows should never be boring and the surprises should follow each other quickly. Many US soaps are examples of this.

Immediate gratification and increased competence seem to be contra-dictory. Increased competence leads to a higher quality, whereas the need for immediate gratification leads to lower quality. Both developments may, however, exist side-by-side for different groups of consumers.

Individualization

The use of media becomes more personal and individualistic. Many households possess a common television set in the living room and other sets in the children's rooms. Most teenagers possess a radio, walkman, cassette recorder and CD-player. Common household possession of this equipment has become the personal possession of individuals.[19] The walkman is the ultimate private radio/cassette player. No agreement is needed any more about which station should be on. And nobody can complain that your choice of music is too loud.

Self-service

CD-players, audio and video cassette recorders, video shops and the Internet provide the option for self-service information and entertainment. Consumers may listen to music and watch movies at the time they like, and are no longer restricted by the time and other restrictions of live perfor-mances. Consumers may also watch only the most important episodes of a series and skip the rest. There is more internal control and internal pacing of use of media and entertainment.

Further changes

Television has brought about the individualization of entertainment. Entertainment has become more passive as well. With *interactive television* more activity and participation in the living room is possible. Viewers may show their preferences, opinions or answers to quizzes through selection buttons and thus actively participate in programmes. They may become a member of a group or a donor to charity funds, ask for additional information on teletext, and order goods or services. Interactive television requires active viewers and participants.

Figure 17.2 *Home concert*

17.4 Time spent on media

People spend a lot of time on media, partly as a substitute for going out. This may be an active and conscious awareness of the media, for example, reading a book or a magazine, intently watching a television programme, or surfing the Internet. Sometimes the medium is in the background, for instance, if the radio is on during work or while someone is driving the car. In table 17.3 the time spent on media is given in minutes per working day.

The average time consumers spend on watching television differs considerably between countries. The British are the champions with over 4 hours watching per day. The Portuguese and Spaniards watch slightly less but still more than the European average of 205 minutes a day. The Czechs, Swiss and Finns watch less than 160 minutes a day. Generally speaking, television is the dominant medium in Southern Europe, whereas print media dominate in Northern Europe.

In table 17.3, the data show how much time persons spend on media and the penetration rate of the media. The penetration rate is the proportion of

Table 17.3 *Time spent on media (minutes per working day)*[20]

	Reading newspapers		Watching television		Listening to the radio	
	Duration (mins)	Penetration rate (percentage)	Duration (mins)	Penetration rate (percentage)	Duration (mins)	Penetration rate (percentage)
Austria	44	63	166	86	195	83
Belgium	68	33	198	87	245	65
Czech Republic	47	66	145	82	244	85
Denmark	59	62	172	81	226	85
Finland	53	84	155	90	232	52
France	47	23	215	87	158	61
Germany	67	68	213	92	185	80
Greece	72	15	208	86	215	39
Hungary	49	65	178	92	210	82
Ireland	48	55	195	92	170	81
Italy	52	27	212	91	125	36
Netherlands	45	54	182	88	178	57
Norway	54	75	162	88	176	62
Poland	53	62	171	91	250	82
Portugal	48	15	225	88	208	50
Spain	55	23	217	91	150	38
Sweden	71	70	190	83	327	74
Switzerland	41	56	160	79	228	69
UK	57	39	252	90	172	55
European averages	57	45	205	89	195	60

people using the medium. The Greeks and Swedes spend most time reading newspapers: more than 70 minutes. But only 15% of the Greeks do so, while 71% of the Swedes read a newspaper. Switzerland has the lowest number of television viewers. Every day only 78% of the Swiss are to be found in front of their screen, devoting on average 160 minutes to this activity. The British spend most time on television: 253 minutes. Television penetration rates are very similar across countries, with an average of 89%. Swedes leave the radio on for more than 330 minutes a day, while Italians listen for only 120 minutes. Radio penetration rates are low in Southern Europe; in Italy, Greece and Spain they are below 40%.

It may be concluded from table 17.3 that newspapers are more popular in Northern Europe, while in Southern Europe television dominates. The British score at the European average on newspaper reading, but are above average in television viewing. Listening to the radio is most popular in central and Northern Europe.

Table 17.4 shows the number and circulation of newspapers and magazines. The circulation is in copies per 1000 inhabitants. Newspaper circulation is high in Denmark, Germany, The Netherlands and the UK, while it is low in Southern Europe. Magazine circulation is high in Belgium, France, Germany and The Netherlands, and low in Southern Europe and Ireland.

National television stations broadcasting diverse programmes in the national languages are the most popular and have a high reach in most countries, especially in Southern Europe. Berlusconi's Italian media empire is an example. National TV stations use vertical segmentation to reach all segments in the same country or language group. Pan-European television stations are mainly categorical, i.e., specializing in music, news or sports.

Table 17.4 *Readership of print media*[21]

	Number of newspapers	Copies per 1000 inhabitants	Number of magazines	Copies per 1000 inhabitants
Belgium	35	175	˙29	1183
Denmark	45	355	31	588
France	103	127	900	1018
Germany	356	343	1200	1539
Greece	132	118	50	154
Ireland	8	189	60	97
Italy	82	118	59	361
Netherlands	47	313	96	1055
Portugal	24	39	200	135
Spain	110	77	200	218
UK	105	393	1150	966
EU total	1051	221	4075	785

They use horizontal segmentation and target similar segments of youth, professionals or businesspeople in different countries. In table 17.5, some pan-European TV stations are listed.

Most pan-European television programmes are in English, because English is understood by about 150 million Europeans, as a first or a second language. Russian is the most frequently spoken first language (mother tongue) in Europe. German is the largest first-language group in Western Europe (in Germany, Austria and Switzerland). Table 17.6 shows the first languages (mother tongues) spoken in Europe and the world. Chinese is the language spoken by most people in the world.

Table 17.5 *Pan-European television stations*[22]

TV station	Themes	Number of households reached (millions)	Languages
Eurosport	Sports	61.1	English, French, German, Dutch, Finnish, Spanish, Swedish
MTV Europe	Music	56.1	English
CNN Europe	News	54.5	English
NBC Superchannel	Lifestyle, business	40.8	English
TNT Cartoon	Cartoons, movies	25.8	English, French, Spanish Norwegian, Swedish
Euronews	News	22.1	English, French, German, Italian, Spanish
Discovery	Documentaries	9.0	English

Table 17.6 *First languages spoken in Europe and the world (in millions of people)*

	Europe	World
Russian	90	130
German	78	118
English	60	426
French	60	115
Italian	57	63
Polish	50	62
Spanish	39	308
Dutch	20	21
Portuguese	10	166
Chinese	–	1200

Reading versus watching

The time spent on reading books, newspapers and magazines is decreasing (see table 17.7). Television seems to push the print media aside. On average, most people spend more hours watching than reading. Note that for older people with secondary and higher education, both the number of hours watching and reading increase, even with a correction for time restrictions. A large proportion of these persons are retired and have more time to spend on media use. The most intensive television viewers are younger people with a primary level of education. The least intensive viewers are people with a high level of education. Reading requires more

Table 17.7 *Time per week (in hours) spent on reading print media and watching television and the reading/watching ratios[a,23]*

Educational level	activity/ratio	1975	1985	1995
Primary education, young	Watching	11.0	13.1	13.9
	Reading	4.4	3.1	2.6
	Ratio	0.40	0.24	0.19
Secondary education, young	Watching	8.5	12.0	13.3
	Reading	5.4	4.2	3.2
	Ratio	0.64	0.35	0.24
Higher education, young	Watching	6.1	9.1	10.4
	Reading	6.6	5.5	4.2
	Ratio	1.08	0.60	0.40
Primary education, old	Watching	11.5	12.5	13.5
	Reading	6.0	5.0	5.1
	Ratio	0.52	0.40	0.38
Secondary education, old	Watching	9.7	11.2	12.1
	Reading	6.9	6.5	6.3
	Ratio	0.71	0.58	0.52
Higher education, old	Watching	7.1	10.0	9.6
	Reading	8.0	8.3	7.7
	Ratio	1.13	0.83	0.80
Total sample	Watching	10.2	11.8	12.4
	Reading	6.0	5.1	4.4
	Ratio	0.59	0.43	0.35

Data from the Social-Cultural Planning Bureau, The Netherlands. To eliminate time restrictions, e.g., a paid job, the data are 'normalized' to 47 hours free time per week.
[a]The reading/watching ratio is the time spent on reading (print media) divided by the time spent on watching (television).
Primary education: elementary school and lower professional education
Secondary education: secondary and medium-level professional education
Higher education: higher professional education and university
Young: born in 1950 or later
Old: born before 1950

Figure 17.3 *Reach of media*

effort than watching television. This explains the high popularity of television with the less educated people. The distinction between watching and reading should not be taken too strictly. Print media now contain more pictures and have become more visual media. In a similar way, subtitles to some television programmes require that consumers read. It is possible that people with a higher education read faster than people with a primary education. In this way, they may read more in a shorter time.

It may be explained as habitual behaviour that older people read more than younger people. Younger people are more accustomed to television than older people. It is a cohort effect that younger people watch more television than older people. It may thus be expected that in the future television will further increase its dominance at the expense of reading.[24]

17.5 Reach of medium and message

Media and messages in the media should reach consumers, otherwise no information exchange will take place. The questions are thus: Which people can be reached using which media? And with which messages in the media are they confronted? Medium and message reach are thus necessary conditions for consumers to be exposed to the media.

Media may only fulfill their functions if attention is paid and appreciation felt for the messages. Attention and appreciation or 'likability' are necessary conditions for advertising to have any effect. We may thus add three functions to the list of media functions: *reach*, *attention*, and *appreciation*.[25] In this way, messages in the media may be transferred. The messages in the media have to attract the attention and evoke positive appreciation. Both advertising and editorial messages should 'stand out' in a positive way. Because consumers do not see all the messages in a medium, message or advertising reach is usually lower than medium reach.

Medium reach

Medium reach is the number of persons who were in contact with the medium during a particular period. 'In contact' means: read or browsed the print medium; watched at least a part of a television programme or saw an outdoor advertisement. 'In contact' thus means 'awake and in front of the medium'. With daily newspapers, the period is normally one day. This is the actual reach. The reach of newspapers is the number of persons who browsed a newspaper on a particular day. Title reach is the number of persons who browsed a particular newspaper, for example *The Times*, on a particular day. Because a newspaper consists of a number of parts, medium-part reach is sometimes distinguished. Then consumers are asked if they saw, for instance, the sports section of *The Times*. In this medium-part, messages including advertisements appear.

Definition

Medium reach is the number of people who have been in contact with that medium during a particular period.

If someone saw a medium-part, it is not certain whether this person also saw a particular message. Therefore, page reach, message reach and advertising reach are distinguished. Page reach is the number of people who saw a particular page of the medium. Message reach is the number of persons who saw the message. This does not necessarily imply that they read the message completely, understood it or agreed with it. This hierarchy of types of reach is given in figure 17.4.

The different types of reach constitute a decreasing series. Medium reach is greater than title reach. Title reach is greater than page reach and message reach. If a particular message, for instance the weekly advertisement of a retailer, appears in different newspapers, message reach may be greater than title reach. By means of media planning, advertisers try to achieve the maximum reach possible in a target group within the available budget.

Reach has been defined as the number of persons that have been in contact with the medium or the message. Messages are often targeted

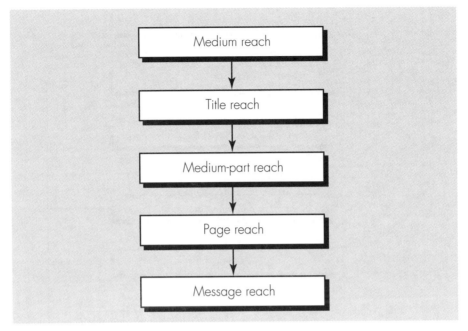

Figure 17.4 *Types of reach*

to specific target groups, for instance, higher educated younger people between 18 and 28 years old with an interest in sports and drinking beer. It is thus relevant what percentage of the target group saw the message. If the number of higher educated people interested in beer, between 18 and 28 years old is 4 million and if an advertisement in *Playboy* and *Penthouse* reaches 1 million of them, the coverage or reach in the target group is 25%.[26]

Scanning and focusing

Consumers often scan the media to see whether it contains relevant information for them. Only if information is relevant do they give any attention to the message. The latter is called 'focusing'.[27] This is represented in figure 17.5.[28] The reach of the message is the first step of the process; the message needs to be seen by the consumer.

In the *scanning* stage, consumers browse media and advertisements, by leafing through a magazine, watching shopwindows and outdoor advertising, zapping television channels and watching commercials. During this stage, programmes and advertisements are selected based on their relevance and attractiveness. In this way, message reach develops. The scanning stage constitutes a cognitive and an affective substage, i.e., the attention and the primary affective reaction (PAR) of acceptance/ appreciation of the message. The selection of messages occurs both on the

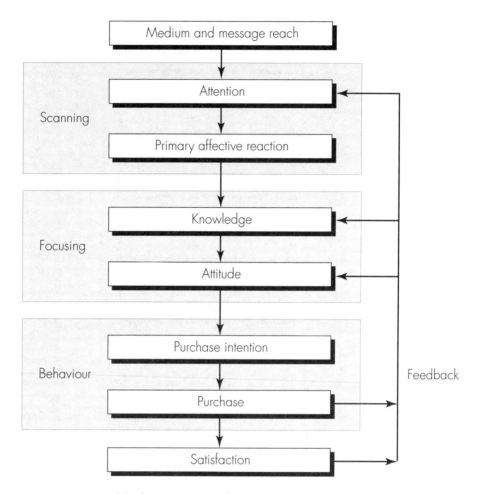

Figure 17.5 *Model of scanning and focusing*

basis of perception and a global affective evaluation: 'Do I like this adver-tisement?', 'Is this product attractive?' or 'Is this information relevant?' The scanning process may take a few seconds. It is necessary because, in many cases, consumers cannot process all the information on offer.[29] The reach of a message in a particular title is therefore lower than the title reach.

If a message passed the scanning stage, more attention will be paid to it. This is called *focusing*. When consumers focus on the content of the message, they try to understand what it means, to relate the information to prior knowledge, and form an attitude on the basis of the content of the message. In the case of high involvement, the focusing stage may be very extended. In situations of low involvement, this stage is almost skipped or is minimal. After the scanning stage, a purchase may be made. Eventually, focusing takes place after the purchase. See the feedback from behaviour and satisfaction to knowledge and attitude in figure 17.5. Focusing may lead to a purchase intention and purchase, if the product in the store is available and there are no attractive competing brands 'on sale'.

In the scanning–focusing model, the traditional effect hierarchies are integrated. Three effect hierarchies can be described:

- *Cognition → attitude → behaviour*. First consumers process information, form their attitude and base their behaviour on this. Often, this is done for important decisions and with a high consumer involvement. It is a 'rational' and well-designed way of making decisions. The focusing stage including knowledge and attitude is very important.
- *Cognition → behaviour → attitude*. A choice is made on the basis of limited information processing. Then, on the basis of product experience and satisfaction, an attitude is formed. The focusing stage is minimal, but the feedback of behaviour and satisfaction to attitude is very important. Primary learning processes such as operant conditioning and observational learning belong to this hierarchy.[30] This sequence is relevant in low involvement situations, high brand awareness and trial purchases.
- *Attitude → behaviour → cognition*. Based on emotions such as a global attitude, consumers select products and brands, and process this information. The primary affective reaction is important, the focusing stage is minimal, but the feedback of behaviour and satisfaction to knowledge is very important. This sequence is relevant in low involvement situations, for example, using the affect referral decision rule.[31]

These three models can be integrated as submodels of the model shown in figure 17.5. These models all start from an individual choice process, without influencing other people. Many decisions are taken at home. A number of people influence each other and together they make a decision.[32] Sometimes the influence of other people is the social norm.[33] Although one may have a positive attitude towards buying a product or service, one may be held back by a negative social norm. An individual might like to buy a sports car, but is held back by the negative social norm of others.

Definition

The hierarchy of effects refers to a fixed order of cognition, attitude and behaviour, depending upon such factors as involvement with the attitude object.

Information overload

The scanning–focusing model is also important, because consumers are confronted with a large information supply in the media. The information supply increased by 50% (books, newspapers and magazines) between

1975 and 1995. In many countries, total broadcasting time of television stations in 1995 is five times higher than in 1983, due to commercial TV stations, such as RTL and SBS. During the same period, free time did not increase, on average. This means that there is less time for consumers to process all information. Consumers have to be selective in their information search and processing and are forced to reject much information.

Recognition and recall scores of commercials declined during the last 25 years. Although recall and recognition are imperfect measures of advertising effect, it is indicative that the scores of table 17.8 decreased. Confrontation scores (a) are the percentages of people who saw the particular advertisements. Reading scores (b) are the percentages of people who read parts of the advertisements. Recognition scores (a + b) are the percentages of consumers who recognize having seen the advertisements. For the measurement of recognition, advertisements are shown to respondents and they are asked whether they recognize having seen these advertisements. During the last 25 years, recognition scores decreased from 53.6% to 36.8%. This is a relative drop of 31%. Reading scores (b) show the steepest decrease, 50% in 25 years. This means that consumers are more and more likely to scan only the pictorial part of advertisements rather than read them (focusing). The index of table 17.8 indicates this decrease. For this index, the period 1965–1970 was set as to 100 and the index shows comparison with the period 1986–1991.

Recall scores are lower, because respondents have to actively remember which advertisements they saw. Recall scores have decreased over the last 25 years, from 11.3% to 8.9%. This is a relative decrease of 21%. The data of table 17.8 refer to black and white advertisements. Recognition scores for colour advertisements are generally higher, but also show a decrease over time.[35]

Message reach

Message reach is defined as the number of people or the percentage of the target group that were confronted with a particular message. For example,

Table 17.8 *Recall and recognition scores of advertisements in magazines*[34]

	1965–1970 (percentage)	1980–1985 (percentage)	1986–1991 (percentage)	Index
Recall	11.3	9.7	8.9	79
Confrontation score (a)	31.9	28.8	26.1	82
Reading score (b)	21.7	10.6	10.7	49
Recognition (a + b)	53.6	39.4	36.8	69
b/(a + b)	44.0	27.0	29.0	72

Data from The Netherlands. Index describes comparison of 1986–1991 measured against 1965–1970 it would be the percentage of people interested in beer between 18 and 28 years who saw an advertisement in *The Times* or the *Daily Telegraph*. Message reach means that the message was seen by consumers. This does not mean that these people consulted, understood, recognized or recalled the message. It does not imply that the message had an effect. Message reach is a necessary condition for a specific effect; it is not the effect itself.

It is, for instance, interesting to know that 200,000 flyers were distributed but it is more interesting to know how many people read this flyer. The reach of the flyer is the number of copies multiplied by the average number of readers per flyer, for example, 4.2. Thus, a flyer in a doctor's waiting room may have a large number of readers. The reach of the flyer in this example would be 4.2 × 200,000: 840,000. But this number says little about the effect of the flyer. Its information could be irrelevant or too difficult to understand. Because of this, little or no knowledge, attitude or behavioural change could occur in the consumers who read the flyer.

17.6 Conclusions

The characteristics, functions and effects of media were discussed in this chapter.[36] Due to restricted space in this book, we could only give the most important characteristics and functions of mass communication, such as medium and message reach.

There are important changes in the use of media, from print media to television, and from public and common to private and personal use of media at home. The benefits of use at home include the greater degree of control over the media. In the modern context, people get together less often to watch media. They are rather individual media users for occasions that suit them best. The type and possibly also the effects of media have changed due to this.

Depending on consumer involvement, different processing strategies of messages take place, with either more or less attention at the focusing stage. Because consumers may be involved in only a limited number of topics and domains, the focusing stage will be often quickly and superficially passed over. In the case of high consumer involvement, the focusing stage gets much more attention.

The reach of media and messages are important data according to which media are selected as conveyers of messages. Reach is a necessary but not sufficient condition for advertising messages to have any effect. Advertising recall is often used as an indicator of advertising effect. This is only correct in a few cases. Not all advertising that is remembered has an effect. And advertising that is not remembered, may have an effect.

Notes

1 Floor, J. M. G. and Van Raaij, W. F. (in preparation) *Marketing Communication Strategy* (Hemel Hempstead, UK: Prentice Hall).

2 See section 10.5.

3 Adapted and extended from McQuail, D. (1983) *Mass Communication Theory. An Introduction* (London: Sage).

4 See section 11.4, figure 11.6.

5 See section 3.3.

6 See section 10.5.

7 See section 14.5.

8 Gerbner, G. (1973) 'Cultural indicators. The third voice' in: Gerbner, G., Gross, L. and Melody, W. (Eds) *Communications Technology and Social Policy. Understanding the New Cultural Revolution* (New York: John Wiley) 553–573.

9 See section 6.3.

10 See section 3.8.

11 Gerbner (1973).

12 See section 9.5.

13 Linder, S. B. (1970) *The Harried Leisure Class* (New York: Columbia University Press).

14 Knulst, W. P. (1989) 'From Vaudeville to Video' *Sociale en Culturele Studies* 12 (Rijswijk: Social and Cultural Planning Bureau) (in Dutch). See also section 13.6.

15 Maslow, A. H. (1954) *Motivation and Personality* (New York: Harper & Row).

16 Linder (1970).

17 Scitovsky, T. (1976) *The Joyless Economy* (New York: Oxford University Press).

18 Postman, N. (1986) *Amusing Ourselves to Death* (New York: Viking).

19 See section 4.5 and section 20.3.

20 IP (1992) *The Europeans* Euro Time Survey: sample size $n = 9,774$. The data were collected in September–October 1991.

21 Shelley, M. and Winck, M. (Eds) (1995) *Aspects of European Cultural Diversity* (London: Routledge) tables 3 and 4. The newspaper data are from 1990 and the magazine data from 1985.

22 Source of the data: *Universal Media*, Amstelveen.

23 Kraaykamp, G. L. M. and Knulst, W. (1992) 'Increasing level of schooling. Decreasing literacy' *Massacommunicatie* 20, 22–37, table 3 (in Dutch).

24 This is a cohort effect, see section 3.4.

25 Pieters, R. M. G. and Van Raaij, W. F. (1992) *Advertising Processes* (Houten: Stenfert Kroese) (in Dutch). They distinguish three functions of advertising: attention, appreciation/acceptance, and information transfer. The first two functions are conditions for the third function. Appreciation and acceptance are also called 'likability'.

26 See also Floor and Van Raaij (in preparation), chapter 22.

27 See Floor and Van Raaij (in preparation), section 5.4.

28 Van Raaij, W. F. (1989) 'How consumers react to advertising' *International Journal of Advertising* 8, 261–273.

29 Erickson, K. A. and Simon, H. A. (1980) 'Verbal reports as data' *Psychological Review* 87, 215–251.

30 See sections 10.4 and 10.5.

31 See section 11.6.

32 Davis, H. L. and Rigaux, B. P. (1974) 'Perception of marital roles in decision processes' *Journal of Consumer Research* 1, 51–61.

Kirchler, E. (1988) 'Diary reports on daily economic decisions of happy versus unhappy couples' *Journal of Economic Psychology* 9, 327–357.

Kirchler, E. (1993) 'Spouses' joint purchase decisions: determinants of influence tactics for muddling through the process' *Journal of Economic Psychology* 14, 405–438. See sections 14.4 and 14.5.

33 For instance the extended model of Fishbein and Ajzen. See Fishbein, M. and Ajzen, I. (1975) *Belief, Attitude, Intention, and Behavior: An Introduction to Theory and Research*. (Reading, MA: Addison-Wesley). See also section 9.4.

34 It concerns 1/1 pages black & white. Measurements by NIPO/Gallup. See Franzen, G. (1992) *How advertising really works* (Deventer: Kluwer Bedrijfswetenschappen) 51 (in Dutch).

35 Franzen (1992) 52. Strangely, the NIPO/Gallup impact score shows a small increase.

36 More information can be found in Floor and Van Raaij (in preparation).

18 SHOPPING BEHAVIOUR

18.1 Introduction

The shopping environment speaks the language of consumption and for this reason has meaning for consumers.[1] In this chapter, the structure of distribution, the shopping centre and the store are described from the consumer perspective. Stores are not only used for purchases but they are also used for finding out about new products and brands on the market. Stores are also important for after-sales service. In the future, shops could be involved in the final stage of the consumption cycle—the re-use of products and the recycling of parts.

Section 18.2 deals with the distribution structure. As well as economic and town planning factors, psychological and sociological factors are important elements of a successful distribution structure. This also applies to the characteristics and functions of shopping centres (section 18.3). Section 18.4 deals with shop characteristics in particular. Consumer shopping behaviour is described in section 18.5. Way-finding and the effects of crowding are discussed in section 18.6. In section 18.7 some conclusions are drawn.

The aim of this chapter is to provide insight into shopping behaviour, including the choice of both shopping centres and shops. Impulsive buying behaviour, way-finding and crowds are also considered.

18.2 Distribution structure

At the most general level, distribution structures differ across countries. This is evident at the level of the North–South axis when comparing developed with less developed countries. On the East–West axis differences exist when comparing market economies with former centrally planned economies. These differences are based on the economic and cultural development of the countries regarding affluence and scarcity. The most differentiated distribution structures have emerged in the traditional Western free-market economies.

However, distribution structures also differ in Western countries. In a comparative study of France and the USA the shopping behaviour of working and non-working women has been compared.[2] Compared with the French women, the American women did their shopping mainly in large supermarkets and less frequently in local shops. This reflects the situation that shopping malls are common in the USA whereas small, traditional shops are more common in France. US women more frequently shopped at department stores and discounters whereas French women looked for boutiques. Another study reported the relative importance of value for money for store choice in the USA as compared with the UK.[3]

Differences in shopping behaviour mainly reflect differences in distribution structure across countries. The large market-share of small, self-employed grocers in France causes a pattern of fragmented purchases. However, it is also possible that differences in distribution structure reflect underlying differences in consumer attitudes and preferences between countries. On the one hand, the built environment shapes behaviour, but on the other hand, it reflects the culture of the society. In the development of distribution structures it is of great importance to recognize and to capitalize on patterns of behaviour and consumers' purchasing power and values.

The distribution structure not only results from cultural factors but also from historic developments. The department store and the shopping centre emerged in the USA and were introduced later in Europe. Distribution structures have their own life-cycles. The classical department store is now over a hundred years old and is in the final stage of its life-cycle. New types of distribution have emerged, such as hypermarkets (e.g., Pryca, Intermarché, Rinascente), discount warehouses (e.g., Aldi, Lidl, Netto, IKEA), fast-food restaurants (e.g., McDonald's, Burger King), discount chemists (e.g., Superdrug), discount toy warehouses (e.g., Toys'R'Us), franchise outlets (e.g., Benetton) and vending machine shops (especially in Japan).[4]

In comparing the developments of distribution structures across different countries, one should be careful as definitions differ across countries. Hypermarket definitions vary the least across countries: they offer large parking areas, and in most countries the floor size exceeds 2500 m^2. The average number of hypermarkets per 100,000 inhabitants in the European Union has increased from 0.71 in 1981 to 1.20 in 1994. This indicates a large-scale trend toward larger stores. Interestingly, its variance across countries has also increased, indicating an increasing gap between innovators (countries with a relatively large number of hypermarkets)

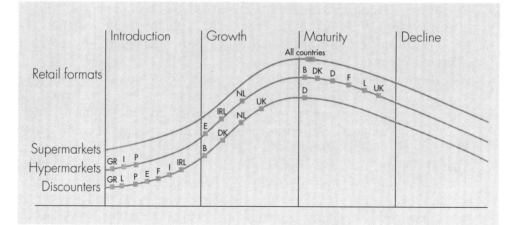

Figure 18.1 *Life-cycles of supermarkets, hypermarkets and discounters in Europe (source: Eurostat)*

and laggards (countries with a relatively small number of hypermarkets).[5] Figure 18.1 shows the situation of various European countries with respect to the stages of the life-cycles of supermarkets, hypermarkets and discounters. It appears that Germany takes the lead with respect to the number of discounters, followed by the other Northern European countries. The Southern European countries are still in the beginning stages of the hypermarket and discounter life-cycles.

The trend toward larger stores in Europe is associated with concentration in the retail sector. In Denmark and the Netherlands, the market share of the biggest three firms in food retailing is 61% and 60% respectively in 1995. In Ireland, it is 43%. In Belgium, France, UK and Germany, it is 30–40%. In Portugal, Spain and Greece it is less than 20%.[6]

18.3 **Shopping centres**

The traditional shopping centre is the 'downtown' city centre. As the cities grew larger, shopping facilities were needed in the suburbs and new shopping centres were planned. The locations, natures and sizes of shopping centres were determined by economic–geographic factors such as density and composition of the population in neighbourhoods and regions. Distribution planning research studies income, age, family size and purchasing power of the population in areas around planned shopping centres.[7] What level of spending on product groups can be expected in the shopping centre? The traffic situation and public transportation facilities are also considered. What is the capacity of supply routes and parking areas? An important question is how far and for how long are consumers willing to travel in order to visit the shopping centre?

Figure 18.2 *Fun shopping*

Shopping centres within a region are competitors. The problem of shopping centre location choice is thus to discover the boundaries of their service areas. When the shopping centre Oosterhof was planned in a suburb of Rotterdam, the issue was whether this would distract customers from the city centre. Parking facilities at Oosterhof were better than in the centre of the city and several retail chains had establishments both at Oosterhof and the city centre. This resulted in pulling customers away from the centre to Oosterhof, as well as attracting new customers from villages in the neighbourhood.

In addition to economic and geographic data, psychological data is important. Shopping is not merely a matter of business. Shopping centres differ regarding atmosphere and attractiveness. Historic city centres with pedestrian areas like Cologne and Copenhagen have different atmospheres than modern city centres like Rotterdam and Frankfurt. For many consumers shopping has become a way of spending their free time. Affective elements like atmosphere thus become important. However, new shopping centres also have advantages such as roofs protecting against wind and rain.

Table 18.1 shows the most important characteristics of shopping centres as reported by the inhabitants of Rotterdam. The explained variances indicate the relative importance of the characteristics. First of all, consumers evaluate shopping centres in general terms of quality, variation, organization, friendliness of personnel, and safety. The second factor concerns the environment—how attractive, peaceful and clean is the environment and what sort of people are around? The third factor concerns efficiency—crowding, walking distance between the shops and distance between home and the shops. The fourth factor is accessibility by car and

Table 18.1 *Importance of shopping centre characteristics*[9]

Factor	Explained variance	Factor loading	Characteristics
General evaluation	45.5%	0.77	Quality of shops
		0.58	Variation of shops
		0.51	Organization
		0.48	Friendliness of personnel
		0.45	Safety
Environment	16.2%	0.58	Traffic noise
		0.46	Kind of people
		0.43	Shelter
		0.37	Clean streets
Efficiency	13.9%	0.68	Walking distance
		0.48	Distance from home
		0.31	Crowding
Accessibility	13.0%	0.50	Parking
		0.48	Public transport
Social aspects	11.5%	0.62	Sociability
		0.42	Friendliness of personnel

public transportation. The last factor comprises social aspects—the sociability and friendliness of personnel. The latter variable is also included in the first factor.

Similar studies in the UK revealed two different sets of factors.[8] At Merry Hill, a shopping mall near Dudley, West Midlands, factors of store variety, comfort and convenience, and general facilities were found to be significant. In the city centre of Worcester, factors of service quality, access, facilities, sociability, choice and variety were found to be important. It appears that, depending on the sample, the shopping environment and the questions asked, different representations of shoppers' values of importance may be found.

Shopping centres compete with each other. Table 18.2 compares six shopping centres in Rotterdam by means of consumer evaluations regarding the five above-mentioned factors. It appears that shopping centre South Square (Zuidplein) dominates on the factors concerning environment, efficiency and accessibility. South Square is a covered shopping centre connected to metro and bus, explaining the favourable judgements in these respects. In terms of general evaluation and social aspects, the Northern Boulevard and Boulevard South are judged favourably. These are friendly shopping centres outside of the city centre. The shopping centres West–North and West–South are judged rather unfavourably. These are old shopping streets which feel unsafe in the evening and which also offer little shelter from the weather. At the time of this survey, Oosterhof had not yet been opened. Rotterdam Centre obtains average scores as compared with the other shopping centres.

The images of shopping centres are based on these perceptions.[10] In essence, a shopping centre's image comprises a set of opinions about the characteristics mentioned, both in an absolute sense and in comparison with other shopping centres.

Table 18.2 *Comparison of six shopping centres in Rotterdam*[11]

Factor	Centre	South Square	West-North	West-South	North Boulevard	Boulevard South
General evaluation	2.9	2.8	2.8	2.9	3.1	3.0
Environment	2.2	3.2	1.7	2.0	2.2	2.4
Efficiency	2.9	3.4	2.9	2.9	3.0	3.1
Accessibility	2.3	2.8	2.1	2.1	1.8	2.2
Social aspects	2.5	2.5	2.5	2.6	3.1	2.9
Weighted average	2.6	3.0	2.4	2.5	2.7	2.7

Note: Five-point scale: 1 = very unfavourable; 5 = very favourable

18.4 Shops

Shops can also be investigated and compared on a number of factors. The following characteristics of shops are important.[12]

- The *location* of the shop with respect to parking areas, public transport and other shops. Solitary shops, shops at street corners and outside shopping streets or shopping centres are gradually disappearing. To older consumers without a car, the disappearance of shops from the neighbourhood is a problem. A location in a shopping centre with many people passing by is favourable to the retailer. Often 'crowd-pullers', for example discounters are placed at the far ends of the shopping centre. The other shops benefit from the people walking from one crowd-puller to another. Frequently, shoppers buy on impulse while walking along the shop fronts.
- The *appearance* of the shop serves to attract the interest of the shoppers. Appearance includes the architecture, flags, shop-windows, posters, items at the entrance like racks with clothes or flowers. The shop-window is a vital element fulfilling an important role for specialty shops. For supermarkets, the shop-window as a display area has disappeared.
- The *shop layout* is considered to be a way of inducing purchasing behaviour within the shop. Offers and packaging should be laid out to attract the consumer's attention. The shop layout determines the consumer's affective reaction and a feeling of familiarity.[13] A small floor-size gives the impression of familiarity, however at the expense of a wide variety of stock. The length of aisles in shops is an important determinant of purchase behaviour.[14] If aisles are too short, customers do not walk up them, but merely look into the aisle to find various items. But this can mean that they overlook purchase offers at the other ends of short aisles.
- The *perceived price level* of a shop does not necessarily coincide with the actual price level. Many shops advertise intensively with a few low-priced products to suggest a generally low price level.
- The *width and depth of the variety on offer*. The width concerns the range of products in a shop. The depth concerns the number of brands and varieties within a group of products. Specialty shops have a small range of products but offer variety within those ranges; whereas discounters offer wide ranges but little depth of stock.
- The *expertise and friendliness of personnel* is especially important in 'service shops' such as clothing and furniture stores, car dealers, travel agencies, banks, and copyshops. In the case of self-service, an accurate and friendly cashier frequently provides the only human contact with the customer.

- The *store atmosphere* results from physical characteristics and subjective perceptions. The store atmosphere can be manipulated to induce certain effects on the behaviour of customers.[15] At the bakery section one smells freshly baked bread. Background music, colours and shop design can influence customers so that they stay longer in the shop and experience their visits as more pleasant.[16]
- The *type of customers* visiting a shop. Customers like to visit shops in which they meet people from their own reference group.[17]
- *Personal service* is a characteristic of specialty shops. For instance, the gift purchase is nicely wrapped, the clothing can be altered to fit, and heavy or large goods can be delivered at home. In contrast, the personal service of discounters is minimal.
- The *perceived quality* of the stock on offer is frequently based on several conspicuous items which are advertised and that establish the impression of high quality of the stock.[18] Many shops whose entire ranges are based on high-quality products exist.
- The *waiting times* in the shop are an increasingly important factor for hurried consumers.[19] Consumers frequently have to wait, for example, at the hairdresser, travel agency, car dealer, builder's merchant, post office, ATM, restaurant, fun park, social service office, hospital and supermarket. Consumers perceive queues to be shorter and are less dissatisfied if

  - the waiting time is made more attractive,
  - they perceive progress in being served,
  - they are not worried about the waiting time,
  - they know how long the waiting will last,
  - the reason for waiting is explained,
  - the rules of waiting are equitable,
  - the customer is waiting in the company of others,
  - the service is considered valuable.

For example, Disneyland Paris offers live music performances to queues waiting for rides, the queues are organized, the waiting times are announced and the queues are (slowly) moving. A number of supermarkets offer quick cashier services for customers buying just a few items.

- *Marketing communication* by shops mainly consists of advertisements and door-to-door flyers and papers. This is meant to attract customers, but at the same time it gives an impression of the prices and the quality of the stock on offer. Within the shop, the decoration, displays and other elements of the interior serve to make the customer's stay in the shop agreeable. To the retailer, the latter forms of communication are methods of increasing sales and turning one-off customers into regular ones.

Store image

The store image is largely based on the characteristics mentioned above. Stores position themselves such that they distinguish themselves from other stores. To consumers, Harrods is a different store than Tesco. The former has a higher perceived quality, the latter a lower perceived price level. Private labels can also contribute to the store image. Private labels—also called own-labels—are brands owned by the retain chain, e.g., Marks & Spencer (St Michael), Sainsbury and Dixons (Matsui). Private labels are gaining market share in Europe at the expense of generic or manufacturer labels.[20] For example, in the UK, market share has increased from 21% in 1986 to 37% in 1992.[21] This effect is mainly due to the relatively low price of private labels,[22] and the greater concentration of retailers, mentioned earlier.[23] A private label is exclusively available in stores associated with the label and contributes to the positioning of the store. In contrast, generic labels with a high distribution coverage do not offer opportunities for store identification, because other stores also sell these labels. Private labels are no longer inferior substitutes purchased mainly by price-conscious consumers. Due to democratization, increased quality and innovativeness, private labels are becoming more popular in the higher social classes too.[24]

Types of stores

Table 18.3 shows the diversity of stores, distinguished by general and specific target groups. A general target group consists of a heterogeneous population. A specific target group consists of consumers interested in a certain product category. The general stockist is characterized by wide product categories, large turnover and low margins for the retailer. Prices are relatively low and relatively few services are provided. The specific stock is characterized by category depth, high prices, high margins and added value in the form of customer service.

Stores serving a general target group are characterized by an undifferentiated approach of the general public and a product-oriented shopping

Table 18.3 *Assortment, target groups and types of shops*

Target group	General assortment	Specific assortment
General	*Intensive general store* Broad, but shallow stock, e.g., department store, supermarket	*Classical specialty store* Narrow, deep assortment, e.g., sports shop, butcher
Specific	*Selective general store* Selected 'spearheads', e.g., photo shop and copy shop within store	*Super specialty store* Small, unique assortment, e.g., golf shop, tie shop

experience. The stock is usually traditional. Stores serving a specific target group approach their customers more specifically. The shopping experience is aimed mainly at the customer lifestyle and shop atmosphere. The stock frequently includes innovations. Specialty shops in many retail areas compete with general shops for market share. Sometimes department stores develop in-store specialty shops, thus becoming selective general stores.

The sports shop and the traditional bakery, butcher and druggist are examples of classical specialty shops. The Häagen Dazs ice-cream shops form a more recent example as do the Tie Rack shops which exclusively sell ties.

Traditional stores, specialty stores and frequently also department stores serve the first three stages of the consumption cycle.[25] However, it is to be expected that some consumers and some firms will separate these stages in the future. The Internet can now serve the first stage of information provision about the supply of goods and services. Discounters mainly serve the second stage, as they neither provide information and advice nor maintenance and repair. Repair shops take care of the third stage.

Buying through mail order, teleshopping and homeshopping provide alternatives to outdoor shopping. In Germany, mail catalogue sales comprise almost 5% of annual spending. In Austria, Sweden, UK, Denmark, France, Switzerland and Norway, this figure varies between 2% and 4%.[26]

A different alternative is home delivery of goods after a telephone order, e.g., pizza delivery. Some supermarkets also provide this service. Home shopping is emerging by means of lifestyle magazines, teletext or the Internet.[27] IBM has launched a pilot shopping service on the Internet—PC Gifts and Flowers—initially selling flowers, balloons, teddy bears and gourmet food. Soon, electronic payment for these services from within the home will become possible. The advantages to the consumer are savings in time and effort, the disadvantages are diminished inspection of the goods available, the obligation to be at home at the time of delivery, and possibly higher prices. The advantages to the retailer are savings in storage costs, handling of goods within the shop and check-out personnel, the disadvantages are reduced opportunities at the point of sale.

Possibly, in the future, shops will be more involved in the final stage of the consumption cycle. Some current examples include shops which take back returnable packages, glass and containers, second-hand shops for clothing and appliances, used-car dealerships and antique shops.

18.5 Shopping behaviour

Shopping behaviour is described here by following the stages of the consumption cycle, i.e., search, purchase, use and disposition.

Searching while shopping

The shop, including shop-windows, product presentations, displays, sales talks and other product information, is an important medium for consumer search. An important advantage of shops is the physical presence of products. The video-cassette recorder can be tested and clothing can be tried on before purchasing. Some fashion specialty stores organize fashion shows for their customers to show their new collections. In addition, more and more information is provided by displays or product description leaflets rather than verbally by salespeople.

Motives for shopping   ·

Obviously, searching and purchasing goods and services are important functions of shopping. In this sense, shopping is instrumental to consumption. However, in addition hedonistic shopping motives can be discerned. Furthermore, motives can be either individual or social.[28] In table 18.4, shopping motives have been categorized into four groups. It is also possible to divide motives into two categories: individual and social.

Individual motives for shopping
- *Learning* about product supply, the new fashion, innovations and the psychosocial meaning of products and brands.
- *Bargain hunting*. Many consumers consider it an interesting and exciting sport to buy items cheaply during sales, at second-hand markets, car boot sales or at other occasions.
- *Physical activity*. For several consumer types shopping can be a necessary form of physical activity, for example, the elderly or people who have sedentary jobs.
- *Entertainment and recreation*. Fun shopping can be entertaining as a variation on housekeeping or work in a paid job. Shopping can stimulate one's daydreams, for example, the furniture and decoration section of a department store.

Table 18.4 *Shopping motives*

	Individual	Social
Instrumental	Learning about supply Bargain hunting	Negotiation
Hedonistic	Physical activity Entertainment, recreation Bargain hunting Role playing Sensory stimulation Avoiding boredom Self-gratification	Social experiences Communication Reference group Status and authority Negotiation

- *Role playing.* Some consumers like to play the role of the critical consumer, expert, concerned mother or poor student. Certain behaviours such as negotiation fit these roles and are imitated and accepted in shops.
- *Sensory stimulation.* This motive comprises variety seeking, for example, by touching and looking at goods, browsing through books and magazines, gaining interesting experiences, sniffing the smell of perfume or the warm bakery, or listening to music in a record shop.
- *Avoiding boredom.* Different from the sensory stimulation motive, the avoidance of boredom, depression and loneliness can instigate compulsive buying behaviour.[29] It is pleasant to purchase items and to have the concentrated attention of salespeople.
- *Self-gratification.* Some consumers like to buy something for themselves if they are in a depressive mood. In such a mood, they like to indulge themselves or to be indulged, for example, by eating cakes or ice-cream, going to the hair-dresser or having a manicure. By doing this, they may overcome their mood.

Social motives for shopping
- *Negotiation.* The pleasure of negotiating with salespeople in purchase situations where there is no fixed price, such as at second-hand markets and when trading-in a car.
- *Social experience.* Gaining social experiences, for example, sitting at an outdoor cafe in summer, looking at people and other people's clothes.
- *Communication.* Talking to other people who have similar interests and hobbies, such as photography or embroidery, for example, with salespeople and other consumers.
- *Reference group.* In some shops, one meets friends and members of one's own reference group. For example, in a record shop one meets people interested in music.
- *Status and authority.* Some consumers like giving orders and being served (as in the hairdressers, in a restaurant or at a bar).

Purchase and provision of services

Shopping is not everyone's hobby. For daily necessities consumers usually consider shopping to be a necessary, important and easy job but not a hobby. Opinions about the pleasure of daily shopping are divided.[30] For more interesting goods, such as clothes, jewellery and cars, shopping can be fun.

Impulsive buying behaviour

Some consumers go to the supermarket with a shopping list and buy everything on their list. The list may contain products, for example, beer, or brands, for example, Boddingtons. If beer is on the list, it does not mean

Figure 18.3 *Run shopping*

that there is no brand preference. To some consumers, beer always means Boddingtons. However, it may also indicate that brand choice is made in the shop. If so, then brand choice is more or less impulsive, depending on supply and pricing. Other consumers use the shelves in the supermarket to prompt their purchases. They walk along the shelves and realize that they need chocolates, cookies or coffee. This method of shopping makes it easier to persuade them to buy more than strictly necessary.[31]

> **Definition**
>
> Impulse buying is purchase behaviour without a (complete) plan to buy, frequently resulting from a sudden urge that cannot be resisted.

Consumers frequently buy products in the shop they did not intend to buy before entering. This is known as impulse buying, and it occurs in different degrees. Table 18.5 shows the possibilities, which are also discussed in the following:

- *No intention*. An impulsive product choice occurs if the consumer has no intention of buying a certain product and yet buys the product. A complete impulse purchase occurs if, in addition, the brand choice is impulsive. The brand choice does not need to be impulsive. For example,

Table 18.5 *Types of impulsive buying behaviour*

	Product impulse	Brand impulse	Description
No intention	Yes	Yes	Complete impulse buying
	Yes	No	Impulsive product choice
Product intention	No	Yes	Impulsive brand choice
	No	No	Planned purchase
Brand intention	Yes	No	Impulsive product choice
	No	No	Planned purchase

one may buy a bottle of sherry on impulse, but if one buys sherry, one may always choose Sandeman.

- *Product intention.* An impulsive brand choice occurs if the consumer plans to buy a product but decides on the brand in the shop. A completely planned purchase occurs if the consumer is brand loyal and always chooses a certain brand when buying a product. For example, someone who puts cornflakes on the shopping list and then chooses Kellogg's because he or she always buys this brand of cornflakes.
- *Brand intention.* An impulsive product choice occurs if the consumer has no intention of buying a product before entering the shop but decides to buy it in the shop. The brand choice need not be impulsive if a clear brand preference already exists. A completely planned purchase occurs if both the product and the brand purchase were planned.

From the above, it appears that three types of impulse buying exist, implying various degrees of impulse buying behaviour. For this reason, it is impossible to assess how many decisions are taken in the store. Each purchase that is not on the shopping list is not necessarily an unplanned purchase.

Types of shopping behaviour

Consumers differ considerably regarding their shopping behaviour, i.e., concerning their sensitivity to shopping characteristics such as price, quality, variety and distance. On the basis of consumer sensitivities, clusters of consumers can be formed, which can be described in terms of socio-demographic characteristics.[32]

- Price-conscious consumers are willing to accept lower quality for a lower price. They frequently buy at discounters.
- Price-unconscious consumers are willing to pay more for better service and they often buy from specialty shops such as the bakery, delicatessen or butcher.
- Lower-income consumers are sensitive to price and distance. They may not own a car and are dependent on shops in the neighbourhood.

- Many consumers with young children at home are sensitive to distance. They cannot leave home easily but at the same time they need food relatively often. For this reason, the distance to the shop is important to them.
- To many consumers with large families with older children a wide variety of goods is important.

Consumers frequently use certain strategies for shopping. Possible shopping strategies are:

- Buy all products at a large supermarket such as Sainsburys, Tesco or Lidl;
- Buy all products at specialty shops, such as the bakery, greengrocer and butcher;
- Buy at the supermarket once a week and buy the remaining items at specialty shops;
- Buy once a week at the discounter such as Aldi and the remaining items at specialty shops;
- Buy at the discounter once a week and the remaining items at the supermarket.

The first two strategies include primary stores only. The latter three strategies include both a primary store and secondary shops for complementary shopping. Secondary shops are frequently used for items that are either not available in the primary shop or that do not have the desired quality. Also, secondary shops are used to buy perishable items, for example, fresh vegetables.

Use and re-use

After-sales service concerns the third stage of the consumption cycle. This regards the proper installation of the products and usage instructions, for example, the installation of a PC, and the maintenance and repair of a car. After-sales service also comprises the sales of supplementary and complementary products such as spare parts.[33]

The fourth stage—in the case of durable goods—includes scrapping and re-use, which can take several forms. To the distribution channel the re-use of products in their original functions is of main importance. Furthermore, the re-use of parts and materials is relevant. The trade of used goods frequently takes place at second-hand markets, which are either institutionalized or informal.[34] Second-hand markets for goods and parts are frequently dependent on volunteers, e.g., the Salvation Army and jumble sales. It is possible that these activities will become of interest to commerce as a reverse marketing channel.[35]

18.6 Way-finding and crowding

Way-finding[36]

Sometimes consumers have difficulty in finding their way around shopping centres. The elderly in particular sometimes spend a long time looking around before they find the shop they want. Consumers use a mental 'map' of a shopping centre or shopping street. Elements of the map can be

Figure 18.4 *Mental map?*

pathways, areas, borders, crossings and recognition marks, such as a statue or special building.[37] A mental map is an internal representation of an external geographical reality.[38] Consumers do not have exact mental maps in their heads but they use elements such as pathways and areas to find their way about and to form an idea of the location. However, little is actually known about how consumers find their way and do not get lost in shopping centres and department stores.

Research has shown which shops and characteristics of the shopping centre are recalled most.[39] Shops at pathway crossings are remembered relatively well. Shops with special or distinguishing architectures were used as reference points in consumers' mental maps, both for traditional shopping streets and modern shopping centres.

The complexity of shopping centres affects the development of mental maps.[40] The traditional shopping street has two dimensions but the shopping centre has three since it has several levels. Obviously, a three-dimensional map is more difficult to construct and remember than a two-dimensional map. Yet way-finding is not more problematic in the shopping centre than in the shopping street. The latter finding was based on consumers' reports of how they would go to a particular shop. These results suggest that either three-dimensional maps are simplified—for example, by constructing two-dimensional maps for each level—or way-finding includes different processes than just the ability to form mental maps.

Products are sometimes hard to find within the supermarket. In general, consumers find products placed at the sides easier than those in the aisles. Frequently, fresh products, dairy products, bread, meat and vegetables, are placed along the sides. These products are purchased relatively often. Relatively fewer consumers walk through the aisles and they are less able to find products there.[41] Both passive and active search strategies of way-finding in the shop have been found.[42] The passive strategy comprises looking at the environment to identify specific products and then reviewing one's shopping list to assess the likelihood of finding any desired products in that area. In the active strategy, consumers first review their shopping lists and then select specific products to locate. In a different study, both knowledge of the store environment and available time increased the number of unplanned purchases in a grocery store.[43]

Crowding

Crowding concerns the physical density of people in a shopping environment.[44] In crowded shops consumers can hardly concentrate and there is a greater chance that they will take wrong decisions. They may leave earlier than planned and develop a negative attitude towards the shop. Customers in a busy shoe section of a department store remembered fewer details concerning the range of shoes and the store design than those in comparable but less busy environments.[45] In crowded grocery stores, customers feel less satisfied with the supermarket, feel less comfortable and have more difficulty finding and choosing items.[46] These effects are smaller if customers are used to crowding and know how to deal with such situations.[47]

Consumers may react to crowding in different ways. It may cause anxiety and aggression.[48] They may adapt to a crowded environment by spending less time shopping, visiting fewer shops before deciding, postponing purchases, avoiding crowded shopping centres, letting others do the shopping, and limiting their interactions with people in the shopping environment.[49] Alternatives for crowded shopping environments are buying through mail order or buying in small, well-known and familiar shops. Crowded and unsafe shopping centres thus may increase loyalty to traditional shops.

A crowded shop causes distraction and time pressure. In these situations consumers tend to simplify their information processing and rely on elimination rules and direct evidence.[50] This implies that they easily reject alternatives with negative characteristics.

Crowding is not always negative, however. An empty restaurant or a desolated shopping centre is not appreciated. Diners often feel ill at ease in an empty restaurant. They may doubt the quality of food and service. In cafés crowding is more acceptable than in banks or shops. A café should be busy as this increases the chances of meeting nice people. In a bank, crowding conflicts with privacy, and speedy, efficient service. A soccer match lacks atmosphere if there are only a few supporters.

In this way, shops, banks, restaurants, cafés, stadia, theatres, aeroplanes, trains, buses, trams and other public spaces each have their own optimal level of crowding.[51] Optimal crowding is associated with the optimal level of stimulation.[52] In these situations the consumer's perceived control is relevant. If consumers feel in control or are told that they are not dominated by the situation, are independent and need not passively wait until being served, crowding is evaluated less negatively.[53] Furthermore, the subjective experience of crowding varies according to the efficiency and effectiveness of the service. One can still be served quickly in a busy McDonald's establishment.

18.7 Conclusions

Simply describing the shopping environment in terms of physical and psychological characteristics is insufficient for a full understanding of consumer behaviour in this situation. Research into the shopping environment should include the conceptual boundaries of the location and the psychological dimensions of the situation in order to develop a taxonomy.[54] The taxonomy may serve both to explain, predict and even manipulate the consumer's shopping behaviour.

Models of shopping environments and their effects on consumer behaviour need to be psychological. A great number of situational aspects may induce psychological, affective reactions of consumers and this influences their behaviour in the shopping centre, department store and shop.

Shopping is both instrumental and hedonistic, respectively routine shopping and fun shopping. The hedonistic function can be both individual and social. One gains new experiences and meets other people. Shopping can be fun and is a form of recreation to many consumers. This is evidenced by the massive stream of consumers at Sunday shop openings.

The instrumental and hedonistic functions of shopping are inhibited by waiting times and crowding. In many cases this is evaluated negatively and causes suboptimal consumer behaviour and feelings of lack of control of the situation.

Notes

1   Sack, R. D. (1988) 'The consumer's world: Place as context' *Annals of the Association of American Geographers* 78, 4, 642–664.
2   Douglas, S. (1976) 'Cross national comparisons and consumer stereotypes: a case study of working and non-working wives in the US and France' *Journal of Consumer Research* 3, 12–20.
3   D. Perkins, cited in East, R. (1997) *Consumer Behavior: Advances and Applications in Marketing* (London: Prentice Hall) 231.
4   Van Raaij, W. F. and Floor, J. M. G. (1983) 'Retailing developments in the Netherlands' *International Journal of Physical Distribution & Materials Management* 13, 128–137.
5   Based on Euromonitor (1995), *European Marketing Data and Statistics* (London: Euromonitor Publications)
    Foodmagazine International (1995) 2, 5–32; 5, 3–40; 1, 19–30; 8, 11–32; 6, 13–31; 3, 5–31; (1996) 1, 13–31.
    Eurostat (1993), *Retailing in the European Single Market 1993* (Luxemburg: Eurostat) 8th edition.
    Nilsson, O. S. and Solgaard, H. S. (1995) 'The changing consumer in Denmark' *International Journal of Research in Marketing* 12, 405–416.
    Grunert, K. G., Grunert, S. C., Glatzer, W. and Imkamp, H. (1995) 'The changing consumer in Germany' *International Journal of Research in Marketing* 12, 417–433.
6   *Foodmagazine International* (1995).
7   See, for example, Wrigley, N. (Ed.) (1988) *Store Choice, Store Location and Market Analysis* (London: Routledge).
8   Hackett, P. M. W. and Foxall, G. R. (1994) 'A factor analytic study of consumers' location specific values: a traditional high street and a modern shopping mall' *Journal of Marketing Management* 10, 163–178.
9   Van Raaij, W. F. (1983) 'Shopping centre evaluation and patronage in the city of Rotterdam' *Papers on Economic Psychology* 27 (Rotterdam: Erasmus University).

10 See section 8.2.

11 Van Raaij (1983).

12 See also Lindquist, J. D. (1974–1975) 'The meaning of image' *Journal of Retailing* 50(winter), 29–38.

13 Giffort, R. (1987) *Environmental Psychology: Principles and Practices* (Boston, MA: Allyn and Bacon).

14 Sommer, R., Herrick, J. and Sommer, T. R. (1981) 'The behavioral ecology of supermarkets and farmers' markets' *Journal of Environmental Psychology* 1, 13–19.
    May, F. E. (1965) 'Buying behaviour: some research findings' *Journal of Business* 39, 379–396.

15 See, for example, Kotler, P. (1973) 'Atmospherics as a marketing tool' *Journal of Retailing* 49(Winter), 48–64.

16 Milliman, R. E. (1982) 'Using background music to affect the behaviour of supermarket shoppers' *Journal of Marketing* 46, 86–91.
    Milliman, R. E. (1986) 'The influence of background music on the behaviour of restaurant patrons' *Journal of Consumer Research* 13, 286–289.
    Kellaris, J. J. and Rice, R. C. (1993) 'The influence of tempo, loudness and gender of listeners on responses to music' *Psychology and Marketing* 10, 15–29.
    Bellizzi, J., Crawley, A. and Hasty, R. (1983) 'The effects of color in store design' *Journal of Retailing* 59, 21–45.

17 See chapter 14.

18 For quality management, see section 5.5.

19 Pruyn, A. and Smidts, A. (1993) 'Customers' evaluations of queues: three exploratory studies' in: Van Raaij, W. F. and Bamossy, G. J. (Eds) *European Advances of Consumer Research* Vol. 1 (Provo, UT: Association for Consumer Research) 371–382.

20 Corstjens, J. and Corstjens, M. (1995) *Store Wars, The Battle for Mindspace and Shelfspace* (Chichester, UK: John Wiley).

21 Nielsen (1994) *Europa Retail Trends 1993* (Diemen, The Netherlands: Nielsen).

22 Glémet, F. and Mira, R. (1993) 'Solving the brand leader's dilemma' *The McKinsey Quarterly* 2, 3–15.
    Glémet, F. and Mira, R. (1993) 'Solving the brand leader's dilemma' *The McKinsey Quarterly* 4, 87–98.
    Hoch, S. J. (1996) 'How should national brands think about private labels?' *Sloan Management Review* Winter, 89–102.

23 Messinger, P. R. and Narasimhan, C. (1995) 'Has power shifted in the grocery channel?' *Marketing Science* 14, 189–223.

24 Doel, C. (1996) 'Market development and organizational change: the case of the food industry' in: Wrigley, N. and Lowe, M. (Eds) *Retailing, Consumption and Capital* (Harlow: Longman) 48–67.

25 See section 4.5.

26 *Gale Country and World Rankings Reporter* (1995) (New York: Gale Research Inc.).

27 OECD (1992) *New Home Shopping Technologies* (Paris: OECD).

28 Tauber, E. M. (1972) 'Why do people shop?' *Journal of Marketing* 36, 46–59.

29 See section 23.5.

30 Source: time budget survey of the Dutch Social and Cultural Planning Bureau (1980).

31 Rook, D. W. (1987) 'The buying impulse' *Journal of Consumer Research* 14, 189–199.

32 Verhallen, T. M. M. and De Nooij, G. J. (1982) "Retail attribute sensitivity and shopping patronage' *Journal of Economic Psychology* 2, 39–55. This is an example of domain-specific market segmentation. See section 24.4.

33 See section 22.5.

34 See Stroeker, N. E. (1995) 'Second-hand markets for consumer durables' (Doctoral dissertation, Erasmus University, Rotterdam).

35 Zikmund, W. G. and Stanton, W. J. (1971) 'Recycling of solid wastes: a channels-of-distribution problem' *Journal of Marketing* 35, 34–39.

36 Hackett, P. M. W., Foxall, G. R. and Van Raaij, W. F. (1993) 'Consumers in retail environments' in: Gärling, T. and Golledge, R. G. (Eds) *Behavior and Environment: Psychological and Geographical Approaches* (Amsterdam: Elsevier) 378–399.

37 Lynch, K. (1960) *The Image of the City* (Cambridge, MA: MIT Press).

38 Olshavsky, R. W., MacKay, D. B. and Sentell, G. (1975) 'Perceptual maps of retail locations' *Journal of Applied Psychology* 60, 80–86.
    MacKay, D. B. and Olshavsky, R. W. (1975) 'Cognitive maps of retail locations. An investigation of some basic issues' *Journal of Consumer Research* 2, 197–205.

39 Hackett, P. M. W. and Foxall, G. R. (1992) 'How consumers structure evaluations of satisfaction within complex service and retail locations: a mapping sentence design study of a modern international airport development' (University of Birmingham, Consumer Research Unit).

40 Moeser, S. D. (1988) 'Cognitive mapping in a complex building' *Environment and Behavior* 20, 29–49.
    Hackett and Foxall (1992).

41 Sommer, R. and Aitkens, S. (1982) 'Mental mapping of two supermarkets' *Journal of Consumer Research* 9, 211–216.

42 Titus, P. A. and Everett, P. B. (1996) 'Consumer wayfinding tasks, strategies, and errors: an exploratory field study' *Psychology & Marketing* 13, 265–290.

43 Iyer, E. S. (1989) 'Unplanned purchasing: knowledge and shopping environment and time pressure' *Journal of Retailing* 65, 40–57.

44 Harrell, G. D., Hutt, M. and Anderson, J. (1980) 'Path analysis of buyer behavior under conditions of crowding' *Journal of Marketing Research* 17, 45–51.

45 Saegert, S. (1973) 'Crowding: cognitive overload and behavioral constraint' in: Preiser, W. (Ed.) *Environmental Design Research* Vol. 2 (Stroudsberg, PA: Dowden, Hutchinson and Ross) 254–261.

46 Langer, E. J. and Saegert, S. (1977) 'Crowding and cognitive control' *Journal of Personality and Social Psychology* 35, 175–182.

47 Harrell, Hutt and Anderson (1980).

48 Harrell, Hutt and Anderson (1980).

49 Harrell and Hunt (1970).
    Milgram (1970).

50 Wright, P. L. (1974) 'The harassed decision maker: time pressure, distractions, and the use of evidence' *Journal of Applied Psychology* 59, 555–561. See also section 11.5.

51 Wicker, A. W. (1984) *Introduction to Ecological Psychology* (Monterey, CA: Brooks/Cole).

52 See sections 8.3 and 9.2 and figure 9.5.

53 Perceived control is the third dimension of the PAD model. See section 12.3.
Hui, M. K. and Bateson, J. E. G. (1991) 'Perceived control and the effects of crowding and consumer choice on the service experience' *Journal of Consumer Research* 18, 174–184.
Langer and Saegert (1977).

54 A taxonomy is a systematic overview of possible shopping situations, categorized into main groups and subgroups based on certain criteria.

19

FINANCIAL BEHAVIOUR

19.1 Introduction

Financial behaviour is an important aspect of consumer behaviour. Financial aspects are included in purchase, rent and maintenance of goods and services. Because of budget restrictions, consumers are confronted with financial considerations, and decisions over saving and borrowing. Financial behaviour comprises budget management, saving, borrowing, investment, insurance, filing tax forms and paying taxes, earning extra income, gambling, speculation, and wealth management. Financial behaviour plays a part in the decision to spend or to save money. It also plays a part in the consideration of paying for a car or other item in cash or buying it on credit. Banks and insurance companies need to understand consumers' financial behaviour to attract consumers with good credit ratings. For the government, knowledge of consumer financial behaviour is relevant in assisting consumers in problematic debt situations. The structurally decreasing saving quota of consumers in several countries is a macroeconomic problem.[1] Although recently, savings have increased, especially in pension funds and other forms of old-age income provision.

In recent years, the saving behaviour of consumers has become increasingly complex. In many transactions, cash payment has been replaced by cheques, credit cards, and electronic payment. Because of the abundance of credit facilities, the financial situation of many households has become less transparent—even to the households themselves.

Section 19.2 gives an overview of different levels of financial behaviour. The financial life-cycle model describes important life events and their respective financial consequences. The financial management of the traditional household implies a distribution of roles and duties between husband and wife. Payment becomes different by the introduction of new payment methods such as credit cards and electronic payment (section 19.3). Saving, borrowing, insurance and investment are considered in sections 19.4, 19.5, 19.6 and 19.7, respectively. In section 19.8 conclusions are drawn. The aim of this chapter is to offer insight into the different varieties of financial consumer behaviour.

19.2 Levels of financial behaviour

The financial behaviour of households and individuals is not only of interest to banks, insurance companies and other financial institutions. It is also important from a consumer protection perspective, to pay attention to cash management, saving and borrowing. One of the aims of governmental consumer policy is to protect low-income households in particular against misleading information concerning credit facilities and any eventual financial mistakes that result.[2]

Four levels of financial behaviour can be distinguished:[3] budget and cash management, creation and maintenance of a precautionary buffer, financing goal attainment, and wealth management.

Budget and cash management

This level of operation includes payment from current accounts. Usually, salary is transferred regularly to a bank account and money is spent on rent, mortgage, energy and other fixed obligations. Furthermore, there is expenditure on food, transportation and recreation. If there is money left at the end of the month, this is called *residual saving*—a form of non-conscious, accidental saving. The temporary overdraft on the salary account could be labelled a non-conscious type of borrowing.

Buffers and precautions

At the second level, consumers attempt to create savings accounts and maintain them as buffers and precautions against unforeseen events. Some-times, these accounts can contain several thousand euros over the long term. In this case a short-term saving account will also be maintained. Some households regularly transfer money to a savings account. A revolving credit account may also be used as a buffer for unforeseen expenses.[4] For instance, the car or the washing machine may suddenly break down and need to be replaced. An accident with financial consequences may occur. The creation and maintenance of a buffer demands self-control in order not to spend the balance on consumption.[5]

Goal attainment by saving or borrowing

Some consumers do not want to use their savings accounts for con-sumption and would rather arrange personal loans.[6] Consumers may save or borrow money for specific transactions; the purchase of a durable good or a holiday trip. Saving for a certain transaction is called *goal saving*. This also includes setting aside money for trading in the car. The payment of consumer credit, used to finance a transaction, may be considered a form of retroactive saving.

Wealth management

The fourth level is reserved for higher incomes and home-owners exclusively. It deals with the creation and maintenance of (family) capital by investment, speculation and real estate.[7] Fiscal benefits, high interest and return (dividend) and avoidance of inflation are important objectives in this respect. Households and individuals with high incomes frequently take advice from tax experts and investment consultants to avoid taxes and to obtain high returns.

Hierarchical model of financial behaviour

These levels of financial behaviour constitute a hierarchical model (see figure 19.1). All consumers are involved in the first level (budget and cash management). Depending on their income level, households become involved in the second, third and fourth levels. Households, involved in a certain level of financial behaviour, will also be involved in lower levels. At the level of goal saving, one usually also maintains a financial buffer and one is involved in budget and cash management.

Definition

The hierarchy of financial behaviour captures the general tendency of consumers to engage in higher levels of behaviour (e.g., wealth management) only after they have dealt with the lower levels (e.g., precautionary saving).

The four levels mentioned are not strictly separated. One can imagine that some consumers save for certain necessary goods first, such as a refrigerator, car, house, and other durables, and build a financial buffer later. Many consumers keep a saving account while they borrow money to purchase durable goods at the same time. This seems irrational since the interest on a saving account is usually lower than the interest on a loan. Yet, it may be sensible to force oneself to discharge a debt without using the saving account.[8] This is a type of behaviour that could be explained by mental budgeting, which was considered in section 4.3.[9]

In a French survey, the four levels were assessed as follows.[10] The first group (20% of French households) is exclusively involved in residual saving. This frequently concerns the young and the single. The second group (33% of households) also values security and saves money as a buffer. The third group (33% of households) have a variety of needs and

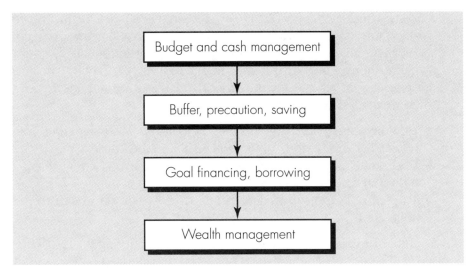

Figure 19.1 *Levels of financial behaviour*

practise goal saving. In particular, they are saving for the purchase and the furnishing of a house. The fourth group includes the wealthy (14% of households) who owned over 400,000 francs in 1981. These households invest relatively little money in savings institutions as they put their wealth in stocks, bonds and real estate. These are mainly highly educated and well-informed individuals.

Financial life-cycle

In economics, saving behaviour has been described by means of the life-cycle model.[11] This model assumes a striving for a permanent level of spending, equal to the average income over the entire life-cycle of a household. Since the highest income level is not achieved immediately, the income at a younger age will be lower than the life-cycle average. At this stage borrowing is prevalent, for instance to pay for education or to buy a house. At a later age, the income is usually higher than the life-cycle average. At this stage, a buffer is created which is spent during the spell thereafter (retirement). If in the meantime an unforeseen income shock occurs, the average level of spending will be adapted. The life-cycle model concerns saving as a precaution for old age but also as wealth management,

Definition

The economic life-cycle model assumes a permanent level of spending, equal to the average income over the entire life-cycle of the household. This implies fluctuating levels of wealth.

namely when savings for old age are invested in shares, life insurances and real estate. This is particularly relevant for people without (sufficient) pension arrangements, such as self-employed entrepreneurs.

Some households are unable to save enough to spend the life-cycle average in their old age. On the other hand, many households do not spend their wealth.[12] The latter may be caused by:

- Liquidity constraints, for instance inability to mortgage 100% of one's house. For this reason, money will be left 'in the house'.
- Uncertainty about the time of death, such that one always has to have money in reserve.
- The felt obligation to bequeath inherited or earned wealth to the next generation.[13]

Table 19.1 shows a list of characteristic events during the household life-cycle. The period until 25 years of age is characterized by saving, between 25 and 45 years by arranging and discharging loans and mortgage, between 45 and 65 years by saving again and beyond the age of 65 by drawing on savings. Given this pattern, it is rational to borrow money around the age of 25 years and to buy a house on a mortgage. In the period between 45 and 65 years of age, the loans can be discharged. In a business cycle with relatively high inflation, owners of a house will be better off than those who have rented a house.[15] Contracting debts in these situations is rational because the value of the purchased house increases. In addition, the interest paid may be deducted from the income tax in several countries. Moreover, the interest received would have been taxed above a certain threshold.[16] Most fiscal systems actually reward borrowing and discourage saving.

Table 19.1 *Financial life-cycle*[14]

Age	Life events	Financial behaviours and services
0–16 years	Go to school	Youth saving plans
16–20 years	Education/work	Student grant
	Independence	Open current account
20–25 years	Cohabitation/marriage	Saving/spending
	Work	
	Durable purchases	Consumer credit
25–35 years	Having children	Family insurance
	Owning a house	Mortgage
	Refurnishing of the house	Consumer credit
35–45 years	Children go to school	Increased expenses for children
	Peak of income	Redemption of the mortgage
45–65 years	Children leave home	Less expenses for children
		Saving and investing
>65 years	Retirement	Drawing on savings
	Life annuity	Wealth management

Table 19.2 *Complexity and perceived risk of bank services*

	Little complexity	Great complexity
Low risk	Current account Saving account Credit card	Liability insurance Damage insurance
High risk	Shares Mutual fund	Consumer credit Life insurance Pension insurance Income insurance Wealth management Mortgage

Most financial behaviours shown in table 19.1 will be dealt with in this chapter. For banks, consumer policy, financial advisors, loan providers and durable goods manufacturers, it is important to know at which stages of the life-cycle these events generally occur.

Financial services vary in complexity and perceived risk. In table 19.2, these services are classified according to these criteria.[17] This table considers risks as perceived by the consumer.

Bank accounts and saving accounts are relatively simple services, not incurring risk. Liability and accident insurance are relatively complex services because of the many accident risks. However, consumers in these cases usually have low risk estimates. Simple services incurring high risk are buying and selling stocks, since the consumer runs the risk of wealth decline and missed opportunities. Complex services incurring high risk are consumer credit, life and income insurance, mortgage, and professional wealth management. These bank services in particular demand 'tailoring' and a trusting relation between the customer and the bank.

There is a tendency to separate bank services into elementary services and then offer new combinations of these elements. For example, this applies to mortgages based on life insurance and saving facilities, and credit cards including travel insurance. Instead of separate bank services, consumers buy packages, tailored to their personal needs.

19.3 Financial management and payment behaviour

This section deals with the financial management of the household. Financial management comprises more than the operational money and cash management. The household is similar to a business in the sense that estimates and budgets may be made and book-keeping may be done. However, in many households, bookkeeping is not systematic and often there is no administration at all. The money management and payment behaviour at the first level of the hierarchy can take many forms. Within traditional households, husbands and wives frequently divide roles and duties in financial matters.

Financial management

Financial management comprises three levels of planning:

- the strategic level of long-term decisions, such as the financial aspects and arrangements concerning choice of education, job, partner and children;
- the administrative level of book-keeping, estimation and budgeting;
- the operational level of shopping, paying bills and taxes.

In many households, one person is responsible for paying bills and other financial management tasks. In the first years of marriage, many financial matters will be dealt with together; after several years, the tasks will be divided and will be taken care of by either partner, usually for the sake of efficiency.[18] However, the varieties of financial management are more complex and depend on who earns the income, who does the shopping and who pays the bills.

Five varieties of financial management may be identified for married couples, depending on the influence of both husband and wife on decision making:[19]

- In *husband-dominant behaviour*, the husband executes the financial management and provides his wife with household money for daily shopping.
- In *husband-syncratic behaviour* financial matters are dealt with together and joint bank and saving accounts exist. The husband pays the bills, takes care of the redemption of the mortgage and executes most financial transactions. This mainly occurs in households with higher incomes.
- In *autonomous behaviour*, husband and wife arrange their own financial matters and have their own bank and saving accounts. Frequently, they have a joint household contract.[20] Only in the case of important purchases do they consult each other. This mainly occurs in households with high incomes, for instance dual-income households.
- In *wife-syncratic behaviour* financial matters are dealt with together and the wife executes the financial transactions. This mainly occurs in households with modal incomes.
- In *wife-dominant behaviour*, the wife arranges all financial matters and provides her husband with pocket money for his own expenses. This mainly occurs in low-income households.

The main breadwinner usually has more influence on financial management than the other household members. Expertise plays a part; someone educated as a book-keeper will be inclined to take care of the financial management. Table 19.3 shows the results from a UK survey. This table shows that the wife has more influence if she earns income herself, especially if this comprises more than 30% of the husband's income. However, the right-hand column shows that wives without any income may also influence the spending of the household income. Autonomous behaviour was not distinguished in this survey. Pocket money for the children is also part of the financial management of the family.

Payment behaviour

Many payments take place in cash. This implies an immediate settlement in case of a purchase of a good or service, for example with the cashier of a supermarket, gas station, cinema, or recreation park. In a number of Western European countries the amount of cash money varied between 3% and 8% of GDP in 1993.[22] Some consumers prefer to pay in cash. Others try to pay as often as possible by credit card or electronically. In the UK, the percentage of cash payments has fallen from 93% in 1976 to 76% in 1992.[23] In several Western European countries, transactions by automatic teller machines (ATMs) doubled between 1989 and 1994.[24] Payment by plastic cards tripled in these countries at the same time. The use of cheques has also declined. See table 19.4 for an overview of methods of payment.

In addition, delayed payments occur where customers receive a bill to be

Table 19.3 *Household financial management related to the wife's income*[21]

Financial management style	Income of wife as a percentage of husband's income		
	>30%	0–30%	0%
Husband-dominant	18	18	26
Husband-syncratic	18	52	43
Wife-syncratic	43	30	15
Wife-dominant	21	0	17

Table 19.4 *Methods of payment*

Direct/indirect payment	Form of payment
Direct payment (payment over the counter)	Cash Bank and traveller cheques Credit card, customer card Banker's card Debit card, chip card, telephone card
Delayed payment (buying on credit)	Cheque Bank transfer Automatic regular transfer Automatic payment authorization Telebanking

Figure 19.2 *Private banking*

paid by cheque or bank transfer. Revolving payments, such as rent or insurance premiums can be transferred automatically by standing order or direct debit. It is possible to authorize the receiver to be paid from the bank account automatically upon delivery of goods or services. A new development is telebanking where bank transactions can be executed at home by means of a PC. Forms of direct payment or payment over the counter are described in the following.

Cash money
Paying in cash is the traditional method of payment. Both the consumer and the receiver incur the risk of theft. Cash payment limits spending to the amount of money the consumer carries. Some consumers use this constraint to control expenditure by carrying only a limited amount for

shopping, thus forcing themselves not to spend more. This is an expression of self-control.[25] In general, small expenses are paid in cash or by debit card, since other methods of payment are too expensive or troublesome.

Cash includes metal coins and paper notes. As a coin represents a higher nominal value, a more expensive type of metal or alloy is used, e.g., a copper penny, a nickel dime or a golden rand. Usually, both the section and the gauge increase with higher nominal values. The German five-marks coin is larger than the one-mark coin. Many consumers have the feeling that a coin of five marks is worth less than the former note. In the UK, it has been found that £1 coins are spent more easily than the £1 notes were.[26] Since ATMs pay out a limited variety of notes, a shortage of certain types of notes may develop in shops and market-places.

In 2002 the euro—European currency unit—will be introduced as cash and many of the old European currencies may gradually disappear. Due to electronic methods of payment, demand for the cash euro will be considerably less than for today's local currency. In addition, because of the large volume of the European market, the total demand for euro coins and notes can be estimated more precisely than demand for today's national currencies.

Cheques

Paying by cheque gives better facilities than payment in cash, especially with unforeseen expenditure. An advantage of cheques is that in the case of theft, the consumer's liability is limited. The use of cheques, however, has been discouraged by bank charges and partly because of this, the use of cheques has decreased in most Western European countries. Although the *per capita* use of cheques is also decreasing in the USA and Canada, it is still about twice as high as in Europe. This is partly due to a different use of cheques; for example, electricity bills are often paid by means of cheques.

Outside Europe, traveller's cheques are used frequently, as these will be reimbursed in case of loss or theft. Since traveller's cheques may be issued in different countries, consumers run the risk of unfavourable exchange rates, which may be balanced against the risk of losing cash money.

Credit card

On a certain evening in 1950, Frank McNamara was dining with some guests in a restaurant in New York. When the waiter presented the bill, McNamara happened not to carry cash money. A discussion followed regarding how to settle the payment. McNamara left his business card and asked the restaurant to send him the bill. The restaurant trusted the business card and the payment was settled this way. This is a form of limited credit facility. McNamara decided that there would be a demand for an organization guaranteeing payments. In this way, the first credit card organization developed—Diners Club. In 1958, American Express came out with a credit card. In the USA and Canada, on average, every citizen has a credit card. In Western European countries credit card possession levels vary from 5–60% of the population.[27]

In a credit card transaction, the seller usually has to pay the credit card company a commission fee of 2–7%. There are credit limitations. To pay larger amounts, authorization from the credit card company has to be obtained, usually by telephone. No interest is charged if the consumer pays the bill of the credit card company within the term of payment of one month—the grace period. If one delays the payment, a high interest rate is charged. Consumers pay much more interest on these debts than with other credit facilities.

In an American survey on the use of credit cards, three types of consumers were identified.[28] The first group pays within the grace period. For this group, the interest rate is not relevant. The second group has problems borrowing elsewhere and uses the easy credit facilities of the credit card. These consumers may easily run into problems of repayment and get into debt because paying by credit card is easy, but repayment is difficult. The third group includes consumers who intend to pay in time but do not succeed in doing so. Eventually, these consumers pay their debts, albeit with an element of added interest. This group is too optimistic about their own abilities to pay. This 'irrational' optimism is 'punished' by means of the high interest rate.

Furthermore, there exists a distinction between travel and entertainment cards, such as American Express and Diners Club, and cards meant for common usage, such as Eurocard–Mastercard and Visa. The travel and entertainment cards are more exclusive and are used for travel tickets, hotel bills, restaurants and exclusive shops. In addition to its green card, American Express issues gold and platinum cards with better credit facilities for 'members' with a high income. Eurocard and Visa can be used in many situations, for example in supermarkets, on toll-roads, phone booths and ATMs. The fee for the credit card companies is lower, namely 2–3%.

For consumers, payment by credit card has several clear advantages. By carrying the card, one always has money to hand. The card can be used internationally, without the need to exchange currency. For example, at an intermediate landing in Paris, one can buy tax-free items at the airport without using French francs. The card is protected against misuse and the user receives a monthly overview of the account. A disadvantage may be that spending money becomes too easy by credit card. Research has shown that consumers spend money more easily and also spend more when paying by credit card than when using other methods of payment. The ownership of a credit card may increase the likelihood and number of impulsive purchases.[29]

Customer card

A customer card is a private-label card, issued by department store chains, mail-order companies, petrol companies, car-rental companies, hotel chains and airlines, such as British Airways and Lufthansa. Usually, it is a combination of a membership card and a credit card. The membership card gives access to shops, a club magazine, special discounts and price offers, and a credit point system, such as an airline frequent-flyer programme. An important aim of the customer card issuer is to create relationships with customers and to increase the level of their custom. For the customer, it is a convenient way of paying afterwards and it gives advantages to loyal customers.

In France, Finland, and UK, on average 20–40% of the population owns a customer card, in Sweden almost everyone has one, and in the USA each person has almost two customer cards on average.[30]

Debit cards

For some payments, debit cards may be used, such as the telephone card, copy card, or parking card. In contrast with credit cards, one pays in advance and the card is devalued during its use. Advanced debit cards can be recharged. A debit card could replace buying separate tickets for public transport.

Electronic payment

The sixth form of payment is electronic. In Belgium in the 1970s, payment systems were developed enabling gasoline purchases 24 hours a day—Bancontact and Mister Cash. These systems have grown into full-bodied payment systems. The banker's card has increased in popularity very fast in the early 1990s. In Belgium and France in 1994, the number of banker's card accounted for 15–20 transactions *per capita*.[31] In other West European countries, and in the USA and Canada, the equivalent figure was less than 10 transactions *per capita*.

The banker's card carries information on a chip. A PIN-code is used for authorization and the amount of the transaction is transferred to the bank by telephone. The PIN-code is a secret four-digit number that is revealed exclusively to the customer. Considerable changes in payment behaviour are expected for payments over the counter. In the near future, electronic payment will increase and the use of cheques will decrease further.

Smart cards

The wallets of many consumers are bulging with plastic cards, including: phone cards, public transportation cards, parking cards, credit cards, banker's cards, customer cards, and air-miles cards. The average consumer owns six plastic cards. A traveling businessperson has even more cards. The

Figure 19.3 *Plastic cards*

more customer cards and credit cards consumers have, the less frequently they use each one.

The most recent development in banking comprises electronic payment by means of computers and smart cards (chip cards). The smart card offers many opportunities for the future. Memory on the card can be assigned to card issuers, such that several card issuers may operate with only one plastic card. For example, a hotel card to open the door of one's room, to pay in the restaurant, to pay for the drinks from the minibar, the pay-TV and the hotel bill. Alternatively, one card may be used for public transportation, the parking place, the library, insurance identification and to contain medical data, such as one's blood group and medicine usage.

In line with the development of phone cards and parking cards, it is expected that smart cards will gradually replace small cash transactions. Several market experiments have been conducted with smart cards:

- In Belgium, the Proton card has been issued which can be used in shops, soft drink machines and public phones.[32]
- In Denmark, the Danmont card was issued in 1994.
- The MONDEX experiment has been started in the UK where 40,000 consumers can use a smart card at 1000 retailers. There are plans to extend the MONDEX project to six countries including Canada, USA and Hong Kong.[33]
- In The Netherlands, a combined banker's card and smart card was issued in 1997.

- Portugal has introduced its Multibanco Electronic Purse in 1995 by issuing 500,000 cards[34] which can be used to pay for 26 services including train reservations, energy bills, taxes and investments in stocks.[35]

One of the consequences of the smart card is a reduction of cash transactions; in the MONDEX experiment a reduction of 25% was accomplished.

The success of the smart card will depend on the market circumstances and cooperation among the banks, as has generally been the case with other payment innovations. The proper timing of the introduction may depend on the consumer's readiness to use the new system and this may be affected by the consumer's previous experiences and willingness to innovate, among others.[36]

19.4 Saving

Saving is heavily influenced by norms and values in society. Saving is generally considered a virtue in western culture. During the Middle Ages, laws existed to limit extreme spending by ordinary people. Saving was preferred, so that the king or the church would benefit if necessary. Obviously, the laws against extreme spending did not apply to the king and the nobility. These opinions have changed and today, everyone has to decide individually about saving or spending their income. Besides, saving does not always have to be a virtue, as spending creates other jobs and incomes. On the other hand, the industry and the government call on consumer savings to finance their projects. For this reason, consumer saving behaviour is important in economics.

Discretionary and non-discretionary saving

Discretionary saving includes all the varieties of saving in which the consumer is free—has discretion—to decide whether or not to save. The saving bank account is an example of a discretionary saving device. Discretionary saving is heavily influenced by economic circumstances and consumer expectations, as indicated by the Index of Consumer Sentiment.[37] Many consumers prefer a form of automatic saving. This is less discretionary because it is harder to cancel the contract. Examples are authorizations to the bank to transfer a fixed monthly amount from the salary account to the saving account. In this way, savings are accumulated with little effort. Of course, consumers may cancel the authorization at any time. Yet, they do not do this easily. The automation of the savings process is a way of beating any lack of will power. Many people know themselves and know that this system helps them to create and maintain a saving balance.[38] Besides, it is easier than making the effort to transfer money time and again, or and in the case of numerous transfers, it may be cheaper to use a standing order.

Usually non-discretionary savings include premium payments for pensions and life insurance, sometimes arranged via collective labour agreements. Surrendering this type of insurance is often not an appealing or sensible thing to do. It is almost a forced type of saving. According to the Dutch National Accounts of 1990, non-discretionary or contractual savings constitute about 65% of total savings.

Table 19.5 shows total net household savings as a percentage of disposable household income in a number of European countries in different years. Household saving rates have increased over time except in Portugal and Germany. Household saving rates differ markedly between countries although this may be partly due to different definitions of these rates. Saving rates have varied dramatically in Sweden, Finland and Norway, but these countries save considerably less than other European countries.

In general, European households save considerably more than US, Australian and Canadian households and the difference appears to be increasing. In the long run, this may influence spending patterns.

Meaning structure of saving

Figure 19.4 shows a meaning structure for saving behaviour.[40] At the first level, concrete saving behaviours are found, such as 'putting money into a

Table 19.5 *Household saving rates in Europe, USA and Japan*[a] *(as percentages of disposable household income)*[39]

	1980	1990	1995[b]	Index (1980 = 100)
Belgium	19.6	18.0	22.0	112
Denmark	8.0	15.7	16.2	203
Austria	10.5	13.8	12.5	119
Spain	10.8	10.5	12.2	116
Ireland	10.9	10.0	12.1	111
Portugal	25.5	17.5	11.8	46
Germany	12.8	13.8	11.0	86
Switzerland	3.3	12.2	10.8	360
Sweden	6.7	−0.6	7.5	112
Finland	5.4	0.4	5.6	104
Norway	3.4	0.9	4.3	126
France[c]	17.6	12.5	13.6	77
UK[c]	13.4	8.4	9.9	74
Italy[c]	23.0	18.2	13.8	60
USA	8.1	4.3	5.0	62
Canada	13.6	9.7	7.2	53
Australia	10.4	7.5	4.3	41
Japan	17.9	14.1	15.7	88

[a] National definitions
[b] Projections
[c] Gross savings

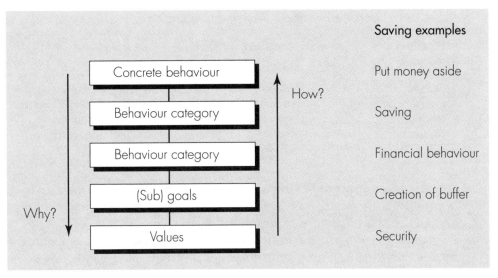

Figure 19.4 *Meaning structure of behaviour*

saving account', 'buying life insurance' or 'paying off a mortgage term'. At the second level, concrete behaviours may be categorized into a category of 'saving'. This behaviour category is part of a wider behaviour category of 'financial behaviour'. Financial behaviour is executed with certain goals in mind, such as the continuity of consumption, the creation of a buffer amount or the realization of a purchase. Finally, these goals are related to (domain-specific) values. Typical values in relation to savings are security, safety, prudence, independence, caution and care for children and heirs. Developing wealth may become a goal in itself. Negative values such as avarice and miserliness may also be associated with saving.

Goals and values are abstract, imply several behaviours and a long-term time perspective. Goals and values remain operative for a long time, sometimes even a lifetime. In contrast, the level of concrete behaviours implies a relatively small number of behaviours and a short-term time perspective. Saving behaviour can be studied at different levels: as concrete behaviour, as a behaviour category and as behaviour goals.

Concrete behaviours answer the *how* question: 'How do you save?' or 'Which type of saving did you choose?' Goals and values include the reasons for behaviour; they answer the *why* question: 'Why do you save?' or 'What are you saving for?'

Expectations

Discretionary saving is particularly sensitive to income expectations and business outlook. Households whose income increased in the previous year and who expect an increase in the next year, will save little. In contrast, if income has remained static or has decreased in the previous year and an

Table 19.6 *Income expectations, saving and spending*[41]

Income in the past year	Income expectations for next year	Consumer behaviour
Increased	Increase	High discretionary spending
Constant or decreased	Constant or decrease	Low discretionary spending
Increased	Decrease	High discretionary saving
Decreased	Increase	Low discretionary saving

increase is not expected in the next year, much will be saved (table 19.6). It appears that in the case of negative income expectations, much is saved and, in the case of positive expectations, little is saved.

In addition, a negative correlation exists between saving and spending—money saved cannot be spent. If savings are high, little will be spent on durables and other discretionary purchases in general. Such purchases can easily be delayed or cancelled. Low savings generally are associated with high spending.

Income expectations influence both saving behaviour and the amount saved. An expected income increase in general implies that less will be saved and more will be borrowed. An expected income decrease implies that more will be saved and less will be borrowed. In the latter case, consumers want to develop a financial buffer against setbacks and do not dare to make large acquisitions, especially not on credit.

For saving, a long-term perspective is needed. Pessimistic expectations and a positive judgement regarding the sense of saving, given the interest rate and inflation, contribute to saving. In the case of a low interest rate and high inflation, it is not rational to save. In the early 1990s, Russian consumers lost confidence in their currency. In these circumstances, they preferred US dollars and German marks to roubles and they invested their money in gold, diamonds, jewellery and other valuables.

Delaying gratification

Saving means delaying gratification and control of impulsivity. Instead of spending money as soon as they get it, consumers prefer to spend more money later. On the one hand, they want to realize their immediate wants and needs. On the other hand, they know that it is good to save and not give in to impulsivity. Thus, self-control is needed. In each individual, a 'doer' and a 'planner' may be identified.[42] The 'doer' is impulsive and strives for immediate gratification of needs. The 'planner' has a long-term perspective and prefers to save and delay gratification of needs.[43]

The 'planner' tries to control the 'doer'. This is accomplished by precommitment, that is by making arrangements that the doer cannot cancel. Automatic saving and pension systems are varieties of non-discretionary saving. Here, the 'planner' beats the 'doer'. George Katona investigated the hypothesis that pensions would diminish voluntary saving because the 'planner' has to control the 'doer' less.[44] However, people participating in a pension system did not save less than those who did not. Katona assumed that people save a fixed proportion of their *discretionary* income (after subtraction of the pension). Total savings (pensions plus voluntary savings) are greater after the introduction of a pension system than before. It appears that people consider the pension as a basis to be supplemented by voluntary saving.

The repayment of a mortgage or a loan is also non-discretionary. This concerns the transfer of external wealth into private wealth and it implies a form of saving afterwards. Other self-imposed rules also can control the 'doer', for example not going shopping while carrying a lot of money or setting limits on the credit facilities made available by the bank. In this way, people make non-smoking contracts with their partners and have their good intentions at the beginning of the year controlled by others. Consumers accept that sometimes they have to give up some freedom in order to achieve an important goal.

Definition

Time preference is the preference for receiving a certain amount of money for current consumption rather than a larger amount at a later point in time.

Delay of gratification is associated with *time preference*. Time preference is a measure concerning the preference for receiving a certain amount of money immediately rather than a larger amount later. How much larger does the amount have to be in order to be preferred to the present amount?[45] Individuals with a positive time preference prefer current consumption to future consumption. They demand a greater difference between amounts now and later in order to delay their consumption. Individuals with a negative time preference prefer consumption later to consumption today. They demand a smaller difference between the amounts in order to delay their consumption. Time preference may be effective even after death. Many people think it is important to bequeath money and goods to their children. In that way, saving is extended to the next generation.

19.5 Borrowing

As indicated above, most loans and mortgages are issued to people between 25 and 45 years of age. At this stage of the life-cycle important acquisitions are made, such as a house, a car and other durables. In addition, in this stage substantial expenses are incurred by the upbringing and the education of children. Credit is often used for durable purchases. Borrowing money nowadays is not for the poor but for the rich.

The theory of self-control also can be applied here. In the first instance, the 'planner' tries to control the 'doer' by not allowing loans for consumption but only for the purchase of goods retaining their value or even increasing in value, such as property. If consumers borrow or take a mortgage though, the mortgagee enforces a regular schedule of repayment.[46] In this way, the impulsive 'doer' is controlled. Thus, the redemption of the mortgage becomes a form of saving.

Otherwise, even concerning an important decision such as the choice of a mortgage, consumers can be impulsive. The 'doer' appears to dominate here. Many consumers choose a mortgage after having visited and asked for a quotation from only one or two banks or building societies. As such important decisions often make a difference of thousands of euros, one would expect that consumers would do more 'shopping around' and would compare price offers.[47] However, more information is gathered concerning the mortgage than other financial services.

In many respects, borrowing is the counterpart of saving. It is frequently associated with the purchase of durable goods. In this case, the goods are purchased on a personal loan or by instalments. Here, too, income expectations have predictive value, especially since borrowing is often discretionary.[48] Consumers will voluntarily decide to take a loan, for example to buy a durable product or to go on holiday. Money is more likely to be borrowed from a position of wealth than one of poverty or necessity.

Borrowing often occurs simultaneously with saving. Some consumers would rather take a loan to make an acquisition than break into their savings accounts. They know their lack of willpower and that they will find it difficult to bring the account up to the earlier level. A pay-back arrangement for a loan is a stronger force than the intention to save.[49]

Table 19.7 shows household indebtedness in proportion to net dis-

Table 19.7 *Household indebtedness as a percentage of disposable income*[50]

	Liabilities		Home mortgages	
	1983	1993	1983	1993
Germany	16	–[b]	10[a]	–[b]
France	58	79	39[a]	48[a]
Italy	8	32	5[a]	15[a]
UK	74	110	47	77
USA	74	97	45	65
Canada	75	101	47	68
Japan	85	112	35	51

[a] Long-term credit   [b] Not available

posable household income for several countries. In all the countries reported, liabilities and mortgages have increased. As table 19.5 shows, this was accompanied by a decrease in saving in these countries.

Problematic debts

Taking a loan or credit is not always without problems. Some households get into debt problems. They cannot discharge their loans, or pay their taxes, rents and energy bills as well as meet their daily household expenses. If one cannot make ends meet some time after having taken a loan, one is tempted to take a second loan and a third, eventually and so on. In the long run it is possible to become entrapped. Sometimes new credit is taken out to restructure an existing debt situation, for example, consumers can take out a personal bank loan to pay off their credit card bills. This may solve the problem in the short run but the financial situation may still deteriorate in the long run.

Factors contributing to problematic debt situations are rooted in the financial behaviour of consumers, the availability of credit (the supply) and expected or unexpected events disturbing the financial balance of the household.[51]

The *financial behaviour of consumers* may leave much to be desired because consumers can lack insight into the consequences of financial decisions. It is easy to forget that a monthly repayment of 1000 euros during five years will make it difficult to meet many other necessary expenses. Alternatively, consumers may not have learned to deal with money. Even if a salary is received, it may be spent too quickly on too many expensive items. Consumers sometimes try to live beyond their means. This is particularly likely when someone has a decreasing income; it may happen that spending is still set at the level appropriate to the former, higher income.

The *supply and ready availability of credit* may tempt consumers to take a loan. Then the 'doer' has beaten the 'planner'. Credit cards, credits by mail-order companies and other supply factors facilitate spending. If the consumer lacks insight into the consequences of this behaviour, financial trouble will follow.

Banks use a system of credit scoring to approve or reject credit applications. Credit applicants can be judged with regards to socio-demographic and other characteristics. A number of attributes distinguish 'good' from 'bad' loans.[52] A good loan is a credit that is paid off according to agreement. A bad loan is a credit that is either not paid off at all or paid off with a delay of two months or more. The characteristics are shown in table 19.8. A loan for items that keep their value, at least to some extent, for example, the house and the car, is better than a loan for items that do not keep their value, for example, holidays or paying off other debts.

Expected and unexpected events may disturb the financial balance of a household. This includes an income decrease because one partner stops

Table 19.8 *Characteristics of good and bad loans*

Household characteristic	Good loan	Bad loan
Employment status	Tenured	Unskilled, different jobs
Income	Fixed income	Variable income
Age	Middle-aged	21–25 years
Marital status	Married	Single
Credit record	Good loan(s)	Bad loan(s)
Type of spending	Keeping value	Not keeping value

working, for example, in case of disease, dismissal or the birth of a child. In addition, illness may cause a reduction in overtime work, night duties and shift work. Also, moves and divorce frequently cause financial difficulties. The acquisition of an expensive house may leave little money for other living expenses. A bit of bad luck can cause a problematic financial situation.

19.6 Insurance

Many types of insurance exist. They can be divided into life insurance and non-life insurance—property, accident, and health insurance. Property insurance serves to cover a financial risk by paying a premium. Some insurances are obligatory, such as liability insurance for the car and, in some countries, health insurance for employees. Other insurances are necessary, such as private liability insurance and building insurance. Some insurance may be superfluous, such as television insurance (frequently covered by furniture insurance), glass insurance (frequently covered by building insurance) or funeral insurance (today, people frequently have means of their own to pay for their funerals, for example in the form of property or entitlement to some salary after death).

To determine whether or not to insure against a certain type of damage, the risk of the damage needs to be estimated. The risk basically consists of two components: the probability of the risk happening and the extent of the likely damage.

The probability of damage is usually small, for example odds of a thousand to one of breaking a leg in the next ten years. If statistics concerning the occurrence of damage are lacking, then consumers have to guess the risk for themselves. People tend to neglect very small probabilities. In the case of a very small probability, for instance odds of a thousand to one, people no longer consider the statistical *probability* but rather the *possibility* that the event will occur.[53] In general, this may cause them to underinsure for small risks.[54]

As said, the risk of a damage may be related to the desire to insure against the damage. Information may be obtained about the risk of damage via the media or acquaintances. Several national statistical bureaux keep records of the chance of becoming a victim of an offence, including theft and burglary (see table 19.9). Damage to cars and theft from and of cars occur relatively often in The Netherlands. For this reason, good car insurance seems to be important. Burglary also occurs relatively frequently. However, insurance against this needs to be measured against the premium to be paid (as for every other form of insurance). Risks may vary considerably across countries, due to circumstances, legal regulations and safety precautions. For example, car theft per 100,000 inhabitants in 1995 varied from 27 in Austria, 32 in Ireland and 48 in Portugal to 1505 in Switzerland, 977 in the UK and 879 in Sweden.[55]

The second component of risk is the extent of damage. For example, in the case of personal accidents, the costs can mount considerably if medical treatment is necessary. The extent of damage or theft may vary considerably. Here, too, personal circumstances may influence the estimate of the damage. Someone with a monthly income of 3,000 euros will judge a broken glass costing 500 euros as less severe than someone with an income of 1,000 euros. In the first case, the damage can be paid for from current income, whereas in the second case recovery of the damage may be problematic. In the second case, one may be more inclined to take glass insurance than in the first case.

From the above, it is clear that subjective estimates of risk have more influence on the decision to take insurance than the expected damage according to statistics. According to expected utility theory in economics, people compare the price of insurance—the premium—to its expected utility—risk covering.[57] If the premium is relatively favourable, people will take out insurance. However, in reality people make subjective estimates of probabilities and here, emotional feelings like fear may play a part. Because of this, risk frequently carries quite different meanings for consumers than the actuarial calculation of risk, as practised by insurance companies.[58] In principle, this could lead to large profits for insurance companies playing on people's feelings. However, the market mechanism corrects this effect to some extent by price competition. A sense of equity prevents consumers from taking insurance from a company that charges very high premiums.

Table 19.9 *Victims of selected types of offence in percentages of the Swedish and Dutch population (1992)*[56]

	Sweden	The Netherlands
Theft of bike	1.4	6.0
Theft of car	0.7	0.3
Theft from the car	–	3.6
Theft out of the car	–	3.3
Damage of the car	–	8.9
Burglary	1.8	2.9

Table 19.10 *Insurance premiums* per capita *in the EU (ECUs)*[59]

	1990	1994
Motor car and motor bikes	145	155
Fire and other damage to property	89	93
Accidents and illness	81	94
Personal liability	28	30
Total non-life insurance	333	372
Life insurance	366	517

Table 19.10 shows the *per capita* insurance premiums paid. Since most of the premiums are paid out, the non-life insurance statistics indicate the expected damage. The premium is roughly the result of the probability times the extent of the damage. Motor car insurance appears as the most important type of non-life insurance. Costs due to accidents and illness in many countries are (partly) covered by the state and consequently the premiums do not reflect the true costs.

Life insurance has become a very important and increasingly widespread type of insurance. Life insurances under some conditions pay out during life, after death or a combination of both. Premiums are usually paid over a large number of years. Alternatively, a lump sum can be paid in the case of single-premium insurance. Interest on the premium is accumulated, such that the capital increases, and in several countries tax advantages may be gained. In the case of old-age benefits and pensions, life insurance is not necessary, except in some mortgage contracts. Frequently, life insurance is taken out to benefit from a life-annuity at a later time, for example after retirement. This serves to supplement retirement benefits and pensions.

In the case of life insurance, yet another psychological aspect comes into play. Life insurance usually pays out after a long time, for example at old age. The willingness to take life insurance at a young age is influenced by time preference.[60] A positive time preference will hamper the contracting of life insurance. A negative time preference will facilitate this. Furthermore, the income position will influence the consumer's ability to pay for life insurance.

Life insurance also may adjust the income stream during the life-cycle of a household. By the acquisition of a money purchase policy, the high income in a certain year is diminished and sometimes less income tax is paid. The benefits of a money purchase policy occur in lower income years, for example after retirement. In this way, part of the income is shifted to years with a lower income (and lower taxes).

19.7 Investing

In a sense, investing is opposite to insurance, since one consciously takes a risk to obtain a higher return on investment than in the case of saving. Risky investment opportunities include stocks, options, future and certificates of deposit. Less risky opportunities include bonds, deposits, property and precious metals. By diversifying over a variety of different investments, the risk of low or even negative return is minimized. The economic portfolio theory assumes that people trade off risk and return. People will take risks but only if the expected return is high enough. Furthermore, investments will be diversified such that the total risk is in line with the risk preferences of the investor.

Consumers putting all their money in saving accounts do not run any risk at all, as the interest is guaranteed by the bank and the capital is safe. If the interest rate increases (or decreases), the saving account earns more (or less) returns. However, the amount saved cannot diminish.[61] This is the ideal opportunity for a risk-averse consumer. Risk aversion may occur if one definitely needs money at a later time for a specific reason, for instance for a 25-year wedding anniversary, for which the money will not become available in a different way.

If a consumer has saved enough to cover necessary expenses later and if he or she has no personal desire to avoid all financial risks, he or she may consider some more risky investment opportunities. The aim is not to put 'all the eggs in one basket' but to look for a balanced portfolio. Mutual funds offer the opportunity to invest in balanced, diversified portfolios associated with greater or smaller risk, according to personal preferences. Turbulent movements on the stock market, such as the 1987 stock-market crash, have made private investors more cautious concerning their investment behaviour. Today, there are 'green' mutual funds, investing in companies not harmful to the environment. Furthermore, bonds are available from welfare or scientific organizations, which hardly give any return. This shows that motives other than purely economic ones may play a part on the stock market.

For investments, other than via a mutual fund, one has to be informed of the latest financial circumstances, the investment and profit outlook of firms and the international business situation. This is difficult for laymen. So consumers may join societies, so-called investment study clubs, for a hobby.[63] Private investors have to take transaction costs (bank charges) into account, when buying or sellling shares, so that the composition of portfolios should not be altered too frequently.

Table 19.11 shows household wealth, expressed as a percentage of net household disposable income. It appears that net wealth has not increased so much in the past decade. Real assets have remained relatively stable as

Table 19.11 *Household wealth as a percentage of disposable income (1993)*[62]

	Real assets	Financial assets	Corporate equities	Net wealth[a]	Index of net wealth (1983 = 100)
France	2.66	2.64	1.29	4.51	117
Italy	3.75[b]	2.73	0.61	5.85[b]	120[b]
UK	3.14	3.62	0.43	5.65	121
USA	2.17	3.82	0.88	5.02	102
Canada	2.71	2.90	0.69	4.60	114
Japan	4.66	3.30	0.33	6.83	126

[a] Total wealth minus debts
[b] 1992

compared with financial wealth. Japan turns out to be the wealthiest state among those reported.

19.8 Conclusions

This chapter has dealt with financial behaviour, including saving and borrowing. Financial behaviour has been associated with goals, values and norms. New developments concerning methods of payment have been considered. Banks have an important advisory function to offer to consumers with regard to their financial behaviour.

Changes in methods of payment and payment behaviour may greatly affect consumer spending and saving. By using cheques, credit and debit cards, and other forms of electronic payment, paying becomes a kind of account administration. In many cases, cash payment is not necessary any more. Overdrafts are common and may be agreed in advance as a form of revolving credit. Because of this, consumers frequently have less insight into their financial situation than when they still paid in cash.

The multi-functional smart card or chip card will replace single cards in the future. The following card functions may be available soon:

- *office card* giving access to buildings, stores, copy machines, coffee machines and canteen payments;
- *shopping card* for daily expenses;
- *identification card* for the library, insurance and public utilities;
- *travel card* for larger expenses concerning travel, hotels and restaurants;
- *debit card* for telephone, parking meters and public transportation.

Saving and borrowing are linked to the business outlook. During a recession, consumer expectations are pessimistic—more will be saved and less borrowed. During an upswing, expectations are optimistic—more will be borrowed and less will be saved. Confidence in the future and time preference are important determinants of saving and borrowing.

Investing is a form of wealth management in which one consciously accepts risks and tries to minimize them. The goal is to create or maintain wealth without paying too much income tax and/or wealth tax. Investing is more risky than saving but in general implies higher expected returns.

Property insurance and life insurance are both risk-averse forms of financial behaviour. In addition, consumers cover certain unacceptable risks by taking insurance for liability and other damage one usually cannot pay from the current income or savings. Life insurance offers benefits either to the consumer during his or her life or to his or her heirs.

Notes

1 Maital, S. and Maital, S. L. (1991) 'Is the future what it used to be? A behavioral theory of the decline of saving in the West' in: Antonides, G., Arts, W. and van Raaij, W. F. (Eds) *The Consumption of Time and the Timing of Consumption* (Amsterdam: North-Holland) 195–214.

2 See section 5.4 for the integral approach to credit problems.

3 See Lindqvist, A. (1981) 'A note on the determinants of household saving behavior' *Journal of Economic Psychology* 1, 39–57.
   Wärneryd, K.-E. (1983) *The Saving Behavior of Households* (Tilburg: Katholieke Hoge-school).
   Van Raaij, W. F. and van Wijck, H. (1984) 'Saving and borrowing behavior' *Bank- en Effectenbedrijf* 33, 280–285 (in Dutch).

4 Revolving or continuous credit is an arrangement with the bank which allows the consumer to overdraw an account to an agreed amount. The agreed amount frequently equals the monthly salary.

5 Thaler, R. (1980) 'Toward a positive theory of consumer choice' *Journal of Economic Behavior and Organization* 1, 39–60.

6 Katona, G. (1975) *Psychological Economics* (New York: Elsevier).

7 For investment, see section 19.7 of this chapter.

8 Katona (1975), chapters 15 and 17.

9 See also Thaler (1980).

10 Babeau, A. (1981) 'Diversité des motivations et évolution des comportements d'épargne' [Diverse motivations and evolution of saving behaviour] *Audition devant la Commission de l'Epargne* (CREP) (in French).

11 Modigliani, F. and Brumberg, R. (1954) 'Utility analysis and the consumption function: an interpretation of cross-section data' in: Kurihara, K. K. (Ed.) *Post Keynesian Economics* (New Brunswick, NJ: Rutgers University Press).
   Friedman, M. (1957) *A Theory of the Consumption Function* (Princeton, NJ: Princeton University Press).

12 Thaler, R. and Shefrin, H. M. (1981) 'An economic theory of self-control' *Journal of Political Economy* 89, 392–405.

13 Modigliani, F. (1988) 'The role of intergenerational transfers and life-cycle saving in the accumulation of wealth' *Journal of Economic Perspectives* 2, 15–40.

Wärneryd, K.-E. (1991) 'The psychology of saving' in: Antonides, G., Arts, W. and van Raaij, W. F. (Eds) *The Consumption of Time and the Timing of Consumption* (Amsterdam: North-Holland) 176–194.

14   Aders, J. H. (1987) 'Economics of the household and financial service' *Symposium on Household Production* Erasmus University, Rotterdam. (in Dutch).

15   Ferber, R. and Lee, L. C. (1980) 'Asset accumulation in early married life' *Journal of Finance* 35, 1173–1188.

16   With a mortgage based on life-insurance, the interest received is not taxed under certain conditions.

17   Van den Berg, C. A. (1993) 'Relationship management: a new perspective in 175 years of consumer banking' in: *Financial Advice to the Consumer: Fiction or Fact?* (The Hague, The Netherlands: NIBE) 5–32 (in Dutch).

18   Ferber, R. and Lee, L. C. (1974) 'Husband-wife influences in family purchasing behavior' *Journal of Consumer Research* 1, 43–50. They speak of the FFO, the family financial officer.

19   Section 13.4. See also Pahl, J. (1989) *Money and Marriage* (London: Macmillan).
Pahl, J. (1990) 'Household spending, personal spending and the control of money in marriage' *Sociology* 24, 119–138.

20   In a marriage contract, property, designated goods and money belong to either the husband or the wife. Property is not joined.

21   Pahl (1990) 124.

22   Bank for International Settlements (1994) *Statistics on Payment Systems in the Group of Ten Countries* (Basel: BIS).

23   Central Statistical Office (1994) *Social Trends 24.*

24   Bank for International Settlements (1994).

25   Thaler (1980).

26   Lea, S. E. G., Tarpy, R. M. and Webley, P. (1987) *The Individual in the Economy* (Cambridge: Cambridge University Press) 340–341.

27   Bank for International Settlements (1994).

28   Ausubel, L. M. (1991) 'The failure of competition in the credit card market' *American Economic Review* 81, 50–81.

29   Feinberg, R. A. (1986) 'Credit cards as spending facilitating stimuli: a conditioning interpretation' *Journal of Consumer Research* 13, 348–356. See also section 19.5.

30   Bank for International Settlements (1994).

31   Bank for International Settlements (1994).

32   Kieviet, R. F. M. (1995) 'The Belgian Proton as an example of the Dutch Chipknip' *Bank en Effectenbedrijf* (April), 16–21 (in Dutch).

33   Motoko, R. (1995) 'The dash to replace cash' *Financial Times*, July 5.

34   Wolffe, R. (1995) 'Banks unzip the first £20m "Electronic Purse"' *Financial Times* July 3.

35   Wise, P. (1995) 'Travel: electronic petty cash' *Financial Times* March 7.

36   Andreasen, A. R. (1991) 'Readiness to change: theoretical, empirical and managerial issues' in: Antonides, G., Arts, W. and van Raaij, W. F. (Eds) *The Consumption of Time and the Timing of Consumption* 138–148 (Amsterdam: North-Holland).

Antonides, G., Amesz, H. B. and Hulscher, I. C. (1997) 'Adoption of payment systems in ten countries' *Proceedings of the 26th EMAC Conference*.

37 See section 3.5.

38 Van Raaij, W. F. (1985) 'Attribution of causality to economic actions and events' *Kyklos* 38, 3–19.

39 OECD (1995) *Economics Outlook 57* (Paris: OECD).

40 See section 7.3.

41 Adapted from Katona (1975).

42 Note that this is a metaphor. There are no 'doers' or 'planners' operating in our heads as little homunculi.

43 See for self-control: Thaler, R. H. and Shefrin, H. M. (1981) 'An economic theory of self-control' *Journal of Political Economy* 89, 392–405.
    See for impulsivity: Ainslie, G. (1975) 'Specious reward: a behavioral theory of impulsiveness and impulse control' *Psychological Bulletin* 82, 463–496. The planner and the doer coincide with the superego and the id in the psycho-analytic theory of Freud. See section 8.3.

44 Katona, G. (1965) *Psychological Economics* (New York: Elsevier).

45 See for methods of measurement: Fuchs, V. R. (1982) 'Time preference and health: an exploratory study' in: Fuchs, V. R. (Ed.) *Economic Aspects of Health* (Chicago: University of Chicago Press) 93–120.
    Antonides, G. (1991) 'Psychological factors in the lifetime of a durable good' in: Antonides, G., Arts, W. and van Raaij, W. F. (Eds) *The Consumption of Time and the Timing of Consumption* (Amsterdam: North-Holland) 162–175.

46 The mortgagor is the consumer who borrows money to buy a house. The mortgagee is the bank which lends the money with the house as security.

47 Antonides, G. and van Raaij, W. F. (1993) 'Financial advice and relationship management' in: *Financial Advice to the Consumer: Fiction or Fact?* (The Hague, The Netherlands: NIBE) 33–66 (in Dutch).

48 See section 3.5.

49 Katona (1975).

50 OECD (1995) *Economics Outlook 57* (Paris: OECD).

51 Dessart, W. C. A. M. and Kuylen, A. A. A. (1986) 'The nature, extent, causes, and consequences of problematic debt situations' *Journal of Consumer Policy* 9, 311–334.

52 Van Nieuwburg, M. J. T. J. (1982) *The Personal Loan: Statistical Methods as an Aiding Device in the Judgment of Credit Applications* (Leyden: Stenfert Kroese) (in Dutch).

53 Kahneman, D. and Tversky, A. (1979) 'Prospect theory: an analysis of decision under risk' *Econometrica* 47, 263–291.

54 Slovic, P., Fischhoff, B., Lichtenstein, S., Corrigan, B. and Combs, B. (1977) 'Preference for insuring against probable small losses: insurance implications' *Journal of Risk and Insurance* 44, 237–258.

55 Eurostat (1995) *Statistical Yearbook 1995* (Luxembourg: Eurostat). Although the figures are not meant for comparison across countries, they do indicate major differences across countries.

56 *Statistical Yearbook of Sweden 1997* (Stockholm: Statistics Sweden).
    Statistical Yearbook 1994 (Voorburg: Dutch Central Bureau of Statistics).

57 Schoemaker, P. J. H. (1982) 'The expected utility model: its variants, purposes, evidence and limitations' *Journal of Economic Literature* 20, 529–563.
58 Actuarial science is the mathematics of insurance, which calculates the probability of damage and determines a risk premium.
59 OECD (1997) *Insurance Statistics Yearbook 1997* (Paris, France: OECD). Data have been adjusted for inflation and purchase power parities (1990= 100). In addition, non-life insurance data have been adjusted for consumer prices (1990=100).
60 See section 8.3.
61 If inflation is high, the purchase power of money (its real value) may decrease, despite the interest earned.
62 OECD (1995) *Economics Outlook 57* (Paris: OECD).
63 See Antonides, G. and van der Sar, N. L. (1990) 'Individual expectations, risk perception and preferences in relation to investment decision making' *Journal of Economic Psychology* 11, 227–245. The study clubs are associated in the Dutch Central Association of Investment Study Clubs.

AGE GROUPS AND ETHNIC CONSUMER GROUPS *20*

20.1 Introduction

In this chapter, several consumer groups are dealt with, including children, young people, the elderly and ethnic minorities. These groups distinguish themselves from other consumers by their age, knowledge, behaviour and cultural backgrounds. It is possible to identify other groups and this has been accomplished by market segmentation studies.[1] However, the groups considered here are distinctive on the basis of both general characteristics and special consumer behaviours, which make them vulnerable to misleading advertising and unfair trading practices, rather than their specific product or brand choices. In the case of ethnic minorities, cultural differences induce different consumption and media behaviours than those of the native population.

Section 20.2 deals with children before their teens; section 20.3 deals with youth: teenagers and adolescents. The elderly, a growing market, are considered in section 20.4. Some example ethnic minorities, mainly Turks, Moroccans and ex-Yugoslavians, are dealt with in section 20.5. Ethnic minorities differ considerably from the native population in their media, purchasing and usage behaviour. In section 20.6 some conclusions are drawn.

The aim of this chapter is to provide insight into the consumption and media behaviour of different age groups and ethnic groups, as compared with the native population.

20.2 Children

Children below twelve years of age constitute about 15% of the population. Older children frequently buy goods with their pocket money. However, most goods are purchased by parents. Parents and grandparents frequently buy toys, sweets and clothing for their children and grandchildren and accompany them to the beach, Disneyland, Europark, Walibi, Legoland, and other attractions.

Children have to learn how to deal with money, how the economy works and what consumption is. Children are educated and socialized by their parents, friends, teachers, television programmes, books and magazines.[2] Children form a 'delicate' consumer group since they are easily influenced, persuaded and misled. Until children are able to read, television and radio are the most important media for information and recreation, in addition to comics and cartoons.

Stages of the learning process

The Swiss psychologist, Jean Piaget, described four stages of cognitive development in children.[3] In each stage, there are limited possibilities for the child's understanding and learning. The lack of language mastery of a baby means that abstract thinking is impossible at that age. However, in later stages, children are still unable to think abstractly. The different stages are shown in figure 20.1.

Sensorimotor stage (age 0–2 years)
At this stage, the baby's behaviour is mainly physical and is determined by reactions to sensory perceptions. Reactions include reflexes, reactions to internal stimuli such as hunger and thirst, and recognition and response to familiar people. At this stage, the child is egocentric; the child is the centre-point of its own, small world. Language has not yet been mastered and because of this, abstract thinking is impossible.

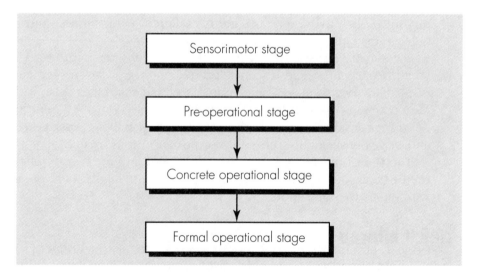

Figure 20.1 *Stages of cognitive development*

Pre-operational thinking (age 3–7 years)
Toddlers and pre-school children are still rather egocentric. They develop the ability to recognize things, to use and to react to symbols and to think about them. Most perception is guided by the supply of stimuli in the environment. The pre-school child concentrates on details and loses sight of the context. Perception guides thinking: children think about what they have perceived. For this reason, thinking is not coordinated and is frequently illogical. Children are easily distracted and find it hard to focus their attention on one issue.

Three-year-olds often think that small creatures live in the television set. In general, toddlers and pre-school children live in a fairyland with much fantasy and they believe that inanimate things are alive. Pre-school children still live in a magical world. Barbie dolls exist like living creatures in the experience of pre-school children.

Concrete-operational thinking (age 8–11 years)
The internal cognitive processes of schoolchildren are stronger and less guided by incidental perceptions. Because of this, thinking is more consistent. Children at this age can read. Thinking is still concrete, as it largely concerns people and objects in the environment. However, abstract issues are hardly understood. Children frequently do not distinguish between the editorial and advertising parts in the media. So they do not think that advertising can possibly be misleading.

Formal-operational thinking (age 11–16 years)
The teenager begins to think as a grown-up and is able to reason abstractly and logically. Ideas, associations and logic become more meaningful. Teenagers can both practise and follow causal reasoning. Perception becomes less important to thinking. Teenagers can also distinguish different aspects and points-of-view concerning a problem. They know the difference between editorial content and advertising in the media.

From the above-mentioned stages, it is clear that children differ from older consumers with regard to the way they process information. Children have limited experience with information processing, have less knowledge of products and use less elaborate processes to transfer information from short-term to long-term memory.[4] They deal with large amounts of information less efficiently and often have difficulty recalling information. However, they perform better than adults at recognition tasks.[5]

Children as consumers

Food, candy and toys are the most important product categories of interest to children and their parents. Advertising directed at children usually stresses the immediate pleasure provided by the product. Children are sometimes sceptical about product claims regarding products they already own. However, promises regarding toys they do not yet own are often believed. Children may then nag their parents into buying these toys. Parents are usually sensitive to the educational elements of toys and, for instance, prefer to buy Lego or Playmobil for their children.

Nowadays, children are taken more seriously than in earlier days. Their opinion counts in matters concerning clothing, food, and the spending of free time. Children have a special sense of humour. For example, some commercials use an absurd 'fantastical' kind of humour that children tend to like. Generally, sound effects are highly appreciated. Surprise effects cause great amusement. Mad and fast is funny; a light protest against the world of grown-ups is highly appreciated.

Children at a young age hardly distinguish between television programmes and commercials. At the stage of pre-operational thinking commercials are short, fast and therefore highly attractive programmes. From the age of eight years on, at the stage of concrete-operational thinking, children know that advertising serves to focus attention on products. They know that advertising stimulates the purchasing of certain products, whereas normal programmes have different objectives. In contrast with adults, who recall printed news better, children aged 9–12 years old recall television news better than printed news, regardless of their reading proficiency.[6]

An important aim and value of children is to grow older, that is to be perceived as older but not yet grown-up. Products are judged regarding their contribution to this value. Childish products are rejected relentlessly. Other values of children include:

- curiosity: discovering and trying out new things;
- achievements, for example by constructive toys and sports;
- competence: fighting spirit and ability, for example, computer games.

To children, as to grown-ups, emotions are important, for example, pleasure, excitement, affection for persons, animals and toys, such as dolls. Games, commercials and programmes with unexpected twists are popular with children.

Children are sensitive to gifts. McDonald's frequently gives away sets of toys, which are collected individually, with its 'Happy Meals'. Many children start collecting things when they go to school, sometimes aided by their parents.

Media Code

Although one has the right to freedom of expression in European countries, the European Commission has published a Green Paper on the protection of minors and human dignity in audiovisual and information services.[7] The general opinion concerns the prohibition of producing,

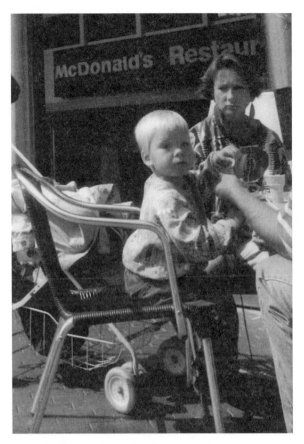

Figure 20.2 *Happy Meal*

distributing, importing and advertising material that is obscene, contrary to sound morals or indecent, child pornography, violent pornography and incitement to racial hatred or violence. In all EU countries, child pornography is prohibited, and in many countries obscene material, incitement to hatred, discrimination and violence, and material detrimental to human dignity is prohibited.

Ways to protect minors against material that may harm their development basically include:

- General prohibition of broadcasting or publishing possibly harmful material. This is the strictest form of protection, which may be problematic because of cultural differences across countries. For example, the Nordic countries in general are tough on violent material but easygoing where sexually-explicit material is concerned, and the Latin countries, tough on sex but less so on violence.
- Limited prohibition of harmful material, for example setting limits on the timing of transmission of programmes or taking into account differences

across countries. Programmes may be classified differently in different countries.

- Technical methods of parental control. This may include subscriptions to pay-as-you-view services and locking systems by means of personal identification numbers (PINs), providing parents with information about the material contents. Regarding the use of the Internet, access to the computer may be restricted to times when parents are present, other possibilities include: memory storage of navigation on the networks, systematic filtering of material and blocking sites on a selective basis.

The European Commission attempts to harmonize the rules regarding the protection of minors in the different member states, which are high on the political agenda.

20.3 Teenagers and adolescents

We define 'youth' as the age group of teenagers attending secondary school, polytechnic or university education. Beyond the age of sixteen, some members of the youth group accept a job or become unemployed. The proportion of children and the youth in the population is expected to decrease from 25% in the early 1990s to about 20% in the year 2050.[8] This process is called 'de-greening'.[9]

Despite the expected decline in volume, the youth market is of interest to marketers because of the budget available to them. Many teenagers and students have small jobs carried out before or after school time or study, for example, newspaper delivery, shop assistant or waiter. Furthermore, the employed members of the youth group have their own income and expenditure patterns.

As compared to the population aged 15 years or over, European youths (aged 15–24) spend relatively large amounts of time on study and professional work, transport, social recreation and active types of leisure (see table 20.1). This reflects both investment of time and a preference for active and social free time. The first is consistent with the economic life-cycle model and the fulfilment of basic needs; the second points to the value of experiences. Relatively little time is devoted to watching television, listening to radio or music, reading, meals, housework, care for others and shopping. It seems that both passive forms of spending free time and household 'duties' are less important at this age.

20.4 Seniors

The proportion of seniors (60 years or older) in the population is expected to increase by about 5% in the next 20 years.[11] This is called the 'greying' of society. Seniors nowadays are far from the image that the phrase 'elderly' can conjure up. Many seniors are dynamic, they are enjoying their lives and

Table 20.1 *Time budgets (minutes) of activities of different age groups Monday to Friday (Europe, 1991)*[10]

	Age groups		
	15–24 (the youth)	15 and over (total adult population)	55 and over (the elderly)
Sleeping/relaxing	535	541	597
Watching tv/listening	297	332	362
Work/studies	339	250	84
Meals	126	163	188
Household work	51	109	155
Social recreation	96	64	60
Transportation	82	66	40
Body care	51	54	56
Reading	37	51	68
Shopping	35	48	67
Care for others	16	45	27
Active leisure	24	18	19
Religious services	2	2	3

finally have the time for travelling, reading, and doing everything they could not do in their busy, working lives. The idea of a 'second youth' or 'third life' is becoming true in the end.

Young seniors are generally not infirm or in need of help. However, many elderly seniors are no longer able to live independently and they need the help of others. In the EU, on average about 5% of seniors live in old people's homes and nursing homes. In addition, home care is provided in many countries. In the Nordic countries, home care is provided for about 20% of the elderly. In other countries, this is below 10%. In general, a higher level of institutional care is associated with a higher level of home care.[12] Because of the higher average lifespan of females, most of the population over 80 years old consists of women.

Characteristic aspects of seniors concern their physical, social and psychological condition. The most important *physical* aspects are infirmity, especially for older seniors. Seniors on average have a relatively low activity level, work relatively slowly and soon become tired. For many of them, their sight, hearing and speed of reaction are deteriorating. They frequently have problems concentrating on particular tasks. On the other hand, many remain functioning on a very high level.

Social aspects mainly include retirement, which has important consequences for time structuring and social contacts. For workers, labour structures the day—rising early and coming home in the evening. Free time is only really free time if there is compulsory work time. An ever-lasting holiday is not a real holiday; it is only a holiday because it contrasts with the working weeks.

Figure 20.3 *Dolce far niente (It's nice to do nothing)*

Work provides a personal identity and gives meaning to life. Being a farmer or bricklayer becomes part of one's identity. As a pensioner one can identify less easily with one's former job than someone who still has the job.[13] Work builds knowledge and skills and it provides social contacts and experiences. Work frequently comes with material advantages, for example the use of facilities and tools for private purposes.[14] Income usually drops on retirement, especially if extra income, compensation for overtime and irregular work, is foregone.

The 'autobiography' of seniors is an important determinant of their view on life and happiness. Their children and grandchildren, their friends and acquaintances, and their former jobs are of great importance. Seniors often remember their experiences during the Second World War. Their life histories determine whether they look back over a well-spent enjoyable life with satisfaction or with a kind of disappointment. Obviously, their current situation also is important, especially the presence of a partner, other family relationships and health. Table 20.1 shows the reduced time budget of seniors for social recreation. Because of the increased budget for free time, seniors spend relatively more time on sleeping and relaxing, watching television and listening to the radio, preparing and consuming meals, household work, reading and shopping.

At this time of life, one partner will die before the other. Widows are often found to engage in husband 'sanctification', i.e., they believe in or experience the continued presence of their spouses, idealise their husbands' memories, 'communicate' with their deceased husbands, take into consideration and frequently comply with their husbands' wishes and advice in making purchase decisions. Husband sanctification was found to be stronger if the spouses used to make syncratic decisions than if they made their decisions autonomously.[15]

The *psychological* aspects of seniors are partly due to the physical and social aspects, including:

- Declining capability to learn.
- Declining ability to adapt to new circumstances and habits.
- Reduced memory, for example, finding it harder to recall one's personal identification number (PIN code).
- Reduced reaction speed, for example, in traffic.
- Reduced ability to perform several tasks simultaneously. Seniors can be easily distracted and frequently have problems concentrating on the main task. For example, seniors are easily distracted by background music.
- Increased vulnerability to manipulation by salespeople. Some seniors are afraid to leave the shop without any purchase.
- Reduced speed of information processing. Many programmes on radio or television go too fast for seniors. The external pacing of these media is too high.[16] Media with internal pacing are more appropriate for seniors, because they can read these media at their own pace.

From this discussion, it is evident that seniors differ from the youth regarding the way they process information. Seniors use less processing effort to transfer information from short-term to long-term memory.[17] They can deal less efficiently with large amounts of information and have problems recalling information.

Seniors currently generally have a relatively low level of education as compared to the rest of the adult population.[18] In former days, it was an achievement to attend secondary or high school. Academic study was only meant for the higher social classes. Many seniors received their education in practical work.

Products and services

Seniors usually own and use fewer durable goods than average, with the exception of the colour television set, which is popular with everyone. However, it appears that at lower levels of ownership, the gap between ownership by older people and the general population increases. For example, in Greece and Portugal—where ownership of colour television sets is about 50%—only about 25% of the older people own a colour television set, whereas in most other EU countries—where ownership levels are over 80%—the gap is almost negligible.[19] The same goes for other durables. The differences in ownership and use can be explained either as a cohort effect or as an age effect, or—most likely—a combination of cohort and age effects.[20]

According to the cohort effect seniors have not owned a number of durables in the past and for this reason, they do not own them presently. Possibly, they consider these goods as luxuries or they feel unable to handle them. According to the cohort effect, younger people will buy these goods and keep using them when they grow older.

According to the age effect, some durable goods do not fit the lifestyle of seniors, and this results in diminished need for them. Possibly, seniors did own these goods in earlier days. For example, they do not need a dishwasher because they do not use many dishes, or they do not need a deep freezer because the children have left home. Many seniors dispose of their cars because they become afraid of driving.

A third reason for lower ownership of these products may be that the relatively low income of the elderly forces them to economize on durable goods. A fourth reason is that seniors tend to be laggards in the adoption of innovations and consequently own fewer 'new' durable goods.

Seniors use many services such as travel, health care, home care, house-keeping, and meal delivery. Food in small packages, spectacles and other paramedical aids, self-medication, papers and magazines are popular products at this age. Media usage is relatively high, both for printed media and television.

Health and housing

Health is one of the most important concerns for the elderly and several physical and psychological aspects of ageing have been considered earlier in this chapter. In addition to health, adequate housing is important for maintaining independence. Table 20.2 shows the satisfaction of seniors

Table 20.2 *Satisfaction of seniors with their health and housing in Europe*

	General[a]	Health[b]	Housing[a]
Ireland	8.23	7.48	8.59
Denmark	7.94	7.00	9.13
Sweden	7.94	7.60	8.87
Netherlands	7.81	7.23	8.23
UK	7.77	7.12	8.64
Norway	7.58	7.32	7.71
Belgium	–	7.26	8.19
Italy	7.24	6.61	8.15
France	7.18	6.82	7.86
West Germany	7.08	5.78	7.65
Spain	7.01	6.24	7.56

[a] 10-point scale (1 = dissatisfied, ..., 10 = satisfied)
[b] 5-point scale (bad = 1, ..., good = 5) multiplied by 2 for comparison purposes

with their lives in general, and with their health and housing situations in particular. It appears that seniors in the former West Germany and the Latin countries are relatively dissatisfied with their situation as compared with those in the Nordic countries, the Netherlands, UK and Belgium.

In Sweden and Norway, health care is the responsibility of municipalities, which focus on home care rather than institutional care.[21] Home care includes shopping, cleaning, cooking, washing and personal care. In addition, home care by relatives and volunteers is subsidized in order to relieve the burden of the helpers. In Ireland, self-aid groups, consisting of seniors helping other seniors, volunteer organizations and assistance by children is popular. These services are subsidized to some extent. In Germany, health care policy is aimed at helping people to live independently as long as possible. A number of organizations provide home care although its volume seems to be insufficient and institutional health care is limited. There has been discussion about the introduction of the *Pflegeversicherung*—a general health care insurance.

In Denmark and Sweden, seniors get special attention in the housing policies of the government, municipalities and non-profit institutions. This includes the building of service flats, adaptation of the existing housing facilities, well-equipped old-people's houses and nursing homes with low personnel/inhabitant ratios. Demented people in Sweden can live in group facilities, i.e., small houses meant for about 6 to 8 people, having their own rooms and 24-hour help available. In addition, several subsidies exist. In Ireland and the UK, volunteer groups, *Staying Put* and *Care & Repair* projects are available to help seniors with the repair, adaptation and improvement of their homes. In Germany, the elderly do not get special attention in housing policy. They are required to pay for any facilities themselves. Nursing homes are generally considered as *Armenasyl* or 'end stations'.

20.5 Ethnic minorities

On 1 January 1993, the population of the European Union included 3.3% of the native populations of non-member countries and 1.5% of Community citizens living in a member state other than their country of origin. The percentage of non-Community foreigners has increased from 2.1% in 1985 to 3.3% in 1993.[22] Seventy-two per cent of those from non-member countries live in Germany, France and the UK (see table 20.3). However, Belgium, Austria, The Netherlands and Sweden also host relatively high numbers of non-Community foreigners. Luxembourg and Belgium have the highest percentages of foreigners from within the Community, mainly due to the offices of the European Union in Luxembourg and Brussels.

Almost half the foreigners from outside the Community come from other European countries, especially Turkey and the former Yugoslavia (see table 20.4). Nineteen per cent comes from the Maghreb countries (Morocco, Algeria and Tunisia). Most foreigners have come to the European Union in response to the need for labour, especially for menial or poorly paid jobs. Usually, they are of an economically active age and have several children, thus compensating to some extent, the effects of greying in the societies they join.

Table 20.3 *Foreign population in the European Union (1992)*[23]

	Non-community foreigners (as a percentage of the total population)	Community foreigners (as a percentage of the total population)
Austria	5.6	1.0
Belgium	3.6	5.6
Denmark	2.5	0.8
Finland	0.5	0.2
France	4.0	2.3
Germany	5.2	2.1
Greece	1.4	0.7
Ireland	0.6	2.1
Italy	0.7	0.2
Luxembourg	3.2	28.9
Netherlands	3.6	1.2
Portugal	0.8	0.3
Spain	0.5	0.4
Sweden	4.0	1.7
UK	2.1	1.4
Total	2.9	1.4

Table 20.4 *Country of origin of non-Community foreigners (1992)*[24]

Country of origin	Percentage of non-Community foreigners stemming from the region
Turkey	23.5
ex-Yugoslavia	10.7
Other European countries	13.0
Morocco	10.2
Algeria	6.0
Tunisia	2.6
Other African countries	7.5
USA	3.4
Other countries	23.1

The country of origin of non-Community foreigners is different for different member states, due to different historical, political and cultural links. For example, Portugal hosts relatively many Cape Verdians and Brazilians, in Belgium there are relatively many people from Zaire, in France relatively many Algerians, in the UK relatively many from India and Pakistan, in The Netherlands relatively many from Surinam.

Other differences are due to the geographical location of the countries. For example, Germany hosts many foreigners from Poland, Italy many from the former Yugoslavia, and Austria many from Romania and the former Yugoslavia.

Many non-Community foreigners are fugitives for political reasons. For example, relatively many Iranians live in Denmark and Sweden, many Somalians live in Finland and many Vietnamese live in Norway.

A substantial proportion of immigrants are natives returning to their country of origin after a few years abroad. In Ireland, Denmark, Greece, Spain and the UK, at least half of all immigrants are returning natives.

Children of naturalized foreigners usually obtain the citizenship of the country where they are born. In the long run, it may become difficult (and probably also less relevant) to assess the membership of ethnic minority groups. After attending local schools and integration into the local society, they may also have largely acquired the local culture. First-generation ethnic groups may acquire the local culture by acculturation, whereas second and third generations mainly become socialized.[25] Generational conflicts in ethnic groups are frequently due to differences in cultural adaptation. At home, the children are brought up with the traditional and religious values of the parents. At school and work, they face the local opinions, norms and values.

Ethnic minority groups usually differ from the population with respect to consumption and shopping. They are more likely to buy from markets and ethnic stores, for example Halal butchers and Turkish bakeries. Because

Figure 20.4 *Ethnic variety*

they travel and transfer money to their country of origin relatively often, ethnic travel agencies and banks have emerged in addition to ethnic video shops, and grocery shops. Their media behaviour is frequently associated with their country of origin. They are more likely to read foreign news-papers and magazines, and watch foreign videotapes and ethnic television programmes.

20.6 Conclusions

This chapter dealt with children, youth, seniors and ethnic minorities. These groups differ with respect to their age, stage of development, culture and consumer behaviour.

In the case of ethnic minorities, several subcultures can be distinguished, each with its own language, religion and culture. Some of these subcultures remain strictly separated from the native population, such as the Chinese. This may be partly due to language problems. People from former colonies may have less problems in this respect, and as a result, may integrate more easily with the native population.

Children and youth are vulnerable groups with respect to manipulative advertising and suggestive sales practices. Seniors too, can easily become victims of persuasive sales techniques, such as door-to-door selling, and sometimes even swindles.[26]

Notes

1 See chapter 24.
2 See section 3.3.

3 Piaget, J. (1954) *The Construction of Reality in the Child* (New York: Basic Books).
  Piaget, J. and Inhelder, B. (1966) *La Psychologie de l'Enfant* (Paris: Presses Universitaires de France).

4 See section 11.5.

5 Roedder John, D. and Cole, C. A. (1986) 'Age differences in information processing: Understanding deficits in young and elderly consumers' *Journal of Consumer Research* 13, 297–315.

6 Walma van der Molen, J. H. and van der Voort, T. H. A. (1997) 'Children's recall of television and print news: A media comparison study' *Journal of Educational Psychology* 89, 82–91.

7 European Commission (October 1996) 'Green paper on the protection of minors and human dignity in audiovisual and information services'.

8 See table 2.3.

9 See chapter 2.

10 IP Group (1991), *Euro Time Survey* (Paris: IP).

11 See table 2.3.

12 Hugman, R. (1994) *Ageing and the Care of Older People in Europe* (London: Macmillan).

13 Warr, P. (1984) 'Job loss, unemployment and psychological well-being' in: Allen, V. L. and van de Vliert, E. (Eds) *Role Transitions* (New York: Plenum) 263–285.

14 Van Raaij, W. F. and Antonides, G. (1991) 'Costs and benefits of unemployment and employment' *Journal of Economic Psychology* 12, 667–687.

15 Turley, D. (1995) 'Dialogue with the departed' *European Advances in Consumer Research* 2, 10–13.

16 See section 17.2.

17 Compare section 11.5.

18 Eurostat and United Nations (1995) *Women and Men in Europe and North America* (Paris: United Nations, and Luxembourg: Eurostat Annex 1, 68.

19 Eurostat (1993) 'Population and social conditions' *Rapid Reports* 1993 (3).

20 See section 3.4.

21 Commission of the European Communities (1993, 1994) 'Older people in Europe: Social and economic policies'.

22 Office for Official Publications of the European Communities (1995) *Migration Statistics 1995* (Luxembourg).

23 Eurostat (1995) *Europe in Figures* (Luxembourg: Eurostat).

24 Eurostat (1995).

25 See section 3.3.

26 Friedman, M. (1986) 'Confidence swindles of older consumers' *Journal of Consumer Policy* 9, 375–387.

PART IV

AFTER-SALES PROCESSES

CONSUMER SATISFACTION AND COMPLAINTS

21

21.1 Introduction

Besides making profit, consumer satisfaction with products and services is a primary objective for many producers, and for other producers it should be a primary objective.[1] In several definitions of marketing the fine-tuning of products and services to meet consumers' desires and needs and therefore increase their satisfaction, takes a central position. For consumers themselves satisfaction is an important result of consumption decisions, contributing to their well-being.

Several stages can be identified in the processes of decision making by consumers who intend to buy products or services. The first stage is problem recognition when the consumer identifies a problem and forms the expectation that a product or service may solve it. The consumer then searches for possible alternatives which are evaluated on the basis of the expectation that they can solve the problem. Here the consumer's main concern is to compare the different performances of brands and types within a product category. After the purchase, satisfaction or dissatisfaction with the product and the brand emerges from its usage and the consumer's evaluation of its performance.

This chapter mainly deals with the issues that arise after a purchase, namely the stage of product evaluation, consumer satisfaction or dissatisfaction, problems and, possibly, complaints. Section 21.2 considers expectations with respect to the quality and the functioning of products and services. Section 21.3 deals with discrepancies between expectations and product performance and the attribution of their causes, possibly resulting in dissatisfaction. Consumer problems and complaints are dealt with in section 21.4. Eventually, complaints may lead to consumer actions, which are considered in section 21.5. Section 21.6 deals with the handling of complaints, outcomes and satisfaction with the complaint procedure.

We have taken the holiday trip as offered by travel agencies and tour operators as our example of a product or service. The general model on which this chapter is based is shown in figure 21.1. The different parts of this figure are considered consecutively in this chapter. Several conclusions are drawn in section 21.7.

The first investigation into consumer satisfaction is already over 30 years old.[2] In the USA attempts were made to develop an Index of Consumer Satisfaction regarding food products.[3] However, it became evident that consumer satisfaction is a relative rather than an absolute measure. Satisfaction after the purchase is partly dependent on expectations held before the purchase. Recently, however, the earlier approach has been tried again and researchers are looking at product evaluations without taking expectations into account. This approach is used to determine consumer satisfaction with product categories and brands in different branches of industry, for instance in Sweden.[4]

The aim of this chapter is to provide insight into the process of dissatisfaction and complaints by consumers in order to contribute to a policy of improving the quality of goods and services, which will in turn improve consumer satisfaction and prevent dissatisfaction.

21.2 Expectations

Consumer expectations are often realistic, but sometimes they are pitched too high. The quality of a product or service does not always meet expectations. As an example, consider the package holiday. This is an ambiguous product as consumers may have difficulty forming a realistic imagination of the trip. Photographs in a travel guide and written or oral descriptions usually form the basis of expectations regarding the trip, although nowadays video material is frequently available. However, the travel agent frequently sells 'illusions'. Other sources of information about the holiday destination are: consumers' own experiences if the holiday destination has been visited before, the experiences of friends, neighbours and colleagues, price—as an indicator of quality—and the reputation of the travel agency or tour operator.

Expectations exist at four levels:

- The *general* level deals with expectations and critique of the operation of the western consumption system—capitalism—for example. One may expect high service levels but also some negative external effects, such as pollution.
- The *category* level deals with the product class, for example holiday trips. Consumers ask themselves what they may expect from a package tour.
- The *brand* level deals with a service provider such as Club Med and with the service organizations—travel agency, tour operator, etc., such as

Thomas Cook or Thomsons Tour Operations. What expectations do consumers have about the expertise and the reputation of these organizations?
- The *transaction* level deals with concrete transactions, for example the expectations regarding a fortnight in Crete.

Holidaymakers compare their expectations with experiences on the trip. If the outcome falls short of expectations, we speak of negative discrepancy. If experiences meet expectations, there is no discrepancy. If the outcomes outperform expectations, there is positive discrepancy. Consequently, discrepancy will induce satisfaction or dissatisfaction. This is known as the *disconfirmation hypothesis.*[5] The discrepancy approach is based on adaptation in perception theory. Stimuli are perceived in comparison with a standard which is based on experience. One has certain expectations in one's perception and compares new stimuli with these expectations.[6] As expectations serve as a reference point in the evaluation of outcomes, evaluations may be asymmetric, in agreement with the asymmetric value function in prospect theory.[7] Indeed it has been found that negative discrepancy causes greater dissatisfaction than a commensurate positive discrepancy causes satisfaction.[8]

Definition

Disconfirmation theory assumes that consumer satisfaction or dissatisfaction results from a positive or negative discrepancy between the outcome and the expectations regarding a purchase.

Although there is some evidence for disconfirmation theory, the perceived performance may also have a direct effect on satisfaction, irrespective of disconfirmation.[9] For durables, satisfaction judgements were found to be exclusively determined by product performance, not by expectations.[10]

Expectations at different levels influence each other. Expectations regarding the product category influence the expectations regarding a brand. Conversely, outcome at the brand level and the transaction level are frequently generalized to the category level. Dissatisfaction with a particular brand induces a brand shift if the brand concerned is considered inferior compared with other brands in the product class. If dissatisfaction about a brand exists but the brand is not considered as inferior in relation to other brands, this will not induce a brand shift in general. For example, many consumers are dissatisfied with their tumble dryer but they do not shift brands because they think that other tumble dryers do not perform better.

Table 21.1 shows three levels at which the discrepancy between expectations and reality can be assessed by consumers.[11] Category level C deals

Table 21.1 *Expectations regarding product category, brands and transactions*

Level	Outcome
Product class, category (C)	Category intention, little brand loyalty
Brand, type (B)	Brand intention, high brand loyalty, satisfaction
Transaction, specific service (T)	Satisfaction

with product classes and categories, brand level B deals with brands and product types and transaction level T deals with specific services. If the category expectations are high and brand expectation is low (C < B), there is a reason to shift brands—indicating low brand loyalty—and consumers will advise others against buying the brand. If category expectations are low and the brand expectation is high (B > C), a high purchase intention regarding the brand concerned exists. Brand loyalty will be high and consumers will advise others to buy the brand. Repeat buying is obvious in this case. In the case of positive discrepancy between expectations and reality, brand expectations especially affect satisfaction. The latter also goes for the expectations regarding a specific transaction or service.

A holiday trip is a complex product including transportation, accommodation, meals and excursions. For this reason, it is difficult to compare the different alternatives exactly and to find the best offer. Frequently, to the consumer it is not clear who is responsible for what. The consumer may first consult a travel agency. For consumers, a holiday is a risky product because it costs a lot of money, emotions are involved, and there is much social communication about it with family members, colleagues, relatives and friends. Holidays involve taking financial and social risks. People may only go on holiday once a year. So, an unsuccessful holiday is a major source of worry.

Because holidays are complex, emotional and risky products, it is unsurprising if consumers form unrealistic expectations regarding their holiday trips. Advertising frequently breeds high expectations regarding the holiday destination, the accommodation, the recreation facilities and even the travel company. This may easily lead to negative discrepancies, disappointment and dissatisfaction. In addition, holiday trips need to satisfy several people at the same time, which will involve compromise and satisficing by the service provider. This may induce further discrepancies. The SERVQUAL model shows several discrepancies in service provision[12] (see figure 21.1).

The SERVQUAL model states that the expected service is influenced by personal experiences, experiences by others, social communication, and marketing communication. All of these sources may breed expectations, and in the case of holiday trips sometimes even illusions. The service provider will have an idea about consumer expectations and this should not

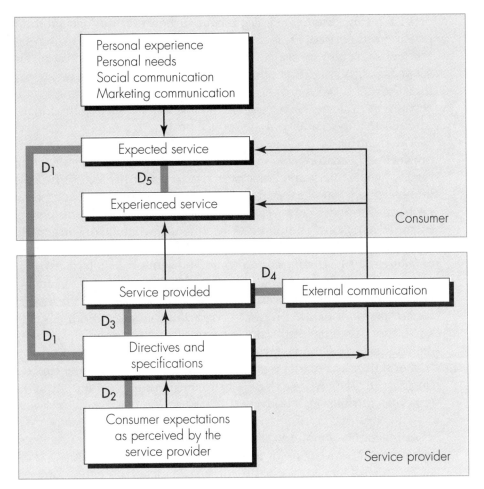

Figure 21.1 *The SERVQUAL model*

deviate too much from the consumers' actual expectations. This expectations gap is indicated by D_1 in figure 21.1.

On the basis of perceived consumer expectations, the management of the service provider develops certain directives and specifications as to how services should be provided. Here, discrepancy D_2 may arise. The directives and specifications have to be translated into the actual performance of the service. Usually, the people who perform a service are not the managers who formulate the directives and specifications. Representatives at the holiday destination are required to behave according to managers' directives, but there may be a discrepancy, D_3, between directed and actual behaviour. Discrepancy D_4 may exist between the actual provision of the service and the communication with the consumer. Benefits may be promised which may not materialize. Representatives who promise to solve certain problems may not be able to fulfil their promises.

As a result, discrepancy D_5 may arise between the expected and the experienced service. D_5 is a consequence of all the other discrepancies. Frequently, service providers aim at maintaining the technical quality of a service. For them, this is often the most important. However, consumers think how and by whom the service is provided is important. Frequently, consumers evaluate a service on intangible aspects such as the friendliness, carefulness and reliability of the service provider.

The example of package holidays clearly shows that the discrepancies between expectations and consumer experiences are a central theme in quality management and consumer satisfaction. This is also the case with durable goods. At the point of purchase, the consumer sometimes has problems forming a clear image about how he or she will use a product, for example, a personal computer. Consequently, when he or she actually tries to use the product, the usefulness, the ease of operation and the frequency of failures may be disappointing compared with pre-purchase expectations.

A positive discrepancy may be attributed either to low consumer expectations (internal attribution) or to an exceptional performance of the service provider or the product (external attribution). Both cases lead to satisfaction. External attribution of a positive discrepancy usually leads to higher satisfaction than internal attribution; see figure 21.2.

A negative discrepancy may be attributed to high consumer expectations (internal attribution) or to bad performance of the provider or the product (external attribution). Both cases lead to dissatisfaction. However, in general, external attribution of a negative discrepancy leads to higher dissatisfaction than internal attribution. At each stage of the process shown in figure 21.2, satisfaction or dissatisfaction may arise.

The realization of expectations manifests itself after the purchase of a

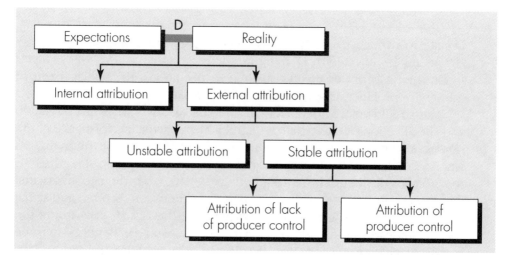

Figure 21.2 *Attribution of the discrepancy D between expectations and outcome*

product or service. From that moment on, the similarity of, or discrepancy between expectations and realizations becomes apparent from the consumption of the product or service. In case of high *a priori* expectations one will be less easily satisfied with the product performance or the service provided. Frequently, there is only imperfect agreement, since expectations are ambiguous in a number of cases, such as holidays. This ambiguity may be caused in different ways:

- Lack of experience with an existing product. The consumer may not know what to expect, for example, when buying a CD-ROM package for the first time.
- The product concerned is new on the market—an innovation—for instance a reclining bicycle.
- At the moment of purchase, the service is not physically present, for example, in-home teleshopping.
- The quality of service varies spontaneously. Not all hairdressers cut in the same style and neither does the same hairdresser perform the same way at different times; the girl at the desk or the checkout is not as friendly every time. In general, the variation in quality is greater with services than with products.

In some cases, expectations can be very precise, for example with standardized products—pre-packed groceries, items of everyday use such as cleaning products—or a house of which the floor plan is known beforehand.

Expectations are influenced by comparisons. A product is always judged in comparison with some standard or criterion, for instance a description in a leaflet, the use of a similar product by one's neighbours or one's own experiences with a similar product. Large individual differences exist regarding consecutive, social and spatial comparison processes.[13]

Knowledge of alternatives leads to more accurate expectations and possibly to less satisfaction if a product does not meet one's expectations. In the case of small differences between alternatives, the consumer remains in a situation of conflict concerning the correct choice.[14] Small differences may lead to cognitive dissonance.

Although expectations and realizations may correspond in the short run, in the long run a discrepancy may arise, for instance due to failures occurring after some time (but sooner than expected). For some products the consequences only become evident in the long run, for example alcohol and tobacco. Consumption of demerit products depends on the time preference of the consumer, since in the short run they offer satisfaction but in the long run they may lead to health problems and dissatisfaction.[15]

Dissatisfaction may appear because of discrepant expectations and realizations. A small discrepancy will lead to dissatisfaction less easily than a large one. Here, the consumer's perceptual threshold plays a part. Some consumers are more critical than others and detect product shortcomings instantaneously, for example a difference in colour, any damage or too long a delivery time. If a discrepancy is perceived, the consumer may not necessarily feel dissatisfaction—he or she may reduce cognitive dissonance in a different way. Slightly disagreeable aspects of a product may be rationalized, thus avoiding dissatisfaction. Reduction of cognitive dissonance also means a reduction of dissatisfaction. If the discrepancy exceeds a certain level, the difference between realizations and expectations may be exaggerated. Then it becomes a matter of a contrast effect which motivates the consumer to take further action.[16]

Perceived quality

The *quality* of products and services has been mentioned several times. Everyone has an idea of what quality is, but it can be hard to define. Quality may be approached from several different perspectives:[17]

- *Transcendental quality* is a kind of innate excellence which is generally recognized. Mozart possessed transcendental quality as a composer. Skill and love for one's profession are indicators of the quality of service provision.[18]
- *Production design quality* is the quality assurance of careful design, production and sale. The product or service has to conform to its design specifications (discrepancy 3 in figure 21.1).
- *Product character quality* is an accurately measurable product characteristic, for example the fruit content of marmalade, the cocoa content of chocolate or the frequency of failure of a Citroën.
- *Value directed quality* is defined in terms of costs or price. A product has a high quality if it functions well at a reasonable price. It concerns the equity of the price-value ratio of the product.
- *Perceived quality* is derived from consumers' perceptions. Products and services have high quality if they meet the desires and the expectations of consumers (discrepancy 5 in figure 21.1).

The definition of perceived quality fits the consumer perspective best. High perceived quality includes fitness for use, durability, safety, comfort, reliability, low frequency of failure, and good performance. Perceived quality is a subjective characteristic determined by objective ones—the quality indicators (product-directed quality). For example, the quality of fruit juice is determined by its freshness and the fruit content. The quality of a car is determined by its failure frequency and driving characteristics. The quality of a textbook is determined by its organization, categorizations and examples fitting the needs of the readers and users (both students and teachers).

Frequently, consumers have certain expectations regarding a product and its use. Sometimes quality is defined by the comparison of expectations and product performance. See figures 21.2, 21.3 and 21.5. If a product performs as expected, we speak of adequate quality. If the product out-performs expectations, we speak of high quality.[19] Because adaptation to quality level occurs, increasing quality levels tend to lead to demand for even higher quality products. Consumers differ in their knowledge and expectations regarding products, which leads to people perceiving different qualities in the same products or services.

The quality of services is hard to guarantee because they are 'produced' at the very moment of order or purchase. A restaurant may buy the ingredients of meals or produce them in advance but the service only takes place when the guests have been seated. Customers do not passively consume services. Frequently the customer has to participate actively, as in the case of piano lessons, to obtain high quality service. Quality indicators are also used for services. This may include measuring tangible service elements such as the toughness of a steak, and the speed of service, or less reliable indicators of quality, such as brand name, price and reputation.

21.3 Dissatisfaction and attribution of its cause

It might be assumed that consumers will be more satisfied the less they know, expect and demand. But clearly, this cannot be the aim of consumer policy. More information may increase inequality across consumers, namely between those who can use the information provided and those who cannot.[20] Some degree of dissatisfaction may be useful in order to strengthen the consumer's position.[21] Creative dissatisfaction frequently causes social change and strengthening of the consumer's position.

Discrepancies, satisfaction and dissatisfaction may be measured at the general, category and micro levels. For marketing and government policy it is desirable to locate the bottlenecks. One can identify four levels of dissatisfaction with increasing specificity.[22]

- Dissatisfaction at the *general level*: this type of dissatisfaction frequently is associated with a critique of the consumption system, for example, dissatisfaction with the use of goods and services (consumption system), dissatisfaction with the availability of goods (shopping system) and dissatisfaction with the choice possibilities (purchase system).
- Dissatisfaction at the *category level* refers to certain product classes such as tumble dryers, mowers and package tours.
- Dissatisfaction at the *brand level* is directed toward specific brands, retailers or organizations.
- Dissatisfaction at the *specific level* refers to certain services and offers, for example, the repair of a car.

Facilitation and inhibition

Not only the level but also the dimensionality of satisfaction/dissatisfaction is important. Satisfaction may consist of more than one dimension. A distinction between facilitation and inhibition can be made.[23] Too high a price may deter consumers (inhibition) but a reasonable price may not be enough to encourage consumers to accept the product.[24] Other product attributes may also be important for consumer acceptance. The lack of a CFC-seal[25] may be a reason for not buying a particular refrigerator (inhibition). In this example a conjunctive decision rule is applied. However, the presence of a CFC-seal is not a sufficient condition to buy the product (no facilitation). Similarly an unfriendly salesperson may constitute sufficient reason for not buying, but a friendly salesperson is not a sufficient reason for buying.[26] For producers it is of primary importance to dispose of inhibition factors. The creation of facilitation factors is of secondary importance.[27]

Likewise there are inhibiting and facilitating factors in consumer satisfaction. Inhibiting factors cause dissatisfaction. The removal of inhibiting factors may prevent dissatisfaction, but does not create satisfaction. Facilitation factors cause satisfaction provided inhibition is absent. See figure 21.3.

"In the case of durable goods we observe more and more that consumers find certain product characteristics obvious, especially for functional performance and values, such as safety. However, if it is lacking, it is an inhibiting factor but if it is present, the producer is not given credit for it." Nelson Foote[28]

An example of dissatisfaction caused by inhibition is dissatisfaction with public transportation. In most northern European countries, travellers are dissatisfied if the train or bus is late or if no seats are available, but they take it for granted if the trip is on schedule and if they can be seated. So, the priority of public transportation management is to avoid or remove inhibition and not the creation of facilitation. A facilitating factor such as providing coffee on the train cannot compensate the inhibition caused by delay or shortage of seats. Only if all inhibiting factors have been removed, might facilitation have a positive effect.

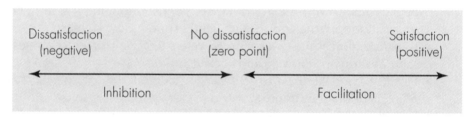

Figure 21.3 *Inhibition and facilitation*

Measurement of satisfaction

Measures of consumer (dis)satisfaction refer to the subject—problems, satisfaction or dissatisfaction—the method—objective or subjective—and the time—before or after the supplier has had the opportunity to solve the problem.[29] Objective indicators of satisfaction are, for instance, quantities purchased, repeat buying and complaints. Subjective methods refer to inhibition, facilitation, problems and dissatisfaction experienced by the consumer. This means asking the consumer about *problems* regarding consumption of goods and services.

Attribution

Dissatisfaction with a holiday trip may occur if reality does not meet the consumer's expectations regarding the trip (discrepancies D_5 in figure 21.1 and D in figure 21.2) and regarding alternatives in the product class. Expectations usually refer to an area of acceptable product performance. If the areas of expectations and reality overlap, no dissatisfaction will occur. A slight disappointment will usually be rationalized—for example, by lowering the level of expectations after the fact. In this case the discrepancy between outcome and expectation is said to be assimilated within the cognitive schema. A great disappointment will cause general dissatisfaction, especially if the consumer attributes the cause to the retailer or manufacturer.[30]

Attribution theory is concerned with the causes to which individuals attribute certain events.[31] Consumers behave as lay-scientists and attempt to detect the causes of events. In this process, three causal dimensions have been distinguished:[32] locus, stability and controllability; see figure 21.2.

Locus of control indicates which party is considered to be the cause of the event: the consumer or the supplier, indicating internal or external attribution, respectively. A car repair may have been carried out wrongly because the driver could not explain the problem to the mechanic exactly (internal attribution) or because the mechanic did not carry out the repair correctly although he or she knew what the problem was (external attribution). *Stability* refers to the duration of a cause. A car repair may be carried out incorrectly because the mechanic has a bad day (temporary cause) or because the mechanic is not good at the job (permanent cause). *Controllability* refers to the degree to which someone has control over the cause. A mechanic who consciously carries out a repair poorly while hoping that the customer will not detect it, controls the cause in a negative way. A mechanic who uses incorrectly adjusted measuring equipment unknowingly and carries out the repair badly because of this, does not control the cause. In the latter case, he or she is less responsible for the results of his or her work.

Figure 21.4 *Explaining the problem*

It has been found that the greatest dissatisfaction and most complaints occur in the case of external attribution and a stable, controllable cause.[33] See figure 21.2. In the case of an external attribution most consumers demand a supplier's apology and compensation for the damage sustained. If the cause is also considered to be stable, consumers prefer their money back to a replacement product or another repair. This is because in the case of a stable cause, the consumer expects the other products or services by the supplier to be as bad. The customer will probably never return to this supplier. If, in addition, the supplier has intentionally harmed and deceived the customer, the customer will probably become angry and may take action against the supplier.

Definition

Attribution theory of consumer satisfaction assumes that the consumer feels greater dissatisfaction the more the discrepancy between outcome and expectations is attributed to external causes (i.e., outside the consumer's control), stable causes and causes under control of the producer.

The model shown in figure 21.2 implies that dissatisfaction and probability of complaints increase if the cause is attributed to the supplier and if the cause is considered to be stable and under the control of the supplier. This does not exclude the possibility of dissatisfaction and complaints in other cases, but this is less likely. The result of the attribution process influences the perception of quality and the degree of satisfaction. When consumers are satisfied they are more likely to make repeat purchases and be loyal to the brand. In the case of dissatisfaction the probability of complaints and actions is greater; see figure 21.5.

Private and public actions will be more likely if the cause is attributed to the supplier and is perceived to be under his or her control. In this case consumer stress—anger, tension and frustration—will be great. It is worth the effort of taking action to reduce the tension.

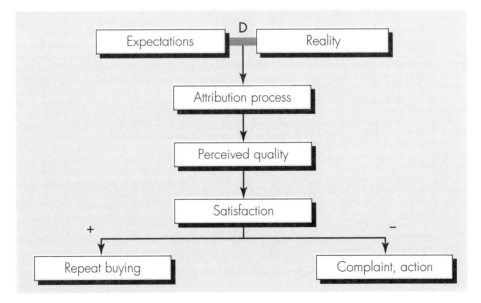

Figure 21.5 *Expectations, perceived quality, satisfaction and consequent behaviour*

21.4 Problems and complaints

There have been many studies conducted in Western Europe and the USA on the subject of consumer problems and complaints. In the USA about 80% of purchases in 1975 were considered satisfactory (no problems reported, not even after prompting); on average this percentage was equal across infrequent purchases, frequent purchases and services. Non-price problems occurred relatively often in the purchases of cars (32%), vacuum cleaners (27%), mail order goods (31%), toys (31%), clothing (28%) and repairs (32%).[34] The most frequent problems reported were total and partial breakage, poor workmanship, design of product, method of supplying service and slow, late or nondelivery.

In general, European countries do not investigate consumer problems and complaints on a regular basis, despite the overabundance of commercial services offered in this respect. However, the Swedish National Customer Satisfaction Barometer (CSB) measures consumer satisfaction on a regular basis. The 1991 CSB score shows an average satisfaction score of 65 on a 0–100 scale across 32 different industries.[35] In 1989 and 1990 the satisfaction score was 64. Group means for nondurable (72) and durable goods (70) are higher than for retailers (65), services (64) and monopolies (64) including pharmacies, postal services, telecommunication services and the police. TV broadcasting received the lowest score (48) and candy/coffee the highest (80). Unfortunately, the repair industry is excluded from this barometer.

A categorization of complaints registered at the Dutch Consumer Union revealed that most problems occur in home decoration and, in descending order of importance, indemnity insurance, tourism/recreation/transportation, governmental service and financial service.[36] The following domains of consumer problems were distinguished—in descending order of importance:[37]

- commercial information and guidance;
- usage costs and product quality;
- after-sales service.

Young consumers generally appear to have more problems with product information, despite (or maybe because of) their relatively high levels of education. Possibly lack of experience plays a part here. Consumers with lower incomes are generally troubled by high usage costs and low product quality. Possibly they buy cheaper products that are associated with more usage problems. Furthermore, men appear to have more problems with services than women.

Concrete problems are the most easy to demonstrate and to formulate. Regarding a holiday trip these problems may include a faulty reservation, a serious flight delay, missing a connection, hotel room not available, noise pollution, or lack of hygiene. Abstract problems such as unfriendly and inattentive service are more subjective, difficult to demonstrate and to prove, and therefore will less often lead to voiced complaints.

The problems associated with consumption have been described. However, the process and results of complaining can lead to satisfaction or further complaints, depending on how the complaint is handled. If the complaint is handled correctly and if the consumer is satisfied with the result, dissatisfaction is likely to decrease.[38] Procedural justice positively affects repurchase intentions.[39]

21.5 Consumer actions

Dissatisfaction may result in a number of different kinds of consumer action. Consumers may engage in private action, public action, or refrain from action; these are shown in table 21.2. However, dissatisfaction is an insufficient condition for complaining, explaining only 15% of the variation in this behaviour.[40] Available time and other resources, experience with complaints, expected benefits from complaining, and the attitude toward complaining behaviour may further affect the likelihood of this behaviour.[41]

No action

There are five possible causes for dissatisfied consumers not taking any action over a complaint:

- Consumers may forget about problems or refrain from action because complaining requires too much effort, the effort does not balance the expected benefits or the expectation of success is low. The latter may

Table 21.2 *Possible consumer actions*

Type of action	Possibilities
No action	Forget about the problem Refrain because of high costs Communication threshold—problem to formulate complaint Action threshold—lack of assertiveness Entry threshold—lack of opportunities Norms threshold
Private action	Boycott of retailer or producer Negative word-of-mouth
Public action	Complaining to the seller Complaining to the ombudsman Taking legal action

occur if the problem is intangible, if any damage is minor and in the case of internal attribution of the problem.

- Consumers may experience a communication threshold because of inability to formulate a complaint verbally or in writing. This relates to the consumer's level of education and experience with complaints.
- Consumers may not reach their 'action thresholds'. The consumer may not take action[42] because of passiveness, lack of assertiveness and aggressiveness[43] or uncertainty about the justifiability of the complaint.
- Consumers may experience barriers or 'entry thresholds' in the form of unwilling retailers,[44] an overloaded consumer organization or high fees for third-party services. Lowering the 'entry threshold' will increase the number of voiced complaints. This does not necessarily indicate increased dissatisfaction or bad product quality but is a result of making it easier for consumers to voice their complaints.
- Personal and social norms may restrict complaining behaviour.[45] The consumer may feel that complaining and making trouble is not an appropriate behaviour.

The concept of marketplace participation has been introduced to explain complaining behaviour.[46] Marketplace participation constitutes one of the roles one should be able to play in society. The factors influencing the no-action strategy may be described by the MAO-model. No action because of high costs indicates lack of motivation (M). Communication and action thresholds are associated with lack of ability (A). Entry and norms thresholds are associated with lack of opportunity (O).

Private action

The customer may engage in private actions such as a boycott of the retailer or the brand (exit behaviour). A consumer may decide: 'I will never return to this restaurant.' The customer may also engage in negative recommendations to friends, relatives and colleagues. Such private action will generally be unknown to the retailer but may harm its reputation. Private actions are usually characterized by low communication, action and entry thresholds.

Public action

The customer may engage in public action, such as voicing a complaint to the seller (second party), to a consumer organization, ombudsman, Trading Standards Office or court (third party). Going to court is associated with a high entry threshold. Obviously, combinations of private and public actions may occur.

In a US study 60% of consumers with a problem took no action, 6% changed seller or brand and 31% voiced complaints to the seller only.[47] In The Netherlands 29% took no action.[48] In both studies taking action was less common in the case of frequently purchased products.

Figure 21.6 *Arbitration committee*

Complainers differ from other consumers in several respects. In general, they are relatively wealthy, better educated and often work in executive functions or liberal professions.[49] A better education is useful in over-coming the communication threshold. The higher income may also indicate the possession of many goods, thus increasing the probability of problems and complaints.[50] In addition the entry threshold may be lower at higher income levels.

21.6 Complaint handling

Consumer complaints can provide great opportunities for firms and retailers for several reasons:[51]

- They provide feedback about product or company performance.
- If appropriately handled, the amount of brand-switching among dis-satisfied consumers may be reduced, in contrast to dissatisfied non-complaining consumers.
- Dissatisfied consumers usually show higher levels of brand loyalty and retaining them is worth the effort.
- The cost of retaining a customer (e.g., via complaint handling) is often low, in relation to attracting a new customer. Volvo estimates that acquisition of a new customer is three times more expensive than keeping a customer.

A direct agreement with the retailer concerned may solve many problems and may help to prevent a problem escalating. Frequently companies have consumer affairs departments to manage their complaints. Many have adopted the policy assuming the customer is in the right and compensating for any damage, as this will help to prevent negative rumours. The damage caused by some problems escalating out of hand is often considered to be greater than the costs of giving speedy compensation to all. In the US study 57% of the complaints were resolved satisfactorily. Complaints about frequently purchased products were resolved more often (66%) whereas complaints about services were resolved less often (44%).[52]

In a study with faked complaint letters to 50 companies in the USA 86% of the companies responded within 90 days. A separate sample of consumers evaluated the letters from the companies as 'very much' or 'somewhat' valuing the customers who sent the letters. Among the specific comments 20% included favourable impressions created by the manufacturer's enclosure of discount coupons, refund cheques and small gifts.[53]

21.7 Conclusions

This chapter dealt with the processes of consumer satisfaction and complaints. This is important both for consumer protection, consumer policy and for the producers of goods and services. This concerns the consumer rights of economic protection and the right to be heard.

The process of dissatisfaction and complaints can be described by means of attribution theory. By using the criteria of attribution theory both the extent of dissatisfaction and the probabilities of consumer actions and complaints can be determined.

Attribution theory may also be applied with respect to complaint handling and compensation. Although even after compensation of the damage to the complainer the relationship with the seller may not be fully restored, product satisfaction and re-purchase intention generally are higher than for dissatisfied non-complaining consumers. In addition, compensation prevents negative social communication regarding the brand, the retailer or the producer. High entry thresholds may be avoided by creating simple procedures for complaint handling.

The perceived quality of goods and services has been studied by means of the SERVQUAL model. It appears that satisfaction and dissatisfaction are associated with discrepancies between consumers' expectations and suppliers' performances regarding the product or service. The five discrepancies described may each cause dissatisfaction.

Notes

1   Kotler, P. and Armstrong, G. (1991) *Principles of Marketing* (Englewood Cliffs, NJ: Prentice Hall) 18.
2   Cardozo, R. N. (1965) 'An experimental study of customer effort, expectations and satisfaction' *Journal of Marketing Research* 2, 244–249. This was the first article about consumer dissatisfaction and complaints.

3   Pfaff, A. (1972) 'An index of consumer satisfaction' in: Venkatesan, M. (Ed.) *Proceedings of the Third Annual Conference of the Association for Consumer Research* 713–737.
Lingoes, J. C. and Pfaff, A. (1972) 'An index of consumer satisfaction' in: Venkatesan, M. (Ed.) *Proceedings of the Third Annual Conference of the Association for Consumer Research* 689–712.

4   Fornell, C. (1992) 'A national customer satisfaction barometer: The Swedish experience' *Journal of Marketing* 56, 6–21.
Fornell, C. and Johnson, M. D. (1993) 'Differentiation as a basis for explaining customer satisfaction across industries' *Journal of Economic Psychology* 14, 696.
Johnson, M. D. and Fornell, C. (1991) 'A framework for comparing customer satisfaction across individuals and product categories' *Journal of Economic Psychology* 12, 267–286.

5   Oliver, R. L. (1980) 'A cognitive model of the antecedents and consequences of satisfaction decisions' *Journal of Marketing Research* 17, 460–469.

6   Helson, H. (1964) *Adaptation Level Theory* (New York: Harper and Row). Oliver (1980).

7   Kahneman, D. and Tversky, A. (1979) 'Prospect theory: An analysis of decision under risk' *Econometrica* 47, 263–291.

8   Anderson, E. W. and Sullivan, M. W. (1993) 'The antecedents and consequences of customer satisfaction for firms' *Marketing Science* 12, 125–143.

9   Anderson and Sullivan (1993).

10   Churchill Jr, G. A. and Suprenant, C. (1982) 'An investigation into the determinants of consumer satisfaction' *Journal of Marketing Research* 19, 491–504.

11   Koelemeijer, K., Roest, H. and Verhallen, T. (1993) 'An integrative framework of perceived service quality and its relations to satisfaction/dissatisfaction, attitude and repurchase intention' in: *Proceedings of the AMAC Conference* Part 1 (Barcelona: ESADE) 683–699. These authors consider the discrepancy between expectation and reality as the perceived quality of a service.

12   Parasuraman, A., Zeitham, V. A. and Berry, L. L. (1985) 'A conceptual model of service quality and its implications for future research' *Journal of Marketing* 49(fall), 41–50.

13   Helson (1964).

14   Hansen, F. (1972) *Consumer Choice Behavior. A Cognitive Theory* (New York: The Free Press).

15   See section 8.7.

16   Poiesz, T. B. C. and Von Grumbkow, J. (1988) 'Economic well-being, job satisfaction, income evaluation, and consumer satisfaction: an integrative attempt' in: van Raaij, W. F., van Veldhoven, G. M. and Wärneryd, K. E. (Eds) *Handbook of Economic Psychology* (Dordrecht: Kluwer Academic Publishers) 570–593.

17   Garvin, D. A. (1983) 'Quality on the line' *Harvard Business Review* 83, 64–75. For quality management, see section 5.7.

18   An interesting philosophical book about quality is Pirsig, R. M. (1974) *Zen and the Art of Motorcycle Maintenance* (Toronto: Bantam Books).

19 Parasuraman, A., Zeithaml, V. A. and Berry, L. L. (1988) 'SERVQUAL: A multiple item scale for measuring customer perceptions of service quality' *Journal of Retailing* 64, 1, 12–40.

20 Renoux, Y. (1973) 'Consumer dissatisfaction and public policy' in: Alloine, F. C. (Ed.) *Public Policy and Marketing Practices* (Chicago: American Marketing Association).

21 Ölander, F. (1977) 'Can consumer dissatisfaction and complaints guide public consumer policy?' *Journal of Consumer Policy* 1, 124–137.

22 Renoux (1973).
    Czepiel, J. A., Rosenberg, L. J. and Akerele, A. (1975) 'Perspectives on consumer satisfaction' in: Curhan, R. C. (Ed.) *Combined Proceedings* (Chicago: American Marketing Association).

23 Herzberg, F., Mausner, B. and Snyderman, B. (1959) *The Motivation to Work* (New York: John Wiley).
    Jacoby, J. (1976) 'Consumer and industrial psychology: prospects for theory corroboration and mutual contribution' Chapter 24 in: Dunnette, M. D. (Ed.) *Handbook of Industrial and Organizational Psychology* (Chicago: Rand McNally) 1044–1045.

24 Gabor, A. and Granger, C. W. J. (1965) 'The pricing of new products' *Scientific Business* 3, 141–150.

25 See note 2 of chapter 22.

26 See section 11.6. In the case of inhibition, non-compensatory decision rules are applied; in the caseof facilitation, compensatory rules are applied. Inhibition especially occurs in the beginning of the decision process to select acceptable alternatives (pre-selection). Facilitation mainly occurs in the second part of the process in order to select the 'best' alternative from the acceptable ones (choice).

27 Avoiding inhibition is associated with informational value and creating facilitation is associated with transformational value (cf. sections 4.3 and 7.4).

28 Statement by Nelson Foote 1961, manager of General Electric at the time.
    Foote, N. N. (1961) *Consumer Behavior: Household Decision Making* Part 4 (New York: New York University Press).

29 Andreasen, A. R. (1977) 'A taxonomy of consumer satisfaction/dissatisfaction measures' *Journal of Consumer Affairs* 1, 1, 11–24.
    Andreasen, A. R. (1977) 'Consumer dissatisfaction as a measure of market performance' *Journal of Consumer Policy* 1, 311–324.

30 Van Raaij, W. F. (1985) 'Attribution of causality to economic actions and events' *Kyklos* 38, 3–19.

31 Folkes, V. S. (1984) 'Consumer reactions to product failure: an attributional approach' *Journal of Consumer Research* 10, 398–409.

32 This distinction has been made by Weiner, B. (1980) *Human Motivation* (New York: Holt, Rinehart & Winston).

33 Folkes (1984).

34 Best, A. and Andreasen, A. R. (1977) 'Consumer response to unsatisfactory purchases: a survey of perceiving defects, voicing complaints, and obtaining redress' *Law & Society Review* 11, 701–742.

35 Fornell (1992).

36 Francken, D. A. and Van Raaij, W. F. (1985) 'Socio-economic and demographic

determinants of consumer problem perception' *Journal of Consumer Policy* 8, 303–314.

37 Based on a factor analysis of reported frequencies of occurrence, see Francken and Van Raaij (1985).

38 Schouten, V. and Van Raaij, W. F. (1990) 'Consumer problems and satisfaction in a retail setting' *Journal of Consumer Satisfaction, Dissatisfaction and Complaining Behavior* 3, 56–60.
Gilly, M. C. (1987) 'Postcomplaint processes: from organizational response to repurchase behavior' *Journal of Consumer Affairs* 21, 293–311.
Halstead, D. and Page Jr, T. J. (1992) 'The effects of satisfaction and complaining behavior on consumer repurchase intentions' *Journal of Consumer Satisfaction. Dissatisfaction and Complaining Behavior* 5, 1–11.

39 Blodgett, J. G. (1994) 'The effects of perceived justice on complainants' repatronage intentions and negative word-of-mouth behavior' *Journal of Consumer Satisfaction, Dissatisfaction and Complaining Behavior* 7, 1–14.

40 Bearden, W. O. and Teel, J. E. (1983) 'Selected determinants of consumer satisfaction and complaint reports' *Journal of Marketing Research* 20, 21–28.
Oliver, R. L. (1987) 'An investigation of the interrelationship between consumer (dis)satisfaction and complaint reports' *Advances in Consumer Research* 14, 218–222.

41 Kolodinsky, J. (1995) 'Usefulness of economics in explaining consumer complaints' *Journal of Consumer Affairs* 29, 29–54.
Richins, M. L. and Verhage, B. J. (1985) 'Cross-cultural differences in consumer attitudes and their implications for complaint management' *International Journal of Research in Marketing* 2, 197–206.

42 Kuhl, J. (1982) 'Action vs. state orientation as a mediator between motivation and action' in: Hacker, W. (Ed.) *Cognitive and Motivational Aspects of Action* (Amsterdam: North-Holland) 67–85.

43 Richins, M. L. (1983) 'An analysis of consumer interaction styles in the marketplace' *Journal of Consumer Research* 10, 73–82.
Slama, M. E. and Williams, T. G. (1991) 'Consumer interaction styles and purchase complaint intentions' *Journal of Consumer Satisfaction, Dissatisfaction and Complaining Behavior* 4, 167–174.

44 Granbois, D., Summer, J. O. and Frazier, G. L. (1977), 'Correlates of consumer expectations and complaining behavior' in Day, R. L. (Ed.) *Consumer Satisfaction, Dissatisfaction and Complaining Behavior* (Foundation for the School of Business, Indiana University, Bloomington, IN) 18–25.

45 Richins, M. L. (1982) 'An investigation of consumers' attitudes toward complaining' *Advances in Consumer Research* 9, 502–506.
Singh, J. (1989) 'Determinants of consumers' decisions to seek third party redress: An empirical study of dissatisfied patients' *Journal of Consumer Affairs* 23, 329–363.

46 Grønhaug, K. and Zaltman, G. (1981) 'Exploring consumer complaining behavior: a model and some empirical results' *Journal of Economic Psychology* 1, 121–134.

47 Best and Andreasen (1977).

48 Francken, D. A. (1983) 'Postpurchase consumer evaluations, complaint actions and repurchase behavior' *Journal of Economic Psychology* 4, 273–290.

49 Liefeld, J. P., Edgecomb, F. H. C. and Wolfe, L. (1975) 'Demographic character-istics of Canadian consumer complainers' *Journal of Consumer Affairs* 9, 73–80.

50 Francken and Van Raaij (1985).

51 Yi, Y. (1990) 'A critical review of consumer satisfaction' in: Zeithaml, V. A. (Ed.) *Review in Marketing, American Marketing Association* (Chicago, IL) 68–123.

52 Best and Andreasen (1977).

53 Smart, D. T. and Martin, C. L. (1992) 'Manufacturer responsiveness to con-sumer correspondence: an empirical investigation of consumer perceptions' *Journal of Consumer Affairs* 26, 104–128.

CONSUMPTION AND THE ENVIRONMENT 22

22.1 Introduction

The natural environment has gradually become more important in consumer behaviour. Environmental pollution is one of the most important issues of concern during the last decade. All kinds of external effects of production and consumption have gradually become visible in the environment. River and sea water has become unsuitable for swimming; forests suffer from acid rain; beaches are polluted with oil with horrifying consequences for birds and other animals; sometimes housing has been built on polluted soil, affecting the health of the inhabitants. Furthermore, inhumanity to animal species has raised consumer concern, for example, fur farms, cosmetic testing, battery hens and factory farming.

Consumers are responsible for 25% or acid rain, the greenhouse effect and the breakdown of the ozone layer. Fifteen per cent of the waste problem is caused by consumers.[1] However, most consumers do not want to give up the living standards that they have attained. Governments have to prevent and to clean up environmental pollution, while the costs are not being reclaimed from the polluters. On the positive side, a number of firms participate in the application of environmental innovations to production processes, with or without government subsidies. Where environmental innovations are associated with higher market prices, consumers have to decide whether or not to buy these products. Examples of environment-friendly behaviour include buying free-range eggs, phosphate-free detergents, lead-free and water-based paints.

Environmental problems not only stem from production but also from the use and disposal of products. Sometimes the use of a product is harmful to the environment, such as speedy driving and fast acceleration of the car, washing at high temperatures, and careless use of products. Product disposal can harm the environment directly, for example disposable products, packaging, CFCs in refrigerators[2] and chemical waste such as paint, batteries and bleaching agents. In several countries in Europe attempts have been made at waste separation in order to recycle materials, for example organic waste, paper, metal, glass and small chemical waste. Products and their parts sometimes are collected at central units for re-use, for example, cars and motors.

Definition

Sustainable consumption aims at fulfilling the needs of the current generation without neglecting those of future generations.

Sustainable consumption has become the aim of environmental policy. The lifetime of goods has to be extended and materials have to be recycled as far as possible; trees used by the paper industry have to be replaced. Sustainable consumption aims at fulfilling the needs of the present generation without neglecting those of future generations. The *Fifth Environmental Action Programme* of the European Union aims at long-term objectives and focuses on a more global approach concerning climate change, acidification and air quality, urban environment, coastal zones, waste management, water resources and protection of nature and biodiversity.[3] Its policy instruments include:

- legislation to set environmental standards;
- economic instruments to encourage the production and use of environment-friendly products and processes, for example, taxation and charges;
- support measures—information, education and research;
- financial measures—funds and subsidies.

More specifically, legislation has covered water pollution, atmospheric pollution, noise, chemical products, waste disposal and the protection of nature.

Several directives deal with the protection of surface and underground water. Quality standards have been set for bathing water, drinking water and water suitable for fish and shellfish life. Several measures have been taken to prevent disposal of toxic substances into the River Rhine, the North Atlantic, the North Sea and the Mediterranean.

Directives have been adopted concerning emission of gases from motor vehicles and power stations, and to phase out the production and consumption of CFCs.

Maximum noise levels have been set or are considered concerning cars, lorries, motorcycles, tractors, aircraft, lawnmowers, building-site machinery, helicopters and rail vehicles.

Since the Seveso accident in northern Italy in 1977, measures have been taken concerning the classification, packaging and labelling of dangerous substances, and the composition of detergents. A European Inventory of Existing Chemical Substances has been drawn up since 1986 listing all chemical products on the market.

The European Union produces more than 2 billion tons of waste every year and has regulated its collection, disposal, recycling and processing by a number of directives. Specific measures concern transboundary shipments of wastes, waste from the titanium oxide industry, waste oils, dumping of waste at sea and radioactive waste.

Several directives have been adopted on the conservation of wildlife and habitats, on banning the importation of products made from the skin of baby seals and on the control and restriction of scientific experiments on animals.

Section 22.2 deals with the consumer's contribution to a better environment in the consecutive stages of the consumption cycle. Section 22.3 considers the processing of information about the environment. Environmental concern and self-perception are dealt with in section 22.4. Section 22.5 deals with disposal and section 22.6 concludes. The aim of this chapter is to provide insight into the factors influencing consumer behaviour with respect to the environment.

22.2 Environmental aspects of the consumption cycle

Environmental consequences of consumption may result from each stage of the consumption cycle. Product choice implies the demand for certain basic materials and production processes. Use and maintenance implies favourable and unfavourable environmental effects. Consumption behaviour consists of problem recognition and information search, buying behaviour, use and disposal. These stages are described here with respect to their environmental aspects.[4]

Problem recognition frequently results from the malfunctioning of products in use, for example product failure, technical or economic obsolescence, and increased energy use. In the case of a house, information search may take several years. In the case of a car, it may take several months and in the case of small products several days or weeks. In the case of impulse buying, information search hardly occurs. While they are seeking information, consumers are sensitive to it. For example, they see advertisements they would normally ignore and consumer advice magazines are considered. The alternatives on offer may differ regarding their environment-friendliness, thus influencing choice at the brand level. Eventually, consumers may decide not to buy at all because of environmental concerns.

In the decision making stage before buying, the environmental aspects of the available alternatives may be considered. For example, consumers may choose between alkaline paint on an oil basis and acrylic paint on a water basis. By using alkaline paint, volatile substances are emitted which are harmful to the environment and the ozone layer. Acrylic paint is less harmful to the environment but it is more expensive and requires some changes in the manner of painting. Acrylic paint dries relatively quickly during warm weather. So, consumers have to trade-off the environmental benefits against the higher price and the need to paint in a different way.

Frequently, price mechanisms are used to facilitate the use of environment-friendly products. Environment-friendly products may be subsidized and harmful products may be charged. In this way, lead-free petrol and the catalytic converter have been introduced. Similarly, acrylic paint may be subsidized by a charge on alkaline paint, making acrylic paint relatively cheap. Environment-friendly characteristics may also be used as differential advantages in the marketing of products, for example, products of the Body Shop.

In the usage stage, maintenance, repair, use frequency and type of use are of interest. For example, the maintenance of a car, the tuning of the engine and the way it is driven may influence the use of petrol. The purpose of use also is of interest. For example, is the car used for short trips which could have been made on foot or bicycle? Is car-pooling encouraged? Product usage stimulates energy use for heating, lighting and movement. Different ways of using products may save energy, for example, by setting the thermostat lower, wearing warmer clothing at home, closing windows and curtains, and cycling instead of using the car.

The final stage is disposal, i.e., selling, giving away or throwing away the

Figure 22.1 *Car boot sales*

product. What is the residual value of the product and is it possible to sell it on the second-hand market? Is it possible to re-use several parts or should the entire product be discarded? Several methods of waste separation exist, including separation of paper, glass, metal, organic waste, and chemical waste. These materials may be recycled and re-used in production processes. Volkswagen facilitates recycling of materials by coding the components in a special way. In the future, car disposal, scrapping and recycling may be managed by the industry.

22.3 Information processing

During the information processing stage consumers search for information, especially in the case of durable goods and expensive services such as holidays. In the case of simple products and services, information search is more limited. Brand loyalty serves to simplify choice processes, especially in the case of daily consumables. Once consumers have decided on a particular product or brand, for example, alkaline paint, it is difficult to change.

Except for the risks considered before,[5] environmental risks may be taken into account. A higher (perceived) risk is usually associated with an increased search for information. The purchase process often proceeds rationally, i.e., search for information in the first place and formation of opinions and buying intentions later. Environmental concern will contribute to the evaluation of environmental attributes in deciding what to buy.

Information about the environmental consequences of behaviour is a prerequisite for environmental concern and environment-friendly behaviour. Table 22.1 shows several opinions regarding the consequences of human behaviour on the environment. It appears that, on average, East Europeans believe more in the harmful effects of human behaviour than both West Europeans and North Americans. The latter are the least convinced of the harmful effects of people on the environment, although this might be changing. The figures suggest that environmental concern may be influenced by the extent of environmental pollution in the countries concerned.

Air pollution by cars, the danger of radioactive waste and the effect of fossil fuels on the environment seem to be commonly known as negative consequences of consumption. Pesticides and chemicals in food consumption are considered less dangerous environmental effects.

Environmental attributes

In general, products and services are not purchased for the sake of the environment. Although special products such as compost bins and catalytic converters are purchased exclusively because of their environmental function, the environment usually shows up as a product attribute in consumer

Table 22.1 *Averaged opinions regarding environmental damage in Europe and the USA (1993)*[6]

	Western Europe	Eastern Europe	North America
Cars are not really an important cause of air pollution in respondent's country	2.04	2.29	1.73
Some radioactive waste from nuclear power stations will be dangerous for thousands of years	3.38	3.39	3.31
Every time we use coal or oil or gas, we contribute to the greenhouse effect	3.17	3.06	3.04
Human beings are the main cause of plant and animal species dying out	3.09	3.24	2.83
The greenhouse effect is caused by a hole in the earth's atmosphere	2.96	3.05	2.70
All man-made chemicals can cause cancer if you eat enough of them	2.68	3.06	2.46
All pesticides and chemicals used on food crops cause cancer in humans	2.47	2.73	2.30

Agreement with the statements was measured on a five-point scale: 1 = strongly disagree, 2 = disagree, 3 = neither agree nor disagree, 4 = agree, 5 = strongly agree.

decision making. Environmental attributes may be included both in conjunctive and compensatory decision processes.[7] Consumers who demanded a minimum level of environment-friendliness may exclude products harmful to the environment from their consideration sets, for example, spray cans. Others trade-off environment-friendliness against other attributes such as price, performance and design. For example, one may take the ratio of price and environment-friendliness into account.

Several environmental attributes may be distinguished, some of which are related to consumer health.

- *Animal-friendliness* refers to the extent that animal well-being is preserved in the production of goods. For example, the Body Shop exclusively sells products developed without animal experiments. Free-range meat is taken from pigs and calves that have not been locked up in narrow pens. Free-range eggs are laid by hens with greater freedom of movement than those kept in battery cages.
- Several products are *harmful to the natural environment*, for instance CFCs in refrigerators breaking down the ozone layer, and PVC in packaging.
- A number of products *deplete natural resources*, such as furniture made from tropical hardwoods, products consuming energy, and products requiring much energy during the production process, for example, vegetables from heated greenhouses.

- Some food is *harmful to one's health*, for example meat from animals that have undergone intensive hormone treatments and fruit or vegetables treated with pesticides. Macrobiotic food has not been treated with chemical means. Frequently consumers are uncertain about the harmfulness of food, for example in the case of genetic manipulation and irradiation. Other products may also be harmful to one's health, for example, asbestos insulation, ozone-emitting printers and exhaust fumes from cars.
- Many consumers like to return to the original taste—the essence—of food. This concerns attributes such as health, taste, *naturalness* and purity, for example high-fibre food without unnatural additives.

Many consumers are environmentally responsible when making decisions concerning products and services. Producers have to account for the consequences of their products for the environment. This is called socially responsible marketing.[8]

Costs and benefits

Choice alternatives are often evaluated in terms of costs and benefits. This includes not only financial but also behavioural costs—time, effort and trouble taken to achieve something. In this respect, public transportation implies higher behavioural costs than using a car. One has to wait, it takes

Figure 22.2 *Train to a better environment?*

more time and frequently it is less comfortable. On the other hand, traffic jams also imply behavioural costs and air pollution. Behavioural benefits of the car include speed, efficiency and comfort. Behavioural benefits of public transportation include relaxation, environment-friendliness and freedom of movement within the vehicle.

Costs and benefits can apply to the consumer or to society. In the latter case, we speak of collective costs and benefits. Frequently, environment-friendly products require behavioural costs but they are beneficial to society in the long run. In contrast, products harmful to the environment produce behavioural benefits—at least in the short run—but incur collective costs.[9] Frequently, societal outcomes only become evident in the long run, whereas individual outcomes occur immediately. Long-term benefits are often traded off against the short-term costs. For example, energy-saving equipment requires an investment which is paid back by lower energy bills. However, not everyone is able and willing to make the investment because the money is needed for different things.

Several eco-labels have been developed to distinguish environmentally-friendly products from those harmful to the environment. Examples are the Grüne Punkt and blue angel in Germany, the white swan in Scandinavia and the CFC seals. In the case of paper towels it has been found that adding an eco-label resulted in greater preference for the brand, both in the US and The Netherlands.[10] Adding an energy label to refrigerators resulted in more energy-efficient decisions than the standard format—kW/24h—in a condition without time pressure.[11] However, in general only half of the sample in a Dutch study recognized and understood eco-labels correctly.[12]

22.4 Environmental concern

Above, it has been assumed that people trade-off costs and benefits of products and brands. However, the weights given to environmental attributes may differ according to the degree of environmental concern. Given a certain level of knowledge about the environmental consequences of production, transportation and consumption of goods and services, environmental concern is defined as an attitude regarding environmental consequences. Strong environmental concern implies great worries over the environmental consequences of consumption, involvement with the environment, internalization of environmental values, and a willingness to change consumption behaviour into an environment-friendly direction. Environmental concern results in searching out and processing information about the environment as well as a relatively high probability of being a member of environmental organizations, such as the World Wildlife Fund (WWF) or Greenpeace.

Environmental concern is influenced by direct personal experiences, other people's experiences and communications by the mass media.

Environmental concern may be shaped on the basis of one's own experience. Experience with products and the harmful effects of consumption serve as feedback to one's knowledge of environmental attributes of products. An example is the Norwegian Mjøsa lake which served as the sewer discharge point of a village. The inhabitants could see the effects that phosphate-containing detergents had directly from the lake's water quality. In this case the feedback loop is very short and powerful. Most Norwegians near the Mjøsa lake have decided to use phosphate-free detergents. Usually, these feedback loops are non-transparent or indirect, since most sewage water is filtered in remote areas and few people know its true costs and effects. Energy monitors that provided immediate feedback on household energy use resulted in 12% energy savings in a Dutch study.[13]

Social communication may also influence environmental concern.[14] For example, neighbours may convince each other of the benefits of home insulation. Furthermore, social communication contributes to the development of social norms, which may serve as restrictions on consumption behaviour that is harmful to the environment.

The mass media increasingly provide information about the environmental costs and benefits of consumption. This may also contribute to the development of social norms in society.

Environmental concern has been measured several times in the 12 countries that have been member states of the European Union since 1986. Table 22.2 shows several indicators of environmental concern in the past

Table 22.2 *Indicators of environmental concern in the EU*[15]

	1986	1988	1992	1995
Protection of the environment and suppression of environmental pollution is:[a]				
• an immediate and urgent problem	74	76	87	83
• more a problem of the future	22	21	11	15
• not really a problem	3	3	2	2
Concern about international environment:[b]				
• the disappearance of some plant varieties, species and habitat in the world	3.2	3.2	3.5	3.4
• the exhaustion of natural resources in the world	3.0	3.1	3.5	3.3
• global warming (greenhouse effect)	3.0	3.2	3.5	3.4
Concern about national environment:[b]				
• pollution of rivers and lakes	3.2	3.2	3.5	3.3
• pollution of seas and coast	3.3	3.3	3.6	3.3
• air pollution	3.1	3.2	3.5	3.4
• industrial waste	3.2	3.3	3.6	3.4

[a] Percentage choosing one of the three alternatives
[b] Average of scores on a 4-point scale where 1 = totally unconcerned, 2 = concerned to a small extent, 3 = moderately concerned, 4 = highly concerned

decade. It appears that environmental concern has increased from 1986 to 1992; in 1995 it decreased somewhat. In general, environmental concern is high, although countries differ in their attitudes considerably. On average, Greece and Italy score the highest regarding protection of the environment and suppression of environmental pollution as an immediate and urgent problem, Belgium, Ireland and France score the lowest. Spain, Italy and Greece on average score the highest with respect to international and national concern and Belgium and Ireland score the lowest. Again the figures suggest that environmental concern is directly linked to the extent of local environmental pollution.

A different survey has included questions concerning the environment and the economy in eight West European countries, six East European countries and six countries outside Europe, in 1993; table 22.3 shows these results. Regarding the first two questions, East Europeans show more concern than both West Europeans and North Americans. However, regarding the other questions, they show less concern (the statements show optimism about the environment).[16] The difference between environmental concern and concern with animals used for medical purposes is striking. On average, people are less concerned with animals used for testing than with the environment as a whole. It appears that people are concerned about the choices made between economic welfare and the environment but less so with the choice between animal and human health.

Environmental concern may result in environment-friendly behaviour, given a number of conditions including the price level, product performance, social norms, knowledge about the environment, etc. Table 22.4 shows self-reported environment-friendly behaviour in the 12 countries that have been member states of the EU since 1986. It appears that

Table 22.3 *Indicators of environmental concern in Europe and North America (1993)*[17]

	Western Europe	Eastern Europe	North America
Almost everything we do in modern life harms the environment	3.19	3.37	3.12
Economic growth always harms the environment	2.96	3.24	2.61
Modern science will solve our environmental problems with little change in our way of life	2.63	2.90	2.39
People worry too much about human progress harming the environment	2.76	3.38	2.61
It is right to use animals for medical testing if it might save human lives	3.40	4.09	3.51

Average of scores on a five-point scale where: 1 = strongly disagree, 2 = disagree, 3 = neither agree nor disagree, 4 = agree, 5 = strongly agree

Table 22.4 *Self-reported environment-friendly behaviour in the EU*[18]

Percentage of people reporting	1986	1988	1992	1995
Not throwing away in the street paper and other trash	79	80	88	91
Having saved energy	–	–	64	67
Having separated household waste	39	42	59	65
Having saved tap water	49	47	57	63
Having used different transportation than the car, if possible	–	–	41	48
Having purchased an environment-friendly product, even when it was relatively expensive	–	–	47	44
Having taken holidays less harmful to the environment[19]	–	–	23	26
Having equipped the car for limitation of pollution	7	9	19	26

environment friendly behaviour has generally increased over time. The most common environment-friendly behaviours reported are not throwing away rubbish in the streets, saving water and energy, and waste separation. Across the different behaviours, the countries vary markedly regarding the extent of environment-friendly behaviours. For example, the former West Germany obtains the highest score for car equipment to limit pollution but the lowest score for preventing rubbish on the street.

Table 22.5 shows several self-reported environmental intentions and behaviours in Western Europe, Eastern Europe and North America in 1993. It seems that economic efforts are made more easily than behavioural efforts—payment is acceptable but changing one's behaviour is relatively painful. Paying taxes appears to be the least preferred method of payment, possibly because the money is added to the general budget, unrelated to consumption that is harmful to the environment. By preferring to pay higher prices it seems that people prefer a direct relationship between products and services that are harmful to the environment and spending.

Sorting materials for recycling appears to be the easiest thing to do. Refraining from meat consumption and car driving appears to be relatively difficult.

Self-perception

Many consumers acquire little information before buying a product and then observe whether they like it after they've bought it. Obviously, this is ill-advised in the case of cars and houses but this trial-and-error strategy may be useful in the case of goods with low risk and low value. Sales promotion techniques are frequently aimed at breaking habitual consumer behaviour and persuading consumers to try a different product. If successful, this induces product experience. The product itself, the packaging

Table 22.5 *Self-reported environmental intentions and behaviours in Europe and North America (1993)*[20]

	Western Europe	Eastern Europe	North America
How willing would you be to pay much higher prices in order to protect the environment?	3.27	3.04	3.35
How willing would you be to accept cuts in your standard of living in order to protect the environment?	3.01	2.61	2.97
How willing would you be to pay much higher taxes in order to protect the environment?	2.80	2.75	2.88
How often do you make a special effort to sort glass or tins or plastic or newspapers and so on for recycling?	3.43	2.27	3.80
How often do you make a special effort to buy fruits and vegetables grown without pesticides or chemicals?	2.71	2.68	2.84
How often do you refuse to eat meat for moral or environmental reasons?	2.40	2.40	2.43
How often do you cut back on driving a car for environmental reasons?	2.23	1.72	2.44

Average ratings on a five-point scale: 1 = very unwilling/not available, 2 = fairly unwilling/never, 3 = neither willing nor unwilling/sometimes, 4 = fairly willing/often, 5 = very willing/always

and product information should then convince the consumer of the value of the new product.

Self-perception refers to the consumer's observations of the following type: 'I have purchased product X, so I am a person who likes X.'[21] If the consumer owns the product and if it meets his or her expectations, he or she will value the product and is likely to develop a positive attitude toward the product.[22] This will induce repeat buying in a subsequent situation. Self-perception may also refer to the environment as a whole, for example: 'I save energy, so I am environmentally conscious.' In this case, the attitude follows behaviour and it may influence various kinds of environment-friendly behaviour.

Definition

Self-perception theory assumes that people use observations of their own behaviour to infer their attitudes toward the object of concern.

Self-perception may be used to set the agenda for environment-friendly products and to increase environmental concern. For example, one may provide confirmed car drivers with a free bus or train ticket together with information about commuting by public transport. Drivers can then personally experience public transport. It might be hoped that the experiences would be positive, as only then drivers may be persuaded to use public transport more frequently. Then, a new habit might develop. This process contributes to the internalization of environmental values.

An example of how 'self-perception' can be manipulated was shown by an experiment carried out in the USA.[23] A petition was to be raised against the construction of a new highway and the destruction of a forest. Going from door to door to gather signatures usually yields a number of positive reactions, but the aim of the experiment was to increase the number by using a smarter strategy. Free posters concerning the environment were offered in a neighborhood. A few days later, it was observed that most inhabitants had hung posters in their windows. Returning home at night, they saw the posters hanging on their own windows and they thought: 'How environment-friendly I am!' The process of self-perception was at work and each person perceived him or herself as environment-friendly.[24]

Several weeks later, signatures and money were collected in the neighbourhood. No connection with the posters was mentioned. The yield in the neighbourhoods owning the posters was much higher than in those without the posters. The posters had set in motion a process of changed self-perception. In such cases, the advice is to divide the action into two stages, one to enable the self-perception change process and the other for collecting the donations. This study is an example of the 'foot-in-the-door' technique.[25]

After two months of a waste separation at source programme at Aalborg, Denmark, 63% of the people reported 'no trouble'. This proportion had increased to 75% after six months.[26] This may be considered yet another example of changed self-perception. In this case, the largest changes were obtained in the older age groups, where old habits might be assumed to be the strongest.

22.5 Disposal behaviour

In the final stage of the consumption cycle, consumers have to decide whether to keep, re-use or throw away a product. This section deals with disposal behaviour with respect to recycling.[27] As unsorted waste cannot be recycled, environment-friendly disposal behaviour implies waste separation in the household (paper, glass, tin and chemical waste), re-use of products for other purposes and the trading in of products.[28]

From the environmental point of view, disposal decisions and the reasons why consumers keep or discard products are of great concern. In the case of a second-hand market, products may be traded in or sold.[29] If products are discarded, this may be accomplished either in an environment-friendly way or not. The determinants of disposal behaviour

Table 22.6 *External and internal motivational factors in disposal behaviour*

External motivations	Internal motivations
Taxes, charges	Environmental knowledge
Environmental actions	Environmental concern
Nearness of containers for recyclable goods	Time preference
Rubbish collection frequency	Social influence

fall into two categories (see table 22.6). External motivational factors usually determine the opportunities to accomplish the desired behaviour. Internal motivational factors refer to the ability and motivation of consumers.[30]

Some of these factors are facilitating, such as containers in the vicinity and a high garbage collection frequency. They enable or facilitate the performance of environmental behaviour. External motivational factors include deposit money, financial incentives, charges, taxes and environmental actions. These factors are mostly helpful in the short run to start off an environmental programme. In contrast, these factors can inhibit environmental behaviour. If the containers are too far away or if rubbish is collected infrequently, the desired behaviour is made impossible, despite the consumers' good intentions.[31]

External motivational factors mainly are economic—money, for instance deposits given back when glass and tins are returned. Also environmental actions, such as competitions involving prizes, may be used as rewards for recycling behaviour. In The Netherlands, several municipalities published kilograms of glass per capita put into containers for a year. This constituted a kind of competition between these municipalities. Charges and other sanctions are also external motivational factors. For example, graffiti 'artists' can be forced to clean up the walls.

Internal motivational factors are mainly psychological and they are effective in the long run. Care for others, for society and nature is at stake, rather than personal advantage. This implies environmental concern, knowledge of the environmental effects of consumption, involvement with the environment and time preference. These factors are important to sustain environment-friendly behaviour. Absence of these factors causes inhibition and the desired behaviour is not established. Knowledge about the environmental effects of consumption can be improved and reinforced by providing general information about the condition of the environment, the consequences of consumption to the environment and specific information about behavioural alternatives available.

Pressure from the social environment is an important factor in stimulating environment-friendly disposal behaviour. Neighbours, friends and relatives influence consumers' behaviours and opinions. Programmes in neighbourhoods, residential areas and clubs have a greater probability of success than programmes aimed at individuals because of the identification with a common goal. Observation and stimulation of each other's behaviour is a necessary condition in these programmes.[32]

22.6 Conclusions

The environment is an important issue of concern to consumers. By refraining from buying products harmful to the environment and by paying attention to environmental aspects consumers can contribute considerably to a clean environment. From the point of view of the environment, the consumption cycle as a whole is important, i.e., environment-friendly purchases, use and disposal behaviours.

In general, environmental concern and the internalization of environmental values is important. However, even more important is the 'translation' of environmental concern into concrete environment-friendly behaviour. Frequently, consumers do not have the necessary information at hand to select behavioural alternatives that avoid or reduce environmental pollution. Consumer advice may help in turning environmental intentions into concrete behaviour.

Environment-friendly behaviour can be stimulated in different ways. One way uses knowledge and attitudes resulting in the desired behaviour. This is feasible in the case of high involvement. In the case of low involvement, behaviour may be influenced directly, for example by means of a self-perception process. In the latter case, attribution and dissonance reduction result in agreement of knowledge and attitudes with behaviour.

In consumer behaviour, opposite objectives exist for the individual and for society. This becomes evident from the costs and benefits of environmental behaviour and from short-term and long-term consequences of behaviour. Environment-friendly behaviour frequently is associated with short-term costs and investment for consumers, whereas the benefits are collective and become visible only in the long run. This hampers the introduction of environment-friendly consumption alternatives.

Notes

1. IOCU (1993) *Beyond the Year 2000. The Transition to Sustainable Consumption* (London: IOCU).
2. Consumption of chlorofluorocarbons (CFC) is largely held responsible for the depletion of the ozone layer, causing skin cancer. It is used in cleaning solvents and in air conditioning and refrigeration. The EU's environmental policy is partially aimed at reducing CFC consumption.
3. European Union (1993) *Fifth Environmental Action Programme*. European Union (1996) *Progress Report on Implementation of the Fifth Action Programme*.
4. See also chapter 4.

5. See section 11.4.
6. Data from the International Social Survey Program, 1993. Western Europe includes Germany, UK, Ireland, Italy, Norway, The Netherlands and Spain; Eastern Europe includes Hungary, Czech Republic, Slovenia, Poland, Bulgaria and Russia; North America includes the USA and Canada. Data were averaged unweighted across the samples.
7. See section 11.6.
8. See section 5.5.
9. See table 8.3.
10. Ottum, B. D., Scammon, D. L. and van Dam, Y. K. (1994) 'The effect of eco-labels on brand choice' in: Ringold, D. J. (Ed.) *Marketing and Public Policy Conference Proceedings* Vol. 4, 109–111.
11. Verplanken, B. and Weenig, M. W. H. (1993) 'Graphical energy labels and consumers' decisions about home appliances: a process tracing approach' *Journal of Economic Psychology* 14, 739–752.
12. Van Dam, Y. and Reuvekamp, M. (1995) 'Consumer knowledge and understanding of environmental seals in the Netherlands' *European Advances in Consumer Research* 2, 217–223.
13. Van Houwelingen, J. H. and Van Raaij, W. F. (1989) 'The effect of goal-setting and daily electronic feedback on in-home energy use' *Journal of Consumer Research* 16, 98–105.
14. See chapter 14.
15. Commission of the European Communities *Europeans and the Environment in 1992; Europeans and the Environment in 1986; Europeans and the Environment in 1995* (Brussels). ICPSR (1988) 'Eurobarometer 25: Holiday, travel and environmental problems' (April 1986). ICPSR (1990) Eurobarometer 29: Environmental problems and cancer' (March–April 1988). ZA (1995) Eurobarometer 37: Awareness and importance of Maastricht and the future of the European Community' (March–April 1992).
    Weighted average across countries.
16. The data from Eastern Europe concerning human progress harming the environment and using animals for medical testing seem to contradict those in table 22.1. We have no explanation for this result.
17. Data from the *International Social Survey Program*, 1993. Western Europe includes Germany, UK, Ireland, Italy, Norway, The Netherlands and Spain; Eastern Europe includes Hungary, Czech Republic, Slovenia, Poland, Bulgaria and Russia; North America includes the USA and Canada. Data were averaged unweighted across the samples.
18. Commission of the European Communities *Europeans and the Environment in 1992; Europeans and the Environment in 1986; Europeans and the Environment in 1995* (Brussels). ICPSR (1988). ICPSR (1990). ZA (1995).
    Weighted average across countries.
19. For example, holidays in one's own country.
20. Data from the *International Social Survey Programme* (1993). See note 17.
21. Self-perception is a kind of attribution. See sections 8.8 and 21.3.
22. This process is similar to the endowment effect, discussed in section 12.5.
23. Scott, C. A. (1977) 'Modifying socially-conscious behavior: The foot-in-the-door technique' *Journal of Consumer Research* 4, 156–164.

24. Self-perception is only one explanation of this phenomenon, based on self-attribution. Another explanation is the reduction of cognitive dissonance, i.e., by changing one's opinions to be consistent with one's behaviour.
25. See section 10.4.
26. Thøgersen, J. (1994) 'A model of recycling behaviour, with evidence from Danish source separation programmes' *International Journal of Research in Marketing* 11, 145–163.
27. Hornik, J., Madansky, M., Cherian, J. and Narayana, C. (1992) *Consumers' Recycling Behavior: a Meta-analysis* (Chicago: University of Chicago).
28. See also section 4.5.
29. Stroeker, N. E. (1995) 'Second-hand markets for consumer durables' (Unpublished doctoral dissertation, Erasmus University, Rotterdam).
30. This refers to the MAO-model including motivation, ability and opportunity. See section 9.6.
31. See section 21.3 for a discussion of facilitation and inhibition.
32. This constitutes a reference group effect. See chapter 14.

23 WELFARE AND OWNERSHIP

23.1 Introduction

'Money doesn't buy happiness.' Yet, many economists assume that goods, services and leisure make people happy, since the economic utility function is usually defined over goods and services, and in some theories also over leisure time. Obviously, the more money is available, the more goods and services can be purchased. So can money buy happiness? Section 23.2 deals with this question regarding welfare and well-being. In a sense, this chapter is a continuation of chapter 4.

Do all goods contribute equally to one's happiness or do some products contribute more than others? Some goods are necessary and can be found in any household, such as the refrigerator, washing machine, furniture and telephone. Other products have a low penetration level, i.e., these goods are owned by relatively few households. Is there a certain order of acquisition of durable goods and if so, what does it look like? These questions are considered in section 23.3.

Does the economic assumption of rationality apply to everyone? Do people always act rationally in their strivings for ever more durables? In other words: is materialism a universal human characteristic? Section 23.4 goes into more detail regarding the concept of materialism and its dimensions. There is also a 'dark side' to consumer behaviour. Section 23.5 deals with compulsive buying behaviour and addiction. Several conclusions are drawn in section 23.6.

The aim of this chapter is to offer some insight into the relationships between welfare, well-being and consumption. How do people cope with their living situation? What positive and negative consequences does consumers' welfare have on their behaviour and well-being?

23.2 Welfare and well-being

Happiness can be considered in different ways. Considering material issues only, such as income, wealth and goods, we speak of *material welfare* or *standard of living*. However, a consumer's needs can be greater than those that can be attained by the available means. *Welfare* implies a certain relation between means and needs.[1] If the means are sufficient to satisfy one's needs, welfare can be said to be high. If the means are insufficient, welfare is low. Finally, *well-being* concerns satisfaction and happiness in a wider sense, including happiness with society as a whole, the environment, health, housing, leisure, friends, marriage and family life. See figure 23.1 for an illustration of how these three concepts fit together. It has been found that social factors are more important determinants of well-being than economic factors regarding income and job.[2]

Welfare

Insight into the welfare of the population is important in the evaluation of income distribution and the assessment of welfare increase by governments. A measurement device has been constructed that can be used in large-scale surveys to assess the individual welfare of households. This is illustrated by the following survey question:[3]

> "Taking into account my own situation with respect to family and job I would call a net household income (including fringe benefits and after subtraction of social security premiums):
>
> —very bad   if it were about £....................
> —bad   if it were about £....................
> —insufficient if it were about £....................
> —sufficient   if it were about £....................
> —good   if it were about £....................
> —very good   if it were about £....................
> per week/four weeks/month/year (please encircle the period you have in mind)."

Figure 23.1 *Standard of living, welfare and well-being*

> **Definition**
>
> The Income Evaluation Question measures people's evaluation of their net-income, taking into account their own living circumstances (i.e., family and job).

This income evaluation question directly refers to the relation between means (income) and needs (bad, sufficient, good). From the answers to this question, the income that is generally perceived to be sufficient can be derived. The answers differ across households. Households with more people generally need larger amounts than those with fewer people, as the income has to be shared with more people. Understanding what constitutes a sufficient income provides information about the desired level of child allowance and the optimal income distribution.[4] It has been found that a relatively high income is needed if the household already has a high income. For example, at a net income of £2,000 per month one may evaluate an income of £1,800 as sufficient, whereas at a net income of £1,500 an income of £1,200 may be evaluated as sufficient. This implies that the welfare associated with a certain income may vary according to the level of the household income. If the household in the above example experiences an income increase from £2,000 to £3,000, the income of £1,800 will soon no longer be viewed as sufficient. This phenomenon is called *preference drift*. Before it happens, the income increase will be valued highly, but afterwards the consumer will become used to it and his or her evaluation of the increased income will become lower because of preference drift.

Finally, consumers look at the incomes of other people. If the incomes in the social reference group[5] are higher than their own incomes, they will be relatively dissatisfied. If a consumer's income becomes higher than the average income in his or her reference group, for example after a promotion, welfare will increase not only to the *absolute* income rise but also due to the *relative* income rise. A change in one's reference group may have similar effects. For example, a secretary changing her job at the sanitation department to one at an accountant's office may evaluate her income as less favourable than before. This phenomenon is called *reference drift*. Reference drift emerges in the process of social comparison. People like to compare with those who are a little higher on the social ladder. For this reason, they remain slightly dissatisfied regarding their own position.[6]

The income evaluation question above deals with the net income, which equals gross income minus income tax and social premiums. The distribution of gross income from salaries, profits, dividends, interest, lease and rent is called the primary income distribution. The distribution of gross

Table 23.1 *Types of income*[7]

Distribution	Elements	
Primary =	Salary + profits + dividends + interest + rent	= Gross income
Secondary =	Gross income + pension + social benefits − direct taxes − social premiums paid	= Net income
Tertiary =	Net income + value of public services + tax advantages − indirect taxes	= Available income

income plus pension and social benefits, minus taxes and premiums, is called the secondary income distribution. The tertiary income distribution equals the secondary income distribution plus the monetary value of public services and tax advantages minus indirect taxes. Public services, mentioned here, are either free or available at a price less than their costs. Households benefit from government services such as education, health care and social work. This constitutes income in kind, see table 23.1.

The above-mentioned ideas pertain to income evaluation. However, they can also be applied to consumption. For example, if (real) prices of goods and services increase, the result will be similar to an income decrease. Welfare will decline but less than expected. Price changes may affect different households in different ways. For example, large families will suffer more from price increases of food and clothes than small families. Price changes of 'public goods' such as audio and video equipment and kitchen appliances will affect large and small families more evenly.[8] In a society with decreasing household size,[9] people will benefit more from cheaper appliances than cheaper food, generally. Stated differently, both consumption and income distribution influence consumer welfare. Declining income may be compensated for by economizing on expenditure.

Economizing

In the case of declining income, (real) price increases or a recession, consumers may be forced to cut back on expenses. The need for economizing may also arise from declining consumer confidence.[10] It may be assumed that economizing is more easily accomplished for discretionary than for non-discretionary spending. A Dutch sample of 500 households has been asked whether it had economized on expenses in the past and, if so, on what type of expenses.[11] The results are shown in table 23.2. In fact, most savings were made on goods and services which were at least partly discretionary.

Table 23.2 *Percentage of households that economized on expenses*[12]

Types of expenses	Percentage of economizers	Discretionary
Clothing	54	Mostly
Energy	53	More or less
Media	41	Mostly
Private transportation	40	More or less
Going out	35	Mostly
Food	35	More or less
Hobbies	33	Mostly
Telephone	25	More or less
Durable goods	25	More or less
Insurance	14	No
Public transport	14	No
Clubs	13	No
Housing	7	No
Education	4	No
Courses	3	No

Table 23.3 *Economizing tactics*

General tactic	Example actions
Price	Visiting cheaper store, discount store Buying cheaper brands Using sales and bargains
Quantity	Buying less Postponement and delay
Quality	Buying higher quality and durability Buying lower quality (lower price)
Lifestyle	Do-it-yourself products Sharing and borrowing Terminating and refraining from consumption

Economizing on expenses can be accomplished in different ways.[13] Table 23.3 shows the possibilities. One may economize on price by buying from cheaper shops, such as discounters, or buy cheaper brands, such as own-labels. One may also engage in bargain hunting and buy items that are on sale. This is the most obvious economizing tactic. A more fundamental tactic is to diminish the volume of consumption, by buying fewer products or smaller quantities, for example 500g of cheese instead of a kilogram, or by postponing purchases, for example by wearing cloths longer and trading-in the car later.

Consumers may also try to improve the relationship between quality and price, for example by purchasing products with a higher quality or a longer expected lifetime. However, this often requires a higher 'up-front' investment than when buying cheaper, lower quality goods. Sometimes a price advantage can be obtained by buying a larger quantity; this also requires an up-front investment. In the long term, costs will decrease but in the short term, costs will increase, thus rendering these economizing tactics unlikely in practice.

The most drastic way of economizing concerns a change in lifestyle. Consumers may produce products or services within the household instead of buying them on the market, for example cutting the children's hair (substitution). Consumers can also choose to hire or lease various products, for example, television or video equipment, or share them with others, for example tools or newspapers. Finally, consumers can terminate the use or the ownership of a product, for example by selling the family car.

Economizing tactics, applied to a number of goods and services, have been scaled in two-dimensional space and shown in figure 23.2.[14] The

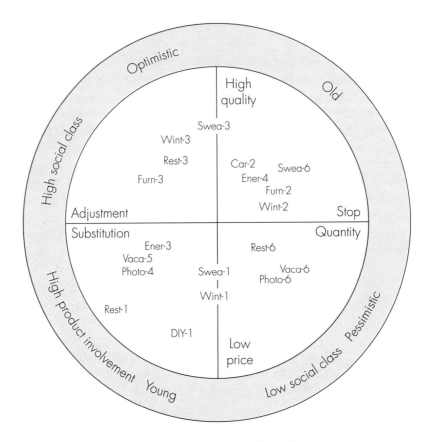

Figure 23.2 *Economizing tactics in a two-dimensional space. 1. Price; 2. Quantity; 3. Higher quality; 4. lower quality; 5. Life-style; 6. Shop; Car = car; Ener = energy; Furn = furniture; Rest = restaurant; Vaca = holiday trip; Photo = photography; DIY = do-it-yourself; Swea = sweater; Wint = winter coat*

horizontal axis of the plane reflects the dimension stopping/buying less *versus* lifestyle adaptation/substitution. The vertical axis reflects the dimension quality/durability *versus* low price/low quality. Furthermore, age, social class, product involvement and consumer confidence were included in the analysis. It appeared that older consumers tend to buy less quantity or stop consumption, and choose higher quality instead of a low price (first quadrant of figure 23.2). Young consumers tend to buy substitutes, change their lifestyles and buy at low prices relatively often (third quadrant of figure 23.2). Young consumers frequently have higher aspirations than the elderly and they want to meet their aspirations by cutting their expenses. Also, young people can more easily change their lifestyle than the elderly, since the latter are more committed to their habits.

With respect to social class, it appeared that the lower social classes tend to stop/buy less and buy at lower prices, possibly due to lower incomes (second quadrant). Consumers from higher social classes tend to choose the approaches of substitution, lifestyle changes and buying higher quality (fourth quadrant). The latter may also be able to perceive more economizing opportunities because of their higher level of education. This indicates that consumers with high incomes invest in high quality goods, whereas consumers with low incomes are forced to buy at lower prices and lower quality. Thus the rich become richer and the poor become poorer.[15]

Product involvement appeared to be associated with the first dimension. For example, consumers with a considerable interest in photography will economize by substitution and lifestyle adaptation, whereas consumers with less interest are more likely to decrease or stop taking pictures. Product involvement determines the choice between terminating and substitution. This implies that a core of interested consumers will remain loyal to the product, although they will adapt their consumption behaviour.

Confident consumers tend to economize by purchasing higher quality, whereas pessimistic consumers more frequently choose to reduce quantity or terminate consumption. Apparently, optimistic consumers are willing to invest in higher quality products, whereas pessimistic consumers lack the courage. Alternatively, optimistic consumers in general have a relatively high time preference, which allows them to spend more on consumption. Pessimistic consumers in general have a low time preference and tend to buy cheaper, thus saving money for future consumption.[16]

Poverty

Economizing may eventually lead to a situation of poverty. Poverty can be defined as a situation in which the available means are insufficient to meet one's needs.[17] Poverty is a situation of low welfare, for example when a household's income falls below the amount associated with the 'sufficient'

Table 23.4 *Poverty ratios for two different poverty lines in the EU[21]*

	Percentage of households falling below the poverty line	
	Expenditure (40% cut-off)	Utility (40% cut-off)
Portugal	15.7	_a
Greece	13.0	_a
Italy	11.2	9.5
Spain	8.6	_a
Ireland	8.4	26.1
France	6.5	27.1
UK	5.8	13.9
Germany	4.7	3.1
Luxembourg	3.5	_a
Belgium	1.9	12.3
Denmark	1.3	23.1
Netherlands	1.1	5.9

aFigure not available or country not included in EU at time of survey

answers to the income evaluation question considered before.[18] As different households answer this question differently, it is evident that poverty is subjective. For one household, a social benefit income suffices, whereas for another it does not. Also across countries, poverty lines may concern different income levels.[19] Poverty is frequently associated with debts.[20] Table 23.4 shows the percentages of households below two different poverty lines. The first poverty line equals 40% of the average expenditure per equivalent adult in a country. The second poverty line is subjective and equals the income level associated with 0.4 on the [0,1] utility scale of the income evaluation question (almost equal to 'insufficient income').

Definition

A poverty line defines the fraction of a population that is considered poor by some definition of poverty.

Looking at the 'objective' poverty ratios in table 23.4, a rough distinction between North and South can be made. In southern Europe, relatively many people are classified as poor, in northern Europe, relatively few people are considered poor. Although the figures in table 23.4 stem from different years, the differences between 'objective' and subjective poverty ratios are mainly due to the definition of the poverty lines. It appears that the 'objective' poverty ratio in Denmark is relatively low, whereas subjective poverty is relatively high. The reverse seems to be true in Italy.

Table 23.5 *OECD list of social indicators*[22]

Social concern	Indicator
Health	
Length of life	Life expectancy
	Perinatal mortality rate
Healthfulness of life	Short-term disability
	Long-term disability
Education and Learning	
Use of educational facilities	Regular education experience
	Adult education
	Literacy rate
Employment and quality of working life	
Availability of employment	Unemployment rate
	Involuntary part-tme work
	Discouraged workers
Quality of working life	Average working hours
	Travel time to work
	Paid annual leave
	Atypical work schedule
	Distribution of earnings
	Fatal occupational injuries
	Work environment nuisances
Time and leisure	
Use of time	Free time
	Free time activities
Command over goods and services	
Income	Distribution of income
	Low income
	Material deprivation
	Distribution of wealth
Physical environment	
Housing conditions	Indoor dwelling space
	Access to outdoor space
	Basic amenities
Accesibility to services	Proximity of selected services
Environmental nuisances	Exposure to air pollutants
	Exposure to noise
Social environment	
Social attachment	Suicide rate
Personal safety	
Exposure to risk	Fatal injuries
	Serious injuries

Well-being

Well-being refers to a general type of happiness, including welfare. A summary of well-being aspects has been listed by the OECD; see table 23.5. Some of the indicators are documented in international statistics. Many of the indicators are associated with consumption, for example income, ownership of goods and housing. In this case, consumption influences welfare, which in turn influences well-being. However, negative external effects of consumption may harm the environment and this may negatively affect well-being. Several types of consumption may increase well-being, for example environment-friendly products, medical consumption, housing and education. Recreational consumption may increase well-being, although leisure time alone is insufficient to attain a high level of well-being; otherwise the unemployed would have the highest levels of well-being.

By means of the OECD indicators, the average level of well-being can be assessed across countries and over time. For example, life expectancy has increased over time but varies considerably across countries. This indicates problems in specific areas in response to which political measures can be taken. This has already occurred in response to the poverty statistics shown in table 23.4. The EU provides subsidies for poor regions in the countries concerned.

The OECD list includes objective indicators of well-being. However, well-being is essentially subjective and can only be partly explained by objective factors.[23] Subjective well-being can be assessed in many different ways. A popular survey question is: 'In general, are you very satisfied, rather satisfied, not very satisfied or dissatisfied with the life you live?' Inhabitants of rich countries in general report higher levels of satisfaction than those living in poor countries.[24] Considering the answers for the same country over several years, it appears that the distribution of the answers is nearly equal. Despite the improvement of economic conditions, well-being has apparently not improved. This is possibly due to the human capacity of adapting to new circumstances. Every time circumstances improve, new desires and needs appear, thus preventing the attainment of the highest level of well-being.[25] This is consistent with the phenomenon of preference drift.[26] Table 23.6 shows subjective well-being measures from the EU, using the question listed above. The well-being levels were assigned numbers 1–4 and averaged per country.

It appears that the northern countries score above 3 while the southern countries score below 3 on the four-point scale. The largest improvement occurred in Italy and the largest decline occurred in Greece.

23.3 Consumption ladder

Welfare concerns the relationship between needs and the means to satisfy them. Since durable goods are important means of satisfying needs, the

Table 23.6 *Subjective well-being in the European Union*[27]

	1983	1993	Index (1983 = 100)
Denmark	3.50	3.60	102.9
Netherlands	3.27	3.39	103.7
Luxembourg	3.29	3.30	100.3
Ireland	3.06	3.14	102.6
UK	3.11	3.12	100.3
Belgium	2.99	3.10	103.7
Germany	2.95	3.02	102.4
Italy	2.66	2.87	108.9
Spain	2.87[a]	2.83	98.6
France	2.82	2.75	97.5
Portugal	2.44[a]	2.64	108.2
Greece	2.66	2.44	91.7

[a]1985
Averaged scores on a scale of 1–4; where high numbers indicate high subjective well-being

question of ownership of these goods and the constitution of the stock of durable goods in households is important. Similar to a hierarchy of needs,[28] a hierarchy of means can be assumed. This captures the idea that greatly needed (i.e., necessary) goods are acquired earlier than less needed (i.e. luxury) goods.

Ownership of goods

Several statistical offices in EU countries document the ownership of durable goods. Tables 23.7 and 23.8 show percentages of households owning particular goods. The percentages show the levels of ownership or penetration levels of the goods. TVs, radios, telephones, vacuum cleaners and washing machines all show very high levels of ownership. Apparently these goods are considered necessary. Lack of these goods indicates low welfare. Goods with a low penetration level in general are luxury goods. Lack of these goods does not necessarily imply low welfare. Differences in taste may also cause the lack of these goods. Not everyone wants or needs a personal computer, tumble dryer or video camera.

Unfortunately, tables 23.7 and 23.8 do not show the development of ownership over time, which would indicate the product life-cycle.[29] From national data, we know that the levels of ownership of TV sets, radios, telephones, vacuum cleaners and washing machines do not increase any more. These goods have reached the top of the product life-cycle. The ownership of tumble dryers, micro-wave ovens, video recorders, CD players and PCs has increased. These goods are in the middle stages of the product life-cycle. The ownership of video cameras is increasing but is still at a very low level. This product is in the first stage of the product life-cycle. Not every

Table 23.7 *Ownership of consumer electronics in Europe (1990/1991)*[31]

| | TV | Radio | Telephone | Percentage of households owning items | | | | | | |
				Cassette recorder	Record player	Personal stereo	VCR	CD player	PC	Video camera
Austria	96	95	85	82	27	30	37	24	11	–
Belgium	97	90	79	75	30	25	42	26	15	6
Denmark	98	98	87	82	60	30	63	48	27	5
Finland	94	96	79	85	62	37	46	19	16	–
France	95	98	94	76	65	37	35	23	14	6
Germany	97	84	89	74	72	31	42	24	16	6
Greece	94	92	75	72	46	17	37	5	6	1
Ireland	98	–	53	73	61	34	38	14	12	2
Italy	98	92	89	64	60	22	25	9	12	4
Luxembourg	98	–	75	69	–	30	39	30	12	9
Netherlands	95	99	96	81	80	33	50	48	25	7
Norway	97	98	89	87	64	43	41	21	16	–
Portugal	92	60	52	36	40	13	22	9	7	4
Spain	98	95	66	67	49	21	40	11	8	4
Sweden	97	93	97	88	64	45	48	17	12	–
Switzerland	93	99	97	82	65	29	41	39	14	–
UK	98	90	88	82	29	37	69	20	19	4

Table 23.8 *Ownership percentages of large electrical appliances in Europe (1990/1991)*

	Vacuum cleaner	Washing machine	Separate fridge	Fridge-freezer	Deep freezer	Dish-washer	Micro-wave oven	Tumble dryer	Spin dryer
Austria	92	86	62	42	61	35	31	6	13
Belgium	92	88	54	53	86	26	21	39	28
Denmark	96	74	52	56	92	36	31	30	5
Finland	93	76	52	49	52	31	53	3	6
France	89	88	98	41	43	32	19	12	66
Germany	96	88	66	43	73	34	36	17	16
Greece	52	74	70	24	27	11	2	–	–
Ireland	87	81	54	43	58	15	20	19	8
Italy	56	96	21	83	89	18	6	10	12
Luxembourg	88	93	55	54	91	50	16	35	13
Netherlands	98	89	98	60	54	11	22	27	30
Norway	90	87	72	34	80	37	34	29	23
Portugal	62	66	27	87	91	14	4	2	7
Spain	29	87	43	51	55	11	9	5	10
Sweden	97	72	57	50	70	31	37	18	6
Switzerland	93	78	11	86	68	32	15	27	12
UK	98	88	99	53	84	11	48	32	7

product reaches a penetration level of 100%. For example, the ownership of dishwashers increased over time but it has stabilized at the current level in most countries.[30] Several goods are in the final stage of the product life-cycle, implying a decreasing level of ownership. For example, separate cassette recorders, record players and spin dryers are being replaced by, respectively, personal stereo equipment, CD players and tumble dryers. In many countries, records can only be purchased at second-hand shops and flea markets.

Order of acquisition

When people first set up a household, they begin to develop a stock of durable goods. On the basis of general need patterns, as based on levels of ownership, it can be expected that necessary goods will be purchased first, following by less necessary (luxury) goods. Furthermore, households owning luxury goods are assumed to own necessary goods also. We expect a structure as shown for five households in table 23.9. A zero indicates absence and a one indicates the presence of the good. Counting the durables in a household gives a score on the ownership scale.[32]

The pattern in table 23.9 has the form of an ownership ladder on which one advances one rung with each acquisition. The example in table 23.9 shows a perfect ladder with the following rank order: vacuum cleaner, washing machine, fridge, and TV set. In practice deviations from the 'ideal' pattern occur, for example a household may own a TV but not a washing machine. Such deviations can be tolerated to some extent without invalidating the idea of an ownership ladder.

Criteria for the existence of an ownership latter have been suggested.[33] On the basis of empirical data regarding the ownership of durable goods in households, the rank order of ownership has been assessed. However, the results of different studies are different and strongly depend on the scaling criteria and the set of goods involved in the study. Usually, second-hand goods are omitted. However, it is plausible to buy a second-hand washing machine first, a new vacuum cleaner next, and finally a new washing machine. Not accounting for second-hand purchases results in problems in the estimation of the rank order of ownership. Table 23.10 shows an

Table 23.9 *Model of acquisition pattern of four durable goods*

Household	Vacuum cleaner	Washing machine	Fridge	TV	Score
1	0	0	0	0	0
2	1	0	0	0	1
3	1	1	0	0	2
4	1	1	1	0	3
5	1	1	1	1	4

Table 23.10 *Acquisition pattern including second-hand goods*

Rung on ownership ladder	Durable good purchased
1	Second-hand vacuum cleaner
2	Second-hand refrigerator
3	Second-hand black-and-white TV set
4	New vacuum cleaner
5	New black-and-white or second-hand colour TV set
6	Second-hand washing machine
7	New washing machine
8	New refrigerator
9	New colour TV set
10	Second-hand deep freezer
11	New deep freezer

ownership ladder, based on Dutch ownership data regarding a limited set of durables, including second-hand goods.[34] First, three second-hand goods appear on the ladder. 'Climbing up' the ownership ladder, results in more new goods appearing.

The ladder of table 23.10 is imperfect, because, in practice, deviating patterns of acquisition occur in some households. However, in general a ladder can be used to predict demand for goods in households which do not yet own a certain item but which own a product one rung lower on the ladder. The rung reached on the ladder indicates the level of welfare and the standard of living of the household.

23.4 Materialism

The symbolic value of consumption was considered in chapter 4. Except for functional characteristics, goods appear to have different characteristics that are important to the consumer's personal identity. High material wealth is frequently associated with positive human attributes, whereas poverty is associated with negative attributes.[35] Wealthy persons are often considered intelligent, responsible, hard working, successful, clever, handsome and creative. In contrast, poor people are often considered lazy, unmotivated, less skilful, less clever, irresponsible, unattractive, and less able to deal with money. These qualifications indicate certain attributions regarding human characteristics. Probably also the 'halo effect' plays a part.[36] By the halo effect, all kinds of characteristics are attributed to a person on the basis of a single perceived characteristic such as wealth or poverty.

Materialism plays a part in the judgement of others, as indicated above. It even plays a part in one's self-judgement. Success and prestige may be derived from the house one occupies and the car one drives. Bandwagon,

Figure 23.3 *Home sweet home*

Veblen and snob effects have already been considered as social effects of consumption.[37]

Although associations with wealth often are based on psychological mechanisms, many people strive for wealth and material property. Now, the question is whether the striving for property (materialism) is a separate human characteristic or that materialism serves higher, abstract goals. The term symbolism has been used to indicate the level of psychic energy associated with the ownership of goods.[38] Symbolism may be associated with higher or abstract goals, as opposed to the functionality of products. So, individual differences in symbolic values may influence consumption. On the one hand, products contribute to one's identity and express one's personality; on the other hand products are instrumental in attaining certain goals, for example time saving or avoiding physical effort. The increased tendency to derive personal identity from consumption means that people have drifted away from one another.[39] Materialism could serve as compensation for a lost sense of community.

Definition

Materialism is the striving for property, characterized by possessiveness, nongenerosity, envy and preservation.

Figure 23.4 *The right car in front of the right house*

Several dimensions of materialism have been distinguished: possessiveness, nongenerosity, envy, and preservation.[40] Furthermore, materialism has been associated with happiness, and with the judgement of individuals on the basis of their possessions.[41]

Possessiveness

Possessiveness is closely related to materialism and concerns the striving for possession and control of property. This is evidenced by concern over the loss of property, preference for ownership over borrowing, hiring and leasing, and a disposition to collect and keep property.

Nongenerosity

Materialism would be associated with less willingness to share or give away goods. This would be evidenced by a less positive attitude toward charity, giving lifts to hitchhikers, lending goods, and the presence of other people in one's house (whether or not in the presence of the inhabitant). This attitude is similar to reverse altruism. In fact, more is known about altruism than about nongeneous materialism.[42]

Envy

Materialism is associated with envy if others possess goods different from one's own. One longs for other's possessions. Jealousy is felt over goods or persons one considers as one's own property. A person may be jealous of his or her partner's friendship with another person, even while not wanting a different partner. Applied to goods, this implies that jealousy regarding one's own goods coincides with the above-mentioned envy and concern about losing one's property.

Preservation

Preservation concerns the conservation of events, experiences, and memories in material form, for example, souvenirs, and collectibles. This aspect of materialism may also lead to the better maintenance of goods, thus extending their lifetimes. Collecting and cherishing antiques, coins and stamps also has a historic function.

Happiness

The human striving for property is frequently considered as insatiable. Recall the preference drift. After obtaining a desired good, the early satisfaction often fades quickly and new desires emerge. This tends to induce a general feeling of dissatisfaction. In fact, different studies have found negative or zero correlations between materialism and happiness.[43]

Materialism has both positive and negative effects. Materialism is said to have positive effects on economies. It causes workers to work harder, and encourages consumers to invest in durable goods, which in turn leads to greater productivity, technological breakthroughs and higher living standards.[44] Negative effects of materialism include spiritual hazards, harm to interpersonal relationships and a negative impact on natural resources.

Characteristics of materialism

Although no unequivocal classification of materialism exists, the individual extent of materialism can be assessed by psychological measurement. Differences in materialism across countries and sociodemographic groups, and the effects of materialism on consumption can also be measured and assessed.[45]

Important differences in materialism between age groups have been found. The young prefer goods that enable them to accomplish something and to be independent, such as cars, motorbikes or audio equipment. These products are strongly associated with their activities, frequently expressing enhanced experience and control of the environment. In the final stage of their education, the yearning for independence emerges, along with a desire for status.

The middle-aged prefer the kinds of products that remind them of their achievements and experiences. Frequently, these are products expressing status and power, such as houses, cars and clothing.[46]

The elderly prefer goods reminding them of the past, such as photographs, films, souvenirs and books. The possession of other goods is of less importance. Frequently, the elderly find the success of their children more important than their own success. Sometimes it seems as if they identify with the lives of their children and grandchildren.[47] As age increases, people give less attention to the future and are more busy with the past. This tends to result in decreased possessiveness as people get older.

Differences in life-style exist between materialists and less materialistic people. A number of differences are shown in table 23.11. Young people in general have less materialistic values than older people; self-realization, environmental concern and social values dominate materialistic values.

Materialism across countries

A cross-cultural study with MBA students revealed significant differences across countries. Table 23.12 shows the summary measures of materialism of a number of different countries. Both affluent and non-affluent, and Western and non-Western countries appear as materialistic and non-

Table 23.11 *Evaluation of several activities and materialism*

Activities/circumstances	More materialistic point of view	Less materialistic point of view
Eating in a restaurant	Special service and expensive menu are central	Pleasure is central
Someone buying an expensive car	Is happy, appreciates a good life	Is rich, in search of status, and foolish
Home with a garden	Good, desirable, top of the world	Requires gardening
Supplementary pension	Thinking ahead	Prudent
Attached to things	Keeping	Disposal
Christmas	Shopping	Relationships, gifts
Charity	Sometimes good, sometimes bad	Good, generous
Birth gift	Makes child happy, grateful	Should be something useful
Helping others	Is not appreciated	Gives a warm glow
A warm glow leads to:	Celebration, taking action	Being happy, singing, laughing
A gift results in:	Purchasing	Sharing with others
Conditions of happiness	Money, success	Good health, success for one's children

Table 23.12 *Materialism of different countries*[48] *(higher scores indicate greater materialism)*

Romania	63.1	Israel	58.9
USA	61.1	Thailand	58.3
New Zealand	60.5	India	57.7
Ukraine	59.9	UK	56.5
Germany	59.2	France	56.5
Turkey	59.1	Sweden	53.2

not allowed in public places. Several airline companies have adopted a non-smoking policy on their continental flights.

Alcohol addiction

Alcohol is a legal product, which is easily available in most countries. Annual average consumption of alcohol varies between 5 and 15 litres of pure alcohol per person in EU and EEA countries. In the Nordic countries the consumption levels are below 10 litres on average, whereas in France, Luxembourg and Portugal consumption is higher than 14 litres on average.[52] Average consumption slightly decreased in the past decade.

Alcohol addiction includes physical and psychological dependency and may result in health problems, (traffic) accidents, drunkenness and problems with one's partner and family. Societal costs include health care of alcohol users and their victims, material damage, police and judiciary. These costs are generally not compensated for by taxes levied on alcohol. However, moderate alcohol consumption is socially accepted. To prevent excessive consumption, several countries have advertising campaigns encouraging people to drink less alcohol.

Drug addiction

Drugs are usually illegal and not easily available. However, some drugs are extremely addictive, such as heroin and other opiates (hard drugs). Other drugs may be less addictive but may also cause health problems, such as barbiturates, LSD, ecstasy, marijuana and other stimulants (soft drugs). Drugs are relatively expensive and many addicts engage in criminal activities to acquire money for the next shot. Hard drugs are often taken by intravenous injections, so contagious diseases such as hepatitis and AIDS are transmitted relatively easily.

Addiction to behaviour

Gambling, card-playing, compulsive buying and even surfing on the Internet are examples of addictive or compulsive behaviour. Workaholics are addicted to their work. Others are regular prostitutes' clients. Kleptomania, an uncontrolled need for theft, can be an addiction. Compulsive behaviour is mainly psychological in origin and causes psychological or financial harm.

Prostitution constitutes a major 'service' activity. Erotic clubs can be found in almost every city, for example, the Rue Pigalle in Paris, Soho in London, and the 'red light district' in Amsterdam. Prostitution is a black market activity as usually neither income tax nor social security premiums are paid (except for 'professional' prostitutes who do pay taxes in some places). For this reason, it attracts women from low-income countries, such as South Asia, South America and Eastern Europe. Frequently, their status is illegal.

Addiction to gambling occurs in all social classes. It is a rather unnoticed and frequently underestimated kind of addiction. No physiological dependency develops and physical symptoms are absent. Addiction to gambling can be evidenced by visits to casinos, gambling at horse races, sports matches, fruit machines, and lotteries. Some of these occasions are organized by the state. Gambling addiction can be financially destructive and may result in debts, divorce, child neglect and diminished self-esteem. The addict may experience manic-depressive symptoms, from a manic 'high' during gambling to a depressive stage with feelings of guilt during abstinence.

Compulsive buying behaviour results from individuals using the satisfaction they gain from the purchase of goods to compensate for feelings of depression, stress, anxiety and boredom. Shopping and purchasing temporarily removes these negative feelings. It also gives the individual the opportunity to appear socially desirable.[53] In this respect, compulsive buying is related to postmodernist values of symbolic consumption. The compulsive buyer experiences satisfaction primarily from the buying behaviour, not so much from the possession of goods. They get attention and appreciation from salespeople. Compulsive buyers frequently buy goods they do not need and they are more often women than men. Compulsive buying is facilitated by the possession of credit cards. Compulsive buyers frequently have problematic debts because of their excessive buying behaviour.[54] Ironically, compulsive buyers long for the attention and affection of salespeople while losing the affection of their family and relatives because of their excessive debts.

In general, compulsive buyers have a great tendency to fantasize, and this often prevents them from considering the consequences of their purchases. Compulsive buying behaviour is associated with a low level of self-esteem, which may be either a determinant or a consequence of the behaviour. Also compulsive buyers score relatively high on materialism, especially on envy and nongenerosity.

They do not differ from normal consumers on scores of possessiveness. In fact, their objective is not to possess goods but rather to relieve emotional tension, and gain attention and appreciation from others. Table 23.13 shows the dimensions of materialism (possessiveness, nongenerosity and envy) supplemented with acquisition. To compulsive buyers and collectors but not to the other types of consumers it is the process of acquisition that is important.

Consumers buying stocks of goods in the face of imminent scarcity (hoarding) may also be considered compulsive buyers. Hoarding is driven by the expected scarcity of necessary goods, such as sugar, during a strike or threat of war. To hoarders, it is the security of the availability of food that is important rather than the act of buying. They score relatively high on possessiveness and nongenerosity but relatively low on envy.

Table 23.13 *Consumer typology based on materialism*

	Acquisition	Possessiveness	Nongenerosity	Envy
Materialist	–	High	High	High
Heavy user	–	High	–	–
Impulsive buyer	–	High	–	–
Compulsive buyer	Important	–	High	High
Addict	–	High	High	–
Hoarder	–	High	High	–
Collector	Important	High	High	–

Compulsive buying differs from impulsive buying.[55] Impulsive buying implies lack of cognitive control of one's behaviour, whereas compulsive buying implies high cognitive control but a strong reaction to one's emotional state. Regarding the impulsive buyer, the 'doer' does not control the 'planner'.[56] Without much thought one buys a soft drink because one is thirsty. The drink quenches one's thirst and the impulse is over. Typically this behaviour relates to small expenses. Impulsive buying is temporary and transitory, occurring, for example in the shop without any preceding buying intention.[57] Impulsive buying may become habitual and may result in compulsive buying. Compulsive buying is a long-term type of addiction and may involve significant expenditure.

The compulsive buyer can also be distinguished from the heavy user. The heavy user buys a large amount of a particular product because of the utility it provides. Heavy use need not be problematic, although it may cause personal problems, for example, excessive beer consumption may result in drunkenness and obesity.

23.6 Conclusions

This chapter has considered the important topics of welfare and well-being. When income increases, welfare and well-being tend to increase. However, this phenomenon is only temporary. People quickly adapt their preferences to the new situation and they tend to compare themselves with other people who have a higher position. Compared with their earlier state, they are better off, but with respect to the new target comparison group, they are still ambitious. New aspirations are bred to climb the societal ladder.

The adaptation of consumption in the case of an (expected) income decline results in economizing behaviour. Minor adaptations include paying attention to prices and buying less. It is possible to economize by buying higher quality goods that offer longer lifetimes. Major adaptations include the change of lifestyle and consumption level. Usually, minor adaptations precede major adaptations since the latter are considered more painful.

The acquisition of durable goods shows particular regularities. A general order of acquisition exists among households. This is called the ownership ladder. Given the existing stock of goods, it is possible to predict the demand for the next good on the ladder.

The concept of materialism, including its aspects of possessiveness, nongenerosity and envy has become popular in the recent consumer literature. Consumption is often associated with materialism. The 'dark' side of consumer behaviour, such as compulsive buying behaviour, can be described by means of aspects of materialism. Compulsive buyers have considerable difficulty in escaping the negative spiral of emotions, needs, need satisfaction and guilt.

Notes

1. Van Praag, B. M. S. (1968) *Individual Welfare Functions and Consumer Behavior* (Amsterdam: North-Holland).
2. Levy, S. and Guttman, L. (1975) 'On the multivariate structure of wellbeing' *Social Indicators Research* 2, 361–388.
3. Van Praag, B. M. S. and Kapteyn, A. (1973) 'Further evidence on the individual welfare function of income: an empirical investigation in the Netherlands' *European Economic Review* 4, 33–62. A survey is a large-scale inquiry that uses questionnaires. See chapter 25.
4. Kapteyn, A. and van Praag, B. M. S. (1976) 'A new approach to the construction of equivalence scales' *European Economic Review* 7, 313–335. Compare the equivalence factors in section 2.3.
5. See section 14.2.
6. Festinger, L. (1954) 'A theory of social comparison processes' *Human Relations* 7, 117–140. Rijsman, J. B. (1974) 'Factors in social comparison of performance influencing actual performance' *European Journal of Social Psychology* 4, 279–311.
7. Kooreman, P. and Wunderink, S. R. (1997) *The Economics of Household Behaviour* (London: Macmillan).
8. See section 13.2 regarding economies of scale.
9. See section 2.3.
10. See section 3.5.
11. Feenstra, M. H. (1990) *Less Money, Less Food?* (Leyden: SWOKA) (in Dutch).
12. Adapted from Feenstra (1990).
13. Van Raaij, W. F. and Eilander, G. (1983) 'Consumer economizing tactics for ten product categories' *Advances in Consumer Research* 10, 169–174.
14. Van Raaij, W. F. (1986) 'Difficultés économiques et comportement des consommateurs: L'exemple néerlandais' *Revue Française du Marketing* 110, 39–50.
15. Dillman, D. A., Rosa, E. A. and Dillman, J. J. (1983) 'Lifestyle and home energy conservation in the United States: The poor accept lifestyle cutbacks while the wealthy invest in conservation' *Journal of Economic Psychology* 3, 299–315.
16. Antonides, G. (1990) *The Lifetime of a Durable Good: An Economic Psychological Approach* (Dordrecht: Kluwer Academic Publishers).

17. Kooreman and Wunderink (1997).
18. For other definitions and operationalizations of poverty, see Hagenaars, A. J. M. (1986) *The Perception of Poverty* (Amsterdam: North-Holland).
19. The poverty line is the income level below which a household is considered poor in a country.
20. See section 19.5.
21. Poverty lines are based on expenditures in 1987–1989. Hagenaars, A. J. M., de Vos, K. and Zaidi, M. A. (1994) *Poverty Statistics in the Late 1980s: Research Based on Micro-data* (Luxembourg: Eurostat). Subjective poverty lines are based on a survey in eight countries of the EU, 1979: van Praag, B. M. S., Hagenaars, A. J. M. and van Weeren, H. (1982) 'Poverty in Europe' *The Review of Income and Wealth* 28, 345–359.
22. OECD (1982) *The OECD List of Social Indicators* (Paris: OECD).
23. Demographic factors together explain only 15 percent of the variance in subjective well-being. Andrews, F. M. and Withey, S. B. (1976) *Social Indicators of Well-being* (New York: Plenum).
24. Veenhoven, R. (1984) *Conditions of Happiness* (Rotterdam: Erasmus Universiteit, dissertation).
25. See section 23.4.
26. See section 23.2.
27. Eurobarometer (1996) *Trends 1974–1994* (Cologne: Central Archive).
28. Maslow, A. H. (1954) *Motivation and Personality* (New York: Harper & Row).
29. See section 4.2.
30. See chapter 16.
31. Euromonitor (1997) *European Marketing Data and Statistics 1997* (London: Euromonitor).
32. Pickering, J. F. (1981) 'A behavioral model of the demand for consumer durables' *Journal of Economic Psychology* 1, 59–77.
    Kasulis, J. J., Lusch, R. F. and Stafford Jr, E. F. (1979) 'Consumer acquisition patterns for durable goods' *Journal of Consumer Research* 6, 47–57.
33. Hebden, J. J. and Pickering, J. F. (1974) 'Patterns of acquisition of consumer durables' *Oxford Bulletin of Economics and Statistics* 36, 67–94.
    Guttman, L. (1944) 'A basis for scaling qualitative data' *American Sociological Review* 9, 139–150.
    Loevinger, J. (1948) 'The technique of homogeneous tests compared with some aspects of scale analysis and factor analysis' *Psychological Bulletin* 45, 507–529.
    Mokken, R. J. (1971) *A Theory and Procedure of Scale Analysis with Application in Political Research* (The Hague: Mouton).
34. Jansen van Rosendaal, E. (1992) 'The pattern of acquisition of durable goods' (Unpublished Master thesis, Rotterdam: Erasmus University).
35. Dittmar, H. (1992) *The Social Psychology of Material Possessions: To Have Is To Be* (Hemel Hempstead: Harvester Wheatsheaf).
36. The term 'halo' refers to a brightly lit nimbus and the halo effect describes the way that one aspect of a person's character may 'drown' out other aspects leading others to make false attributions.
37. See section 14.2.
38. See section 4.3.

39. Belk, R. W. (1985) 'Materialism: Trait aspects of living in the material world' *Journal of Consumer Research* 12, 265–280.

40. Belk (1985). Ger, G. and Belk, R. W. (1996) 'Cross-cultural differences in materialism' *Journal of Economic Psychology* 17, 55–77.

41. Richins, M. L. and Dawson, S. (1992) 'A consumer values orientation for materialism and its measurement: scale development and validation' *Journal of Consumer Research* 19, 303–316. Richins, M. L. and Rudmin, F. W. (1994) 'Materialism and economic psychology' *Journal of Economic Psychology* 15, 217–231.

42. See, for example, Latané, B. and Nida, S. (1981) 'Ten years of research on group size and helping' *Psychological Bulletin* 89, 308–324.
Antonides, G. (1996) *Psychology in Economics and Business* (Dordrecht: Kluwer Academic Publishers).
Lea, S. E. G., Tarpy, R. M. and Webley, P. (1987) *The Individual in the Economy* (Cambridge: Cambridge University Press).

43. See Richins and Rudmin (1994).

44. Richins and Rudmin (1994).

45. Belk (1985).

46. See section 4.4.

47. Compare the vicarious reinforcement in observational learning processes; section 10.5.

48. Ger and Belk (1996).

49. Eurostat (1995) *Statistical Yearbook 1995* (Luxembourg: Eurostat).

50. Eurostat (1991) *Social Portrait of Europe* (Luxembourg: Office for Official Publications of the European Communities).

51. Smokepeace Europe (1997) 'Fact and figures' http:\\www.smokepeace-europe.com.

52. Eurostat (1995).

53. Elliott, R. (1994) 'Addictive consumption: function and fragmentation in post-modernity' *Journal of Consumer Policy* 17, 159–179.

54. O'Guinn, T. C. and Faber, R. J. (1989) 'Compulsive buying: a phenomenological exploration' *Journal of Consumer Research* 16, 147–157.

55. Valence, G., d'Astous, A. and Fortier, L. (1988) 'Compulsive buying: concept and measurement' *Journal of Consumer Policy* 11, 419–433.

56. See also sections 19.9 and 19.5. For self-control, see Thaler, R. H. and Shefrin, H. M. (1981) 'An economic theory of self-control' *Journal of Political Economy* 89, 392–405.
Hoch, S. J. and Loewenstein, G. F. (1991) 'Time-inconsistent preferences and consumer self-control' *Journal of Consumer Research* 17, 492–507.

57. See also section 18.5

PART V

APPLICATIONS

MARKET SEGMENTATION AND PRODUCT DIFFERENTIATION

24

24.1 Introduction

Market segmentation and product differentiation are two sides of the same coin. On the demand side, heterogeneous markets can be divided into homogeneous submarkets. On the supply side, homogeneous products can be differentiated into products tuned to these homogeneous market segments.

This chapter looks at the demand side, at target groups and market segments. These are groups of consumers that have some common characteristics relating to their consumption behaviour. A focused marketing and marketing-communication policy can be aimed at these segments. The supply side is also taken into consideration, including product differentiation, positioning of products and brands, and brand extensions.

The concept of 'target group' is discussed in section 24.2. After that, the different levels of market segmentation are considered. Section 24.3 examines the general level characteristics which are more or less permanent over the different product domains. The domain-specific level is considered in section 24.4 which looks at characteristics that are of special importance for a particular behavioural domain. The brand-specific level (section 24.5) concerns characteristics which are especially important for brands in a specific product class or product group. On the basis of variables on these three levels, market segments can be formed which satisfy certain conditions as discussed in section 24.6. The three levels are related to the structure of meaning explained in section 7.3.

Sections 24.7 and 24.8 deal with the supply side, with positioning and brand extensions, respectively. In both approaches, meaning structure analysis is used. In section 24.9, some conclusions are drawn.

The orientation in chapters 24 and 25 is from the viewpoint of the producers and retailers of products and services. These can be commercial products, but also governmental services, hospitals, charities and other non-profit organizations.

24.2 Target group

The target group is the group of consumers, decision makers or companies towards whom the marketing and information policy is directed. Information and advertising objectives are not only aimed at reaching buyers, but also influential people. 'Influentials' are people who exert influence on the eventual buyers and users of the product or service. A campaign for exclusive cigars is not only directed towards cigar smokers (marketing target group), but also to household members and colleagues of the cigar smokers (advertising target group). The latter people should accept smoking and know the exclusiveness of the brand. A cigar smoker is only really satisfied, when his or her social environment also values his or her choice of cigars.

In the development of marketing and information policy, it is important to understand the target group. 'All car drivers' or 'all consumers' are too general categories to be of value and give direction to marketing and information policies. There are many ways of describing target groups. Here we consider three levels: the general, domain-specific, and brand-specific level; see figure 24.1.

At the general level, target groups and market segments are described with general, more or less permanent characteristics of people. These are person and household characteristics, socio-economic and demographic variables, such as age, gender, level of education, income, region, city, residential area and postal code.[1] These characteristics can be determined objectively. Most psychographic variables also have a general level: values

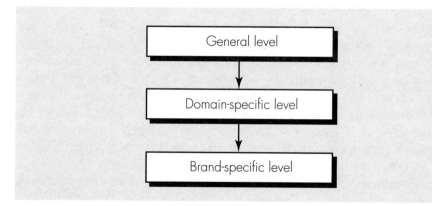

Figure 24.1 *Levels of segmentation*

and lifestyle.[2] Psychographic characteristics are subjective and can only be measured by questionnaires filled out by respondents.

Objective and subjective variables may be connected to a product domain. Buying and selling behaviour, knowledge and attitude regarding products, and the stage of the decision-making process regarding products and services, belong to the domain-specific level. The domain-specific level is usually the most suitable one for market segmentation and target group determination.

Brand-specific variables concern the purchase and use of certain brands. Objective characteristics like brand loyalty and frequency of use of brands are useful for a target group determination. Brand loyalty can also be an attitude and then belongs to the subjective variables such as brand knowledge, preference and buying intention. Brand-specific variables are also suitable for research in product improvement and development. Brand loyalty is an important variable in marketing at the specific level.[4]

Market segmentation

Segmentation variables should be measurable and the target groups formed should be accessible in the market, for example, by way of the media they consult or through their postal codes. The target groups formed by these variables should be large enough to be worth a separate marketing approach. The target groups should also differ sufficiently to justify separate approaches.

There are many variables by which consumers can be described and grouped: see table 24.1. The variables used to form a segment are called

Table 24.1 *Types of segmentation variables*[3]

	Objective	Subjective
General level (general characteristics)	Income, age, level of education, city of residence, postal code, behavioural patterns	Lifestyle, personality, instrumental values, terminal values
Domain-specific level (behavioural domain)	Usage frequency, substitution, complementarity, observable behaviour	Interests, opinions, perception attitude, domain-specific values
Brand-specific level (brand choice and preference)	Brand loyalty (behaviour), usage frequency, actions	Brand loyalty (attitude), preference, evaluation, brand knowledge, beliefs, buying intention

Table 24.2 *Types of segmentation analysis*

	Purchase/use behaviour	Person characteristics
Forward segmentation	Active	Passive
Backward segmentation	Passive	Active
Simultaneous segmentation	Active	Active

'active variables'. Variables used to further describe and characterize the segments are called 'passive variables'. Cluster analysis is often used to group the respondents and thereby create target groups. It is beyond the scope of this book to discuss these multivariate techniques of data analysis.

Three forms of segmentation exist (see table 24.2):

- In *forward segmentation*, segments are formed on the basis of differences in purchase and use behaviour. After that, differences between the segments regarding their attitudes, preferences, values, lifestyles and other personal characteristics of consumers are studied. The advantage of forward segmentation is that segments that are homogeneous in terms of their purchase and use behaviour are created. It is relatively easy to form a product and communication package around these homogeneous segments.
- In *backward segmentation*, target groups are formed on the basis of personal characteristics. The groups thus formed are then characterized further according to purchase and use behaviour. The advantage of reverse segmentation is that in this way segments can be formed on the basis of general variables such as age and area of residence, with which the segment is easily accessible. However, it is not given that these segments will be homogeneous in their purchase and use behaviour.
- *Simultaneous segmentation* is a combination of both methods. Segments are formed by the relationship between personal characteristics and behaviour.[5] For example, consumers are clustered according to their holiday behaviour and opinions on holiday travel. Segments are then further defined by level of education, age and other personal characteristics, and possibly by specific characteristics such as the chosen destinations and travel agencies.

Meaning structure

The three segmentation levels can be linked to a meaning structure.[6] Product characteristics, consequences and values are identified in the meaning structure. This corresponds with brand-specific, domain-specific and general segmentation levels, respectively. In figure 24.2, a division is made at these three horizontal levels:

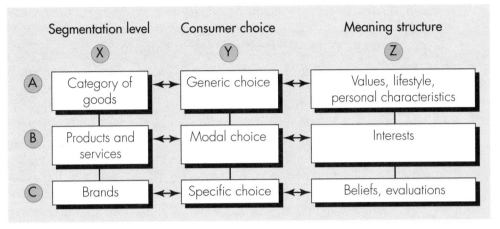

Figure 24.2 *Structure of the levels of segmentation, consumer choice and meaning structure*

- The *general* level (A), i.e., the use, evaluation and values of categories of goods, services, savings and behaviour patterns, and additionally, personal characteristics. This corresponds to the generic level of decision making. At this level, segments of heavy consumers of certain product categories may be classified, such as heavy consumers of food, consumers of electronic equipment, travellers, savers, etc. In the meaning structure, this is the level of the values.
- The *domain-specific level* (B), i.e., the use of and interest (domain-specific value) in products and services. This corresponds to the modal level of decision making. At this level, the type of product may determine market segments. For example, users of public transport and car drivers may be distinguished. In the meaning structure, this is the level of the consequences and benefits.
- The *brand-specific level* (C), i.e., the use and the characteristics of certain brands. This corresponds to the specific level of decision making. Preferences for product attributes may determine market segments. For example, price-buyers, design-buyers, and function-buyers may be distinguished. In the meaning structure, this is the level of product characteristics.

Three vertical areas are further defined:

- Area of the *segmentation levels* (X): category of goods (AX), products and services (BX) and brands (CX).
- Area of *consumer choice levels* (Y): generic decisions (AY), modal decisions (BY) and specific choice (CY).
- Area of the *levels of meaning structure* (Z): General values, lifestyles and other personal characteristics (AZ), interests and opinions (domain-

specific values; BZ) and beliefs and evaluations regarding product characteristics and brands (CZ). Sociodemographic characteristics such as income, education, age and personality also belong to AZ.

At level A, scientifically interesting relationships exist between consumption patterns (generic decisions), values and person characteristics. These relationships are usually too general for marketing applications. At level C, interesting relationships can be found between evaluations and behaviour towards particular brands. These relationships are important for brand/product development, but are usually too specific for meaningful market segmentation. The middle level of abstraction (B) is generally the most useful for segmentation; this level is judged to be optimal not only for consumer behaviour, but also in personality and social psychology. In personality psychology, research at the domain-specific level is called the interactionist approach to behaviour and situations.

Definition

Level error refers to attempts at explaining behaviour at one of the segmentation levels (categories, products or brands) by using variables from a non-corresponding level of the meaning structure (values, interests or beliefs).

Using the wrong level of analysis is a commonly made error, i.e., trying to use general person characteristics and values (AZ) to predict modal and specific consumer behaviour (BY, CY). In studies of this type, the researchers have found only weak relationships at best. It is unlikely that a meaningful segmentation will be obtained, if the level correspondence is incorrect.

24.3 General segmentation level

At the general level of segmentation, geographical, socio-economic and psychographic (lifestyle) characteristics are used. Product ownership is also a segmentation characteristic at the general level.

Geographical characteristics

Geographical characteristics are normally stable for long periods of time, for example area of (permanent) residence, Nielsen area, province/state, district, city area, zip code area, and level of urbanization. Some companies deal specifically with *postal-code segmentation.*[7]

A market can often be divided into regions. Large differences exist between the north and the south, the west and the east of Europe. Not only countries differ. Regional Europe may be a useful 'vertical' segmentation. Regions such as Bavaria, Basque, Catalonia, Corsica, Galicia, Provence, and Sicilia differ from other regions in culture and language. This is called 'vertical' segmentation, because all the people in a region are taken as a segment.

On the other hand, there are brands for which the same market approach is used in all countries ('global marketing'). Wrigley chewing gum, Mexx clothing and Pepsi Cola use the same international commercials in every country. In all countries, these brands attract similar target groups. This is called 'horizontal' segmentation, because similar people in different countries and regions are taken as a segment.[8]

Socio-economic characteristics

Socio-economic characteristics can relate to a person or a household. Examples are: gender, age, marital status, length of time spent living together, size and composition of the household, phase in the family life-cycle, religion, occupation and occupational status, social class, level of education and income. These characteristics are to a large degree permanent. Sometimes these properties are not attributed to a person but to a household, for example household composition and income.[9]

A market could, for example, be segmented on the basis of the variables *time* and *money*.[10] There are consumers with plenty of free time and those with little free time, and there are consumers with high and with low discretionary incomes.[11] With the use of these criteria, four segments can be distinguished. See table 24.3.

In table 24.3, some characteristics are shown in each of the four segments. Most households are located in segment A. These are generally young households with minimum to modal incomes. Households in segment B are generally older with unemployment or disability benefits. Segment C comprises people busy with their careers with high, often dual incomes, but little time for shopping. Comparatively few households are located in segment D. These are generally older people at the end of their career, with good pensions, possibly with early retirement. Segment D is expected to increase in the future. The division into four segments is quite

Table 24.3 *Segmentation by time and money*

	Little free time	Plenty of free time
Low discretionary income	A <35 years old, 'minimum/modal income'	B >50 years old, 'social-security benefit'
High discretionary income	C 35–50 years old, 'dual income'	D >50 years old, 'good pension'

simple. The segmentation can be further refined to nine segments, where amongst others, students constitute a separate segment.

For many companies, this is a useful market segmentation. The primary target group of teleshopping (a system where goods can be ordered by telephone and are delivered at home) consists, for example, of consumers with little time and high incomes (segment C). These consumers like to buy all sorts of good things. However, they have little time to stop by the supermarket.

Psychographic characteristics

Psychographic characteristics are attitudes, interests and opinions not directly related to specific product characteristics or functions. Examples are: fashion interest, opinions on the roles of men and women, political preferences, attitudes towards food and cooking, attitudes towards household jobs, willingness to experiment, purchasing orientation, pleasure in shopping, attitudes towards money and saving, environmental consciousness, job orientation, religion, social orientation, self-perception, and optimism/pessimism.

Divisions into lifestyle groups are often made on the basis of psychographic, socio-economic and demographic variables, supplemented with activities. VALS is a well-known American classification.[12] In comparison to a socio-economic description, psychographics gives a rich and lively characterization of the target group. In this way, we get a better understanding of the target group. The richness and liveliness of the descriptions can be exploited in advertising and information extension.

Product ownership

Product ownership is sometimes included in the general characteristics. This mainly concerns the ownership of some strategic products such as home, garden, car, caravan, pets, sports or hobby equipment.[13] On the one hand, these strategic products are indicators of household prosperity. On the other hand, these products lead to the purchase of complementary goods. Home and garden owners buy articles necessary for the upkeep of the home and garden. Car owners buy petrol, and some of them a caravan. Owners of a dog or a cat buy pet food. Strategic products can also be seen as indicators of domain-specific attitudes and interests.

24.4 Domain-specific segmentation level

Domain-specific variables are often the most interesting for market segmentation.[14] This implies that behaviour, interests and opinions which are directly related to a certain product class, can be taken as segmentation variables ('active variables'). If market segments are thus formed, they can be further described with other ('passive') variables to get a richer description of the segments.[15] The segments formed are a basis for the marketing and communication strategies. At the domain-specific level, we can identify product ownership and use, timing of consumption, consumer roles, and search styles.

Product ownership and use

The purchase and usage frequency of a product may be very different for each consumer. A market can be segmented into non-users, ex-users, potential users, first-time users, light users, average users and heavy users. The group of heavy users is usually quite small, but responsible for the largest part of the total consumption.

Figure 24.3 *Heavy user*

A common rule is the *80/20 rule*. A small number of consumers (20%) accounts for 80% of the sales.[16] This is even stronger for imported beer in the USA. Only 6% of American households accounts for 85% of the total consumption of imported beer. Many producers therefore aim their advertising at heavy users with the objective of making them into or keeping them as customers. The 80/20 rule will already count for a group of non-users. Many women for example do not drink beer and many men do not use cosmetics. For toothpaste, which is used by both men and women, the 80/20 rule will not be applicable.

The *judicial form* of the product ownership may play a role. A product can be bought, sold, hired, leased, acquired or stolen. It is for example obvious to divide the house market into renters and owners of homes. Car drivers can buy or lease their car, privately or via their employer. Goods can be sold for own use or as a present. In the collective campaign to promote the giving of flowers, both givers and receivers of flowers form the advertising target group.

Timing of consumption

The timing of consumption may be different across consumers. Some consume a heavy breakfast, others take extensive lunches, and still others like lavish dinners. For example, when do they use cheese, only at breakfast or also at lunch, dinner or as a snack? Do they drink wine or water with the dinner? This is important for the choice of advertising themes, broadcasting schemes of advertising, and media choice.

Consumer roles

For marketing, it is important to know the consumer roles played in the household.[17] Women relatively frequently buy fast-moving consumer goods. Mothers buy clothes for their children. Gifts are purchased for someone else. Husbands frequently take the role of financial planning. Each of these roles implies taking decisions within the domain concerned.

Search styles

Consumers differ with respect to the extent of the information search they carry out. For example, some consumers shop extensively before buying, others buy on impulse, and still others browse product catalogues. Such groups require different marketing approaches. Obviously, the first group is attracted by product displays and sales people. The second group may be attracted by shop windows and the third by direct mail and other advertising. Sometimes, marketing efforts themselves may be commercialized. In such a case it is possible to speak of an information market. Examples are publications by consumer organizations, such as *Consumer Reports*, videoclips, CD-ROMS containing product information, such as *Car Almanac*, department store catalogues and teleshopping catalogues.

24.5 Brand-specific segmentation level

At the brand-specific level, segments of different brand loyalty, and different preferences regarding product characteristics may be formed. Furthermore, markets can be segmented on the basis of the knowledge, the attitude and the behaviour towards the brand.

Brand loyalty

In the purchase and use behaviour for a certain brand, five groups can be distinguished: brand-loyal users, brand switchers, new users who have never before used a brand in the product category, users who are loyal to another brand, and non-users.

In the above classification, *brand loyalty* fulfils an important role. On the one hand, brand loyalty is a type of behaviour, namely the frequent or regular purchase of a certain brand. On the other hand, brand loyalty is an attitude, a preference for a certain brand, which manifests itself in purchasing behaviour.[18] Brand loyalty and brand switching are most easily studied with fast moving consumer goods.

A coffee example may clarify this. Brand-loyal users use only one brand of coffee. They have a favourable opinion about their brand. Brand-loyal users can be further divided into the type of coffee they use: regular, mocca or decaffenated. Brand switchers will use other brands, for instance, they buy brands that are on sale. New users are, for example, students living on their own or new householders who buy coffee for the first time. There are also coffee drinkers who are loyal to another brand. And finally there are the non-users, who do not drink any coffee at all.

Besides brand loyalty, there is store loyalty. This concerns buyers who regularly visit a certain shop (retail chain) and are convinced that this is the best shop for their interests if, for example, low price or high quality are concerned. It is possible to substitute shop loyalty for brand loyalty. Hennes & Mauritz, McDonald's and The Body Shop are also brands.

Brand-loyal users

These consumers are already convinced of the advantages of their brand. To them, advertising is a support and confirmation which helps to maintain their brand loyalty. Their brand loyalty is especially tested by the introduction of competing brands. Sometimes brand loyal users are urged to make more use of a product, for instance when new usage occasions are suggested.

'Single-brand loyals' almost always use the same brand. Besides this, there are consumers who are 'multi-brand loyal'. They regularly alternate between two or three brands. The goal of a marketing strategy can be to change these multi-brand loyals into single-brand loyals. Multi-brand loyalty is also a form of brand switching within a limited consideration set of brands.

Brand switchers

Brand switchers often have a preference for a product, but know, value and use other brands as well, sometimes four brands or more. They perceive advantages and disadvantages in the different brands. They may change brands as a result of attractive promotions or availability in the store.

For most brands, brand switchers from the largest group. It is useful to distinguish some subgroups:

- The 'searchers', who have not found their favourite brand yet and test the advantages and disadvantages of the different brands by trial and error. In a later stage, they may become brand-loyal users.
- The bargain-seekers, who always buy the cheapest product regardless of the brand, because they do not perceive any differences between the brands, or because they spend their money economically.
- The occasional buyers, who buy different brands for different occasions, for example, an expensive brand of coffee for visitors and a cheap brand for use at home alone.

New users

These tend to be young people who have to make the choice between different brands by themselves for the first time. Or they are foreigners who have come to live in a country. For new products such as the personal computer, there are many new users in the beginning and middle phases of the life-cycle. The new users possibly do not yet have clear brand preferences and are easily influenced by advertising. They are also influenced by their parents, colleagues and acquaintances or people of the same age.

Loyal users of a different brand

These consumers are difficult to influence into trying another brand. They will only occasionally try another brand if there is a sale or other form of attractive promotion. The tracing of consumers who drive a certain type of car via licence plate registration is for example common practice in the car industry. These consumers can then be approached through direct-marketing communication. In this way, Ford sent invitations to loyal Opel drivers for a test drive and was successful in converting Opel drivers.

Non-users

Non-users are not usually selected as a marketing target group because the chance is very small that this group can be persuaded towards product use. Cigarette commercials are aimed at smokers to influence their brand preference. Non-smokers are not a target group of tobacco advertising. Only if the non-users have never heard of the product or brand, or if the price has always been too high for them, may they become potential users. Many Europeans may not consider a holiday in the USA because they think that it will be too expensive. Only after the value of the dollar and the prices of plane tickets have dropped noticeably, does a Florida holiday become a realistic option for many Europeans.

Preferred product characteristics

Consumers attach different weights to product characteristics. These differences can form the basis for market segmentation. The toothpaste market is an interesting example.[19] This market can be segmented on the basis of four preferred product characteristics: the taste and appearance of the toothpaste, white teeth, prevention of teeth decay, and price. People who attach much importance to white teeth are generally young (predominantly teenagers). They are also more geared towards social contact than others. This segment also contains many smokers who worry about tar on their teeth. They form a target group for brands such as Macleans and Ultra Brite. Other users are more interested in the price and may consider an own-brand product. Other consumers may be more concerned with prevention of tooth decay, and will be attracted to Colgate's message about 'total protection'. The brand Signal, on the other hand, has been designed to have a more appealing taste and appearance. This kind of information is important in the formulation of the advertising strategy. If one were to introduce a new product aimed at the 'white teeth' segment, the emphasis in its marketing and advertising would need to be on the success that brand-users achieve with their social contacts. The campaign should be positioned in media aimed at young people.

Knowledge, attitude and behaviour towards the brand

The following data can be collected through research:

- To what extent is the consumer aware of the brand (unaided and aided recall)?
- In which phase of the choice process is the consumer? What does the consumer know about the product and the brand? Does the consumer know how the brand differs from other brands? What feelings does the consumer have about this? Does the consumer own the product of a different brand?
- The involvement of the consumer in the choice process.
- The extent to which cognitive and affective factors dominate in a purchase decision.
- How many consumers have tried the brand? What is their opinion about the brand?
- For how many people has there been a repeat purchase?

- What part of the sales can be attributed to loyal customers? Why did they become loyal customers?
- How often do consumers buy and use the product and the brand?

Using this information, one obtains a picture of the positioning of the brand in the mind of the consumer. If the answers to these questions are known, it can be determined what the primary objective of the marketing policy should be. Is the aim to increase brand awareness? Is it to change attitudes? Is it to try to move more consumers towards a trial purchase? Or is it to reinforce loyal buyers in their purchasing behaviour?

Knowledge and attitude regarding brands at the brand-specific level are related to the purchasing and usage behaviours at the domain-specific level. They comprise: brand awareness, interest or involvement with brands, brand attitudes, expectations of brands, buying intentions, purchasing and shopping behaviour. The concepts are not only used to describe target groups, but are often also advertising objectives.[20]

Brand awareness

There are two types of brand awareness. First, brand awareness is the active awareness of a brand name. Secondly, brand awareness is the passive recognition of a brand from a series of brand names. In a service shop, in a restaurant and for a telephone order, active brand awareness is required. In a self-service shop, passive brand recognition is often enough to choose, for example, the 'film with the yellow box'. The passive recognition does not necessarily have to be based on a brand name, like Kodak, but can also be based on colour, logo, packaging or even its place in the store. Bars and restaurants are often known by their locations.

Interest and brand knowledge

Consumers differ in the extent to which they are interested in products and services. It is a 'specialization' of consumers in certain domains.[21] Some people are crazy about cars and know all car brands and types, while others are particularly interested in clothing. A highly involved advertising target group can be reached with informative, sometimes even technical advertising. A less involved target group often needs an emotional approach to become interested in the brand. Highly involved people often read special-interest magazines in their domain, whereas less involved people may be reached through general-interest magazines.

Attitudes

Attitudes towards a brand also differ. Depending on the brand, consumers have a series of beliefs about specific product characteristics. Footwear may be judged by fit, grip, the support it may offer to feet, colour and price. The separate brands each have a score on these characteristics. Furthermore, the characteristics are evaluated according to their importance. The attitude is calculated as the sum of these properties, weighted with evaluations and/or importance.[22]

Although the 'general attitude' regarding two brands or product types can be the same, beliefs constituting the 'overall attitude' may differ considerably. It can uncover the strong and weak characteristics of a brand as perceived by the consumer. Groups of consumers with the same attitude structure probably exist. This gives a starting point for an advertising campaign to confirm or change attitudes.

Attitude and *image* are strongly related. The image of a product or brand is either a simple or a well-structured attitude. In the first case, the image is based on little brand knowledge. In the second case, it is based on extensive product and brand knowledge.

Expectations

Expectations about brands are partly formed on the basis of people's own experiences, the experiences of others, and on the basis of advertising. Consumers compare actual brand performance with the expectations they had. If the brand is deficient compared to these expectations, dissatisfaction results and complaints are possibly filed with the supplier, producer or consumer organizations.[23] Expectations are partly a basis for segmentation to locate dissatisfied customers and solve their problems. Some companies have separate divisions of Consumer Affairs or Customer Services. To prevent or reduce dissatisfaction, marketing communications should avoid creating unrealistic or overly high product expectations.

Buying intentions

The buying intention or buying plan is another variable to define target groups. It is often effective to aim advertising at people with buying plans in order to influence the brand choice within these buying plans. Especially the timing of the advertising is of importance. Consumers in a transitional phase of their lives, as when they are approaching a move, marriage or birth of a child, often have concrete buying plans.[24] A 'congratulation service' can strongly influence the purchasing decisions in such a transitional phase.[25] Buying intentions may also be derived from the ownership ladder.[26] Good timing of the message to the consumers with buying intentions can be achieved with direct-marketing communications.

Purchasing and shopping behaviour

Not only brand preferences, but also the purchasing and shopping behaviours of consumers determine which brand they eventually choose. Some consumers regularly buy on mail order, others go on extensive shopping trips. Some consumers usually buy at discounters, others appreciate atmosphere, advice and good service and are prepared to pay more for these aspects. It is often useful to classify target groups by store choice and store loyalty. This is particularly important in the case of cooperative advertising (joint advertising of producer and retail chain) and the added value (service and atmosphere) which the shop can add to the product or brand.

24.6 Conditions for market segmentation

For scientific research, market and communication research, segments have to fulfil certain conditions of size and homogeneity.[27] These conditions are discussed in the following.

Typification of segments

There are two parts to the identification of segment types:

- *Identification*: it should be possible to determine the size and composition of a segment.
- *Measurability*: the segmentation variables should be clearly and concisely measurable. In addition, objective characteristics are preferable.

Homogeneity

The definition of segments calls for three aspects to be considered:

- *Homogeneity*: is the segment homogeneous enough? Are the people within the segment similar enough? The same marketing approach can be applied to a homogeneous segment, assuming that these consumers will react in the same way.
- *Heterogeneity*: is there enough heterogeneity between the segments? Do consumers from one segment react differently than consumers from another segment? If this is not the case, they can be handled by the same marketing approach and the segments may be merged.
- *Stability*: is the segment stable over time? If consumers are allocated to a certain segment, do they still belong to the same segment after several years? A problem with much lifestyle research is the instability of segments obtained in this way.

Usability

Another important characteristic for a market segment definition is its usability:

- *Reachability*: can the segment be reached using marketing communications? Which media should be selected to reach the segment? Suppose the aim is to reach people highly involved in environmental problems. Which magazines do these people read and to which organizations do they belong?

- *Size*: is the segment large enough to be eligible for a separate market application? It is not cost-effective to use a separate marketing approach for segments that are too small.

Strategic criteria

There are two aspects to identifying the strategic importance of a segment:

- *Potential*. Does the segment have enough purchasing power to justify a separate strategy? Suppose a campaign for selective car use is concerned. Which households have the highest chance of being convinced by the campaign not to use their car for short journeys?
- *Attractiveness*. Are the segments attractive to the information provider and advertiser, for instance, as a reference group for other consumers?

When can segments be used?

If a segment satisfies the previously listed conditions, it is worth applying a separate marketing and communication policy and considering different prices, conditions, communication and distribution arrangements for the segment. Product differentiation is based on market segmentation.[28] Products, messages and services can be differentiated for each of the different segments. In most segmentation studies, consumers are classified in only one segment. In principle, however, it is possible to classify one consumer in more than one segment and thereby create overlapping segments.[29]

24.7 Positioning

The first part of this chapter dealt with market segmentation, i.e., the demand side of the market. In this section and the following we deal with the supply side of the market, positioning and brand extension being relevant topics.

The first step in the positioning of brands and products is categorization. A producer should examine the category in which consumers place a brand or a product. The other brands and products in the category are the competing brands and products. Is 'Yofresh' categorized as a normal margarine or as a subcategory of yogorines? Is Bavaria Malt a normal beer without alcohol or do consumers form a subcategory of malt beer? Is Nescafé perceived as regular coffee or does it belong to the subcategory of instant coffee?

Definition

Positioning refers to the consumer's perception of a brand amongst other brands. Positioning mainly results from marketing communication regarding brands, social communication and personal experience.

The second step is the positioning of the brand or product within a category. Producers position their brands with the objective of attaining a prominent place for their brands amongst other brands in the minds of consumers. Positioning is the result of this activity. Positioning is therefore linked with consumers' perceptions. Producers try to influence positioning. For example, Aldi and Ikea are perceived as cheap stores and Harrods as an expensive department store. This is an example of positioning on the price dimension. It is however, to a certain degree, also a quality dimension. Consumers compare brands and weigh them against each other on the basis of price and quality.

Positioning can be linked to the meaning structure; see figure 24.4. Assuming that product advantages or 'benefits' of products are central to the consumer, the positioning starts from these benefits. They can be linked to characteristics or to values. If the benefits are linked to characteristics, this is called informational positioning (A). If the benefits are linked to values, this is called transformational or value positioning (B). Positioning can also occur both ways, if the benefits are linked to both characteristics and to values (C):[30]

A   Informational positioning: benefits → characteristics
B   Transformational positioning: benefits → values
C   Two-way positioning: characteristics ← benefits → values
D   Execution positioning: benefits → advertising property.

Informational positioning

In informational positioning (A), the benefits of brand use are linked to the functional characteristics of the product. An example is the positioning of Freedent sugar-free chewing gum. Freedent prevents an 'acid attack' and tooth decay after a meal (consequence), because it has a pH-reducing effect (functional product characteristic). This positioning strategy is often used with new products and products with a problem-solving character. However, informational positioning can also be used for enriching products.

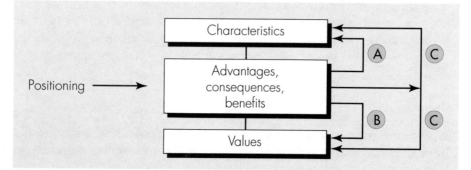

Figure 24.4 *Three positioning strategies (compare with figure 7.3)*

The property causing this enrichment is then emphasized.[31] If a product has a unique selling point (USP), informational positioning is advisable. It is often used in situations in which consumers are motivated to process information, for example with durable consumer goods.

Transformational positioning

Transformational positioning (B) is sometimes called value, image or lifestyle positioning. Here the benefits of the brand are linked to the goals, values or lifestyle of the consumer. All sorts of goods and behaviours in the life of the consumer which symbolize these values may be shown in commercials. These can be reasons for consumers buying the brands. This positioning strategy is often used with enriching products and brands which one buys for pleasure such as soft drinks, and with products which differ little with respect to product benefits, for example cigarettes and beer. Value positioning can also be applied to problem solving products as some insurance companies do in their life insurance campaigns. The values are then mainly related to safety, security and peace of mind, as life insurance may prevent or solve problems.

Transformational positioning is not always based on the linking of product benefits with values. Sometimes brands are connected to values without clear product benefits being mentioned. The brand symbolizes values. Coffee may represent sociability without specifying which product characteristics create this benefit.

Two-way positioning

In two-way positioning (C), product/brand benefits are linked with both the product characteristics and the values of the consumer. An example is the positioning of Green Persil. In the communication, it is explained that Green Persil does not contain phosphates (product characteristic), so the environment is preserved (product benefit), and that by using Green Persil, the consumer is acting as a responsible and environmentally-conscious citizen (values). Two-way positioning is strong, as it uses the whole means–end chain of the meaning structure.

Execution positioning

Execution positioning (D) is a positioning from the advertising campaign. This form of positioning is often chosen in strongly competing markets where brands differ very little or not at all. In advertising, therefore, there is not much of a distinguishing message about the brand to be given. The distinction from the competition is then mainly an advertising property. In the communication, the brand or the product is linked to a unique element or symbol. Symbolic signs can become advertising properties, for example Fido Dido for Seven-Up. Advertising properties can be a sign or cue for a product characteristic or value linked to the brand. In this way, the Snuggle bear stands for the softness of the fabric softener.

A clear positioning of a brand is preferable for consumers, because they then know of what 'use' the brand is to them. But the positioning should be honest, i.e., it should correspond with reality. If as a result of marketing-communication campaigns, consumers think that a certain shop is inexpensive, when in reality it is not, the positioning is misleading rather than useful in making the right decision.

24.8 Brand equity and brand extension

Brands

Brand names have a number of functions for consumers. Historically, they are trade names with which the producer makes itself known. It is often the name of the founder or owner of the company. Examples are Johnson & Johnson, Ford, Hewlett Packard, and Philips. These trade names became a sign that marks out all the products of a particular producer. Many brands lead lives of their own, with their own schemas and brand images. The brand is now a recognition sign for the consumer and often a guarantee for a certain level of quality.

The brand can be an *umbrella brand*. This means to say that all products of the producer concerned are brought on the market under this brand name. Almost all Philips products carry the brand name Philips. Private labels of store chains are also umbrella brands. Many different products have the brand St Michael. The advantage of an umbrella brand is that with good experiences with the brand, consumers can generalize this to the other products under the same brand name. It is, of course, a disadvantage when consumers have bad experiences with some element of the brand.

In the case of fast-moving consumer goods, on the other hand, the different products usually have separate brand names. Unilever and Proctor & Gamble both use a policy of *separate brands*. In this way, Unilever has different brands of margarine on the market for different target groups. Unilever has three divisions on the consumer market. The brand associations of food products (first division) are totally different from the associations with household cleaning products and detergents (second division), and articles for body care including cosmetics (third division). Separate brands have the disadvantage for consumers that experiences with a certain brand cannot be generalized to the other brands of the same producer.

An in-between form of branding is *endorsement*. Examples of endorsement are for example 'Skoda by Volkswagen' or 'Seat by Volkswagen'. Skoda and Seat remain separate car brands with their own models and marketing. Volkswagen is a part-owner of these brands and supports these brands with its expertise. Another example is Pickwick tea, which is a brand endorsed by Douwe Egberts.

Besides brand name and recognition sign, the brand is a sign for a certain quality or other characteristics of the products. A brand can bring about positive emotions and a schema of associations. The brand name is sometimes the only difference between products which are technically practically identical. For example, petrol is a fairly homogeneous product. Brands such as Shell, Esso, Mobil and Texaco form the distinction, besides the differences in services offered, customer loyalty incentives (gifts, points etc.) and the shops at the petrol stations.

The brand, as a formal category, evokes certain associations. 'Whummies' is a suitable brand name for salty snacks but not for detergents. On the other hand, Jif is suited for a cream cleanser but works less well for snacks. Each brand has its own associations which can be developed further. A brand such as Radio obviously calls up associations with radios. It is however a brand of clothing. Diesel and Radio can be registered as brands for clothing, but not as brands for engines and radios. Although evoking the wrong associations, these brands seem to be good brand names for clothing.

Brand names need to satisfy judicial and psychological criteria in order to be admitted and to be suitable as a brand. The following are some criteria for good brand names:

- Generic names cannot be brand names. The words car, umbrella or salty snack cannot be registered as brands, for cars, umbrellas and salty snacks, respectively. However, a generic name for a different category is allowed, so Radio is allowed to be a clothing brand. The opposite does occur, so a brand name can become a generic name for a category or product class. Consider for example aspirin, xerox and hoovers.
- Brand names need to be sufficiently distinct to prevent brand confusion. The Dutch Philips and Phillips, an American oil company, are not distinct enough, but allowed. It helps that these are brands from completely different product categories and geographic areas. To prevent confusion, Philips has long used the name Norelco in North America.
- Brand names need to be easily pronounceable and legible. The cosmetics brand '2nd Debut' is hard to decode and pronounce for non-English speaking people. The insurance company 'Equity and Law' is also difficult for them. English and American people have trouble with the German shampoo 'Schwarzkopf' or the German–Belgian brand Agfa–Gevaert. Names like Disney, Omo, Rolex, Shell and Volvo on the other hand, are easily pronounced and recognized in many languages.
- Some brand names can be very attractively visualized, like Camel and Shell. The brand name Bull's Blood is traditional and not very tactfully

chosen as a name for a Hungarian red wine. And how can 'Bird's eye', a Unilever deep freeze brand be attractively visualized?

- Expressiveness of brands. Some brand names are not very original and say very little, like Automatic for coffee machines or Euro Light for snacks with few calories.

Brand equity

A brand is not only a neutral reference to a product. By employing a product policy, R&D, marketing communication, personal recommendation and PR, a brand can attain an added value which is translated into a higher price for the branded product as compared with the generic product. The brand then represents fame, quality and security. The brand acquires expressive value for the user and an equity for the brand owner. By their brand use, users communicate their preference, expertise, wealth and/or status. The values represented by the brand are transferred to the user.

Definition

Brand equity is the value of a brand, resulting from brand awareness, brand loyalty, perceived quality, associations with the brand, and the brand schema.

The determinants of brand equity are as follows (see also figure 24.5):[32]

- *Brand awareness* includes awareness and evaluation of the brand ('the brand is a friend'). Brand awareness indicates a certain reputation and brand-loyal customers. This facilitates the acquisition of new customers.

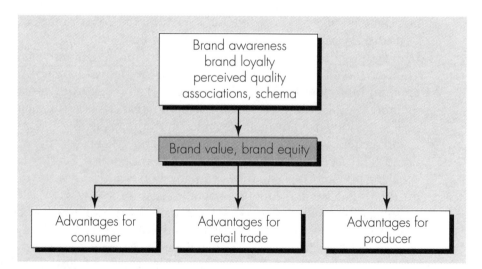

Figure 24.5 *Determinants and consequences of brand equity*

- *Brand loyalty*: for brand-loyal users, marketing costs are lower. It gives the producer and retailers the confidence of future sales. Moreover, a higher price is asked for a well-known brand in comparison with a generic brand.
- *Quality*: perceived high quality is a reason for buying and satisfaction.
- *Associations*: marketing communication enriches the schema with favourable associations, especially product benefits. From these associations and quality, a favorable positioning of the brand can be achieved. Brand extensions are also possible.

Brand equity is not only advantageous to the consumer. It also has advantages of security, continuity and a certain profit margin for the retailer and the producer.

Brand extension

Brand extension is the introduction of a new product under an existing brand name. If the existing brand is well-known and brings positive associations to mind, its fame and associations can be carried over to the new product. Moreover, the introduction of a new product under an existing brand is cheaper and more effective for the producer than the introduction of a new brand. Mars Almond and Mars Ice Cream are, for instance, brand extensions of Mars. Apparently this is successful, because Snickers and Twix ice creams are now sold as well. These are extra products for sales in the summer, when fewer 'normal' Mars, Snickers and Twix are bought.

Figure 24.6 *Brand extension*

There must be a certain logic for the brand extension to be successful. In this respect, the consumer-oriented approach can be distinguished from the manufacturer-oriented approach.[33] In the manufacturer-oriented approach, the success of potential brand expansions is judged by the degree of production transfer, marketing transfer, substitutability and transfer of the brand image or brand concept. For example, Mars caramel sweets could benefit from production transfer, Mars chewing gum could benefit from production transfer and substitutability, and Mars sports drink could benefit from image transfer. In the consumer-oriented approach, the logic follows from the meaning structure of goods and services. Table 24.4 shows three levels of brand extension. Incidentally, brand extension can occur on more than one level simultaneously. For example, products in a line extension may also possess the same benefits.

Characteristics level
At the characteristics level, brand extensions extend into variants of taste, colour, shape, etc. Classic Coke, Cherry Coke and Coca-Cola Light exist besides the normal Coke. Danone has yoghurt in different flavours. Besides normal Ariel, there is Ariel Ultra and next to Carlsberg, there is Carlsberg Light. There are Pampers nappies for boys and girls of different ages. The different colours, flavours and variants are substitutes for each other. The choice set of consumers becomes more extensive. The product is differentiated and offered to different target groups. This form of brand extension is called 'line extension'. This type of brand extension requires little change of the brand schema, i.e., assimilation. In the manufacturer approach, it is assumed that the extension will be successful because consumers think that the characteristics of the extension will have the same quality as the parent brand.

Consequences level
At the consequences level, brand extension is based on the same function, the same consequence or the same 'benefit' for the consumer. Under the

Table 24.4 *Levels of brand extension*

Type of brand extension	Meaning structure	Marketing-technical elements
Line extension, technical substitute	Characteristics level	Production transfer
Similar or complementary consequences, usage in similar situations	Consequences level	Marketing transfer, substitutability
Similar target group or lifestyle	Value level	Brand image transfer, brand concept transfer

name Lean Cuisine, different products which all contain few calories and are good for slimming, are brought onto the market. So there is Lean Cuisine margarine, cheese, paté, cream milk and smoked sausage. These products all share the common characteristic that they are less fattening than other products. Lean Cuisine also is associated with a certain lifestyle: if you take good care of yourself and your figure, you will have more self-confidence and be happier. In the manufacturer approach, the expected success of these extensions is due to the transfer of marketing expertise, i.e., using the same marketing knowledge for similar products, and sub-stitutability, i.e., substitutes have similar consequences.

Lifestyle and values
Brand extensions can also be based on the same lifestyle and values. Dunhill was originally a cigarette brand, but the brand Dunhill is now also used for completely different products such as expensive lighters, jewellery and watches. Ray Ban was originally a brand of sunglasses, but now this brand is also seen on skis and ski clothing. There are brand Porsche sun-glasses. Swatch is planning to release artistic and lively coloured city cars under the brand Smart, produced by Mercedes. These brand extensions appeal to a certain target group striving for certain values and a certain lifestyle and who use these brands to express their identity. From the manu-facturer's viewpoint, these extensions are expected to benefit from the transfer of brand image.

Extending brands successfully
Brand extensions are not always successful. A good brand extension must adhere to certain conditions:[35]

- *Favourable existing schema*. There must be a positive schema con-cerning the formal category of the original brand. In this case, positive associations can be conveyed. An Apple PC is seen as a user-friendly PC of high quality.
- *Favourable forward transfer*. A positive schema should be generalizable to the new product. The new product receives the existing brand schema (transfer) plus a label with new product attributes. It is a formal cate-gorization with some functional labels. For example, Apple copiers may also be seen as user-friendly and of a high quality, according to some customers.
- *Favourable backward transfer*. Negative schemas should not be trans-ferred, from the existing product to the new one, or from the new product to the existing one. If photocopiers are seen as frequently defective products, a negative schema may be carried over to Apple Macs. Kleenex toilet paper might convey negative associations to Kleenex tissues. Miller Light beer had a negative effect on Miller High Life because

of the schema ('almost water') of light beer. The new product under the same brand name is then created at the expense of the existing product (cannibalism).

It is not advisable to place a famous brand name of complex products on a trivial product, an IBM stapler for example or a Philips bathroom wash basin. This is called trivialising. The new product then detracts from the reputation of the famous brand and from the quality and complexity of the existing products brought out under that brand. It is a case of undesirable backward transfer. It is just as unadvisable to use a famous brand name of a simple product for a complex product, for example, 'Heineken computers'. The brand name then does not achieve the association of complexity and durability that is needed for the new product.

In general, an existing brand name must not be used for products with entirely different associations. With these conditions in mind, it is interesting to examine whether the following brand extensions are favourable or unfavourable to the new and to the existing product under the same brand: McDonald's theme parks, McDonald's photo printing service, Heineken soda water, Swatch city cars, Akzo Nobel contraceptive pill, and Heinz peanut butter. Which levels do these brand extensions have? Are these brand extensions likely to evoke positive associations for the consumer? Which of these brand extensions would have a chance of success?

24.9 Conclusions

This chapter has tried to create a picture of the levels and usability of market segmentation from a marketing perspective. By the use of market segmentation, homogeneous target groups for the marketing approaches of companies and other organizations can be determined. In particular, the domain-specific approach, which is drawn from product benefits, has many perspectives.

In the segmentation procedure, it is important to distinguish between active and passive variables. The segments are formed on the basis of active variables and are further described and 'enriched' with the use of passive variables. Not every segment is worth a separate marketing approach. Segments must satisfy certain conditions of homogeneity, usability and strategic criteria in order to be eligible for this.

Positioning and brand extension are two important strategies for a supplier of goods and services to bring brands to the attention of consumers in a favourable and efficient manner.

For producers, positioning is the attaining of a prominent position of a brand in relation to other brands in the minds of consumers. The benefits of a product or brand for consumers are the starting point here. These benefits are linked to values and to characteristics, including price and quality.

Brand extension allows the possibility of a fast and relatively inexpensive market introduction of a new product. The extension has to do with the characteristics, consequences and values of the original product or brand. The extension should fit the brand schema. There is a danger that the existing brand name transfers the wrong associations to the new product. Another danger is that the existing product schema is damaged by the extension. Only if both these risks are avoided or minimized will brand extension be successful.

Notes

1. See chapter 2.
2. See section 16.3.
3. Van Raaij, W. F. and Verhallen, Th. M. M. (1994) 'Domain-specific market segmentation' *European Journal of Marketing* 28, 49–66.
4. See section 11.6.
5. Van Raaij and Verhallen (1994).
6. See chapter 7.
7. See section 2.3.
8. Van Raaij, W. F. (1998) 'New media for new consumers' *Journal of Marketing Communications*.
9. See chapter 2.
10. Lakatos, P. A. M. and Van Kralingen, R. (1985) *Toward 1990. A Matter of Time and Money* (Amsterdam: Elsevier).
11. Discretionary income is the part of the income that can be spent freely, after deduction of obligatory expenditure on home rent, mortgage payments, insurance premiums, saving plans and other contractual obligations.
12. VALS stands for: Values and Lifestyles. See for VALS-1: Mitchell, A. (1983) *Nine American Lifestyles: Who We Are and Where We Are Going* (New York: Macmillan). For VALS-2 see: Riche, M. F. (1989) 'VALS 2' *American Demographics* 25. See also section 16.3 and figure 16.4.
13. Arndt, J. (1976) 'Reflections on research in consumer behavior' *Advances in Consumer Research* 3, 213–221. See also section 1.4.
14. Van Raaij and Verhallen (1994).
15. 'Active' means that these variables play a role in the forming of the clusters (segments). 'Passive variables' are used to further describe the clusters already formed.
16. Twedt, D. W. (1964) 'How important to marketing strategy is the heavy user?' *Journal of Marketing* 28, 1, 71–72.
17. See section 13.4.
18. Jacoby, J. and Chestnut, R. W. (1978) *Brand Loyalty. Measurement and Management* (New York: Ronald Press).
19. Haley, R. I. (1968) 'Benefit segmentation' *Journal of Marketing* 32 (July) 30–35.
20. Floor, J. M. G. and van Raaij, W. F. (in preparation) *Marketing Communication Strategy* (Hemel Hempstead, UK: Prentice Hall), Chapter 7.
21. See section 14.4.

22. Fishbein, M. and Ajzen, I. (1975) *Belief, Attitude, Intention, and Behavior: An Introduction to Theory and Research* (Reading, MA: Addison-Wesley).
23. See section 21.4.
24. Andreasen, A. R. (1966) 'Geographic mobility and market segmentation' *Journal of Marketing Research* 3, 341–348.
25. A congratulation service visits young mothers who have just given birth and households which have just moved. The service offers a package of user goods and information on baby care, shops and nearby provisions.
26. See section 23.3.
27. See chapter 2.
28. Smith, W. R. (1956) 'Product differentiation and market segmentation as alternative marketing strategies' *Journal of Marketing* 21, 3–8.
29. Oppedijk van Veen, W. M. and Verhallen, Th. M. M. (1986) 'Vacation market segmentation: a domain-specific value approach' *Annals of Tourism Research* 13, 37–58.
30. See section 6.4.
31. See section 7.1.
32. USP stands for 'unique selling point' or 'unique selling proposition'.
33. Aaker, D. A. (1990) 'Brand extensions: the good, the bad and the ugly.' *Sloan Management Review* 31, 4, 47–56.
    Aaker, D. A. (1991) *Managing Brand Equity* (New York: The Free Press).
    Aaker, D. A. and Keller, K. L. (1990) 'Consumer evaluations of brand extensions' *Journal of Marketing* 54, 27–41.
    Kapferer, J.-N. (1992) *Strategic Brand Management. New Approaches to Creating and Evaluating Brand Equity* (London: Kogan Page).
34. Nijssen, E. J., Antonides, G. and van Leeuwen, B. (1997) 'A conceptual framework of fit for brand extension' (Working paper, Erasmus University, Rotterdam).
35. Aaker (1991); Kapferer (1992).

CONSUMER RESEARCH 25

25.1 Introduction

This chapter deals with consumer research. Western Europe is a research-minded part of the world. Much consumer and market research into the opinions and behaviour of consumers and business buyers is conducted. Europe is responsible for 45% of all market research expenditure, whereas the USA and Japan account for 34% and 8%, respectively.[1] This chapter focuses on consumer research, which comprises 72% of all market research (in Europe, in 1995). Market research into consumers is not only useful for companies that market consumer goods or consumer services; it is also useful for environmental and consumer policies, charities, preventive healthcare plans and other areas of policy making.

This chapter is structured according to the four 'P's of the marketing mix: product, price, promotion (marketing communication) and place (distribution). Consumer research into distribution has been discussed in chapter 18. Market segmentation, positioning and brand extension, as important applications of theories of consumer behaviour, were dealt with in the previous chapter.

Only those types of consumer research linked to the previous chapters of this book will be discussed here. It is, of course, impossible to comprehensively cover consumer and market research in the course of one chapter. Many complete books have been published about this subject.[2]

In section 25.2, the functions of consumer research for producers of goods and services play the central role. The history of consumer and market research is described in section 25.3. The methods of consumer and market research are discussed in section 25.4. In sections 25.5, 25.6 and 25.7, product, price and communication research respectively are discussed. Section 25.8 gives an insight into the ethics of consumer research. In section 25.9 some conclusions are drawn.

The objective of this chapter is to connect the theories of consumer behaviour as discussed in this book, to the practice of consumer and market research.

25.2 Functions of consumer research

Consumer research is part of market research. Market research is the collection, analysis and reporting of data necessary for better control of the processes in the market. Consumer research is the collection, analysis and report of information to be used for policy decisions in relation to consumer behaviour. These can apply to various forms of consumer behaviour: effects of media and advertising, financial behaviour, consumption cycle including orientation, purchase and use of products and services, household production, and disposal of products. In fact, nearly all the subject areas of this book could be considered by consumer research.

Consumer research can be descriptive, explanatory and predictive. This distinction was discussed in the first chapter of this book.

- *Descriptive*. In descriptive research, the best possible inventory of consumer behaviour is made. Who buys what, when and by what means? This concerns, for example, demand estimates and brand loyalty.
- *Explanatory*. Consumer behaviour is explained, for example, with the help of motivation, knowledge and attitudes. Insight into the determinants of behaviour can thus be obtained.
- *Predictive*. In predictive research, statements are made about future behaviour of consumers and the expected effects of policy decisions in marketing.

This information is necessary for *marketing*, the development and improvement of products and services, as well as communication about it. Research can give insight into the motives of consumers for purchasing and using certain products, services and brands. Often these reasons are linked to the benefits obtained from the product use. The reasons for carrying out consumer research are usually connected to a desire to increase the demand for these products and services. This information is also necessary for *demarketing*. This is the reduction of the demand for products and services, for example, harmful products such as tobacco, alcohol and drugs. From an environmental policy perspective, the government may wish to 'demarket' products such as cars and thus encourage the use of public transport.

Policy-makers strive for the reduction of risk and uncertainty about the effects of their decisions, as a result of which they are able to make decisions with more confidence. As a matter of fact, consumers also do this. Comparative product testing could be considered market research for the benefit of consumers.

Macro-marketing environment

Marketing managers and other policy makers need to take into account the macro-marketing environment.[3] The macro-marketing environment restricts and restrains marketing policies. Policies have to operate within these macro-marketing boundaries. The macro-marketing environment consists of sociodemographic, economic and cultural developments such as the development of income, employment, number of households, development of supply and demand, media, marketing communication in its broadest sense, marketing and distribution structures, consumerism and the consumer policy of the government. Values, standards and ethics also belong to the macro environment.[4] In marketing policies, the macro environment can only be changed slightly if at all. It is thus necessary to take the environment into account and to anticipate sociodemographic and cultural developments.

Market structure studies

Studies of market structures include, among other things, the positioning of brands. How do consumers 'perceive' the market and the brands on this market? This concerns the position of brands in relation to competitive brands. The adjustment of this position is called positioning.[5] In general, the similarities and differences between brands are established here as perceived by consumers. Brands may be placed in a multidimensional space according to their degree of similarity. Brands close together in this perceptual space are competitors. Positioning also concerns the naming of dimensions in this perceptual space. These are the dimensions on which brands are judged by consumers.

Association networks or schemas with regard to brands and in particular the means–end chains of meaning structures are another subject of market research.[6] They are applied in marketing, for example in market segmentation, positioning and brand extension.[7] A frequently used method for investigating meaning structures, is 'laddering.'[8]

As a third component of marketing structure studies, market segmentation and target group definition should also be mentioned.[9] As a consequence of market segmentation and target group definition, products are differentiated to cater to these segments.

25.3 History of market research

Although there were a number of consumer studies before the Second World War, consumer research really started to flourish in the 1950s and 1960s. Manufacturers had a relatively easy time shortly after the War. Although raw materials were difficult to find, it was not difficult to sell the finished goods. Due to the economic development, increased competition, and consumer discretionary income, consumers have become more powerful in the 1990s. Producers of goods and services have to compete for consumers. Consumers have become more demanding concerning product quality, performance, and value for money. This is why it is important for manufacturers and retailers to know more about consumer preferences and choices in order to sell products and services.[10]

The history of consumer research was described in chapter 1.3. Related to this is the history of market and marketing research. Market research agencies in Europe developed after the Second World War. Some of these agencies focus their activities on large-scale data collection, whereas other agencies focus on qualitative research, often focusing on consumer motivation.[11]

In the 1950s, the first standard, syndicated services in market research started, such as the store audit and the consumer audit.[12] A *retail-store audit* is a study of brands available in stores and their rates of circulation. For producers this information is important to find out quickly whether a new product, a product improvement or a sales promotion is successful. A. C. Nielsen is the most important supplier of these standard services. Factors measured by store audits are:

- market size and trends for all brands in a category;
- sales and market share of brands;
- sales effects of sales promotion;
- sales effects of pricing policies.

A *consumer audit* consists of a panel of households keeping diaries on their purchases and the prices they paid. This is a different way of checking the success of new products, product improvements and sales promotion actions. GfK (Gesellschaft für Konsumforschung) is the most important supplier of these standard services. Factors measured with consumer audits are similar to the factors measured with store audits. Of course, both store and consumer audits should give approximately the same results.

In the 1960s, new standard syndicated services such as *omnibus research* came into being. This is the regular 'multi-client' study. A market research agency may, for example, decide to perform an omnibus study on smoking habits and the purchase of cigarette brands. The research consists of a common part and specific parts. For example, both the tobacco industry and anti-smoking activists may have questions included in the specific part of this omnibus and obtain the exclusive rights to the answers of these questions.

The 1970s were characterized by the introduction of telephone surveys with a CATI (Computer-assisted Telephone Interviewing) system. The 1980s saw a further development of telephone and computer-assisted inter-viewing. In CAPI (Computer-assisted Personal Interviewing) the pollsters

Table 25.1 *The ten largest European market research agencies (1995)*[15]

Agency	Turnover in million Ecu	Offices in EU countries	Country of origin and ownership
1 A.C. Nielsen	558	14	Dunn & Bradstreet, USA
2 IMS International[16]	262	11	Dunn & Bradstreet, USA
3 Gesellschaft für Konsumforschung	228	11	GfK, Germany
4 Sofrès Group	174	7	Finalac Group, France
5 Research International	130	13	WPP Group, UK
6 Infratest/Burke	116	9	Infratest, Germany
7 Ipsos Group	109	7	Ipsos, France
8 Taylor Nelson AGB	78	3	Taylor Nelson, UK
9 MAI Information Group	67	4	MAI, UK
10 Millward Brown International	61	7	WPP Group, UK

are equipped with portable PCs. The questionnaire is programmed as a branched programme, and respondents are only asked questions that are relevant to them. The questions can be answered directly by respondents or pollsters. Next to CATI and CAPI, CAPAR came into being. In CAPAR (Computer-aided Panel Research) the respondents are equipped with a PC and modem at home. At the weekends they receive a questionnaire, the answers to which are sent via the modem to the market research agency. CAPAR telepanels are an important development of the 1990s.

Market research expenditure

The world expenditure on market research in 1995 is about 7.9 billion Ecu. The European market share of 45 per cent is approximately 3.6 billion Ecu. Germany (875 million Ecu), the UK (730 million Ecu) and France (619 million Ecu) account for nearly two-thirds of European research turnover.[13] Other European countries with large shares are Italy, Spain, The Netherlands, Sweden, Belgium, Switzerland and Austria.

Consumer goods industry dominates with 51% of all market research expenditure. This is followed by services (14%), public sector (10%), wholesale and retail (7%), advertising agencies (5%), and research organizations (5%). Seventy-two per cent of market research is consumer research; 28% business-to-business research.[14]

There are over 1,500 market research companies and consultancies in Europe, including over 400 in the UK. Table 25.1 shows the largest market research chains, their turnover in Europe, the number of offices in EU countries and the ownership of the companies.

25.4 Methods of market research

Methods of market research discussed here include: the analysis of existing or 'secondary-source' data ('desk research'), qualitative, experimental, omnibus, model and survey research.

In figure 25.1, the different forms of market research are placed in two dimensions. The vertical dimensions shows small-scale versus large-scale research. The horizontal dimension indicates development versus the testing of hypotheses.

Desk research
Desk research is the collection and analysis of secondary-source data from databases and customer registrations by firms. It accounts for less than 5% of research expenditure. Organizations that manage such databases are the central bureaus of statistics, chambers of commerce, university libraries, government departments, and trade organizations. Desk research cannot answer all marketing questions. Sometimes the information is outdated or it may not be exactly what is needed. A new type of 'desk research' is the

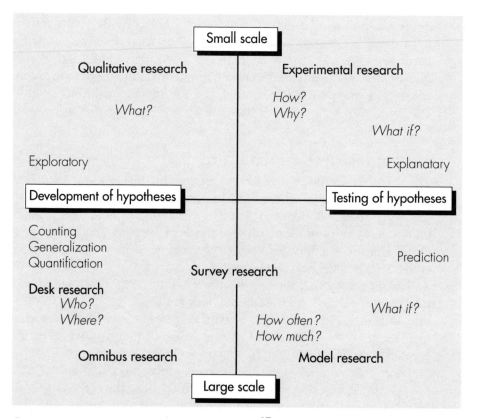

Figure 25.1 *Major types of market research*[17]

analysis of supermarket scanning data. These huge data sources can be analyzed to find patterns of purchasing behaviour and the effects of sales promotions. In the future, scanning data could supplement or replace retail-store and consumer-audit data.

Qualitative research

This kind of research is characterized by its small scale and exploratory character. This type of research accounts for 9% of research expenditure (see table 25.2). The research refers to how specific behaviour occurs, what happens and why. Through in-depth interviews and focus group discussions the motives of why consumers do or do not purchase specific brands are investigated. Group discussions account for two-thirds of qualitative research expenditure, and in-depth interviews for about one-third (table 25.2). In terms of number of participants, group discussions have a 'market share' of 57% and interviews of 43%.

Projective techniques are also part of qualitative research. In projective techniques, people are asked to give the answers they think that 'other people' would give. Direct questioning could evoke resistance and defensive barriers especially on 'sensitive subjects', whereas projective techniques may overcome these barriers. Consumers reveal their opinions by 'projecting' them into the opinions of 'other people'.

Qualitative research particularly focuses on insights into purchase motives and barriers against buying specific products or brands. Motivation research (see chapter 1.3) has become popular again, probing for the less

Table 25.2 *Expenditure and number of interviews/participants by types of research*[18]

	Expenditure (percentage)	Percentage of interviews/ participants
Ad-hoc quantitative		
Face to face	26	51
Mail	4	16
Telephone	12	33
Other	2	
Total	44	100
Ad hoc qualitative		
Group discussion	6	57
Interview	3	43
Total	9	100
Standard		
Omnibus (syndicated)	5	
Panel	29	
Other	13	
Total	47	
Grand Total	100	

conscious and less socially acceptable motives why consumers prefer products and brands. In qualitative research, ideas are developed that can be tested in quantitative research, with adequate sampling of respondents.

Experimental research

Experimental research is based on certain hypotheses formulated in advance. Here the *how* and *why* questions come up as well. This research checks to see under which conditions and circumstances certain reactions occur. Hypotheses are developed to explain individual or group behaviour and are then tested. Test markets or split runs are examples of field experiments. In a test market, a new product is tested before it is launched on the whole market. In split runs, the response rates of two or more variants of a direct-mail letter or advertisement can be tested.

Omnibus research

This form of research involves large-scale syndicated studies. In a large random survey, questionnaires are sent out, for more than one client at the same time ('multi-client research'). Omnibus research is most often at the extent of certain activities such as frequency of purchase, media reach and opinion polls. It accounts for 5% of standard research (table 25.2).

Model development

Research focused on the construction of marketing models makes use of large databases. This is mostly concerned with links at aggregate levels, such as marketing structures, competition analysis and models for the introduction of innovations. These models are of less importance for the understanding of consumer behaviour.

Surveys

In figure 25.1, survey research is placed below the centre, in the direction of large-scale research. It is also called quantitative research, although experimental, omnibus, panel and model research are also quantitative. This type of research accounts for the majority (more than 90%) of research expenditure. Survey research is a tool used both for omnibus and panel research. A survey uses a questionnaire that can be taken face-to-face by mail or by telephone or telepanel. In the case of a mail or panel survey, respondents themselves answer the questions. In the case of a telephone or face-to-face survey, the interviewer fills out the questionnaire with the answers of the respondents. The answers to the questions are coded for efficient processing of the data. Estimation of market range and effects as well as testing of hypotheses are possible by means of quantitative research.

Intermediate research types exist. A survey with open questions is positioned between quantitative and qualitative research. Research into

Figure 25.2 *Face-to-face interviewing*

individual choice processes is an intermediate type between qualitative and experimental research. Field experiments and test markets are an intermediate type of experimental and omnibus research.

Standard *versus ad hoc* research

In table 25.2, expenditure on types of research is shown. An important difference is *ad hoc versus* standard research. With *ad hoc* research, specific measurement and analysis methods for the research problem have to be developed each time. *Ad hoc* or tailor-made studies account for 53% of research expenditure (see table 25.2) (44 + 9 = 53%).

Standard research can be used for many more-or-less standard purposes and questions. Panel and omnibus research are the major types of standard research. Standard research accounts for 47% of all market research. Most panel and omnibus research uses questionnaires. Fifty-nine percent of all *ad hoc* quantitative research is conducted with face-to-face interviews and 27% with telephone interviews. The second column shows that the proportion of face-to-face interviews is relatively low compared with expenditure, whereas the proportion of telephone interviews is relatively high compared with expenditure. Telephone interviewing is thus more cost-effective than face-to-face interviewing.

Cross-section versus panel

Cross-section and longitudinal research are not separated in figure 25.1. Usually, in cross-section research, a random sample of subjects is drawn that is used only once. Only a one-time measurement is taken of the respondents. With panel research, respondents are asked to participate several times, so changes in their behaviour and opinions can be observed directly.

Longitudinal panel studies are, for example, family budget research and purchase diaries (consumer audit). This type of research is done with regular questionnaires, diaries, and 'on-line'. In the latter case, a group of households answer questions at home by using a PC. The advantage of a panel is that personal characteristics are known from the first contact. Thus, selections can be made, for instance on lifestyle or the possession of strategic products.

Monitoring of consumer behaviour takes place in longitudinal research, with the aid of panels or repeated surveys. With a panel, the same group of consumers is interviewed on different occasions. This enables the analysis of changes at the individual level. With repeated surveys, a different random sample is used for each measurement occasion. Thus only the changes of averages and dispersions in the random samples can be determined. Monitoring or tracking is particularly important to determine the developments and changes of consumer behaviour and advertising effects over the years. Scanner data, obtained through cash registers in stores, can also be used to monitor consumer behaviour.

An example is the MDI study in The Netherlands.[19] This study examines the social issues people are concerned with. For most consumers, environmental pollution has been the most important issue since 1990. Next to that, in later years, issues about danger in the streets (criminality), industrial pollution, health care and ethnic minorities have risen; see table 25.3.

Table 25.3 *Involvement in social issues*[20]

| | Percentages of people defining each issue as important | | | | |
	1981	1985	1990	1991	1992
Environmental pollution	31	25	57	57	59
Danger on the streets	36	35	46	47	53
Industrial pollution	32	26	50	46	50
Health care	20	25	42	47	49
Minorities	21	19	27	34	49

25.5 Product research

Research is regularly conducted into both new and existing products and their packaging. The 'extended product' includes package, price, communication, and distribution. This concerns the total product as marketed: the product as sold in the store and as advertised.[21]

The launching of a new product entails considerable costs and risks.[22] Early in the process of product development, concept tests are done to verify future product acceptance by consumers. Just as pre-tests with advertising, a concept test is a check into the comprehension and acceptance of the idea by consumers. However, the success or failure of the product cannot be fully predicted by a concept test, just as a pre-test cannot accurately predict an advertising effect. However, a concept test of a product characteristic, such as a new taste or colour, can have predictive value. Also, in the case of a discontinuous change or innovation, a concept test is useful to detect problems with the product or service.[23]

Experimental research often comprises a test of food products. It concerns taste and usage tests, and often comparative research of several brands. These can be either 'blind' tests of products without brand names, or product tests in which the brands are known to the respondents. Frequently, consumers report taste differences in 'branded' product tests, which they do not discover in blind tests. The explanation is that either the

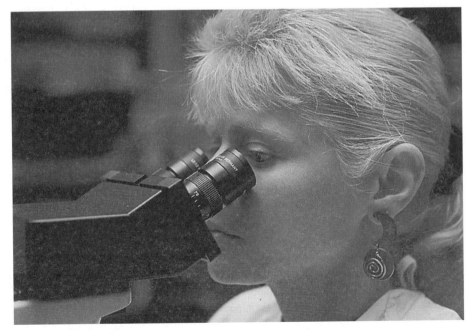

Figure 25.3 *Product test*

brand has a suggestive influence on the taste perception and/or consumers are more sensitive to taste differences when brands are known.

Packaging

The package is an important part of the product. Research into packaging of products includes the following aspects:

- the functionality of packaging—its easy use in handling and opening;
- the recognizability and attention-grabbing quality of packaging, especially on the shelf in the shop, surrounded by other packages;
- the degree to which the package reflects and represents the 'personality' of the product;
- ecological and other social effects of the use of packaging materials.

Research contributes to the prediction of the success of new products. It is especially important to study the acceptance of the product by early buyers closely. Success mostly depends on the acceptance of repeat purchases by this group, at least for fast-moving consumer goods. The product is by then, of course, in an advanced stage of product development.

Estimates can be made about the market share of the new product with the help of market research. Many models exist for obtaining these estimates, such as Demon, News and Sprinter.[24]

25.6 Price research

Price is an indicator of the cost and quality of a product or service. What price is acceptable to consumers? Do clear minimum and maximum levels of acceptable prices exist? Below what (minimum) level does the product become too cheap such that consumers question its quality? Above what (maximum) limit does the product become too expensive for consumers? Consumers may feel that a product does not warrant its price. Between the minimum and maximum levels an acceptable or 'fair' price exists. Prices also need to be considered in the light of prices of competing brands.[25] This type of research is not only relevant for new products. Existing products' prices can also be compared with those of competing brands.

This does not mean that products within the acceptable price range will be purchased without question. It only means that a price within the acceptability range is not a barrier against its purchase.

An acceptability range often has 'round' prices. For example, some consumers may have a maximum price of £20,000 for a car. Brands and models with a higher price will be rejected following a conjunctive decision rule. Many products are priced just below a limit, such as £19,995. This is called 'psychological pricing'. The product seems cheaper when priced just below the round figure.

Within the acceptability range, the price is weighed against the quality

Figure 25.4 *Money evaporates quickly*

and advantages of the product. Here the rule is 'value for money'. A higher price is only acceptable if product quality is correspondingly high.[26] For example, consumers are willing to pay more for chocolates of national brands such as Cadbury or Mars than for own-label chocolate products.

Weber's law may be applied to perceived price differences. It is not a direct application of this law because price differences can always be perceived.[27] It is an application regarding the acceptability of price differences. According to Weber's law the just observable difference (∂I) in price (I) is a constant fraction (k) of the original price: $\partial I / I = k$. This relates to both price increases and reductions. A price reduction of 5 Ecu on a price of 100 Ecu has the same result as a reduction of 0.50 Ecu on the price of 10 Ecu. A reduction of 50 Ecu on the purchase of a bike can be decisive, while this is not the case with the purchase of a car. The fact that in both cases the consumer saves the same amount (or does not spend it) is generally ignored.

According to Weber's law, products with a higher price can be increased more in absolute price than products with a lower price. Obviously, proportional increases are viewed as reasonable: $I + \partial I$. This does not apply to prices which, after an increase, will go beyond the limits of the acceptability range.

25.7 Communication research

An important type of research is that which concerns the effects and results of marketing communication (promotion). Separate advertising messages are often pre-tested to remove possible communication barriers. The achieved results of communication campaigns can also be verified.[28]

In communication research, seven types of research may be distinguished.[29]

- *Fundamental communication research* covers scientific research into the effects and results of marketing communication. This type of research does not focus on direct applications, but on knowledge and insight into the attention, appreciation and information processing of consumers with regard to advertising. This knowledge is of general importance to advertisers, agencies, consumers and anyone involved in governmental consumer policies.
- *Media-reach research* is in fact the largest type of continuous market research. It concerns media reach and contact frequency. How many people in the target group are reached with a medium or a combination of media? How often do consumers see certain titles?[30] Via which titles can advertisers best and/or cheapest reach their target groups? Data from media-reach research form the basis for media planning and selection. Also the consumers' relationships with media, appreciation of magazines, and research among subscribers and other readers concern many market research agencies. The latter is called readership research.[31]
- *Communication-strategy research* covers research into the positioning of a brand among competing brands and the way this positioning can be changed favourably by means of marketing communication. About which themes, focused on which target group and through which media are messages communicated to reach the desired objectives?
- *Concept (development) research.* A certain theme and a certain proposition are chosen for a campaign. A proposition is the offer to the

consumer including a reason (often a product benefit) to buy a certain product. 'Milk gives energy' is such a proposition. After a certain theme or proposition is chosen, it is important to 'translate' the proposition into a concept. A concept is a creative 'translation' of a proposition into 'consumer language', for example: 'Milk. The White Motor'. Concept research is usually qualitative and verifies whether a concept is understood and comes across as sound and sympathetic to the target group.

- A *pre-test* involves research into a particular advertisement or commercial that will be placed in the media. Thus it is possible to detect, at an early stage, incorrect interpretations, mistaken associations and unexpected conclusions made by consumers, as well as other barriers in communication. Generally, pre-testing comprises qualitative research in which individual respondents can freely associate and react to advertising messages with pros, cons and neutral arguments. This is called cognitive response analysis.[32]

    The expected results of promotions and direct marketing actions may be investigated on a small scale, for example in a test market. How many consumers will react to the offer? It is very important to know this before a promotion is fully launched because of the need to order products and to be prepared to handle the logistics of dispatching. When the World Wildlife Fund makes a special offer on a nature book about Indonesia, it is very desirable to have an estimate of the number of people that will order this book. A miscalculation can lead to dissatisfaction amongst customers who were expecting to receive this book before a certain day, for example Christmas.

- A *post-test* is research into the reach, notion and appreciation of a concrete advertising message placed in the media. When several messages are developed within an advertising or public-relations campaign, it is possible, on the basis of a post-test, to obtain an indication of which messages should be used more frequently. Possibly some advertising messages are more successful and therefore allow for a higher contact frequency.

- *Campaign evaluation*. Changes in the images of brands, companies and organizations, i.e., banks, can be investigated, for example changes due to a certain policy or advertising campaign. This type of research strongly resembles the research into positioning within the market structure. Often it is longitudinal research monitoring changes over time with regard to consumers' knowledge, attitudes, intentions and behaviour.

25.8 Ethics

Ethics are linked to standards and values. Rules and conditions are imposed on the behaviour and operational procedures of market researchers, marketing managers, advertising agencies, advisers, product designers and other professionals concerned with consumers. With their professional methods these people can influence the behaviour, spending and well-being of consumers. In ethics, restrictions are put on the acceptability, decency and desirability of market offerings and procedures. This means, for example, that various practices are unacceptable, including: misleading advertising and public relations, hiding product defects, publishing individual data obtained from market research, or using this individual data for selling purposes.

Consumer rights, developed within the framework of consumer policy, have an ethical foundation.[33] Currently, consumers need to be well-informed, to have a free choice and to be informed and to be heard concerning damage and any other problems. Consumers' safety and health may not be endangered. If certain products, such as tobacco and alcohol, could endanger their health, consumers must be informed so they are able to make a deliberate decision about moderate, or even immoderate, use of these products.

Consumer research is focused on providing information and insight into consumer reactions and behaviour. Most consumer research is done within the framework of marketing management of companies, but can also be done by governmental or consumer organizations. Consumer research makes use of individual data but is not geared to provide information about individual consumers. It is not about Mrs. East or Mr. West, but about a segment, target group or population.

People differ in their standards and values. Therefore they have different opinions about what is tolerable or intolerable in consumer research. Some people are strongly opposed to capitalism and on this ground reject all consumer research as it is seen as contributing towards the functioning of the market system. In these postmodern times, this seems a one-sided and ideologically biased point of view. Others accept the ideas of social order and free enterprise. On these grounds they are open to more types of consumer research. Still others are hedonistically oriented, they perceive consumption and prosperity as a way to fulfilment in life and on these grounds are happy to talk about their consumption behaviour.

Codes of behaviour

Codes of behaviour are prescriptive professional ethics, a collection of rules and regulations that professionals have to adhere to. Codes of behaviour are designed to protect consumers and also to protect researchers against malicious members of their own profession. Codes of behaviour are developed by trade organizations, e.g., the ICC/ESOMAR code for marketing and opinion research. These trade organizations can sanction members caught violating the codes. Professional organizations guiding the behaviour of members in this way in the general interest are implementing self-regulation.[34]

Apart from the ICC/ESOMAR code for marketing and opinion research, there are ICC international codes of marketing and advertising practice.[35] The International Chamber of Commerce, with headquarters in Paris, is a non-governmental organization that serves world business and has a consultative status with the United Nations. ICC submits policy recommendations on behalf of world business to the Group of Seven (G7) Economic Summit. International codes of advertising, sales promotion, direct marketing, environmental advertising, and general marketing practice exist.

Basic principles of the advertising code are that all advertising should be legal, decent, honest and truthful. Advertising should be identified as such, in order not to be confused with editorial messages. Advertising to children should not exploit their inexperience and credulity. Advertising to children should be truthful and avoid harming them. Advertising should not suggest that the possession of products will give a child an advantage over other children. It should not include any direct appeal to children to persuade their parents or others to buy the advertised products for them.[36]

These ethical codes of behaviour are also influenced by privacy laws. Marketing research agencies restrict themselves regarding the acquisition, storage, analysis, and use of data received from respondents.[37]

Acquisition

Personal data can be obtained through interviews, questionnaires, observation of people and by using public registers and publications. Pollsters need to legitimize themselves and mention both the research agency and the client. Respondents must be told about the nature and the aim of the survey before they begin. In addition, pollsters need to point out that participation in a interview or questionnaire is voluntary. Respondents may be informed about the aim of the survey immediately after the interview, in cases where the results of the interview may be strongly influenced by this information. Respondents have the right to refuse cooperation and not to answer questions. When the aim of the survey can only be revealed after the interview, respondents are entitled to destroy the information they have given.

Experimental subjects may not be put into a dangerous situation and their health and well-being may not be threatened. They may not be misled about the aim of the experiment, and must be informed before or afterwards about the aim of the experiment.

Storage and use

Market research agencies 'decapitize' personal data within 6 months of obtaining it. This means that names, addresses, dates of birth and telephone numbers of the respondents are separated from the data file. Year of birth and place of residence may remain part of the file. In any case, the data can no longer be traced to individuals. The client of the market research agency should never be given personal data.

Data processing
In the *processing of data* links to individuals should be avoided, unless they are members of panels. With panels it is necessary to connect individual results to the different measuring occasions. Quotes in the reports must be given anonymously, unless the respondent agrees to the publication of the quote stating his/her name.

These measures are meant for protection of the privacy of respondents and to prevent abuse of personal data. This way companies cannot use data from market research for (direct) marketing activities, to canvass subscribers or for other (sales) aims. Furthermore 'consumer research' may not be used as cover for sales and promotion activities. A so-called 'survey' into information needs, which is really designed to sell encyclopedias, is not allowed.

Advertising code of behaviour

Particularly with advertising, but also with public relations, ethical questions about misleading, irritation, waste and manipulation are asked. Advertising is instrumental to selling products and services. Thus advertising can give incorrect, incomplete and one-sided representations of these products and services.

Deception
Products and services nearly always are presented more favourably and better than they actually are. Advertising can suggest product advantages that do not really exist. Consumers may know this and bear in mind that advertising exaggerates. Nevertheless, consumers can make a non-optimal purchase decision on the grounds of misleading, exaggerated and false claims.[38]

Irritation
Advertising is hurtful and insulting if women are portrayed as sex objects or consumers treated as idiots. Irritation can also occur with a continuous repetition of, for example, highly similar laundry detergent commercials.

Waste
Advertising is wasteful when an 'arms race' of advertising campaigns starts with advertisers who bid against each other and do not want to fall behind their competitors. For example, criticism exists on the waste of paper in direct mail campaigns.

Manipulation

Misleading is an aspect of manipulation. Manipulation is seen as the influence on consumers to urge them into a certain purchase or perform certain user behaviour that is not in their interest, but in that of the producers. Some see advertising as an instrument in the hands of producers to control the market for their products.[39]

With advertising, the sale and use of environmentally damaging products can be boosted because the campaign fails to mention the negative environmental effects. On the other hand, environment-friendly behaviour can be stimulated by advertising and public relations. Advertising is the most visible element of the marketing mix and is therefore an easy target for people who wish to criticize the development and marketing of products and services.

25.9 Conclusions

Consumer and market research have been discussed with reference to theories explained in previous chapters. This chapter has offered only a brief outline of the issues because it is impossible to treat all aspects of consumer research within a single chapter. The different methods of analysis, for example, have not been discussed.

Uncertainty about the success of a new product or effects of an advertising campaign can be reduced by careful consumer research. A complete failure can often be averted. However consumer behaviour and advertising effects cannot be predicted in any absolute sense.

Market research methods offer a broad range of possibilities. This means that researchers have to choose the best research method for each case. In the early stages, research is exploratory and often qualitative. In later stages, it becomes confirmatory and quantitative. Interest in longitudinal research is increasing. This type of research examines questions of great importance to the progress of knowledge about consumer behaviour. Longitudinal research can yield important new insights particularly regarding communication effects.

Research into consumer behaviour is bound by ethical rules and regulations. It is important in the interest of consumers and the market research business to prevent the abuse or improper use of consumer research. Therefore, codes of behaviour have been formulated in many areas. Knowledge about consumer behaviour may not be used against the interest of consumers.

Notes

1. ESOMAR (1996) *Annual Study on the Market Research Industry 1995* (Amsterdam: ESOMAR (European Society for Opinion and Marketing Research)).

2. Churchill, Jr, G. A. (1987) *Marketing Research. Methodological Foundations* (Chicago: The Dryden Press), 4th edition.
   Green, P. E. and Tull, D. S. (1966) *Research for Marketing Decisions* (Englewood Cliffs, NJ: Prentice-Hall).
   Luck, D. J. and Rubin, R. S. (1987) *Marketing Research* (Englewood Cliffs, NJ: Prentice-Hall) 7th edition.
   Parasuraman, A. (1986) *Marketing Research* (Reading, MA: Addison-Wesley).
   Tull, D. S. and Hawkins, D. I. (1976) *Marketing Research. Meaning, Measurement, and Method* (New York: Macmillan).
3. Leeflang, P. S. H. and Van Raaij, W. F. (1995) 'The changing consumer in the European Union: a "meta-analysis"' *International Journal of Research in Marketing* 12, 373–387.
4. See chapters 2, 3, 4 and 5.
5. See section 7.3 and section 24.7. Also see Ries, A. and Trout, J. (1986) *Positioning: The Battle for Your Mind* (New York: McGraw-Hill).
6. See chapter 7.
7. See chapter 24.
8. Reynolds, T. J. and Gutman, J. (1984) 'Advertising is image management' *Journal of Advertising Research* 24, 27–36.
9. See chapter 24.
10. Katona, G. (1960) *The Powerful Consumer* (New York: McGraw-Hill).
11. Dichter, E. (1964) *Handbook of Consumer Motivations* (New York: McGraw-Hill).
12. Hamilton, J. (1989) *What Is Market Research?* (Amsterdam: ESOMAR).
13. East Germany is included in the figure for Germany.
14. ESOMAR (1996).
15. ESOMAR (1996), Table 15, p. 41. Only the European turnover of these companies is given in this table.
16. IMS stands for Institute for Medical Statistics.
17. Verhallen, Th. M. M. and Vogel, H. (1982) 'Techniques of qualitative research 1' *Tijdschrift voor Marketing* 16, 28–32 (in Dutch).
18. Data from ESOMAR (1996).
19. MDI stands for Multi Dimensional Involvement. The MDI study is performed by NSS Market Research, The Hague, The Netherlands.
20. This table is taken from NSS Marketing Research (1993) *Peilpunten* (The Hague: NSS). Similar results have been found in other European countries.
21. See section 7.3, Figure 7.4.
22. See chapter 15.
23. Tauber, E. (1975) 'Why concept and product tests fail to predict new product results' *Journal of Marketing* 39, 69–71.
24. DEMON: DeVoe, J. K. (1965) 'Plans, profits, and the marketing program' in: Webster, F. E. (Ed.) *New Directions in Marketing* (Chicago: American Marketing Association).
   NEWS: New Product Early Warning System.
   SPRINTER: Urban, G. L. (1974).
25. Gabor, A. and Granger, C. W. J. (1965) 'The pricing of new products' *Scientific Business* 3, 141–150.

Gabor, A. and Granger, C. W. J. (1966) 'Price as an indicator of quality: report of an inquiry' *Economica* 33, 43–70.

26. Stapel, J. (1972) "Fair" or "psychological" pricing' *Journal of Marketing Research* 9, 109–110.

27. See section 6.3.

28. Floor, J. M. G. and van Raaij, W. F. (in preparation) *Marketing Communication Strategy* (Hemel Hempstead, UK: Prentice Hall).

29. See chapter 13 for advertising research and chapter 17 for media research. Floor and Van Raaij (in preparation).

30. A medium title is a specific 'brand' of a medium, for example, *The Times* is a medium title of the category newspapers.

31. See section 17.5.

32. See section 9.6.

33. See section 5.6.

34. The ICC/ESOMAR International Code of Marketing and Social Research Practice is a European code of behaviour for marketing and social scientific research, developed by the International Chamber of Commerce, Paris, and ESOMAR, the European Society for Opinion and Marketing Research, Amsterdam. The third revision of the code is dated 1995.

35. ICC (1995) *International Codes of Marketing and Advertising Practice* (Paris: International Chamber of Commerce). The *International Code of Advertising Practice* has been revised in 1997.

36. See section 20.2.

37. ICC/ESOMAR (1995) *International Code of Marketing and Social Research Practice* (Amsterdam: ESOMAR).

38. Russo, J. E., Metcalf, B. L. and Stephens, D. (1981) 'Identifying misleading advertising' *Journal of Consumer Research* 8, 119–131.

39. Galbraith, J. K. (1958) *The Affluent Society* (Harmondsworth, UK: Penguin Books). Galbraith, J. K. (1973) *Economics and the Public Purpose* (Harmondsworth, UK: Penguin Books).

EPILOGUE

Several themes that link the chapters of this book will now be briefly discussed. These related issues include: societal trends, rational decision making, emotions, social interaction, segmentation, consumption, production, welfare and well-being.

Societal trends

Demographic developments,[1] such as the 'greying' of society, individualization and the increasing number of small households have been described. Increasing attention to the environment and to the preferences and potential of individuals has also been noticed. Because of these factors, consumption patterns may shift even more.

The market for the elderly will become more important and marketing activities will increasingly be aimed at senior citizens, because they will have greater budgets available. A greater need for products for the elderly will emerge and entrepreneurs will capitalize on this need. For example, they may develop lightweight equipment that helps to compensate for failing bodily functions, and deliver services that compensate for declining household productivity.

Because of declining household sizes, products will have to become available in smaller portions and be adapted to personal tastes and possibilities. The postmodernist trend will probably lead to even greater product differentiation.[2] The volume of consumption may decrease and products will need to be converted to offer greater differentiation and higher quality. Problems with products and services will be even less acceptable because consumers will be more dependent on them. Failing equipment and ill-functioning products and services will become matters of the past.

High quality products should provide not only more utility to the consumers but they should also be produced, consumed and disposed of in a more environment-friendly way.

All this makes high demands on the production, distribution and marketing of products and services in the future. This offers opportunities for well-educated personnel. However, because of the shrinking size of the active population, the work force may find this task a burden.

Rational decision making

The rational model of decision making, based on information, perception and preference formation has a number of limitations which will become more significant, given the societal trends. The consumer information overload will increase because of increasing product differentiation and more opportunities for advertising in the media.

Consumers will show increasing tendencies to apply simplifying decision rules[3] while at the same time avoiding risky purchases. One way to do this is via the product trial. An advantage of product trials for the supplier is that they can 'break' consumption habits through the process of cognitive dissonance.[4] Particularly in a greying society, breaking habits will become an important marketing objective.

Decision making not only deals with functional but also with psycho-social product characteristics. Consumers want to know whether the product or brand is suitable for them, what other people think about the product and whether the product or brand contributes to their image. Products and brands have become a means of communicating for people. In a sense it is 'rational' to appreciate this kind of communication.

Emotion

The symbolic value of products has become more important, especially with expressive and publicly consumed products. In the case of information overload and the reduced ability to process information, emotions play a part in decision making.[5] Advertising plays on emotions so as to build a favourable image of the product. In sales, emotions may help consumers to 'break the barrier'. Emotions can play a part in the relationships between suppliers and consumers, and in creating brand loyalty and store loyalty. Emotions also play a part in consumption, for example, in protecting the ego or gaining social esteem.

Connected to emotions, cognitive processes play a part, for example, by attributing emotions to particular causes.[6]

Social interaction

Social influence is less a one-way traffic than previously assumed.[7] Because of greater access to information, people have generally become less dependent on information from others. However, other people may have become more important with respect to the motives for purchasing a product. Is this product conspicuous? Isn't this outfit dull? Isn't this coat too cheap? What will the neighbours think about the new car? Emotions can play unexpected roles in social interaction.

Social influence is important within households.[8] To what extent do products contribute to the well-being of the household members and to what extent are the members involved in purchase decisions? How do social networks outside the household influence decision making within the household? These questions go beyond the theories and the evidence presented in this book.

Segmentation[9]

Sociodemographic developments may change the needs and preferences of a population indeed, but the personality characteristics concerned appear to be insufficient to describe target groups for marketing purposes. The chapter dealing with age groups and ethnic groups discussed several implications for the consumption of these groups.[10] For many products, these implications are still too broad. For example, the process of acculturation may contribute to the convergence of consumption patterns of ethnic minority groups and the indigenous population. However, adaptation of consumption patterns of the indigenous population may likewise contribute to converging consumer behaviours. It would be interesting to study the behaviour of mixed households in this respect.

In former days, mainly young and unsettled people travelled to far countries. Nowadays the elderly are travelling all over the world. This process can hardly be described by means of simple market segmentation. As the lifestyles of the segments are also changing, in the long run they will be inadequate to predict consumption patterns. It is equally plausible to argue that lifestyles are explained by consumption patterns. Insofar as consumption is stable, current consumption may be explained from earlier consumption. However, because of the fast pace of societal changes and successive product innovations, consumption patterns can hardly be called stable.

Does segmentation make sense? There are at least two possible answers to this question. To a supplier who wants quick success, it is important to gain insight into the potential market in a certain product domain. To such a supplier, segmentation is of great importance, even if the segmentation is only valid in the short term.

However, for a long-term strategy of the firm such segmentation is not sufficient. In this case, a more profound domain-specific segmentation of perceived product benefits is necessary. Factors that should be included in this approach are preferences for products and brands within a particular domain, product attributes and prices of brands and types (taking perceptions and fairness into account), product benefits, and the emotional values of products and brands. This book tries to provide insight into the relevant factors.

Consumption and production

Consumption is not an isolated issue. The consumption possibilities are closely connected with the financial position of a household, labour market participation and free time. Also family planning and child care influence the possibilities of consumption.[11]

Consumption goods and services can be acquired in different ways, i.e., by household production (or by volunteer workers such as neighbours and relatives), supplied by the government or by the market sector. The growth and shrinkage of these sectors is a continuous process.[12] The government sector is an uncertain factor in this process. On the one hand, the withdrawal of the government implies that this sector is shrinking. On the other hand, we expect increasing demand for government services by the elderly, implying that this sector will grow. Furthermore, we expect a shrinking household sector because of increasing labour market participation of the working population (for the size of the working population will decrease because of an outflow of the elderly) and a growing market sector (taking over the tasks of the other sectors).

Welfare and well-being

Welfare, via wealth, is closely connected with consumption. Currently, much wealth is owned by the elderly and accumulated by the middle-aged. According to the economic lifecycle theory many of the elderly will spend their savings in the future.[13] Also, wealth transfers will take place in the form of donations and bequests.

To the extent that transferred wealth is not saved, both consumption and welfare will increase. It would be a good conclusion of this book if welfare could increase well-being. However, problems have been indicated with respect to the environment, exhaustion of raw materials and energy, care for the elderly and child care. Several additional problems exist, such as relational problems (divorce), the third-world problem (and Eastern Europe), wars and illnesses and other detriments to well-being.[14] It would be fortunate indeed if welfare could be increased without harming well-being and if it could be durable welfare, i.e., not diminishing the world stock of raw materials and fossil fuels.

Notes

1. See section 2.3.
2. See section 3.8.
3. See section 11.5.
4. See section 9.5.
5. See, for example, the Elaboration Likelihood Model in section 9.6.

UNIVERSITY OF CHESTER, WARRINGTON CAMPUS

6. See section 21.3.
7. See section 14.4.
8. See section 13.4.
9. See section 24.
10. See chapter 20.
11. See chapter 13.
12. See section 13.6.
13. See section 19.2.
14. See section 23.2.

AUTHOR INDEX

Index compiled by Annette Musker

SUBJECT INDEX